2016-17 EDITION

Indian Economic Development Since 1947

Also by the same author :

2016-17 Edition

INDIAN ECONOMY: ECONOMIC DEVELOPMENT AND POLICY

Specially designed to serve as a text book for Indian economy (Course 05) for B.A. Programme, and Honours other than Economics, including B.Com (Hons.)

27th Edition: 2016-17 (Revised)

INDIAN ECONOMY SINCE INDEPENDENCE

Revised year after year, now into its 27th Edition, this unique book is widely accepted as the core text for graduate/post-graduate courses in Indian economy, in various universities across India. The book is essentially, a collection of select articles by some of India's topmost economists and experts. These highly recommended original readings are well-supported by editorial notes and excerpts from Plan documents, that together present a comprehensive and critical analysis of Indian economy since independence: 1947-2016.

17th Edition: 2016-17 (Revised)

INDIAN ECONOMY: PERFORMANCE AND POLICIES

Recommended text for undergraduate students in several universities across India and is widely used by candidates preparing for IAS and other competitive examinations.

UMA KAPILA, author/editor of several other books, has taught Indian Economy to undergraduate students for over forty-two years. She retired as Reader from the Department of Economics, Miranda House, University of Delhi. Presently, she is Senior Editor, Academic Foundation.

An Honours Graduate from Miranda House, University of Delhi and M.A. and Ph.D. from Delhi School of Economics, Dr. Uma Kapila has also served on the Planning Commission Study Group on "Agricultural Strategies in the Eastern Region of India for the Seventh Five Year Plan" (Perspective Planning Division).

Dr. Uma Kapila is the author of the book *Oilseeds Economy of India* (1982) published by the Institute of Economic Growth, Delhi. She is also the author/editor of textbooks on Indian economy, one meant for B.A. (Hons.) Economics and the other for B.A. (Programme) and B. Com (Hons.) and Hons. other than Economics. She has edited, and co-edited with Raj Kapila, a number of books on India's economy, banking and finance. Detailed information on these publications is readily available at the publisher's website: *www.academicfoundation.org*

2016-17 EDITION

Indian Economic Development Since 1947

Reference Text for BA (Hons) Economics (Course 15), University of Delhi

EDITED BY

UMA KAPILA

ACADEMIC FOUNDATION
NEW DELHI

www.academicfoundation.org

2016-17 Edition
© 2016.

ACADEMIC FOUNDATION

Delhi Sales Office:
4772-73 / 23 Bharat Ram Road,
(23 Ansari Road), Darya Ganj,
New Delhi - 110 002.
Phones : +91-11-23245001 / 02 / 03 / 04.

Corporate Office:
No. 35, Sector 7,
IMT Manesar,
Gurgaon - 122050.
Phones : +91-124-4215070 / 71.

Fax : +91-11-23245005
E-mail : books@academicfoundation.com
www.academicfoundation.org

Cataloging in Publication Data--DK
Courtesy: D.K. Agencies (P) Ltd. <docinfo@dkagencies.com>

Indian economic development since 1947 / edited by Uma
Kapila. -- 2016-17 edition.
pages cm
Contributed articles.
"Reference text for BA (Hons) economics (course 15),
University of Delhi."
ISBN 9789332703735

1. India--Economic policy--1947- 2. India--Economic
conditions--1947- I. Kapila, Uma, editor.

HC435.2.I53 2016 DDC 338.954 23

Typeset, printed and bound by The Book Mint, New Delhi.
www.thebookmint.in

Syllabus

Course 15 - Indian Economic Development Since 1947 - II

Department of Economics, Delhi School of Economics,
University of Delhi

Notes:

1. *Internal Assessment:* There will be two tests of 10 marks each and 5 marks will be allotted for attendance
2. *Examination Pattern:* Students would be required to answer any 5 out of 8 questions. Distribution of questions should be roughly proportional to the amount of reading material under each topic.
3. *Readings with an asterisk* mark are for teachers only.

Topic-wise revised reading list for 2016

Unit I. Macroeconomic Policies and Their Impact:

Fiscal policy; trade and investment policy; financial and monetary policies; labour regulation.

1. Panda, Manoj (2015). "Macroeconomic Development and Challenges for Growth", in Mahendra Dev (ed.), *India Development Report 2015*.
2. Kohli, Renu (2014). "Financial Globalization in India", in Ashima Goyal (ed.), *The Oxford Handbook of Indian Economy in the 21st Century*. Delhi: OUP, Ch. 8.
3. Balakrishnan, Pulapre (2014). "The Great Reversal: A Macro Story", *EPW*, May 24.
4. Kanagasabapathy, K., Vishakha G. Tilak, and R. Krishnaswamy (2013). "A Rethink on India's Foreign Trade Policy", *EPW*, August 3.
5. Dhar, Biswajit (2015). "India's New Foreign Trade Policy", *EPW*, May 24.
6. Bhagwati and Panagariya (2012). "A Multitude of Labour Laws and their Reforms", in *India's Tryst with Destiny*. Noida: Collins Business, Ch. 8.

For Teachers

1 * Pal, Rupayan and Bibhas Saha, "Labour Market: Balancing Freedom and Protection", in Ashima Goyal (ed.), *The Oxford Handbook of Indian Economy in the 21st Century*, OUP, Delhi, Ch. 30,

2. * Deakin, S. and A Haldar (2015). "How Should India Reform its Labour Laws?", *EPW*, March 21.
3. * Chakraborty, Achin (2015). "Reforming Labour Markets in States: Revisiting the Futility Thesis", *EPW*, May 16.
4. * WTO (2015). "Trade Policy Review-INDIA", Relevant sections of the (a) Secretariat report (especially Ch. 3 on *trade policy and facilitation*), (b) Government report. (*www.wto.org*)

Unit 2: Policies and Performance in Agriculture

Growth; productivity; agrarian structure and technology; capital formation; trade; pricing and procurement.

1. Dev, Mahendra (2012). "Agricultural Development", in K. Basu and A. Maertens (eds.), (2012), *New Oxford Companion to Economics in India* (referred to as NOC hereafter). pp. 12-14.
2. World Bank Group (2014). "Overview", in *Republic of India, Accelerating Agriculture Productivity Growth*, (*http://documents.worldbank.org/curated/en/2014/05/23789323/indiaaccelerating-agricultural-productivity-growth*)
3. World Bank Group (2014). "The Context and Conundrums of Contemporary Agriculture", in *Republic of India, Accelerating Agriculture Productivity Growth*. World Bank Group, Washington, Ch. 2.
4. Rao, Chandrasekhara and Mahendra Dev (2010). "Agricultural Price Policy, Farm Profitability and Food Security", *EPW*, June 26.

Unit 3: Policies and Performance in Industry

Growth productivity; diversification; small scale industries; public sector; competition policy; foreign investment.

1. Nagaraj, R. (2011). "Industrial Performance, 2001-2008", in Nachane (ed.), *India Development 2011*.
2. Nayak, Pulin (2012). "Privatisation", in NOC.
3. Bhattacharjea, Aditya (2010). "Of Omissions and Commissions: India's Competition Laws", *EPW*, 28 August, sections 1 and 3 only. (Briefer account in A. Bhattacharjea, 2012, Antitrust Law, in NOC.)
4. Kumar, Nagesh (2014). "FDI and Portfolio Investment Flows and Development: A Perspective on Indian Experience", in Uma Kapila (ed.), *Indian Economy Since Independence* (26th edition), 2015-16. Delhi: Academic Foundation, Ch. 40.
5. Mazumdar, Dipak and Sandeep Sarkar (2009). "The Employment Problem in India and the Phenomenon of the Missing Middle", *Indian Journal of Labour Economics*.

Unit 4: Trends and Performance in Services

1. Rupa Chanda (2012). *Services Led Growth* in NOC.

Contents

PART III

INDUSTRY

PART IV

SERVICES

Preface

READERS of Indian economy may wonder and ask this question: what was the need for this new book "Indian Economic Development since 1947" when already there is "Indian Economy since Independence" (in its 27th edition/2016) by the same editor?

This new book has been designed specially to meet the requirements of the revised course content of BA (Hons) Economics students of the University of Delhi by including most of the recommended readings. While "Indian Economy since Independence" is a much more comprehensive volume on India's economic development since Independence, the new book is confined only to the present restructured course under four units.

Starting with macroeconomic policies and their impact such as fiscal policy, trade and investment, financial and monetary policies and labour regulations (Section I), it is followed by sector specific policies and performance with respect to three sectors viz., agriculture, industry and services. In Section II (agriculture), policies and performance relating to growth and productivity; agrarian structure and technology; capital formation;trade, pricing and procurement have been discussed and analysed by experts in the respective fields in addition to the editorial notes. Section III covers policies and performance in industry: growth, productivity, diversification, small scale industry, public sector, competition policy and foreign investment. Section IV is devoted to trends in performance in services sector.

As performance of any sector is crucially dependent on productivity growth, we have added a chapter on productivity growth performance authored by Profs K.L. Krishna and B. Goldar. The authors have revised and updated this essay adding a section for the benefit of students. I would like to express my deep sense of gratitude to the authors in particular to Prof Krishna who has always been accessible and is ever helpful.

I am extremely grateful to the contributors who have very kindly agreed to the inclusion of their essays in this book. I would also like to mention that some of the contributors have taken the trouble of revising and updating their essays. I owe a deep debt of gratitude to all the authors for their contributions viz.: Aditya Bhattacharjea, Pulapre Balakrishnan, Biswajit Dhar, S. Deakin and A. Haldar, K. Kanagasabapathy, Achin Chakraborty, Mahendra Dev, R. Nagaraj, Nagesh Kumar, Dipak Mazumdar, Sandeep Sarkar and Chandrasekhara Rao.

I am also thankful to various organisations, institutions and journals like World Bank, WTO, Indira Gandhi Institute of Development Research (IGIDR), and Economic and Political Weekly for granting permission to reproduce relevant chapters/articles from their publications.

It is my sincere hope that the book will serve the needs of students and teachers.

— Uma Kapila

July 2016

Contributors

Pulapre Balakrishnan .... *Professor of Economics, Ashoka University, Kundli, Haryana.*

Aditya Bhattacharjea .... *Professor and Head, Department of Economics, Delhi School of Economics, University of Delhi, Delhi.*

Achin Chakraborty .... *Professor and Director, Institute of Development Studies, Kolkata.*

Simon Deakin .... *Professor of Law, University of Cambridge, England.*

S. Mahendra Dev............. *Director (Vice Chancellor), Indira Gandhi Institute of Development Research, Mumbai.*

Biswajit Dhar................ *Professor, Centre of Economic Studies and Planning, School of Social Sciences, Jawaharlal Nehru University, New Delhi.*

Bishwanath Goldar .... *ICSSR National Fellow, affiliated to IEG; Chairman, Standing Committee on Industrial Statistics; Chairman, Working Group on Producer Price Index (PPP), Government of India.*

Antara Haldar .... *University Lecturer, Empirical Legal Studies, University of Cambaridge, England.*

K. Kanagasabapathy.......... *Independent Economic Consultant; formerly Director EPW Research Foundation, Mumbai.*

Uma Kapila.................. *Reader (Retd.), Department of Economics, Miranda House, University of Delhi. Presently, Senior Editor, Academic Foundation, New Delhi.*

Vijay Kelkar................. *Chairman, India Development Foundation, New Delhi. Formerly Chairman 13th Finance Commission, Govt. of India.*

K.L. Krishna................. *Chairman, Madras Institute of Development Studies, Chennai; Member, Centre for Development Economics, Delhi School of Economics, Delhi.*

R. Krishnaswamy .... *EPW Research Foundation, Economic and Political Weekly, Mumbai.*

Nagesh Kumar............... *Head, UN-ESCAP South and South-West Asia Office, New Delhi.*

Dipak Mazumdar. .... *Munk Center for International Studies, University of Toronto; Visiting Professor, Institute for Human Development, New Delhi.*

R. Nagaraj.................. *Professor, Indira Gandhi Institute of Development Research, Mumbai.*

Manoj Panda .... *Director, Institute of Economic Growth, University of Delhi, Delhi.*

N. Chandrasekhara Rao...... *Professor, Institute of Economic Growth, University of Delhi, Delhi.*

Sandip Sarkar................ *Professor, Institute for Human Development, New Delhi.*

M.H. Bala Subrahmanya...... *Professor & Chairman, Department of Management Studies, Indian Institute of Science, Bangalore.*

Vishakha G. Tilak............ *EPW Research Foundation, Economic and Political Weekly, Mumbai.*

Part I

Macroeconomic Policies and Their Impact

1

UMA KAPILA

Indian Economy

Then and Now

The Colonial Regime

The pre-Independence period was a period of near-stagnation for the Indian economy. At the time of Independence, Indian economy was caught up in a *vicious circle of poverty* characterised by one of the lowest per capita consumption and income levels among the countries of the world. Low income levels resulted in low levels of saving and capital formation and therefore, low productivity and low level of income and this vicious circle perpetuated poverty in the country. Further, the size of the market being limited because of low incomes, entrepreneurs had little incentive for making investments in diversified fields and therefore, the productivity in the economy continued to be low thereby perpetuating low incomes and mass poverty.

Judged in terms of per capita incomes and standard of well-being, the Indian economy remained more or less stagnant during the colonial regime. Quoting from the First Five Year Plan document: "This is primarily because the basic conditions under which an economy can continuously expand have been lacking. The impact of modern industrialism in the latter half of the 19th century was felt in this country initially through imports of machine-made goods from abroad which reacted adversely on the traditional pattern of economic life, but did not create the impulse for development along new lines. The transition that followed was characterised not by expansion of industry and a diversification of the economic structure but by a decay of India's traditional arts, crafts and industries and by an increasing pressure of population on land. This retrogression led to a decline in productivity per person engaged in agriculture, the adverse effects of which were perhaps softened to some extent by the shock absorbing capacity of the old institution of the joint family. The result was a continuous increase in under-employment. In such an environment there could be little economic or social progress. Whatever surpluses might have been available in the system under these conditions were directed to the purchase of imports, partly of better finished products from abroad and partly of equipment for the new transportation system designed primarily in the interests of foreign commerce. The responsibility for promoting modern commerce and industry came to be concentrated in the hands of certain classes in the urban areas, and up to the end of the nineteenth century the only major large-scale industries which had taken root in the country were textiles. Little attention was paid to improvement of agriculture or to the needs of the rural areas." (First Five Year Plan, p. 28)

The India of 1947

Indian economy at the time of Independence was overwhelmingly rural and agricultural in character with nearly 85 per cent of the population living in villages and deriving their livelihood from agricultural and related pursuits using traditional, low productivity techniques. The backwardness of Indian economy is reflected in its unbalanced occupational structure with 70 per cent of working population engaged in agriculture. Even with this large proportion of population engaged in agriculture, the country was not self-sufficient in food and raw materials for industry. The average availability of food was not only deficient in quantity and quality but also precarious as exhibited in recurrent famines. Illiteracy was as high as 84 per cent; majority of children (60%) in the 6-11 age group did not attend school. Mass communicable diseases were widespread and in the absence of a good public health service, mortality rates were very high (27 per thousand). An average Indian born between 1940 and 1951 could expect to live for barely 32 years. Epidemics and diseases like small pox, plague, cholera, malaria and other fevers carried away millions every year. Thus, the economy was faced with the problems of mass poverty, ignorance and diseases which were aggravated by the unequal distribution of resources between groups and regions.

The India of 1947, under British rule, showed all the signs of what is today called an underdeveloped country.

The low degree of economic development can be judged from the relative importance of various industrial activities in terms of their contribution to national income and the workforce engaged in these activities (Table 1.1).

Table 1.1

Distribution of National Income and Workforce Sectorwise

(Per cent)

	Sector	*National Income (1948-49)*	*Workforce (1950-51)*
1.	Agriculture, animal husbandary, forestry, fisheries	49.1	72.3
2	Mines, manufacturing industries, small enterprises	17.1	10.7
3.	Trade, transport and communications	18.5	7.7
4.	Other services, professions, administration, domestic services	15.7	9.3
	Total	100.0	100.0

Source : Bettlehem Charles, India Independent (p. 2).

As can be seen, agricultural activities contributed nearly 50 per cent to India's national income. Mines, factories and small craftsmen's work contributed only one-sixth, even lower than the figure for trade, transport and communications, and hardly greater than that for other services.

Regarding the occupational distribution, 72 per cent of the total working force was occupied in agriculture. Less than 11 per cent of the working force was employed in all the forms of industry, whereas the organised industries employed only about 2 per cent, a figure lower than the number of administrative workers (2.7%). Less than 8 per cent was employed in trade and transports, less than 10 per cent in other services. These statistics speak for low level of industrialisation.

The Agrarian Scene

Stagnating Agriculture

Colonialism became a fetter on India's agricultural and industrial development. Agriculture stagnated and even deteriorated over the years, especially during the first half of the 20th century when the full impact of colonialism began to be felt. Per capita agricultural production declined at a rate of 0.72 per cent per year during 1911-1941 (Blyn, 1966). The situation was worse insofar as per capita foodgrain output was concerned: during the same period, it declined by 29 per cent, i.e., at a rate of 1.14 per cent per year. Even though the per capita non-foodgrain output grew by 14 per cent, it failed to make up for the decline in foodgrain output (Blyn, 1966).

Whatever the absolute growth in agricultural output, it occurred mainly because of the increase in crop-acreage. The rate of increase in all-crop yield per acre was near-zero during 1911-1941. While all-crop and food grain yields declined by 0.02 and 0.44 per cent per year, non-food grain yield went up by 1.15 per cent per year (Blyn, 1966). The increase in yield of non-food grains was basically at the cost of food grain yields, as cultivators shifted better and irrigated land and capital resources to commercial crops in order to earn cash.

Causes

(i) Regressive Agrarian Structure: The stagnation in agriculture is basically explained by the fact that colonialism transformed the agrarian structure in India and made it extremely regressive. As is well-known, the zamindars in zamindari areas failed to invest in land and relied on rack-renting, while the peasant proprietors fell into the clutches of the moneylenders and lost control over their lands. Sub-infeudation, tenancy and sharecropping increasingly dominated both the zamindari and ryotwari areas.[1]

(ii) Internal Drain of Capital: Further Agricultural surpluses were siphoned from agriculture without any quid pro quo, thereby subjecting it to an internal drain of capital. Throughout the 18th and 19th centuries, high land revenue demand ate into the peasant's surplus and even his subsistence. But the government spent very little on improving agriculture as was done, for instance, in Japan. The landlords, old or new,

1. By 1947, nearly 70 per cent of the total cultivated land in British India was owned by zamindars and landlords. According to Nanavati ("Minute of Dissent", in the Famine Inquiry Commission—Final Report, Government of India, Calcutta, 1945), in ryotwari areas between 30 to 50 per cent of the land was in the hands of the landlords and most of the rest was heavily under debt. In 1951, 27.8 per cent of rural agricultural families consisted of peasant proprietors while tenants, sharecroppers and labourers made up the remaining families. (Chandra, Bipan, 1979).

took no interest in agriculture beyond collecting rent. They found rack-rent and usury far more profitable than making productive investment in land. The moneylenders and merchants used their increasing share of agricultural surplus to intensify usury or to take possession of land to become landlords.

(iii) Poor Technology: Another reason for the stagnation of productivity in agriculture was the near absence of change in its technological basis or its productive technique and inputs. As Blyn points out, the type of equipment used changed very little till 1941. Modern machinery was conspicuous by its absence. Improved seeds covered about 1.9 per cent of all crop-acreage in 1922-23 and 11.1 per cent in 1938-39, these being largely confined to non-food cash crops.

It is also to be noted that commercialisation did not change the unit or organisation of productive activity (e.g. capitalist farming) or lead to improved technology—only better soil and available water and other resources were diverted from food crops to commercial crops.

The State of Indian Industry and its Structure

Another aspect of India's economic backwardness was the state of its industry in spite of her vast industrial resources. India's iron ore deposits estimated at 21 thousand million are a quarter of the total world deposits, manganese deposits are the third largest in the world. India also possesses deposits of chromium, gold, bauxite and various non-ferrous metals, which are important raw materials for atomic industries. Finally, gypsum also exists, as does mica, the latter deposit being one of the largest in the world. India is equally rich in her energy potential. India's resources as a whole would give her a leading position in world industry, in particular the steel and engineering industries and the chemical industries based on coal (Bettleheim, 1968).

Given this potential, we may now examine the state of India's industrial development immediately after Independence.

India's industrial situation in 1948 was the result of a long period of change in which modern industry replaced the traditional crafts.

Foreign trade statistics best show the effects of 'deindustrialisation'. India, still an exporter of manufactured products at the end of the 18th century, becomes an importer. From 1815 to 1832, India's cotton exports dropped by 92 per cent. In 1850, India was buying one quarter of Britain's cotton exports. All industrial products shared this fate.

The ruin of the traditional trades and crafts was the result of the British commercial policy. Restrictions were imposed upon Indians exporting to the West, while favours were granted to British exporters, who flooded the Indian markets.

Modern industries began to develop during the second half of the 19th century but their progress was exceedingly slow and stunted. Up to the very end of the colonial period, the level of industry and technology remained low. During the 19th century, industrial development was confined to cotton and jute textiles. The iron and steel industry developed after 1907 while the sugar, cement and paper industries and a few engineering firms came up in the 1930s.

Still, as late as 1946, cotton and jute textiles accounted for nearly 30 per cent of all workers employed in factories (Kumar, 1984).

According to the Census of Manufacturing in 1951, which covered the larger enterprises, of the total value added in manufacturing, 56.8 per cent originated in cotton and jute textiles, 6.6 in sugar, 8.4 in engineering, 7.6 in steel, 4.1 in chemicals and 2.1 in cement.

Consequently, even though modern industry developed quite fast after 1918—its rate of growth being 3.8 per cent per annum—it had little impact on the overall economic situation for its share in the national income at the end of British rule at 7.5 per cent was quite insignificant. In 1913, it was 3.8 per cent (CEHI, 1984). Modern industry perhaps barely compensated for the displacement of traditional handicrafts (Chaudhuri, 1979).

In 1951, only about 2.3 per cent of the labour force was employed in modern industries. According to the Planning Commission, the number of persons engaged in processing and manufacturing (including artisanal industries) fell from 10.3 million in 1901 to 8.8 million in 1951, even though the population increased by nearly 40 per cent. Moreover, in 1951, of the total industrial output, at least 60 per cent was by the unorganised, small enterprises (Jalan, 1972).

An important index of India's industrial backwardness was the virtual absence of capital goods and machine industries. In 1950, India met 90 per cent of its needs of machine tools through imports. Lopsided industrial development was yet another striking feature. Industries were concentrated only in a few regions and cities of the country resulting in wide regional disparities in income. But there were some major changes in the Indian economy especially during the thirties and forties that did impart a certain strength to it and provided a basis for post-independence economic development. One positive feature was the growth of the means of transport and communication. The development of roads and railways unified the country and made rapid transit of goods and persons possible. However in the absence of a simultaneous industrial revolution only a commercial revolution was produced which further colonised the Indian economy—railway lines being laid primarily to link India's inland raw material producing areas with the ports for exports and to send imported manufactures from the ports to the interior. Another positive feature was the development of the small but Indian owned industrial base consisting of several consumer goods industries such as cotton, jute textiles, sugar, soap, paper and matches. There was also after 1914, rise of a strong indigeneous capitalist class with an independent economic and financial base. However, these positive features of Indian economy have to be seen in a wider historial context. The development of Indian industry and capitalism was still relatively stunted and severly limited occurring within the framework of a colonial economy. This industrialisation took place without India undergoing an industrial revolution as Britain did.

Similarly, modern banking and insurance were grossly under-developed. In 1946, class A and B banks had 4,644 offices or one office for 90,000 inhabitants. Underdeveloped banking and insurance meant that the Indian entrepreneurs could not mobilise the available capital. Also, British-controlled banks starved Indian industry of funds and favoured British-owned and controlled enterprises.

The growth of foreign trade and the rapid construction of railways which could have been the positive factors, unfortunately became instruments for the underdevelopment of the Indian economy. Under conditions of free trade, imports displaced indigenous handicrafts and artisanal industries and prevented the rise of new industries. In the absence of a simultaneous industrial revolution, railways had only introduced a commercial revolution and further colonialised the Indian economy. The layout of railway lines and the railway freight rates policy promoted the export of raw materials and distribution of imported goods for they encouraged traffic with ports as against traffic between inland centres. The railways also did not have any forward or backward linkages. They had encouraged the steel and machine industry, not in India but in Britain. They had served as a social overhead not for Indian but British industry and their external economies were exported back to Britain.

Till the late 1930s, foreign capital dominated the industrial and financial fields and controlled the foreign trade network as also part of the internal trade that fed into exports.

It is important to keep in view, in this respect, that foreign investment rarely marked a transfer of capital to India from abroad. It was far less than the unilateral transfer of capital or the 'drain' from India. Three other characteristics of foreign investment were important.

(i) It contributed to 'the guided underdevelopment' of India by concentrating on the production and export of raw materials and foodstuff.

(ii) It went into sectors which catered to foreign markets and not to India's home market.

(iii) "The multiplier effects in terms of income, employment, capital, technical knowledge, and growth of external economies of these investments were largely exported back to the developed countries." (Jalan, 1992).

We may sum up India's economic profile at the time of Independence as: stagnating per capita national income, abysmal standard of living, stunted industrial development and the bulk of the population dependent on stagnating, low-productivity semi-feudal agriculture (Jalan, 1992).

The end result of colonial underdevelopment was the pauperisation of the people especially the peasantry and the small artisan. Extreme poverty, disease, hunger and starvation were the lot of the ordinary people. The frequent famines in some part or the other in the country was the order of the day. The last major famine in 1943 carried away nearly 3 million people in Bengal.

When India attained its independence in 1947, many sceptics doubted that such a country marked by crushing poverty, bewildering diversities and weak institutions could long endure. Much before the British Raj ended in the subcontinent, Winston Churchill had remarked that India was little other than an "abstraction ... a geographical term. It is no more a united nation than the Equator" (Tellis, 2014: 3).

India's first prime minister, Jawaharlal Nehru and many others in the post-independence leadership deeply believed that the combination of liberal democracy, civic nationalism and socialist economics was essential to successfully building a modern Indian state. Given this belief, the Indian constitution oriented the formal democratic process towards more substantive aims: "to create social, economic and political institutions which will ensure justice and fullness of life to every man and woman", as Nehru framed it in his immortal "Tryst with destiny" midnight address on the eve of India's independence (Ibid.: 5). The Indian constitution's preamble aimed "to secure to all its citizens JUSTICE, social, economic and political; LIBERTY of thought, expression, belief, faith and worship; EQUALITY of status and of opportunity and to promote among them all, FRATERNITY assuring the dignity of the individual, and the unity and integrity of the Nation" (Ibid.: 8).

Immediately after the attainment of Independence, Government's main concern in economic policy was to control persistent and severe inflationary pressures and to alleviate shortages of essential food items which had been aggravated by the partition of the country in 1947. The Industrial Policy Resolution of 1948 marked a fundamental departure from the earlier policy of laissez-faire. According to the new Policy Resolution, the government was to have a major role in initiating and regulating development in one of the key sectors of the economy. The Directive Principles of State Policy, incorporated in the Constitution, defined the broad objectives of socio-economic policy. They mentioned the right of citizens to an adequate means of livelihood, regulation of ownership and control of the material resources of the country to subserve the common good and the avoidance of concentration of wealth and means of production. Finally, the concept of co-ordinated planning of development programmes under the auspices of the Central government, was accepted and the Planning Commission was set up in March 1950 to make an assessment of the material, capital and human resources of the country and to formulate a Plan for the most effective and balanced utilisation of the country's resources.

A New India

Despite that grim beginning as Drèze and Sen (2013) remarked, "newly independent India rapidly went on to have a cluster of significant political and economic successes. Its bold decision to go straight from centuries of colonial rule to resolutely democratic government, without a pause, has proved to be sound and sustainable.

After more than sixty years of largely successful democratic governance, India has earned its status as a leading democratic country.

On the economic front, as the country became independent and India has now been able to establish a new position as one of the fastest-growing economies in the world. Table 1.2 presents a summary picture of the growth of the gross domestic product (GDP), from the colonial time to the present.

Table 1.2

Growth Rates of India's GDP at Constant Prices

(% per year)

	GDP	*Per capita GDP*
Colonial period		
1900-1901 to 1946-47	0.9	0.1
Early post-independence period		
1950-51 to 1960-61	3.7	1.8
1960-61 to 1970-71	3.4	1.2
1970-71 to 1980-81	3.4	1.2
Recent Decades		
1980-81 to 1990-91	5.2	3.0
1990-91 to 2000-01	5.9	4.0
2000-01 to 2010-11	7.6	6.0

Sources: Sivasubramonian (2000) and Government of India (2012a); for details, see Chapter 2, Table 2.1.

Growth rate of Indian economy has slackened very recently—partly due to global slump, but India is still—even with its diminished growth rate below 6 per cent per year—is one of the fastest-growing economies in the world. The country's growth potential remains strong and robust and it can be a major source of strength for India—particularly if the fruits of economic growth are well utilised for the advancement of human lives and the development of human freedom and capabilities (Drèze and Sen, 2013).

Along with economic progress, there has also been significant social change. Life expectancy in India today (about 66 years) is more than twice what it was in 1951 (32 years); infant mortality is about one fourth of what it used to be (44 per thousand live births today as opposed to 180 or so in 1951); and the female literacy rate has gone up from 9 per cent to 65 per cent. There have certainly been major improvements in the miserable levels of social indicators that prevailed at the time of India's independence (see Table 1.3). All this is in contrast with the predictions of doom, gloom and famine that were often made about India in the 1950s and 1960s. It is also a substantial political achievement that many of the leaders of democratic politics have tended to come from neglected groups—women, minorities and disadvantaged castes. However, enormous inequalities remain, and many divisions have not diminished at all, but the fact that some significant changes have occurred even in the political arena of hierarchy must be a reason to believe that more—much more—should be possible.

Table 1.3

India: Then and Now

	1951	*2011*
Gross domestic product (GDP) at constant prices (1951=100)	100	1,766
Per capita net national product at constant prices (1950-51=100)	100	511
Estimated life expectancy at birth (years)	32	66
Estimated infant mortality rate (per 1,000 live births)	≈ 180	44
Total fertility rate (children per woman)	5.9	2.4
Literacy rate[a] (%)		
Female	9	65
Male	27	82
Estimated proportion (%) of the population below the poverty line[b]		
Rural	47	22[c]
Urban	35	20[c]

Note: a Age 5 years and above for 1951, 7 years and above for 2011.

b Based on national poverty lines applicable prior to Tendulkar Committee Report (₹ 49 and ₹ 57 per person per month at 1973-74 prices in rural and urban areas, espectively).

c 2004-05

Source: See Statistical Appendix, Table A.5. The fertility rate estimate for 1951 (strictly speaking, 1950-5) is from the United Nations Population Division (2011). In the last row, the 2007-08 figures are from the International Institute for Population Sciences (2010a), Table 2.8, and the 1951 figures are estimated from census data presented in Vaidyanathan (1983), Table 13.3

A Short History of Fast Growth

As already stated, India's GDP preceding independence was mainly stagnant and sometimes declining, even economic growth of 3.5 per cent per annum in the decades immediately following independence was, in fact, a big leap upwards. But the fact remains that 3.5 per cent per year (translating, at that time, into something like 1.5 per cent per year in per capita terms) is painfully slow for the purpose of rapid development and poverty reduction. The modesty of Indian economic growth, which lasted from the 1950s through the 1970s, gave way to considerable quickening in the 1980s, with a higher rate of expansion at 5 per cent per year. And then, following the economic reforms of the early 1990s (led by Manmohan Singh, then Finance Minister and later Prime Minister of India), the economy settled down to faster progress, establishing a new norm of rapid growth, very near the top of the world league. The robustness of high growth in India is undoubtedly connected with the economic reforms of the 1990s, which have built a solid foundation for continuing economic growth. After hovering between 5 and 6 per cent, the growth rate took a further hike upwards to 7 per cent, and then further up, even crossing 9 per cent between 2005 and 2008 for some years. Given India's long-standing income poverty, a phase of fast economic growth was certainly needed, and despite the recent slow-down (which still leaves India as the second fastest-growing large economy in the world), India clearly has made huge progress in this respect.

So where does India stand now after all this? The economic growth rate is, of course, agreeably high (even at its current lower level, after having hovered above 8 per cent for five out of six years from 2005-06 onwards), but the sharing of its benefits is still remarkably unequal, Poverty rates have come down, but not close to what could have been achieved had the distributional side (including the provision of essential services) got more attention. Some failures are huge, like widespread undernourishment in general and child undernutrition in particular—India is among the world's worst performers in this respect (even compared with many countries that are considerably poorer in terms of real GDP per head). Another big failure remains the provision of public health care to the bulk of the population. And there is also the continuing scandal of a quarter of the population (including nearly half the women) remaining effectively illiterate in a country with such high-tech achievements in education based on excellent specialised training and practice. A democratic country can hardly want to become part California and part sub-Saharan Africa (Drèze and Sen, 2013).

Looking ahead, two major problems facing the Indian economy can be summed up as follows: (i) removing the sharp disparities that divide the country into the privileged and the rest, while continuing to encourage overall economic growth and expansion, and (ii) bringing more accountability to the running of the economy, particularly in the delivery of public services and the operation of the public sector (Drèze and Sen, 2013).

The essays that follow in Part I, by Manoj Panda, Pulapre Balakrishnan, Uma Kapila, K. Kanagasabapathy, Vishakha G. Tilak and R. Krishnaswamy, Biswajit Dhar, Simon Deakin and Antara Haldar and Achin Chakraborty, look into the macro story—macro economic policies relating to monetary, fiscal, foreign trade policies, labour laws and their impact on development.

The essays in Part II, contributed by Mahendra Dev, Chandrasekhara Rao, World Bank group and Kapila, are devoted to policies and performance in agriculture, issues relating to growth and productivity, agrarian structure and technology, capital formation, trade, pricing and procurement.

Part III, with contributions from R. Nagaraj, Aditya Bhattacharjea, Nagesh Kumar, K.L. Krishna, Bishwanath Goldar, Balasubramonian, Vijay Kelkar, Dipak Mazumdar and Sandip Sarkar, looks into growth productivity and diversification in industry, privatisation policy, small industry, public sector and foreign investment.

Part IV is devoted to services sector: trends and performance of the key sector in India's economic development.

References

Bettleheim, Charles (1968). *India Independent*. ch.3.

Blyn, G. (1966). *Agricultural Trends in India, 1891-1947*. Philadelphia: Pennsylvania University Press.

Cambridge Economic History of India (CEHI) (1984). Volume 2, Dharma Kumar (ed.). Indian Reprint. Delhi: Orient Longman.

Chandra, Bipin (1979). *Nationalism and Colonialism in Modern India*. Delhi: Orient Longman.

Chandra, Bipin, Mridula Mukerjee and Aditya Mukerjee (1999). *India After Independence*. Viking.

Chaudhuri, P. (1979). *The Indian Economy: Poverty and Development*. Delhi: Vikas Publishing House.

Drèze, Jean and Amartya Sen (2013). *An Uncertain Glory: India and its Contradictions*. Allen Lane: Penguin.

Government of India, Planning Commission, *First Five Year Plan (1951-1956).*

Jalan, Bimal (1992). *The Indian Economy: Problems and Prospects*. New Delhi: Viking. p.8.

Tellis, Ashley J. (2014). "Completing Unfinished Business: From the Long View to the Short", in Bibek Debroy, Ashley J. Tellis and Reece Trevor (eds.), *Getting India Back on Track: An Action Agenda for Reform*. Random House India.

2

PULAPRE BALAKRISHNAN

The Great Reversal

A Macro Story

THE central macroeconomic development in India over the past decade has been the replacement of historically high growth rates by persistently high inflation. Thus, we would find that the period 2003–04 to 2013–14 may be divided into two more or less equal phases—the first, a period of high growth with low inflation, and the second, one of low growth with high inflation. As the reduced volatility that had characterised much of the economies of the Organisation for Economic Co-operation and Development (OECD) for over a decade preceding the global financial crisis has been termed the 'Great Moderation', the development in India may be termed the 'Great Reversal'. Any proposal for a return to high growth and low inflation can only be based on an understanding of what caused this turnaround in the first place. This essay seeks to provide one.

I

The Facts

By 2007–08, the Indian economy had grown at a rate of over 9 per cent per annum for three consecutive years. The last time the growth rate had exceeded the 9 per cent mark was in the late 1980s, and that too in a single year. At that time, it was so unexpected that it did not provide cause for comment. This time though, the repeated outcome had given rise to the expectation in some circles that it was only a matter of

---

I thank Bharat Ramaswami and Chetan Ghate for extensive comments, and Govinda Rao, Gurbachan Singh, Rathin Roy and Arvind Subramanian for discussions. Ashish Aggarwal assisted with the graphics. None is implicated, however.

time before the double-digit growth barrier would be breached. But this did not materialise. In an unexpected reversal we now have a situation in which growth has been trending downwards, and appears to have settled at less than 5 per cent for the past two years. At the same time, midway through the decade, inflation may be seen as having shifted gear forward. Since 2008-09, wholesale price inflation (WPI) has mostly been much higher than in the first half of the decade.

So the principle stylised fact of the past decade is that somewhere in its middle a macroeconomic reversal took place. This would be evident from a viewing of the data on growth and inflation in Table 2.1, and is summarised by the mean values of growth and inflation for each half of the decade presented in Table 2.2. This switch in regimes, so to speak, is graphically reproduced in Figure 2.1 by the trend lines fitted to the annual data. The behaviour of the time series of these variables prompts the following observation. First, the steady decline in growth since 2008-09, except over the period 2009-2011 when it was possibly shored up by the 'Mukherjee Stimulus', suggests something systematic at work. Second, the pattern of slowing growth and rising inflation presents us with the possibility of a third factor driving both.

Table 2.1

Macroeconomic Outcomes: 2003–2013

Year	*Growth (%)*	*Inflation (%)*	*Fiscal Deficit (%)*	*Agriculture Growth (%)*	*Relative Price of Food*	*FDI (₹ bn)*
2003–04	8	5.5	4.3	10.8	100	198.3
2004–05	7.1	6.5	3.9	0.1	96.4	269.47
2005–06	9.5	4.4	4	5.5	97.7	394.57
2006–07	9.6	6.5	3.3	4.1	100.5	1,026.52
2007–08	9.3	4.8	2.5	6.3	102.7	1,394.21
2008–09	6.7	8	6	–0.3	103.7	1,907
2009–10	8.6	3.6	6.5	0.4	115.1	1,578
2010–11	8.9	9.6	4.8	9.5	121.5	1,324
2011-12	6.7	8.8	5.7	5.3	119.6	1548.16
2012-13	4.5	7.4	4.9	0.9	122.5	1465.82

Note: *Inflation* is the rate of change in the wholesale price index; *relative price of food* is an index of the ratio of the wholesale price of food to that of allcommodities computed by the author; fiscal deficit is that of the Centre in relation to GDP; FDI is in billions of rupees.

Sources: *FDI* inflows from Reserve Bank of India: 'Handbook of Statistics on the Indian Economy', Table 155, *www.rbi.org.in,* accessed on 19/4/14 and the rest fromPlanning Commission: Data Tables, Table 5, *www.planningcommision.nic.in/data,* accessed on 27/3/14.

Table 2.2

The Macroeconomic Reversal: A Summary

Variable/Period	*2003–08*	*2008–13*
Growth (%)	8.4	6.7
Inflation (%)	5.5	7.5

Source: Same as Table 2.1

Figure 2.1

The Trend in Growth and Inflation Growth

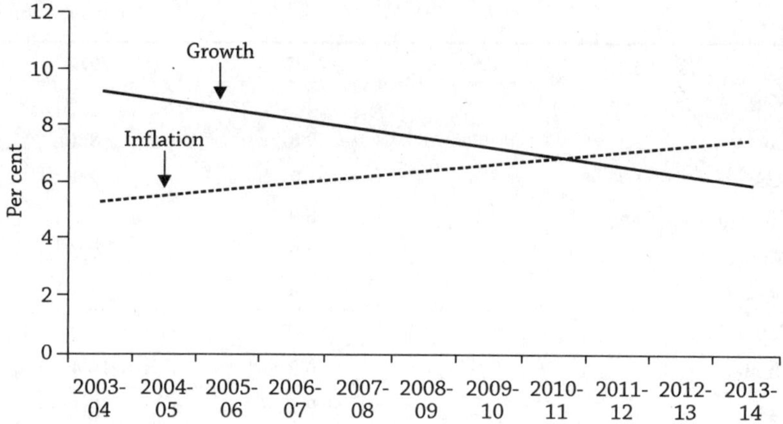

Source: Data presented in Table 2.1.

II

Relevance of Global Factors

It could not have escaped attention that the commencement of the slowing of growth in 2008–09 had followed closely in time the global financial crisis which originated in the United States in 2007–08. However, it also cannot be ruled out that this is merely a coincidence. The experience of the rest of the world over this period may hold out a clue when trying to separate out the impact of the crisis on India's economy. With this in mind, annual data on growth and inflation in India and some selected regions of the world economy are presented in Table 2.3. Comparison can now be made over two points in time, being the year of the onset of the crisis and the most recent year for which comparable data for all countries was available to us at the time of writing. With respect to growth, we find that while growth had declined in all the regions for which data is presented, it has fallen quite dramatically in China and even more so in India. Growth in India has contracted much more than in the rest of the world as a whole and China on its own. This, despite India's share of world trade being lower and the share of exports in its gross domestic product (GDP) being less than in the latter.

Table 2.3

Inflation and Growth: Cross-country Since 2007

(in %)

	2007	*2012*
Growth		
India	9.8	3.2
US	1.7	2.9
Emerging economies	8.9	5.1
China	14.2	7.7
World	5.4	3.2
Inflation		
India	6.2	10.4
US	2.9	2.1
Emerging economies	6.5	6.0
China	4.8	2.7
World	4.1	3.9

Source: Planning Commission; see *www.planningcommision. nic.in/data/database/1203/table_291.pdf* (accessed on 27 March 2014); source cited IMF, World Economic Outlook Database.

With respect to inflation, on the other hand, we find that it has fallen in all parts of the world, including in China, but risen substantially in India. The data suggest the following: Global factors are likely to have had an impact on growth in India, but domestic factors clearly have been at work too. By comparison, the rise in inflation in India must owe largely to factors specific to this country, as it has actually declined elsewhere.

Of course, that growth in India has slowed more than in other countries is not by itself clinching evidence that global factors cannot account for all of the decline. For instance, if following the global financial crisis international investment flows had diverted funds from

India to the rest of the world, then this would have slowed growth in India. The magnitude of the effect would, however, depend on the share of foreign investment in total investment in the country. In consideration of this line of argument, data on investment flows into India have been presented in Table 2.1. Note that the figures are in rupees as that represents the demand injection when the rupee is depreciating. We find that it is only in one year, i.e., 2010–11, following the onset of the global crisis that foreign direct investment (FDI) inflows register a decline. So, a systematic diversion of the existing FDI flows from India to the rest of the world is not evident. However, it is the case that the rate of increase in these inflows declined after 2007–08. Considering the full range of the evidence, while we cannot rule out an external influence in the form of a slower rate of accretion of FDI, given its share in total investment in India this influence is unlikely to have been great. While on the issue of cross-border investment flows, it may be worthwhile to make the following point. It has repeatedly been suggested, especially in the media, that 'policy paralysis' within the central government has led India's corporates to invest outside India. Now, while there certainly has been outward investment from India, its trajectory has actually been strictly downward since the onset of the global slowdown. FDI outflow in 2012–13 was less than half of what it was in 2007–08, when it had peaked.[1] In fact, it has been slowing at an increasing rate. It may then be concluded that while it is not unimportant for India to retain potential investment outflows, this form of capital flight is unlikely to have caused the growth slowdown.

So, if the contribution of external factors to both the growth slowdown and accelerating inflation is unlikely to have been substantial, what could have contributed to these developments? I now turn to an explanation.

III

Accounting for the Regime Change

The regime switch whereby the combination of high growth and low inflation is replaced by its obverse, namely low growth and high inflation attracts the question as to whether in this period inflation and growth could have been jointly determined, possibly by movements in an independent third factor. It is proposed here that agricultural growth could have been such a factor. In Table 2.1 are found data on annual agricultural growth. Two observations may be made on its recent history. First, the latter half of the ten years for which data has been gathered in the table, i.e., the period 2008–09 to 2012–13, commenced with two years of near-zero agricultural growth. Specifically, the first year witnessed negative growth in output, and the second, a barely positive one. Second, this five-year period was also one of fluctuation in agricultural output. Thus, after a smart recovery midway through, the period ended with low growth once again. With such severe fluctuation, one is advised to be circumspect while projecting a measure of average performance.[2] Nevertheless, a comparison between the two halves of the decade in terms of the average annual agricultural growth is yet made. When we go with the mean, we find the following: it is 5.4 per cent for the first period and 3.2 per cent for the second. When we go with the median the difference is accentuated. It is 5.5 per cent for the first period and a mere 0.9 per cent for the second. These statistics indicate a wide swing downward in the average growth of agriculture during the decade. Finally, to attempt another characterisation, there was only one 'bad' year in its first half compared to three in its second. So, howsoever it is viewed, the latter half of the decade is distinctly one of lower agricultural growth.

As agricultural growth may be treated as exogenous in the short run, we may imagine the economy as having faced repeated agricultural supply shocks in this period. There is substantial guidance from theory on what to expect in such situations. For instance, we know from the first set of models developed in the 1970s to understand the macroeconomic impact of the oil shocks of the period that a negative supply shock in the agricultural sector of the economy can, in the presence of real-wage resistance in the non-agricultural sector, give rise to a higher inflation rate (Gordon 1975). We also know from the work of Kaldor (1976) that slow growth of agriculture in relation to the growth of demand for its product generated from the non-agricultural sector of the economy leads to inflation and a slowing of the latter sector. This is precisely what we find has happened[3] in India since 2008–09. Data on industrial production, not presented in the article, show that having steadily declined from 2010–11, it has more or less ground to a halt by now. Of course, it is not necessary that all of this is related to the slower agricultural growth. In fact, we can assert right away that this is unlikely, for the slowdown in industrial growth is too dramatic.

We have so far implicitly focused on the impact on non-agricultural output of a slow-growing demand from surplus farmers who benefit from the rising agricultural prices. However, adverse agricultural production shocks can also impact industrial output growth via the adverse distributional effect it has for the rest of the population. For households whose income growth does not keep pace with the rising price of food, higher expenditure on food must crowd out spending on industrial goods. We cannot over look this possibility at a time when the relative price of food has steadily risen (Table 2.1).

The upshot of the argument so far is that the slower growth and higher inflation economy-wide witnessed are related to the adverse supply shocks in agriculture. Of course, this need not be the whole story and I shall now turn to other factors that matter. Before that, however, the following is worth narrating. If it at all comes as a surprise that agriculture continues to exert such a strong influence in India even as its share is continuously declining, it may be added that in the first seventeen years since 1991 annual changes in the economy-wide growth rate are more closely aligned with changes in the annual rate of change of output in agriculture than in any other sector of the economy (Balakrishnan 2010).

IV

The Role of Macroeconomic Policy

We have considered the likely impact of supply shocks, but what could have been the role of macroeconomic policy? I start with fiscal policy.

As a component of aggregate demand, the fiscal deficit merits attention. However, in this period its role could actually have been no more than passive in a manner to be explained below. Note from Table 2.1 that the deficit is distinctly higher on average since 2008–09, but appears to not have had any success in buoying up growth except briefly. In fact, components of non-agricultural growth that may be expected to be most closely aligned with movements in the fiscal deficit, namely industrial production, have actually slowed.[4] As for inflation, the rising relative price of food (Table 2.1) signals an inflation originating in a sectoral imbalance rather than in an 'inflationary gap' due to excess aggregate demand, for we would expect that the latter would affect all prices equally, thus leaving the relative price unchanged. Year-to-year changes in the inflation rate are more closely related to changes in agricultural output than to the fiscal deficit. This is particularly true in the second half of the decade, when the inflation rate had accelerated. Altogether then, the diagnosis of an 'overheating' economy that was put forth[5] as inflation began to accelerate around 2008–09 appears to be off the mark. In any case, a positive relationship between the fiscal deficit and the inflation rate is fully compatible with a fiscal deficit that is endogenous with respect to inflation. That is, as inflation gathers pace, public expenditure may be expected to rise almost immediately, while tax revenues increase only with a lag. Despite the possibility of the deficit being endogenous with respect to inflation, it can be seen from Table 2.1 that year-on-year movements in the deficit are mostly inversely correlated with inflation after it accelerates in 2008–09, weakening further the case for an inflation driven by the fiscal deficit. However, the question as to why a higher fiscal deficit was unable to shore up the growth rate remains, and we turn to it now.

Once we are made aware of its composition, we would no longer be surprised that the on-average higher fiscal deficit since 2008 has not had the effect of halting the slide in growth. In fact, a change in the composition of the deficit may have actually contributed to the very slide. The one element of macroeconomic policy across the decade that appears quite closely linked to growth is public capital formation. Note from Table 2.4 that public capital formation rose steadily up to 2008–09, and declined more or less continuously since. It is of interest that this decline in capital formation in the public sector took place as the fiscal deficit expanded, that of the centre more than doubling in certain phases (see Table 2.4 and 2.1, respectively). This implies that at this time government expenditure was not financially constrained in the aggregate. This raises the question as to whether the Mukherjee Stimulus that had followed the global financial crisis was motivated by a desire to shore up growth of the economy. Only further research than what has been attempted here can establish whether the government was primarily motivated by wanting to increase consumption, both its own and that of the private sector via subsidies.

Table 2.4
Capital Formation

Year	Capital formation		Public savings
	Public	Private	
2003–04	6.6	18.7	1.3
2004–05	7.4	23.8	2.3
2005–06	7.9	25.2	2.4
2006–07	8.3	26.4	3.6
2007–08	8.9	28.1	5.0
2008–09	9.4	24.8	1.0
2009–10	9.2	25.4	0.2
2010–11	8.4	26.0	2.6
2011–12	7.7	25.9	1.2
2012–13	8.1	23.9	1.2

Source: *Economic Survey 2013–14*, Table 1.6: Gross domestic savings and gross capital formation (as per cent of GDP at current market prices); *www.indiabudget.nic.in/es2013-14/3estat.pdf* (accessed on 13 February 2015).

The decline in public capital formation after 2008–09 suggests that either the government misjudged the drivers of growth, assuming growth would continue regardless of the composition of its own spending, or it cared only to increase consumption in the economy regardless of the consequences. If the latter is true, then the strategy failed to reckon with the constraint that for the economy as a whole consumption cannot continue to grow without contemporaneous growth in income, and that in the absence of productivity growth, income cannot continue to grow faster without raising the level of investment. It is of interest that private capital formation behaved quite differently from the public. While it is on average substantially lower in the second half of the decade, it does not display the more or less steady downward trend that the latter does, having instead fluctuated from year to year. Overall, there is evidence to suggest that the public sector has contributed to the growth reversal by reducing its capital formation after 2008–09. If crowding in prevails, declining public capital formation may have acted as a drag on the private. To emphasise a point already made, the decline in public capital formation took place at a time when the fiscal deficit expanded substantially, suggesting that the government just chose to prioritise consumption expenditure.[6] In Figure 2.2 are plotted the annual movements in growth and public capital formation (as a share of GDP). A public investment cycle that tracks the growth cycle may be noticed. Not all fluctuations are matched, however, but this is to be expected as investment is not the only factor that drives growth in the short run, agricultural supply shocks being particularly relevant. Here it is important to note that while private investment has fluctuated, its trend could have been influenced by growth due to the presence of the accelerator. By comparison we would expect public investment to be relatively autonomous of growth, especially at a time when the fiscal deficit is expanding, thus easing the financing constraint for government.

Figure 2.2

Growth and Public Capital Formation

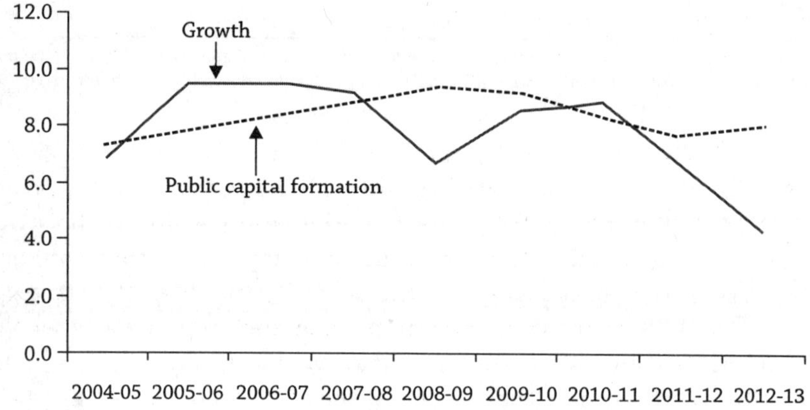

Source: Data presented in Tables 2.1 and 2.4.

V

Inflation Targeting

Though inflation targeting has only recently been brought into the public consciousness by the Reserve Bank of India (RBI), India's central bank has always been known to be concerned about inflation. In fact, we find that this time around it responded with alacrity. Quick on the heels of the second consecutive year of near-zero agricultural growth, the policy (repo) rate was raised in March 2010. Over the next twenty months, it was raised thirteen times in succession. The increase in the policy rate was unable to prevent an acceleration of inflation in 2010–11, after which it has softened somewhat, but yet remains far higher than it was in the first half of the decade. This need not surprise us, as it is only to be expected when an economy is hit by a supply shock. Only, some part of the inflation may be seen as policy-induced though, as the central government has consistently raised the minimum support price (MSP) for cereals. That this had an effect is apparent when we note that, at least in phases, inflation has been led by the price of cereals at a time when stocks of rice and wheat were accumulating with the government. So, while the second United Progressive Alliance government (UPA-II) may have been unlucky with the weather, it has also stoked inflation in an effort to woo the support of the farmers. More research is necessary to establish the precise role of farm-price setting in the recent bout of inflation in India. However, I do not pursue it here, as both the mechanism involved and the facts of the case are well known.[7]

We know from theory (Kaldor 1974) that a 'monetary solution' for inflation caused by a supply shock can lead to output loss. The sector of the economy mostly likely to have been affected by the increases in the policy interest rate—the repo—is manufacturing. The growth of industrial production has steadily contracted from 2010–11 onwards, and has been barely positive in the past two years. While this bears the unmistakable signature of restrictive monetary policy following a supply shock, we cannot be sure as to how much of the impact can be credited to monetary policy. It can be seen from Table 2.4 that contraction of public capital formation, which may be expected to have an even more immediate impact on industrial production than a restrictive monetary policy, had been in place for at least two years by then, and continued apace. As already stated, by 2012–13, annual public capital formation had more than halved. However, some impact of the restrictive monetary policy may be assumed, as we find evidence of a rise in the weighted average lending rate[8] over 2011–12. But, this is not the most interesting thought that should remain with us after having studied the episode. It is that if macroeconomic policy has brought about a decline in the inflation rate by engineering a growth slowdown, then the inflation rate may be expected to rise as growth resumes. Supply-side inflation must be tackled at the source. Aggregate demand management cannot serve as a permanent solution in the context.

A slight diversion may be ventured upon here to make a methodological point relevant to establishing the impact of macroeconomic policy. It is often asserted that when the inflation rate is at least as high as the interest rate so as to leave the real interest rate unchanged, changes in the monetary policy stance cannot be deemed to have been effective. But, things can turn out differently in a dynamic context. We know from Keynes' *General Theory of Employment, Interest and Money* that the potential investor compares the interest rate with the marginal efficiency of capital (which is the internal rate of return). As the marginal efficiency of capital shrinks with slowing growth, interest rate hikes can be contractionary in their impact by inducing a postponement of investment. The recent experience in India is compatible with such an analysis. Moreover, the repeated cries of industry bodies following the interest rate hikes as and when they have occurred suggests that monetary policy has had a role in the growth slowdown.

V

Some Considerations for Near-Term Polilcy

If the revival of growth is going to be on the agenda of the government that will assume office very soon, increasing public capital formation would have to be part of the plan. The decline in public capital formation since the end of high growth in 2007–08 has been steep. But, as may be seen in Table 2.4, so has been the decline in public savings. Therefore any plan for substantially increased capital formation in the public sector would require the government to increase its savings, requiring in turn a combination of increased revenues and reduced expenditure on subsidies. The rationalisation of public food stocks and the elimination of regressive subsidies such as those on diesel would work in the direction of the latter objective. The government also appears to be losing revenue due to the practice of foregoing taxes once levied. This needs to be reviewed. Generally, improved management of the public finances would have to be part of a credible strategy of public sector-led revival of the economy.

Poor agricultural performance over the past five years points to the relevance of agriculture being brought into the centre of public policy. Of course, this would require the use of both macro and micro approaches. The macroeconomic element would, once again, have to revolve around public capital formation. There has been long-term decline in public capital formation as a share of agricultural GDP. In a cross-country comparison, it is low in India. At the same time, however, it is effective governance that will determine whether increased spending will translate into capital assets on the ground.[9] But the question of food production is important. Note that the relative price of food has increased by over 20 per cent over the past decade. This is unusual for an economy that embarked on a developmental strategy over sixty years ago. As pointed out, this is at least partially the result of government intervention in the grain markets. But, there is agricultural production beyond foodgrains, and this component has been ignored in public policy. The consequence has been that the production of food, such as milk and vegetables, has lagged behind the growth of demand and contributed to inflation. It is not known widely enough that public capital formation in agriculture has been on a downward path for over two decades, and by 2010 had collapsed to less than a third of its level in 1993.[10] It can hardly come as a surprise then that agricultural growth is less than satisfactory. So long as this situation continues, agricultural production is likely to remain an important factor determining growth and inflation in the economy.

There has been little discussion of the external sector in this essay beyond arguing that external developments have very likely had less to do with the slowing growth and rising inflation of the past five years. This is not to downgrade the importance of trade for the economy. Properly approached trade can be a source of export earnings and, thus, growth. However, macroeconomic reforms may have run their course here. The best, and the most, the government can do is to improve the infrastructure related to the supply chain for exports. Poor infrastructure leaves Indian firms uncompetitive globally. On the other hand, the government's approach to trade appears somewhat simple-minded. It celebrates 'openness' per se, but we can see that openness by itself provides no solution in the present situation.[11] However, an aspect of the UPA-II government's recent management of the external sector deserves praise. Faced with a surging current account deficit in mid-2013, the Ministry of Finance responded immediately with a rising import duty on gold. The effect has been almost immediate, with a drastic lowering of the trade deficit and thereby containment of the current account itself.[12] This, despite only a mild increase in the duty rate.

The government's action has come in the face of criticism from quarters that decry intervention of any kind in the economy. Actually, the UPA-II government needs to be congratulated for taking an entirely practical approach here, one that has worked. It must now follow up this action by reflecting on the consequence for macroeconomic stability of subsidising imported oil and gas. Macroeconomic instability affects the poor severely when the contraction comes, even though they may not have gained that much from the subsidies to start with. As for the importance of resorting to direct intervention when required, it may be recollected that when the country was faced with a balance of payments crisis in 1991, it was the swift resort to import compression by the RBI that saved the day as we had waited for the more *kosher* International Monetary Fund-sponsored macroeconomic stabilisation programme to work its way through. Similarly, in mid-2014, when fresh macroeconomic options will be considered, policy must be guided by a concern for outcomes. Thus, while it is true that import controls introduce an incentive for smuggling, this is not a reason to avoid them when absolutely essential. The prevention of smuggling requires improved surveillance and exemplary punishment of offenders. In the case of the duty on gold, smuggling may well have increased, but the fact of the rupee having held its own, when it has not actually appreciated, suggests that smuggling is not occurring on a scale large enough to put pressure on the balance of payments and thus weaken the rupee. Short-term measures could have high value in extraordinary situations without being valid in all situations. Thus, the only long-term solution to the current account deficit is to increase exports. Here, the reach of macroeconomic policy is limited.

Notes

1. The source is the same as that cited for FDI inflow in Table 2.1. The flows were measured in USD, however.
2. This was considered to be less of a problem in the exercise underlying the figures in Table 2.2 as both GDP growth and inflation have fluctuated less than has agricultural production, notably since 2008.
3. For econometric evidence on the presence of this relationship in India, see Balakrishnan (1991).
4. See the industrial growth data at *http://mospi.nic.in/Mospi_New/upload/iip/IIP_main htm?status=1&menu* (accessed on 24 September 2014).
5. See Goyal (2013) where this account by the International Monetary Fund (IMF) is contested by the author on grounds of declining manufacturing growth. We might add that the fiscal deficit been contracting while inflation accelerated, casting doubt on the 'overheating' hypothesis.

6. It is important to note that the capital formation under scrutiny here is of the entire public sector—that is inclusive of the public enterprises—and not just of the government. Therefore it would not be appropriate to conclude that the reduced public capital formation is directly related to increased spending on the welfare programmes introduced under UPA-II. For evidence that spending on the MGNREGS, the government's flagship welfare programme, though substantial had peaked by 2009–10, see Himanshu *et al.* (2014). However, it would be correct to say that the UPA-II was less engaged with capital formation than UPA-I. For evidence on high public investment in infrastructure under UPA-I and its virtual collapse under UPA-II, see Balakrishnan and Parameswaran (2013). It is very likely the increased government expenditure showing up as a rising fiscal deficit was due to the food, fertiliser and oil subsidies.
7. For data on the increase in minimum support prices for foodgrains in recent years, see Singh (2014).
8. For statistical tables relating to banks in India, see *http://rbi.org.in/scripts/AnnualPublications* (accessed on 16 April 2014). Here it is worth noting, however, the view of some of India's leading commercial bankers that the connection between the base (lending) rate and the repo is tenuous as the former depends upon the deposit rate. Thus when there is competition for deposits, the lending rate will rise irrespective of what happens to the repo. (See The Hindu. 2013. 'Lending Rate Hinges on Deposits and Not on Repo Rate: Chaudhuri', an interview with Pratip Chaudhuri, Chairman, State Bank of India. Thiruvananthapuram edition. 1 October.) If Chaudhuri is right, then observing a rise in the lending rate following a rise in the repo rate cannot by itself constitute clinching evidence of the transmission having taken place.
9. See Balakrishnan et al. (2008) for evidence on how substantially increased spending on irrigation has not translated into commensurate expansion of area irrigated.
10. See Planning Commission. 'Gross Capital Formation in Agriculture and Allied Sectors', Data Table 9. *www.pc.gov.in/data/datable* (accessed on 16 April 2014).
11. See the entry in the Economic Survey 2011–12, p. 4, that following the reforms of 1991 trade has come to account for over 50 per cent of India's GDP. It is interesting to note that this had appeared at a time when inflation was close to double-digits and manufacturing growth was slowing quite dramatically.
12. The magnitude of the decrease is worth noting. In the first nine months of 2013–14, the current account deficit stood at 2.3 per cent of GDP, down from 5.2 per cent for the same period in the previous year. See, *The Hindustan Times*. 2014. 'CAD Narrows to $4.2bn in Q3'. New Delhi edition. 6 March.

References

Balakrishnan, P. (1991). *Pricing and Inflation in India*. New Delhi: Oxford University Press.

———. (2010). *Economic Growth in India: History and Prospect*. New Delhi: Oxford University Press.

Balakrishnan, P., R. Golait and P. Kumar (2008). "Agricultural Growth in India since 1991". DRG Study no. 27. Mumbai: Reserve Bank of India.

Balakrishnan, P., and M. Parameswaran (2013). "The Mechanism of Economic Growth in India". Unpublished paper. Thiruvananthapuram: Centre for Development Studies.

Gordon, R.J. (1975). "Alternative Responses of Policy to External Supply Shocks". *Brookings Papers on Economic Activity* 6: 183–206.

Goyal, A. (2013). "Propagation Mechanisms in Inflation: Governance as Key", in S. Mahendra Dev (ed.), *India Development Report 2012–13*. New Delhi: Oxford University Press and IGIDR.

Himanshu, A. Mukhopadhyay, and M.R. Sharan (2014). "The National Rural Employment Guarantee Scheme in Rajasthan: Rationed Funds and Their Allocation across Villages". Unpublished paper. New Delhi: Indian Statistical Institute.

Kaldor, N. (1974). "The Role of Industrialisation in Latin American Inflations", in D.T. Geithman (ed.), *Fiscal Policy for Industrialisation and Development in Latin America*. Tampa: University of Florida Press.

———. (1976). "Inflation and Recession in the World Economy", *Economic Journal* 86: 703–14.

Singh, G. (2014). "Inflation Targeting in India: Right and Wrong". *http://ideasforindia.in/article.aspx?article_id= 248* (accessed on 23 April 2014).

This essay is a slightly different version of author's EPW article May 24, 2014.

3

MANOJ PANDA

Macroeconomic Developments and Challenges for Growth

Introduction

The overall macroeconomic picture in India has not been bright since 2011. After a phase of high growth that lasted over 2003 to 2010, the Indian economy has grown consecutively for 3 years at a rate lower than its long term average over last 4 decades. The aspirations of various sections of the population for a better level of living has risen considerably, partly due to the high growth phase. But, the performance of the economy has been disappointing to many due to slowdown in income growth coupled with erosion of purchasing power due to high inflation, particularly those of food items. Adequate and proper diet for its entire billion plus population is a major challenge before the nation. Major initiatives have been taken to improve the welfare of the weaker sections of the population, though other means of reaching the poor more efficiently is being debated. The government needs fiscal space for incurring priority expenditure. Policy choices also need to take into consideration the regulatory activism noticed in recent years. India needs to be prepared to take advantage of the emerging global trade scenarios. Macroeconomic management against this backdrop has been a challenging one. The new government, which is elected on a development agenda, must focus on innovative strategies to put the economy back on a sustainable and inclusive growth trajectory.

After the global economic crisis in 2008, the world economy witnessed subdued growth for several years, it now seems to have

The author is thankful to Aaditya Sharma for updating the database and help in preparation of tables and figures.

recovered and expected to grow at about 3.5 per cent in 2014 and world trade is likely to grow by above 4.5 per cent. While better external demand for emerging economies such as India would help growth, big ticket reforms would be needed to take full advantage of the recovery. Moreover, international situation continues to remain vulnerable. The modest recovery in the Eurozone has been accompanied by fear of a deflationary situation.

India's GDP[1] in US dollar terms stood at close to 2 trillion in 2013. Given its population of above 1.2 billion, India's average level of living is the lowest when compared to other BRICS countries. Its per capita income at US$ 1600 was just a quarter of that of China or South Africa and way below that of Russia or Brazil. When adjusted for purchasing power parity (PPP)[2], India's per capita income is about PPP$4000, but the relative ranking of India among BRICS remains the same. A GDP growth rate of about 7-8 per cent per year would be required to meet aspirations of Indians for a better level of living over the next three decades. In order to meet this, policy design in India must be guided by such a long term goal for the economy. Against this backdrop, this chapter attempts a review of recent macroeconomic developments and discusses some policy issues from the point of view of medium term prospects. Section II below documents the major developments in the economy in recent years. Possible policy agenda for recovery of growth trajectory is discussed in section III followed by concluding remarks in Section IV.

Macroeconomic Developments

GDP Growth

Figure 3.1 depicts the exponential trend growth rate in GDP for each of the last two decades. Despite the slowdown since 2011-12, the economy clearly witnessed a higher trend growth rate of 7.5 per cent in national income during the decade 2004-05 to 2013-14 compared to 5.8 per cent during the previous decade. But, on a 5-yearly basis, average growth rate dropped to 6.7 per cent during 2009-10 to 2013-2014 from 8.4 per cent during 2004-05 to 2008-09 (Figure 3.2). This drop was primarily driven by the industrial sector whose growth fell by as much as 4 percentage points to 5.2 per cent. Services growth fell by less than 2 percentage points to 8.1 per cent. The current pessimism is on account of the fact that GDP has grown at sub-5 per cent for two consecutive years. In particular, the industrial sector, which has hardly grown in the last two years, has been a major concern.

Figure 3.1

Trend Growth Rate in Real GDP

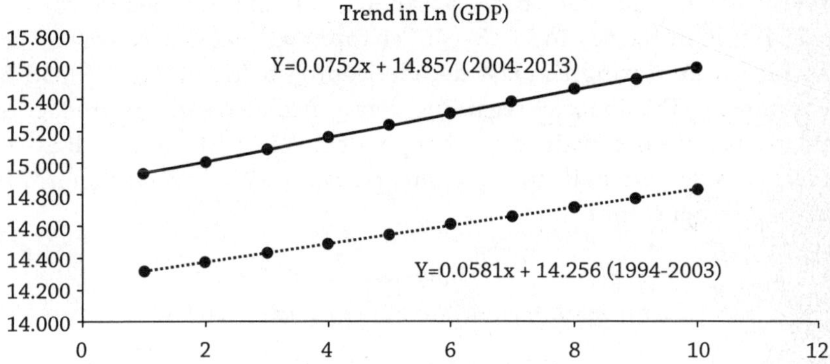

Figure 3.2

5-Yearly Average Growth by Sectors during 1994-2013

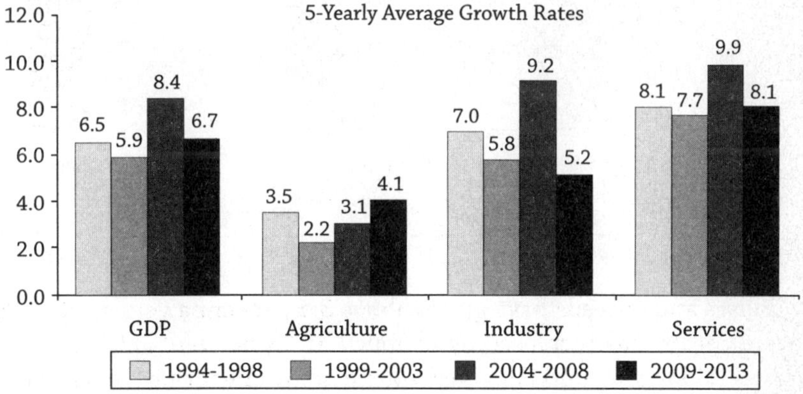

Agriculture

Agriculture recorded 1.4 per cent growth in 2012-13 and picked up to 4.7 per cent in 2013-14. Indeed, one satisfactory point to note in the otherwise gloomy picture is that agricultural value added growth improved to reach above 4 per cent during the last 5 years, the highest on a 5-yearly average basis since 1994 (Figure 3.2). Similar achievement, if continued, could help in relaxing supply constraint in agriculture and help in restoring sectoral balances.

Composition of agricultural production is changing in favour of non-grain crops (Figure 3.3). Food grain production has continued to grow at above 2 per cent per year from 108 million tonnes in 1970-71 to 264 million tonnes in 2013-14. Per capita availability of cereals has not picked up during the last decade leading to rising stocks held by government. This 'puzzle' regarding divergence of trends in production and availability is explained by changing demand pattern as well as the incentive structure built in the grains trade intervention mechanism by the government.

Figure 3.3

Growth in Agricultural Production Index

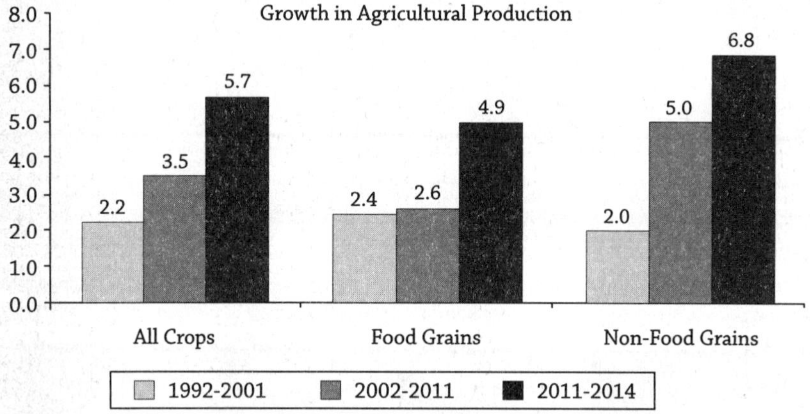

Pulses and oilseeds have grown above 3.5 per cent a year since 2000-01 and cotton has increased by as much as 13 per cent. Livestock has been an important supplementary source of income for farmers in India. Dominated by small farmers and women workforce, livestock sector is more equitable in its income distribution impact. Horticulture has emerged as an important component of crop cultivation in recent time. Agricultural investment had fallen during 1990s, but has improved in recent years to above 20 per cent of agricultural GDP.

Indian agriculture is marked by transformation from dependence on food imports to a net exporter of grains over the years, thanks to the success of green revolution initiated during late 1960s. Rural economic landscape has drastically changed after independence in all parts of the country except some remote areas. Non-agriculture has been a significant source of rural income. Yet, agriculture cannot be neglected for: (a) ensuring a decent level of living to the rural population most of whom are still primarily engaged in agriculture, (b) meeting the changing domestic demand pattern for food and agro-based products, and (c) managing food inflation. While India has largely succeeded in its fight against incidence of hunger, malnutrition continues to be widespread. Since scope for cultivable area expansion is very limited, agricultural growth largely depends on increase in yield. Investment on irrigation and adoption of technology has helped to raise yield and to reduce volatility arising from variations in weather over the last half a century. But, the slow agricultural growth in recent decades has been a matter of major concern. The acceleration recorded in last 5 years will not be sustainable without improvement in land and labour efficiency.[3]

Industry

Industrial sector performed fairly well during 2002-2007 registering a value added growth rate of above 9 per cent per annum. It fell to 4.4 per cent in 2008-09 in the wake of the global financial crisis, but recovered quickly in 2009-10 and grew between 7.6 per cent and 9.2 per cent over the next 3 years. Against this, the growth of industrial value added below 1 per cent for 2 years in succession during 2012-13 and 2013-14 has been a matter of concern. Indeed, such a situation occurred for the first time in several decades (Figure 3.4).

The fall in industrial growth since 2012-13 has been primarily due to mining and manufacturing components (Figure 3.5). Electricity and construction showed moderate growth. The fall in manufacturing in the last two years was widespread across most of its subsectors. Use-based classification of manufacturing data reveals that capital goods and consumer durables have been hard hit with negative growth, while basic goods and intermediates have recorded positive but low growth of 1.5-3.1 per cent (Table 3.1). The weak industrial performance has been due to a combination of several factors. Investment sentiments were hard hit during 2012-13 and 2013-14 due to policy uncertainties and high interest rate. Steady deceleration of investment is due to

Figure 3.4

Annual Growth in Industrial Value Added

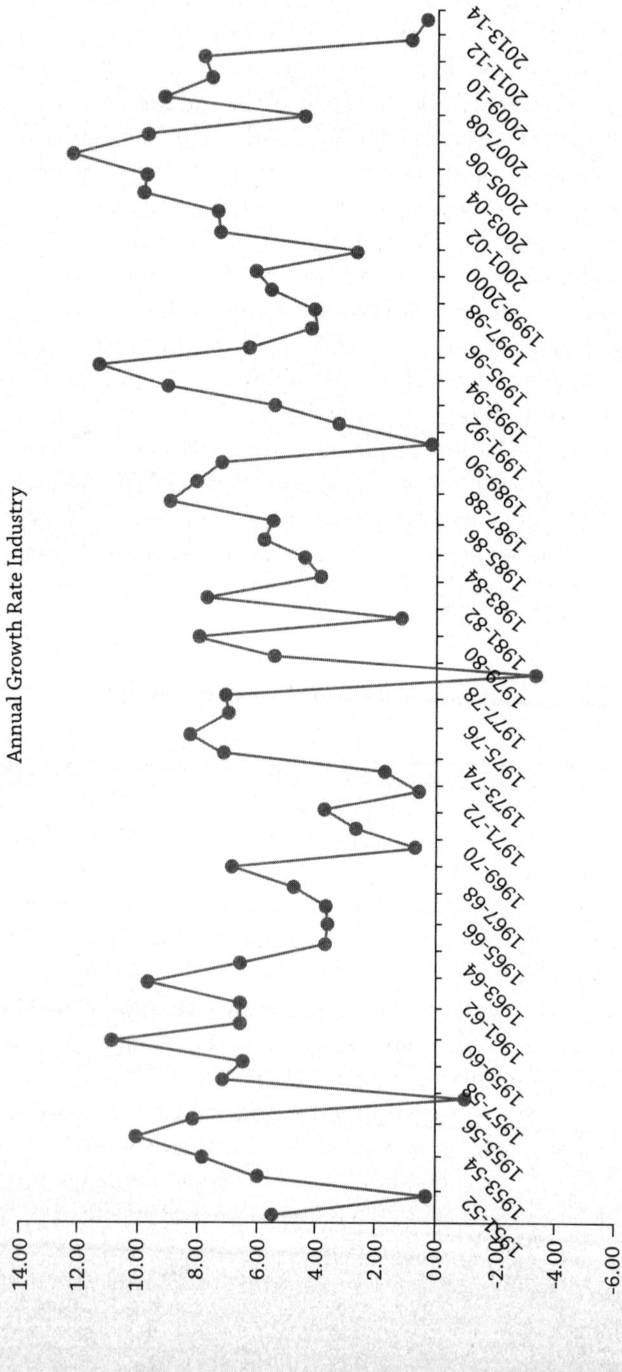

slow progress in completion of ongoing projects and drop in new investment. Negative growth in production of consumer durables reflects fall in domestic household demand and failure to take advantage of revival of global market for consumer durables. Other factors include infrastructure bottlenecks, rising input cost, and restrictive imports (e.g. gold needed for gems and jewellery exports). Within industry, several subsectors like coal, steel, cement and refinery production, and road construction sectors recorded lower growth. Corporate sector's earning and profitability remained weak, while debt rose putting stress on the banking sector's non-performing assets. Responding to the changing demand pattern, the small and medium enterprises (SMEs) have consistently been performing well with above 10 per cent growth. SMEs play an important role in generating non-agricultural jobs in a situation of limited employment opportunities created by their large counterparts.

Figure 3.5

Annual Growth in Index Number of Industrial Production

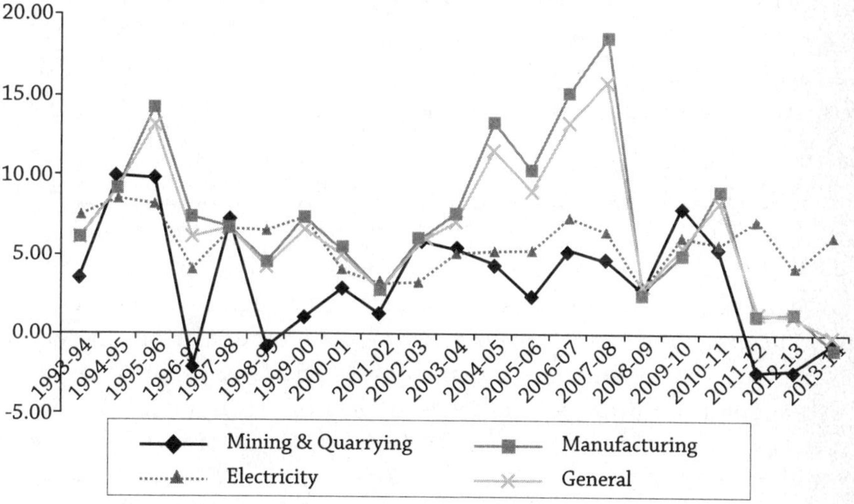

Lack of clarity regarding policies governing production and allocation of natural resources such as iron ore, coal and natural gas affected supply of steel, refinery and power. Mineral based sectors such as steel, aluminium, and thermal electricity are facing problems in receiving adequate supply of raw material due to inordinate delays in environmental clearance. Iron ore and coal mining volume declined following stay order by court on mining activities in some areas due to possibility of corruption and lack of clearly spelt out regulatory provisions. Natural gas production in KG-6 basin fell due to delay in pricing decision.

Table 3.1

Annual Growth Rate in Index Number of Industrial Production by Use-Based Classification

	Basic Goods	*Capital Goods*	*Intermediates*	*Consumer Goods*	*Consumer Durables*	*Consumer Non-durables*
2001-02	2.7	-3.4	1.6	6.0	11.5	4.1
2002-03	4.8	10.5	3.9	7.1	-6.3	12.0
2003-04	5.5	13.6	6.4	7.2	11.6	5.8
2004-05	5.5	13.9	6.1	11.7	14.3	10.8
2005-06	6.7	15.7	2.5	12.0	15.3	10.9
2006-07	10.3	18.3	11.9	10.1	9.1	10.5
2007-08	7.0	18.0	9.0	6.0	-1.0	8.5
2008-09	2.6	6.9	-1.9	4.7	4.5	4.8
2009-10	7.2	39.6	18.4	9.0	28.7	2.8
2010-11	6.3	9.5	8.9	7.5	21.0	2.2
2011-12	19.9	-5.0	-8.6	8.0	2.3	-3.2
2012-13	2.9	-9.2	1.2	1.9	0.7	2.1
2013-14	1.5	1.3	2.6	-1.0	-9.6	12.1

Services

The service sector consists of activities such as trade, hotels, restaurants, tourism, transport, storage, communication, banking, insurance, business services, real estate, social and personal service, public administration and defence. It has been the major driver of economic growth in India since early 1970s[4] with its share in GDP rising from 38 per cent in early 1970-71 to 57 per cent in 2013-14. The service sector in India employs 28 per cent of the labour force and accounts for about 5 per cent of world trade in services. Trade, transport, tourism and personal services contribute substantially to employment generation, while software development has been a major exporting sector during the last two decades. Being the fastest growing segment of the economy, this sector also attracts substantial foreign investment, particularly in the high technology segment. Subsectors like banking, insurance, real estate, and business services have continued to perform well in recent years, while trade, hotel and restaurant, and transport recorded deceleration.

Over the years, the subsector 'banking, insurance and business services' has emerged as the largest segment within the service sector and its contribution to GDP has risen from below 10 per cent in 1985-1986 to 20 per cent in 2013-14. This is followed by 'trade, hotel and restaurant' and 'community, social and personal services' in terms of contribution to GDP. Business services, which include information technology and information technology enabled services (IT-ITES), have recorded steady growth even after the global crisis contributing to above 5 per cent of GDP and creating large volume of jobs for skilled and semi-skilled man power.

Table 3.2

Annual Growth in India's Services GDP at Factor Cost

	Annual Growth in Services GDP (%)				
Sector	*2009-10*	*2010-11*	*2011-12*	*2012-13*	*2013-14*
Trade Hotels and Restaurants	7.8	9.0	1.2	4.5	3.0
Transport, storage and Communication	14.8	14.7	9.4	6.0	6.1
Financing, insurance, Real estate and Business Services	9.4	10.4	16.5	10.9	12.9
Community, Social, and Personal Services	12.0	4.5	4.9	5.3	5.3
Construction	7.0	8.0	10.8	1.1	1.6
Total services (excluding constructions)	10.5	9.3	6.6	6.9	6.8
Total services (including constructions)	10.0	9.2	7.1	6.2	6.2
Total GDP	8.4	8.4	6.7	4.5	4.7

Source: Reserve Bank of India, Handbook of Statistics, 2014.

India has witnessed a communication revolution during the last two decades when the sector posted an average growth rate of 20 per cent. Although communication has a small direct contribution to GDP, development of a quick and effective communication system has a very significant impact on the society and livelihood of the people in different parts of the country.

Indian ships carry out an increasingly smaller portion of the country's imports and exports cargo. This share has declined from 40 per cent three decades ago to below 10 per cent in recent years. This trend can be reversed to increase the share substantially and save foreign exchange.

Savings and Investments

The gross domestic savings rate varied in the narrow range of 22 per cent and 25 per cent of GDP during the 1990s, but posted a steady rise after 2001-02 reaching a peak of 36.8 per cent in 2007-08 (Table 3.3). A rise in domestic savings rate by 11 percentage points over 7 years was viewed as a major structural change in the economy similar to that witnessed in several East Asian economies that experienced high growth. But, savings dropped after the global crisis, though it remained above 30 per cent. All three components of savings—household, corporate and government—contributed to the decline in total savings rate. Public sector savings[5] have contributed the most to the drop in aggregate savings. It fell from 5 per cent of GDP in 2007-08 to just above 1 per cent in 2012-13 due to reduced savings of public enterprises and higher growth of expenditure relative to revenue. Corporate savings fell due to low growth and lower profit margins of the stagnant industrial sector. Household savings rose to 25 per cent of GDP in 2009-10 but fell thereafter to stabilise around 22 per cent. Household financial savings, which grew over the 1990s and 2000s and overtook physical savings for a few years, has dropped to a third of the total household savings. There is thus a compositional shift in household savings from financial to physical savings in recent years.

Movement in capital formation rate has closely followed the total domestic savings rate. It has stayed above the domestic savings by 2-4 percentage points of GDP indicating dependence on foreign savings or net capital flows. Investment rate has remained above 30 per cent during the last decade with a peak at 38 per cent in 2007-08. Fixed investment, the most important component in capital formation, too rose to 33 per cent in 2007-08, but fell thereafter to 28 per cent in 2013-14, a level similar to 2004-05. As Figure 3.6 shows, it is the investment component in final demand that absorbed most of the real demand shock in India during slow down phase. It fell substantially during 2008-09 following the global crisis, recovered partially over the next 3 years, but has witnessed virtually zero growth during the last two years constraining new capacity creation in the production process.

Figure 3.6

Growth in Capital Formation and Final Consumption Expenditure

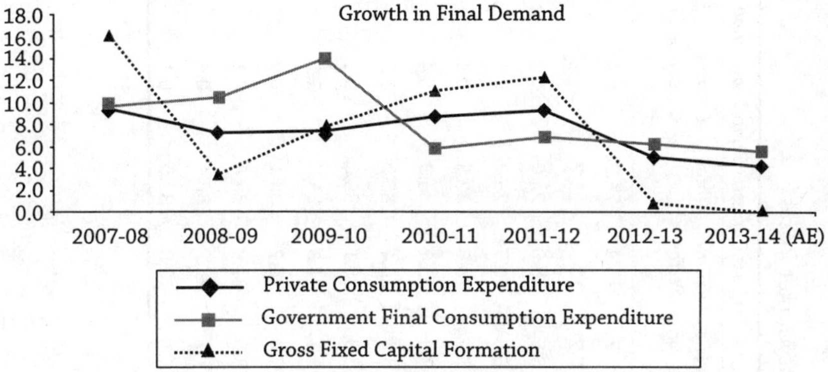

Public sector investment rose by 0.5 per cent in 2008-09 due to expansionary fiscal policy, but declined for the next 3 years in succession and rose marginally in 2012-13. Private sector investment, on the other hand, has remained lower by 3-4 per cent of GDP since 2008-09 when it reached 28 per cent. Investment sentiment deteriorated due to a host of factors such as regulatory barriers, land acquisition problems, cost of credit, uncertain policies, consumer demand decline, and lower business expectations about revival. Restoration of the investment rate would be an important factor in the long term revival of the economy along with productivity rise. The recently prepared report (RBI, 2014) on the total factor productivity (TFP) growth reports that the Indian economy improved its TFP growth rate from 1.1 per cent during 1980-1999 to 2.3 per cent during 2000-2008 led by manufacturing, electricity and services sectors. The findings reconfirm the role of input accumulation as well as productivity growth in explaining GDP growth in India.[6]

Fiscal Developments

The combined expenditure of the Central and state governments rose by about 2 per cent of GDP in 2008-09 from 26.3 per cent in 2007-2008 (Table 3.4) and stayed above that level in the next 2 years due to the expansionary fiscal policy followed by the government to overcome the global crisis. The Central government accounts for a little more than half of the combined Central and state government expenditures and the states together the rest. The government also provided substantial tax

Table 3.3

Savings and Capital Formation (As % of GDP at Current Market Prices)

Year	Gross Domestic Savings				Gross Fixed Capital Formation			Gross Domestic Capital Formation				
	House-hold Sector	Private Corporate Sector	Public Sector	Total Savings	Public Sector	Private Sector	Total	Public Sector	Private Sector	Total	Errors and Omissions	Adjusted Total
2000-01	21.4	3.7	-1.3	23.8	6.7	16.1	22.8	7.2	16.4	24.2	0.1	24.4
2001-02	23.2	3.3	-1.6	24.9	6.8	18.3	25.1	7.2	17.8	25.7	-1.3	24.3
2002-03	22.3	3.9	-0.3	25.9	6.6	17.1	23.8	6.5	18.0	25.0	-0.2	24.8
2003-04	23.2	4.6	1.3	29.0	6.7	17.9	24.6	6.6	18.7	26.2	0.7	26.9
2004-05	23.6	6.6	2.3	32.4	6.9	21.8	28.7	7.4	23.8	32.5	0.4	32.8
2005-06	23.5	7.5	2.4	33.4	7.3	23.0	30.3	7.9	25.2	34.3	0.4	34.7
2006-07	23.2	7.9	3.6	34.6	7.9	23.4	31.3	8.3	26.4	35.9	-0.2	35.7
2007-08	22.4	9.4	5.0	36.8	8.0	24.9	32.9	8.9	28.1	38.0	0.1	38.1
2008-09	23.6	7.4	1.0	32.0	8.5	23.8	32.3	9.4	24.8	35.5	-1.2	34.3
2009-10	25.2	8.4	0.2	33.7	8.4	23.3	31.7	9.2	25.2	36.1	0.2	36.5
2010-11	23.5	7.9	2.6	34.0	7.8	24.0	31.7	8.8	24.9	35.8	-0.1	36.8
2011-12	22.3	7.2	1.3	30.8	7.1	24.7	31.8	7.7	28.7	36.4	-0.4	35.0
2012-13	21.9	7.1	1.2	30.1	7.8	22.6	30.4	8.1	23.9	32.0	0.1	34.8

Source: *Economic Survey*.

Table 3.4

Receipts and Disbursements of Consolidated General Government

(as % of GDP)

	1990-91	2000-01	2006-07	2007-08	2008-09	2009-10	2010-11	2011-12	2012-13	2013-14 (BE)
Total Receipts	26.8	28.7	26.2	26.7	27.8	28.5	27.6	27.2	27.8	28.5
Revenue Receipts	18.6	18.1	20.4	21.3	19.8	18.7	20.3	18.8	20.2	20.9
Tax Receipts	15.4	14.6	16.9	17.6	16.5	15.2	16	16.0	16.8	17.6
Non-Tax Receipts	3.2	3.5	3.6	3.7	3.4	3.5	4.2	2.8	3.4	3.3
Capital Receipts	8.2	10.5	5.8	5.4	8.0	9.8	7.4	8.5	7.6	7.5
Disinvestment proceeds	0.0	0.1	0.1	0.9	0.0	0.4	0.3	0.2	0.2	0.5
Recovery of Loans & advances	0.6	0.5	0.0	0.1	0.3	0.2	0.1	0.3	0.2	0.1
Total Disbursements	28.8	28.5	25.8	26.4	28.4	28.6	27.5	26.9	28.1	28.4
Revenue Disbursements	22.8	24.8	21.7	21.5	24.1	24.4	23.5	22.9	23.9	23.9
Capital Disbursements	3.9	2.9	3.7	4.5	3.9	3.8	3.4	3.2	3.5	4.2
Loans and Advances	2.0	0.9	0.4	0.4	0.4	0.4	0.6	0.7	0.6	0.4
Revenue Deficit	4.2	6.6	1.3	0.2	4.3	5.7	3.2	4.1	3.7	2.9
Gross Fiscal Deficit	9.4	9.6	5.4	4.1	8.3	9.3	6.9	7.6	7.4	6.9

Source: Economic Survey, 2013-14, Ministry of Finance, Government of India.

relief to encourage private consumption expenditure. These measures meant that fiscal deficit as a percentage of GDP, which had come down to 4.1 per cent in 2007-08 due to adoption of FRBM, more than doubled to 8.3 per cent in 2008-09 and rose further to 9.3 per cent in 2009-2010 (Table 3.4). The extent of fiscal imbalance after the global crisis was similar to that prevailed during the 1991 crisis. The fear was that continued high level of fiscal imbalance may get reflected in a balance of payments crisis in an open macro economy environment. Fiscal consolidation measures resumed subsequently brought down the deficit figures in a gradual manner to reach 4.5 per cent in 2013-14. Since scope for tax revenue increase was limited due to growth slowdown, the burden of the consolidation process fell mostly on government expenditure. Composition of government expenditure shifted away from capital expenditure.

Subsidy by central government has risen considerably from 1.4 per cent of GDP in 2007-08 to about 2.5 per cent recently. Petroleum and fertiliser subsidies have remained high despite partial decontrol of their prices. Food subsidy which has gone up sharply due to rising difference in procurement price by the Food Corporation of India (FCI) and issue price in public distribution system (PDS). While the subsidies were introduced over time to meet certain social welfare objectives, a major concern has been on the large leakages in the delivery system, often amounting to half or more of the subsidy amount. The recently introduced food subsidy bill is expected to further add to the subsidy bill.

Fiscal deficit creates debt liability for the government. While the accumulated debt liability has been rising in volume, it has fallen as a percentage of GDP because nominal GDP has been rising faster than nominal interest rate. Both real growth and inflation are contributing factors in reducing the debt burden.

Foreign Trade

The foreign trade regime witnessed historic changes after the reforms in the 1990s and played significant role in bringing about structural changes in the Indian economy. Expansion of trade volume and capital flows have been the major drivers of enhancing growth and efficiency during the last two decades. India's exports witnessed a 16-fold rise in between 1990 and 2013 when it reached US$ 312 billion. Yet, India is a small player in the world merchandise trade transactions and Indian exports accounted for only 1.7 per cent of world exports. Imports too grew 18-fold from 24 billion in 1990-91 to 450 billion in 2013-14. Merchandise trade accounted for 42 per cent of India's GDP in 2013-14, imports 25 per cent and exports 17 per cent (Table 3.5).

Indian merchandise exports and imports grew by an average rate of 30 per cent in 2010-11 and 2011-12 indicating recovery of trade after the global crisis. But, the recovery did not last long and exports contracted by 1.8 per cent in absolute terms in 2011-12 and grew only moderately by 4.1 per cent in 2013-14. Merchandise imports grew by about 30 per cent in 2010-11 and 2011-12 leading to a big jump in trade balance. Corrective measures taken by the RBI helped to contain imports growth to 0.3 per cent in 2012-13 and to contract by 8.3 per cent in 2013-14. It is noteworthy that petroleum products have emerged as the most important exports category in recent years with a share of 20 per cent in total exports followed by gems and jewellery with share of 13 per cent. Engineering goods, pharmaceuticals and chemicals are other major items in the exports basket. The import basket is dominated by petroleum, oil and lubricants (POL) accounting for a third of the total imports followed by capital goods, gold, electronic goods and chemicals.

One structural feature of Indian trade is that while our exports fall with contraction in global trade, imports remain relatively stable due to essential nature of certain imports like crude oil. This generated large volume of trade deficit going above 10 per cent of GDP in 2012-13. Despite global slowdown, software exports continued to rise and reached US$ 67 billion in 2013-14. Total surplus on invisible transactions amounting to 5-6 per cent of GDP has been a major source of financing of trade deficit. But, the jump in trade deficit to 10 per cent and current account deficit (CAD) to 4.7 per cent of GDP in 2012-13 in the wake of the Euro zone crisis raised serious concern about stability of the foreign exchange market. Several measures were taken to curb non-essential imports such as gold and encourage capital flows helping trade deficit to fall below 8 per cent of GDP in 2013-14. CAD improved from US$ 88 billion in 2012-13 to US$ 32 billion (1.7 per cent of GDP) in 2013-14, a level well within net capital flows of US$ 48 billion during the year.

Foreign exchange reserves of India had reached $309 billion by end of 2007-08. It dropped by US$ 57 billion in 2008-09 due to the global crisis, but recovered slowly later to fluctuate between US$ 290 and 300 billion in recent years. The reserves are currently adequate to provide imports cover of about 8 months as against above one year before the global crisis. This fall in reserves relative to imports in an uncertain

Table 3.5

Major Balance of Payment Parameters

(%)

	2013-14	2012-13	2011-12	2010-11	2009-10	2008-09	2007-08	2006-07	2000-01	1990-91
Exports/GDP	17.0	16.5	16.5	15.0	13.4	15.4	13.4	13.6	9.9	5.8
Imports/GDP	24.8	27.0	26.6	22.4	22.0	25.2	20.8	20.1	12.6	8.8
Receipts/GDP	12.4	12.1	11.7	11.1	12.0	13.7	12.0	12.1	7.0	2.4
Invisible Payments/GDP	6.3	6.3	5.7	6.5	6.1	6.2	5.9	6.6	4.9	2.4
Net Invisibles/ GDP	6.1	5.8	5.9	4.6	5.9	7.5	6.1	5.5	2.1	-0.1
Current Receipts/ GDP	29.4	28.5	28.1	26.1	25.3	29.1	25.4	25.6	16.9	8.0
Current Receipts/Current Payments	94.3	85.7	87.0	90.2	89.9	92.6	95.0	96.0	96.4	71.5
Current Account Balance/GDP	1.7	-4.7	-4.2	-2.8	-2.8	-2.3	-1.3	-1.0	-0.6	-3.0
Foreign Investment/ Exports	11.2	17.8	16.3	23.6	35.9	14.8	37.3	23.1	14.9	0.6
Foreign Investment/GDP	1.9	2.9	2.7	3.5	4.8	2.3	5.0	3.1	1.5	0.0
Import Cover of Reserves (In months)	7.8	7.0	7.1	9.5	11.1	9.8	14.4	12.5	8.8	2.5

Source: Reserve Bank of India.

global scenario constrains RBI's ability to intervene in the exchange market to contain volatility. India's external debt of $425 billion is about a fifth of GDP in 2013-14 and debt service ratio is 5 per cent which are within comfort zones. Short term debt was 22 per cent of total external debt.

Money Market

During the expansionary fiscal policy phase money supply grew by 16-17 per cent during 2009-10 and 2010-11 (Figure 3.7). It fell in the following two years when fiscal correction measures were undertaken. Reserve money and broad money grew only by 14.4 per cent and 13.3 per cent respectively during 2013-14. Bank credit too increased by about 14 per cent. The money multiplier stood at 5.5 without exhibiting any change. The possibility of tapering of quantitative easing in the United States in mid-2013 led to capital outflows and volatility in the foreign exchange rate in second quarter of 2013-14. The Reserve Bank of India took exceptional measures to restore stability by containing liquidity. With restoration of normalcy, RBI rolled back exceptional measures and focused on controlling inflation.

Figure 3.7

Growth in Money Supply

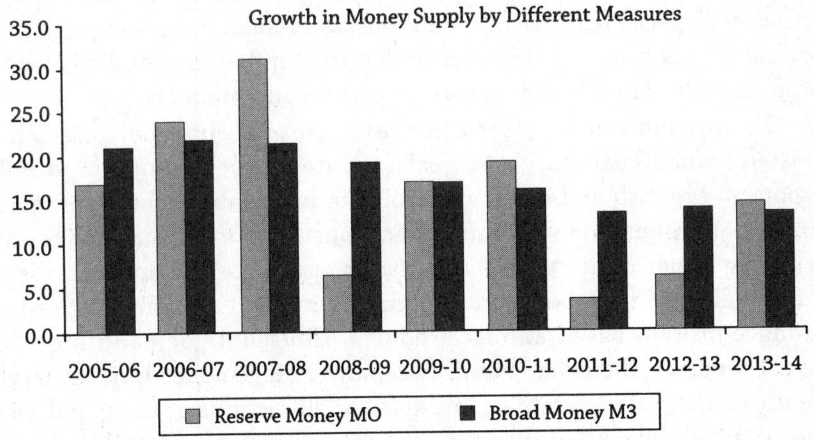

Inflation

Along with growth slowdown, prevalence of high rate of inflation was the second most important concern for policy makers in recent years. In fact, given its mandate, the Central Bank was primarily concerned with controlling inflation on the grounds that inflation beyond a threshold would be counterproductive for long run sustainability of growth itself. On an annual average basis, wholesale price index (WPI) has remained in the range of 7-10 per cent in 4 years out of last 6 years. Moderate inflation of 4-6 per cent was recorded in 2009-10 and 2013-14 only. Consumer price index for industrial workers (CPI-IW) or CPI for agricultural labourers (CPI-AL), on the other hand have posted 8-14 per cent inflation since 2008-09 except for 2011-12 when it was about 6.5 per cent. On a quarterly basis, both CPI-IW and CPI-AL remained above 8 per cent in 22 out of 24 quarters ending with last quarter of 2013-14 (Figure 3.8). Both the indices touched 14-16 per cent range in mid-2010-2011. Since food has got a larger weight in CPI than WPI, persistent food inflation is the primary reason for CPI inflation to remain above WPI inflation for most period (Figure 3.9).

Food prices in India have increased faster compared to India's own history as well as global movement. Food inflation affected the global economy including India in 2007-08, though transmission of global inflation into Indian economy was only partial. But, unlike the global experience, it reoccurred in 2009-10 and has continued since then.[7] There are several special features of food inflation in India. Detailed analysis in several papers from the RBI[8] shows that food inflation in India is led by protein and vitamin based high value agricultural products.

The consumption pattern in India across all income classes has shifted from cereals to non-cereal food items such as milk and milk products, egg, fish and meat, and fruits and vegetables which are major sources of protein and vitamins. Direct consumption demand for cereals is falling in per capita terms[9] and rise in aggregate demand for cereals is basically due to population growth and indirect demand for feed to produce protein based animal products. Household demand for non-cereal food, on the other hand, is rapidly rising induced by relatively elastic demand along with income gain for all sections of the population in the last decade either directly due to the growth process or indirectly due to the poverty reduction schemes. Availability of a variety of 'new' food products in the local market due to integration of global food

Figure 3.8

Quarterly Inflation by Wholesale and Consumer Price Index Numbers

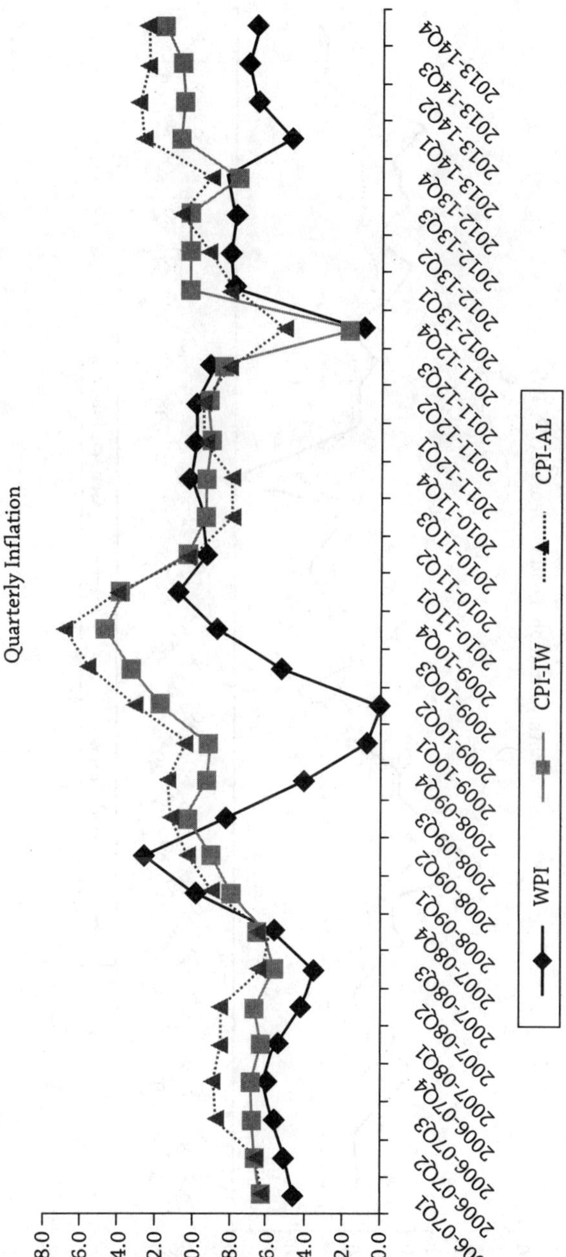

Figure 3.9

Monthly Inflation: Food Versus General (CPI-IW)

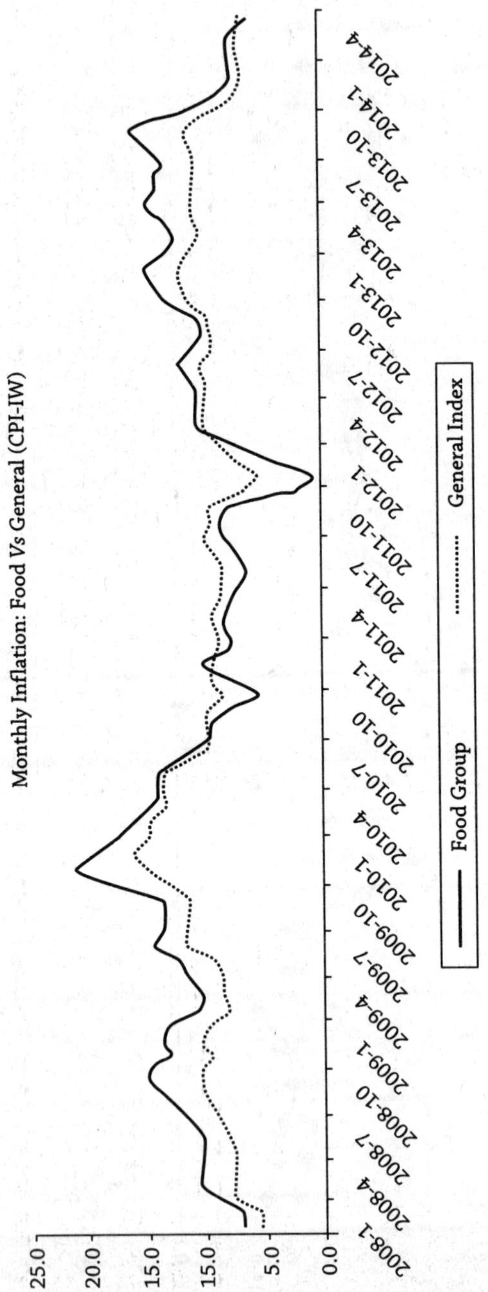

market has also been another factor in the food diversification process,[10] particularly for the growing middle class.

Production pattern also shifting towards protein based items, but significant excess demand persists creating upward pressure on prices. Supply of the non-cereal products has not kept pace with demand over the years. Operating around this medium run excess demand situation, there have been other factors such as weather conditions, input prices, and speculative trade contributing to widening of the demand-supply gap. Stagnant agricultural output in 2008-09 followed by an absolute fall of 4 per cent in 2009-10 due to weather conditions was a major supply side factor for food inflation in these two years.

Lastly, some analysis cite wage hike as a reason for food inflation. Figure 3.8 illustrates real wage movement for ploughing and unskilled labour obtained by deflating Labour Bureau's nominal wage data by CPIAL. Nominal wage rates in rural areas rose but did not keep pace with CPIAL and real wage rate fell during 2001 to 2007, but, it rose after that till 2012 resulting in an increase by 25-30 per cent compared to 2001. While food price rise might have partly contributed to cost push inflation through the wage component, the real wage increase must be judged against real per capita income rise of above 80 per cent during 2001 and 2012.

Figure 3.10

Real Wage Rate in Rural India

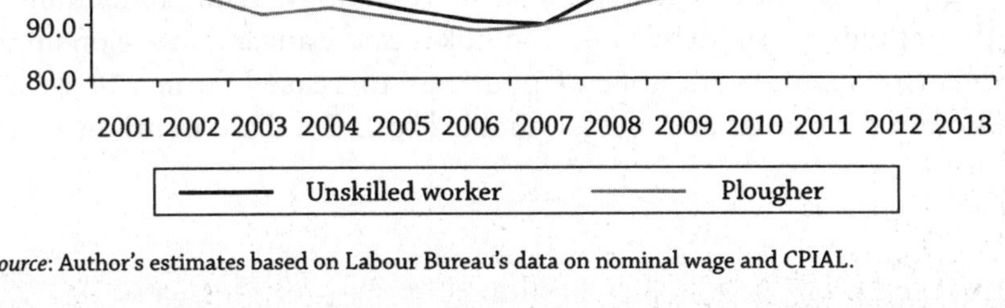

Source: Author's estimates based on Labour Bureau's data on nominal wage and CPIAL.

Poverty Incidence

Estimates of poverty in India are based on National sample Survey (NSS) consumption expenditure data. Using the method recommended by the Tendulkar Committee (2009), the percentage of population below poverty line (PL) or head count ratio fell from 41.8 per cent in 2004-05 to 25.7 per cent in 2011-12 in rural areas and from 25.7 per cent to 13.7 per cent in urban areas during the same period. In absolute number the poor numbered 217 million in rural areas and 53 million in urban areas in 2011-12 by this methodology.

The Rangarajan Committee (2014), which has submitted its report recently, attempts to construct a normative consumption basket for measuring poverty in 3 steps. First, it reworks out the calorie, protein and fat requirement for an average Indian. The calorie requirement works out to 2155 and 2090 calories per person per day in rural and urban areas respectively. Protein and fat norm similarly vary in the range of 48-50 and 26-28 grams respectively. The Committee finds out a food basket that meets the requirement of the 3 major nutrients allowing the calorie norm to be in a band of +/-10 per cent. The rural calorie requirement in particular is found to be much lower compared to earlier estimates. Second, the Committee considers actual expenditure of the median fractile class as the norms for certain non-food items like clothing, rent, conveyance and education. Third, for all other non-food items, actual expenditure of the fractile class that meets the nutritional needs are taken as requirement for constructing poverty line. Summing up all the 3 components, the poverty line works out to ₹972 in rural areas and ₹1407 in urban areas for the year 2011-12. The Committee then estimates that 30.9 per cent of rural population and 26.4 per cent of the urban population were below poverty line in 2011-12. This meant that poverty declined by 8.7 per cent in both rural and urban areas between 2009-10 and 2011-12 compared to 8.1 per cent and 7.2 per cent reduction by the Tendulkar methodology. While reductions by both methods recommended by Tendulkar and Rangarajan are of similar order, the absolute number of poor has increased from 217 to 261 million in rural areas and almost doubled to 103 million in urban areas.

Table 3.6

Poverty Estimates in 2009-10 and 2011-12

Year	*Poverty Ratio*			*No of Poor (Millions)*		
	Rural	*Urban*	*Total*	*Rural*	*Urban*	*Total*
			Expert Group (Rangarajan)			
2009-10	39.6	35.1	38.2	325.9	128.7	454.6
2011-12	30.9	26.4	29.5	260.5	102.5	363
Reduction (%age points)	8.7	8.7	8.7	65.4	26.2	91.6
			Expert Group (Tendulkar)			
1. 2009-10	33.8	20.9	29.8	278.2	76.5	354.7
2. 2011-12	25.7	13.7	21.9	216.7	53.1	269.8
3. Reduction (%age points)	8.1	7.2	7.9	61.5	23.4	84.9

Source: Rangarajan Committee Report.

The conclusion that poverty fell during the last decade by both methods is reassuring because it meant the poor did benefit from high economic growth of the last decade. Based on estimates of Generalised Lorenze curve, Dutta and Panda (2014) come to a stronger conclusion that the result regarding reduction of incidence of poverty is independent of the poverty line at the all-India level. As they state, the controversy surrounding the poverty line debate in 2012 generated more heat than light. It must be added that such a strong result is not uniformly found at the state level; all sections of the population did not benefit in some states from the overall growth process during these years.

Policy Challenges for High Growth

According to the Central Statistical Organisation's August 2014 estimate, the Indian economy witnessed a growth of 5.7 per cent in the first quarter of 2014-15. More importantly, there was a pickup in growth of manufacturing and investment, though the construction sector which employs large number of casual labour has not picked up. There are good news on other counts. Inflation has also showed signs of moderation. Trade deficit has improved and rupee has remained stable. These may be early indications that the worst of the slowdown phase might have been over and the economy might be turning to a revival phase. Yet, there is no scope for complacency. Strong policy initiatives need to be adopted for accelerating the economy back to 8 per cent growth in about two years. Some key policies for reviving and maintaining the growth trajectory are discussed below.

Both faster rate of capital accumulation and efficiency gains contributed to the high growth phase. Revival of the savings and investment rates in the economy would be critical for economic recovery. Private and public savings each need to rise by 2-3 percentage points of GDP. Households should be encouraged to save more in financial instruments. Early adoption of tax reforms already in the pipe line such as goods and service tax and enlargement of tax base could help in raising revenue and generate public savings apart from contributing to efficiency. Corporate sector would make investment decisions when it witnesses the economy back on the growth path and is assured of long term growth prospects. The subdued investment sentiment needs to be addressed to raise confidence of investors on the policy environment. Two crucial areas that recently generated big concern among private investors are land acquisition act and environmental clearance mechanism. There is a need to have a relook at them to strike a balance among various stakeholders. One way of moving forward on the land issue might be to pay part of the land cost directly to the landowner and the rest in the form of other instruments such as equity. The land owners can then have a long term stake in the industry set up on their land and benefit from future value of the asset. Environmental regulations should not turn out to be prohibitive type for setting up of industry. Regulatory framework must be sensitive to the aspirations of the various sections of the society to develop economically.

The dynamism seen in the agricultural sector during the green revolution seems to have been lost and needs to be revived. Policy package for agricultural growth includes commercially viable technology development for neglected crops such as pulses and maize, infrastructure development to build up cold storage and transportation of perishable goods, organisation of supply chains to link rural producers with urban consumers, and relaxation of Agricultural Produce Market Committee (APMC) rules. These are well recognised in policy circles. Faster diversification into high value crops and livestock could raise productivity in the agricultural sector and help in fighting food inflation.

Given the prevalence of high inflation despite achieving targeted 4 per cent average agricultural growth during last 5 years, it seems that 4 per cent growth target[11] will not be able to eliminate excess demand situation in agriculture. The target might need an upward revision for meeting changing demand pattern towards high value crops and controlling food inflation.

Major policy changes are needed to quicken the crop diversification process. While implementation of the food security act might need additional volume of rice and wheat through public distribution system, steps need to be taken to enhance efficiency in the system.[12] The minimum support price system for rice and wheat is obstructing faster diversification of agriculture by distorting the market based incentive structure. It has led to a situation where production continues to increase even as per capita availability of cereals is nearly stagnant contributing to rising public stock. In order to help dynamism in agriculture, the procurement policy objective need to be confined to checking price volatility. Other instruments may be used to achieve minimum income objective, where needed. The system also involves substantial wastage, leakages and diversion. A concerned Supreme Court has directed that grains should be released to the poor instead of wasting. In the context of high inflation of cereals, the government could have used release of public food stocks into the market as an instrument to control inflation.

Another institutional reforms required relates to promotion of land lease market which is very thin in India. The green revolution helped farmers to generate surplus and invest on education of their children who have subsequently migrated from rural areas. But, despite migration, the next generation continues to hold land due to expected higher return on land value. In this situation, promotion of the lease market with security of medium term tenure, without affecting the ownership, could incentivise private investment and help introduction of technological change in agriculture. The states need to launch a proper tenancy registration system that could help tenants to claim government benefits when calamities occur.

Turning to long term transformative process, the industrialised economies have historically witnessed structural transformation in their growth process due to large scale reallocation of resources from rural agriculture to urban non-agriculture. As growth took off, share of agriculture in these economies fell rapidly in terms of both GDP and employment leading to convergence in labour productivity between agriculture and non-agriculture. A stylised feature of Indian agriculture has been that while its share in GDP has come down to less than 15 per cent, about half the population continue to depend on agriculture for livelihood. This has contributed to growing differential (above 5:1) in per worker productivity between the non-agricultural sector and the agricultural sector. The decline in share of agriculture in employment has been slow because there has not been fast enough labour absorption in the urban economy. A new welcome development revealed by Census data has been a decline in number of cultivators from 127.3 million in 2001 to 118.7 million in 2011 indicating a shift from farm to non-farm employment. The NSSO data also show a fairly large drop by 7.4 percentage points in agricultural workers during 2004-11. As Dev (2014) points out further evidence is needed to conclude if this development indicates 'a paradigm change towards a possible Lewisian turning point'.

It is instructive to note that China has also found it difficult to rapidly reduce share of the labour force in agriculture in its growth process, but it indicates a movement towards convergence in labour income in agriculture and non-agriculture. It has succeeded in raising agricultural income per worker through enhancing productivity and efficiency. Technological change and diversification have played key role in this process.

Binswanger-Mkhize (2013) states that rural-urban migration in India has been 'far less than could have been expected in a rapidly growing economy'. In his view, rural non-farm sector has 'emerged as the largest source of new jobs' in India and has been 'much more dynamic' since mid-1980s in terms of contributions to both GDP growth and employment creation. These jobs are created in activities such as construction, trade, transport and communication. World Bank (2010) notes that 'non-farm employment increased more in regions where urban income grew faster' confirming rural-urban linkages. Another feature pointed out by Binswanger-Mkhize is that more and more households are engaged in agriculture on a part time basis, spending the other part of their time in rural non-farm activities. This process may, of course, eventually result in full time non-farm activities in rural or urban areas for a predominant section of the population.

India is not an atypical case witnessing service led growth in the last few decades. However, given the size of its huge labour force and the need to divert labour from agriculture as discussed above, future strategy should focus on encouraging labour intensive manufacturing growth for achieving the inclusive growth. The National Manufacturing Policy 2011 aimed at increasing share of manufacturing in GDP to 25 per cent and creating 100 million new jobs within a decade.[13] The policy specifically tried to promote labour intensive manufacturing and stressed growth of small and medium enterprises (SME) which play an important role in generating non-agricultural jobs. A major initiative under this policy was development of several national investment and manufacturing zones (NIMZ) and industrial corridors such as those from Delhi to Mumbai, Chennai to Bangalore, and Amritsar to Kolkata. Quick execution of some of these projects would have a signalling effect on the investment climate. Policy support in terms of technology, skill development, and credit availability need to be enhanced for SMEs. The regulatory structure must be re-examined to meet the present needs of the society. Laws from the colonial days that have become obsolete over time may be dropped and focus should be on encouraging compliance rather than high penalty. Separation of land into commercial and residential purpose discourages setting up of micro enterprises. Mixed use of land may be permitted to encourage those industries that do not involve health hazards.

Our labour laws stand on the way of expansion of labour intensive large scale manufacturing[14] because exit provisions have been found to be nearly prohibitive. Without provision for closure of nonviable industries within a reasonable timeframe, risks are high that capital may be locked idle for decades. In the absence of labour market flexibility and effective utilisation of the labour force, India may not be able to fully gain from its potential demographic dividend in the form of a larger fraction of population in the working age group. The current laws protect only about 10 per cent of labourers employed formally in organised sector and is not in the overall interest of the labour class. In the absence of broad political consensus, governments have been reluctant to carry on labour reform in the past. The new government with a clear majority for one party is in an eminent position to generate consensus and undertake big-ticket reform for manufacturing growth. Acceptable deal might include protecting existing employees under the old provisions.[15]

India accounts for more than half of global outsourcing market in IT-ITES sector. Maintaining cost competitiveness in the face of increased competition from other Asian countries and tackling the protectionist tendency in the industrialised countries will be the major challenges in near future. An area where India needs to tap its service potential at the global level relate to research and development (R&D). India has a qualified scientific research community compared to other emerging countries, but it lags behind in university-industry collaboration and must focus on more active commercially viable uses of R&D. While quality of education at the top end of higher educational institutions is well recognised, concerns have been expressed on the quality at the average level of our higher educational

In international circles, India is counted among the major emerging economies. Compared to other BRICS countries, India's per capita income is the lowest and hence it has more pressure to attain high growth. In order to attract global capital for fast expansion of the manufacturing sector, it must improve its competitiveness. According to the Global Competitiveness Report for 2013-14 prepared by the World Economic Forum, India ranks 60 among 120 countries in terms of the overall competitiveness index and stands lower than Brazil, China and South Africa (Table 3.7). It ranks way below other BRICS countries in

Table 3.7

Global Competitiveness Index

		Brazil	*China*	*India*	*S. Africa*	*Russia*
OVERALL INDEX		56	29	60	53	64
Basic Requirement						
1.	Institution	80	47	72	41	121
2.	Infrastructure	71	48	85	66	45
3.	Macroeconomic Environment	75	10	110	95	19
4.	Health and primary Education	89	40	102	135	71
Efficiency Enhancer						
5.	Higher education and training	72	70	91	89	47
6.	Goods market efficiency	123	61	85	28	126
7.	Labour market efficiency	92	34	99	116	72
8.	Financial market development	50	54	19	3	121
9.	Technological Readiness	55	85	98	62	59
10.	Market size	9	2	3	25	7
Innovation and Sophistication Factors						
11.	Bussiness sophistication	39	45	42	35	107
12.	Innovation	55	32	41	39	78

Source: World Economic Forum, 2013

terms of specific factors such as infrastructure, environment, health and primary education, and labour market efficiency. It does relatively well in terms of two factors, financial market development and business sophistication, but does not score higher rank compared to other BRICS countries in terms of any of the other indicators considered in the report.

China is entering into a high wage phase in its development process and likely to lose its competitive advantage in production of labour intensive manufacturing and shift to mid-technology industries. This scenario is likely to bring in large changes in global production and trade structure of consumer goods. India can capture a good deal of the consumer goods supply potential to the Western markets provided it improves its competitiveness. Major reforms in the labour laws may thus be seen as historical need to take advantage of the emerging opportunities in the global market, as China did for the last 4 decades.

Conclusion

The economy has witnessed a downturn in economic activities during the last 3 years after a high growth phase during 2004-2011. The agricultural sector has displayed moderate diversification and needs to adopt further diversification and technological up gradation. The virtual stagnation noticed in the industrial sector needs urgent policy action. Exports are likely to go up due to expected acceleration in global demand. While current account balance has improved to prudential level, fiscal deficit level is still high. Quick clearance of projects by regulatory authorities, initiation of measures for next round of reforms and a relook at the land acquisition act will help to boost investment sentiments. In order to attain the raised aspirations of the people, India needs to return to the high growth path witnessed earlier.

The new government at the Centre is in a strong position to carry out factor market reforms covering land and labour markets and set the stage for realising additional growth in the coming decades. Institutional reforms include the food procurement and distribution system, tenancy laws, changes in industrial laws including labour laws. Technological change and efficiency increase will be critical for sustaining high growth. There are signs that rural economy in India is going through a transformative process with non-farm income generation process playing a major role, even though rural-urban migration is moderate. A strategy of fast expansion of labour intensive manufacturing activities could help in restoring high growth trajectory and spread the benefits of growth to a large spectrum of the population. It could also help India to capture a significant portion of the vast world market likely to be vacated by China in consumer goods. Without improving its competitive edge, India will not be able to take sufficient advantage of the changing scenario in the global market.

Notes

1. Gross Domestic Product (GDP) is the value of all goods and services produced for final use within a country.
2. Purchasing power parity (PPP) estimate adjusts the market price based nominal dollar estimates by taking into account differences in cost of living and reflects standard of living across countries on a comparable basis.
3. A detailed report being prepared by the World Bank (2014) attempts to draw attention to problems at regional level in the country and suggests several efficiency enhancing measures for various crops.
4. The industrial sector was the major driver of growth during the 1950s and 1960s when several large public sector undertakings were set up.
5. Public or government savings refer to total income less current expenditure of the consolidated government; revenue includes surpluses of public enterprises passed on to the government.
6. According to a CRISIL Research (2014), contribution of TFP growth to overall GDP growth has considerably reduced during the downturn.
7. See, Bandara (2013) for a survey of food inflation in India.
8. As Mohanty (2013) states: 'The protein inflation has assumed a structural character'.
9. A decreasing trend in per capita calorie intake has also been noticed across most sections of the population.
10. Pingali and Khwaja (2004) had termed this feature as 'diet globalisation'.
11. Apart from Plan documents, Parikh et.al. (2013) too estimate that 4 per cent growth for agriculture would meet the demand generated by 8 per cent GDP growth.
12. See, for example, Ganesh-Kumar *et al.* (2007) for issues in reorganising the system.
13. India's 483 million labour force is growing by about 8 million a year.
14. See, Panagariya (2008) for a strong case for labour market reform for industrialisation.
15. History has several examples of such 'Pareto optimal' deals with a grand fathering clause as a way of compensation for potential adverse effect to a party.

References

Bandara, Jayatilleke S. (2013). "What is Driving India's Food Inflation? A Survey of Recent Evidence", *South Asia Economic Journal* 14(1).

Binswanger-Mkhize, Hans P. (2013). "The Stunted Structural Transformation of the Indian Economy: Agriculture, Manufacturing and the Rural Non-Farm Sector", *Economic and Political Weekly* XLVIII(26-27).

CRISIL Research (2014). *Of Growth and Missed Opportunity*. CRISIL, Mumbai.

Dev, Mahendra S. (2014). "The Challenge of Employment in Globalising India", *Economic and Political Weekly* XLIX(31).

Dutta, Bhaskar and Manoj Panda (2014). "Social Welfare and Household Consumption Expenditure in India—2004-05 to 2011-12", *Economic and Political Weekly* XLIX(31).

Ganesh-Kumar, A., Ashok Gulati and Ralph Cummings Jr. (2007). *Foodgrains Policy and Management in India: Responding to Today's Challenges and Opportunities*. Indira Gandhi Institute of Development Research, Mumbai and International Food Policy Research Institute, New Delhi.

Mohanty, Deepak (2013). "Indian Inflation Puzzle", Speech delivered at *Late Dr. Ramachandra Parnekar Outstanding Economics Award*, Mumbai.

Panagariya, Arvind (2008). *India: The Emerging Giant*. New York: Oxford University Press.

Parikh, Kirit S. Prabal Ghosh and Hans P. Binswanger-Mkhize (2013). "Double-Digit Inclusive Growth: Not without Robust Agricultural Growth", *Economic and Political Weekly* XLVIII(51).

Pingali, P. and Y. Khwaja (2004). *Globalisation of Indian Diets and the Transformation of Food Supply System*. Food and Agricultural Organisation, Rome.

Planning Commission (2014). *Report of the Expert Group to Review the Methodology for Measurement of Poverty* (Chaired by C. Rangarajan), Planning Commission, Government of India.

Reserve Bank of India (2014). "Estimates of Productivity Growth for the Indian Economy", (KLEMS Report prepared by B.N. Goldar, Deb Kusum Das *et al.*), Mumbai.

World Bank (2010). *Perspectives on Poverty in India: Stylized Facts from Survey Data*. Washington.

World Bank (2014). "India-Accelerating Agricultural Productivity Growth", (Work in Progress), Sustainable Development Department.

World Economic Forum (2013). *The Global Competitiveness Report 2013-14*. Geneva.

4

UMA KAPILA

Monetary, Fiscal and Budgetary Developments

Policies and their Impact

Monetary Policy

The Reserve Bank of India (RBI) formulates, implements, and monitors monetary policy. On 20 February 2015, the Government signed an agreement with the RBI on a monetary policy framework, which is intended to meet the challenge of an increasingly complex economy.[1] The main objective of monetary policy to be operated by the Reserve Bank will primarily be to maintain price stability while keeping in mind growth objectives. As per the agreement, the RBI will aim to bring inflation below 6 per cent by January 2016 and the target for financial year 2016-17 and all subsequent years will be 4 per cent with a band of +/- 2 percentage points. Inflation is the year-on-year change in the monthly Consumer Price Index – Combined expressed in percentage terms. The RBI is required to publish the operating target(s) and establish an operating procedure of monetary policy through which the operating target will be achieved so as to explain the deviation from the target band for three consecutive quarters from 2016-17.

The RBI has recently been focusing on containing inflation and tightening its monetary policy stance, although in 2015 this stance was slightly eased. In May 2011, following the change in policy stance to fix only one rate, the repo rate was increased to 7.25 per cent.[2] The rate was then increased several times, to 8 per cent on 28 January 2014. On 15 January 2015, the rate was lowered by 0.25 percentage point to 7.75 per cent, and on 4 March 2015 it was brought down by 25 basis points to 7.5 per cent. In the Sixth Bi-Monthly Monetary Policy statement of 2014-15 issued on 3 February 2015, the statutory liquidity ratio (SLR) of scheduled commercial banks was lowered by 0.5 percentage points from

22 per cent to 21.5 per cent of their net time deposit liabilities (NDTL) with effect from 7 February 2015. In addition, export credit refinance was withdrawn and replaced with system-level liquidity.[3]

Regarding other monetary policy measures, banks were required, inter alia, to meet at least 99 per cent of the cash reserve ratio (CRR) on a daily basis, and limit the provision of liquidity under the Liquidity Adjustment Facility (LAF) to 0.5 per cent of the bank's own NDTL; the statutory liquidity ratio (SLR) of scheduled commercial banks was lowered by 0.5 percentage points from 22 per cent to 21.5 per cent of their NDTL in February 2015.[4]

Reforms in India's monetary policy are gradually being adopted in accordance with an RBI expert committee's recommendation in January 2014[5], such as the adoption of the CPI, instead of the wholesale price index (WPI)[6], as the key measure of inflation, and making a transition from a quarterly to a bi-monthly monetary policy cycle since April 2014.

The agreement on monetary policy framework signed between the Government and Reserve Bank of India (RBI) in February 2015 has shaped the monetary policy stance in 2015-16. The RBI further eased its monetary policy stance during the year 2015. Headline inflation based on the consumer price index (CPI) fell to below 6 per cent much ahead of the January 2016 target. The RBI reduced the statutory liquidity ratio by 0.50 per cent to 21.50 per cent in February 2015 and further eased the policy repo rate during the year to 6.75 per cent, in all making a substantial cut of 125 basis points (bps) between January 2015 and September 2015 (Table 4.1). In the bank's latest monetary policy review held on 2 February 2016, the policy repo rate remains unchanged.[7]

The easing of the policy repo rate has been accompanied by a pick-up in the growth rates of reserve money (M0) and narrow money (M1) in 2015.The growth in M0 has been higher owing to pickup in growth of currency in circulation and in bankers' deposit with the RBI, while the increase in M1 has been due to a higher rate of growth in demand deposits with banks. In terms of sources of reserve money, net foreign exchange assets (NFA) have been a major determinant of the growth, modulated by net domestic assets. There was a seasonal pick-up in M0 growth to above the 14 per cent mark to accommodate the festive demand at end-December 2015; it has since moderated to a 12 per cent level. However, the growth of broad money (M3) has not picked up (Table 4.2).

Table 4.1

Revision in Policy Rates

Effective Date	*Bank Rate/ MSF Rate* (%)*	*Repo Rate (%)*	*Reverse Repo Rate (%)*	*Cash Reserve Ratio (% of NDTL)*	*Statutory Liquidity Ratio (% of NDTL)*
09-08-2014	9.00	8.00	7.00	4.00	22.00
15-01-2015	8.75	7.75	6.75	4.00	22.00
07-02-2015	8.75	7.75	6.75	4.00	21.50
04-03-2015	8.50	7.50	6.50	4.00	21.50
02-06-2015	8.25	7.25	6.25	4.00	21.50
29-09-2015	7.75	6.75	5.75	4.00	21.50

Notes: *: Bank Rate was aligned to MSF rate with effect from February 13, 2012. NDTL is net demand and time liabilities.

Source : RBI.

Table 4.2

Year-on-Year Change in Monetary Aggregates as on December of Each Year

(%)

		2015	*2014*	*2013*	*2012*	*2011*	*2010*
1.	Currency in circulation	13.0	9.6	11.1	12.0	12.4	18.2
2.	Cash with banks	11.0	15.6	8.3	17.3	12.8	31.5
3.	Currency with the public	13.0	9.3	11.2	11.8	12.4	17.7
4.	Bankers' deposits with the RBI	17.9	7.4	9.0	-15.3	12.1	35.3
5.	Demand deposits	11.9	10.4	7.4	0.1	-0.1	22.4
6.	Time deposits	10.6	10.9	16.3	12.6	19.2	18.4
7.	Reserve money (M0) (1+4)	14.3	9.4	10.7	4.6	12.2	22.1
8.	Narrow money(M1)(3+5)	12.8	10.0	9.8	6.8	6.7	19.6
9.	Broad money (M3) (6+8)	11.0	10.7	14.8	11.2	16.0	18.7

Source: RBI.

Consistent with the accommodative monetary policy stance since January 2015, the RBI has been actively managing monetary policy tools to ensure adequate liquidity in the system and accordingly the weighted average call rate (WACR), or the operating target of monetary policy, remained closely aligned to the policy repo rate. The RBI conducted variable rate repo and reverse repo (overnight and term) auctions in order to address the day-to-day liquidity requirements arising out of frictional factors, besides regular liquidity operations. The WACR declined by130 bps in response to the 125 bps cut in repo rate by the RBI since January 2015, pointing to perfect transmission at the first leg of the term structure. However, post the 29 September 2015 rate cut, call rate remained above repo rate for some time, implying tightening of liquidity conditions. Other short-term money market rates, in particular market repos and call money, also co-varied with the WACR. The revised liquidity management framework put in place by the RBI since 5 September 2014 has helped in containing volatility in the WACR. Under the new framework, the RBI used variable rate repo/ reserve repo auctions of varying tenors as well as outright open market operations, apart from the normal liquidity operations under the liquidity adjustment facility (LAF) to manage liquidity.

Bank Credit

Bank credit is an important indicator of economic activity. The high growth observed in the 2003-08 period was accompanied by a surge in monetary aggregates and credit growth, which usually exceeded the 20 per cent mark year on year. After being impacted sharply by the global financial crisis and the fiscal stimuli over the period 2008-10, credit growth remained at around the 15 per cent mark till February 2014. Subsequently, it has slowed down.

Box 4.1

What Explains the Incomplete Passthrough of Monetary Policy?

According to the February 2016 policy statement, the RBI has shifted to an accommodative policy stance.

Without doubt, policy rates have been reduced substantially: in 2015, there were no less than four rate cuts cumulating to 125 basis points, including a 50 basis point cut at the October meeting. But there has been much less "accommodation" in bank lending rates, which have only fallen by around 50 basis points. What explains the failure of passthrough from policy rates to bank rates?

Many commentators have emphasized that transmission is limited by high administered and small savings rates. The argument is that banks worry that if they cut their deposit rates, customers will flee to small savings instruments. Recognizing this, the government has reduced rates on some small savings schemes to make them more responsive to market conditions. But it is also clear from the chart that the small saving schemes don't always constrain passthrough. For example, the June rate cut was followed by a large reduction in deposit rates whereas the much larger October cut was barely passed on at all. And the small saving schemes cannot explain why the reductions that have taken place in deposit rates have not led to commensurate reductions in lending rates.

Source: *Economic Survey 2015-16*, Vol. I.

Fiscal Policy

Fiscal policy is a critical component of the policy framework for achieving sustained annual growth of 8-10 per cent with macroeconomic stability. High deficits, unproductive expenditure and tax distortions have constrained the economy from realising its full growth potential.

As Economic Survey 2014-15 remarks, it is worth examining India's recent fiscal past, to see if there are lessons for the country's future fiscal trajectory. A look back at recent history is especially warranted now because India today is in a very similar situation to that in the early 2000s, with comparable fiscal deficit (4% of GDP) at a broadly similar state of the macroeconomic cycle. Today, like then, inflation is close to 5 per cent. Today, like then, the current account deficit is manageably low. And, today, like then, the economy is poised to attain a faster growth trajectory. So, it is worth asking: What are the lessons from recent fiscal performance in India?

Recent Fiscal Performance

India's macroeconomic improvement has been nothing short of dramatic—inflation has been cut in half to about 5 per cent today, rural wage growth has declined from over 20 per cent to below 5 per cent, and the current account deficit has come down from over 6.7 per cent of GDP (in Q3, 2012-13) to an estimated 1.0 per cent in the coming fiscal year.

Key fiscal indicators for the central government are summarized in Table 4.3. At least three phases of policy can be distinguished since the early 2000s: 2002-2007; 2008-2011; and post-2012.

Two noteworthy conclusions can be drawn from this period. First, nearly all the improvement in the fiscal indicators stemmed from rapid growth, which averaged about 8 per cent in this phase. Second, and one with important lessons for the future, was the ratcheting up of overall expenditures. Until 2005-06, the expenditure to GDP ratio declined in line with rising growth but in the following two years, it increased—at a time when growth averaged 9.5 per cent. In other words, real expenditures grew at a staggering 10 per cent.

The second and difficult phase of Indian fiscal history began with the Lehman crisis in 2008-09 and lasted four years. In this period nearly all the positive trends of the previous six years were reversed. The fiscal deficit increased by about 4 percentage points, shared equally between revenue reductions (owing to large indirect tax cuts) and

Table 4.3

Select Fiscal Indicators (as per cent of GDP)

	Particulars	*2002-03*	*2003-04*	*2004-05*	*2005-06*	*2006-07*	*2007-08*	*2008-09*	*2009-10*	*2010-11*	*2011-12*	*2012-13*	*2013-14*	*2014-15*
	1	*2*	*3*	*4*	*5*	*6*	*7*	*8*	*9*	*10*	*11*	*12*	*13*	*14*
1	Real GDP growth [g] (in per cent)	3.9	8	7.1	9.5	9.6	9.3	6.7	8.6	8.9	6.7	4.5	4.7^	5.9
2	CPI Inflation # (in per cent)	5	4.1	4	3.7	6.8	5.9	9.2	10.6	9.5	9.5	10.2	9.5	7.2
3	Inflation from GDP Deflator (in per cent)	3.7	3.9	5.7	4.2	6.4	5.8	8.7	6.1	9.0	8.5	7.2	6.9	
4	GDP at market price in ` lakh crore	25.3	28.4	32.4	36.9	42.9	49.9	56.3	64.8	78.0	90.1	101.1	113.6	128.8
							Central Government							
5	Total Revenue ## (before devolution)	12.8	14.6	13.9	12.3	13.1	14.8	12.6	11.9	13.4	11.6	12.0	12.2	12.8
6	Gross Tax Revenue	8.5	9.0	9.4	9.9	11.0	11.9	10.8	9.6	10.2	9.9	10.2	10.2	10.6
7	Total Expenditure (including tax devolution)	18.5	18.9	17.8	16.2	16.4	17.3	18.5	18.4	18.2	17.3	16.8	16.8	16.9
	Major Subsidies	1.6	1.5	1.4	1.2	1.2	1.3	2.2	2.1	2.1	2.3	2.4	2.2	1.9
	Food	1	0.9	0.8	0.6	0.6	0.6	0.8	0.9	0.8	0.8	0.8	0.8	0.9
	Fertilizer	0.4	0.4	0.5	0.5	0.6	0.7	1.4	0.9	0.8	0.8	0.6	0.6	0.6
	Petroleum	0.2	0.2	0.1	0.1	0.1	0.1	0.1	0.2	0.5	0.8	1.0	0.8	0.5
	Tax devolution to States	2.2	2.3	2.4	2.6	2.8	3.0	2.8	2.5	2.8	2.8	2.9	2.8	3.0
	Revenue Expenditure	13.4	12.8	11.9	11.9	12.0	11.9	14.1	14.1	13.4	12.7	12.3	12.3	12.2
	Capital Expenditure	2.9	3.8	3.5	1.8	1.6	2.4	1.6	1.7	2.0	1.8	1.6	1.7	1.8
	Non-Defence	2.4	3.3	2.5	0.9	0.8	1.6	0.9	1.0	1.2	1.0	1.0	1.0	1.0

contd...

...contd...

	1	2	3	4	5	6	7	8	9	10	11	12	13	14
8	Fiscal deficit	5.7	4.3	3.9	4	3.3	2.5	6	6.5	4.8	5.7	4.8	4.6	4.1
9	Revenue Deficit	4.3	3.5	2.4	2.5	1.9	1.1	4.5	5.2	3.2	4.4	3.6	3.3	2.9
10	Primary Deficit [pd]	1.1	0	0	0.4	-0.2	-0.9	2.6	3.2	1.8	2.7	1.8	1.3	0.8
11	Total outstanding liabilities	66.9	66	65.5	63.9	61.4	58.9	58.6	56.3	52.1	51.7	51.7	50.9	49.8
12	Average cost of borrowing [n] (in %)	7.5	7.3	7.2	7	7.3	7.6	7.6	7.5	7.4	7.8	7.7	8.3	--
13	Average cost of borrowing [r] (in %)	3.8	3.4	1.5	2.8	0.9	1.8	-1.1	1.4	-1.6	-0.7	0.5	1.4	--
14	Debt Dynamic Wedge [g-r-pd]	-1.0	4.6	5.6	6.3	8.9	8.4	5.2	4.0	8.7	4.7	2.2	2.0	--

Note: ^: Provisional; n=nominal; r= real

Back series from the Urjit Patel Committee Report, RBI. CPI Data for 2014-15 is up to November, 2014.

Total revenue consists of GTR, non-tax revenue, recovery of loans and other receipts.

1. Data for 2013-14 and 2014-15 for central government is revised estimates and budget estimates respectively.
2. Total outstanding liabilities are derived by adding 'other liabilities' (that includes national small savings fund, state provident funds and other accounts to the government's public debt. External liabilities of the Centre is at current exchange rate.
3. Data on GDP at current market prices and GDP growth numbers at factor cost are from CSO's National Accounts series of 2004-05.
4. The exact formula for the Debt Dynamic Wedge is: $\Delta d_{(t+1)} = p_{(t+1)} + [(r_t - g_t)/(1+gt)]\, d_t$ where p_t is the primary deficit as per cent of GDP,; r_t is the real rate of interest; g_t is the real growth rate; d_t is debt to GDP ratio

Source: *Economic Survey 2014-15.*

expenditure increases. In the initial years (2008-09 to 2011-12), current expenditures (public consumption) increased dramatically due to the rising subsidy bill (up by 1 percentage point of GDP); the increase in pay and allowances because of implementation of the Sixth Pay Commission recommendations (0.4% of GDP); and schemes that built in permanent entitlements such as MGNREGA (0.3% of GDP). Meanwhile, the quality of spending suffered as non-defence capital expenditure stagnated while current expenditures rose by about 2 percentage points on average during the period.

In the third and most recent phase, from 2012-13 to 2014-15, which was characterized by a sharp growth slowdown, the fiscal position finally began to be repaired. The fiscal stimulus provided in the post-Lehman phase was unwound, with equal contributions from revenue increases and expenditure reductions, bringing the deficit close to the level prevailing in the early 2000s, at a comparable stage of the business cycle.

India experienced a near-crisis during July/August 2013, as the conjunction of the U.S. Federal Reserve's decision to taper its monetary stimulus and India's growing current account deficit, high inflation, and still-large fiscal deficits caused capital to flee the country. This episode underscored the final and most critical lesson, namely that India needs to create additional fiscal space, in order to ensure macro stability and to create buffers for economic downturns in the future (*Economic Survey 2014-15*).

Medium-Term Fiscal Framework

The 2016-17 fiscal stance needs to be assessed in two contexts. Most obviously, it needs to be evaluated against the likely short-term outlook for growth and inflation. At the same time, it also needs to be framed in a medium-term context. That's because the most fundamental task of budget policy is to preserve fiscal sustainability. The government needs to be in a strong position tomorrow to repay the debts it is incurring today. And it needs to be seen to possess this strength.

Governments adopt various targets to achieve and signal fiscal sustainability. These include the overall deficit, the primary deficit, the revenue deficit, and the debt-to-GDP ratio. In principle, sustainable ratios are very much time, country, and history-contingent (Reinhart, Rogoff, and Savastano, 2003). But pinning down a relationship between these contingencies and targets is difficult to do scientifically. Accordingly, countries often adopt targets established by others. For example, countries in other regions adopted targets of 3 percent of GDP for the fiscal deficit and 60 percent for the debt-to-GDP ratio as these had been adopted by Eurozone economies under the Stability and Growth Pact (SGP).

The clearest sign that a government is on a sustainable path is the direction of its debt-to-GDP ratio. If this ratio is declining, then the government's fundamental fiscal strength is improving. For much of the period since the 2008-09 the government has run large annual deficits in order to reflate the economy. Initially, the impediment was the large annual deficits that the government incurred as it sought to reflate the economy. These deficits were eventually curtailed, but macro imbalances nonetheless continued to grow, leading by 2013-14 to the second impediment: a sharp exchange rate depreciation that inflated the rupee value of foreign debts.

As a result, overall government debt continued to grow as fast as GDP, keeping the debt ratio of the consolidated government (Centre plus states) near 67 per cent of GDP. This ratio is high compared to some countries in emerging Asia—India's credit rating peers. Accordingly, the government is determined to break the post-GFC trend, and finally put the debt ratio on a downward path toward more comfortable levels.

For this reason, there are strong arguments to stick to a path of aggressive fiscal consolidation as envisaged at the time of the last budget. Such a low deficit would not only curtail the debt accumulation, but would also offer some wider advantages. To begin with, it would mean that the government would be delivering on a commitment, thereby reinforcing its credibility, which is one of the most precious assets that any authority can command. Conversely, it is far from clear why such a commitment would be abandoned when the economy is growing at more than 7 per cent. Such rapid growth would seem to provide ample revenues for the Budget, while enabling the economy to withstand the reduction in government demand. So, credibility and optimality seem to argue for adhering to the 3.5 percent of GDP target.

However, there are also arguments on the other side. With respect to feasibility, two factors complicate the fiscal task in 2016-17 and beyond:

- The Seventh Pay Commission has recommended that government wages and allowances be increased significantly. Full implementation of this pay award—which the government will decide on—would add about ½ percent of GDP to the Centre's wage bill.

- Public investment may need to be increased further to address a pressing backlog of infrastructure needs. Such an increase would merely return spending to its 2010-11 level of around 2 percent of GDP, well below the level in other emerging markets.

Taking these factors into account, the Centre's deficit could swell substantially. As a result, achieving the original could prove difficult unless there are tax increases or cuts in expenditures. There is some scope to increase receipts from disinvestment and spectrum auctions to realize which will require effort.

Second, even the desirability of a strategy of aggressive fiscal consolidation could be questioned. This is because the current environment is fraught with risks, which threaten all the engines of India's growth, as explained earlier. It would consequently seem important for the government to "purchase insurance" against these downside risks—rather than reduce fiscal demand significantly and take the chance of precipitating their realization. Data uncertainty reinforces the need for purchasing insurance.

But if the deficit target were to be relaxed, two questions would need to be answered. First, what would happen to interest rates? The lower the fiscal deficit, the lower the borrowing requirement, and possibly the lower the interest rate on government securities, which would be very helpful to companies facing debt servicing difficulties. International empirical research, however, suggests that the impact of deficits on longterm rates is typically small and uncertain. The reason for this is straightforward: long-term rates are basically determined by expectations of the future path of short-term rates. And this expected path typically depends largely on the long-term outlook for growth and inflation-and, not necessarily on the current year's fiscal deficit.

Summing up the cyclical considerations, small differences in the degree of fiscal adjustment may not have much impact on interest rates. Which means that any positive effects from a large adjustment ("austerity") coming from lower interest rates could be offset by the direct negative impact on aggregate demand.[8]

The golden rule of fiscal policy is that governments are expected to borrow over the cycle only to finance investment and not to fund current expenditures. This implies that achievement of the government's fiscal consolidation should ideally take place over the business cycle and short-term targets should be set accordingly.

Legacy/Credibility

Reinforcing these considerations are legacy issues. India's FRBM Act as well as the Kelkar Committee (2012) established the principle of aiming to bring the centre's fiscal deficit down to 3 per cent of GDP. Adhering to this objective is essential for maintaining credibility and also to bring India closer in line with its emerging market peers. States are a constant while governments come and go. In this regard, if every new government decided to change the rules of the game, volatility and uncertainty would be the rule and the overall credibility of the state and the country would suffer as a result.

Moreover, even if there were good reasons to change the rules of the game, there is a signalling problem. Fiscally responsible governments may not be able to credibly convey to the market early in their tenure that they are indeed fiscally responsible. In this situation, until they can establish a track record, governments will be required to adhere to previous commitments.

Accordingly, the medium-term fiscal strategy should be based on two pillars. First, the fiscal deficit should be reduced over the medium-term to the established target of 3 per cent of GDP. Second, and mindful of the experience of the past decade, efforts to achieve this objective should be based on firm control over expenditures, most notably by eliminating leakages in subsidies and social expenditures.

Further, switching from public consumption (via the rationalisation of subsidies) to public investment will, for any given level of overall spending, mitigate long-run inflationary pressures because the latter will add to capacity and boost the aggregate supply potential of the economy. Also, asset sales to finance investment is consistent with boosting growth without adding to aggregate demand pressures in the short run.

India's tax-to-GDP ratio stood at 7.4 per cent in 2013-14 and is estimated to stand at 7.6 per cent in 2014-15 (Table 4.4); the authorities consider this ratio to be low and in need of improvement by, for example, broadening the tax base.[9] The authorities consider that India has a complex tax system that suffers from problems in structure (e.g. tax exemptions, tax rebates, uneven tax treatment of similar economic activities) and administration.[10] Parliament is still in the process of approving the goods and services tax (GST) as well as a direct tax bill, which is envisaged to remove a large number of cesses and tax exemptions.[11]

Table 4.4

Central Government's Tax Revenue, 2010-15

(₹ billion and %)

	2010-11	*2011-12*	*2012-13*	*2013-14*	*2014-15a*
Total tax revenue, net of states' share (₹ billion)	5,698.7	6,297.6	7,402.6	8,360.3	9,772.6
(% of GDP)	7.3	7.0	7.3	7.4	7.6
			(% of total tax revenue)		
Direct taxes	55.3	54.9	53.4	54.4	53.7
Corporation taxes	37.7	36.3	34.4	34.0	33.0
Personal income taxes	17.5	18.5	19.0	20.4	20.4
Indirect taxes	43.4	44.1	45.7	44.8	45.8
Customs	17.1	16.8	16.0	15.1	14.8
Excise duties	17.4	16.3	17.0	15.4	15.1
Service taxes	9.0	11.0	12.8	14.2	15.8

Note: a Provisional estimates.

Source: WTO Secretariat, based on information provided by the Indian authorities.

If expenditure control is maintained, revenue increases will flow straight through to the flow and stock fiscal aggregates. This effect should be large, since accelerating growth and the introduction of the GST in 2016-17 could raise India's tax-GDP ratio from the current level of 17.5 per cent to close to 20 per cent for the general government. Moreover, debt dynamics will then work strongly in India's favour. Simple calculations suggest that if growth averages 9 per cent over the next three years, and real interest rates remain broadly where they are, overall debt-to-GDP ratios (more precisely, the ratio of total outstanding liabilities to GDP) for the central government could decline to around 40 per cent in 2017-18 from the current level of 49.8 per cent and would be associated with a similar decline in the general government debt. This would create the buffers to insure against future downturns.

Conclusions

Current expenditures on a downward path and the quality of spending improving through a switch away from public consumption to investment, India's improved growth, introduction of the GST, and the associated revenue buoyancy can comfortably ensure the attainment of medium-term targets. This buoyancy is assured by history because over the course of the growth surge over the last decade, the overall tax-GDP ratio increased by about 2-2.5 percentage points even without radical tax reform.

For India, the key to achieving medium-term fiscal targets resides in expenditure control, the failure to do so during the boom growth years between 2005-06 and 2008-09, playing a major role in the loss of macroeconomic control and the near-crisis of July/August 2013.

Another cost of the failure to maintain expenditure, and hence fiscal control was the quality of spending, with public investment being the casualty and public consumption the beneficiary. This, in turn, has affected India's medium-term growth potential.

These trends need to be reversed, and the nation's public finances need to be set back on the path toward fiscal deficit of 3 per cent of GDP, as planned in FRBM (Amendment) Act 2012. To do this, concrete actions will be needed to control expenditure via subsidy reductions, improve its quality in altering the mix between public consumption and investment in favour of the latter, and move India toward the golden rule of borrowing only for public investment. Broadly, the increase in fiscal space, including that gained from subsidy reductions and higher disinvestment proceeds should be devoted to public investment.

Even with these measures, progress toward the medium-term target may be limited in the upcoming fiscal year by a number of new and exceptional factors, such as implementing the recommendations of the Fourteenth Finance Commission, clearing the compensation obligations to the states for the reduction in the central sales tax, and the need to modestly ramp-up investment.

In a recent paper[12] Chakraborty(s), based on their analysis, have concluded that a revenue led fiscal adjustment will be key to fiscal prudence in 2016-17. Since there has been an increase in tax GDP ratio by almost one percentage point between 2014-15 and 2015-16, there are challenges to maintaining that level of tax effort in 2016-17. However, a revenue led fiscal consolidation is always better than the blanket cut in expenditure to adhere to fiscal deficit target. Also the fiscal policy space for further reduction in government expenditure is limited. Further contraction in public expenditure can have a negative impact on growth and revenue mobilisation.

Notes

1. Ministry of Finance online information. Viewed at: *http://finmin.nic.in/reports/MPFAgreement 28022015.pdf.*
2. Since 3 May 2011, the RBI has been using the repo rate (RBI's lending rate to commercial banks) as the only independently varying policy rate. The RBI implements monetary policy through the use of several direct and indirect instruments. The main direct instruments used to conduct monetary policy include the cash reserve ratio (CRR), the statutory liquidity ratio (SLR), and refinance facilities. The RBI uses the liquidity adjustment facility (LAF), as its main indirect instrument which enables it to adjust short term liquidity through repo and reverse repo auctions. The RBI also makes use of open market operations.
3. The export credit refinance was reduced in phases. It was 50% of eligible export credit outstanding as at 2 June 2014.
4. IMF (2014).
5. Reserve Bank of India online information. Viewed at: *http://rbi.org.in/Scripts/Publication ReportDetails.aspx?ID=743.*
6. The RBI had traditionally been using the WPI as the key inflation measure.
7. *Economic Survey 2015-16*, Vol.II.
8. *Economic Survey 2015-16*, Vol.I.
9. Budget Speech 2014-15 and Ministry of Finance (2014).
10. Ministry of Finance (2014).
11. The Government's continued intention is to introduce a GST and to consolidate the Income Tax Act 1961 and the Wealth Tax Act 1957 in a Direct Tax Code (Trade Policy Review, April 2015).
12. EPW, April 2016.

References

Basu, Kaushik (ed.) (2004). *India's Emerging Economy: Performance and Prospects in the 1990s and Beyond*, Ch 1. Oxford University Press.

Chakraborty, Pinaki, Lekha Chakraborty (2016). "Beyond Fiscal Prudence and Consolidation", *Economic and Political Weekly* (April). Mumbai.

Ministry of Finance, *Economic Survey* 2012-13, 2013-14, 2014-15, 2015-16.

OECD (2011). *Economic Survey India*. New Delhi: Academic Foundation.

Patnaik, Ila (2014). "Maintaining Macroeconomic Stability", in Bebek Debroy, Tellis and Trevor (eds.) (2014), *Getting India Back on Track: An Action Agenda for Reform*. Random House India.

World Trade Organisation (2015). *Trade Policy Review, India, Report by the Secretariate*. April 2015.

5

K. KANAGASABAPATHY, VISHAKHA G. TILAK and R. KRISHNASWAMY

A Rethink on India's Foreign Trade Policy

OVER the last decade, India's foreign trade—exports and imports—has undergone a significant transformation both in terms of composition of commodities and direction. However, foreign trade expanded over the period with dominance of import growth *vis-à-vis* exports resulting in widening of the negative trade balance. The trade policy announced on 27 August 2009, in the backdrop of the economic crisis, kept the short-term objective of arresting and reversing the declining trend of exports and sought to provide additional support to those sectors badly hit by the recession in the developed world. Accordingly a policy objective of achieving an annual export growth of 15 per cent with an annual export target of $200 billion by March 2011 was set, and in the three years up to 2014, the country was expected to come back on the high export-growth path of around 25 per cent per annum [Government of India (GoI), 2009]. Unfortunately, the growth target set for the years after 2012 turned out to be too ambitious as exports declined sharply in financial year (FY) 2012-13. It is also recognised that in a fast-growing economy, a rapid increase in exports is the only option available to maintain the current account deficit (CAD) at reasonable levels (GoI, 2011).

Against this backdrop, this note primarily attempts to review the developments in India's trade over the last decade *vis-à-vis* global trends. Secondly, the note analyses the changing composition and direction of India's exports and imports (in terms of $). One significant feature has been that India's exports never kept pace with imports during the high trade-growth phase. After analysing possible reasons, the note finally attempts to bring out some strategic steps that might be needed to correct the growing trade imbalance.

India's Place in Global Trade

India was one of the fastest growing economies in the last decade, its merchandise trade growth expanded more or less in tandem with global trade. India's trade over the period showed remarkable increases, as its share in world trade went up from 0.80 per cent in 2002 to 2.13 per cent in 2013 (Figure 5.1). But unlike its east Asian counterparts, India's merchandise trade grew mainly due to increased imports than that of exports. As a result, the trade deficit accelerated from a near balance in 2000-01 to as high as $191.7 billion in 2012-13 (Figure 5.2).

Figure 5.1

*Share of India's Total Trade to World's Total Trade**

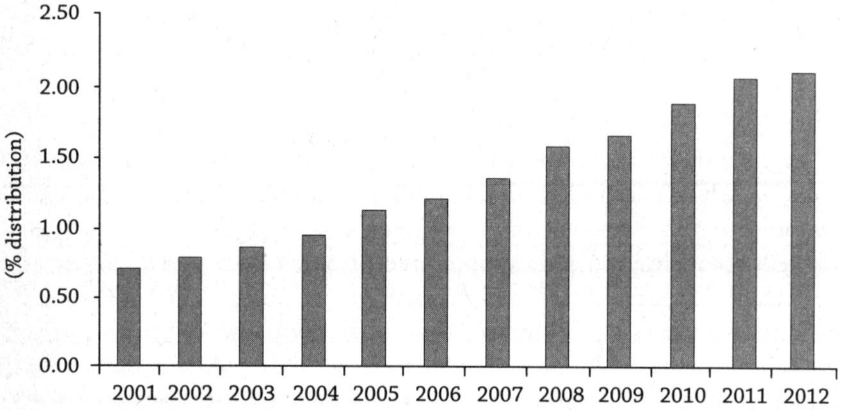

Note: * in terms of $ million.

Source: United Nations Conference on Trade and Development (UNCTAD).

Elasticity of Trade to GDP

An attempt has been made to work out crude elasticities of trade to gross domestic product (GDP) over the period 2002-2012 for India and the world (Table 5.1). It is generally observed that India's elasticity was significantly lower compared to world trade during the whole of the period—both during the pre-crisis period as well as the post-crisis periods. It is therefore the higher growth of GDP in India *vis-à-vis* that

Figure 5.2

Trend in India's Export, Imports and Trade Balance

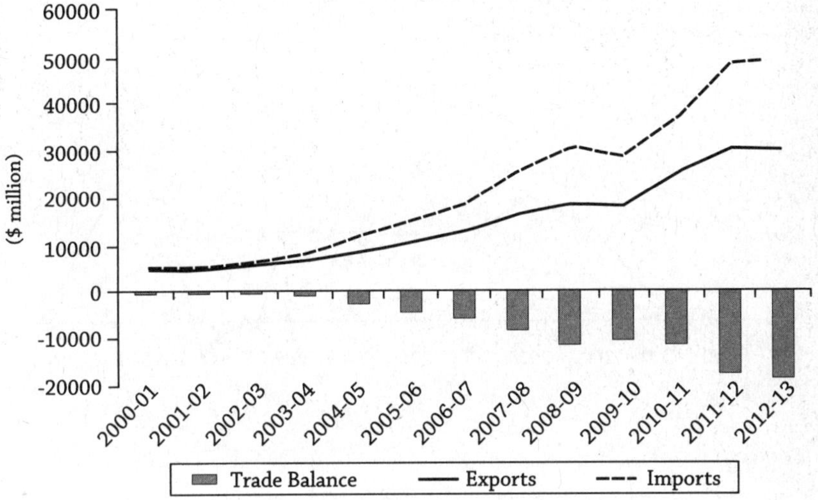

Table 5.1

Crude Elasticities of Trade to Real GDP Growth (Average Growth Rate Per Annum %)

Period	*Trade*		*GDP*		*Crude Elasticities*@	
	India	*World*	*India*	*World*	*India*	*World*
2002-2008	30.4	16.4	8.0	3.3	3.8	5.0
2009-2012	13.4	4.7	7.1	1.7	1.9	2.8
2002-2012	23.6	11.7	7.7	2.7	3.1	4.4

Note: @ Average growth in trade/average real GDP growth.

Source: World Bank and United Nations Conference on Trade and Development (UNCTAD).

of the world which has helped India's share in world trade grow over the decade. But, since the crisis of 2008, not only has India's trade elasticity come down significantly to 1.9 from 3.8 in the pre-crisis period, the real GDP growth is also converging more or less to the world's GDP growth rate (Figure 5.3). Looking at both, lower GDP growth and lower elasticity of trade to GDP, the trade outlook for the near term is indeed bleak and requires some special attention and strategic policy direction.

Figure 5.3

Trade Growth of India and World along with Real GDP Growth (Constant 2005 \$) of India and World (%)

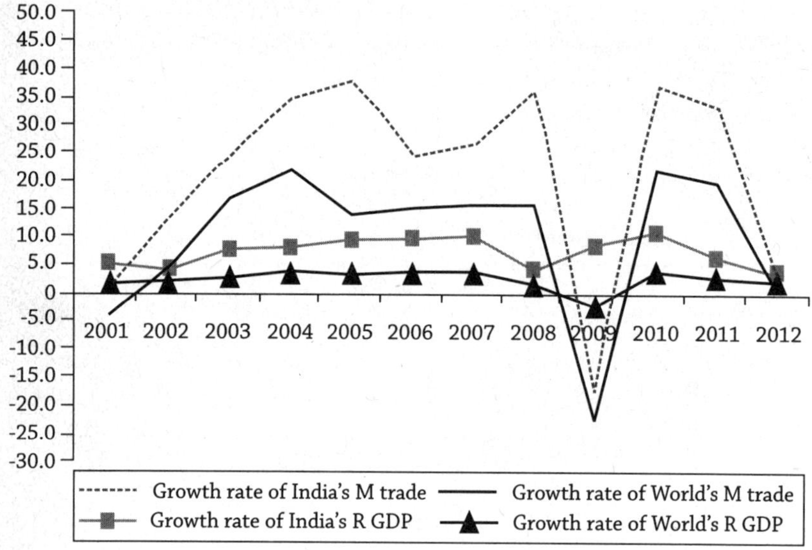

Direction and Composition

Both in terms of direction and composition of commodities, India's trade still remains highly skewed despite some diversification seen in the last few years. This is reflected in the concentration of trade with a few countries, and in a few commodity groups. This tendency is evident both with respect to exports and imports. This makes India's trade vulnerable. The trade policy objective of diversification is yet to be achieved. Apart from this, what is also evident is the widening trade imbalance, which is biased towards imports rather than exports.

Direction of India's Trade

Direction of trade data reveals that India's trading partners are about 230 countries globally. But, of these, more than 60 per cent of trade volume (in \$) is with 23 countries. Among these 23 countries, India depends on only 4 countries, *viz.*, United Arab Emirates (UAE), China, US and Saudi Arabia, for more than 51 per cent of trade. Such an overdependence makes India's trade performance vulnerable to any changes that take place in these few countries.

India has been consistently maintaining trade deficits with most of the top trading partners. In terms of trade volume, the top 10 countries in order of importance in 2012-13 were: the UAE, China, the US, Saudi Arabia, Switzerland, Germany, Singapore, Hong Kong, Indonesia and Japan, accounting for 48 per cent of total trade. India had a negative trade balance with 6 of these countries, *viz.*, China, Saudi Arabia, Switzerland, Germany, Indonesia and Japan, far in excess of the positive balance with the remaining 4 countries. Among the top 23 countries accounting for about 60 per cent of total trade volume, India's trade balance remained negative along with as many as 14 countries [*Economic & Political Weekly* (EPW), 2013]. China has emerged as one of the important trading partners of India over the years, but the benefits are skewed towards China. In the first five months of 2013, India's trade deficit with China is reported to have increased by 34 per cent to reach $12 billion.

Exports have no doubt become more diversified in terms of trading partners with a shift from developed economies towards developing ones, with China becoming one of the top three trading partners. Directional changes in exports were also seen clearly in the post-crisis period. India's exports to Europe, America, and Commonwealth of Independent States and Baltic shrunk after the economic slowdown hit in the year 2008. On the other hand, India's exports to Asian and African countries went up after the crisis. India has thus shifted focus from traditional markets in European and American countries to Asian countries.

The highest and most drastic shift in the direction of India's imports was seen from Asia, which was 29.22 per cent in total imports in 2002-03, which increased to reach 60 per cent of India's total imports in the year 2012-13. India's imports from northeast Asian countries (consisting of China, Japan and Hong Kong) have consistently remained higher with about 12 per cent share. Decline in imports from Europe (from European Union countries) has been seen in the post-crisis period. Imports from America also bettered on account of augmented import from Latin American countries, while imports from North America came down after the crisis.

Composition of India's Trade

Exports: Compositional changes in India's export basket have been taking place over the years. A gradual shift in India's manufacturing exports was seen from labour-intensive sectors like textiles, leather and manufacturing, handicrafts, and carpets, to capital and skill-intensive sectors. Share of primary products in India's exports fell over the years from 15.90 per cent in FY 2000-01 to 14.20 per cent in FY 2012-13 (Table 5.2).

Table 5.2

Share of Export of Principal Commodities Group (%)

Commodity	*2000-01*	*2007-08*	*2008-09*	*2009-10*	*2010-11*	*2011-12*	*2012-13*
Primary products	15.90	15.60	13.50	13.70	12.00	13.40	14.20
Plantation	1.48	0.60	0.58	0.59	0.56	0.59	0.58
Agri and allied products	8.80	8.31	7.84	7.06	6.91	8.96	10.61
Marine products	3.16	1.06	0.83	1.17	1.04	1.13	1.15
Ores and minerals	2.62	5.61	4.26	4.88	3.45	2.75	1.85
Manufactured products	83.00	84.60	86.50	86.30	88.00	86.60	85.80
Leather and mnfrs	4.41	2.15	1.94	1.88	1.56	1.57	1.62
Gems and jewellery	16.75	12.07	15.33	16.27	16.13	14.67	14.45
Sports goods	0.15	0.08	0.08	0.08	0.07	0.07	0.07
Chemicals and related products	14.01	13.72	12.99	13.66	12.29	12.87	14.15
Engineering goods	12.87	20.68	21.85	18.21	19.84	19.14	18.89
Electronic goods	2.54	2.15	3.87	3.15	3.30	3.06	2.81
Projects goods	0.06	0.09	0.08	0.06	0.03	0.03	0.05
Textiles	24.26	11.33	10.43	10.71	9.24	8.89	8.78
Handicrafts	1.50	0.31	0.16	0.13	0.10	0.09	0.07
Carpets	1.32	0.58	0.42	0.41	0.41	0.28	0.33
Cotton raw incl waste	0.11	1.36	0.35	1.15	1.16	1.41	1.22
Petroleum products	4.29	17.42	14.87	15.77	16.52	18.32	19.98
Unclassified exports	1.66	2.49	4.13	4.83	7.40	6.18	3.39
Total	100	100	100	100	100	100	100

Source: DGCIS, Kolkata.

Contribution of the top 10 commodities was on an average at 62 per cent, for the period starting from 2003-04 up to 2012-13. Petroleum (crude and products), gems and jewellery, transport equipment, machinery and instruments, and electronics goods are among the top 10 commodities. Export of gems and jewellery increased steadily in value terms. Export of petroleum also grew consistently but for a dip recorded in FY 2008-09. Transport equipment was the persistent performer among this group. Rather, most of the commodities in this band improved performance each year except in 2008-09, when impact of crisis surfaced leading to a moderation in exports.

About 58 per cent to 60 per cent of India's export earnings are generated from four commodity groups, *viz.*, garment, gems and jewellery, engineering goods, and petroleum products. The share of engineering goods which reached 21.85 per cent in 2008-09 dipped to 18.9 per cent in 2012-13. The share of gems and jewellery came down to around 14 per cent from 17 per cent. The jewellery industry is an import-based industry and hence sufficient credit in foreign currency is a must for easy and continued availability of raw diamond. Export of ready-made garments saw a substantial fall during the period. The share of ready-made garments dipped to 4.3 per cent from about 12.5 per cent mainly due to competition from China, Bangladesh, Turkey and Vietnam. This sector is labour-intensive and offers maximum scope for export and employment growth.

Imports: India is a net importer of crude oil for its energy needs and has faced rising petroleum imports. In recent times, global oil prices are more or less stable, but India's petroleum bills have gone up mainly due to an increase in demand for petroleum in volume terms.

Presently, the share of petroleum import is about 35 per cent of total imports. Similarly, the import of hi-tech capital good imports whose share now is about 18 per cent may also go up. This is unavoidable for a developing economy. But, the share of gold import which was averaging at about 7 per cent of total imports jumped to about 11.5 per cent in the last couple of years (Table 5.3). As a result, import bill increased from $4 billion to $58 billion between 2000-01 and 2011-12.

Strategic Rethink

Since India is facing a widening trade deficit with major trading partners, bilateral trade negotiations should emphasise some element of reciprocity. Now, the position seems to be one-sided favouring the partner's interests more than India's.

Manufacturing exports have the lion's share in total exports over the years. It constituted 85 per cent of the total merchandise exports in FY 2003-04 which increased over the period to 86 per cent in 2012-13. The manufacturing sector has sustained its share but growth somehow looks restricted.

Table 5.3

Share of Imports of Principal Commodities Group (%)

Commodity Group	*2000-01*	*2007-08*	*2008-09*	*2009-10*	*2010-11*	*2011-12*	*2012-13*
A) Bulk Imports	41.82	44.62	45.58	42.92	40.60	43.63	46.35
of which: Petroleum Crude and Products	31.32	31.70	30.84	30.22	28.66	31.67	34.43
B) Pearls, Precious and Semi-Precious Stones	9.62	3.16	5.53	5.65	9.36	5.76	4.59
C) Machinery	8.22	18.00	13.50	12.55	11.20	10.58	9.89
D) Project Goods	1.50	0.51	1.05	1.63	1.66	1.79	1.33
E) Others	38.84	33.71	34.34	37.24	37.17	38.24	37.83
of which: Gold and Silver	9.28	7.05	7.39	10.33	11.52	12.59	11.34
Total	100	100	100	100	100	100	100

Source: DGCIS, Kolkata.

As noted by Kumar and Gupta (2008), the lack of a focused approach in identifying, sustaining and building the country's competitive advantage, the concentration of exports in low value categories and relatively poor inflow of foreign direct investment (FDI), especially in export-oriented industries are responsible for the relatively weak performance of India's manufacturing exports.

Exports have shifted towards technology-intensive manufacturing exports with an increased share of engineering goods, petroleum products, chemical and related products from labour-intensive traditional sectors like textiles, gems and jewellery, leather, jute, carpets, and handicrafts. There is scope to improve efficiency of these sectors which can contribute to enhance their share in manufacturing exports. Boosting exports of these sectors has the added advantage of increasing employment as these are labour-intensive industries. These sectors are facing peculiar problems. These include securing availability of raw material and alter native markets for gems and jewellery, corporatisation and compliance of environmental standards for leather, techno logy upgrades for improved productivity, balance between the domestic and export requirements for jute, and ways and means to handle variations in international demand for carpets and handicrafts.

If we want to enhance our performance in these traditional sectors we need to tide over existing shortcomings by ensuring adequate availability of raw material, skill development, manufacturing parks/clusters, tapping potential markets, appropriate brand promotion, providing financial/fiscal incentives, capacity building for export, continuation of existing schemes, etc. Micro, small and medium enterprises (MSMEs) have made substantial contributions to the Indian economy, and exports from this sector have been accorded high priority in India's export promotion strategy. The sector faces a number of problems such as low levels of technology and innovation, inadequate access to concessional credit, poor marketing, and branding, packaging and complicated government procedures. Addressing these problems is expected to improve their production capability and exports. Emphasis of the strategy is on skill development and training, standardisation and quality, access to affordable credit, impetus for innovation, and brand building.

The share of MSMEs in total exports is spread across different product segments. In case of items like textiles, leather goods, processed food, engineering goods, and gems and jewellery, export performance has been commendable over the years. Sectors like sports goods are almost 100 per cent export-oriented. In view of this, export promotion from MSME sector has been accorded high priority in India's export promotion strategy which includes simplification of procedures, incentives for higher production of exports, preferential treatment to MSMEs in market development fund, simplification of duty drawback rules, higher value addition, skill development and training, thrust on standardisation and quality, access to affordable credit, impetus for innovation, etc., would be essential elements of the strategy (GoI, 2011).

The focus on gold and oil alone to restrict imports tends to obscure other important impediments which are also structural and policy-induced. India has the third largest coal reserves in the world, yet it has imported substantial quantity of coal for internal consumption, and thus share of coal and coke in total import rose from about 2.2 per cent to 3.4 per cent between 2000-01 and 2012-13. Similarly, one-third of fertiliser consumption is imported as there was inadequate production capacity within India. Share of fertiliser in total imports is still about 2 per cent. India is also among the larger edible-oil-consuming countries, but it still imports edible oil from countries like Malaysia and Indonesia for domestic consumption. The ban on iron ore mining in several states has meant that steel producers have to import ore. The share of metalliferrous ores and products in imports doubled to 3 per cent during the period. Similarly, the shares of import of many conspicuous consumption goods are also increasing.

Thus, the faster growth of imports is getting more and more skewed in favour of gold and avoidable imports of some commodities and luxury items. Such items cover more than 25 per cent of India's import bill. Import substitution in several commodities should be explored.

To conclude, after the eruption of the sub-prime crisis in the US which was followed by the European crisis, it was inevitable to change our focus towards non-traditional markets to keep our exports alive, which have taken a major hit after the crisis and still remained shaky. There is a dire need to scale up exports in the wake of unabated and inevitable high imports.

References

EPW (2013). "Current Statistics, 'Direction of Trade'", *Economic & Political Weekly* 48(29): 129-30.

Government of India (2009). "Foreign Trade Policy", Ministry of Commerce and Industry, 27 August.

———. (2011): "Report of the Working Group on 'Boosting India's Manufacturing Exports,'" *Twelfth Five-Year Plan (2012-17)*, Ministry of Commerce and Industry, Government of India.

Kumar, Rajiv and Abhijit Sen Gupta (2008). "Towards a Competitive Manufacturing Sector", *Working Paper* No. 203, ICRIER, February.

Economic & Political Weekly xlvIiI(31). 3 August 2013.

6

BISWAJIT DHAR

India's New Foreign Trade Policy

Pluses and Minuses

THE long-awaited foreign trade policy (FTP) of the National Democratic Alliance (NDA) government evoked much interest both because it was the first comprehensive statement on the government's priorities in the external sector, and also, perhaps more importantly, it would show if the present government has set its sights differently from the United Progressive Alliance (UPA) government.

It was the UPA government that tabled the first FTP in 2004, replacing the export–import policy. This seemed to suggest a change in the thinking of the policymakers—they had finally understood that it was necessary to move beyond export–import procedures and incentives for improving foreign trade performance, and that it was imperative for FTP to consider policies for improving production efficiencies and reducing transaction costs. In other words, FTP had to extend beyond the decisionmaking confines of the Department of Commerce, and the department had to develop a broader framework that provided the scope for coordinating with a number of administrative ministries to make the foreign trade sector more vibrant. But despite tabling two five year FTPs, the UPA government did little to change the orientation of policymaking in trade.

The NDA government has attempted a new approach in its FTP by tabling two documents. While the main document follows the UPA government's practice of detailing export–import procedures, the new government has made a detailed foreign trade policy statement (FTPS) that articulates its overall thinking on the external sector, covering two key dimensions. First, the policy statement spells out the government's strategy for addressing some of the structural and institutional issues that are relevant for improving the performance of the foreign trade sector. Second, the government has given some idea about its thinking on the ways in which it would make trade and economic integration agreements with major trade partners work better for Indian enterprises. The second dimension is important because India has concluded a number of economic integration agreements with trade partners over the past decade, but most of them have not delivered the expected results.

'Whole-of-Government' Approach

It must be said to the credit of the Department of Commerce that it recognises that "foreign trade policy can neither be formulated nor implemented by any one department in isolation" and that "a 'whole-of-government' approach will be required." The FTPS speaks of a "major path-breaking" initiatives that the department has taken "to mainstream State and Union Territory (UT) Governments and various departments and ministries of the Government of India in the process of international trade." Yet, another reflection of a possible change in thinking in the commerce department is an important statement made in the FTPs—"the biggest challenges that India's foreign trade faces today are from within the country." To meet these challenges, the FTPS underlines the need for "Setting Our House in Order."

There is no doubt that bold print of the FTP shows a welcome departure from past thinking. The proposed involvement of other departments and ministries of the central government as well as state and union territory governments, and the recognition of "behind the-border" constraints faced while engaging in foreign trade should be regarded as steps in the right direction. However, the details of this strategy spelt out in the FTPS have several limitations, and there is a strong case for looking at them anew.

The "whole-of-government approach" lists the possible areas of engagement with state and union territory governments, but is silent about the manner in which departments and ministries of the central government would be involved in supporting conduct of foreign trade. As for states and union territory governments, the FTPS mentions that they "can play a crucial role in promoting exports and rationalising non-essential imports." This statement is quite intriguing since governments in member-countries of the World Trade Organization (WTO) have little policy space to either promote exports or restrict "non-essential imports." One of the key objectives of the WTO is to minimise government interference in the conduct of foreign trade and, therefore, members are not allowed to provide subsidies and other incentives for promoting exports. As for "rationalising non-essential imports" (appears to be a euphemism for "restricting imports"), it should be pointed out that state and union territory governments do not have any instruments for doing so. Imports can only be restricted by using customs duties, which can only be imposed by the central government. Further, India had the right to restrict imports of "non-essential" products using quantitative restrictions because of a weak balance of payments (BoP) situation, which it did until 2000. However, this right had to be given up in 2001 after a WTO Dispute Settlement Panel ruled that India no longer faced BoP problems and therefore had no basis to continue with these restrictions.

The other dimensions of involving state and union territory governments that are listed in the FTPS are essentially statements of intent. These include assistance that the Department of Commerce is providing state and union territory governments to prepare export strategies and set up an "Export Promotion Mission to provide an institutional framework to work with State Governments to boost India's exports." It is not entirely clear from the FTPS how these initiatives will give the necessary impetus to state and union territory governments to participate more vigorously in export promotion.

Three Issues Highlighted

What are the steps that the FTPS suggests for "setting our domestic house in order?" It suggests this can be done by addressing three sets of issues. The first is to make better use of telecommunications and information technology (IT) infrastructure, especially the internet, in trade transactions. The second is to remove the anomalies caused by the "absence of a uniform system of indirect taxation in India." The existing system, according to the FTPS, prevents exporters from getting "a rebate or drawback on all indirect taxes paid on the exported product and the inputs that went into its production, significantly inflating the final price of the exported product and making it less price competitive". And the third is the "liberalisation, rationalisation and simplification of labour laws." The FTPS insists,

> Recent initiatives by the Central Government and some State Governments ...must be taken to their logical conclusion in order to make Indian labour more productive and efficient, which will, in turn, contribute to enhancing the global competitiveness of India's products.

Given the huge burden of inefficiencies that plague the domestic manufacturing sector, which often begin at the shop-floor, the three areas identified by the FTPS seem to convey yet again that the policymakers are not fully cognisant with what it takes to make India a globally competitive production hub. What is really needed is actualising the "whole-of-government" approach, which can provide a comprehensive view about the needs of the manufacturing sector for enhancing its competitiveness. This approach, which was a feature of policies adopted by most of the successful countries in East Asia, is essential for repositioning Indian industry on the world stage.

SEZ Failure

Special economic zones (SEZS) are another area where successive governments have ignored the steps necessary to make them function effectively. Although the FTPS says that exports from SEZs increased significantly from ₹22,000 crore in 2005–06 to ₹4,94,077 crore in 2013–2014, there is a facet of these zones that the government needs to consider. Since the notification of rules under the SEZ Act in 2006, 435 SEZ had been formally approved by the Board of Approvals until March 2015. Of these approved SEZS, 189 have been functional. Importantly, all but 20 of these SEZS were established before 2010 and only three after 2013. The past few years have also witnessed a spate of cancellations of the approvals granted for setting up SEZS. Since July 2014, approvals for 82 SEZS have been withdrawn by the Board of Approvals. India's experience with SEZS thus seems to be at considerable variance with that of China, where SEZs have contributed immensely to the country's export growth over the past several decades. One possible way forward for the Government of India would be to understand the process countries such as China follow for establishing of successful SEZS and consider applying good practices wherever they are possible under Indian conditions.

Regional Trade Agreements

As mentioned, the FTPS provides an account of the Government of India's position on its economic integration agreements with partner countries. The commerce and industries minister has commented on more than one occasion that these agreements have not been particularly beneficial to India's interests and that they must be comprehensively reviewed. Perhaps in the continuation of this position, the FTPS indicates that two sets of initiatives should be taken—one, to make these agreements work better for Indian enterprises through focused programmes; and two, to explore opportunities in countries where India has a relatively small footprint, including through economic integration agreements.

The South Asian Free Trade Agreement (SAFTA), one of the older free trade agreements that India is a party to, has remained largely dormant. The government has proposed reinvigorating SAFTA by building regional value chains in several sectors that are of considerable interest to the countries in the region, which include textiles, engineering goods, chemicals, pharmaceuticals, auto components, and plastic and leather products. Successful implementation of this proposal would go a long way towards furthering the cause of South Asian regional integration.

India's free trade agreement with the Association of Southeast Asian Nations (ASEAN), which has been operational since 2009, has not brought the desired benefits. The present government has therefore proposed reworking the contours of its engagement with its eastern neighbours by focusing on trade integration with the CLMV (Cambodia, Lao PDR, Myanmar and Vietnam) countries. As a part of this strategy, it has decided to support the development of manufacturing hubs by the Indian private sector in these countries.

The government has indicated that it will actively consider enhancing India's economic engagements with the African region by assisting countries there to develop their productive capacities in both agriculture and manufacturing. Such a programme would not only complement the development cooperation initiatives that were taken by the UPA government, but also enable these initiatives to yield better results.

Although the FTPS is an important statement of the government's intent to improve the performance of the foreign trade sector, the results are not likely to be delivered if the operational framework is not made functionally more robust. There are a number of weaknesses in the proposed framework and the government would need to address them. There is a greater urgency for so doing because the FTPS sets an ambitious target of increasing India's exports of merchandise and services to $900 billion by 2019–20, which would raise the country's share in world exports to 3.5 per cent from the 2 per cent it is now.

Economic & Political Weekly I(16). 18 April 2015.

7

SIMON DEAKIN and ANTARA HALDAR

How Should India Reform Its Labour Laws?

Introduction

Labour law reform has come on the political agenda in India, particularly in the wake of the elections in May 2014 of the Narendra Modi-led government at the centre. India's labour laws are decades old and are said to suffer from rigidities which are holding back economic development. Worker-protective labour laws, it is argued, are deterring investment and stalling the growth of formal employment. India's labour laws are set at an inappropriately high level for a developing economy, which would otherwise be in a position to use low-cost labour as a source of comparative advantage. The strict regulation of employment terminations ("retrenchments") in Part V B of the Industrial Disputes Act (IDA) 1947 (as amended in 1976) has been a particular focus of criticism. Critics of this law argue that as it targets larger plants and enterprises for regulation, it discourages the growth of firms, and contributes to labour informality.

Viewed in a comparative perspective, India's recent focus on labour law reform is not unique: other middle-income countries have been having similar debates about the form and content of labour regulation. While these debates sometimes lead to deregulation, there is no worldwide trend towards the weakening of worker-protective labour laws (Adams and Deakin 2015). Although the discourse of the World Bank and other international financial institutions remains focused on the need for flexibility in labour markets, there is an emerging view at the country level that labour flexibility is not a sufficient condition for economic development, and perhaps not even a necessary one. Instead the focus is increasingly on how to build institutions for managing labour market risks in the transition to a formal economy (Marshall and Fenwick 2015). In this paper we seek to locate the debate over the future of labour law in India in the context of global trends, as seen through the lens of recent theoretical and empirical contributions to the study of labour regulation, and in relation to India's own experiments in regulatory reform, in particular the "Gujarat model." Section 2 outlines the movement of labour market theory away from equilibrium-based models, with their emphasis on labour law as a distortion of competition, towards an evolutionary understanding of labour market institutions, which takes a more nuanced view of their efficiency effects. Section 3 reviews empirical evidence on the operation of labour law systems, including India's. Section 4 looks at the Gujarat model and its combination of labour law deregulation, financial incentives for business and infrastructural investment. Section 5 contains the conclusions.

Developments in the Theory of Labour Regulation

Beginning in the 1980s and gathering strength during the years of the "Washington Consensus", the economic critique of labour law was part of a wider case against regulation, which saw state interference as the source of distortions and inefficiencies in the operation of markets. This argument depended critically on the validity of its main premise, which is that markets, if unregulated, will move naturally or spontaneously to an equilibrium state. Neoclassical economics, which is the foundation of this view, has been highly effective in describing, and mathematically modelling, a state of the world in which, through perfect competition, supply and demand are equalised, and the aggregate wealth (or, in some versions, well-being) of market actors is thereby maximised. In such a world, any outside interference with free exchange will, by definition, have negative effects on economic welfare. This follows axiomatically from the assumptions of individual rationality (consistent preferences coupled with maximisation) and market equilibrium which underlie neoclassical models (Becker 1976).

It is one thing to model pure competition as a possible state of the world, and another to assume that it is the norm. Since the mathematical formalisation of the competitive market economy reached its apogee in the middle decades of the 20th century (Arrow and Hahn 1971), economic theory has directed its attention towards understanding how market exchange comes to be established in the first place, a very different question. This research agenda has gradually coalesced around the idea that perfect competition is a highly unusual state of affairs that it is not often, if indeed ever, replicated in real-life market economies (Coase 1988). Meanwhile, the processes by which markets are instituted and sustained are still poorly understood, with historical research pointing to a range of causally relevant institutions (North 2005).

The reorientation of the social sciences away from the study of markets in equilibrium towards analysis of the dynamics of institutions and institutional change has significant implications for labour markets in general and for the experience of developing countries in particular. A long tradition in economics, dating at least from Adam Smith (1776), recognises that power is unevenly distributed within the employment relationship. Modern institutional economics generally avoids using the term "power" but recognises that labour markets are far from perfect. Labour market outcomes are skewed by transaction costs arising from uncertainty and incompleteness of contracting (Williamson, Wachter and Harris 1975) and by externalities arising from asymmetric information (Shapiro and Stiglitz 1984). Characteristic features of labour market regulations in industrial market economies can be understood as evolved responses to the coordination problems associated with the distinctive form of the employment contract (Deakin and Sarkar 2008). These include social insurance (Esping-Andersen 1996), employment protection (Acharya, Baghai-Wadji and Subramanian 2014) and worker representation (Rogers and Streeck 1995). The right to strike, in addition to being framed as a human right deriving from the principle of freedom of association, can also be analysed as a counterweight to the managerial prerogative which law and custom together vest in the employer, with results that may, in principle, be conducive to the efficient operation of the market (Moore 2014).

This point of view does not imply that labour market regulation is always and everywhere efficient. In the context of industrial economies with established institutions, there is a debate to be had over the appropriate form of regulation and over the degree of worker protection which is compatible with the use of the market as a mechanism of resource allocation. There may be trade-offs between equity and efficiency under certain circumstances, and complementarities between a fairer distribution and sustainable economic growth in others (Deakin and Wilkinson 2005). In the final analysis these are empirical questions which cannot be addressed through theoretical reasoning alone, but a theory grounded in the experience of real-life economies is to be preferred to one based on axiomatic reasoning.

In developing economies, the debate takes a distinct form. Where the institutions which might underpin a formal labour market are still in the process of emerging, the issue for policymakers is, or should be, whether labour laws are likely to advance that process, or to hinder it (Marshall 2015). On the one hand, there is a case against transplanting into a developing country context laws which were designed for mature industrial systems. In particular, laws which presuppose the existence of a formal economy in which wage dependence is the norm may have little relevance for economies in which the majority of the population relies on access to the land or the family for subsistence.

On the other hand, the transition to a wage-based economy with formal labour market relations does not occur in an institutional vacuum. Loss of access to traditional means of subsistence is compensated for by new forms of mutualisation and protection for the working population. In the global North, the transition to an industrial economy occurred coterminously with the evolution of institutions for managing and diffusing labour market risks, including laws on wage regulation, poor relief and apprenticeship, which anticipated later features of modern welfare states in Europe and North America (Deakin and Wilkinson 2005). Thus the claim that developing countries have no need of laws to underpin emerging labour market institutions, whatever other arguments might be made in its favour, is not supported by the historical record of the countries which were first to industrialise. On the contrary, it was largely through the legal framework that labour capacity, which is not a "natural commodity" (Marx 1847; Polanyi 1944), acquired the form needed to sustain the complex economic relations and deep division of labour of a market economy (Deakin and Supiot 2009).

Middle-income countries today are very far from being pure subsistence economies. The characteristic pattern is for a formal economy consisting of a minority (of varying size) of the working population to coexist with a larger informal sector. In the informal sector, workers and households tend to rely for subsistence on a combination of waged work and access to the land and family incomes. Employment in the informal sector is irregular and discontinuous, as well as being insecure in the wider sense of providing limited access, at best, to collective mechanisms for sharing and diffusing labour market risks. In economies with this type of mix, it is far from clear that labour laws are irrelevant to the operation of the economy. Even when reliance on wage labour is partial or incomplete, laws which regularise the hiring process, protect the right to wages and permit workers to self-organise for the purpose of collective bargaining, can address needs of workers in the informal sector for greater income security. Similarly, bringing informal enterprises into the coverage of social insurance systems can help mitigate the economic risks to which informal sector workers are exposed.

Much has been made of the argument that poverty in developing countries is the result of the failure of the legal system to recognise the interests of the poor in land and other tangible assets which could, with appropriate legal title, be used as collateral (De Soto 2000). The limited success of land titling programmes to date suggests that the simple equation of legal rights with developmental capacity is misplaced (Haldar and Stiglitz 2013).

While there may be many reasons in practice for the failure of land titling to realise hoped-for economic benefits, the insight that the legal system plays a significant role in supporting economic exchange in middle-income countries is not necessarily mistaken (Chen and Deakin 2015). But it is striking that the proponents of legal formality in credit and capital markets should have had little to say about the role the legal system could play in promoting access to labour markets in middle-income countries. There is an inconsistency in regarding credit as an institutional commodity when labour power is seen as a natural one, requiring nothing more than the free play of market forces. This omission is the more surprising since extending wage protection and social insurance systems has the potential to benefit a far higher proportion of the working-age population in these countries than can be reached through land titling schemes.

Empirical Evidence on the Economic Effects of Labour Laws

Just as theory has moved on since the high point of the "Washington Consensus," the same trend can be observed in the empirical literature on labour regulation. In the late 1990s and early 2000s a small but influential literature appeared to have settled the debate in favour of the supporters of deregulation and labour market flexibility. Fallon and Lucas (1999), using a cross-national panel data analysis, found evidence of a negative relationship between worker-protective labour law and labour demand in a number of countries, including India. This finding was repeated in the larger panel data set of labour laws across the world constructed by Botero *et al.* (2004). Of most significance for India was the study carried out by Besley and Burgess (2004), which found evidence of a negative impact on employment and investment of the adoption of worker-protective laws at the sub-national (state) level. This study has been used to support claims that labour laws are one of the factors contributing to the relatively small size of the formal economy in India, which in 2014 accounts for less than 10 per cent of the total labour force.

Much has been written on the Besley–Burgess study. On one view, the methodology used to measure differences in state-level labour laws is insufficiently robust to justify clear conclusions being drawn from their analysis (Bhattarcharjea 2006, 2009; Jha and Golder 2008). On another, once the Besley–Burgess index is corrected for coding errors, the same negative impact of labour laws is found (Ahsan and Pagés 2009). Even so, the results of the original study do not survive once account is taken of limited effectiveness, including court delays and difficulties of accessing the judicial system, in the enforcement of labour laws in India (Fagernäs 2010). The econometric method used to test for correlations between the scores in the index and outcome variables measuring employment and investment has also been called into question (D'Souza 2010). There is evidence that insofar as there is a correlation between worker protective labour laws and economic indicators, changes in the law are endogenous to those in the wider economy. Thus for the most part, Indian labour law has largely been responsive to wider factors in the economy, rather than a determining cause of them (Dutta Roy 2004; Deakin and Sarkar 2011).

An obstacle to achieving a better understanding of the role of labour law in economic development has been the lack of data that can track changes in the legal framework over time in both developed and developing countries. The most widely used index for employment protection law is the Organization for Economic Cooperation and Development's (OECD). Employment Protection Index (EPI) (OECD, various years). However, it does not cover many developing countries, and while its ambit has recently been extended to include some systems outside the OECD, it does not provide a continuous time series for these countries. India and China, for example, are coded from 2008 only, and Brazil from 2010. The World Bank's Employing Workers Index (EWI) provides longitudinal data on dismissal regulation (among other things) going back to the 2000s (World Bank, various years), but has been subject to criticism for its methodology (Manuel Report 2013), in particular its focus on the regulations governing a standard employment relationship of full-time, permanent work which is not typical, in practice, for emerging markets. In both the EPI and EWI, data are based on mixture of survey evidence and analysis of legal materials, making it hard to discern the source of the codings.

The Centre for Business Research Labour Regulation Index (CBR–LRI) is a data set constructed by researchers at Cambridge University (including one of the present authors) which provides a continuous time series on country-level changes in labour law going back to the early 1970s (or late 1980s/early 1990s in the case of former socialist systems) (for explanations of the methodology used in the construction of the data set, see Deakin, Lele and Siems 2007; Adams and Deakin 2015). The data in CBR–LRI are based on content analysis of legal texts and other primary sources of labour law rules, using a coding algorithm designed to capture gradations of labour protection (so that on a 0–1 scale, a higher score indicates a greater degree of protection for the worker). As such, the data set can only capture cross-national variations in the formal (de jure) law, but it can be combined with other indices, including the World Bank's Rule of Law Index (World Bank 2015), to give a more complete picture of the operation of the law (Deakin and Sarkar 2008; Deakin, Malmberg and Sarkar 2014; Deakin, Fenwick and Sarkar 2014).

Table 7.1 sets out the scores in the CBR–LRI sub-index on dismissal protection for India (variables 25–31 out of a larger index consisting of 40 individual indicators). The explanations for the codings are provided at the point when the law changes (or from 1970, if it was in force at that point). The indicators cover the normal content of rules governing employment protection, including those regulating the minimum period of notice that the employer must give; entitlement to redundancy or severance pay; qualifying or arbitration periods; procedural and substantive standards relating to terminations; notification of dismissal; redundancy selection; and priority in rehiring. The provisions of the IDA 1947 as amended in 1976 are reflected in the high scores attributed to India for this part of the sub-index.

Some sense of India's position in comparison to other developed and developing countries can be obtained from Figures 7.1 and 7.2. India's dismissal laws are at the more protective end of the scale when compared to developing countries such as Germany and the UK, although they are not stricter than those of France. In relation to middle-income

Table 7.1

Dismissal Protection in India, 1970–2013

Variable	*Template*	*Score*	*Explanation*
Legally-mandated notice period (all dismissals)	Measures the length of notice, in weeks, that has to be given to a worker with three years' employment. Normalise the score so that 0 weeks = 0 and 12 weeks = 1.	1970–75: 0.33 1976–2013: 1	From 1970 the rule was one month or 4.3 weeks: Industrial Disputes Act (IDA) s 25F. From 1976 it was three months for an employee with one year's service in an establishment employing 300 workers, reduced to 100 from 1984: IDA s 25N, eventually declared constitutional in 1992 (Meenaskhi Mills 1992), although before then it was effectively in force in a number of states.
Legally-mandated redundancy compensation	Measures the amount of redundancy compensation or severance pay payable to a worker made redundant after three years of employment, measured in weeks of pay. Normalise the score so that 0 weeks = 0 and 12 weeks = 1.	1970–2013: 0.5	IDA s 25F provides that for a retrenchment to be lawful, compensation must be paid at the rate of 15 days' average pay for every year of service.
Minimum qualifying period of service for normal case of unjust dismissal	Measures the period of service required before a worker qualifies for general protection against unjust dismissal. Normalise the score so that three years or more = 0, 0 months = 1	1970–2013: 0.67	One year qualifying period for procedural protection and right to compensation for retrenchment (s 25N IDA).

contd...

.contd...

Variable	*Template*	*Score*	*Explanation*
Law imposes procedural constraints on dismissal	Equals 1 if a dismissal is necessarily unjust if the employer fails to follow procedural requirements prior to dismissal. Equals 0.67 if failure to follow procedural requirements will normally lead to a finding of unjust dismissal. Equals 0.33 if failure to follow procedural requirement is just one factor taken into account in unjust dismissal cases. Equals 0 if there are no procedural requirements for dismissal. Scope for gradations between 0 and 1 to reflect changes in the strength of the law.	1970–2013: 1	Under the IDA, disciplinary proceedings must precede dismissal for misconduct. The workman must be informed of the alleged misconduct in writing and be given an opportunity to respond. Various formalities must be followed. See Industrial Employment (Standing Orders) Central Rules 1946, and extensive case law (*Barot vs State Transport Corporation* (1966), *Brooke Bond India vs Choudhary* (1969), *Chandulai vs Pan Am* (1985)).
Law imposes substantive constraints on dismissal	Equals 1 if dismissal is only permissible for serious misconduct or fault of the employee. Equals 0.67 if dismissal is lawful according to a wider range of legitimate reasons (misconduct, lack of capability, redundancy, etc). Equals 0.33 if dismissal is permissible if it is "just" or "fair" as defined by case law. Equals 0 if employment is at will (i e, no cause dismissal is normally permissible). Scope for gradations between 0 and 1 to reflect changes in the strength of the law.	1970–2013: 0.33	The court will intervene where there is lack of good faith, a breach of natural justice, an error of fact, or in the case of a perverse finding: Industrial Employment (Standing Orders) Central Rules 1946; extensive case law beginning with *Indian Iron and Steel Co* (1958)); IDA s11A, inserted in 1976.
Reinstatement normal remedy for unfair dismissal	Equals 1 if reinstatement is the normal remedy for unjust dismissal and is regularly enforced. Equals 0.67 if reinstatement and compensation are, de jure and de facto, alternative remedies. Equals 0.33 if compensation is the normal remedy. Equals 0 if no remedy is available as of right. Scope for further gradations between 0 and 1 to reflect changes in the strength of the law.	1970–2013:0.33 1976–2013: 0.67	IDA 1947, s 11A, inserted in 1976, formally gave labour courts the power to grant reinstatement as the ordinary remedy for dismissal, although the courts have been reluctant to grant it e.g., where to do so would be contrary to industrial peace (Tulsidas Paul 1964).

.contd...

.contd...

Variable	*Template*	*Score*	*Explanation*
Notification of dismissal	Equals 1 if by law or binding collective agreement the employer has to obtain the permission of a state body or third body prior to an individual dismissal. Equals 0.67 if a state body or third party has to be notified prior to the dismissal. Equals 0.33 if the employer has to give the worker written reasons for the dismissal. Equals 0 if an oral statement of dismissal to the worker suffices. Scope for further gradations between 0 and 1 to reflect changes in the strength of the law.	1970–1975: 0.67 1976–2013: 1	Between 1970 and 1975, under s 25F IDA, the employer had to notify the state authorities, give one month's notice in writing, and pay compensation to the employee. Under s 25N IDA, inserted in 1976, government permission and three months' notice were required for retrenchments in establishments of 300 or more employees, reduced to 100 from 1984.
Redundancy selection	Equals 1 if by law or binding collective agreement the employer must follow priority rules based on seniority, marital status, number or dependants, etc., prior to dismissing for redundancy. Equals 0 otherwise. Scope for further gradations between 0 and 1 to reflect changes in the strength of the law.	1970–2013: 1	The employer should follow the rule of seniority implied by the "last in, first out" rule: s 25G IDA.
Priority in re-employment	Equals 1 if by law or binding collective agreement the employer must follow priority rules relating to the re-employment of former workers. Equals 0 otherwise. Scope for further gradations between 0 and 1 to reflect changes in the strength of the law.	1970–2013: 1	There is a right to priority in re-employment on the part of retrenched workers: s 25H IDA.

Source: CBR Labour Regulation Index (Deakin, Lele and Siems 2007; Adams and Deakin 2015).

Figure 7.1

Dismissal Laws in Selected Developed Countries

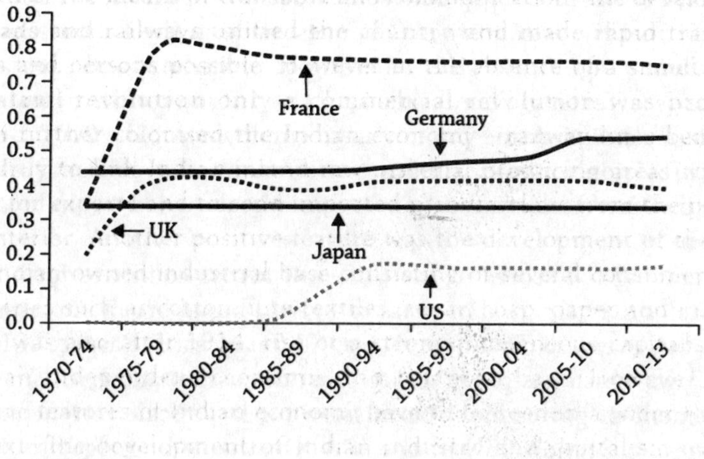

Source: See Table 7.1.

Figure 7.2

Dismissal Laws in Selected Developing Countries

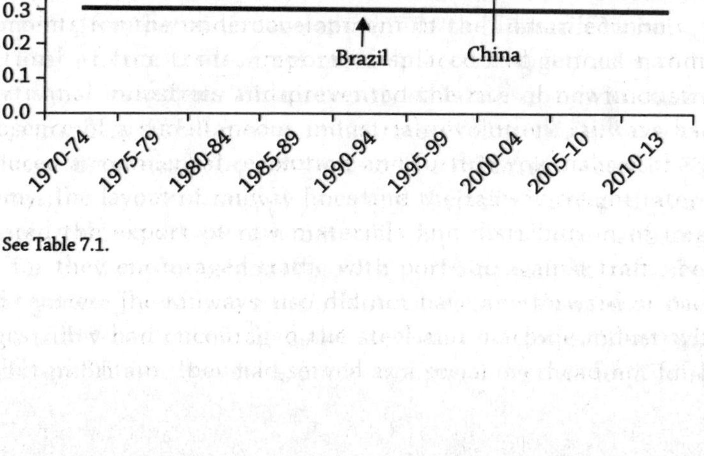

Source: See Table 7.1.

countries (Figure 7.2), India has again scored more highly for worker protection, but the reforms made in China by the Labour Contract Act 2007 have removed the gap between these two countries, at least as far as the formal law is concerned. Changes made in the Labour Contract Act include a significant strengthening of procedural and substantive standards affecting dismissals and the introduction of rules on redundancy selection and priority in re-employment. The 2007 law also makes provision for trade unions to be consulted over dismissals and for the union to seek rectification of a dismissal carried out in breach of procedure.

Averaging the scores in the CBR–LRI across countries for a range of variables over a period of years can give a broad-brush impression of trends, but may also gloss over relevant differences. The aspect of Indian labour laws which has given rise to most discussion and criticism is the requirement of government permission for large-scale retrenchments, contained in Section 25N of the IDA. On the coding algorithm used in the CBR–LRI, this change, made in 1976, makes Indian labour law among the most workerprotective in the world, but it by no means is the only country with a high level of legal protection for workers in matters of dismissal.

Table 7.2 sets out in summary form the content of similar laws in other developed and developing countries. Nearly all have a notification law of some kind. France required administrative permission for dismissals between 1975 and 1986. This requirement was repealed in 1986 and replaced by an obligation to notify a state body, while also leaving intact the right of a dismissed worker to seek compensation or (less usually) reinstatement before a labour court. In Germany, notification of dismissal to the works council is required, and failure to comply with the process laid down for notification can lead to the nullification of the dismissal under certain circumstances.

When administrative permission was needed in France, prior to 1986, it was normal for it to be granted if the employer could demonstrate a prima facie case for the dismissal and if procedural requirements were followed. The move away from administrative oversight was accompanied by a strengthening of protection for the worker in the context of individual claims and by a growing role for collective worker voice on issues of dismissal. Thus it is not clear that the change of approach gave employers more leeway over dismissals than they had before. In some ways they may have had less once the certainty of administrative approvals was no longer available. In Germany, although the works council can, in principle, exercise a veto power over a dismissal, this very rarely happens in practice. Works council approval is sometimes used by employers to provide legitimacy for dismissals which might otherwise have been questioned.

Thus in the European approach, laws on notification of dismissal generally do not constitute an absolute bar on employment terminations. Rather, they serve to proceduralise the dismissal decision, in the sense of subjecting it to standards of fairness whose application is worked out on a case by case basis. It is an open question whether such laws hinder or assist employers. One view is that by legitimising dismissals, their overall effect is to strengthen managerial prerogative (Collins 1995).

In the Indian context, the requirement of state permission contained in Section 25N of the IDA may have been operated somewhat more strictly than its equivalents in western Europe. Empirical research (Ahsan and Pagés 2009) suggests that the law has in the past provided a disincentive to employers to increase numbers in employment over the threshold at which the requirement is triggered (300 workers from 1976; 100 from 1984). A case may therefore be made for modifying the IDA's notification requirements.

However, as we have seen, it is unusual for labour law systems to make no provision of any kind for notification. When formal administrative permission for terminations was removed in France in the mid-1980s, this was against the backdrop of a dismissal law which in other respects continued to provide significant procedural and substantive safeguards against dismissal, enforceable through recourse to the labour court (the conseil de prud'hommes). In Germany, the involvement of collective employee representatives in the dismissal process provides a check on the employer's termination power. In the Indian context, given the delays affecting court claims and the absence of a codetermination law or its equivalent, there can be no guarantee that the repeal of Section 25N would allow a similar shift from one mode of regulation to another.

Table 7.2

Rules on Notification of Dismissals in Selected Countries, 1970–2013

Country	*Score*	*Explanation*
Brazil	1970–89: 0	Under Art 477 of the Code on Labour Law, amended in 1990, a termination will only be valid if certain formalities are observed, including submission of a termination form to the Ministry of Labour.
China	1986–94: 0.5 1995-2007: 0.75 2008-13: 1	Under the Provisional Regulations on Labour Relations (1986), the employer had to consult the trade union and make a report of the dismissal to the administrative authorities and to the labour office. Labour Law 1994 Art 30 gave the trade union the right to make representations to the employer in a case where it considered termination to be inappropriate. The Labour Contract Law 2007 refers to notification to both the union and the public authorities in the case of both collective and individual dismissals. If the employer violates the law the trade union has the right to require rectification and the employer must consider the trade union's view and notify it of how it handled the matter.
France	1970–72: 0 1973-74: 0.33 1975-85: 1 1986-2013: 0.67	Under Law 75–5, the authorisation of a state body was required for economic dismissals, including individuals ones (Labour Code Art L 321–7). From 1986, this was replaced by a duty to notify the relevant state body. See now LC Art L 1233–115. Act No 75–5, codified as LC Art L122–14–1, provided that written reasons had to be given to the employee. See now LC Art L 1232–6.
Germany	1970–71: 0.5 1972: 0.67	Until 1972: §§ 65, 66(1) BetrVG (Works Constitution Act) stipulated that notification to the works council was necessary, but it was controversial whether violation of this norm affected the validity of dismissal (see Söllner, Arbeitsrecht, 3rd edn, 1972, p 164). § 102(1) BetrVG of 15 January 1972 (BGBl. I 1972, 13): violation does affect validity.
India	1970–75: 0.67 1976-2013: 1	Between 1970 and 1975, under s 25F Industrial Disputes Act, the employer had to notify the state authorities, give one month's notice in writing, and pay compensation to the employee. Under s 25N IDA, inserted in 1976, government permission and 3 months' notice were required for retrenchments in establishments of 300 or more employees, reduced to 100 from 1984.

contd...

.contd...

Japan	1970–2013: 0	There is no legal requirement for notification of dismissals.
Russia	1992–2013: 0.33	Notification in writing to the employee (see now Art.180, Labour Code).
South Africa	1970–2013: 0.33	Notification to the worker has been the norm in respect of individual dismissals under successive versions of the Labour Relations Act.
UK	1970–71: 0 1972-2013: 0.33	The normal rule since the inception of the unfair dismissal jurisdiction in 1971 (see now Employment Rights Act 1996) is that the employee must be given written reasons in writing.
US	1970–88: 0 1989-2013: 0.67	Written notice must be given to the exclusive representative or bargaining agent of affected employees or to unrepresented individual workers under the provisions of the Workplace Adjustment, Retraining and Notification Act 1988.

Source: See Table 7.1.

Reform of Part V B of the IDA should also take account of the growing empirical literature on the operation of employment protection laws in Europe and North America. Although this is a developing field, the literature by no means points to a deregulatory agenda (for an overview, see Adams and Deakin 2015). In studies making use of the CBR–LRI data set, dismissal protection is seen to encourage innovation based on workers' firm-specific skills and knowledge (Archarya et al 2014). Worker-protective dismissal regulation is generally correlated with improvements in productivity. In some countries (notably the United States), this results in reduced employment growth, as tighter controls over dismissal raise hiring costs, but in others (notably Germany), where dismissal laws operate alongside laws mandating vocational and educational training, these disemployment effects have been avoided (Deakin and Sarkar 2008). The provisional conclusion to be drawn from this literature is that dismissal laws may be conducive to employment growth where they operate alongside institutions to promote investment in human capital. Dismissal protection, along with laws mandating employee voice at work and collective bargaining over wages and terms and conditions, has also been shown to favour more egalitarian outcomes, in terms of the relative shares of wages and profits in national income (the "labour share"), and by reference to the Gini coefficient, which is a general measure of economic inequality (Deakin, Malmberg and Sarkar 2014; Deakin, Fenwick and Sarkar 2014).

The Gujarat Model

The "Gujarat model" of development has become a byword in development and economic policy circles since Narendra Modi's election as prime minister on 16 May 2014. The focal point of Modi's electoral campaign was the promise that he would do for India as a whole what he did for his home state, Gujarat. Over his decade-long period at the helm since 2001, the state acquired the reputation of being unparalleled in its "pro-business" approach, by offering a package of improved infrastructure (especially roads, but also ports) and good governance (reduced corruption and a streamlined bureaucracy, often achieved by means of innovative use of technology as in the case of the Jan Vikas Kendra simplifying certification processes, or the E-Jamin scheme for digitising land records). Land and labour were offered on favourable terms to businesses, including through the creation of special economic zones (SEZs) which were set up via forced land acquisition on a large scale. Under the Gujarat Industrial Disputes (Amendment) Act 2004 and the Gujarat Special Economic Zone Act of the same year, the bulk of national labour law was disapplied in the SEZs. In particular, Part V B of the IDA was replaced by a more liberal regime for employment terminations, under which the requirement of administrative authorisation for dismissals was replaced by a limited right to compensation for workers with a year or more of continuous employment. Further incentivisation was provided through "assistance packages" for investments over a certain amount. The Gujarat government currently advertises "path-breaking labour laws" alongside "facilities and fiscal benefits" (mostly exemptions from taxes and planning rules) for firms relocating to its SEZs (Government of Gujarat 2014).

There is, however, considerable dispute with respect to the nature of the Gujarat model. During the general election campaign, industry and investment, infrastructure and power were presented by its supporters as the key features of the model. Industrial growth appears to have jumped to 12.65 per cent per annum in the period 2005–09, from 3.95 per cent in the period 2001–04. Agricultural reform, channelled mainly through improvements in infrastructure (power, water, roads), also appears to have worked, with annual average growth rates in agricultural production of 10.97 per cent, the highest of any Indian state between

2001 and 2010. Improvements in healthcare and women's empowerment are also emphasised by the model's supporters, although gains on these fronts are more contentious.

Managing to outcompete several other Indian states in bids for international and domestic investment, Gujarat has established itself as a major industrial hub and manufacturing centre, becoming home to major industrial houses like Reliance and Essar, and developing a special competence in automobiles with investments from Maruti Suzuki and the Tatas. The obvious contrast to the Gujarat model in policy terms is West Bengal, ruled for the majority of the history of post-independence India by the Communist Party that was elected to power on the back of a widespread land redistribution policy, and associated with extremely stringent labour laws and support for trade unions. The weak economic performance of West Bengal, despite its illustrious history, rich endowment of natural resources and advantages of geographical location, has become a cautionary tale of the ills associated with an overprotective government apparatus. The contrasting approaches of the two states were underscored dramatically by the defection of the Tata Nano car factory from West Bengal to Gujarat in 2008, in the wake of violent protests about forced land acquisition in the Singur region.

The Gujarat model can also be contrasted with the Kerala model that has long been prominent in development discourses. Unlike the Kerala model, that became famous for its high attainment in human development-type welfare indicators (notably 100 per cent literacy), the Gujarat model is more focused on traditional models of economic success, particularly high growth rates. Indeed, it was the contrast between these two trajectories of development that was the focal point of the Sen–Bhagwati debate (Dreze and Sen 2013; Bhagwati and Panagariya 2012) in the run-up to the general elections.

Thus the Gujarat model seems to exemplify the wisdom of the "rule of law" orthodoxy, providing empirical evidence of the idea that a process of rationalising institutions and a regime of deregulation, focused on a minimal institutional structure providing clarity and certainty in the realms of property and contract, will bear fruit in terms of economic growth and prosperity. Indeed, it is this perspective that has informed the national government's initial labour law reforms of October 2014, which include streamlining databases of companies, modifying procedures for reporting on compliance with labour regulations, and reducing the discretion of inspectors. So far, the government has not proposed a more fundamental change to Part V B of the IDA, but this remains an option for the future in what appears to be a cautious approach to the sequencing of reforms.

Before Gujarat is accepted as an undisputed "gold standard" for Indian economic policy, however, there are a few points that should be considered. To begin with, an extensive literature indicates that the dynamics of institutional replication are more complex than they may initially appear (Berkowitz *et al.* 2003a, 2003b). The apparent success of a certain set of economic policies in the context of Gujarat may be due to local factors such as a longestablished entrepreneurial tradition in that state and advantages of geographical location that do not apply in other contexts.

The more fundamental question, however, is whether the transposition of the model onto the national platform would be desirable even if it were achievable. On this front, the first thing that is worth noting is that the key point on which the model has built itself is reform in land, labour and credit markets. As Polanyian scholarship emphasises, land, labour and money are not "pure commodities." Attempts to construct a market economy require the creation of institutional capacity and not simply the removal of government controls (Polanyi 1944). In this context it is unclear what is distinctive about the Gujarat model, and what it offers beyond a policy of liberalisation and deregulation combined with subsidies for plant relocations which can by their nature be only temporary.

Nor is it clear that Gujarat's deregulatory approach should be credited with the growth it has achieved. Other Indian states, including Maharashtra, have grown as quickly as Gujarat or even surpassed it. Thus the idea of the Gujarat model is a unique path to unparalleled growth may be questioned.

Finally, while adopting the model in Gujarat may have led to positive outcomes in terms of growth, the model entails some questionable trade-offs: there may have been gains in the aggregate, but this says little about how those gains are divided up (for instance what proportion of them accrues to labour). Serious questions and concerns remain about the inclusivity of the model, and about social indicators (on health, education, infant mortality, and women's literacy) lagging behind the economic ones. Gujarat's scores on the Human Development Index place it below the national average, so that it is still classified as a "less developed state." The Union Ministry of Health and Family Welfare estimates that the shortage of doctors in Gujarat is 34 per cent, compared with the national average of 10 per cent, while one child in three in Gujarat is reported to be malnourished on 2013 estimates.

Conclusions

The Gujarat model emphasises the streamlining of governance structures as the pathway to development, with the deregulation of labour laws a key element of this process. The state appears to have reaped significant benefits from this approach in terms of attracting investment and augmenting growth. It is consequently a noteworthy model, and its successes are worth studying. However, implicit in the model are a range of normative and policy choices that need to be examined carefully before adopting it as a template for the entire country.

In particular, it is not clear that a policy of deregulation and subsidisation of business through fiscal exemptions is sustainable over the longer term. This strategy may produce some quick wins for state governments keen to attract inward investment, but it will not lead to sustainable growth unless it is coupled with investment in institutional capacity. For the labour market, this means supporting the institutions through which human capital is created and sustained, in particular, education and training systems, and social insurance. Without such changes, it is unlikely that access to the formal employment will become a reality for more than a small minority of Indian workers, as it is at present. There may be a case for modulating the strict controls over employment terminations set out in Part V B of the IDA. However, removing all regulation of the termination decision and leaving workers with a limited financial claim following dismissal is unlikely to encourage investment in firm-specific skills. Such an extensive deregulation of dismissal protection would do little to help firms remain competitive over the long run. For India to embed the Gujarat approach to labour law at national level at a time when other middle income countries, including China, are strengthening employment protection rights, would raise many questions over the direction of policy.

The Gujarat model also poses some difficult questions over potential trade-offs between equity and efficiency. Weakening workers' rights is generally regressive in distributional terms, and economic growth without social cohesion comes at a wider cost. For India's policymakers, labour law reform poses the question of whether growth is to be seen as an end in itself or a means to other ends.

References

Acharya, V., R. Baghai-Wadji and K. Subramanian (2014). "Labor Laws and Innovation", *Journal of Law and Economics* 56: 997–1037.

Adams, Z. and S. Deakin (2015). "Quantitative Labour Law", in A. Blackham and A. Ludlow (eds.), *New Frontiers in Empirical Labour Law Research*, Oxford: Hart, forthcoming.

Ahsan, A. and C. Pagés (2009). "Are All Labor Regulations Equal? Evidence from Indian Manufacturing", *Journal of Comparative Economics* 37: 62–75.

Arrow, K. and F. Hahn (1971). *General Competitive Analysis*. New York: Houghton Mifflin.

Becker, G. (1976). *The Economic Approach to Human Behaviour*. Chicago: University of Chicago Press.

Besley, T. and R. Burgess (2004). "Can Labour Regulation Hinder Economic Performance? Evidence from India", *Quarterly Journal of Economics* 199: 91–134.

Bhattacharjea, A. (2006). "Labour Market Performance and Industrial Performance in India", *Indian Journal of Labour Economics* 49: 211–32.

———. (2009). "The Effects of Employment Protection Legislation on Indian Manufacturing", *Economic & Political Weekly* 44: 55–62.

Berkowitz, D., K. Pistor and J-F Richards (2003a). "The Transplant Effect", *American Journal of Comparative Law* 51: 163–203.

———. (2003b). "Economic Development, Legality and the Transplant Effect", *European Economic Review* 47: 165–95.

Bhagwati, J. and A. Pangariya (2012). *India's Tryst with Destiny: Debunking Myths That Undermine Progress and Addressing New Challenges*. New Delhi: Collins Business.

Botero, J., S. Djankov, R. La Porta, F. Lopez-de-Silanes and A. Shleifer (2004). "The Regulation of Labor", *Quarterly Journal of Economics* 119: 1340–82.

Chen, D. and S. Deakin (2015). "On Heaven's Lathe: State, Rule of Law, and Economic Development", forthcoming, *Law and Development Review*.

Coase, R.H. (1988). *The Firm, the Market and the Law*. Chicago: University of Chicago Press.

Collins, H. (1995). *Justice in Dismissal*. Oxford: Oxford University Press.

D'Souza, E. (2010). "The Employment Effects of Labour Legislation in India: A Critical Survey", *Industrial Relations Journal* 41: 122–35.

Dutta Roy, S. (2004). "Employment Dynamics in Indian Industry: Adjustment Lags and the Impact of Job Security Regulations", *Journal of Development Economics* 73: 233–56.

De Soto, H. (2000). *The Mystery of Capital*. New York: Basic Books.

Deakin, S., P. Lele and M. Siems (2007). "The Evolution of Labour Law: Calibrating and Comparing Regulatory Regimes", *International Labour Review* 146: 133–62.

———. (2007). "Shareholder Protection: A Leximetric Approach", *Journal of Corporate Law Studies* 7: 17-50.

Deakin, S. and P. Sarkar (2008). "Assessing the Long-run Economic Impact of Labour Law Systems: A Theoretical Reappraisal and Analysis of New Time Series Data", *Industrial Relations Journal* 39: 453–87.

———. (2011). "Indian Labour Law and Its Impact on Unemployment, 1973-2006: A Leximetric Study", *Indian Journal of Labour Economics* 53: 607–29.

Deakin, S., P. Sarkar and A. Singh (2012). "An End to Consensus? The Selective Impact of Corporate Law Reform on Financial Development", in M. Aoki, K. Binmore, S. Deakin and H. Gintis (eds.), *Complexity and Institutions: Markets, Norms and Organizations*. Basingstoke: Palgrave Macmillan.

Deakin, S., C. Fenwick and P. Sarkar (2014). "Labour Law and Inclusive Development: The Economic Effects of Industrial Relations Laws in Middleincome Countries", in M. Schmiegelow (ed.), *Institutional Competition between Common Law and Civil Law: Theory and Policy*. Frankfurt: Springer.

Deakin, S., J. Malmberg and P. Sarkar (2014). "Do Labour Laws Increase Equality at the Expense of Higher Unemployment? The Experience of Six OECD Countries, 1970-2010", forthcoming, International Labour Review, 153: 1-27.

Deakin, S. and A. Supiot, eds. (2009). *Capacitas: Contract Law and the Institutional Foundations of a Market Economy*. Oxford: Hart.

Deakin, S. and F. Wilkinson (2005). *The Law of the Labour Market: Industrialization, Employment, and Legal Evolution*. Oxford: OUP.

Dreze, J. and A. Sen (2013). *An Uncertain Glory: India and Its Contradictions*. Princeton: Princeton University Press.

Esping-Andersen, G. (1996). *Welfare States in Transition: National Adaptations in Global Economies*. London: Sage.

Fagernäs, S. (2010). "Labor Law, Judicial Efficiency and Informal Employment in India", *Journal of Empirical Legal Studies* 7: 282–321.

Fallon, P. and R. Lucas (1993). "The Impact of Changes in Job Security Legislation in India and Zimbabwe", *World Bank Economic Review* 5: 395–413.

Government of Gujarat (2014). "Path-breaking Labour Laws", *http://www.imd-gujarat.gov.in/policy/path_breaking_labour_laws.html* (last consulted on 30 December 2014).

Haldar, A. and J. Stiglitz (2013). "Analysing Legal Formality and Informality", in D. Kennedy and J. Stiglitz (eds.), *Law and Economics with Chinese Characteristics: Institutions for the Twenty-First Century*. Oxford: Oxford University Press.

Jha, P. and S. Golder (2008). "Labour Market Regulation and Economic Performance: A Critical Review of Arguments and Some Plausible Lessons for India", *Economic and Labour Market Papers* 2008/1, ILO, Geneva.

Manuel Report (2013). *Independent Panel Review of the Doing Business Report*. Washington DC: World Bank.

Marshall, S. (2015). "Revitalising Labour Market Regulation for the Economic South: New Forms and Tools", in S. Marshall and C. Fenwick (eds.), *Promoting Decent Work: The Role of Labour Law*. Oxford: Hart.

Marshall, S. and C. Fenwick eds. (2015). *Promoting Decent Work: The Role of Labour Law*. Oxford: Hart.

Marx, K. (1847). *Wage Labour and Capital*, Marx Engels Internet Archive, *https://www.marxists. org/archive/marx/works/1847/wage-labour/*

Moore, M. (2014). "Reconstituting Labour Market Freedom: Corporate Governance and Collective Worker Counterbalance", *Industrial Law Journal* 43: 398–428.

North, D. (2005). *Understanding the Process of Economic Change*. Princeton: Princeton University Press.

OECD (various years). *Employment Outlook*. Paris: Organization for Economic Cooperation and Development.

Polanyi, K. (1944). *The Great Transformation: The Political and Economic Origins of Our Time*. Boston: Beacon Press.

Rogers, J. and W. Streeck (1995). *Works Councils: Consultation, Representation and Cooperation in Industrial Relations*. Chicago: University of Chicago Press.

Shapiro, C. and J. Stiglitz (1984). "Equilibrium Unemployment As a Worker Discipline Device", *American Economic Review* 74: 433–44.

Smith, A [1976] (1999). *The Wealth of Nations. Books I-III*, ed. with an introduction by A. Skinnner, London: Penguin.

Williamson, Oliver E., Michael L. Watcher and Jeffrey E. Harris (1975). "Understanding the Employment Relation: The Analysis of Idiosyncratic Exchange", *The Bell Journal of Economics* 6(1): 250–78. (Spring).

World Bank (2015). *Rule of Law Index*, available at: *http://databank.worldbank.org/data/views/variableselection/selectvariables.aspx?source= worldwide-governance-indicators* (last consulted on 30 December 2014).

———. (various years): Doing Business Reports, Washington DC: International Bank for Reconstruction and Development.

Economic & Political Weekly I(12). 21 March 2015.

8

ACHIN CHAKRABORTY

Reforming Labour Markets in States

Revisiting the Futility Thesis

THE "need" for reforming the labour market in India has been forcefully articulated by protagonists of economic reform ever since major reform measures were implemented in several sectors of the economy in the 1990s to make a decisive break from the past. Industry and business interests, the corporate media, and a section of economists have been repeatedly complaining about the so-called rigidity in the labour market in India allegedly because of a bunch of protective legislations that has made the retrenchment of workers difficult, and has been clamouring for labour market reform.

In the Constitution, labour belongs to the concurrent list, which means that both the centre and the states can legislate in the area and the central law will prevail in case of any contradiction. As there are major central laws on labour, individual states can amend them. Once a state legislature passes a bill, the union government forwards it to the president for assent. If the president assents, it becomes a law in the state.

A number of states have made amendments in the provisions of the Industrial Disputes Act (IDA), 1947 and other acts relevant to labour. But, by and large, those amendments have had very little impact on the general perception of industry and business that labour laws in India are rather stringent. Indian labour laws, as alleged by both domestic and foreign investors, provide a high degree of protection to labour since retrenchment of workers and closure of an unviable unit requires prior permission of the state government for companies employing more than 100 workers. This leads to the complaint that firms lack the flexibility to adjust to changed economic circumstances in the post-reform era.

Much has been written on this and other aspects of labour market reform. One might wonder if anything new could be added. The motivation of this article is the recent initiatives in reforming the major laws to do with labour. Late last year, we saw Rajasthan drastically amend the IDA, the Contract Labour Act, 1970, and the Factories Act, 1947, which finally received the president's assent in November. The most important was the changes in the IDA that will now allow companies in Rajasthan employing up to 300 workers to lay them off or close down the unit without seeking government approval. By the central government's amendment to the IDA passed in 1982 (made effective in 1984), only companies employing up to 100 workers were allowed to do so. Further, the threshold of the number of employees required for applying the Factories Act has been increased from 10 to 20 in electricity-powered factories and from 20 to 40 in factories without power. A third major amendment says that a union now has to record a membership of 30 per cent of the total workforce to be recognised, up from 15 per cent earlier. Initiatives of this kind ostensibly aim at improving what is called the "ease of doing business." Rajasthan Chief Minister Vasundhara Raje chose to clarify the government's motivation with the explanation that the reforms would create "a fertile habitat for jobs creation." It can be anticipated that other states, in particular where the Bharatiya Janata Party (BJP) is in power, will follow Rajasthan's footsteps. Madhya Pradesh (MP) has already passed a similar bill, and Haryana and Himachal Pradesh (HP) are reportedly contemplating similar amendments.

Critiques of labour market reform that aim at increasing labour market flexibility usually argue from a normative rights-based position which gives priority to job security as the most important aspect of workers' rights. In this article we take a different route. We elaborate on what we call the "futility argument" to establish that it would be wrong to claim that such reforms would achieve what the advocates of reform expect them to achieve, given the realities of the Indian labour market. We first make an attempt to present a critical review of the issues in labour market reforms against the backdrop of the recent trends in the labour force participation and formal/informal employment in organised/unorganised sectors in India. In particular, drawing on a variety of evidence we try to examine if reforms aimed at making the labour market more flexible would succeed in raising the rate of economic growth and generating employment at a faster rate.

How Rigid Is the Labour Market?

That the Indian growth story has so far been one of jobless growth is now widely known. Despite a marked acceleration in growth of the gross domestic product (GDP) in the post-liberalisation period, employment growth has been falling in the last three decades. Using various rounds of National Sample Survey Office (NSSO) data, it has been estimated that average annual employment growth was about 2.4 per cent in the 1970s.[1] This continued in the 1980s, but declined in the 1990s. Between 1999–2000 and 2004–05, there was a spectacular jump in employment growth to 2.8 per cent, which is hard to explain. However, the most recent rounds of data provided by the NSSO show a sharp deceleration in the growth rate of employment in recent years. The compound annual growth rate (CAGR) of employment from 2004–05 to 2011–12 fell to a mere 0.5 per cent from the earlier 2.8 per cent. As a matter of fact, from 2004–05 to 2009–10, in which GDP grew at unprecedented rates, employment collapsed to virtually zero.

There have been gradual changes in the structure of employment as well. The share of the primary sector in total employment has, for the first time, fallen below 50 per cent. It declined from 58.5 per cent in 2004–05 to 48.9 per cent in 2011–12. At the same time, the share of the secondary and tertiary sectors in total employment increased to 24.3 per cent and 26.8 per cent, respectively, in 2011–12 from 18.1 per cent and 23.4 per cent, respectively, in 2004–05. Self-employment continues to dominate, with a 52.2 per cent share in total employment. India's total labour force in 2011–12 is estimated to have been about 484 million, following the definition of "usual status" (principal plus subsidiary). This is only about 40 per cent of the total population. The overall low labour force participation reflects the disproportionately low labour force participation rate among women. In rural areas, the female work participation rate has remained stagnant. Such trends clearly point to the need for diversification in rural livelihoods from agriculture to non-agriculture activities.

Given these overall trends in employment and labour force participation, the most remarkable feature of the 480 million- odd workforce is that more than 90 per cent of them belong to the category of informal workers. It is worth noting that the National Commission for Enterprises in the Unorganized Sector (NCEUS) made a very important distinction between the unorganised sector and informal workers. This distinction helps us understand the changing nature of formal/ informal work across the organised/unorganised sectors. The NCEUS followed the standard definition of the unorganised sector comprising all unincorporated private enterprises owned by individuals or households engaged in the sale and production of goods and services operated on a proprietary or partnership basis and with less than 10 workers (with electricity; less than 20 without electricity). It defined informal workers as "those working in the informal sector or households, excluding regular workers with social security benefits provided by the employers, and the workers in the formal sector without any employment and social security benefits provided by the employers."

Table 8.1 has been taken from recent Economic Survey (2014–15). It shows that the share of the organised sector in the total workforce increased from 13 per cent to 17.3 per cent between 2004–05 and 2011–12, which looks like a significant improvement. But it would be misleading if we ignored the formal/informal distinction. Not all workers engaged in the organised sector can be considered formal workers. Among those employed in the organised sector, a high 48 per cent belonged to the category of informal workers in 2004–05. And this share increased to 54.6 per cent in 2011–12 (Table 8.1).

Table 8.1

Distribution of Formal and Informal Workers in Organised and Unorganised Sectors

(%)

	2004–05			*2011–12*		
	Organised	*Unorganised*	*Total*	*Organised*	*Unorganised*	*Total*
Formal	52	0.3	7.3	45.4	0.4	8.1
Informal	48	99.7	92.7	54.6	99.6	91.9
Total	13	87	100	17.3	82.7	100

Source: Economic Survey 2014–15.

The trends in formal and informal employment inevitably raise the question of how rigid India's labour market is. The evidence available shows that even though no significant changes have been made in the labour laws in the last two and a half decades, regimes of employment, instead of remaining static, have adapted in covert ways to accommodating more and more workers without any modicum of security. This has been made possible by even employers in the organised sector increasing their reliance on casual and contract workers. We thus have the peculiar paradox of a so-called rigid labour market that has within it the mass of workers who can be hired and fired at will.

The mobility of people seeking work from rural to semi-urban and urban areas has increased over time. Very few of them end up securing a regular job in the organised sector. Yet, NSSO data typically show very low rates of open unemployment in India. Since the large majority of the people who desperately move out of agriculture end up in a variety of informal and seasonal employment, it is reasonable to believe that there are varying levels of underemployment between those who are fully employed and those who are not. The NSSO data cannot fully capture the extent of underemployment. Can labour market reforms reverse the process of growing underemployment and informalisation? It is unlikely.

The crucial stumbling blocks are usually said to be the relatively small share of manufacturing in the economy and the low employment intensity of services. Indian agriculture contributes roughly 14 per cent to GDP, but employs 49 per cent of the workforce. Services contribute close to 60 per cent of GDP but employ only 27 per cent of the workforce. While the contribution of manufacturing to GDP is 16 per cent, it employs only 13 per cent of the workforce. Since wage earnings of informal workers are typically much lower than those of formal workers, increasing informalisation means a decreasing share of labour in total value added, and an increasing share of capital. From the macroeconomic point of view, this can effectively create a demand problem in the economy, which, in turn, could affect growth prospects in output and employment. Unless incomes at the lowest end of the employment spectrum are protected, demand for mass consumption goods may not rise.

Therefore, the kind of trend—the shift of the labour force from agriculture to non-agriculture—that we observe in the Indian economy can hardly be seen as a positive development dynamic since most of them end up in the unorganised or informal sectors where earnings are low, work conditions are generally dismal, and the fear of termination is always there. One can argue that a desirable solution would be to create more formal employment in the organised sector, but the terms of contract should not be such that they create disincentives for employers to expand employment. But this is easier said than done. While at the policy level it is assumed almost as a truism that more relaxed labour laws will expand employment, neither economic logic nor the evidence is able to support this.

The Logic of Flexibility

Two papers based on the empirical information on changes in laws on labour in India, which have had the most influence in policymaking circles, are Fallon and Lucas (1993) and Besley and Burgess (2004), particularly the latter. They have since drawn a significant amount of attention from the research community as well. Scholars have re-examined their findings and ended up either refuting or further strengthening their conclusion. Before we present a brief review of this literature based on the evidence, we take a quick look at the theoretical arguments for labour market flexibility.

It was common in the theoretical literature of the 1980s and 1990s to explain unemployment in developed countries in terms of a simple model of a non-clearing labour market, where employment and real wage were given by the intersection of a downward-sloping demand curve for labour and an upwardsloping wage-setting curve, with a labour supply curve to the right of this interaction. In this model, while the labour supply and labour demand curves have usual interpretations, the wage-setting curve was novel. But it has no unique interpretation, and has been interpreted differently in different models. For example, in the efficiency wage theory of Shapiro and Stiglitz (1984), it can be interpreted as a no-quitting or noshirking locus, or in the insider–outsider (I–O) theory of Lindbeck and Snower (1990), it may represent an insider's wage claims.

In this kind of theoretical set-up, the persistence of unemployment may be shown by making the positions of the labour supply, labour demand, and wage-setting curves depend on past levels of labour market activity. In the I–O model, labour turnover costs play an important role in a firm's employment decisions and in enabling insiders to gain market power in the wage setting process. Job security regulations also play an important role in this model, which provides the justification for a policy of lower regulation to enhance labour market flexibility. However, if the prevailing wage rate is found to be above the so-called market-clearing rate, I–O is not the obvious explanation. Even if there are no job security regulations, firms may find it unprofitable to cut wages given involuntary unemployment. Different variants of the efficiency wage hypothesis argue that labour productivity depends on the real wage paid by a firm. Therefore, even if the labour market is competitive, firms may choose to pay wages at a rate above the market clearing one for several expected benefits—less shirking by employees because of the higher cost of job loss, lower turnover, improved morale, and so on. Thus, we are in a curious situation. The same empirical observation of involuntary unemployment together with a wage settled above the reservation wage of the unemployed is consistent with two alternative theories, one of which has labour market flexibility as a policy implication while the other has no such implication.

The I–O model of wage setting is therefore not the only explanation for the persistence of involuntary unemployment in the theoretical literature, even though policy advocacy for labour market flexibility is the logical outcome of the model. There are other explanations that have little to do with rigid institutional rules that make labour retrenchment difficult. Shapiro and Stiglitz (1984), for example, show how the information structure of employer–employee relationships, in particular, the inability of employers to observe workers' on-the job effort in a costless way, explains involuntary unemployment as an equilibrium phenomenon. In their model, unemployment results from imperfect monitoring of effort. In equilibrium, all firms pay the same wage above the market-clearing rate, and unemployment, which makes job loss costly, serves as a device for worker discipline. Having gone through these theoretical insights, one might argue that the models to explain the persistence of unemployment in Europe and the United States (US) and their implications for a policy to ensure labour market flexibility have little relevance in the Indian context. At the other extreme, excellent papers have been written to argue for the "benefits from rigid labour markets" in the Western context (Agell 1999).

Having gone through the theoretical models of involuntary unemployment, particularly those based on a strong positive relationship between wage and productivity, such as the efficiency wage models, one would naturally think that they are irrelevant because wage–productivity relations are rather blurred in the Indian context for rigidities in the labour market. This would be a mistake. It seems that the wage–productivity nexus is important in some sectors of the economy, but not in others. For the primary sector, where the efficiency wage hypothesis is relevant, job rationing and voluntary payment of wages in excess of market clearing may be found. In the secondary sector, where the wage–productivity relationship is weak or non-existent, we should observe fully neoclassical behaviour. The existence of the secondary sector does not, however, eliminate involuntary unemployment because the wage differential between primary and secondary sector jobs will induce unemployment among jobseekers who choose to wait for primary sector job opportunities.

Turning to empirical studies in the Indian context, we observe that the focus of most of them is the IDA, 1947, in particular Chapter VB where the minimum number of workers to qualify for exemption from government's approval to effect any lay-off or closure has been specified. This chapter was inserted by an amendment to the act in 1976, which stipulated that firms employing 300 or more workers would require the government's permission to retrench or lay off workers, or to close down a unit. This was ostensibly to protect workers from arbitrary dismissal and to avoid the political repercussions of large-scale job loss due to closure of firms. However, it was subsequently found that more effective protection of workers' interests would need a further reduction in the minimum size of the unit for exemption. In 1982, a further amendment was made to reduce the minimum number of workers from 300 to 100. Fallon and Lucas (1993) used these episodes of change in the IDA to examine the effect of the legislations on employment. Besley and Burgess (2004) used information on various legislations by states to amend the IDA. Bhalotra (1998) raised a number of questions on the method in Fallon and Lucas (1993). Her own finding suggests that the apparent increase in labour market flexibility in the 1980s, despite the tightening of the job security legislation, could be attributed to a growing trend towards subcontracting output to small firms, which were outside the scope of the law, and to firing workers, which occurred despite the provisions of the law. Bhattacharjea (2007) made a thorough critique of the methodological strategy adopted in these empirical studies and persuasively showed how weak the ground was to claim that "pro-worker" states lagged behind "pro-employer" states in terms of generation of employment.

What Flexibility Cannot Achieve

It is hard to see how making amendments to the IDA and other acts, as Rajasthan has done, will push manufacturing forward with increasing output and employment. Bardhan (2014) cites the example of the garments industry, which is known to be very labour intensive. By combining the Annual Survey of Industries (ASI) and NSSO data, he estimates that about 92 per cent of garment firms in India employ eight or fewer workers. Surely the firms could have expanded if they had wanted to, at least the labour laws would not impose any constraint until they become 100-worker firms. But that 92 per cent of them have not grown beyond their present size implies other factors are at play, which are far more important than the labour laws that are assumed to be rigid. The problems may have to do with issues such as inadequate credit and marketing opportunities, bad infrastructure, erratic power supply, bureaucratic hassles, and so on.

At the other end, amending labour laws is unlikely to have a major influence on the further growth of industries such as the pharmaceutical sector, which has been considered one of the most successful in India, mainly through a favourable patent regime that facilitated reverse engineering and innovation. One might ask, what are the constraints that inhibit Indian manufacturing from following the path that the pharmaceutical industry has taken? Reverse engineering does not yield an immediate improvement in productivity. Therefore, firms with the objective of maximising profits in the short term are unlikely to carry it out. More importantly, Indian business generally chooses to compete on price with a high degree of reliance on reduced wage costs by using contract labour. With contract labour, there is a high degree of attrition, which means that it does not make much sense to develop skills through in-house training. Nathan *et al.* (2014) find evidence that firms that compete on quality and product innovation have a stable workforce, whereas those that compete on price utilise a flexible workforce. Continuous improvement in productivity is needed to remain competitive, and this requires a stable workforce that has a stake in fostering improvements in productivity. For productivity growth to translate into higher wages, incomes, and improved living conditions, it is necessary to build strong and well-functioning labour market institutions (Amjad *et al.* 2015).

Finally, mitigating the growing problem of "graduate" unemployment requires an approach different to amending the IDA. The rate of unemployment among graduates, including those who were technically trained in 2011–12, was 18 per cent. If this information is combined with the largely anecdotal evidence of a labour shortage in industry and the steady increase in nominal wages in the organised sector, the disconnect between growing enrolment in higher education and forming appropriate kinds of skills becomes apparent.

What is perhaps needed is education reform rather than the kind of labour reform that Rajasthan has enacted. The National Skills Development Corporation is not a panacea, but it is a move in the right direction. The corporation needs to work closely with industry. A bargaining process between trade unions and enterprises needs to produce the terms of separation that unions agree to in accepting loss of job security. Social security for workers needs to be strengthened rather than weakened in the name of labour market flexibility. There cannot be a blanket argument against contract labour (firms should be allowed the flexibility to take on short-term employees) but the wide gap between employment conditions for contract and regular workers has led to increasing incidents of industrial strife that has vitiated the environment for manufacturing.

The large-scale violence at the Manesar plant of Maruti Suzuki and Honda Motorcycle and Scooter India a few years ago, and similar incidents reported elsewhere show that labour institutions in India are ineffective in resolving conflicts and facilitating collective bargaining. The growing sense of injustice and discontentment among the industrial labour force in recent times needs to be faced with sensitivity and caution while thinking about labour market reforms. While industry and business hail Rajasthan's initiative in amending the laws, the fact is that the state has the highest number of child labourers after Uttar Pradesh and Andhra Pradesh, according to the United Nations Children's Fund's (UNICEF) Child in India 2012 report.

Admittedly, labour market reforms are not all about increasing the freedom to hire and fire. They are also about the social security provisions and conditions of work on the side of workers, and avoiding unnecessary bureaucratic hassles on the side of firms. The recent *Economic Survey* (2014–15) lists the reform measures that the central government has undertaken, which seem to be about either improving workers' benefits or saving industry from the unnecessary hassles of an inspector raj.

Raising the statutory wage ceiling under the Employees Provident Fund and Miscellaneous Provisions (EPF&MP) Act to ₹15,000 per month from 1 September 2014, introducing a minimum pension of ₹1,000 under the Employees' Pension Scheme 1995, amending the Apprenticeship Act, 1961, and so on are ostensibly to benefit workers. A unified labour portal called Shram Suvidha Portal has been launched for the "timely redressal of grievances and for creating a conducive environment for industrial development." The filing of a single selfcertified and simplified online return under this scheme instead of the earlier practice of filing 16 separate returns, and transparent labour inspection processes are expected to reduce the hassles for the industry (see Government of India 2015: 137, Box 9.3). But all these are too little to attract attention as far as the contested terrain of labour market reforms is concerned. However, highlighting these measures in the Economic Survey while underplaying the push towards more flexibility in hiring and firing seems aimed at giving the impression of a kind of "labour reform with a human face," perhaps to facilitate far wider and deeper reforms. Such subtleties were not visible a few years ago. The Economic Survey for 2005–06) said,

> Various studies indicate that Indian labour laws are highly protective of labour, and labour markets are relatively inflexible. These laws apply only to the organised sector. Consequently, these laws have restricted labour mobility, have led to capital-intensive methods in the organised sector and adversely affected the sector's long-run demand for labour. Labour being a subject in the concurrent list, State-level labour regulations are also an important determinant of industrial performance. Evidence suggests that states, which have enacted more proworker regulations, have lost out on industrial production in general (209).

These lines were clearly a reflection of uncritically accepting the findings of papers such as Besley and Burgess (2004), which claimed to have established a connection between state-level labour regulations and industrial performance. Over time, the influence of these studies has waned because other findings have questioned the connection. Interestingly, while the Economic Survey (2014–15) seems to have sobered in its view of the benefit of deregulation and maintained a strategic silence on a more flexible labour market, some of the BJP-ruled states seem eager to take the plunge. Of course, one should not read too much into this difference between the views of some states and the Ministry of Finance, which was responsible for producing the *Economic Survey*, but the difference may not be accidental. As states compete with each other to attract investment, they find labour market reform a convenient way of signalling their investor friendliness. Given the ruling coalition's weak position in the upper house of Parliament, any major reform initiative is unlikely to go unchallenged. The states, on the other hand, may garner political support for certain reforms within their territories by invoking the imperatives of interstate competition. As a consequence, the central government can conveniently absolve itself of the responsibility of amending labour-related laws.

Concluding Remarks

In his monograph "The Labor Market as a Social Institution", Solow perceptively observes,

> Wage rates and jobs are not exactly like other prices and quantities. They are much more deeply involved in the way people see themselves, think about their social status, and evaluate whether they are getting a fair share out of the society ... Social institutions define acceptable and unacceptable modes of behavior in the weighty context like the labor market (1990).

Yet, the arguments for flexibility in the labour market are usually couched in the language of market clearing through a downward movement of the wage rate. Hence, the wage rate is considered essentially no different from any other price as far as its market-clearing role is concerned. So-called competitive pressures tend to draw economies around the world into "a race to the bottom." Policymakers have been racing to make their markets more competitive and increase incentives to invest. Labour markets are being subject to changes intended to enhance flexibility and lower labour costs. Social security measures are perceived as inimical to competitive advantage and growth. That the inevitable result of all this has been widening gaps in income and well-being is now accepted by many with greater equanimity than before. However, hardly any commentator in the business media seems to appreciate the idea that there is no inherent trade-off between dynamic efficiency and basic income security for the working poor despite a long stream of theoretical literature on this supported by strong empirical evidence (Chakraborty 2006). It needs to be emphasised that job security is not the only means by which income security can be achieved. But in the absence of any protective security, that would at least partially compensate for income loss due to job loss, and workers have no other option but cling to the demand for job security. Unfortunately, even with all the power that workers can still wield, they will hardly succeed in their struggle to resist losing jobs, whether the market is reformed by legislative means or not.

Note

1. Estimates are from various rounds of the National Sample Survey and Economic Survey 2014-15, Vol II, p 135.

References

Agell, Jonas (1999). "On the Benefits from Rigid Labour Markets: Norms, Market Failures, and Social Insurance", *Economic Journal* 109.

Amjad, Rashid, Sunil Chandrasiri, Dev Nathan, Selim Raihan, Sher Verick and Anam Yusuf (2015). "What Holds Back Manufacturing in South Asia", *Economic & Political Weekly* 50 (10).

Bardhan, Pranab (2014). "The Labour Reform Myth", *Indian Express*, 23 Aug, *http://indianexpress.com/article/opinion/editorials/the-labour-reform-myth/*.

Besley, T. and R. Burgess (2004). "Can Regulation Hinder Economic Performance? Evidence from India", *Quarterly Journal of Economics* 119: 91–134.

Bhalotra, S. (1998). "The Puzzle of Jobless Growth in Indian Manufacturing", *Oxford Bulletin of Economics and Statistics* 60: 5–32.

Bhattacharjea, Aditya (2007). "Labour Market Regulation and Industrial Performance in India: A Critical Review of the Empirical Evidence", *Indian Journal of Labour Economics* 49(2): 211–32.

Chakraborty, Achin (2006). "The Primacy of Politics", Seminar, December.

Fallon, P. and R.E.B. Lucas (1993). "Job Security Regulations and the Dynamic Demand for Labor in India and Zimbabwe", *Journal of Development Economics* 40: 241–75.

Government of India (2015). *Economic Survey, 2014-15*, Ministry of Finance, New Delhi.

Lindbeck, Assar and Dennis Snower (1990). "Demandand Supply-Side Policies and Unemployment: Policy Implications of the Insider-Outsider Approach", *Scandinavian Journal of Economics* 92 (2): 279–305.

Nathan, Dev, J. Jeyaranjan and Harishwar Dayal (2014). "Better Workforce Practices: Contract and Other Flexible Labour", A Study for the Planning Commission, CII, and GIZ, Institute for Human Development, New Delhi.

Shapiro, Carl and Joseph Stiglitz (1984). "Equilibrium Unemployment as a Worker Discipline Device", *American Economic Review* 74 (3): 433–44.

Solow, Robert (1990). *The Labor Market as a Social Institution*. Cambridge, MA: Blackwell.

Sood, Atul, Paritosh Nath and Sangeeta Ghosh (2014). "Deregulating Capital and Regulating Labour: The Dynamics in the Manufacturing Sector in India", *Economic & Political Weekly* 49(26, 27).

Economic & Political Weekly I(20). 16 May 2015.

Part II

Indian Agriculture: Policies and Performance

9

Editorial Notes

Indian Agriculture

Policies and Performance

PART II, chapters 9 to 13, is devoted to a discussion on Indian agriculture: growth, productivity; agrarian structure and technology; capital formation; trade; pricing and procurement. Chapter 9 (editorial notes) provides a broad coverage of Indian agriculture covering briefly the major aspects particularly the agrarian structure and technology. S. Mahendra Dev's essays chapter 10 looks in to the issue of agricultural growth since 1947 more particularly since the economic reforms period—the 1990's; the policy reforms needed to achieve the goals of higher growth, equity and sustainability covering price policy, subsidies and investment, land issues, irrigation and water management, agriculture market reforms, research and extension, credit and domestic market reforms and diversification. The next two chapters, chapters 11 and 12 from World Bank Report, "Accelerating Agriculture Productivity and Growth" look in to the dynamics of agriculture productivity with an international perspective on India's structural transformation both at the macro and micro level; the growth prospects and policy intervention for higher productivity and growth. The issues relating to food grain management and food prices have been discussed in chapter 11 (chapter 2 of World Bank Report). Further, agricultural price policy, farm profitability and food security have been discussed in detail in chapter 13 (Rao and Mahendra Dev).

Introduction

Agriculture is the mainstay of Indian economy because of its high share in employment and livelihood creation, notwithstanding, its reduced contribution to the nation's GDP (gross domestic product). It is the most important sector of the Indian economy from the perspective of poverty alleviation and employment generation. The share of agriculture in national income has been declining from 56.5 per cent in 1950-51 to 39.6 per cent in 1980-81, 26.3 per cent in 2001-02 and only 13.9 per cent of the GDP at 2004-05 prices in 2013-14. According to the new series of national income released by the CSO, at 2011-12 prices the share of agriculture in total GDP is 18 per cent in 2013-14. As against a growth target of 4 per cent for agriculture and allied sectors in the Twelfth Plan, the growth registered in the first year at 2011-12 prices was 1.2 per cent, 3.7 per cent in 2013-14, and 1.1 per cent in 2014-15 (Table 9.1).

Table 9.1

Agriculture Sector: Key Indicators
(At 2004-05 Prices) and New Series Data at 2011-12 Prices

(%)

Item	*2007-08*	*2008-09*	*2009-10*	*2010-11*	*2011-12*	*2012-13*	*2013-14*	*2014-15*
1. Growth in GDP in Agriculture & Allied Sector	5.8	0.1	0.8	8.6	5 (-)	1.4 (1.2)	4.7* (3.7)	(1.1)
Share of Agriculture & allied sectors in total GDP	16.8	15.8	14.6	14.6	14.4 (18.4)	13.9 (18.0)	13.9* (18.0)	(NA)
Agriculture	14.3	13.4	12.3	12.4	12.3 (12.0)	11.8 (11.7)	NA (11.8)	(NA)
2. Share of agriculture & allied sectors in total Gross Capital Formation (GCF)	6.4	7.8	7.3	6.3	7.0 (8.6)	7.1 (7.7)	NA (7.9)	(NA)
Agriculture	5.9	7.2	6.7	5.8	6.5 (7.4)	6.5 (6.5)	NA (6.6)	(NA)
3. GCF in Agriculture and Allied sectors as per cent to GDP of the sector	16.1	19.4	20.1	18.5	20.8 (18.3)	21.2 (15.5)	NA (14.8)	(NA)
4. Employment in the agriculture sector as share of total workers (Census 2001)			58.2		54.6			(NA)
5. Agri exports (incl. marine products) as per cent of total exports			8.2	8.0	10.1	11.8	11.9 (P)	(NA)

Note: Figures in bracket show the new series data at 2011-12 prices.

Source: Central Statistical Organisation (CSO) and Department of Agriculture and Cooperation. *Economic Survey* 2012-13, 2013-14, 2014-15.

Agriculture's share in GDP has thus declined rapidly in the recent past. This is explained by the fact that whereas overall GDP has grown by an average of 8.62 per cent during 2004-05 to 2010-11, agricultural sector GDP has increased by only 3.46 per cent during the same period. The role of the agriculture sector, however, remains critical as it accounts for about 54.6 per cent of employment in the country (as per 2011 census). While it still accounts of 54.6 per cent of total employment, there has been a decline in the absolute number of cultivators which is unprecedented, from 127.3 million (Census 2001) to 118.7 million (Census 2011). This is indicative of a shift from farm to non-farm employment, causing real farm wages to rise by over 7 per cent annually in recent years (*Economic Survey 2013-14*).

Moreover, this sector is a supplier of food, fodder and raw materials for a vast segment of industry. Hence the growth of Indian agriculture can be considered a necessary condition for 'inclusive growth'. More recently, the rural sector (including agriculture) is being seen as a potential source of domestic demand, a recognition that is even shaping the marketing strategies of entrepreneurs wishing to widen the demand for goods and services.

Linkages between Agriculture and Other Sectors

The linkages between agriculture and other sectors of the economy have been extensively investigated in the development literature. In the early analysis, agriculture was assumed to play the role of providing food, fibre, labour and raw material for the development of industry and services (Rosenstein-Rodan, 1943). It was also held that surplus resources available in the agriculture sector could be transferred for rapid industrialisation as well as for tertiary sector growth. In the subsequent analysis, the intersectoral linkages, both from the demand and supply sides, gained prominence. In India, it was earlier viewed that the supply side linkages of the agriculture sector had weakened, while the demand side linkages remained strong (Sastry *et al*., 2003).

There could be a number of developments contributing to the gradual weakening of the relationship between the performance of the agriculture sector with the rest of the economy (*RBI Annual Report 2009-10*):

- Services sector has increasingly driven the growth of the economy backed by the services exports.

- The consumption of services by the manufacturing sector is on the rise; similar linkages are yet to be observed for the agriculture sector.
- The manufacturing sector is moving away from traditionally agro-based industries towards the machinery, consumer goods and construction based activities, which cater to the market segments characterised by high income elasticity.
- Supply side linkages are also weakening due to increasing linkages of industrial sector with the rest of the world.
- Given the surplus labour in the agriculture sector and low agricultural productivity, demand linkages are getting muted.
- The share of 'food and beverages' in private consumption expenditure has been declining.

Any sustained fall in the growth of agriculture for more than four to six quarters tends to affect the performance of the industrial sector as well as the growth of overall private consumption.

Empirical estimates indicate that there is a weakening of inter-sectoral linkages in the post-reform period in India (Table 9.2). Major dilution in the strength of the relationship has occurred in the case of linkages between: (i) industry and services sector and (ii) industry and agriculture sector. As per the latest input-output matrices, the share of agro inputs in manufacturing has declined from 20 per cent in 1993-94 to 5 per cent in 2006-07. At the same time, the services sector linkages have increased relatively more with the rest of the world than the domestic economy as evident from an increase in the proportion of services exported to total output of the services sector by nearly four-fold from about 3.2 per cent in 1990-91 to more than 12.0 per cent in 2009-10.

However, any policy maker trying to alleviate India's poverty cannot neglect the fact that the *World Development Report 2008* clearly says that "GDP growth originating in agriculture is at least twice as effective in reducing poverty as GDP growth originating outside agriculture."

The approach paper to the Twelfth Five Year Plan (2012-2017) itself recognises that a one per cent growth emanating from the agriculture sector would be atleast two to three times more effective in reducing poverty than the same growth coming from non-agriculture sector (Gulati, 2012). In the case of China it was 3.5 times as efficient and in case of Latine American countries especially Brazil, it was 2.7 times as efficient (World Bank, 2008).

Table 9.2

Inter-Sectoral Linkages

	Correlation Matrix			*Input- Output Table Leontief Inverse***			*Inter-Sectoral Elasticities@*		
	Agr.	*Ind.*	*Serv.*	*Agr.*	*Ind.*	*Serv.*	*Agr.*	*Ind.*	*Serv.*
				Period I					
Agriculture	-	0.27	0.42	-	0.20	0.06	-	0.41	#
Industry	0.27	-	0.54	0.13	-	0.27	0.23	-	0.80
Services	0.42	0.54	-	0.15	0.52	-	0.25	0.88	-
				Period II					
Agriculture	-	0.07	0.05	-	0.05	0.02	-	0.29	#
Industry	0.07	-	0.38	0.07	-	0.15	0.23	-	0.23^
Services	0.05	0.38	-	0.08	0.16	-	0.21	0.56	-

Note: Agr.: agriculture, Ind.: industry, Serv.: services.

Period I: correlation matrix (1966-1990), I-O Table (1993-94) and elasticity (1951-1990); Period II: correlation matrix (1991-2008), I-O Table (2006-07) and elasticity (1991-2008).

** : Coefficient represents requirement of row variable for producing one unit of column variable.

@: Represents percentage change in column variable with one per cent change in row variable.

: Statistically insignificant; ^: Lagged impact.

Source: *RBI Annual Report 2009-10.*

The power of agriculture in reducing poverty is observable in the Chinese case, especially during 1978-1984, the initial years of reform. China began its reform process with agriculture: by moving from the commune-based system to the household responsibility system, and by revising agricultural prices upwards by more than 20 per cent, the results were spectacular. The agricultural growth rate jumped to 7.1 per cent per annum during 1978-1984, up from 2.5 per cent during the pre-reform period of 1966-1977. This was followed by a dramatic reduction of poverty: from 33 per cent to 15 per cent in the early reform period between 1978 and 1984. Farm incomes in China grew by almost 14 per cent per annum. It is this high growth in farm incomes that boosted demand for manufactured goods produced by Town and Village Enterprises, kick-starting the manufacturing revolution in China (Gulati and Fan, 2008: 6). Much of this can be ascribed to the bottom-up approach of reforms adopted by China—that is, starting from the agricultural sector. This is unlike India, which chose a top-down approach—that is, initiating reforms in the non-agricultural sector. As a result, the process of poverty reduction has been held hostage to the 'trickle down' effect.

With more than 54 per cent of the workforce still dependent on agriculture for their livelihood, agriculture in India has a far-reaching impact on poverty reduction as well as on rural development. Agriculture forms the resource base for a number of agro-based industries. Thus, it would be more meaningful to view agriculture not as farming alone but as a holistic value chain, which includes farming, wholesaling, warehousing (including logistics), processing and retailing. Also, the fact that an average Indian spends more than 50 per cent of his monthly expenditure on food establishes the centrality of agriculture in the context of food security concerns (GoI, 2006a). These factors together determine the critical importance of agriculture in general, and food in particular. Also, for the economy to grow at 8-9 per cent, it is important that agriculture should grow at 4 per cent. The growth target for Agriculture in the Twelfth Five Year Plan remains at 4 per cent as in the Eleventh Plan. This target is not only necessary to achieve the overall GDP growth target of 8 per cent per annum without undue inflation, but it is also an important element of 'inclusiveness' since the global experience of growth and poverty reduction shows that GDP growth originating in agriculture is at least twice as effective in reducing poverty as GDP growth originating outside agriculture.

The Institutional Context

It is important, at the very outset, to understand the institutional, demographic and sociopolitical context within which agricultural growth has been taking place. The prevailing framework had a profound impact on the pattern of agricultural development. This, in turn, has necessitated special strategies and policies for employment generation and poverty removal in rural areas. The thrust of policies, in the first decade of planning (1951-1961) was on institutional and agrarian reforms. In an agrarian economy like India with great scarcity and unequal distribution of land, coupled with a large mass of below poverty line (BPL) rural population, there are compelling economic and political arguments for land reform. Not surprisingly, it received top priority on the policy agenda at the time of Independence. In the decades following Independence, India passed a significant body of land reform legislation. The Constitution of 1949 left the adoption and implementation of land

and tenancy reforms to state governments (Ghatak, 2007). The two basic objectives of land reforms were: (i) to remove such impediments on agricultural production as arise from the character of agrarian structure in rural areas and (ii) to reduce or eliminate exploitation of landless and small cultivators through measures of land redistribution.

Land reform legislation in India consisted of four main categories: abolition of intermediaries who were rent collectors under the pre-Independence land revenue system; tenancy regulation that attempted to improve the contractual terms for tenants, including crop shares and security of tenure; a ceiling on landholdings with a view to redistributing surplus land to the landless; and finally, attempts to consolidate disparate landholdings.

Economic Arguments in Favour of Land Reform

The most obvious argument in favour of land reform is equity. In a land-scarce country with a significant section of BPL rural population, the case for ensuring that everyone has access to some minimum amount of land seems compelling from this point of view.

Also, small farms tend to be more productive than large farms. This inverse farm size-productivity relationship is widely documented. Another empirical evidence is that owner-cultivated plots of land tend to be more productive than those under sharecropping tenancy.

The intermediaries were abolished within a few years after Independence and the actual tillers accounting for about 40 per cent of the cultivated area became owners. This, according to C.H.H. Rao, provided a major incentive for investment and the growth of agriculture in large parts of the country.

As regards the ceiling on land holdings and distribution of surplus land among the landless, there were two rounds of land reform legislation—one in the 1950s and another in the early 1970s. However, due to numerous exemptions provided in the law and due to the lack of political will, the objective of this reform could not be fulfilled and not much surplus land could be acquired by the government for distribution among the landless. According to G. Parthasarthy (2003), Indian land reform conceived as a programme of conferment of rights of ownership on tenants and as public distribution of the land of the big owner in favour of the small farmer and the landless has, by and large, been a failure. The only exception to this sad record is the abolition of intermediaries. However, its indirect effects on the agrarian structure have been marked, though the character of these effects is varied depending upon the responses generated in varying situations of tenurial relationships.

The direct effects of the redistribution to alter the structure of ownership holdings and of cultivation holdings were only marginal except in select pockets. The indirect effects were, however, quite significant. The major indirect effects were in respect of absentee ownership. The quantitative significance of these could not be precisely measured. But there is enough evidence in a number of studies to indicate the varying trends. Broadly speaking, the absentee landowner was of less importance in the early 1970s than in the early 1950s. His importance waned much more in the dry areas than in the irrigated areas in which land is much more valuable. Transfers of land, under the forewarning impact of tenancy and ceiling legislation, to the resident landowners was on a much larger scale in the dry than in the irrigated areas. The result of shifts in land from the absentee to resident landowner was a decline in tenancy.

The forewarning effects of tenancy and ceiling legislation had also some effects on the structure of ownership holdings among the residents. The greed of the big landowner to acquire more land was kept in restraint, and the transfer of land should have been effected mainly to the middle group, who were below the declared level of ceiling. Decline in tenancy, resulting in transfers of tenanted land at least in part to the owner cultivator groups, resulting in the drift of tenants into landless, combined with demographic pressures and poor absorption of the growing numbers in non-agriculture had led to a rise in the class of rural proletariat even in the absence of expansion of the large farm. Where tenants had not been evicted, tenancy was pushed underground with informal arrangement and security of tenure.

The emerging agrarian structure revealed that less than one-fourth of the rural households controlled more than 70 per cent of the land, another one-third less than 30 per cent and the rest two-fifths, among whom the majority are the landless agricultural labour. Rich peasants preferred to avoid conflicts with labour on wage issues during crucial peak operations and rather chose to use tractors and other mechanisation devices adding to the poverty of the landless.

According to (late) S.K. Ray, on balance, there seems to be some reasons to conclude that agrarian reorganisation in India has failed to make any considerable impact on the socioeconomic conditions of the working cultivators. Indeed, the record so far is so depressing and frustrating that even an able administrator like Appu, who championed and spent a considerable part of his career in administering land reform programmes, noted:

> Thus the programmes of land reform implemented since Independence did not lead to any significant redistribution of land, or, the removal of all the obstacles to increasing agricultural production. Of the three programmes considered in this study, the laws for the abolition of intermediary interests were implemented fairly well. But in the case of tenancy reform and ceilings on holdings, the policies adopted were ambivalent and there were large gaps between policy and legislation and between legislation and implementation. We have seen that as result of the implementation of the tenancy laws, tenants became owners of or acquired rights in only about 4 per cent of the operated area. The enforcement of ceilings led to the redistribution of less than 2 per cent of the operated area. Thus these two measures taken together led to the redistribution of only about 6 per cent of the operated area (Appu, 1995: 217).

It is against the background of the last four decades experience that the need to reformulate the land policy of India should be considered. Even persons emotionally attached with land reform programmes agree that the scope for improving implementation through legislative measures is now very limited. They point out the socioeconomic and political environments in which these programmes were introduced have changed so dramatically, that it would be almost impossible to carry out the reforms. Appu described the changed environment as follows:

> ...If the political will in favour of meaningful land reform was weak at independence and weaker still later on, it is non-existent today. Land reform has practically disappeared from the agenda of most political parties. This, in my view, is the inevitable consequence of the great changes that have taken place in the social and economic fields. With the abolition of intermediary interests the erstwhile superior tenants belonging mostly to upper and middle castes acquired a higher social status. Rise in agricultural productivity, rising land values and higher incomes from cultivation have added to their economic strength. Substantial landowners who wield great authority in rural India are bitterly opposed to ceilings on agricultural holdings. They are able to

> have their way because no serious efforts have been made to organise the landless and the land poor and enlist their support in favour of reforms. As for tenancy reform is concerned, there is a certain commonality of interest between all landowners—large, medium, small and even marginal. They are all passionately attached to their land and all of them are opposed to conferring benefits on insecure tenants. In the first round of land reform only the intermediaries were adversely affected. They were few in number and were weak politically. They had also made themselves obnoxious by aligning themselves with the colonial power. So it was easy enough to abolish intermediary interests. And it was done without hurting them much. But injuring the interests of the present class of landowners is an entirely different proposition. No political party that wishes to win elections and come to power can afford to do that. At the time of independence this class of landowners did not wield much political and economic power, and with a modicum of political will the reforms could have been implemented. But now it has become almost impossible to carry out the reforms (Ibid.: 232-3).

The National Commission on Farmers has placed the unfinished agenda in land reform first in its list of five factors central to the present agrarian crisis, and states:

> The first and foremost task of the National Policy for Farmers should be in the area of land reform with particular reference to tenancy laws, distribution of ceiling surplus land, attention to common property and wasteland resources and the consolidation of holdings. Following the conferment of land rights to women under the Hindu Succession Amendment Act (2005), the provision of appropriate support services to women farmers has become urgent. Joint Pattas are essential for women to get access to credit. Also, there should be stringent restrictions on the diversion of prime farmland for non-farm purposes.

Since migration and feminisation are increasing trends, land reforms that make tenancy legal and give well defined rights to tenants and to women are now more necessary than ever, not only to reduce distress but also to increase agricultural growth. Facilitating leasing of land for cultivation is necessary to prevent cultivated land from turning fallow due to migration of owners to urban areas. Lack of recognised tenancy rights makes it difficult for *de facto* tenants to get credit from formal sources. Tenants without legal rights do not have proper incentive to develop the land and this explains part of the yield gap. Similarly, a woman without property title is unable to get credit when the male member is away. Giving access to land and homesteads not only reduces poverty but is the most powerful way to bring dignity in the lives of today's excluded. This, along with the more general need to record land titles properly where these are weak is also one way to deal effectively with encroachment and non-participation that plague watershed and wasteland development programmes.

The New Technology

It was becoming clear by the mid-1960s that there was no alternative to technological change in agriculture for achieving self-sufficiency in food grains. Even those countries in Asia which could carry out radical land reforms and built up an adequate infrastructure for agriculture had taken to the path of modernising agriculture. Japan took the lead in this direction and China followed suit even after successfully experimenting with structural changes and mobilisation of a growing labour force for capital construction in agriculture.

Between 1951 and 1966, grain production rose at a rate of 2.8 per cent per annum, a rate that failed to keep up with population growth at more than 2 per cent per annum (India, Ministry of Agriculture, 2004). Thus, from the mid-1950s India began to rely on imports of food grains to feed its growing population. In 1956, India signed the agreement of Public Law 480 (P.L. 480) with the United States to receive food aid, mostly in the form of wheat (Gulati and Fan, 2008).

A series of tragic political and natural circumstances increased foreign food dependency. After two wars (with China in 1962 and Pakistan in 1965), India found itself in a deadlock because large amount of resources had to be channeled to meet defence needs and as a result, rural investments were sacrificed (Fan *et al.*, 2004).

Then two consecutive droughts (1965-66) plunged the country into an unprecedented food crisis, with food grain production and yield declining by 19 per cent and 17 per cent, respectively, in 1966 (India, Ministry of Agriculture, 2004). The country's food security was so precarious that India and the rest of South Asia were predicted to be heading for a famine that would claim 10-20 million lives by 1975 (Paddock and Paddock, 1967). To avoid massive starvation, food grain imports (mainly wheat) increased to 10 million tonnes (mt), with internal wheat production hovering near 12 mt in 1966-67. Against the backdrop of the Cold War, food aid was used to 'twist the arms' of recipient countries to seek compliance, and India fell prey to this policy when on one occasion, the US shipments were abruptly stopped for 48 hours at the height of the drought (Gulati, 2000). India's leaders then realised the high level of political risk inherent in relying on foreign sources for food security and resolved to achieve self-sufficiency in grain production, no matter what it cost. The history of the goal of food self-sufficiency that would shape Indian agricultural policy for the next 40-odd years can be traced back to this period, especially the government's harsh experience with food aid then (Gulati and Fan, 2008).

Three Phases of Green Revolution

Gulati and Fan (2008) identify three phases of the Green Revolution.

The First Phase, 1966-1972

To end its dependence on P.L. 480, India, prompted by the Minister of Agriculture at that time, C. Subramaniam, adopted a new agricultural strategy to boost grain production accompanied by remunerative support price for farmers. In January 1965, the Agricultural Prices Commission was set up to recommend a minimum support price (MSP), followed by the Food Corporation of India (FCI) to take charge of the logistics of procuring major agricultural commodities (Gulati, 2003). In the same year, India took a bold step by allowing the introduction of new high-yielding seed varieties (HYV) of wheat from Mexico created by CIMMYT (Centro International de Mejoramiento de Maizy Trigo), an international institute for research on maize and wheat.

The new seeds could yield more than double the existing levels and thus, had the potential to dramatically increase wheat production and food grain supply. At first, there was extensive opposition to the import of large quantities of the HYV seeds, owing partly to the potential inequalities they could create in agriculture and partly also to their lower gluten content and less than optimal baking qualities. However, with the support of Prime Ministers Lal Bahadur Shastri at first and Indira Gandhi later, Subramaniam overcame public resistance. In 1966, India ordered the import of 18,000 tonnes of HYV wheat seeds that were distributed in the highly irrigated areas of Punjab, Haryana and western Uttar Pradesh where the past investments in irrigation had paid rich dividends. Under the new agricultural policy, the spread of HYVs was supported by public investments in fertilisers, power, irrigation and credit (Fan *et al.*, 2004). The outcome of the experiment was miraculous, leading to a veritable green revolution (Gulati and Fan, 2008).

The total amount of food grains harvested increased from 74 mt in 1966-67 to 105 mt in 1971-72, and that year India became self-sufficient, with grain imports declining to nearly zero (India, Ministry of Agriculture, 2003).

These outcomes would not have been possible without the favourable pricing policy that provided farmers with adequate incentives, the dynamism of the national research system that proceeded to indigenise the new seeds to tackle their shortcomings (Gulati, 2003), and the availability of inputs including canal water, fertilisers, power and credit. In view of the strategic importance of these critical inputs, it was the responsibility of the government to ensure that farmers had affordable access to them. Subsidies thus became an instrument of agricultural policy in the late 1960s and acquired greater importance in the 1970s (Gulati and Narayanan, 2002a). The role of credit began to be important after 1969 following the nationalisation of banks.

Improved agricultural production resulting from modern input and technologies 'trickled down' to the poor and led to a rise in farmer income, while output growth and increased grain supplies caused a decline in real food grain prices, benefiting the poor. Thus, rural poverty declined significantly in this phase, from 64 per cent in 1967 to 56 per cent in 1973 (Datanet India Pvt. Ltd., 2006). Several government anti-poverty programmes were also introduced during the Fourth Five Year Plan in the early 1970s (Gulati and Fan, 2008).

Debacle and the Second Phase, 1973-1980

After the nationalisation of the banks, Prime Minister Indira Gandhi took other steps to extend the role of the state in key areas of economic management. In agriculture, private wholesale traders came under attack because, due to their speculative motives, they were regarded as responsible for fluctuations in food grain prices and supplies. Thus, in 1973-74, the government took over the wholesale trade in wheat which proved a disaster and therefore, it was soon abandoned. Wheat procurement was hindered by limited supply resulting from droughts in several states in 1972-73.

Following two consecutive droughts in 1972-73, food grain production decreased by 7.7 per cent (India, Ministry of Agriculture, 2003), and India slid back into the trap of food grain imports of an average of about 4 mt a year from the United States between 1973 and 1976 (FAOSTAT, 2004).

After the oil shock, the government increased fertiliser subsidies to prevent a drop in consumption following the rise in fertiliser prices (Schumacher and Sathaye, 1999). In 1977, the retention price scheme was introduced for urea, the predominant fertiliser in Indian agriculture. During the 1970s, other input subsidies grew in importance within the state budget (Fan *et al.*, 2004), and the subsidy bill excluding fertilisers grew from ₹ 10 billion at constant prices to ₹ 33.2 billion, or from 0.5 per cent to 4.0 per cent of agricultural GDP between 1973 and 1980 (Gulati and Narayanan, 2002a). Also during this period, groundwater irrigation increased in importance, with its share rising from 0.55 per cent to 19.5 per cent between 1960 and 1975 (Datanet India Pvt. Ltd., 2006) on account of private investment in tube wells by farmers who reinvested the income from the earlier burst in food grain production. As a result, power subsidies for water pumping grew dramatically, reaching 44 per cent of the total input subsidy at the start of the 1980s (Gulati and Narayanan, 2002a).

The extension of HYV technology from wheat to rice, favoured by the growth of tube wells, spread the Green Revolution to new areas, marking a new phase in the expansion of domestic production. From 1972-73 to 1979-80, production as well as yields of food grains showed remarkable growth, at 3.1 per cent and 2.5 per cent, respectively, and rural poverty declined from roughly 56 per cent to 50 per cent (India, Ministry of Agriculture, 2004).

The Third Phase, 1981-1990

In the 1980s, India consolidated its status as a food self-sufficient country. Rice production soared to 63.8 mt in 1986, up from 37.0 mt in 1964. Wheat output grew, too, from 12 mt to 47 mt in 1986, a year in which India had her first 25.4 mt of grain buffer stocks (India, Ministry of Agriculture, 2004). When in 1987 the 'worst drought of the century' struck the country, food needs could be easily met without any loss of lives (Gulati, 2003).

During this phase, the HYV technology spread eastward to states like West Bengal and Bihar, which experienced surpluses in rice, with output over the 1980s growing at 5.0 and 3.7 per cent, respectively (Datanet India Pvt. Ltd., 2006). However, in the rest of the country the Green Revolution ran out of steam by 1985 once the new seed varieties had been widely adopted in the main producing regions. Yields for rice and wheat that had grown, respectively, by 3.5 per cent and 4.5 per cent per annum between 1967-68 and 1984-85 slowed down to 2.3 and 2.4 per cent per year between 1985-86 and 1999-2000 (IFPRI, 2004). With the HYV technology exhausting its impact in the mid-1980s, input subsidies were steadily increased to continue sustaining food grain production growth. By 1991, input subsidies had grown to 7.2 per cent of agricultural GDP as compared to 4.4 per cent in 1980 and 2.0 per cent of total GDP from 1.5 per cent in 1980 (Gulati and Narayanan, 2002a).

Throughout the Green Revolution, Indian agriculture laboured under a strictly regulated policy regime characterised by wide restrictions on production through licensing requirements and barriers to entry, as well as controls on pricing, movement and private trading of agricultural produce. On the external front, too, the sector was burdened with various tariff and non-tariff barriers to agricultural trade flows (Gulati and Fan, 2008).

The high level of protection accorded to industry produced high industrial prices and adverse terms of trade (ToT) for agriculture, reducing the relative profitability of the primary sector. Agriculture was overall net taxed (disprotected) on account of the overvalued rupee, which produced an anti-export environment for agriculture. The objectives of this framework were broadly dictated by the dominant strategy of the pre-reform era, that is, food self-sufficiency resulting from domestic supplies, aiming to: (i) ensure inexpensive food for consumers, (ii) protect farmers' incomes from price fluctuations, and (iii) keep the balance of payments (BoP) in check (Gulati and Fan, 2008).

Reform Period

Starting in 1991, India adopted a series of sweeping macroeconomic and structural reforms in industry, the exchange rate and foreign trade and investments (World Bank, 2003b).

These policy changes led to a higher rate of economic growth, with GDP recording an impressive 6.5 per cent per year growth between 1991-92 and 1996-97 compared to 5.2 per cent in the 1980s.

Overall, the reforms helped accomplish the shift from a closed to a more liberalised and open system. This is reflected in the change of indicators such as FDI inflows and the ratio of trade to GDP.

Although the reforms were implemented in off-farm activities, they affected agriculture in at least two important ways (Landes and Gulati, 2003). First, the higher rate of economic growth and the consequent rise in per capita incomes resulting from the 1991-1993 reforms had a significant impact on food demand. Higher per capita incomes, growing at 4.5 per cent per annum in this phase as opposed to 3.6 per cent in the 1980s (WDI, 2004), led to the diversification of food demand into non-food grain crops such as fruits and vegetables, as well as meat—mainly poultry—and dairy products. Second, the lowering of industrial protection significantly improved the incentive framework for the sector through improvement in the domestic ToT between agricultural and industrial prices, which rose from 0.9 to 1.2 between 1991 and 2000 (Gulati and Fan, 2008).

Improved ToT for agriculture in turn resulted in an increase in the profitability of the primary sector relative to industry and led to an increase in private investments, which are now double the public investment in agriculture. These were increasingly directed to the production of horticultural produce, poultry, fish, milk and eggs in response to booming consumer demand for these high-value agricultural products, leading to a remarkable growth in output of these commodities during the 1990s relative to the previous decade (WDI, 2004).

As a result of these developments, agricultural GDP went up from 3 per cent in the 1980s to 4.1 per cent in the aftermath of reforms between 1991 and 1996 (Datanet India Pvt. Ltd., 2006). However, the higher growth rates did not initially translate into a significant decline in rural poverty, which actually increased during 1991-92, reaching a peak of nearly 43.5 per cent in 1992 (Datanet India Pvt. Ltd., 2006). It declined thereafter, fluctuating at the pre-reform level of 35-39 per cent by the mid-1990s. Factors contributing to the lack of poverty reduction included the fiscal contraction imposed by macroeconomic stabilisation and the concentration of growth in the off-farm sector (Waldman, 2003). Especially in services, the partial liberalisation of financial and investment policies in the early 1990s meant that poorer areas with lower levels of human development and infrastructure found it difficult to switch from farm to rural non-farm activities and thus, could not benefit much from the reform-induced growth. The difference between richer and poorer areas in the capacity of the off-farm activities to create employment also implied an increase in both urban and rural inequality, with the Gini coefficient measuring 0.38 in 1997 as against 0.31 in the early 1990s (Gulati and Fan, 2008).

Deceleration in Agriculture Growth

There was a notable deceleration in the rate of growth of agricultural production during the 1990s, a fact highlighted by a number of studies in recent times (Mallik, 1997; Rao, 1998; Thamarajakshi, 1999; George, 1999; Pulapare, 2000).

Growth of agricultural GDP decelerated from over 3.5 per cent per year during 1981-82 and 1996-97 to only around 2 per cent during 1997-98 and 2004-05 (Table 9.3). This deceleration, although most marked in rainfed areas, occurred in almost all the states and covered almost all the major sub-sectors, including those such as horticulture, livestock and fisheries where growth was expected to be high. Consequently, growth of agricultural GDP has been well below the target of 4 per cent in Ninth, Tenth and Eleventh Plans.

Table 9.3

Average GDP Growth Rates—Overall and in Agriculture
(Per cent Per Year at 1999-2000 Prices)

Period	*Agriculture & Allied Sectors*	*Total Economy*
1. Pre-Green Revolution 1951-52 to 1967-68	2.54	3.69
2. Green Revolution Period 1968-69 to 1980-81	2.44	3.52
3. Wider Technology Dissemination Period 1981-82 to 1990-91	3.52	5.40
4. Early Reforms Period 1991-92 to 1996-97	3.66	5.69
5. Ninth Plan 1997-98 to 2001-02	2.50	5.52
6. Tenth Plan Period 2002-03 to 2006-07	2.47	7.77
Eleventh Plan Average (2007-2012)	3.3	7.7

Source: *Eleventh Five Year Plan 2007-2012*, Vol. III, 2008.
Mid-term Appraisal Eleventh Five Year Plan, 2010.

Table 9.4

Compound Growth Rates of Area, Production and Yield Indices of Principal Crops during 1980-1990, 1990-2000 and 2000-2011

Crop	(Base: TE 1981-82=100)						(Base: TE 1993-94=100)		
	1980-81 to 1989-90			1990-91 to 1999-2000			2000-01 to 2013-14*		
	Area	Production	Yield	Area	Production	Yield	Area	Production	Yield
Rice	0.41	3.62	3.19	0.68	2.02	1.34	0.00	1.82	1.82
Wheat	0.46	3.57	3.10	1.72	3.57	1.83	1.35	2.65	1.29
Coarse Cereals	-1.34	0.40	1.62	-2.12	-0.02	1.82	0.25	2.96	2.79
Total Pulses	-0.09	1.52	1.61	-0.60	0.59	0.93	1.59	3.72	2.10
Sugar cane	1.44	2.70	1.24	-0.07	2.73	1.05	1.34	2.10	0.75
Total Oilseeds (nine oilseeds)	1.51	5.20	2.43	-0.86	1.63	1.15	2.35	4.71	2.31
Total Food grains	-0.23	2.85	2.74	-0.07	2.02	1.52	0.43	2.32	2.91
Cotton	-1.25	2.80	4.10	2.71	2.29	-0.41	3.22	13.53	9.99

Notes : * Growth rates are based on the second advance estimates (AE) 2011-12 released on 03 February 2012; total oilseeds include nine oilseeds, cotton seed and coconut.

Source : Department of Agriculture and Cooperation.

The Twelfth Five Year Plan (2012-13 to 2016-17) had envisaged a growth target of 4 per cent for agriculture and allied sectors, necessary for the Indian economy to grow at over 8 per cent. During the last three years, the growth rates in agriculture have been fluctuating at 1.5 per cent in 2012-13, 4.2 per cent in 2013-14, and (-) 0.2 per cent in 2014-15. According to the CSO (Central Statistics Office) estimates released on 8 February 2016, the growth in the 'agriculture, forestry and fishing' sector is estimated at 1.1 per cent in 2015-16. The estimates of GDP for the second quarter (July-September) of 2015-16, 'agriculture, forestry and fishing' sector also reported a growth well below the 4 per cent target, at 2.2 per cent. The shortfall in growth in agriculture is explained by the fact that 60 per cent of agriculture in India is rainfall dependent and there have been two consecutive drought years in 2013-14 and 2014-15. Moreover, there are issues of expansion in irrigation and its efficiency, growth of capital formation in the sector has been declining and there is volatility in the markets, especially of prices, altering and distorting cropping patterns of some crops. This suggests that for the agriculture sector to achieve a target of 4 per cent, a significantly different approach has to be followed (*Economic Survey 2015-16*, Vol. II).

Emerging Imbalances

Although the discussion so far suggests that agricultural performance did improve during the Eleventh Plan, experience of the Eleventh Plan also points to emerging imbalances in agriculture which call for a long-term strategic reorientation.

Cereals Production and Build up of Stocks

There has been a major imbalance between production and consumption of cereals, particularly rice and wheat on the one hand which led to rising stocks and rising consumption of edible oils and pulses which led to imports.

An important and related issue is the likely future demand for food. The Twelfth Plan Working Group on Crop Husbandry, Demand and Supply Projections, Agricultural Inputs and Agricultural Statistics has made projections for food grains and other food items by the terminal year of the Twelfth Plan, that is, 2016-17 which would suggest that present levels of cereals production already exceed likely demand at the end of the Twelfth Plan. These projections are based on actual past patterns of observed demand and the fact that cereals consumption per capita has declined since at least mid-1990s. Also there are very high levels of malnutrition in India and, although there are many reasons for this, deficiencies in calorie intake remain one of the most important. With cereals supplying over 50 per cent of total calorie intake even now, falling cereals consumption is the main reason why per capita calorie intake has not increased despite rising incomes. It is not just that the share of cereals in total food expenditure is falling, even poor people are reducing the share of income spent on all foods in order to meet other non-food needs.

Agricultural production must diversify so as to satisfy both tastes and nutrition. In particular, MSP policy should be more restrained for rice and wheat and made more effective in case of pulses and oilseeds where India is a net importer. Although MSP for pulses and oilseeds has been increased substantially in recent years, farmers are still not encouraged enough to put in the effort and resources required to substitute for current imports of these commodities. This is primarily because procurement efforts in these commodities, which are currently not part of Public Distribution, simply do not offer farmers the certainty that they have from procurement effort in rice and wheat.

High Value Commodities: The Future Sources of Growth in Agriculture

The agricultural production basket comprises of (i) food grains (wheat, rice, coarse cereals and pulses) and commercial or cash crops (cotton, sugar cane, oilseeds and other crops); and (ii) high value commodities such as fruits and vegetables, livestock (milk, meat, poultry and eggs), and marine products. As compared with food grains, commercial crops—particularly cotton and sugar cane—have performed well over time.

The high value segment holds the key to future sources of growth. This is primarily due to their higher expenditure elasticity compared to food grains. The share of high value agriculture in total agriculture (crops, livestock and fisheries) has increased from 37.2 per cent in TE 1982-1993 to 46.8 per cent in TE 2007-08, indicating a distinct shift in production pattern (Gulati, 2008).

Rapid economic growth, rising income levels, and changing demographics have triggered a significant change. The rising number of nuclear families and the increasing number of women professionals are fuelling the change in consumption habits and preferences in favour of semi-processed and processed foods, as well as setting trends in eating out. It is being projected that, in the years to come, nearly 80 per cent of the consumption boom is likely to come from rising income levels (McKinsey and Company, 2007).

Many studies indicate that the high growth in the high value commodity sector has given a push to the growth accomplished by the primary sector at large. The high value commodities (HVCs) achieved a growth rate of 4.1 per cent, while that of non-HVC was just 2.3 per cent for the period 1981-2009. There is also a wide debate on the decision allowing foreign direct investment (FDI) in organised retailing to link producer to markets and thereby improve farm profitability and growth (Chengappa, 2013).

Secondary Agriculture: A Driver for Growth of Primary Agriculture

Secondary Agriculture includes "all practices and process which add value to primary agricultural commodities by using efficient technologies, market information and consumer preference". It should be noted that the term value addition in agriculture is a process of increasing the economic value and consumer appeal of an agricultural commodity. It is basically an alternative production and marketing strategy (Chengappa, 2013).

Potential of Secondary Agriculture

The secondary sector is regarded as a sunrise sector for the Indian economy, owing to its immense untapped potential. The impetus for development of secondary agriculture has been due to increasing consumers demand for value added goods like ready-to-eat, ready-to-serve, convenience food. This is again favoured by the growth of organised retail which makes the processed food easily available to the consumers. Secondly, the fast depletion of natural resources used for industries has created a demand for utilisation of non-conventional renewable agro-bioresources. Thus, demand-side factors are key drivers for creating market opportunities for end products of primary agriculture through the growth of secondary sector (Ibid.).

Reforming the Three 'I's: Investments, Incentives, and Institutions

Thus, in response to new demand patterns, developed markets and infrastructure, a change in approach from farming towards a new agri-system will be needed. While India has a large production base, the lack of infrastructure and organised market structure stand in the way of successful diversification. A World Bank (2007b) study shows that for horticulture produce, farmers typically receive about 12-15 per cent of the price paid by the retail consumer in the export market. Further studies conducted by the World Bank (2007c) on value chains of mango and *litchi* in Bihar show that a significant amount of the consumer price is lost in transport and wastage, and farmers receive 34 and 42 per cent of that price, respectively. This can be further increased if the supply chain can be compressed and the wastage minimised (Gulati, 2010).

It is interesting to observe that many policy makers do realise that the future sources of growth in agriculture will increasingly come from the so-called high value segment (fruits and vegetables, livestock, and fishery), yet the overbearing question of food security (basically staples) dominates the policy agenda. If one looks at the overall public resources being spent on agriculture, one is amazed to observe that three-fourth of the resources go primarily as subsidies on inputs like fertilisers, irrigation and power. Only one-fourth of the resources go as public investment in agricultural, and roughly 90 per cent of this is on major and medium irrigation. Moreover, over time, input subsidies in real terms have gone up much faster than investments in agriculture. This has severe implications for policy regarding the allocation of public resources (Ibid.).

The IFPRI research on marginal returns in terms of agricultural GDP from a unit of public expenditure across various categories within agriculture reveals that the returns are the highest on public expenditures devoted to agriculture R&D, followed by rural roads, education and irrigation, and lowest from fertiliser subsidies (Table 9.5).

Table 9.5

Returns in Growth to Investments and Subsidies

	1960s-1970s	*1980s*	*1990s*
Returns in agricultural GDP (₹ per Re. Spending)			
Roads	19.99	8.89	7.66
Education	14.66	7.58	5.46
Irrigation Investment	8	4.71	4.37
Irrigation subsidies	5.22	2.25	2.47
Fertiliser subsidies	1.79	1.94	0.85
Power subsidies	12.06	2.25	1.19
Credit subsidies	18.77	3	4.26
Agricultural R&D	8.65	7.93	9.5

Source: Fan *et al*. (2008).

The culture of proliferating subsidies is not only crowding out public investment in agriculture but also distorting cropping patterns, leading to environmental stress. For example, in Punjab, more than 75 per cent of blocks are overexploited in terms of groundwater. One of the key reasons for this overexploitation is the spread of paddy cultivation encouraged by free power (GoI, 2007a). Gujarat's Jyotigram experiment—wherein they have separated the feeder lines for agriculture—has shown that the situation can be improved (Shah and Verma, 2008). There are also technical solutions to distributing power subsidies directly to farmers through 'smart cards' that enable electronic meters to work (Gulati and Narayanan, 2003).

It is interesting to note that while public investment in agriculture is critical and important, in reality it forms only less than 25 per cent of the total investment in agriculture; 75 per cent comes from the private sector (GoI, 2008d). Moreover, the private sector responds much better to the incentive structures in agriculture. Thus, reforming the incentives in agriculture is as, if not more, important as public investments in agriculture.

Reforming Incentives

Price and Marketing Policy

Gulati maintains to reform incentives in agriculture, the first policy action has to be getting the 'prices right'. While the reduction of tariffs on manufactured products, the correction of exchange rate of the rupee, and the relaxation of export controls on several agricultural products since 1991 have helped reduce 'implicit taxation' on agriculture (Pursell *et al.*, 2009), there are still occasional interventions by the government (like export bans on wheat and rice, or limits on the stocking of grains by private trade in 2008) that dissuade the private sector to invest in agri-system. However, the main government intervention in agricultural markets currently comes through its policy of MSPs for some 24 odd crops, although in practice this mainly works for rice, wheat, sugar cane and cotton, wherein there is some significant degree of procurement. Over time, this MSP has become *de facto* a procurement price, and discourages farmers to diversify into high value crops that do not have such a support/procurement price. To make the system more market oriented, it is critical to de-link the support price from procurement price, where the latter can be changed (up or down) depending upon market conditions, and in full competition with private trade within the same marketing year. This call for the abolition of all levies (on rice or sugar); the free movement of goods across the country; and the abolition of stocking limits, export bans, bans on future markets, etc., on private trade.

Reforming Institutions

While rationalising subsidies and incentives can pave the way towards greater investments, both public and private, it is important to bring about certain institutional reforms that create an enabling environment for private sector participation with a view to promoting efficiency.

Marketing and Warehouse Facilities

Improving marketing conditions and encouraging private sector participation require reforming the Agricultural Produce Marketing Committee (APMC) Act and abolishing the Essential Commodities Act (ECA). What started as a protective regime to restrict the exploitation of farmers in marketing their produce and ensuring a fair price has resulted in excessive government control. Cleaning up these archaic provisions can trigger private sector investment in developing regularised markets, logistics and warehouse receipt systems, futures markets, and in infrastructure (such as cold storage facilities, quality certification, etc.) for imports and exports. This is particularly relevant for the high value segment that is currently hostage to high post-harvest losses and weak farm-firm linkages.

Reforming Land and Credit Markets

The land and credit markets are intricately linked, and improving the marketability of land will enhance access of farmers to institutional credit. According to the 2003 estimates of NSSO, farmer households with less than 2 hectares of land accounted for 80 per cent of the indebted farmer households, and availed nearly 50 per cent of their loan requirements from non-institutional sources. What aggravates their plight is that nearly 38 per cent of it is acquired at a staggering interest rate of 30 per cent (GoI, 2007b). One could think of bringing the traditional moneylenders into the organised network as non-banking financial intermediaries (NBFIs), wherein National Bank for Agriculture and Rural Development (NABARD) can take the responsibility of refinancing them—suppose at an interest rate of 7 per cent, while they can still charge farmers up to 12 per cent rate of interest.

To sum up two decades of economic reforms have at least corrected two things that are critical to agriculture: (i) that the so-called 'anti-agriculture bias' emanating from overvalued exchange rates and high rates of protection to industry has been largely removed, and this was done very early in the reform process; and (ii) the gross capital formation in agriculture, which had dipped to its lowest levels to 6.99 per cent of agri-GDP in 1994-95, was revived and it touched a high of 21.2 per cent in 2012-13 at 2004-05 prices. These are commendable achievements of the reform process and will go a long way to strengthen the base of Indian agriculture. The third noteworthy feature of Indian agriculture in an open economy environment is its gradual integration with the global economy. The exports plus imports of agricultural commodities as a percentage to agri-GDP increased steadily from about 5 per cent in 1991-92 to roughly 13 per cent in 2010-11. Although still much below the desired land. Nevertheless, the fact is that Indian agriculture today is almost three times more integrated with the global economy than it was 20 years back. This is for the first time in the history of independent India that Indian agriculture has given a net trade surplus of more than $25 billion, in FY2014. Its agri-exports crossed $42 billion *vis-à-vis* imports of about $17 billion indicating that Indian agriculture is quite export competitive and India's agri-export basket is quite diversified.

In a nutshell, Indian agriculture has demonstrated its strength in the domain of external trade. In light of that, a purposive and rational tweaking of the trade policies would go a long way in harmonising gains with the rational utilisation of our resources. For this, India needs to have an open trade policy where exports and imports both are open, and tweak these only with mild duties (10-15%) whenever needed. This would bring rich harvest to farmers in a sustainable manner and also protect the interests of consumers, giving a win-win situation. And the time to do that is now.

The challenge for agriculture tomorrow comes not as much from opening it up to global markets, as from policies that still use severe export controls (be it rice, wheat, sugar, or even cotton) and do not permit a single unified national market for agri-produce. Other concerns are the high and distorted structure of taxes and fees on agri-goods in certain states, levies that are still distorting the evolution of markets, the failure to give a clear signal on market reforms that can connect the farmers' organisations to organised processors and retailers without going through the anarchic *mandi* system, and failure to give the right signals to agri-scientists and entrepreneurs on new technologies related to GM crops for commercialisation. These reforms imply institutional reforms, and require strong political will at the centre. Only then can one hope that Indian agriculture will cross the barrier of 4 per cent growth on a sustainable basis and bring the much-needed prosperity in rural areas.

Farm profitability is central to achieving rapid and inclusive agricultural growth. The reports of the Commission for Agricultural Costs and Prices (CACP) show low net farm revenue for many crops, particularly rainfed. Diversification towards higher value crops and livestock remains the best way not only to improve farm incomes and accelerate growth, but also to reduce stress on natural resources which form farmers' production base. This needs better infrastructure and emphasis on integrated farming systems, combining crops and livestock, including small ruminants, for different location-specific endowments. This also requires innovative institutional and contractual arrangements so that small holders have the requisite technology and market access (*Twelfth Five Year Plan*, Vol. II).

Challenges and Outlook

Although India has made impressive progress in increasing its agricultural production in the past 60 years, Indian agriculture is facing a serious crisis. The crisis is clearly evident in falling share of agriculture in GDP with little decline in the workforce depending on agriculture; progressive diminution of agricultural holdings and impoverishment of the large majority of the farmers who cannot make two ends meet from their agriculture income. With 14 per cent share in GDP, agriculture is supporting nearly 52 per cent of country's workforce. Very large numbers of farmers, nearly 83 per cent, are having holdings of less than two hectares, and their number is increasing. Except in some special circumstances, e.g., the holdings growing vegetables or other high-value crops, these holdings are economically non-viable. Most of the farmers are having negative, or at best a meagre income from agriculture. The challenge facing agriculture, and in a way for the economy as a whole, is to increase production on vast number of small agricultural holdings and enable a sizeable number of workers to shift from agriculture to non-agricultural sectors. In most of the circumstances, increase in productivity in agriculture is a precondition for the growth in the non-farm employment, particularly in rural area (Vyas, 2012).

Although India is one of the leading producers in the world of many major crops like paddy, wheat, pulses, sugar cane, spices and plantation crops, the comparison in terms of yield levels is not creditable, achieving a much lower rank in many of these crops. Further, studies indicate that there are wide yield gaps among various crops across the country. Agriculture production can be substantially increased if we address this yield gap by adopting technological and policy interventions. Improvement in yields holds the key for India to remain self-sufficient in food grains and also make a place for itself in many agricultural crops and products in the international market.

Since most of the growth in agriculture in future will come not from food grains, but from sectors such as horticulture, dairying and fisheries, where the produce is perishable, much greater attention needs to be paid to the logistics of transporting produce from the farm to the consumer, with minimum spoilage. This requires active involvement of the private sector. To facilitate such involvement, state governments must amend the Agricultural Produce Marketing Committee (APMC) Acts which at present prevent private sector buyers from dealing directly with producers. Some states have amended their APMC Acts, but the rules are either not notified or are not designed to encourage entry of private players.

As international trade in agricultural commodity is likely to be liberalised further, a greater preparedness is required to face the competition in the international market. In order to compete in the world trade and exploit the full potential of trade liberalisation, India should streamline its domestic reforms, infrastructure and institutions (Dev, 2012).

The rural economy needs to be viewed as comprising of a continuum of interrelated economic activities. Farming needs to be dovetailed with viable off-farm and non-farm activities. Farmers need to be facilitated to take up value addition such as processing of agricultural produce, horticulture, pisciculture, poultry, development of non-farm rural enterprises or what is termed as secondary agriculture which is regarded as the sunrise sector for the Indian economy owing to its immense untapped potential. The future sources of growth in agriculture lie in the high value segment and reforming the three 'I's—Investments, Incentives and Institutions.

On domestic and international marketing, the plethora of government interventions that were used to build a marketing set-up have actually served as barriers to trade. Removing market distortions will create greater competition in markets, promote efficiency and growth, and facilitate the creation of a national agriculture market. Since agriculture provides the backward linkage to agro-based industries and services, it has to be viewed holistically as a seamless farm-to-fork value chain, comprising farming, wholesaling, warehousing, logistics, processing, and retailing including exports.

We have to relate policies, programmes and delivery systems to the reality of a small farm dominated agrarian structure on the one hand, and changing demand pattern for agricultural produce on the other. Then alone we will be able to face the challenge of transforming a stagnant and impoverishing agriculture to a just, efficient and dynamic sector.

References

Bisaliah, S., S. Mahendra Dev and Syed Saifullah (2013). "Capital Formation, Agriculture Growth and Poverty in India", in *Investment in Indian Agriculture*. New Delhi: Academic Foundation.

Chengappa, P.G. (2013). "Secondary Agriculture: A Driver for Growth of Primary Agriculture in India", *Indian Journal of Agricultural Economics* 68(1). January-March 2013.

Dev, Mahendra (2012). "Agriculture Development" in Kaushik Basu and Annemie Maetrey (eds.) (2012), *The New Oxford Companion to Economics in India*. New Delhi: Oxford University Press.

Ghatak, Maitreesh (2007). "Land Reform", in Kaushik Basu (ed.) (2007), *The Oxford Companion to Economics in India*. New Delhi: Oxford University Press.

Government of India, *Economic Survey* various issues including 2010-11, 2011-12, 2012-13, 2013-14, 2014-15, 2015-16.

Gulati, A. and Shenggen Fan (2008). *The Dragon and the Elephant—Agricultural and Rural Reforms in China and India*. New Delhi: Oxford University Press.

Gulati, Ashok (2010). "Accelerating Agricultural Growth: Moving from Farming to Value Chains", in Shankar Acharya and Rakesh Mohan (eds.) (2010), *India's Economy: Performance and Challenges*. New Delhi: Oxford University Press.

———. (2012). "Indian Agriculture in an Open Economy: Will it Prosper", in Isher Judge Ahluwalia and IMD Little (eds.) (2012), *India's Economic Reforms and Development: Essays for Manmohan Singh* (Second Edition). New Delhi: OUP.

———. (2012). "Reforming Agriculture", in Uma Kapila (ed.) (2012), *Two Decades of Economic Reforms*. New Delhi: Academic Foundation.

———. (2014). "Revamping Agriculture and the Public Distribution System", in Bibek Debroy, Ashley J. Tellis and Reece Trevor (eds.) (2014), *Getting India Back on Track: An Action Agenda for Reform*. Random House India.

Jeromi, P.D. (2002). "Is Indian Agriculture Approaching the Limits to Growth", in *Economic Developments in India*, Vol. 58. New Delhi: Academic Foundation.

Jha, Shekhar (2007). "Food Procurement Policy", in Kaushik Basu (ed.) (2007), *The Oxford Companion to Economics in India*. New Delhi: Oxford University Press.

Parthasarthy, G. (2003). *Economic Reforms and Rural Development*. New Delhi: Academic Foundation.

Planning Commission (2002). *Tenth Five Year Plan* 1997-2002.

———. (2005). *Mid-term Appraisal of the Tenth Five Year Plan.*

———. (2006). *Towards Faster and More Inclusive Growth, An Approach to the 11th Five Year Plan*, December.

———. (2012). *Faster, Sustainable and More Inclusive Growth: An Approach to the 12th Five Year Plan* (Draft).

———. (2007). *Agricultural Strategy for Eleventh Plan: Some Critical Issues*, May.

———. (2008). *Eleventh Five Year Plan 2007-2012*, Vol. III.

———. (2010). *Mid Term Appraisal, Eleventh Five Year Plan 2007-2012*.

———. (2012). *Twelfth Five Year Plan 2007-2012*, Vol. II.

Radhakrishna, R. (2008). *India Development Report 2008*, Indira Gandhi Institute of Development Research, Ch. 3. New Delhi: Oxford University Press.

Rao, C.H.H. (2005). *Agricultural Growth, Farm Size and Rural Poverty Alleviation in India*. New Delhi: Academic Foundation.

———. (2005). *Agriculture, Food Security, Poverty and Environment, Essays on Post Reform India*. New Delhi: Oxford University Press.

Rao, C.H.H. and A. Gulati. "Indian Agriculture: Emerging Perspectives and Policy", in Uma Kapila (ed.), *Indian Economy since Independence* (2000-01 edition). Academic Foundation.

Reserve Bank of India, *Report on Currency and Finance 2001-02*.

Rosenstein-Rodan (1943). "Problems of Industrialisation of Eastern and South-Eastern Europe", *Economic Journal*. 53: 202–11.

Sastry, D.V.S, Balwant Singh, Kaushik Bhattacharya and N.K. Unnikrishnan (2003). "Sectoral Linkages and Growth Prospects: Reflections on the Indian Economy", *Economic and Political Weekly* 38: 2390–7.

Subramaniam, Vijay and Michael Reed (2009). "Agricultural Inter-Sectoral Linkages and its Contribution to Economic Growth in the Transition Countries", *ageconsearch.umn.edu/ bitstream*.

Vaidyanathan, A. (2003). *India's Economic Reforms and Development*. New Delhi: Academic Foundation.

———. (2006). "Farmers' Suicides and the Agrarian Crisis", *Economic and Political Weekly* XLI(38), September 23.

———. (2007). "Irrigation", in Kaushik Basu (ed.) (2007), *The Oxford Companion to Economics in India*. New Delhi: Oxford University Press.

Vyas, V.S. (2003). *Agrarian Structure, Economic Policies & Sustainable Development*. New Delhi: Academic Foundation.

———. (2012). "Challenge of Transforming Indian Agriculture", in Uma Kapila (ed.) (2012), *Two Decades of Economic Reforms*. New Delhi: Academic Foundation.

———. (2012). "Challenge of Sustaining Food grains Production", Foundation Day Lecture 2012, New Delhi: National Academy of Agricultural Sciences, June 5.

Vyas, V.S. and Ratna Reddy (2002). "Economic Reforms in Indian Agriculture: Recent Experience and Long-term Issues", in *India's Economy in the 21st Century*. Raj Kapila and Uma Kapila, (eds.) (2002), 2nd Revised Edition. New Delhi: Academic Foundation.

World Bank (2007). *World Development Report 2008: Agriculture for Development*. Washington, D.C.: International Bank for Reconstruction and Development.

World Bank Group (2014). Republic of India Accelerating Agricultural Productivity Growth.

[illegible]

[illegible]

[illegible]

[illegible]

[illegible]

[illegible]

[illegible]

[illegible]

[illegible]

[illegible]

[illegible]

[illegible]

[illegible]

[illegible]

[illegible]

[illegible]

[illegible]

[illegible]

10

S. MAHENDRA DEV

Agricultural Development in India

Performance, Issues and Policies

AGRICULTURE plays a pivotal role in the Indian economy. Although its contribution to gross domestic product (GDP) is now around one-seventh, it provides employment to nearly 50 per cent of the Indian workforce. Also, the forward and backward linkage effects of agriculture growth increase the incomes in the non-agriculture sector. The growth of some commercial crops has significant potential for promoting exports of agricultural commodities and bringing about faster development of agro-based industries.

Thus agriculture not only contributes to overall growth of the economy, but also reduces poverty by providing employment and food security to the majority of the population in the country, and thus it is the most inclusive growth sectors of the Indian economy.

The objective of this paper is to examine the performance and policy issues in Indian agriculture since Independence with emphasis on the reform period. It is divided into three sections. First section deals with performance, while section two briefly examines policies since Independence. The last section is devoted to a discussion of issues and policy changes needed for higher growth, equity and sustainability in agriculture.

Performance of Agriculture

One of the paradoxes of the Indian economy is that the decline in the share of agricultural workers in total workers has been slower than the decline in the share of agriculture in the GDP. For example, the share of agriculture & allied activities in the GDP declined from 57.7 per cent in 1950–51 to 14 per cent in 2012-13 (Table 10.1). The share of agriculture in total workers, however, declined slowly from 75.9 per cent in 1961 to 48.9 per cent in 2011-12 (Table 10.1).

Table 10.1

Share of Agriculture in GDP and Employment: All India

Year	*Share in GDP (%)*		*Share of Agriculture, forestry and fishing in Total Employment (%)*
	Agriculture, forestry and fishing	*Agriculture**	
1950-51	57.7	50.2	--
1960-51	53.0	47.3	75.9
1980-81	39.7	35.8	--
2004-05	18.9	15.9	56.4
2009-10	14.6	12.3	51.3
2011-12	14.4	12.3	48.9
2012-13	13.9	11.8	--

Source: 'National Accounts Statistics of India: 1950–51 to 2002–03', *Economic and Political Weekly Research Foundation*, December 2004, Mumbai; Brochure on the New Series of National Accounts, Base Year 2005; K. Sundaram, (2001, 2007); *Economic Survey* 2013-14; NSS data on Employment and Unemployment Surveys.

Between 1961 and 2012-13, there was a decline of 39 percentage points in the share of agriculture in GDP, while the decline in share of agriculture in employment was of only 27 percentage points. As a result, the gap between labour productivity in agriculture and non-agriculture increased rapidly.

In terms of growth, the performance of agriculture in the post-Independence era has been impressive as compared to the pre-Independence period. The all crop output growth of around 2.57 per cent per annum in the post-Independence period (during 1949-50 to 2007-08) was much higher than the negligible growth rate of around 0.4 per cent per annum in the first half of the last century. As a result, India achieved significant gains in food grains and non-food grain crops.

The highest growth rate of GDP from agriculture & allied activities of 4.1 per cent per annum in recent years was recorded in the 12th Five Year Plan period (Table 10.2). Decadal average of 1980s also recorded high growth rate of more than 3 per cent per annum. The deceleration in the growth rate of GDP from agriculture between the first half of the 1990s and the later period is glaring. It is disquieting to note that during the 1997-98 to 2004-05, agriculture growth was only 1.6 per cent per annum (Table 10.2). The growth rate was less than 3 per cent during the 9th and 10th the Five Year Plans before recording 4.1 per cent per annum during 12th plan period.[1] Significant fluctuation in growth of agriculture is a matter of concern. Figure 10.1 provides growth rates for the components of agriculture & allied sector since 1980-81.

Extensive cultivation has characterised Indian agriculture during the pre-1965 era, and intensive cultivation in the post-Green Revolution period. There has been significant increase in the use of modern inputs in Indian agriculture. During the period 1950-51 to 2009-10, the percentage of net irrigated area to net cultivated area increased from around 17 to 45. During the same period, fertiliser consumption showed a significant rise from less than 1 kg/ha to 144 kg/ha. Similarly, the percentage of area under high yielding varieties (HYVs) to cereals cropped area has risen significantly. The share of agriculture in electricity consumption also rose from 4 per cent in 1950-51 to nearly 30 per cent in recent years. All this led to a significant increase in agricultural output over time.

Table 10.2

Growth Rates in Agriculture GDP: All India

Period	*Growth Rate (per cent per annum)*
1950-51 to 1964-65	2.51
1967-68 to 1980-81	2.20
1980-81 to 1990-91	3.07
1992-93 to 1996-97	3.85
1992-93 to 2001-02	2.76
1997-98 to 2004-05	1.60
9th Five Year Plan (1997-2002)	2.50
10th Five Year Plan (2002-2007)	2.40
11th Five Year Plan (2007-2012)	4.10
2012-13	1.40
2013-14	4.70

Note: GDP is in 1980-81 constant prices from 1950-51 to 1980-81; in 1993-94 constant prices for the period 1980-81 to 2004-05; in 2004-05 constant prices for the period 2004-05 to 2013-14.

Source: National Accounts Statistics, various years, CSO, Government of India (GoI).

Figure 10.1

Growth in Agriculture Sector

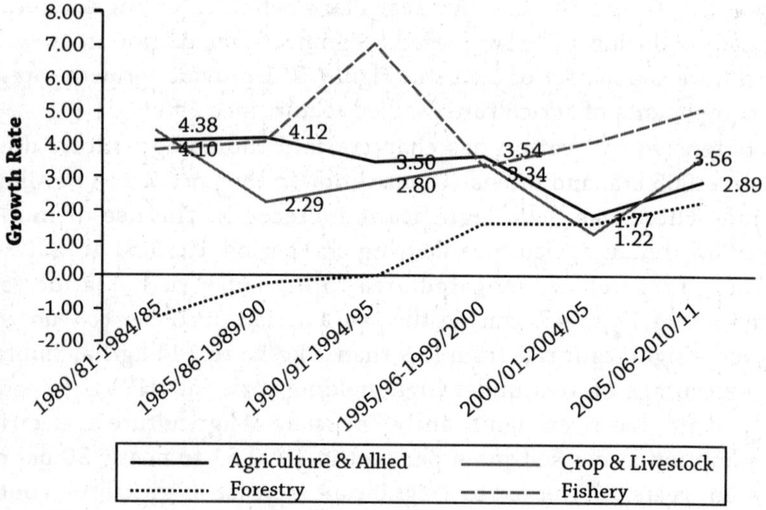

Source: National Accounts Statistics, CSO.

Output of all crops increased at a compound growth rate of 3.15 per cent per annum during 1949-50 to 1964-65, significantly led by area expansion (Table 10.3). There has not been any significant increase in agricultural growth in the post-Green Revolution period. However, the sources of growth have changed from area expansion in the pre-Green Revolution period to yield growth in the later periods. Yield growth at 2.56 per cent per annum was high in the 1980s. However, it declined

Table 10.3

Compound Growth Rates of Area, Output and Yield: All India

Period	*All Crops*			*Food Grains*			*Non-Food Grains*		
	Area	*Output*	*Yield*	*Area*	*Output*	*Yield*	*Area*	*Output*	*Yield*
1949-50 to 1964-65	1.58	3.15	1.21	1.35	2.82	1.36	2.44	3.74	0.89
1967-68 to 1980-81	0.51	2.19	1.28	0.38	2.15	1.33	0.94	2.26	1.19
1980-81 to 1989-90	0.10	3.19	2.56	-0.23	2.85	2.74	1.12	3.77	2.31
1990-91 to 1999-2000	0.27	2.29	1.33	-0.07	2.02	1.52	1.18	2.69	1.09
1994-95 to 2010-11	0.46	3.24	2.91	0.19	2.23	1.87	1.13	3.84	2.65

Source: Various Issues of *Agriculture at a Glance*, Department of Agriculture & Co-operation, Ministry of Agriculture, GoI.

significantly to 1.33 per cent in the 1990s. During the period 1994-95 to 2010-11, yield growth has increased as compared to the decade of the 1990s. In general, output and yield growth for non-food grains is higher than those for food grains.

It is interesting to look at the trends in outputs, value added, inputs and factor productivities since Independence. These trends are given in Table 10.4. The following conclusions can be drawn from the table:

- Growth of total value of output in agriculture (crop and livestock) during the 11th Plan at 3.8 per cent per annum was the highest as compared to earlier periods since Independence. It was also the highest for pulses, fibres, all crops and livestock. The growth rates for all the crop aggregates are higher for 11th Plan as compared to those of 9th and 10th Plans.
- Growth in intermediate inputs for agriculture & allied activities was the highest for 11th Plan at 4.3 per cent per annum compared to 3 per cent and 2.4 per cent respectively for 9th and 10th Plans. The growth rates for all the inputs were higher in 11th Plan compared to those for 9th and 11th Plan. In other words, the high growth rate is accompanied by high input growth which is not sustainable.
- Apart from intermediate inputs, there was increase in net capital stock in agriculture & allied sector. Public sector capital stock rose at 3.6 per cent while private sector capital accelerated to 7.5 per cent per year in 11th Five Year. Rise in capital stock in 11th Plan was much faster than those for earlier two plans. However, public investment stagnated during 11th Plan while private investment increased significantly (Table 10.5). One of the reasons for increase in private investment could be rise in terms of trade in agriculture. The total investment in agriculture as per cent of agricultural GDP rose significantly from 16 per cent in 2007-08 to 21 per cent in 2012-13 (Table 10.5). However, the growth rate was around 4 per cent in 11th Plan with a capital output ratio of 5:1. There is a need for increase in efficiency of investment.
- Land and labour productivity increased significantly in the 11th Plan period compared to the earlier plans. In fact, labour productivity recorded the highest rate of growth at 4.8 per cent per annum. This is the highest since independence. But, capital productivity declined during 11th Plan period (Table 10.4).

Table 10.4

Growth of Output, Inputs and Productivity: All India
(period averages of annual growth rates)

	Pre-Green Revolution 1951-52 to 1967-68	*Green Revolution 1968-69 to 1980-81*	*Wider Coverage 1981-82 to 1990-91*	*Early Liberalisation 1991-92 to 1996-97*	*Ninth Plan 1997-98 to 2001-02*	*Tenth Plan 2002-03 to 2006-07*	*Eleventh Plan 2007-08 to 2011-12*
1	2	3	4	5	6	7	8
I. Value of output (2004-5 prices)							
Cereals	4.2	3.4	3.5	2.4	1.5	1.0	3.0
Pulses	3.0	0.7	3.4	0.8	0.3	1.8	4.2
Oilseeds	3.2	1.8	7.4	4.4	-2.5	7.4	4.5
Sugar	3.3	4.1	4.2	2.4	9.4	1.7	2.2
Fiber	4.4	2.5	5.3	6.5	-5.6	15.1	10.7
Non-horticulture crops	3.2	2.7	3.0	2.1	1.7	2.1	2.8
Horticulture	2.6	4.2	3.1	5.7	3.8	2.6	4.7
All Crops	3.0	3.0	3.0	3.1	2.3	2.1	3.4
Livestock	1.0	3.3	4.8	4.0	3.6	3.6	4.8
Crops and Livestock	2.5	3.0	3.3	3.3	2.6	2.5	3.8
Fishing	4.7	3.1	5.7	7.1	2.7	3.3	3.6
Forestry	1.7	-0.2	0.3	0.3	2.7	1.3	2.3
Agriculture & Allied	2.3	2.4	3.0	3.1	2.6	2.4	3.6

contd...

...contd...

1	2	3	4	5	6	7	8
II. Value of Inputs (2004-05 prices)							
Seed	1.5	1.1	2.3	1.6	-0.6	1.4	4.1
Feed of livestock	1.9	4.0	0.1	0.9	3.9	0.7	3.3
Organic manure	0.0	1.3	0.7	0.5	1.6	2.9	3.3
Fertilisers and peticides	18.2	9.3	8.7	2.0	3.9	4.8	6.7
Diesel oil	26.0	13.1	8.7	4.3	5.1	5.1	5.8
Electricity	18.5	15.2	12.9	14.4	-4.1	2.6	8.0
All Inputs Crops and Livestock	2.4	4.5	2.2	1.9	3.0	2.5	4.4
Inputs for Fishing	4.6	3.3	5.4	6.5	2.7	1.5	3.5
Inputs for Forestry	1.7	-0.2	0.1	0.3	2.6	1.3	2.3
All Inputs Agriculture & Allied	2.3	3.9	2.1	1.9	3.0	2.4	4.3
III. Gross value Added (2004-05 prices)							
Crops and Livestock	2.7	2.7	3.7	3.7	2.5	2.5	3.5
Fishing	4.7	3.0	5.8	7.2	2.7	3.6	3.7
Forestry	1.7	-0.2	0.4	0.3	2.8	1.3	2.3
Agriculture & Allied	2.5	2.4	3.5	3.7	2.5	2.4	3.3
IV. Factor Inputs into Agriculture							
Land (gross cropped area)	1.3	0.4	0.8	0.3	-0.1	0.6	0.3
Labour	1.8	1.1	0.5	2.3	0.3	0.5	-1.5
Net fixed capital stock	2.3	3.6	2.8	3.1	3.4	4.7	6.0
Of which: public	---	---	3.9	2.0	1.4	2.3	3.6
Of which: private	---	---	1.4	4.3	5.1	6.6	7.5
V. Partial Factor Productivities (2004-05 prices)							
Land productivity	1.2	2.0	2.7	3.3	2.6	1.8	3.1
Labour productivity	0.7	1.4	3.0	1.4	2.2	1.8	4.8
Capital productivity	0.2	-1.1	0.7	0.6	-0.9	-2.4	-2.7

Source: 12th Five Year Plan, GoI, Vol. II, p.6.

Table 10.5

Gross Capital Formation (GCF) in Agriculture, Forestry and Fishing (2004-05 prices)

	GCF in Agri. as % of GDP in Agri.		
Year	*Public Sector*	*Private Sector*	*Total*
10th Plan			
2002-03	2.0	12.2	14.2
2003-04	2.3	10.1	12.4
2004-05	2.9	10.6	13.4
2005-06	3.5	11.2	14.6
2006-07	3.7	11.2	14.9
11th Plan			
2007-08	3.6	12.6	16.1
2008-09	3.1	16.3	19.4
2009-10	3.4	16.7	20.1
2010-11	2.8	15.7	18.5
2011-12	2.8	18.0	20.8
2012-13	3.0	18.1	21.2

Source: Obtained from 12th Five Year Plan and *Economic Survey 2013-14*, GoI.

The aggregate output growth at national level hides a great deal of variation in the performance of different crops and regions. While wheat has recorded high and accelerated rates of yield increases, others like coarse cereals and pulses have not. Food grains and non-food grains recorded the highest growth rates in output as well as yields in the 1980s. In the 1990s, growth rate decelerated for both food grains and non-food grains. Increasing commercialisation of agriculture started in a significant way in the 1980s. There are two revolutions in the last decade in the form of BT cotton and hybrid maize. Production increased significantly in these two crops.

There are large regional disparities in output across regions (see Vaidyanathan, 1994). Certain regions such as Punjab, Haryana, western Uttar Pradesh, parts of Andhra Pradesh and Tamil Nadu have benefited more during the initial phase of the Green Revolution than others. This had accentuated regional disparities in the immediate post-Green Revolution period. An important feature of the 1980s and the early 1990s, however, is that there has been much more equitable spread of agricultural growth. According to Bhalla and Singh (1997), the period

1980-1983 to 1990-1993 marks a turning point (in terms of growth) in India's agricultural development. After performing poorly during the early years of the Green Revolution, many of the states where poverty is widespread—Assam, Bihar, Odisha, Madhya Pradesh and West Bengal—have shown significant growth in the 1980s. Oilseeds have also gained in the dry belt of Rajasthan, Madhya Pradesh, Karnataka and Maharashtra.

Growth rates in the post-reform period are given in Table 10.6. The all-India growth rate recoded 4.1 per cent during 2005-06 to 2011-12 compared to 3.3 per cent during 1994-95 to 1999-2000 and 1.7 per cent during 2000-01 to 2004-05. Some of the states with large rainfed areas such as Jharkhand, Chhattisgarh, Rajasthan, Gujarat, Maharashtra, Karnataka and Andhra Pradesh registered growth rate of 5 and above in the latest five year period compared to earlier five year periods (Table 10.6).

Table 10.6

Growth Rates of GDP in Agriculture across Major States: 1994-95 to 2011-12

States	*1994-95 to 1999-2000*	*2000-01 to 2004-05*	*2005-06 to 2011-12*
Andhra Pradesh	2.8	4.7	5.0
Bihar	3.1	7.4	3.3
Chhattisgarh	-2.1	4.6	7.3
Gujarat	5.2	9.1	5.5
Haryana	2.1	2.7	4.2
Jharkhand	4.3	5.0	8.0
Karnataka	4.1	-2.9	5.1
Kerala	1.9	1.7	-0.2
Madhya Pradesh	1.6	2.2	4.4
Maharashtra	3.1	1.6	5.3
Odisha	0.0	3.5	3.1
Punjab	2.5	1.8	1.8
Rajasthan	5.5	10.9	5.5
Tamil Nadu	1.8	-0.5	4.6
Uttar Pradesh	3.5	1.0	2.8
Uttarakhand	2.4	3.3	2.0
West Bengal	4.1	2.4	2.6
All India	3.3	1.7	4.1*
High Irrigated States	3.2	1.7	2.7
Medium Irrigated States	1.8	3.1	4.2
Low Irrigated States	2.8	1.5	4.5
High Productivity States	2.9	2.5	2.1
Medium Productivity States	2.4	2.1	3.7
Low Productivity States	2.6	2.5	5.1

Source: 12th Five Year Plan, GoI.

The 11th Five Year Plan gave emphasis to existing technology and reducing yield gaps rather than new technology. The increase in growth rates since 2005-06 has been higher in states with low productivity and low irrigated states. In relatively high irrigated states such as Punjab, Haryana, Uttar Pradesh (UP), West Bengal and high productivity states such as Kerala, the growth was lower since 2005-06. The low irrigated and low productivity respectively 4.5 per cent and 5.1 per cent during 2005-06 to 2011-12 registered. During the same time, high irrigated and high productivity states recorded respectively 2.7 per cent and 2.1 per cent respectively.

During the post-reform period, in response to the growing domestic and export demand for non-cereal items of food, there has been a discernible shift in the allocation of resources in Indian agriculture in the recent period away from cereals, particularly coarse cereals, to dairy farming, poultry, edible oils, meat, fish, vegetables, fruits, etc. These enterprises, being labour intensive, are suited to small holders and lead to a rise in wage employment. Besides they are environment friendly, as they are generally less land and water intensive, and there is also a rise in incomes of farmers growing high value products. The deceleration in agricultural growth during the period 1997-98 and 2004-05, although most marked in rainfed areas, occurred in almost all states and covered almost all sub-sectors, including those such as horticulture, livestock and fisheries where growth was expected to be high (GoI, 2007).

However, there have been some positive developments in the last decade. Eleventh plan period recoded 4.1 per cent agricultural growth. Total foodgrain production was 264.4 million tonnes in 2013-14. Pulses production was 19.6 million tonnes during the same year. Exports in agriculture rose significantly. Both public and private investment in agriculture increased. Total investment in agriculture was 21 per cent of agriculture GDP. There were large expenditures on programmes like Rashtriya Krishi Vikas Yojana (RKVY), National Horticulture Mission (NHM), National Food Security Mission (NFSM) and Agricultural Technology Management Agency (ATMA). Apart from revolutions in BT cotton and hybrid maize, there has been some increase in high value agriculture. Terms of trade for agriculture improved. Some of the lagging regions like Bihar showed relatively high growth in recent years. Similarly, Gujarat recorded high growth of 9 per cent per annum during 2001-02 to 2007-08. There is also now recognition of climate change issues in India.

Policies Since Independence

At the outset, it may be mentioned that agriculture is a 'state subject' under the Constitution of India. However, the central government plays a crucial role in shaping agricultural policies. Although Indian agriculture is in private hands, government policies have greatly influenced its pace and character. Broadly, agricultural development policies over time can be divided into four sets of policy packages: (a) institutional reforms; (b) public investment policies; (c) incentive policies; and (d) reforms and globalisation policies. The relative importance of the first three sets has varied over time.

Thus, during the first three Five Year Plans (1950-1965), the institutional reforms and public investment packages dominated. The central and state governments enacted a number of laws regarding land reforms. These laws mainly relate to three aspects: abolition of *zamindari* system, land ceiling and redistribution of land, and tenancy reforms. The government was successful in abolishing the *zamindari* or intermediary system after paying compensation to the *zamindars*. The land ceiling laws were not effective, although there was redistribution of some land to the beneficiaries. The tenancy reforms were more successful in two states, West Bengal in the east and Kerala in the south, than in others. West Bengal succeeded in giving ownership rights to tenants, particularly sharecroppers (bargardars). Some efforts were made to consolidate fragmented holdings in India since Independence. In some parts of north and north-west India, these efforts were relatively successful.

There was significant public investment in agriculture during 1950-1965. To achieve the objective of self-sufficiency in food grains, there was massive investment particularly in constructing irrigation reservoirs and distribution systems. Another important policy during this period was the expansion of institutional credit which helped reduce informal sources that had been exploitative in respect of interest rates and terms and conditions.

During the 1967-1990 period, incentive policies for adoption of new technology and public investment policies dominated government strategy in agriculture. After the humiliating experience with import of food grains in the mid-1960s, there was a vigorous drive for achieving self-sufficiency in food grains by stepping up public investment in irrigation and introduction of new technology through incentives. There was a need to increase domestic food production at a faster rate by much higher productivity without upsetting the agrarian structure. Luckily at that time new high-yielding dwarf varieties of wheat and rice were available in Mexico and the Philippines respectively. Yields increased significantly for wheat initially and later for rice. This breakthrough is popularly known as the 'Green Revolution.' The productivity improvement associated with the Green Revolution is best described as forest- or land-saving agriculture. It may be noted that without the Green Revolution it would not have been possible to lift the production potential of Indian agriculture.

As mentioned earlier, inter-regional variations increased in the initial phase of the Green Revolution as it was limited to a few states like Punjab, Haryana, and UP. However, unlike in the first decade of the Green Revolution, the experience in the 1980s indicates that the Green Revolution is spreading to new areas, particularly to the eastern and western regions; the new technology is being increasingly adopted by the small farmers; there is a decline in the relative prices of food grains; and the real wages in agriculture have started rising, especially in the less developed regions (Rao, 1994: 63).

Incentive policies focused on both inputs and output. Subsidies for inputs like irrigation, credit, fertilisers, and power increased significantly in the 1970s and 1980s. The objective of the subsidies is to provide inputs at low prices to protect farmer interests and encourage diffusion of new technology. Similarly, on the output side, there has been a comprehensive long-term procurement-cum-distribution policy in the post-Green Revolution period. The government announces the support prices at sowing time and agrees to buy all the grains offered for sale at this price. To support these operations, institutions like the Food Corporation of India (FCI) and the Agricultural Prices Commission (APC) were established in the mid-1960s.

In the post-reform period, economic reforms in India since 1991 have improved the incentive framework and agriculture has benefited from reduction in protection to industry. The structural reforms and stabilisation policies introduced in India in 1991 initially focused on industry, tax reforms, foreign trade and investment, banking and capital markets. The economic reforms did not include any specific package specifically designed for agriculture. It was viewed that freeing agricultural markets and liberalising external trade in agricultural commodities would provide price incentives leading to enhanced investment and output in that sector, while broader trade liberalisation would shift inter-sectoral terms of trade (ToT) in favour of agriculture (Balakrishnan, 2000)

On the positive side, the reforms have improved ToT for agriculture and opened up new opportunities such as benefits from trade and specialisation, widening choices in new technology including bio-technology, increase in private investment in irrigation and marketing infrastructure like storage and transport. It is viewed that protection to industry in the form of import substitution policies like tight import controls and high import duties have hurt the agriculture till 1991. Disprotection to industry since 1991 are supposed to correct this bias and increase terms of trade for agriculture. "This would create a potentially more profitable agriculture, which would be able to bear the economic costs of technological modernization and expansion" (Manmohan Singh, 1995: 2).[2]

Agricultural growth was 3.7 per cent per annum in the first six years of the reform period (1991-1997). The ToT in agriculture improved during this period due to dis-protection to industry, devaluation of rupee and increase in minimum support prices (MSPs). Then the growth rate started declining since mid-1990s. The ToT deteriorated during this period. Agricultural growth has picked up again and growth was more than 4 per cent during the period 2004-2008. There seems to be a revival in ToT again during this period. Thus, the favourable ToT in agriculture has some impact on agriculture in the post-reform period. Similarly, private investment in agriculture improved in the post-reform period, although there has been stagnancy in the late 1990s. ToT for agriculture based on GDP implicit price deflators indicate the ToT increased significantly since 2004-05. Particularly, the ToT for agriculture increased significantly in 2007-08 and 2008-09, and they are the highest in the last two decades.

Trade reforms are expected to have positive impact on agriculture. There has been significant increase in agricultural exports after economic reforms were initiated. Agricultural exports rose from $3.2 billion in 1991-92 to $6.86 billion in 1996-97 but thereafter it declined. Increase in exports initially was due to significant reduction in the import duties and devaluation of Indian rupee. The economy-wide reforms seem to have benefited agriculture because of increasing business transactions between agriculture and rest of the economy over time (Mishra and Rao, 2003). Sharp reduction in global commodity prices and East Asian crisis could be the principal reasons for decline in agricultural exports in the late 1990s. They picked up again from 2004-05 and continued till the financial crisis in 2008.

Trade liberalisation in agriculture has been faster towards the end of 1990s in tune with WTO agreements. The impact of trade liberalisation on agriculture works through various channels such as volatile prices, problems in imports and exports, impact on livelihood and other employment opportunities. For farmers, perhaps the single most adverse effect has been the combination of low prices and output volatility for cash crops. Some prices such as those of cotton and oilseeds declined for long periods. Plantation crops like tea, coffee and rubber were also affected. This reflected not only domestic demand conditions but also the growing role played by international prices consequent upon greater integration with world markets in this sector.

But, monitoring of the imports for 300 sensitive products has indicated that such imports constitute only a small proportion of total agricultural imports in the country (GoI, 2003). Thus, the concern of significant imports due to trade liberalisation has not been proved. India has considerable flexibility to counter flooding of the Indian market by cheap agricultural imports through imposition of tariffs (bound rates) under World Trade Organization (WTO). The major food and agricultural policies initiated in India are those of: Procurement policy, buffer stocking, public distribution system, public investment, input subsidies and government support to research. Clearly, India does not have to change any of these policies because of Agreement on Agriculture (AoA). However, implementation of the WTO's AoA since 1995 has brought out the inadequacies inherent in the agreement.[3] The ongoing negotiations in the WTO on the AOA provide an opportunity for India to rectify these inadequacies and inequalities.

One problem with trade is that volatility in domestic agricultural prices will increase with globalisation. Several studies have shown that volatility in global prices is higher than domestic commodity prices (Nayyar and Sen, 1994; Chand and Jha 2001; Sekhar, 2004). In a closed economy, lower output is normally accompanied by some price increase. With liberalisation, we had a situation of lower production with lower prices. This pattern reflected the effect of the growing integration of Indian agriculture with world markets, resulting from trade liberalisation. There is a need for extreme vigilance so as to be able to take timely measures, within the existing tariff bindings to arrest heavy import of certain commodities (Rao, 2005).

To sum up on trade reforms, slowing of agriculture growth occurred at a time when the economic reforms were undertaken in the country. It has been concluded by some that this slowing is linked directly to structural macro reforms in the country and globalisation. This view is limited and the slowing in agriculture is not due to industrial and trade reforms including joining of WTO. Slowing down of agriculture growth could be attributed to the structural factors on the supply side such as decline in public investment, credit, technology, etc. rather than trade and industrial reforms. The adverse effects of structural reforms were more to do with the manner in which reforms were undertaken in the country rather than intrinsic to structural reforms. Also, there have been positive effects on agriculture in terms of improvements in terms of trade, private investments, technology and specialisation in agriculture. The negative effects can be reduced with a focus on supply side factors in agriculture.

The 11th Five Year Plan focused on 'faster and inclusive growth.' An important aspect of 'inclusive growth' in the 11th Plan is its target of 4 per cent per annum growth in GDP from agriculture & allied sectors. A detailed agenda for action is spelt out in mid-term appraisl of 11th Five Year Plan covering improved access to water, improvement in the supply of good quality seeds, replenishment of soil nutrients, improvements in agricultural research and extension, reforms in land tenancy and improvements in agricultural marketing which is particularly important for perishable produce.

According to 12th Plan document, the 11th Plan has made the following four conscious choices:

- It emphasised on existing technology and reduce yield gaps.
- It decentralised plan funds to encourage initiatives at state and lower levels.
- Spending more on public investment and food security in disadvantaged regions.
- Focus should be more on farm incomes than production. Stress should be on service delivery with encouragement of group activity. Land and tenancy reforms should be put back on agenda.

The 12th Plan's main focus is on small farmers and resource poor farmers.

Among other things, the 12th Five Year Plan focuses on the following:

- Bringing scale through development of farmer producer organisations.
- Emphasising technology, both on the research and development sides.
- Stressing standards and protocols and standard operating procedures in every scheme.
- Improving statistics and evaluation.
- Initiating a shift towards sustainable and climate-resilient agriculture, not only through NMSA but more generally by laying emphasis on rainfed areas and bringing about shifts of water-intensive rice cultivation from water-stressed North-West India to Eastern India.
- Preparing for faster growth through a more diversified agriculture, with investment in the necessary modern infrastructure required for perishable products.

The *Economic Survey 2013-14* provides some idea about the likely policies of the new NDA government which came to power in May 2014. According to the survey, the major challenges include: low productivity levels, soil degradation due to declining fertiliser-use efficiency, market distortions that prevent the creation of a national common market; changing role of government in production and distribution in the current scenario of bumper production and stocks; phased shifting to direct transfer of fertiliser and food subsidies. Agriculture has to be viewed holistically as a farm-to-fork value chain, comprising farming, wholesaling, warehousing, logistics, processing and retailing including exports. For establishing a national common market, the government advocates several reforms.

Issues and Policies for Higher Growth, Equity and Sustainability

There are three goals of agricultural development. These are: (a) achieve 4 per cent growth in agriculture and raise incomes by increasing productivity (land, labour), diversification to high value agriculture and rural non-farm by maintaining food security; (b) sharing growth (equity) by focusing on small and marginal farmers, lagging regions, women, etc.; (c) third is to maintain sustainability of agriculture by focusing on environmental concerns (see Dev, 2008).

What policy reforms are needed to achieve the above goals? There are basically seven areas which need focused reforms in the short and medium terms. These are: (a) price policy; (b) subisidies and investments; (c) land issues; (d) irrigation and water management; (e) research and extension; (f) credit; and (g) domestic market reforms and diversification. Institutions have to be developed in all these aspects.

Price Policy

The APC was established in 1965 to recommend remunerative prices to farmers. Later it was renamed the Commission for Agricultural Costs and Prices (CACP). The aim is to evolve a balanced and integrated price structure in the perspective of the overall needs of the economy and with due regard to the interests of producer and consumer. Assurance of a remunerative and stable price environment is essential for increasing agricultural production and productivity, since the marketplace for agricultural produce tends to be inherently unstable, which often inflicts undue losses on growers. This is also important for inducing farmers to raise productivity through higher investment and use of modern inputs.

MSP for major agricultural products are fixed by the government each year, taking into account recommendations of the CACP. At present, 25 items are covered under the MSP regime, including all important cereals as well as pulses, oilseeds, cotton, jute and sugar cane.

For any improvement in farm income, it is necessary to keep in check the cost of production. To facilitate this, there should be continuous upgrading of technologies in agricultural operations. India's crop production should be made competitive with that of major producing countries. The cost of cultivation—one important determinant for setting MSP—has been registering increases, particularly for diesel (used for irrigation) and human labour. As the labour component constitutes a sizeable portion of the total input cost of production, the increase in wage rates affects the overall cost. In particular, the implementation of the National Rural Employment Guarantee Act (NREGA) has raised the cost and curtailed the availability of agricultural labor, especially during peak season. Many labourers previously engaged in farming operations are switching to work provided under NREGA.[4] This trend necessitates increasing use of farm implements and machinery in crop production. In view of the predominance of small and marginal farm holdings, agricultural policy needs to support provision of small farm implements and tools, elevating farm production and productivity.

What should be the role of price policy? Price policy needs to balance the needs of producers against those of consumers. A minimum-support policy has long been in favour of cereals like rice and wheat; corrections have been made in recent years by increasing MSP for protein-rich crops like pulses. As a result, production has increased. Similar incentives must be given for other nutrient-rich foods, like fruits, vegetables, milk, meat and fish, to increase supply. On the other hand, consumers have to have access to these foods at reasonable prices to increase consumption.

Subsidies versus Investments

Another issue that needs to be focused on for agricultural growth relates to reducing pressure of subsidies, and escalating investment. As discussed in the earlier sections, agricultural subsidies encourage inefficiency in the use of the resources which leads to environmental degradation. There is a trade-off between subsidies and investments, and it is being shown that returns to investment are three times higher than on the subsidies (Fan, Gulati and Thorat, 2009). Hence it is important to rationalise subsidies and enhance investments.

About 90 per cent of the public sector investment for agriculture covers investment for irrigation in the CSO data. This does not give a correct picture and under-estimates the investment in agriculture. Many researchers have expanded this series by using broader series of investment that also includes expenses such as rural development and rural infrastructure (Chand, 2001; Gulati and Bathla, 2002). In the early 1980s, the share of public sector investment and private sector investment (including household sector) in gross capital formation in agriculture was almost equal but from the early 2000s, the share of private sector was much higher than the share of public sector. These analyses are based on CSO data which make assumptions for corporate private investment on the basis of term loan. However, the entire term loan may not be utilised for the capital formation. Bisaliah and Dev (2011) have used CACP cost of cultivation data for analysing private investment. They have shown that there is not much improvement in private investment for agriculture in the selected states. It was estimated that only 10 per cent of the investment is from corporate bodies and rest 90 per cent of investment is made by the farmers on their farm. There is a shift in the composition of on-farm investment from animal capital towards irrigation and farm machinery. A sudden increase in corporate private investment was seen in the year 2011 but it was mainly due to two major projects, Sankhrail Agro and Agro Allied Products in West Bengal and Lunej Demonstration Project in Gujarat (Reddy, 2011). Most of these corporate private investments are coming in food processing and dairy sub-sectors.

Land Management

Good soil ensures proper retention and release of water and nutrients, promotes and sustains root growth, and maintains soil biotic habitat. Indian soils are gradually degrading because of soil erosion, loss of organic carbon, nutrient imbalance, compaction, salinisation, etc. The prevailing policies of MSP and input subsidies have encouraged inappropriate use of fertiliser and water (Pingali and Shah, 1999), led to inefficiency of production, and caused hindrance in production of crops that are not effectively covered under MSP. Highly subsidised chemical fertilisers lead to nutrient imbalance and deficiency of micro-nutrients. The subsidy has increased from ₹ 60 crore in 1976-77 to ₹ 61,264 crore in 2009-2000. The recommended dose of nitrogenous, phosphatic and potassium (N, P and K) fertilisers has the ratio of 4:2:1. In 2005-06, it was 5.27:2.2:1 and after government measures, has improved to 4.55:1.96:1 in the year 2008-09 (GoI, 2010). Adoption of HYV has led to increased use of the pesticides, which results in soil and water contamination in case of inefficient and careless application.

There are many issues on land in agriculture. Some argue that small size of farm is responsible for low profitability of agriculture. Chinese and the experience of other East Asian countries show that it is not a constraint. On land market, the Report of the Steering Committee recommended the following:

> Small farmers should be assisted to buy land through the provision of institutional credit, on a long term basis, at a low rate of interest and by reducing stamp duty. At the same time, they should be enabled to enlarge their operational holdings by liberalizing the land lease market. The two major elements of such a reform are: security of tenure for tenants during the period of contract; and the right of the land owner to resume land after the period of contract is over (GoI, 2007).

Basically, we have to ensure land leasing, create conditions including credit, whereby the poor can access land from those who wish to leave agriculture. There are some emerging land issues such as increase in demand for land for non-agricultural purposes including special economic zones (SEZs), displacement of farmers, tribals and others due to development projects. There is a need for careful land acquisition. Land alienation is a serious problem in tribal areas.

Irrigation and Water Management

Water is the leading input in agriculture. Development of irrigation and water management are crucial for raising levels of living in rural areas.[5] Major areas of concern in irrigation are: decline in real investment, thin spread of investment, low recovery of costs, decline in water table, wastages and inefficiencies in water use and non-involvement of users. Both investment and efficiency in use of water are needed. Major areas of reforms needed in irrigation are: stepping up and prioritising public investment, raising profitability of groundwater exploitation and augmenting groundwater resources, rational pricing of irrigation water and electricity, involvement of user farmers in the management of irrigation systems, and making groundwater markets equitable (Rao, 2005). In a recent study, Shah *et al.* (2009) indicate that the impact of the drought of 2009 is expected to be less severe than the drought of 2002 due to groundwater recharge in the last few years. Groundwater can be exploited in a big way in Eastern region. Watershed development and water conservation by the community are needed under water management. New watershed guidelines based on Parthasarathy Committee's recommendations were accepted by the Central Cabinet in March 2009. The implementation has to be stepped up in order to obtain benefits in rainfed areas. National Rainfed Area Authority has big responsibility in matters relating to water conservation and watershed development. Assets created under NREGS can help in improving land and water management.

Agriculture Market Reforms

Assured market and remunerative prices are very important for agricultural growth. The MSP policy should lead to diversification in cropping patterns toward non-cereals. The development of markets and post-harvest infrastructures were not able to keep pace with growth of agricultural production over time. In many states, agricultural markets are underdeveloped, and farmers have to sell even rice and wheat crops at much below the MSP price. Because of market imperfections, there is strong asymmetry in transmission of price between retail, wholesale and farm level.

Over time, farmers have diversified production towards high value crops, especially fruits and vegetables (Joshi *et al.*, 2007; Chand, 2008; Dev, 2008a). The share of fruits and vegetables in total value of crop output increased from 16 per cent in 1980-81 to 28 per cent in 2009-10 (NAS, CSO) with its share in total gross cropped area being about 6.1 per cent in 2009-10 (MoA). The share of food grain crops in total value of output was only 42.5 per cent (CSO, 2011) although it occupied about 60 per cent of the gross cropped area in 2009-10. Therefore, for per unit of land, value of output from fruits and vegetables is about 5 times that of the food grains. The percentage area under sugar cane, cotton, and fruits and vegetables increased in the post-reform period as compared to the pre-reform period.

The diversification of agriculture is primarily led by diversification of diet. However, to sustain the diversification towards high value commodities and leverage it towards benefiting the farmers, good infrastructure in terms of assured market, better road connectivity, cold storage, post-harvest technology, etc., and supportive policy to attract private players are required. Participation of private sector is very crucial for development of these sub-sectors of agriculture, as huge investments are required to improve and upscale backward and forward linkages with the farmers (Gulati and Ganguly, 2009). Farmers can hedge against price risk by opting for contract farming, in the context of increasing number of supermarkets and food processing companies (Birthal *et al.*, 2007; Singh, 2008).

Further, vertical integration of services related to farming, warehousing and other logistic, processing, and retailing can help direct farm-firm linkages by lowering the transaction and transportation costs and strengthening the supply chain to enhance value addition. Earlier such direct linkages were not permitted as agricultural produce transaction outside the regulated markets (*mandi*) was restricted. Nevertheless, to promote diversification of agriculture and participation of private players, an amendment to APMC act known as 'APMC Model Act' was enacted in the year 2003. This amendment allowed direct transaction between the producer and the retailer in several states through various institutional mechanisms such as cooperatives, producer's associations and contract farming. Reservations on many products for small scale industry were recently relaxed, and fiscal incentives such as reduction in excise and corporate taxes were given to food processing industries (Birthal *et al.*, 2007). However, the Model Act is not yet fully effected by all the state governments. Only very few states have amended the legislation significantly, for example, Andhra Pradesh, Karnataka and Maharashtra, etc., and several other states have acted but have not notified the rules. States like Jammu & Kashmir (J&K), Meghalaya, Puducherry, UP, Uttarakhand, and West Bengal are yet to amend their APMC Act. The rules proposed under Warehousing (Development & Regulation) Act 2006 still need to be notified for introduction of a regulated system of warehouse (CACP, 2011). Further, it is being reported that most of the markets lack basic infrastructures and charge very high taxes and commissions on fresh and processed agri-produce.

In India, major share of food retailing is still confined to unorganised sector with small traders, *kirana* stores, hawkers and wet markets. However, organised food retail is slowly becoming popular and the top 10 Indian food and grocery retailers have grown at average annual rate above 70 per cent per annum during 2002-2007. This trend is likely to continue for next 10-15 years (Gulati and Ganguly 2009).

With the presence of supermarkets, concept of rural business hubs is emerging. It is like a rural mall where agri-input suppliers and service providers come close with the farmers to meet their demands. It also offers facility for procuring consumer durables, medical services, grocery, etc. Given the fact that demand of high value chains (HVCs) is increasing, the demand for input services have also risen. Private players like ITC (Choupal Saagar), DSCL (Hariyali Kisan Bazaar), Tata (Kisan Sansar) and Future Group (Aadhaar) are some key players operating in this segment of agri-food systems.

To reap the benefit of increased production and diversification towards HVC, good and improved infrastructure is required in the form of road connectivity, cold storage, irrigation, etc. To encourage participation of private partners, policy framework should not be a hindrance. Therefore, there is need to implement the APMC Model Act, Warehousing Act and cut down on taxes and commissions on fresh produce to give a boost to high value agriculture. To ensure the inclusion of small farm holders in the new supply chain, tenancy reforms and clear regulations for contract farming should be evolved and implemented. Food retail trade is a major economic activity and needs attention to ensure livelihood of the poor.

Technology, Research and Extension

A new and efficient technology is essential for agricultural growth. Studies have shown that at least one-third of the future growth in productivity should come through innovations in crop technologies. Generally, private sector research and seed industry focus on crops and varieties with massive commercial market and scope. Public sector research needs to take into the account the farmers' need for the crops as per the prevailing agro-climatic conditions.

Seeds are the carrier of technology and hence play a vital role in improving and sustaining the growth of agriculture, specially under the constraint of scarce and fixed land and water resources. The technology of HYVs seed production was a major contributor in making India self-sufficient in food grains during the Green Revolution period. It has been estimated that the direct contribution of quality seeds in total production is about 15-20 per cent depending upon the crop. This can be further raised up to 45 per cent with efficient management of other inputs (*seednet.gov.in*). There is a proposal for a new Seed Bill 2011, with main objective of increasing production and supply of quality seed to meet future requirement for sustainable agriculture production. However, this bill still is being debated. Singh and Chand (2011) are of the view that the proposed bill can be passed and later some modification can be incorporated. The role of private sector in technological innovation, dissemination and adoption of same to the farmers' field cannot be ignored, as we have experienced in the case of Bt cotton and hybrid maize. Such a spectacular performance especially in case of Bt cotton was possible due to private companies' active participation.

One of the reasons for low growth in total factor productivity in India, as compared to countries like Brazil, Indonesia and China, relates to less focus on science and technology in agriculture in India in comparison to these countries. Public sector investment for agriculture research and development (R&D), and education in India is only 0.6 per cent of the agricultural GDP which needs to be raised to at least 1.0 per cent, as is being invested by most of the developing countries. The resource conservation technologies such as zero tillage, laser level, system of rice intensification, non-pesticide management, etc., are some emerging technologies which need to be first understood and analysed for local adaptation, and then adopted by the farmers at the field level.

As the National Commission on Farmers mentions, there is a knowledge gap in the existing technology. Therefore, extension becomes crucial for improving agricultural productivity. In view of high variability in agro-climatic conditions particularly in unfavourable areas, research has to become increasingly location-specific.

Credit

Public policy is aimed at 'social' and 'development banking' in the form of meeting rural credit needs and reducing the role of informal sector credit. A large number of small and marginal farmers and other vulnerable groups remain excluded from the opportunities and services provided by the financial sector.

It is true that there have been some improvements in flow of farm credit in recent years. However, the government has to be sensitive to the four distributional aspects of agricultural credit. These are: (a) not much improvement in the share of small and marginal farmers; (b) decline in credit-deposit (CD) ratios of rural and semi-urban branches; (c) increase in the share of indirect credit in total agricultural credit; and (d) significant regional inequalities in credit.

Ultimately, the credit expansion programme is successful only if the productivity of the small and marginal farmers improves. We have to recognise that credit expansion for farmers can't be sustained by the banking system alone as there is a need for other measures like public investment in irrigation, research and extension, infrastructure in rural areas, proper seeds and fertilisers, good marketing system for better price, etc. Small and marginal farmers face many risks in cultivation. Credit expansion should take into account the risk element of farmers while framing policies. The agricultural officers must provide 'farm advisory' services that will help in making agriculture an integrated activity with appropriate backward and forward linkages (Rangarajan, 2005).

Climate Change

Climate change is a major challenge for agriculture, food security and rural livelihoods for millions of people including the poor in India. Adverse impact will be more on small holding farmers. Climate change is expected to have adverse impact on the living conditions of farmers, fishers and forest-dependent people who are already vulnerable and food insecure. Rural communities, particularly those living in already fragile environments, face an immediate and ever-growing risk of increased crop failure, loss of livestock, and reduced availability of marine, aquaculture and forest products. In order to have climate change sensitive and pro-poor policies, there is a need to focus on small farmers. Agriculture adaptation and mitigation could provide benefits for small farmers. The coping strategies would be useful to have long-term adaptation strategies. There is a significant potential for small farmers to sequester soil carbon if appropriate policy reforms are implemented. The importance of collective action in climate change adaptation and mitigation is recognised. Research and practice have shown that collective action institutions are very important for technology transfer in agriculture and natural resource management among small holders and resource dependent communities.

There is a need for climate-smart agriculture which contributes in:

> (i) promoting sustainable increase in agricultural productivity by incorporating climate change perspective (including drought), (ii) building adaptive capacity and resilience to production portfolio to climatic risks without compromising food security, and (iii) minimizing green-house gas emissions and maximizing carbon sequestration by improved management practices (Joshi and Aggarwal, 2014: 1).

Joshi and Aggarwal suggest four measures for climate-smart agriculture. These are: (a) climate-smart technologies, (b) capacity building of key stakeholders, (c) information and communication technology (ICT)-based weather advisory and (d) weather index insurance. Efforts need to be made to transform each village a climate-smart to synergise these interventions.

Small Farmers

Small holdings agriculture which is the focus of this paper is important for raising agriculture growth, food security and livelihoods in India. It may be noted that Indian agriculture is the home of small and marginal farmers (85%). Therefore, the future of sustainable agriculture growth and food security in India depends on the performance of small and marginal farmers. Agricultural census data show that there were about 138 million agricultural holdings in India in 2010-11. Around 117 million were small and marginal farmers. Average size has declined from

2.3 ha In 1970-71 to 1.16 ha in 2010-11. Although small and marginal farmers account for 85 per cent of total farm hhs, their share in operated area is around 44 per cent. Thus, there are significant land inequalities in India.

The role of small farms in development and poverty reduction is well recognized (Lipton, 2006). The global experience of growth and poverty reduction shows that GDP growth originating in agriculture is at least twice as effective in reducing poverty as GDP growth originating outside agriculture [World Development Report (WDR, 2008)]. Small holdings play important role in raising agricultural development and poverty reduction.

There are many challenges for small holding agriculture in India. They face several challenges in the access to inputs and marketing. They need a level playing field with large farms in terms of accessing land, water, inputs, credit, technology and markets. Small holdings also face new challenges on integration of value chains, liberalisation and globalisation effects, market volatility and other risks and vulnerability, adaptation of climate change, etc. (Thapa and Gaiha (2011). Inspite of challenges, there are many opportunities in the technological and institutional innovations which can enable marginal and small farmers to raise agricultural productivity and increase incomes through diversification and high value agriculture.

National Commission on Enterprises for Unorganized Sector (NCEUS, 2008) suggests special programmes for small and marginal farmers. Principal activities proposed under this include promotion of marginal-small farmers' groups, enabling greater access to institutional credit, training and capacity building, support for strengthening and non-farm activities, gender-focused activities and planning for development of marginal and small farmers.[6]

Conclusion

There are seven deficits in Indian agriculture. These are: (a) investment and infrastructure deficit; (b) land and water management deficit; (c) research and extension (technology) deficit; (d) market deficit; (e) credit deficit; (f) diversification deficit; and (g) institutions deficit. Focus has to be on small and marginal farmers and resource poor regions. The strategies so far concentrated on rice and wheat in irrigated areas. The future growth will need to rely on a dual strategy of diversification into non-cereal high value crops like pulses, fruits, vegetables, milk, meat, etc., and focus on rainfed areas and small farmers. The focus should also be on Eastern region.

Apart from high growth, efficiency (cost reduction) is also needed in globalised world. Group approach among farmers should be encouraged in order to get inputs at cheaper rates and marketing of output at higher prices.

The four central government's special programmes *viz.*, NFSM, RKVY, NHM and ATMA would be useful, if implemented properly, in improving growth and equity in agriculture. The medium and long term measures relating to supply side can also improve drought-proofing and de-risking agriculture.

Reforms should be undertaken for the growth of the rural non-farm sector. The rigidities in rural non-farm employment have to be removed in order to bring about rural transformation. The very low educational levels in rural areas limit access to better-paid employment, leaving rural workers with low skills, low productivity, and, therefore, probably low wage jobs. Education, infrastructure, credit, etc., have to be improved in order to raise the productivity of rural non-farm employment. The policy changes in the food and agricultural sector and in the rural non-farm sector are expected to reduce rural poverty through rural transformation.

'Business as usual approach' may not help higher growth in agriculture. A big push is needed for reforms in supply side for agriculture. Similarly demand factors also have to be addressed. Sustainability issues are becoming important in recent years. Given the short run and structural long-term problems in agriculture, the government should give large push to core issues to make cultivation viable and profitable. There is a need to concentrate on delivery systems also. India's large numbers of farmers can benefit if there are right policies and effective implementation.

Notes

1. See Deokar and Shetty (2014) for recent high growth in agriculture.
2. Also see Ahluwalia (1996).
3. See Alagh (2006) on WTO and agriculture.
4. These observations are based on field-level visits by the author as chairman of CACP.
5. On land and water management, see Vaidyanathan (2006).
6. Also see Swaminathan (2007) and Vyas (2004).

References

Ahluwalia, M.S. (1996). "New Economic Policy and Agriculture: Some Reflections", *Indian Journal of Agricultural Economics* 51(3).

Alagh, Y.K. (2006). "Indian Economic Strategies after Doha", in R. Radhakrishna, S.K. Rao, S. Mahendra Dev and K. Subbarao (eds.), *India in a Globalising World: Some Aspects of Macroeconomy, Agriculture and Poverty, Essays in honour of C.H. Hanumantha Rao*. New Delhi: Academic Foundation

Balakrishnan, P. (2000). "Agriculture and Economic Reforms: Growth and Welfare", *Economic and Political Weekly*, March 4-10

Bhalla, G.S. and Gurmail Singh (1997). "Recent Developments in Indian Agriculture: A State Level Analysis", *Economic and Political Weekly* 32(13), 29 March–4 April.

Birthal, Pratap Singh, P.K. Joshi, Devesh Roy and Amit Thorat (2007). "Diversification in Indian Agriculture towards High-value Crops: The Role of Smallholders". *IFPRI Discussion Paper* 727. Washington D.C.: International Food Policy Research Institute (IFPRI).

Bisaliah, and S. Mahendra Dev (2011). "Private Investment in Indian Agriculture: Farm Level Evidences and Policy Directions". Paper presented in the workshop on *Policy Options and Investment Priorities for Accelerating Agricultural Productivity and Development in India* organized by IGIDR, Mumbai and IHD, New Delhi at India International Centre, New Delhi from November 10-11.

Commission on Agriculture Cost and Prices (2011). *Report on Price Policy for Kharif Crops 2011-12*. P. 30. *http://cacp.dacnet.nic.in/RPP/Kharif_Report-2011-12.pdf*

Chand, Ramesh (2001). "Emerging Trends and Issues in Public and Private Investments in Indian Agriculture: A Statewise Analysis", *Indian Journal of Agricultural Economics* 56(2): 161-84.

Chand, Ramesh and Dayanath Jha (2001). "Trade Liberalisation: Agricultural Prices and Net Social Welfare", in S.S. Acharya and D.P. Chaudhari (eds.), *Indian Agricultural Policy at the Cross Roads*. New Delhi: Rawat Publishers.

Chand, Ramesh, S.S. Raju, and L.M. Pandey (2008). "Progress and Potential of Horticulture in India", *Indian Journal of Agricultural Economics* 63(3): 299-309.

Deokar, B.K. and S.L. Shetty (2014). "Growth in Indian Agriculture: Responding to Policy Initiatives since 2004-05", *Economic and Political Weekly* 49 (26&27).

Dev, S. Mahendra (2008). *Inclusive Growth in India, Agriculture, Poverty and Human Development*. New Delhi: Oxford University Press.

______. (2008a). "Structural Reforms and Agriculture: Issues and Policies". Keynote paper for the 92nd *Annual Conference of the Indian Economic Association*, 27th-29th December, Bhubaneswar, Odisha.

Fan, Shenggen, Ashok Gulati and S. Thorat (2008). "Investment, Subsidies, and Pro-poor Growth in Rural India", *Agricultural Economics* 39: 163-70.

GoI (2007). *Report of the Steering Committee on Agriculture for 11th Five Year Plan*. New Delhi: Yojana Bhavan.

Gulati, Ashok and Kavery Ganguly (2009). "Transforming Agri-food System: Role of Organized Retail in India". *Mimeo*, International Food Policy Research Institute.

Gulati, Ashok and S. Bathla (2002). "Capital Formation in Indian Agriculture: Trends, Composition and Implications for Growth". *Occasional Paper* 24. Mumbai: National Bank for Agriculture and Rural Development.

Joshi, P.K., A. Gulati and R. Cummings (2007). "Agricultural Diversification in South Asia: Beyond Food Security", in P.K. Joshi, A. Gulati and R. Cummings (eds.), *Agricultural Diversification and Smallholders in South Asia*. New Delhi: Academic Foundation. pp 46-86.

Joshi, P.K. and P.K. Aggarwal (2014). "Prepare for Negative Impacts of Climate Change", *Mimeo*, International Food Policy Research Institute

Lipton, M. (2006). "Can Small Farmers Survive, Prosper, or be the Key Channel to Cut Mass Poverty", *Journal of Agricultural and Development Economics* 3(1): 58-85.

Mishra, V.N. and Govinda Rao (2003). "Trade Policy, Agricultural Growth and Rural Poor: Indian Experience, 1978-79 to 1999-00", *Economic and Political Weekly*, October 25.

Nayyar, Deepak and Abhijit Sen (1994). "International Trade and Agricultural Sector in India", in G.S. Bhalla (ed.), *Economic Liberalization and Indian Agriculture*. New Delhi: Indian Studies for Industrial Development.

NCEUS (2008). "A Special Programme for Marginal and Small Farmers", A Report prepared by the National Commission for Enterprises in the Unorganized Sector, NCEUS, New Delhi.

Parthasarthy Committee Report (2006). Report of the Technical Committee on Watershed Programme in India. New Delhi: Department of Land Resources, MoRD, GoI.

Planning Commission, GoI (2010). *Mid-term Appraisal of 11th Five Year Plan*, Chapter 4. p.85. *http://planningcommission.nic.in/plans/mta/11th_mta/chapterwise/chap4_agri.pdf*

Rangarajan, C. (2005). "Agricultural Credit: Reaching the Marginalised Farmers", Lecture delivered at the Bankers Conference (BANCON), Kolkata, Nov. 12.

Rao, C.H.H. (1994). *Agricultural Growth, Rural Poverty and Environmental Degradation in India*. New Delhi: Oxford University Press.

______. (2005). *Food Security, Poverty and Environment, Essay on Post Reform India*. New Delhi: Oxford University Press.

Reddy, Bhaskar (2011). "Private Investment in Agriculture". Paper presented in the Workshop on *Policy Options and Investment Priorities for Accelerating Agricultural Productivity and Development in India*. Organized by IGIDR, Mumbai and IHD, New Delhi, at India International Centre, New Delhi, November 10-11.

Sekhar, C.S.C. (2004). "Agricultural Price Volatility in International and Indian Markets", *Economic and Political Weekly*, October 23.

Shah, Tushar, Avinash Kishore and P. Hemant (2009). "Will the Impact of the 2009 Drought be Different from 2002", *Economic and Political Weekly* 44(37).

Singh, Harbir and Ramesh Chand (2011). "The Seed Bill 2011: Some Reflections", *Economic and Political Weekly* 46(51): 22-25.

Singh, S. (2008). "Marketing Channels and their Implications for Smallholder Farmers in India", in E.B. McCullough, P.L. Pingali and K.G. Stamoulis (eds.), *The Transformation of Agri-food Systems: Globalization, Supply Chains, and Smallholder Farmers*, Rome: FAO and London: Earthscan, pp.279-310, Chapter 14.

Singh, Manmohan (1995). "Inaugural Address", *Indian Journal of Agricultural Economics* 50(1).

Sundaram, K. (2001). "Employment and Poverty in 1990s, Further Results from NSS 55th Round, Employment-unemployment Survey, 1999-00", *Economic and Political Weekly*, 11 August, pp.3039-49.

______. (2007). "Employment and Poverty in India, 2000-2005", *Economic and Political Weekly*, 28 July, pp.3121-31.

Swaminathan, M.S. (2007). *Agriculture Cannot Wait: New Horizons in Indian Agriculture*. Academic Foundation, National Academy of Agricultural Sciences.

Thapa, G. and R. Gaiha (2011). "Smallholder farming in Asia and the Pacific: Challenges and Opportunities", Paper presented at the *Conference on New Directions for Small Holder Agriculture*, 24-25 January 2011. Rome: IFAD.

Vaidyanathan, A. (1994). "Performance of Indian Agriculture since Independence", in K. Basu (ed.), *Agrarian Questions*. New Delhi: Oxford University Press.

______. (2006). *India's Water Resources: Contemporary Issues on Irrigation*. New Delhi: Oxford University Press.

Vyas, V.S. (2004). "Agrarian Distress: Strategies to Protect Vulnerable Sections", *Economic and Political Weekly*, December 25.

WDR (2008). "Agriculture for Development", *World Development Report*. Washington, D.C.: World Bank.

October, 2014.

11

Accelerating Agricultural Productivity Growth in India

Overview

IN the past 50 years, Indian agriculture has undergone a major transformation, from dependence on food aid to becoming a consistent net food exporter. The gradual reforms in the agricultural sector (following the broader macro-reforms of the early 1990s) spurred some unprecedented innovations and changes in the food sector driven by private investment. These impressive achievements must now be viewed in light of the policy and investment imperatives that lie ahead. Agricultural growth has improved in recent years (averaging about 3.5 per cent since 2004/05), but at a long-term trend rate of growth of 3 per cent, agriculture has underperformed relative to its potential. The pockets of post-reform dynamism that have emerged evidently have not reached a sufficiently large scale to influence the sector's performance. For the vast population that still derives a living directly or indirectly from agriculture, achieving "faster, more inclusive, and sustainable growth"—the objectives at the heart of the Twelfth Five Year Plan—depends critically on simultaneous efforts to improve agriculture's performance and develop new sources of employment for the disproportionately large share of the labor force still on the farm.

Maintaining India's hard-won food security and achieving shared prosperity are proving to be ambitious goals. In the past, India's unwavering focus on food production helped it to achieve self-sufficiency, but a legacy of that effort is a complex web of policies and institutions that now arguably constrain more robust, sustainable agricultural growth, limit the performance of agricultural markets,

World Bank Group (2014). *Republic of India Accelerating Agricultural Productivity Growth*. May 21. Chapter: Overview. pp. xvii-xxxix.

and discourage much-needed diversification. The natural resources that support productive agriculture (namely land and water) are declining in quality, and competition for them is intensifying. Rainfall remains a major source of volatility in Indian agriculture. Heavy public investments, particularly in irrigation and technology, have helped to offset the worst effects of weather, but the deceleration of growth in the late 1990s and early 2000s, persistent increases in food prices in recent years, and declining water tables have revived concerns over food security. Climate change will almost certainly magnify the challenges and expectations for agriculture. India is a large, heterogeneous country. One study alone cannot address the multitude of issues surrounding agriculture, certainly not in sufficient depth to be meaningful. This study was designed through a broad-based consensus to focus on strategic issues related to agricultural productivity. It gives particular attention to the dynamics and sources of productivity growth, the sustainability of growth, and areas where the potential for growth has been overlooked, all with a view to informing the debates on strategic priorities and policy interventions.

The scope of this study is broad in the sense that it marshals considerable empirical evidence and analyses to address those issues. Yet the scope is restricted in the sense that the study does not address all of the issues. A wealth of knowledge exists (and continuing analytical work proceeds) on other major strategic issues—water and irrigation management, food grain management, and public expenditures on agriculture, for example—and the findings of this study must be seen in that context. The lack of sufficient quality data, and often the lack of access to such data, also prevent some issues from being explored in greater depth. Finally, some important issues require more focused and dedicated analysis, such as food safety and quality standards, agricultural trade, and food price increases. This relationship between longer-term strategic issues and contemporary concerns, such as water resource management and food prices, are highlighted in this study through the prism of productivity, but they too require further analysis to fully address the underlying issues.

The Conundrums of Contemporary Agriculture

Contemporary Indian agriculture presents a number of seeming contradictions and conundrums. India's traditional breadbaskets face the food security–sustainability tradeoff. The irrigated rice- and wheat-producing areas appear to be facing diminishing returns to the technology that sparked the green revolution. These areas are singularly focused on increasing production, often at the cost of mining the natural resource base, placing the hardwon productivity gains of the past—and the future—at risk. Other parts of the country face a dilemma of another sort. Although they are far less agriculturally developed, these Low-income States (LIS) could unleash considerable growth in agricultural productivity, yet weak public investments, undeveloped markets and weak institutional and governance capacity have long stood in the way.

A major puzzle seems to be the co-existence of widespread undernourishment and rising food prices on the one hand, and record production levels of food and overflowing stocks on the other. Across India, diversification into higher-value crops and livestock products has proceeded too slowly to increase agricultural growth appreciably. The supply of high-value commodities has not kept pace with demand generated by rising incomes and urbanization, resulting in rapid increases in their prices. Cereal prices have again started to rise, adding to an agricultural conundrum in which per capita availability of food is falling even as per capita production of cereals is at all-time highs and rising, and domestic markets are effectively insulated from global market pressures. Rising Minimum Support Prices (MSPs) create a cereal supply response, but the increased production is diverted to stock silos rather than benefiting consumers through lower prices. Thus MSPs drive domestic cereal prices—especially producer prices—higher, while a combination of trade and storage policies stabilize them. The resulting low risk-to-return ratio for cereals creates strong incentives for farmers to produce cereals rather than other (more risky) crops, limiting diversification and income growth, putting further pressure on prices—this time through the higher-valued non-cereal commodities.

The short-term welfare impacts appear to be contained, as rural wages have risen rapidly in recent years, compensating for rising prices. Rising real prices benefit the net-selling farmers, and rising real wages are good for workers, but both trends have implications for the sustainability of the ensuing growth. The critical question is whether the changed incentives afforded by rising real output prices are accompanied by growth in productivity—are the sources of that growth sustainable?

Trends in Agricultural Performance at the National and Subnational Level

Over the past six decades, agriculture grew at a steady but modest 3.0 per cent, changing imperceptibly but becoming relatively more stable. After almost two decades of sustained expansion (with growth peaking in the early 1990s at about 3.6%), growth decelerated from 1996/97 to 2004/05. This prolonged slowdown was widespread, with few exceptions. The most recent period—from 2004/05 onwards—shows a marked, equally widespread return to growth of 3.5 per cent per year.

Performance and rainfall. What started agriculture on its long decline after 1997, and what spurred the equally decisive turnaround after 2004? Explanations for the slowdown include slow generation of new technologies, poor dissemination of existing ones, weak and inefficient institutions, poor governance, and inadequate investment in public goods. Irrigation, terms of trade, and technology are the major determinants of agricultural GDP growth. These factors are crucial for long-term growth, but their immediate role in the postreform slowdown and the subsequent recovery is less obvious. Because the slowdown coincided with the agricultural policy reforms of the mid-1990s (following the general economic reforms of the early 1990s), a natural conclusion often drawn is that the reforms triggered the weakness. The influence of rainfall on Indian agriculture is widely acknowledged—60 per cent of it remains rainfed—but rainfall's role in patterns of growth has not been fully explored.

At the district level, a credible association emerges between rainfall shocks and productivity (defined as value of output per hectare). Aggregated up to the national level, these data show a strong association of an unusual sequence of sustained negative rainfall shocks and the prolonged stagnation in productivity growth between 1999 and 2004. The weather-induced weakness provides an explanation for the deviation in trends for several key indicators during the early 2000s, including the slowdown in wages identified in previous studies. By extension, poor rainfall in the more recent years may partly account for the sluggish supply response in noncereal crops, which are found to be more susceptible to such shocks, and perhaps partly explain the upward pressure on their prices.

The sensitivity of crop productivity to rainfall varies considerably across districts, reflecting the availability of irrigation to compensate for annual rainfall deficits. Over the long run, districts in the Semi-Arid Temperate Zone are generally less vulnerable to rainfall shocks and relatively more productive on average. But the sustained rainfall shocks between 1997 and 2004 hit those districts the hardest, with a large aggregate and cumulative impact on agricultural productivity. The cyclical as well as random anomalies that are characteristic of rainfall in the Indian sub-continent call for both ex ante risk mitigation and ex post adaptation/management strategies.

Coming back to the question of role of policy reforms in agriculture's performance, a key question is what growth rates might have prevailed had rainfall been normal from the 1960s to 2010. A simple simulation reveals a sharp deviation between the actual and the counterfactual (simulated assuming normal rainfall, all else remaining the same) trends starting in the mid-1990s, suggesting that had rainfall been normal, the growth trajectory would have been significantly different and may possibly have been higher than the actual observed trend, potentially ushering in a much-desired, positive structural change. An important implication of these findings is that there is little evidence to suggest that the policy reforms of the mid 1990s had a significant adverse impact on agriculture, as may be tempting to infer from the observed growth trend. Another, perhaps more important, implication is the urgency of improving agriculture's resilience to the shifting trends in anomalous weather patterns over the near to medium term, and the anticipated intensification of the spatial and inter-annual variability of rainfall over the very long term.

Dynamics of agricultural productivity growth. Wide differences in performance across states in the 1980s appear to have disappeared since 2004/05, suggesting that growth may now be more inclusive, with lagging states starting to grow at par with other states. But within states (and agro-ecological zones), performance has varied widely across districts over time. A few districts have done well but most have not, and the relative rankings across districts are mostly preserved with persistent large differences. The lagging districts are not growing fast enough yet to achieve real convergence. For example, in 2007–08, productivity was 50 times higher in the most productive versus the least productive districts. Within LIS, increased growth in some districts widened inequality—the exception being Odisha—but in the more advanced agricultural states, lagging districts are catching up with the others, indicating convergence in growth rates.

Messages and Implications

> There is little evidence to support the assertion that the policy reforms of the 1990s likely had a negative impact on agriculture. At the same time, the long-term strategic public investments in technology and irrigation have been very successful in increasing food production and mitigating the worst effects of rainfall shocks. The large aggregate and cumulative impact of a series of negative rainfall shocks between 1999-2004 serves a very important purpose—as a harbinger of the potential impacts of changing weather patterns over the short to medium term and the highly uncertain climate change outcomes over the long term. The experience underscores the urgency to address the current strategic issues. It highlights the critical importance of more efficient water management practices to weatherproof agriculture; develop strategies and make investments to mitigate climatic variability and increase resilience amid climate change (climate-smart technologies, sustainable irrigation, water harvesting and watershed development); improve markets and marketing to allow real-time risk sharing across states and districts in response to emerging market signals; and diversify and stabilize sources of income (outside the crop sector) through livestock and productive nonfarm employment. It is essential to quantify the costs and benefits of alternative ex ante risk-mitigation strategies and ex post risk-sharing strategies—issues for further detailed study.

To more closely examine performance and drivers of productivity, districts are classified by growth typology based on their initial (1970s) yields (high or low) and their subsequent performance (relatively stable or fast-growing) over the study period (1970–2008). Most growth in agricultural productivity occurred in northern and southern districts. Agro-ecological conditions and rainfall anomalies by themselves do not sufficiently explain the disparities among districts. What sets the growth districts apart from the others is better access to irrigation (and fertilizer use, which is influenced by irrigation). In addition to intensification, diversification into nontraditional and highervalue crops is also a major driver of growth in the high performers. For example, the low-yield/growth districts, unlike the low-yield/stable districts, switched area from low-value crops to higher-value crops such as cotton, horticultural crops, and soybeans.

District-level indicators to explain changes in agricultural productivity are limited, but the available data convey some important information. Markets per capita declined in low-yield districts relative to the others, likely reducing producer incentives and productivity growth. Road density has improved in the laggard districts, bringing them on par with the other districts. But while roads continue to show significant positive impact in the high-yield areas, they have not yet translated into improved productivity in the lagging districts, calling attention to the importance of complementary investments. A slightly higher share of the population in low-yield districts was rural to begin with; this indicator of urbanization has changed relatively slowly in the districts where yields were initially low but shows no obvious links with the pace of growth within the low- or high-yield cohorts. Similarly, literacy remains marginally lower in the lowyield districts, but this basic measure of human capital development has also improved more rapidly in those districts, again without a clear association with productivity growth.

Messages and Implications

At the subnational level, growth has been pervasive—but not sufficiently broad-based. While the pace of agricultural growth appears to be converging somewhat across states, at the district level the expansionary phase of the 1980s and early 1990s was not very inclusive. A few lagging districts "caught up" with the better-performing districts, but a substantial number fell further behind, despite registering positive but low levels of growth.

Differences across districts are rooted in strategy and the enabling environment—and that is where policy attention is needed. Weather alone does not explain the differences in performance as weather shocks affected the productive districts disproportionately. At the same time, the findings caution against a "silver bullet" approach, highlighting the complementarity of policies and investments tailored to particular circumstances. For example, roads and improved seeds alone do not account for differential performance among districts.

The main drivers of productivity at the district level—and hence the key entry points for action—appear to be markets and irrigation.

contd...

.contd...

Market density has fallen more in the low-yield/stable districts than in the others, likely constraining productivity growth (through producer incentives). Irrigation and the associated adoption of fertilizer have contributed to significant changes in productivity in the growth districts. Improved seeds, the other key element of the green revolution technology, have spread faster and wider, but by themselves they have not narrowed the productivity differentials across districts. The rapid expansion in irrigation occurred mainly through groundwater extraction, well-known among policy instruments as a double-edged sword. The recurrent theme of sustainable water management emerges as a policy priority, with the important lesson from the faster-growing districts, consistently appearing across the low–high yield typologies, that diversification needs to be prioritized for a possible win-win strategy. That said, some areas will inevitably have limited prospects for irrigation, and their agro-ecological endowments may limit the scope for certain types of agriculture. Localized strategies will be needed for these areas to identify viable opportunities, including livelihood options outside of agriculture.

An International Perspective on India's Structural Transformation

The slow pace of India's structural transformation (that is, the decline in the share of labor in agriculture relative to the decline in the share of agriculture in aggregate GDP) is reflected in the large gap in productivity between agricultural and nonagricultural workers. The widening of this gap is a worry for policy makers. The low productivity of a large proportion of the labor force places a heavy tax on overall well-being and shared prosperity. But how atypical is India's experience?

Evidence suggests that developing countries are now taking longer to reach their "turning point"—the point at which the inter-sectoral labor productivities start to converge. The implication is that the development context is changing, and it is increasingly harder to absorb labor outside agriculture. India seems to be experiencing this phenomenon and is behaving no differently than the average developing country (in a cohort of 88 developing countries). Consequently, India must pay particular attention to accelerating the pace of labor absorption outside of agriculture, and it must redouble efforts to increase labor productivity within agriculture. Making agricultural labor more productive is imperative in any case, because a declining farm population will have to meet the consumption and raw material requirements of a growing nonfarm population.

Messages and Implications

Technology has been a consistent driver of productivity in all four countries. Investing in technology is a globally proven and tested strategy for promoting productivity growth. Brazil, India, and China are among the largest investors in public research, and all have benefited significantly from such investment. China's and Brazil's investments, however, have been relatively more effective, making them global leaders in agricultural innovation. In Indonesia, the benefits of technology have also been pivotal, but they have accrued through open trade rather than domestic research.

A second major driver was agricultural diversification, both for domestic and export markets, supported by appropriate technology, policy, institutional reforms, and investments. Brazil, Indonesia, and China all benefited significantly more than India from openness in trade.

The backbone of China's and Brazil's more rapid transformation has been a more predictable enabling and policy environment. With a strong record of implementation, continuous innovation in public sector management for agriculture and rural development, and more effective decentralization in decision making, they have achieved significantly greater productivity growth. For example, major and fundamental reforms have greatly increased water-use efficiency in Chinese agriculture. Conducive policies paid significant dividends in production efficiencies and diversification, and better access to technology, whether from the international public research system, national research organizations, or the private sector (notably in relation to genetically modified crops).

In this context, comparisons among four large developing countries, Brazil, Indonesia, India, and China, are useful. Starting with comparable conditions in 1961, China and Indonesia achieved more success in reducing poverty and improving rural well-being. Brazil was relatively more advanced from the start and has continued to perform well. While Brazil has reached and China has almost reached their turning points, structural transformation in India and Indonesia has been slower. If the status quo prevails, their turning points are projected to be at least two decades away.

China is a more relevant comparator in terms of the scale of farming. The main difference with India is that despite having a larger share of its workforce in agriculture, China has seen much higher growth in agricultural value-added, with significantly more rapid technological change and diversification, and a much greater reliance on efficiency than input use as the main driver of growth. With more rapid increases in labor productivity, living standards among China's agricultural population improved much faster.

A Micro-level Perspective on India's Structural Transformation

A unique longitudinal study at the village level in Bihar, one of India's poorest states, draws attention to major changes at the micro level. Semi-feudal production relations—long associated with Bihar's agriculture—have virtually disappeared, while numbers of poor peasants, shares of casual landless agricultural labor, and the proportion of nonagricultural households all increased. Nonagricultural income, dominated by remittances, is the main source of income for all economic classes. Poor peasants have similar sources of income, but they largely

Messages and Implications

Even villages in poor and backward areas, typical of Bihar, are experiencing significant agricultural and socioeconomic change. Nonagricultural incomes, particularly remittances, dominate household incomes. But agriculture, with a steady increase in yields (faster than the national average for rice and wheat), has not been stagnant. Real incomes appear to be rising, along with agricultural productivity, and agricultural diversification is yielding significant benefits. Structural transformation is more challenging in Bihar than elsewhere in India. Despite high levels of migration (Bihar is unusual in this respect), a substantial proportion of the population remains in agriculture; consequently, the person-land ratio is significantly worse, keeping the productivity of agricultural labor low. Concerns about the sustainability of migration as the major engine of continued growth call for more rapid nonfarm and on-farm diversification as sources of income growth.

undertake nonagricultural production activities. The middle and big peasants have a higher share of agricultural income, but it is still less than half their total income.

Another aspect of structural transformation is the significant diversification in men's occupations. Levels of migration out of the village are high, and migration income is the largest share of household income. At least initially, migration seems to have been a response to the lack of opportunity in local labor markets. Migration affects rural production systems by pushing up local wages, promoting labor-saving cultivation techniques, and increasing the feminization of agricultural labor markets.

Did the Drivers of Growth Change Qualitatively in the 2000s?

To assess whether the recent recovery in agricultural growth can be sustained, it is vital to learn whether the drivers of growth changed qualitatively in the mid-2000s. Agricultural growth is increasingly driven by the rising shares of high-value commodities in value terms, but food grains still occupy two-thirds of the cropped area, and the shares of rice and wheat are unchanged. Except for cotton, yields of high-value crops have not increased significantly, raising concerns about the sustainability of their growth. A decomposition of growth confirms these apprehensions.

Messages and Implications

> *Two worrying trends emerge from the analysis:* The contribution of yields to productivity is declining, and prices have emerged as the main driver of growth toward the end of the 2000s. In 2010, 55 per cent of the increase in the real value of output resulted from price increases. This finding raises concerns about the sustainability of the recent growth spurt: Farmers (specifically the net-sellers) gain from higher prices, but without underlying improvements in productivity, the current growth may be short-lived.

Yields dominated growth until the mid-1990s, as green revolution technology spread. Diversification has been a consistent but moderate contributor to growth. Since the 1980s, diversification consistently accounted for about one-quarter of growth, somewhat less than might be expected from a rapidly transforming agriculture. Prices contributed increasingly to growth in the 1990s, and in recent years they have again become the main driver. Area and yields rebounded early in the recovery (after 2003), but since 2007, area expansion has slowed as expected. Importantly, yields' contribution to growth diminished considerably, and diversification remains modest despite rapidly changing diets and rising commodity prices.

Evolution of Productivity at the National, State, Household, and Farm Levels

Given India's binding land constraint, agricultural growth depends on making land (for crops) and animals (for livestock products) more productive. In the case of land, productivity, often equated to yields, can be enhanced through intensification (using more inputs per hectare), through technological advances (better inputs), and/or improved efficiency (using inputs more effectively). Total factor productivity (TFP) captures the contributions of technology and efficiency and provides a summary measure of the health of the production system. For growth to be ecologically and economically sustainable, TFP must improve.

To build a convincing body of evidence, TFP is assessed using multiple sources of data, at different levels of aggregation, and employing different methodologies. The various analyses consistently demonstrate that productive resources are being used highly inefficiently.

At the national level. Analyses based on different methodologies and data sources suggest that the recovery in recent years has been robust, with TFP growing at its fastest rate. Previous studies noted decelerating growth after the mid-1990s, but a longer time horizon (and hindsight) demonstrate, as discussed earlier, that this unusually long slowdown coincided with an anomalous rainfall pattern. It also means that the recent growth in TFP needs to be interpreted with caution: the period of analysis is short, and the recent growth partially reflects a rebound from a sharp decline in the previous period (reaching the lowest point in 2003). It will be important to track performance with data from additional years to ascertain if the growth is robust.

Irrigation, an important long-term driver of growth, appears to be contributing less to output growth in the 2000s, perhaps reflecting limits on expansion. Increased inputs have historically contributed the most to output growth, but in the 2000s, TFP has been the main source. Other emerging trends are a rise in labor productivity and capital deepening in the most recent period.

When TFP growth is decomposed into the contributions of technology and efficiency, the key finding is that technical change has consistently been the primary driver of productivity growth over the past three decades, growing fastest during the past decade (showing sustained growth even during the slowdown period). In contrast, efficiency has stagnated over the long run. It improved in the 1980s but has started to decline in recent years, indicating that the gap between actual production and the realizable potential (production frontier) is widening.

Another important finding is strong divergence in TFP growth for the traditional crops (cereals, pulses, oilseeds, cotton, and sugarcane) from that of the agricultural sector—which includes higher-valued horticulture and livestock subsectors, both of which are important for inclusive growth, and both of which have been major drivers of agriculture valueadded in recent years. Yet neither subsector has commanded the attention of policy and public expenditure to the same extent as the traditional crops. Given the magnitude of the resources tied up in traditional crops, their low TFP growth (0.28%) contrasts starkly with the sector-wide estimate (1.77%).

The continued reliance on subsidized inputs as the main driver of growth in traditional crops, with declining efficiency, is reason for serious concern. Intensification in the lagging states where input use has been lower may be less worrisome, but the continued or accelerated use of inputs (often imbalanced applications of nutrients and overexploitation of groundwater) in the advanced states demands corrective action.

Messages and Implications

> For traditional crops, which receive most of the resources devoted to agriculture, TFP growth has stagnated. Technical change has been the primary driver of productivity growth, while efficiency has stagnated and appears to be declining in recent years. The fact that three-quarters of the growth is still driven by inputs for the bulk of the sector (traditional crops) raises concerns about the quality and sustainability of agricultural growth.

At the state level. TFP varies widely across states, across crops, as well as across states for the same crops. The biggest gains are associated with new technologies for cotton and maize, but the impact of even these new technologies is not uniform across states. Among staples, rice TFP has improved in recent years for several states, but wheat TFP has slowed considerably, with the exception of reform-driven Gujarat. Sugarcane and cotton offer a telling comparison. Sugarcane experienced consistent declines in TFP growth across all major producing states, while cotton experienced consistent gains. The two differ in that there is substantial government intervention and significant subsidies for sugarcane, whereas the cotton sector has rapidly transformed since the private sector introduced Bt cotton technology in 2002.

What explains the wide variation in TFP across states? As a residual measure, TFP subsumes many unobserved factors, making it difficult to assess the role of important policy levers. An analysis of the determinants of TFP, using state-level estimates and controlling for some of the confounding factors, gives results with significant policy implications.

Messages and Implications

> At the state level, policies and institutions strongly influence productivity growth, along with diversification and technology. TFP is negatively affected by excessive or imbalanced input use, arguably driven by input subsidies. Ironically, instead of the intended impact of boosting productivity, subsidies may now be having quite the opposite effect, jeopardizing future productivity prospects. These results have major implications for the environment, productivity, and sustainable growth. An immediate area for action is more effective extension services. Extension services appear to have made little impact on productivity, even in traditional crops, but if they can help farmers to close the existing yield gaps, they could bring about substantial productivity gains.

The analysis confirms the importance of statespecific factors (broadly reflecting the policy, institutional, and governance environment) for productivity growth. Beyond these, diversification (even within the more restricted group of traditional crops) and technology—primarily agricultural research—are the main drivers of productivity growth. Contrary to general perceptions, the analysis shows that the contribution of research has not diminished over time.

In contrast, the impact of agricultural extension is considerably less visible. Persistent yield gaps, even for rice and wheat, suggest that extension has not enabled producers to benefit from current technology—even though traditional crops have long been a priority of public extension services. This result strongly suggests that the most immediate action to enhance productivity, and to counter "technology fatigue," is to increase the effectiveness of extension services.

A telling result is that rural electrification has a large and highly significant negative impact, strongly suggesting that the large subsidies for electricity use in agriculture are adversely affecting TFP, probably by contributing to declining water tables (by promoting the unsustainable extraction of groundwater). Similarly, the negative and statistically significant impact of nutrient mix on TFP strongly supports the contention that subsidies promote indiscriminate applications of nitrogen that harm soils.

At the household level. Using a completely different data source, the household-level analysis corroborates the major emerging finding that productive efficiency is low. It also shows that this inefficiency entails very high costs in terms of forgone farm income. Depending on the agro-ecological region, the average farmer is about 30–90 per cent less efficient than the "best in class"—those farmers who are her/his peers within the study sample.

Messages and Implications

> Household-level analysis finds that inefficiency is high and very costly in terms of farm income. Although much of the debate on Indian agricultural productivity has focused on technical or technical production issues, these findings suggest significant scope to improve returns through more economically rational choices. The role of policies, institutions, and the enabling environment, which is central to micro-level economic choices, needs be brought to the front and center of the debate if India's farmers are to move to a more profitable agriculture.

The micro-data confirm findings from the secondary data that technical change, rather than economic efficiency, has played the major role in productivity growth. Technical change has generally been good in recent years, with large gains in the formerly lagging semi-arid topics. Average efficiency fell significantly in the humid and arid zones, indicating that the average farmer is unable to keep up with the fast moving technological frontier, and is falling farther away from it. Arid areas have been the most vibrant, catching up with the meta-frontier at a rapid rate and closing their historical technology gap with the rest of the country.

The cost of inefficiency in terms of farmers' net returns or profits is high. A staggering 68 per cent of potential short-run profits (on average) are lost relative to the optimal economic profit that was feasible in 2007 (albeit a slight improvement over the 73 per cent lost in 1999). These losses can be attributed equally to technical and allocative inefficiencies, highlighting the roles of extension services and the policy environment in shaping farmers' choices. Smaller producers are more efficient, with higher allocative efficiency, whereas larger producers showed higher technical efficiency.

Changes in farm-level technical efficiency vary significantly by state. Farmers in Bihar represent the case of the "poor but efficient" producer—they operate at low input-output levels, but their input use is efficient (Schultz 1953). Punjabi farmers are equally efficient, but they represent the high input-output case. The absence of any obvious agro-ecological or geographical correlation with performance suggests that policies and the enabling environment at the state level play a strong role in determining efficiency outcomes.

In the most widely grown crops (rice and wheat), efficiency is lessening, and it is declining significantly for pulses and oilseeds. Only "other crops"—an aggregate of crops other than the cereals, pulses, and oilseeds— show marginal improvement in technical efficiency. Across households there is significant dispersion in efficiency levels for all crops.

Finally, an important finding is the difference in economic efficiency at the crop and wholefarm level. Higher allocative efficiency at the individual crop level suggests households are using resources (inputs) reasonably efficiently given the relative prices they face. But when it comes to the whole-farm level, allocative efficiency plunges, indicating that the bulk of economic inefficiency stems from farmers' crop choices. Household decisions to allocate resources are determined by the relative prices of crops and their associated risk levels, both of which are influenced considerably by the policy and institutional (especially market) environment.

What is driving inefficiency at the farm level? Among the range of factors explaining productivity and efficiency, the empirical analysis confirms the inverse land-productivity relationship, but smaller farms are less technically efficient. Another important finding is that at the margin family labor is less productive relative to hired labor, suggesting overuse of family labor (possibly because too many family members remain on the very small farms that are now more prevalent). Finally, as farm sizes decline through subdivision, land fragmentation is becoming a problem, with direct consequences for productivity through lower efficiency.

Younger and more educated households generally are more efficient at farming. The higher productivity of the newer generation of farmers suggests that greater access to productive land may be beneficial in terms of overall agricultural productivity and more efficient resource use.

Among public investments, the importance of access to *pucca* (paved) roads, technology, and extension services is reaffirmed by empirical results. An important insight on governance is the impact of women's participation in Gram Sabha meetings, which raises productive efficiency.

Messages and Implications

Reforming the policy and regulatory framework governing land lease and rental markets is a high priority to sustain productivity and growth in farm incomes. The empirical findings reaffirm the wellestablished importance of factors like roads, technology, and irrigation while providing new insights. The findings on land fragmentation and the association of profitability with farm size ultimately suggest that some small farms may be getting too small to remain efficient or viable, despite the technical relationship between farm size and yield. Together with the findings that perhaps too much family labor remains and is used on small (and ever smaller) farms, these findings lend new urgency to reforming the tenancy laws and legalizing land lease markets. More efficient lease markets can help to consolidate land in the hands of the more productive farmers, perhaps by improving access to land for younger and more educated farmers, and can provide inefficient or unviable farmers the security to seek off-farm work without fear of losing their primary asset.

Are smaller farms still efficient and viable? The 25 years of household panel data from NCAER surveys provide a rare insight into the relationships between farm size (land owned by households) and three levels of farming returns: gross value of output per hectare, gross-margins per hectare (revenues less paid out costs, so in essence returns to family labor and land), and profits (revenues less paid costs and imputed costs of family labor—in other words, the returns to land only). The data show a significant and dramatic shift in the relationship between farm size and net revenues or profits per acre—from a strong inverse relationship in 1982 to an increasingly positive relationship in 1999 and 2007.

Given that most farms in India are under one hectare, these findings are significant—politically as well as economically—for growth and poverty reduction. The argument of "small and efficient" still applies from a technical perspective of higher yields or productivity (that is, the value of output per acre), as found in the productivity analysis discussed earlier, but the shift in the returns to farming indicates that "small and efficient" does not necessarily translate to more income (profits). The main reason behind this reversal is that the higher value of output per hectare is neutralized by very high family labor costs. These trends re-emphasize the point that family labor is overused on the farm.

Technology, Yield Gaps, and Growth Prospects

Many factors contribute to productivity growth (including infrastructure, markets, and education). Among these factors, technology plays a central role by helping to increase yields. Changes in yields are a joint outcome of contributions by research and extension. Research generates new technology that moves the production frontier (the yield potential) upward and outward. Extension assists farmers to better exploit the available technology— through access to new technology and advice to improve technical proficiency in using it—and in essence to close the "yield gap" (which is the difference between actual and potential yields). A combination of simulation models, research data, and actual yields helps to identify the yield gaps and how they have evolved over time. The analysis focuses on rice and wheat, for which abundant data are available, and which are an appropriate choice, given the heavy historical focus on these green revolution crops.

The all-India weighted averages show significant scope for increasing yields of both crops with technology that is already available. But India's biophysical heterogeneity argues against taking such a blanket assessment at face value. Indeed, the states vary considerably in their potential yields, their progress in closing the yield gaps, and the size of the remaining yield gaps. Some states have made good progress in rice in the last 15 years. Growth in wheat yields has slowed in most states, although Gujarat, Karnataka, and Maharashtra substantially narrowed their yield gaps.

Given that no country in the world has reduced its yield gap below 20 per cent, 30 per cent may be a realistic target. Some states are approaching this 30 per cent target with current technology and face limited prospects for further improvement. Maharashtra and Gujarat seem to have exhausted their potential with the current wheat technology, whereas Punjab and Haryana have limited room to increase yields. West Bengal and Punjab are close to their potential for paddy, but most other states have significant scope for yield improvement. In interpreting these findings, two important caveats need to be kept in mind. One is that the attainable yield, used here as the benchmark for the yield gap, assumes that no biotic or abiotic stresses are present—rarely true in practice. Second, these are physical or output maximum potentials, not economically optimal potentials. Depending on the local policy and institutional environment, reducing the physical yield gaps may not be economically viable (as actual or observed farm yields may more accurately reflect).

The movement of the production frontier, or realizable yields, shows that the potential for wheat has continued to rise as new, better-yielding varieties are released, but rice potential has stagnated. Yet between 1995 and 2010, yield gaps widened for wheat and narrowed for rice. Growth in actual yields is similar for the two crops; the different trends in their yield gaps originate in the much faster rise in realizable yields for wheat—36 kilograms per hectare per year for rainfed wheat and 54 for irrigated wheat—whereas realizable yields for rice have stagnated since 1995, increasing by only 6 kilograms per hectare per year.

How do yield gaps in India compare to those in other major grain-growing areas of the world? The wheat yield gap in Punjab resembles the average across the other major production areas, with similar scope for doubling current yields. The yield gap for irrigated rice in Punjab is larger than the global average: Yields in Punjab need to rise by 75 per cent to close the gap, whereas on average global yields need to double. The comparators for rainfed rice are limited, but the data show that Madhya Pradesh rainfed yields must grow by 150 per cent to close the current yield gap.

Messages and Implications

Yield gaps offer an opportunity, but their persistence reflects challenges in technology services. Yield gaps have narrowed over time, more for wheat than rice. But substantial gaps remain for both crops in rainfed as well as the green revolution areas, signaling potential for further gains and lending weight to the need to resolve the "extension problem." Research too has challenges to confront: dedicating more effort to crops other than rice and wheat, and working with a rapidly emerging private sector to align research priorities to tackle a changing climate and to address the multiple biotic and abiotic stresses prevalent in the LIS.

Investing for innovation and change requires institutional innovation. Technology capital is a critical input to accelerate agricultural productivity. India is among the world's preeminent investors in agricultural R&D. Yet success is more than the sum of public funding. The quality of innovation and the capacity of institutions to reconfigure and reorient themselves to a rapidly transforming agriculture are critical. To remain relevant and stimulate transformative change, the impressive institutions that ushered in the green revolution must take action:

- *In agricultural research*, public investment is increasing, but a number of reforms have also been proposed to reconfigure the research system to meet current needs and challenges. The issues of relevance, efficiency, and effectiveness of the research system are well understood, but bold action is needed to implement the reforms. At the same time, private sector investment in research is rapidly increasing, with significant potential to contribute to rapid growth in productivity and incomes, including in the poorer semi-arid parts of the country. To fully exploit this potential, the remaining constraints to private investment need to be removed.
- *In agricultural education*, the state agricultural universities face multiple crises in fulfilling their mandate to build the needed human capacity for technical innovation and undertake crucial adaptive research and extension activities. The crises in governance, resources, effectiveness, and ethics is widely

contd...

.contd...

acknowledged. These issues are revisited in the Bhubaneswar Declaration. The proposed roadmap for improving India's higher education system calls for fundamental changes but requires unwavering political will and commitment to overcome the ingrained resistance to change.

- *In agricultural extension*, the Agricultural Technology Development Agency models a decentralized, demand-driven approach for advisory and extension services to respond to local demands, priorities, and constraints. The lack of skilled, dedicated personnel in the agency, along with weak research-extension links, limited outreach to farmers, and limited operational flexibility, have yielded disappointing outcomes. Priorities are to renew and improve the focus on community outreach, reinforce organizational autonomy, and improve staff quality. Reforming current service delivery and promoting a pluralistic system is an urgent priority.

Certainly yield is not the only metric of research achievements. Research also aims to develop varieties capable of withstanding specific growing conditions (evolving pests and diseases, for example) and supporting other local priorities (tastes or the timing of growing cycles, for example). Future research will need to emphasize varieties capable of adapting to the pressures of climate change. For example, early maturing varieties may be better adapted to rising temperatures, which are expected to reduce yields significantly. Varieties specifically suited to the needs of crop-livestock systems or agro-processors will also be in increasing demand.

Livestock Subsector: Significant Opportunities and Policy Priorities

The livestock subsector has grown at twice the rate of the food grain subsector. Continued income growth and demographic change in India will heighten demand for livestock products and offer significant opportunities to increase production and incomes. Mixed crop-livestock farming systems predominate among smallholders and are an important tool to target rural underemployment (particularly of unskilled and family labor), diversify risk, and stabilize income throughout the year. Livestock production is more inclusive than crop agriculture, with livestock ownership more widespread than land ownership. Women and other socioeconomically marginalized groups stand to benefit the most from better livestock productivity.

The potential. India has the world's largest livestock herd. It is unlikely to have a substantial dairy surplus for export, but it is already a leading exporter of bovine (buffalo) meat and a highly competitive exporter of mutton and pork. Expanding markets for processed meat and halal-certified products provide additional opportunities for export growth. Growth in meat output has mainly come at the extensive margin—from growth in livestock numbers. Substantial scope remains for improvement at the intensive margin.

More than two-thirds of livestock output is from the dairy industry. India leads the world in milk production, but milk yields are about half the world average. Formal milk processing has expanded rapidly, driven by deregulation of the dairy industry in the early 1990s. Even so, less than 20 per cent of milk is formally processed.

The challenges. Despite this potential, India's public expenditure on livestock is low, declining, and ineffectively targeted. The impact of public programs must be monitored to inform policy, develop a strategy for the sector, and enhance service delivery. Most public funding goes to administrative rather than productivity-enhancing activities. Allocations for the smaller species (small ruminants, poultry, and pigs) that yield more benefits for smallholders remain low and have declined. The limited public expenditure on livestock must be rationalized between public and private goods.

The policy interventions. Policy interventions to raise productivity in the livestock subsector must target services and institutions for technology, marketing, and animal health. The National Dairy Plan is a multi-pronged approach along those lines that would work for the meat industry as well as poultry and pig production. Aside from encouraging commercial and large-scale operations, attention must be given to technologies, institutions, and policies enabling smallholders to produce more efficiently and sustainably and compete profitably in a price- and quality-conscious market.

The states urgently require better strategies to meet local requirements for animal breeding (cattle, small ruminants, pigs), improved nutrition and feed (to realize the gains from breeding), improved animal health systems with better livestock support services (including disease surveillance), and policies to attract private investment.

Messages and Implications

> Aside from additional and better-targeted public spending, priority actions include strengthening the institutions for technology, animal health, and smallholder marketing. The prospective socioeconomic and environmental gains from the livestock subsector offer substantial scope for economic and green growth. Measures that increase livestock productivity can enhance incomes, mitigate the environmental impact of livestock production, and enable livestock to adapt to India's challenging and changing climate. In this context, it is imperative to rely on intensification for growth. Improvements in breeds, feeds, and animal management and productivity are the other critical elements of any strategy to mitigate the environmental impacts of growth in the subsector.

Investments in market infrastructure and quality standards are integral to the efficient distribution of livestock products, value addition, and food safety. Much of the investment will come from the private sector. Aside from encouraging such investment, the public sector must implement measures that help smallholders improve their bargaining power and build their capacity to absorb production and market risks.

Strategy and policy for the livestock sector must incorporate a range of environmental issues. Improvements in animal management and productivity are critical for mitigating greenhouse gas emissions and relieving pressure on land and water. Stocking rates in many areas are 5–10 times the recommended levels, and water use per liter of milk exceeds the world average in most intensive and semiintensive systems. Producers must aim to maintain vegetative groundcover, reduce soil erosion and down-slope sedimentation, improve water infiltration and groundwater recharge, and increase pasture production. Greenhouse gas emissions per head of cattle depend greatly on animal breeds and the type of feed provided. Climate change will affect livestock productivity through a higher incidence of heat stress, drought, and flooding. A large number of adaptation strategies exist, but greater and better implementation is needed.

Investments in Agriculture for Growth and Sustainability

Private and public expenditures to expand productive capacity. Private investment in agriculture has increased rapidly since the mid-1990s. It accounts for more than 80 per cent of the investment in agriculture and largely consists of on-farm investments, primarily in irrigation pumps and to a lesser degree in machinery. Overall investment on the farm remains low, and farmers prefer to allocate more of their disposable incomes to financial savings and expanding business capital.

Shares of public and private agricultural investments in capital formation are declining, however. For a sector deemed to be a priority, agriculture's diminishing share of public investment appears contradictory. When public expenditure is defined more broadly—to include expenditures in the sector (through agricultural programs and institutions) and expenditures for the sector (for complementary public investments like rural roads and electricity)—it is clear that agriculture does indeed command a much higher priority. Based on those criteria, public expenditures were equivalent to one-third of agricultural GDP in 2009, up from about one-fifth in 1995, about half of which was from the central (union) government. Infrastructure accounted for the largest share (34%) of these expenditures, with input support services following at 26 per cent. Input support services (essentially private goods and subsidies) have grown the fastest (22% per year). In sharp contrast, research, education and extension services, which have been shown to have the largest returns among public expenditures in India, had a combined share of less than 2 per cent.

Even those estimates do not capture the totality of subsidies supporting agriculture. A fuller (but still not exhaustive) accounting of subsidies (including food, fertilizer, irrigation, power, and others) shows that they dwarf public investments, irrespective of how the latter are defined. A vivid example is the pervasiveness of subsidies in two of the largest government programs or "missions" directed to increasing agricultural productivity (the National Food Security Mission and the Rashtriya Krishi Vikas Yojana). A review of their implementation in three states shows that 88-98 per cent of funds under the NFSM and 42-87 per cent under RKVY, depending on the state, were directed toward the provision of inputs or other private goods. Private irrigation investments, public subsidies, and declining productivity. Two related trends in public and private investment are the rapid growth in private irrigation and the large and growing volume of subsidies in public expenditures. The importance of irrigation for agricultural growth is clear. But the dominant mode of private irrigation development—groundwater extraction—may not be sustainable in its current form. Distorted incentives encourage excessive extraction and highly inefficient use of water. Power and credit subsidies are the major drivers of groundwater extraction. Marginal returns to these subsidies in terms of improved productivity and poverty reduction were high in the 1960s and 1970s but are now significantly lower than returns to investments in rural roads and technology services.

The political economy of subsidies in India has relegated expenditure efficiency as well as budgetary implications to the extreme margins of public decision making. Yet concrete evidence is emerging that current policies will have an outsized negative impact over the long run. For example, electricity subsidies lead to an increase in the area planted to water-intensive crops such as rice and sugarcane but also lead to a large negative impact on groundwater levels. A fall in groundwater level by 1 meter is found to reduce production of food grains by 8 per cent, water-intensive crops by 9 per cent, and cash crops by 5 per cent. A 10 per cent reduction in the average electricity subsidy would reduce groundwater extraction by 6.7 per cent.

Messages and Implications

Although the budgetary implications of the large share of subsidies have little apparent weight in public policy decisions, policies intended to increase production and productivity clearly impose substantial costs in terms of resource degradation and lost future productivity. Consistent with the priority placed on agriculture, public spending has grown rapidly since the early 2000s and now equals onethird of agricultural value added. But only a small fraction of the public expenditure goes toward expanding the productive capacity of agriculture (to public investments or contribution to capital formation). Subsidies dwarf public investments. The substantial costs of these choices are also being borne now. If public policies that encourage these outcomes are not rationalized, they will further reduce productivity and returns to farmers—outcomes that are diametrically opposite to their intent.

Contrary to their intended objectives, electricity subsidies set a vicious circle in motion, jeopardizing agricultural productivity over the long run. Together with other policies such as MSPs, these distorted incentives have altered crop composition to favor water-intensive crops, particularly in the Northwest and Mid-West, which are experiencing the most severe groundwater crises. This relationship is evident in the strong correlation between the "virtual water export" from the Northwest and public procurement of rice. These policies urgently demand attention—especially in the interests of curbing the mounting risks occasioned by climate change.

Consequences of imbalanced nutrient use. The current and long-term costs of imbalanced fertilizer use on productivity are widely recognized, but the associated changes in land productivity may not be equally well appreciated. The evidence suggests that productivity drops beyond a certain ratio of nitrogen to phosphorous. While the all-India median level is still below that threshold, half of the farmers in the breadbasket states (Punjab and Haryana) are above the threshold. In other words, they have reduced their productivity from the peak response level. Even in Bihar most farmers operate on the decreasing part of the response curve.

Marketing and Market Reform: Unfinished Business

India has long intervened in its agricultural markets. Regulations have eased since the 1990s, but reforms have been slow, uneven, and frequently reversed. When reforms are introduced, even partially, the private sector responds swiftly and dynamically—witness the emergence of contract farming, electronic exchanges, ICT-based market information systems and kiosks, and myriad value chain improvements. Yet the consensus is that the marketing, trade, value addition, agroprocessing, and food safety capacity required by a diversified, vibrant, and modern agricultural sector has not materialized as expected. Government intervention continues. Parastatals dominate food grain markets, and private agricultural trade is heavily regulated.

The traditional chain, passing through agricultural wholesale markets and traditional urban retail, dominates the marketing of agricultural commodities, but it is inefficient, lacks integration, and is plagued by trader collusion in the regulated and restricted markets. Even so, alternatives—modern retail and the processing and food service sectors—are emerging, and even traditional value chains for staples are evolving, with changes in factor markets, innovations that shorten supply chains, wider access to information through mobile phones, and increasing downstream demand for quality and brand differentiation.

Innovations to improve marketing efficiency and link small and marginal producers to more remunerative value chains have been attempted on a limited scale, with mixed results. Firms or other private and public entities generally have preferred large and medium farmers for contract farming; established or corporate retail chains have preferred the more advanced agricultural states to the states where most poor smallholders reside. The main factors influencing those preferences appear to be difficulties in enforcing contracts, high transaction costs, and challenges in meeting quality standards. Initiatives to integrate small farmers to value chains failed to introduce or adapt appropriate technology over time, although producer companies appeared more effective than cooperatives at linking smallscale producers to markets.

Alternative market channels—traditional private sector traders, state-sponsored cooperatives, and Rural Business Hubs (a modern private sector innovation)—also show very mixed results. By and large, the benefits and costs differed little among the alternatives. The alternatives showed no clear improvement in smallholders' access to inputs or outputs, and smallholders experienced no significant price or quality discrimination in any market channel. What emerges is that medium and larger farmers have better access to state-sponsored cooperatives, indicating that subsidies (either through access or merely through the scale effect) are not as pro-poor as intended. Cooperatives are more beneficial in the more remote or backward areas of the states studied, where the private sector is thin or nonexistent.

This evidence from the ground level provides a useful backdrop to two pervasive regulations that have "stifled" agriculture and remain in effect for the most part: the Agricultural Produce Markets (Development and Regulation) Act—APM(D&R) Act—and the Essential Commodities Act (ECA). The issues related to these regulations are well recognized, including zoning and storage restrictions, market fragmentation and inefficiency, and the requirement to sell all produce at a limited number of licensed, regulated markets in often nontransparent transactions. The regulations discourage private investment in storage, handling, and marketing infrastructure; they also constrain contract farming or direct purchases by agro-processers and prevent improvements in value chain efficiencies.

To address the major problems, the government introduced a "Model Act" in 2003 and urged state governments to amend their legislation and regulations accordingly. Most states amended their legislation, but the extent and implementation of reforms remain limited. An in-depth study, including field assessments in five states, finds a largely unfinished agenda. Despite attempts to modify the ECA, its essential provisions remain intact. The multiplicity of control orders issued by multiple agencies (at the central and state levels) creates uncertainty and raises transaction costs. The lack of transparency prevails, restricting trade and maintaining market segmentation.

Different states interpret and implement reforms in different ways, prompting a need to rethink market governance. Agriculture is a state subject, but inter-state trade and commerce is under the Union list. For efficient markets, it is critical to establish common norms and ensure transparency and predictability of rules and regulations to facilitate private trade and investment. While overregulation is clearly a hindrance, the other extreme of an absence of any regulation is also

Messages and Implications

In most cases, market reforms have not been implemented in full or in earnest, with provisions and omissions that effectively retain the status quo and restrict private investment and trade. India remains a segmented agricultural market; reforms to lift restrictions on movement, stock, and trade remain limited. Different states interpret and implement reforms and regulations in different ways, suggesting a need to rethink market governance. It may be advisable to place agricultural marketing on the Concurrent List and establish common norms for taxation and other charges/fees to make the system more transparent and predictable.

State governments face a conflict of interest with the proposed market reforms. Reform of APMCs have fiscal implications for state government, and as such have revenue implications. To overcome this obstacle, a cost-sharing strategy will need to be devised. Another conflict of interest is that state departments or marketing boards both run and regulate markets. An independent market regulator could level the playing field between the state and private markets.

not desirable. Markets need to be orderly and governed well to create a healthy environment for transactions, calling for an independent market regulator.

Beyond the Farm: Exploiting the Potential for Food Processing

Urbanization, the shift to nonfarm activities, rising incomes, women's increasing participation in the labor force, and changing consumption habits will create an outpouring of demand for processed foods. Food processing provides a natural entry point for India's sluggish "manufacturing" sector to move into predominantly agricultural areas and create much-needed off-farm employment. Food processing has among the largest multiplier effects across the economy. It can stimulate higher agricultural productivity through better and more stable farm prices, reduce wastage by transforming produce unsuitable for wet markets into value-added consumables (increasing returns to farmers), and promote diversification.

Food industry structure and investment. Like all manufacturing, the food-processing industry has a dualistic structure, with a relatively small (in number of units) but capitalintensive organized segment coexisting with a pervasive, mostly rural, and more laborintensive unorganized segment. Rural firms are less capital intensive, less productive, and dominated by small family enterprises.

Shares of food processing in all manufacturing in terms of employment and numbers of units have been stable in most states over time, while the share of output has increased. Both the organized and unorganized segments have experienced capital deepening and declining labor intensities. The organized segment has generated jobs with an increased number of units, but the unorganized segment has lost enterprises and jobs over time. The remaining enterprises are larger in scale, with rapidly growing output per unit and slower but still growing employment per enterprise.

Labor productivity has risen fast, keeping pace with labor productivity in the non-food sector, but the associated rise in wages (also relative to the non-food sector) has restrained growth in employment, encouraging further capital intensity and scale of operating units. The preference for higher capital intensity and labor-saving technology reflects the perpetuation of informality and a reluctance to hire labor, perhaps due to labor laws and other factors in the business environment.

The significance of these trends for employment and transformation, even in the more rural food-based industry and in the more populous and poorer states, cannot be overstated. Encouraging new businesses to enter and existing businesses to expand employment more rapidly than in the past will create employment, but only with greater attention to the enabling environment and barriers to entry for smaller firms, especially in the lagging states.

Patterns and drivers of private investment in food manufacturing. Three major findings emerge from the analysis. First, the organized food industry is more prevalent in less industrially developed states with higher shares of income from agriculture; the unorganized segment is more prevalent across states, regardless of the level of development. Second, food manufacturing is more dominant in states with a higher per centage of poor people. Individuals tend to diversify out of agriculture by starting small nonagricultural enterprises or operating such enterprises alongside their agricultural ventures for supplemental income. Third, industrial investments in individual states are highly concentrated in specific sectors. Among the factors explaining investment patterns, the main results of interest for policy are backward linkages to agriculture, credit, and public infrastructure. The food industry's concentration in agricultural states clearly suggests that "location matters." Locations with higher agricultural productivity attract more private investment and employment in food processing. Finally, the findings on access to credit and infrastructure reconfirm their well-known importance as determinants of investment.

Productivity growth in the food-processing industry. TFP growth (TFPG) rebounded sharply after 2000, following a decline in the 1990s. For the unorganized segment, TFPG was positive but much lower than in the organized segment. The strong, positive correlation between TFPG for the organized and unorganized segments across states indicates that states doing better in one segment also do better in the other, suggesting a better overall investment climate for food processing in some states. Key determinants of productivity differences across states include backward linkages to agriculture, infrastructure, and investor friendliness. Beyond the backward linkages, other agglomeration economies appear not to be significant.

Messages and Implications

> A dual focus on agricultural productivity and creating an appropriate investment climate to attract private investment is needed to promote more rapid rural transformation. States where agriculture is dominant have significant potential to attract private investment in the food industry. Higher agricultural productivity also attracts private investment in food processing, placing a premium on supportive investments in (for instance) irrigation, roads, and better functioning markets. Active promotion of this relatively more labor-intensive industry, through appropriate incentives, in states with low per capita income, high dependence on agriculture, and high incidence of poverty will help create off-farm jobs, which will absorb more people from agriculture and promote structural transformation. These arguments are even more relevant with respect to the unorganized segment of the industry, which is more widespread and has higher potential to absorb labor but currently suffers from low productivity. High levels of efficiency in many states signal that the food industry is well placed to compete in a more liberalized marketplace, with potential scope for foreign direct investment as well as exports. Policies to improve the investment climate for agro-processing, both for the organized and unorganized segments, is thus a high priority.

The unorganized segment does not appear to grow through a complementary relationship (for example, through outsourcing or subcontracting) with organized food manufacturing. Both the organized and unorganized segments seem to be operating below optimal scales. The significantly suboptimal scale of operation in the unorganized segment suggests strong disincentives for employing labor in an otherwise efficient industry.

Transforming Agriculture in LIS: Challenges and Priorities for Bihar and Odisha

The eastern states offer enormous agricultural opportunities if their natural resources are managed judiciously, in a framework of appropriate policies and institutions and supportive infrastructure. Sufficient water, a suitable climate, and significant scope to improve yields make the eastern states a valuable resource for sustaining national food security, and their potential for high-value horticulture and livestock production portend a rapid economic transformation. Analysis in two of the poorest states, Bihar and Odisha, reveals the challenges and priorities involved in realizing this scenario and contributing to the inclusive growth agenda for LIS.

Challenges to productivity and diversification. In both states, low crop and livestock yields are typical, with large differentials across districts. Rapidly diversifying production has translated to faster growth and poverty reduction. Despite these seeming similarities, the two states have experienced distinct growth patterns. Diversification was strong and consistent in Bihar, with prices playing a lesser role in growth. Improved yield spurred growth in Odisha in the early 2000s, but now growth is led primarily by prices. As noted earlier, price-led growth raises concerns about its sustainability, given that yields are declining. In contrast, growth in Bihar appears more robust.

Small, fragmented holdings prevail in both Bihar (72% are under 0.5 hectare) and Odisha (60% smaller than 1 hectare). Tenancy and sharecropping arrangements discourage investment, while fragmented holdings and the small scale of operations are a drag on efficiency and constrain output marketing. Inevitably, transaction costs and market risks tend to be high.

Low input use intensity and efficiency limit productivity growth, although fertilizer use has grown faster than the national average in Bihar, approaching the levels in more advanced states. As in those states, fertilizer use is imbalanced, taxing productivity. The high level of biotic and abiotic stress from many sources—pests, diseases, drought, floods, acidic and sodic soils—means a very high level of agricultural risk, and likely constrains the adoption of new technology, reduces the efficiency of input use, and discourages productive investments.

Marketing remains a challenge. Relatively low and volatile prices result from thinly spread and underdeveloped markets; market density is low, and few markets have sophisticated infrastructure such as cold storage facilities. Bihar's bold abolition of the APM(D&R) Act seems to have unintentionally left a void in market governance, with allegations of noncompetitive behavior. Markets have been taken over by private entities; farmers continue to pay market fees but receive no services, and public and private investment in market infrastructure is nil. In Odisha the Act is intact, but most markets still have no mechanism for price discovery and price determination.

Bihar, Odisha, and other LIS historically received much less public funding for irrigation and infrastructure than other states. Allocations remain lower than the all-India average—inconsistent with the objective of inclusive growth. Both states improved road density, but other infrastructure deficiencies persist, particularly in rural electrification. Farmers invested in the more costly diesel pumps in Bihar, where irrigation intensity (at 62% of net sown area) now surpasses the all-India average (45%). Odisha's irrigation intensity remains low. Bihar has significant potential for surface water irrigation; Odisha already sources irrigation water from canals.

Messages and Implications

The top priorities for Bihar and Odisha are to tackle the multiple biotic and abiotic stresses, develop markets, and promote livestock development. Small holdings make it a priority to enable people to leave agriculture or diversify into higher-value agriculture. Technological solutions range from sustainable crop management strategies (for overcoming soil acidity and sodicity, multi-cropping, reducing water use, and conserving other resources) to better seed quality and faster seed replacement, and research on abiotic stresses (together with private companies).

Collective action—through producer organizations, cooperatives, farmer associations, or self-help groups—is important for scale economies and linking smallholders to value chains. Bihar has successful approaches that can be scaled up (for dairy, vegetables), and Odisha is innovating with farmers' markets and cluster approaches for specific horticultural crops. These initiatives need to be set within an overall framework conducive to private investment in marketing, agro-processing, and land development. Establishing a regulatory framework for fair, transparent, and efficient markets with free movement of goods and services is essential.

Livestock is a "quick win" for inclusive growth, nutritional outcomes, and employment. Priority actions include focusing research on diseases and production constraints; policy and other support for small ruminant, pig, and poultry production; and incentives for private investment in processing, value chains, feed production, and veterinary services.

12

The Context and Conundrums of Contemporary Agriculture

INDIAN agriculture has been widely studied.[1] Without going into a detailed review, this section highlights salient features of the current agricultural economy to provide an understanding of the background and context for the analyses that follow.

India's Food Security Puzzle

For India, the priority for agricultural policy and strategy historically has been to achieve food security. The performance of agriculture is thus most often assessed by Indian policy makers in terms of its success in achieving national food security—essentially self-sufficiency in food, specifically cereals (rice and wheat). By this yardstick, Indian agriculture has achieved significant success, given the rising per capita production of cereals between the 1960s and now (Figure 12.1).

The rapid increase in cereal production seen throughout the 1970s and 1980s came from growth in yields driven by the green revolution; net cultivated area has remained largely unchanged since the 1970s. Irrigation development has increased gross cultivated area, but the prospects to bring new land into cultivation appear limited. Following a sluggish decade from about the mid-1990s, production growth appears to be back on track.

Figure 12.1 also shows how per capita cereals availability (defined as production net of change in stocks and trade) has declined in recent years. After rising in the 1980s and 1990s, cereals availability has fallen to levels near those of the 1960s, causing concern among policy makers (GOI 2013a), who are also concerned by the persistence of hunger at a time when food production is at an all-time high. This disparity is as much of a puzzle as the incomecalorie puzzle—the consistent decline

World Bank Group (2014). *Republic of India Accelerating Agricultural Productivity Growth*. May 21. Chapter 2. pp. 7-13.

in the consumption of calories seen since the 1980s, across all income categories, despite rising incomes.[2]

Figure 12.1

Per Capita Availability and Production of Cereals (grams/day)

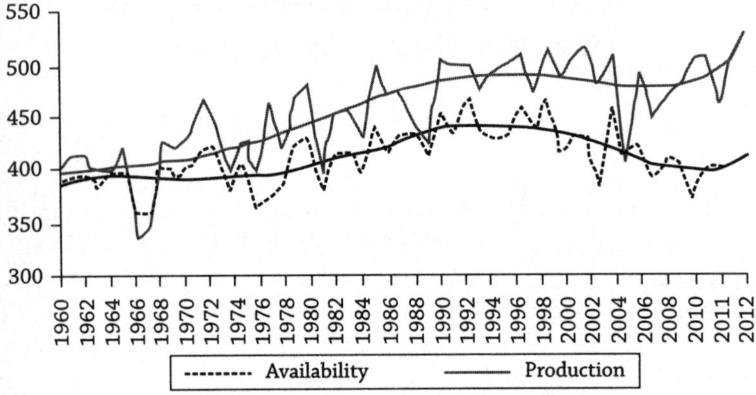

Source: Authors, using DES, MOA data.

Since the 1980s, Indian diets appear to have become more diverse (Figure 12.2). Per capita consumption of grain (cereals and pulses) has fallen as consumption of other commodities has increased. This

Figure 12.2

Percentage Change in Per Capita Consumption (kg/l/no.), 1983/84–2009/10

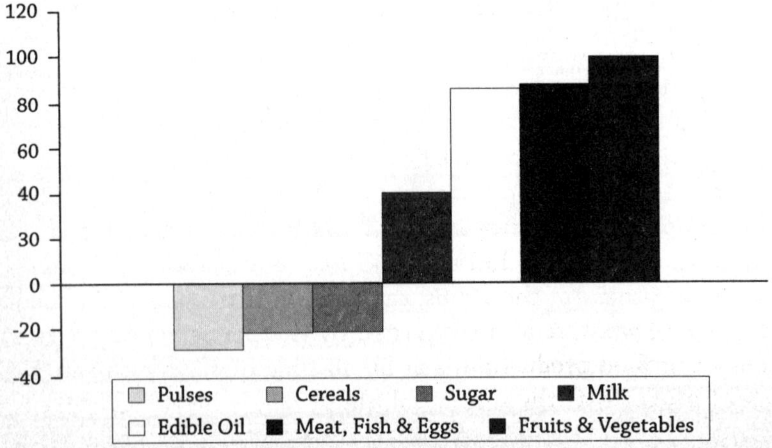

Source: NSS data 1983/84, 2009/10, national aggregates.

trend is consistent with theory, which suggests that the consumption of low-income-elasticity commodities declines as incomes rise.[3] The "puzzle" is that calorie intake has fallen consistently, even at low levels of income and in both rural and urban areas, despite the high incidence of undernutrition—that is, a basic calorie deficiency, without even accounting for the full extent of malnutrition.[4]

Persistent Food Price Rise

The previous discussion suggests that food insecurity may stem more from a lack of access to food than from the unavailability of food. One explanation for this outcome could be the persistent increase in food prices compared to prices of non-food commodities for most of the 1980s to the present, except for a brief period the mid-2000s (Figure 12.3).

Figure 12.3

Food Prices Relative to Prices of All Commodities

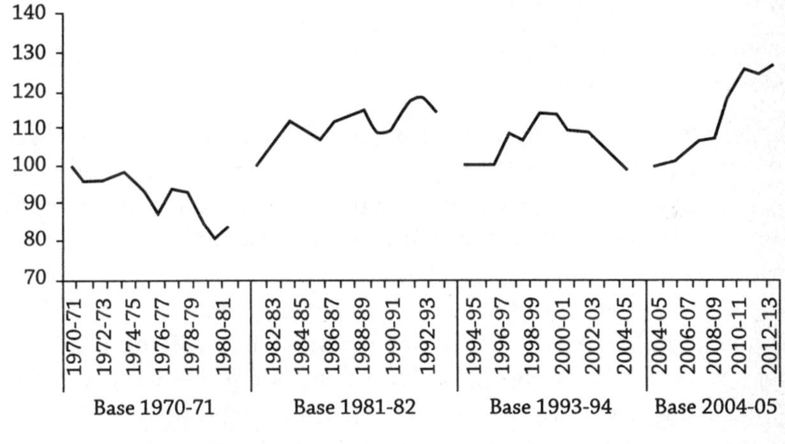

Source: Authors, using RBI online database. Ratio of Food Articles to All Commodity indices, Annual Average WPI, preserving the base years for each time period.

A significant share of the food price increase in recent years has been driven by high-value agricultural commodities, reflecting rising demand with changing dietary preferences as incomes and urbanisation increase. This so-called "protein inflation" is thought to reflect a structural problem (Mohanty 2011) caused by a lag in the supply-response for the commodities increasingly in demand (Dev 2013a). The components of the Wholesale Price Index (WPI) confirm that high-value agricultural commodities (fruits, vegetables, and milk and other livestock products) account for the bulk of food price rise (Figure 12.4).

Figure 12.4

Contribution to Food Price Rise (%)

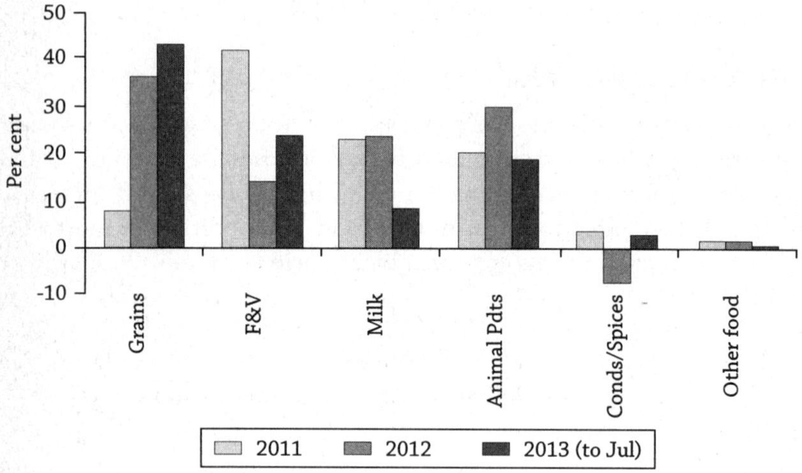

Source: Authors, using CSO data.

Nevertheless, rising prices for food grains have been annoyingly persistent (2010 and 2011 are exceptions). After 2011, food grains reemerged as the largest single contributor to the food price rise, driven by the prices of cereals and the sheer size of cereals' continuing large share in the consumption basket. Real prices of staples have been rising since the early 1990s. This trend seems to follow that of the real Minimum Support Prices (MSPs) for rice and wheat (Figure 12.5), which have been empirically shown to drive domestic prices for these cereals (Bathla 2011; Acharya *et al.*, 2012).

Farmers (the net-sellers) benefit from rising real prices, which translate directly to higher incomes. Food price increases driven by support prices may be masking underlying inefficiencies, however, as sluggish growth in productivity (yields) may be driving up the costs of cultivation (cost per quintal), which in turn provide the rationale for pushing up MSPs (Rao and Dev 2010). In any case, rising prices can have significant consequences, particularly on the welfare of the poor (a large proportion of whom are landless) and of small-scale farmers (who are net buyers of food) (Deaton 1989; Ivanic and Martin 2008, Ivanic, Martin and Zaman 2011, Anderson, Ivanic and Martin 2014).[5]

Figure 12.5

Real Minimum Support Prices

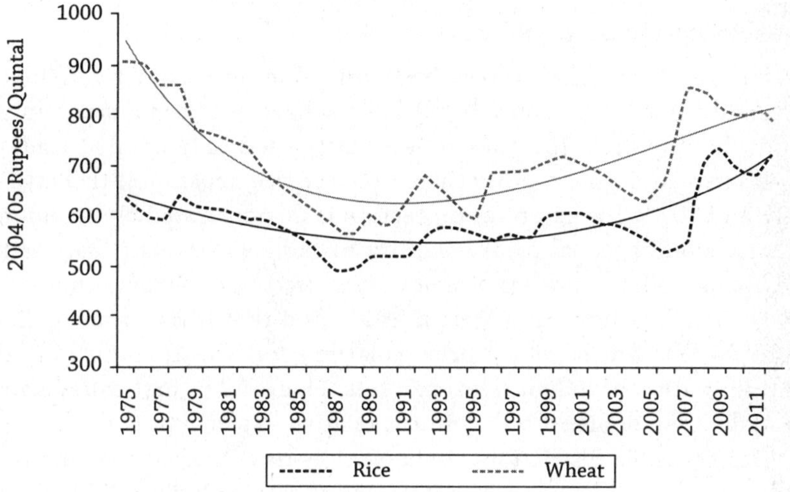

Source: Authors, using DES, MOA data.

Estimates of nutrient demand elasticities reaffirm the intuitive conviction that higher prices affect the nutrients consumed, possibly contributing to malnutrition as households (rural and urban) reduce calorie and protein consumption through own and cross-price effects (Gaiha *et al.*, 2012).[6] Given that cereals contribute 64 and 54 per cent of calories (Gaiha *et al.*, 2012, using 2009/10 NSS data), an increase in the cereal price may reduce food intake as households struggle to meet expenses other than food (Deaton and Dreze 2009). National Sample Survey (NSS) data show that households are spending less of their incremental income on food and more on durable goods and services (health and education).

It is understandable that real prices of food other than cereals would rise with rising incomes and demand, but the recent sharp upward trend in cereal prices is puzzling, especially because per capita cereal consumption is falling, cereal production is growing steadily (notwithstanding the annual fluctuations caused by adverse weather), and food stocks remain at all-time highs. Analysts have raised questions about the irony of amassing large food grain stocks when prices of staples are high (Chand *et al.*, 2010). Two sources of "leakage" from a purely domestic supply-demand regime could influence prices: trade (through imports or exports, if external prices are higher than domestic prices) and stocks (through excessive diversion of grain into silos or ill-timed procurement/release operations).

Trade Policy and Cereal Prices

India's trade policies have been unstable but restrictive (Gulati, Jain, and Hoda 2013), so export-led prices have not been a factor in the rise in food prices.[7] The government has periodically banned trade in staples (rice and wheat) other than aromatic rice, most recently between 2008 and 2011. The extent of protection is demonstrated by the limited transmission of global price volatility to Indian markets (Imai, Gaiha, and Thapa 2008; Rajmal and Misra 2009; Dasgupta, Dubey, and Satish 2011). Gouel, Gautam and Martin 2014) find that Indian trade policies offset 94 per cent of global price volatility for wheat, confirming the great insulation of Indian cereal markets. Figure 12.6 (first panel) shows the stability in domestic wheat prices relative to global prices.

Despite trade restrictions, Indian prices have tracked the long-term trend in global prices, but without the short-term volatility (GOI 2013b). India has also generally maintained domestic prices between import and export parity prices, making commercial trade economically unviable in most years (Figure 12.6). This alignment of domestic and external prices has been achieved as a managed policy rather than a market- or trade-determined outcome, with the government using the global price trend as a key determinant of MSPs (Acharya *et al.*, 2012).

As noted, farmers benefit from cereal prices that appear globally competitive but do not experience the volatility of global prices. The two policies—trade and MSP-driven storage (discussed later)—are inconsistent, however, in the sense that the restrictive trade policy pushes prices down (favoring consumers), while the MSP-based storage policy effectively creates a floor price (favoring farmers). Despite prices being competitive, produce cannot find its way out to external markets, so national cereal stocks are ballooning, because the government is obligated to buy whatever farmers have to offer—at least in the traditional, politically influential grain-basket states. As might be expected, bulging food stocks entail a significant budgetary cost for the government (GOI 2013a). This experience is not unique to India; the United States, European Union, and Australia have faced identical situations. In those instances, governments with open-ended public procurement systems and large food stocks subsequently either abandoned their programs or adopted alternative mechanisms with significant added costs to reduce the pressure to buy (such as acreage set-aside schemes). Finding viable and more cost-effective options for managing food grains is clearly a priority. Such analysis is beyond the scope of this study, but it is the subject of a separate ongoing technical study (Gouel, Gautam and Martin 2014).

Figure 12.6

Relationship between Domestic and External Wheat Prices in Surplus Producing Areas, 2005 ₹/MT (first panel) and Distortion in Agricultural Incentives (second panel)

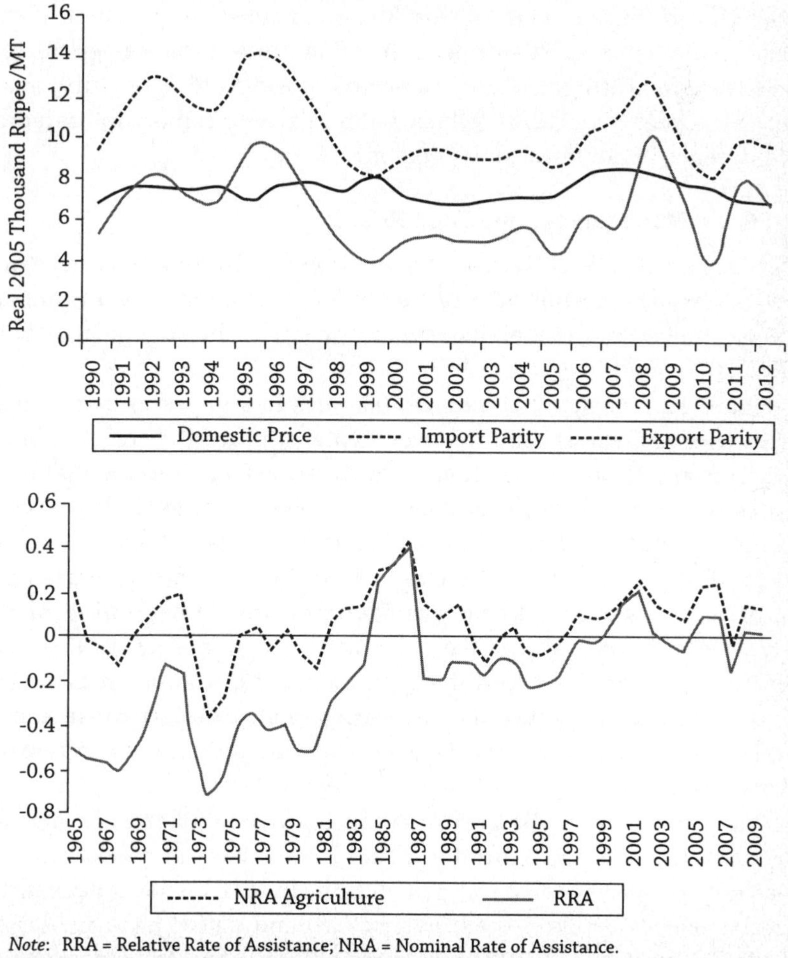

Note: RRA = Relative Rate of Assistance; NRA = Nominal Rate of Assistance.

Source: Authors, using Anderson and Nelgen (2012) database.

More good news for farmers comes with the shift away from a bias against agriculture (implicit tax) in domestic incentives toward a more supportive regime, as indicated by the trend in the Relative Rate of Assistance to agriculture (Figure 12.6, second panel) (Pursell, Gulati and Gupta 2009, Anderson and Nelgen 2012). The implicit taxation of agriculture observed in the 1970s–90s has steadily improved to a more neutral and often more favorable (subsidy) regime in the 2000s. Other than the explicit output price policy, the farmers are also benefiting more significantly through input subsidies and other forms of support, as reflected in the positive and rising Nominal Rate Assistance (NRA) for agriculture since the late 1990s. The gross subsidy equivalent of this assistance amounts to 30–40 per cent of the total value of agricultural production, indicating the significance of subsidies to agriculture apart from the border distortions (which seem relatively minor) indicated by the difference in domestic and global prices.

Food Grain Management and Food Prices

In principle, stock operations should be an infra-marginal transfer; as such, they should not be a cause for food price increase. In practice in India, however, stock-management appears to be suboptimal (Basu 2011).[8]

Figure 12.7 depicts net exports (exports less imports) of the main cereals (rice and wheat) and net procurement (procurement less offtake by various programs such as the Public Distribution System). The figure also shows the extent to which food prices (Food Articles Index) deviate from the overall Wholesale Price (All Commodities) Index. Net exports and food prices show no obvious correlation, but net procurement and price changes increasingly appear to coincide beginning in the early 1990s. Simple statistical tests confirm that after 1995, stock operations are correlated with food prices (the association with exports is not statistically significant), suggesting that procurement in excess of releases and sales is diverting grain from the market to already overflowing silos.[9]

The impact of public grain management operations can also be gauged by the sheer magnitude of the current level of stocks and the share of procurement in total production. In 2013, stocks peaked (in June) at over 77 million tons, almost two and half times the highest established norm of 32 million tons (for midyear). As a share of

Figure 12.7

Cereal Trade, Procurement, and Food Price Index, 1988–2012

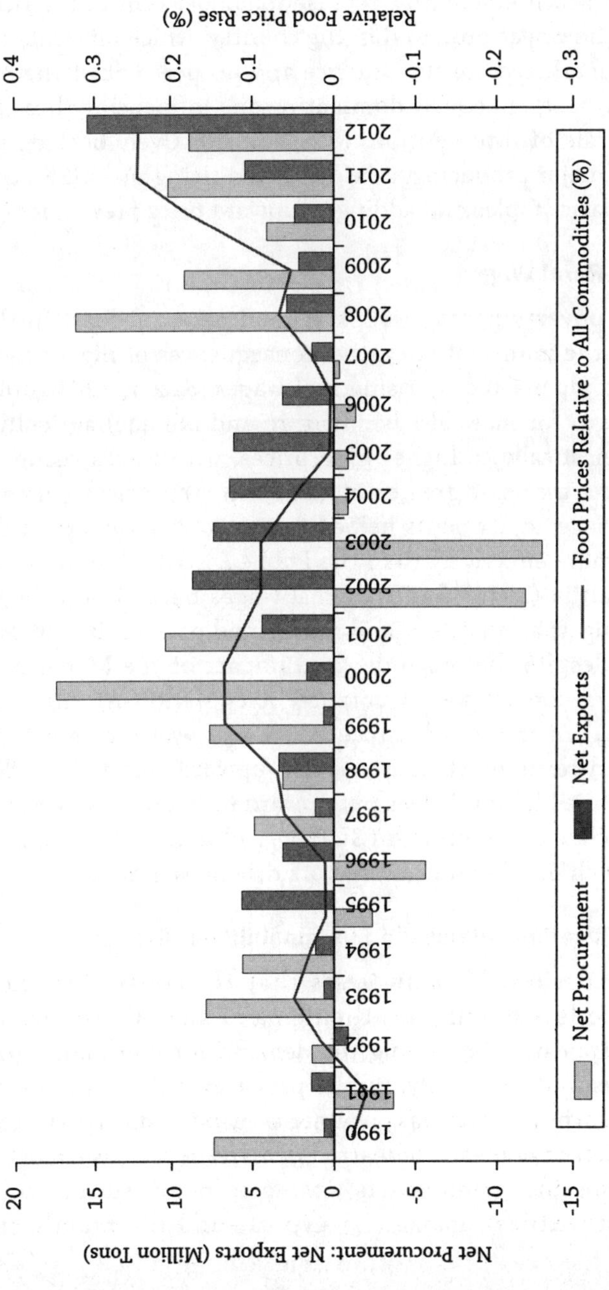

Source: Authors, using DES, MOA, and UN COMTRADE data.

production, government procurement has increased steadily over time. Government procurement now represents 32 per cent of the rice and 46 per cent of the wheat produced in the country, which amounts to 42 per cent of the marketed surplus for rice and 66 per cent of the marketed surplus for wheat, effectively dominating and influencing these markets. Given the scale of intervention, MSP has effectively become the floor price in the major producing areas, with the rising real MSP pushing up the cost of basic staples and adding to upward price pressures.

Rising Real Rural Wages

From a poverty perspective, the good news (at least in the short run) is that the immediate negative consequences of higher food prices have been compensated by rising real wages. Jacoby (2013) finds that nominal wages for manual labor (within and outside) agriculture have responded elastically to higher food prices, with wages rising faster in rural districts that saw greater increases in crop prices between 2004 and 2009. Wage adjustments helped to protect the welfare of the poor, apparently more effectively than the Public Distribution System. Gulati, Jain, and Saltija (2013) find that real wages have risen over the long term, growing at a consistent and more rapid pace in the 1990s than in the 2000s, despite the much-debated impact of the Mahatma Gandhi National Rural Employment Guarantee Act (MNREGA). After falling in the early part of the decade since 2000, real wages rose sharply after 2006/07 and resumed their long-term upward trend. The study also finds that while MNREGA does put upward pressure on wages, the "pull" factors associated with growth (GDP, agricultural GDP, or construction-GDP) are much more significant factors driving wages.10

Persistent Questions about the Sustainability of Growth

The discussion above suggests that the constraints to growth appear to be less binding on the demand side. Consumer incomes and habits appear to be driving the demand for highvalue agricultural commodities and, ironically, public procurement maintains a steady source of absorption (even as consumer demand is shrinking) for cereals. A combination of domestic industrial demand as well as export demand has driven specific "green shoots" in the economy, such as cotton (for exports and textiles), maize (for exports and the rapidly emerging domestic poultry industry), and soybeans (for exports of soy de-oiled cake as animal feed).

These developments aside, the overall production structure of the sector has changed relatively slowly, with the main cereals (rice and wheat) continuing to dominate the area allocation. The slow transformation, even in the face of strong growth in demand (for example, for horticultural commodities), reflects the incentives facing farmers. The price policy, specifically the MSPs for rice and wheat, has been highly successful, inducing a supply response for cereals by keeping prices high, while trade and storage policies have been equally successful in stabilising prices (at least in the major grain-basket areas for these crops). The resulting low risk-return ratio for cereals creates strong incentives for farmers to emphasise cereals in their crop portfolios—as reflected in area allocation—rather than venturing into crops that offer relatively higher returns but also face relatively greater market price risks.

Rising real prices are good news for farmers (who are net-sellers of food) and rising real wages for those engaged in wage labor (on and off the farm), but both trends have implications for the sustainability of the ensuing growth. The critical question is whether the changed incentives afforded by rising real output prices are accompanied by growth in agricultural productivity. Rising real wages have potential implications for employment both on and off the farm, as they are likely to induce greater mechanisation on the farm and more capital intensity off the farm. Understanding developments in the underlying productivity (total as well as factor) is important to assess whether they are underpinned by a sustainable, virtuous circle of growth—as the next chapters will attempt to discern.

Notes

1. For technical background and discussions of some contemporary issues in Indian agriculture, see GOI (2007, 2012); Dev (2008); Gulati and Ganguly (2010); Kotwal, Ramaswamy, and Wadwha (2011); Ferroni (2013); and Chand and Bajar (2012).
2. See Deaton and Dreze (2010); Gaiha *et al.* (2012).
3. Using a quadratic AIDS demand model, which allows a nonlinear expenditure effect on demand, Ganesh-Kumar *et al.* (2012) estimate expenditure elasticity for rice, wheat, and pulses to be negative, while they are positive for other commodities and greater than 1 for livestock products (eggs, chicken, meat, and fish). Similar estimates were obtained by Kumar *et al.* (2011).
4. The debate continues on the level and trends in calorie consumption in India.

5. Using 2003-04 data, Rawal (2008) estimated 42 per cent of rural households to be landless (that is, they own no land other than the homestead).
6. Gaiha *et al.* (2012), using NSS data, find price effects to have weakened over time from 1993-94 to 2009-10, but the negative elasticities remain significant.
7. On the import side, oilseeds and pulses are major imports, which are likely transmitting global prices to domestic prices for these commodities.
8. The government is obligated to buy at the MSP. Procurement remains biased in favor of the traditional "grain baskets" in the country, but there is no defined, rules-based "release" policy, effectively making it very inefficient and cumbersome to release stocks when necessary—whether to release excessive stocks or to moderate rising prices, as the case may be.
9. Other than the large exports in 2012, when the most recent ban was lifted, notable exports were in the early 2000s when the previous ban (1996–2000) was lifted. Those exports were triggered by subsidised stock releases (Below Poverty Line prices) for direct exports (Ganesh-Kumar *et al.*, 2010). The situation in the early 2000s was also an outcome of excessive stock accumulation during the previous ban of 1996–2000. Net procurement, on the other hand, was lowest in 2002/03 owing to the severe drought at the time (though stocks continued to be released for exports).
10. Gulati, Jain, and Saltija (2013) find that MNREGA does have a significant impact on wages, but the broader growth "pull" factors are 4–6 times more effective in raising incomes.

13

S. MAHENDRA DEV and N. CHANDRASEKHARA RAO

Agricultural Price Policy, Farm Profitability and Food Security

AGRICULTURAL price policy plays an important role in achieving growth and equity in the Indian economy in general, and the agriculture sector in particular. The major underlying objective of the Indian government's price policy is to protect both producers and consumers. Achieving food security at both the national and household levels is one of the major challenges in India today. Currently, the food security system and price policy basically consist of three instruments: procurement prices/minimum support prices (MSPs), buffer stocks and public distribution system (PDS). Agricultural price policy is one of the important instruments in achieving food security by improving production, employment and incomes of the farmers. There is a need to provide remunerative prices for farmers in order to maintain food security and increase the incomes of farmers. There has been a debate on price *versus* non-price factors in the literature. However, a review of literature shows that they are complements rather than substitutes (Dev and Ranade, 1998; Rao, 2004; 2006; Schiff and Montenegro, 1997).

In the post-reform period, it was viewed that reforms in non-agriculture would shift the terms of trade (ToT) in favour of agriculture and lead to enhancement of private sector investment, which, in turn, would raise growth in agriculture (Singh, 1995). The favourable ToT in agriculture have had some impact on agriculture in the post-reform period as the periods of improving ToT like in the early 1990s and more recently after 2004 onwards, witnessed a robust growth in agricultural production in general, and in food grains in particular (Dev, 2009). However, the slackening of the efforts in non-price factors has affected the growth of production in the recent period [Government of India (GoI), 2008].

Food inflation of around 18-19 per cent in 2009 is a concern for the poor and vulnerable. Several factors such as shortages in domestic supplies due to a poor monsoon in 2009, the rise in international prices, shortages in global supplies mainly due to diversion of significant food grains to biofuels, increase in demand due to higher growth, implementation of the National Rural Employment Guarantee Act (NREGA) and the loan waiver scheme, inefficiencies in the marketing system, speculation, etc., have been responsible for the price rise in cereals, pulses, sugar, fruits and vegetables, milk, etc. An increase in domestic supplies of agricultural production is important to provide food to the poor and others at reasonable prices. An increase in supplies is also necessary for the success of the PDS, which is supposed to be an important instrument for food security at the household level. Prices and supply-side non-price factors can enhance yields and provide higher incomes for the farmers apart from providing food security for the poor.

Agricultural price policy has come under serious attack in recent years for recommending higher support prices than warranted by the costs of production (CoP) and supposed distortion of the market, leading to food deprivation. It is also blamed frequently for the spikes in prices of food items that reached their peaks in 2009. Rice and wheat are the most state-protected crops and the millions of farmers are dependent on incomes from these crops, grown in an area of nearly 75 million ha or more than 40 per cent of the gross sown area. An analysis of costs and returns in these crops gives some idea about the profitability of Indian agriculture and provides insights into the working of price policy.

Against this background, the overall objective of this paper is to examine the effectiveness of price policy in helping farmers get sufficient profits to promote investment, technology and productivity, thereby to the food security of the country. The specific objectives are to find out the trends in the movements of costs, prices and returns in rice[1] and wheat farming to throw light on the impact of price policy on the profitability of farming in two of the most cultivated and consumed food crops in the country. It also tries to bring out the causes that necessitated the recent increases in support prices and their relation to food security of the country.

The data generated under the cost of cultivation scheme (CS) of the Directorate of Economics and Statistics, Ministry of Agriculture, are used for the analysis in this paper. The data, collected annually under this scheme, cover all the major crops. This mine of data is largely unexplored for policy relevant research and encompasses 9,000 farmers every year. These data help in analysing the economics of cultivation of different crops as well as to see the effectiveness of macro policies like price policy (Sen and Bhatia, 2004; Raghavan 2008). The costs and returns are calculated for all-India using these data to see the emerging trends in profitability. The weights based on area and productions of respective crops are developed to combine the data from states. We have used the area-based weights for all the variables except the CoP. The growth rates used are based on semi-log trend and deflation is done using consumer price indices (CPIs) for agricultural labourers of individual states. The study analyses the data for rice and wheat for a period of more than 25 years from 1981 to 2007-08 for all major growing states. However, 2006-07 is the last year for which the data for different states are available for rice and 2007-08 for wheat. The study is divided into two periods, roughly synchronising with the pre-liberalisation and post-liberalisation eras. The first period starts with 1981 and ends with 1992-93 and the second period covers the years from 1994-95 to 2007-08.[2] The costs and other data under the CS data are comparable over time except for a minor change in the valuation of family labour. Since 1991, family labour is now valued at casual labour wages and not those of attached labour. Nevertheless, this does not alter the overall conclusions of the paper.

The rest of the paper is structured into six sections. The first section presents the costs in cultivation and production of rice and wheat, while the second section gives the movements of MSPs and prices realised. The third section examines the relationship among the CoP, support prices, prices realised and wholesale prices. The fourth section examines the trends in returns at all-India and across different states and the fifth section brings together all these threads to identify the causes for higher support prices in recent years. The sixth section provides concluding observations.

Trends in Costs and Yields

The trends in C2 cost of cultivation (CoC) per hectare and C2 CoP per quintal and A2 CoC for the period 1981-82 to 2007-08 for rice and wheat crops are examined here. The A2 (paid out costs) include the value of hired labour (human, animal, machinery), value of seed (both farm produced and purchased), value of insecticides and pesticides, value of manure (owned and purchased), value of fertiliser, depreciation on implements and farm buildings, irrigation charges, land revenue, cesses and other taxes, interest on working capital and also miscellaneous expenses (artisans, etc.,) and rent for leased-in land. The C2 costs include paid out costs plus imputed value of family labour, rental value of owned land and interest on value of owned fixed capital assets. There have been debates that rice should be given an MSP as similar to wheat as the costs of both the crops are similar. We examine this issue here by looking at the trends in ratio of rice costs to wheat costs. The total CoP per unit of rice and wheat, which include imputed values of land, labour and capital, shown in Table 13.1, reveal that the unit costs of the former are somewhat lower than those of the latter. However, the situation seems to have changed after 1994-95 and there are several years in which the paddy CoP per unit exceeded that of wheat. This was particularly noticeable after 1999-2000.

The ratio of paddy CoP to that of wheat is lower than the ratio of their CoC because of the higher yields in paddy. The ratio of A2 CoC of rice to wheat was higher than the corresponding ratio of C2 CoC as shown in Table 13.1. This may be because of the lower imputed values of land, labour and capital in case of paddy compared to wheat. The conclusion is that the costs of rice have been similar to those of wheat since the mid-1990s. The ratio came down to 0.90 and 0.91 in the case of CoP in the years 2005-06 and 2006-07. On the whole, the demand that the MSP of rice should be closer or slightly below than wheat, based on the cost data, may need a sympathetic hearing. However, it may be noted that although the cost is a major one, it is not the only one factor in determining MSP.

The growth rates in the real CoP declined in the background of a robust gain in per hectare yields in the first period, while these costs went up in real terms in the second period (Table 13.2). As can be seen from the table, the growth rate in yields (per annum) came down from 2.67 per cent to 0.86 per cent in rice and from 2.54 per cent to 0.52 per cent in wheat in the first and second periods, respectively. The growth in yield outstripped the growth in CoC during the 1980s enabling the cost per quintal to go down. The reverse can be noticed for the later period. Another important point to be noted is that the CoC has grown at a lower rate in the recent period indicating that the lower profitability might have discouraged farmers to invest in higher use of inputs and technology.

Table 13.1

Different Costs in the Production of Rice and Wheat at All-India Level

Years	Rice (₹)			Wheat (₹)			Ratio of Paddy Cost to Wheat Cost		
	CoP/ Quintal	CoC/ Hectare	A2 CoC/ Hectare	CoP/ Quintal	CoC/ Hectare	A2 CoC/ Hectare	CoP/ Quintal	CoC/ Hectare	A2 CoC/ Hectare
1981-82	99	2,892	1,705	122	3,260	1,946	81	89	88
1982-83	116	2,824	1,680	125	3,475	2,065	93	81	81
1983-84	108	3,351	1,959	135	3,462	2,039	80	97	96
1984-85	113	3,582	2,107	133	3,752	2,121	85	95	99
1985-86	118	3,718	1,966	123	3,959	2,335	96	94	84
1986-87	124	3,717	2,240	132	4,058	2,391	94	92	94
1987-88	144	4,653	2,828	146	4,826	2,777	99	96	102
1988-89	147	5,704	3,636	168	5,636	3,292	87	101	110
1989-90	172	6,340	3,539	172	5,769	3,361	100	110	105
1990-91	185	6,526	3,734	197	6,872	3,800	94	95	98
1991-92	218	7,884	4,161	204	7,693	4,303	106	102	97
1992-93	238	7,684	3,957	238	8,808	4,823	100	87	82
1994-95	279	11,212	6,369	294	10,990	5,446	95	102	117
1995-96	306	11,207	6,324	318	11,681	6,100	96	96	104
1996-97	338	12,651	6,703	361	13,760	6,927	94	92	97
1997-98	370	13,581	7,246	381	13,236	6,853	97	103	106
1998-99	398	15,495	8,710	383	14,316	7,268	104	108	120
1999-2000	442	16,978	9,275	415	16,459	8,038	106	103	115
2000-01	448	17,365	9,798	450	17,132	8,751	99	101	112
2001-02	469	18,655	10,619	466	17,279	9,058	101	108	117
2002-03	530	19,193	10,949	499	18,837	10,027	106	102	109
2003-04	483	19,583	10,988	498	18,925	10,195	97	103	108
2004-05	529	20,670	11,776	537	19,810	10,975	98	104	107
2005-06	529	21,182	11,845	592	21,847	11,584	89	97	102
2006-07	546	22,059	12,543	586	23,847	12,681	93	93	99
2007-08	NA	NA	NA	617	25,575	13,166	-	-	-

Source: Estimated by the authors based on Commission for Agricultural Costs and Prices (CACP) data at current prices.

Table 13.2

Trend Growth Rates of Different Costs and Yields in Rice and Wheat All-India

Period	*Rice*			*Wheat*			
	Madhya Pradesh	*Punjab*	*All-India*	*Haryana*	*Madhya Pradesh*	*Punjab*	*All-India*
CoP (Constant Prices)							
1981-82 to 1992-93	2.95	-1.52	-0.13	-6.17	1.77	-2.58	-1.96
1994-95 to 2006-07	3.31	-0.50	1.46	2.08	0.97	0.65	1.41
CoC (Constant Prices)							
1981-82 to 1992-93	4.14	-1.55	2.32	-0.56	3.74	0.55	1.36
1994-95 to 2006-07	-0.51	2.18	1.92	2.21	2.94	1.35	1.96
A2 CoC (Constant Prices)							
1981-82 to 1992-93	4.62	-3.31	3.40	-1.29	4.31	-0.22	0.72
1994-95 to 2006-07	-0.33	2.23	2.15	3.01	2.74	1.22	2.45
Yield (Qtls/ha)							
1981-82 to 1992-93	1.13	-0.10	2.67	3.73	2.46	2.16	2.54
1994-95 to 2006-07	-3.63	2.76	0.86	0.21	2.02	0.87	0.52

Note: The second period extends up to 2007-08 for wheat.

Source: As in Table 13.1.

Which states are relatively efficient in CoP relative to all-India average? The states of Himachal Pradesh (HP), Andhra Pradesh (AP) and Punjab are the efficient producers of rice in the triennium ending 2007 (Table 13.3). The farmers of AP and Punjab could produce a quintal of rice at 27 per cent and 23 per cent lower cost respectively than that of the all-India average and they have improved the efficiency of production by reducing the CoP relative to all-India average during the study period. The obverse is true in case of Assam and Madhya Pradesh (MP) produces rice at 30 per cent higher costs. Also, farmers from Assam and Tamil Nadu are expensive in rice production, which may be impinging seriously on their profitability. Rajasthan, Punjab and Haryana are the efficient producers compared to all-India average for wheat. Here, Jharkhand, West Bengal and Chhattisgarh produce wheat at whopping 87 per cent, 57 per cent and 49 per cent respectively higher cost than all-India.

Trends in MSPs and Prices Realised by Farmers

In this section, we examine the trends in MSPs and the prices realised by farmers. The CACP reports provide implicit prices which are derived from the CS data for different states. Implicit price is the ratio of value of the output of main product per hectare to the yield per hectare. It is known the CoP given by the CS are the reported data by the farmers. In other words, the implicit prices reflect the prices realised by the farmers.

Table 13.3

CoP of Different States in Relation to All-India Average for Rice and Wheat (per quintal, for different triennium)

State	*Rice (%)*			*Wheat (%)*		
	TE 1984-85	*TE 1996-97*	*TE 1984-85*	*TE 2006-07*	*TE 1996-97*	*TE 2007-08*
Andhra Pradesh	93	92	73	-	-	-
Assam	88	114	126	-	-	-
Bihar	110	109	96	-	114	102
Chhattisgarh	-	-	94	-	-	149
Gujarat	-	-	-	-	133	100
Himachal Pradesh	102	-	50	121	130	109
Haryana	111	124	106	103	78	84
Jharkhand	-	-	-	-	-	187
Kerala	-	-	119	-	-	-
Karnataka	92	-	105	-	-	-
Madhya Pradesh	102	109	138	95	122	116
Odisha	84	96	104	-	-	-
Punjab	105	96	77	98	92	84
Rajasthan	-	-	-	104	85	77
Tamil Nadu	-	-	128	-	-	-
Uttar Pradesh	102	80	96	98	86	87
Uttarakhand	-	-	-	-	-	103
West Bengal	119	117	121	-	-	157
All India	100	100	100	100	100	100

Source: As in Table 13.1.

Changes in MSP

The changes in MSP show that the increase in rice and wheat prices are the highest during the period 2000-01 to 2009-10 as compared to those of earlier decades (Table 13.4). The rice prices for the common variety increased from ₹ 510 to ₹ 1,000 (while the wheat prices rose from ₹ 580 to ₹ 1,080 during this period. In the 1990s, the rate of increase in

Table 13.4

Trend Growth Rates (% Per Year) in MSPs for Rice and Wheat in Real Terms

Period	*Rice*	*Wheat*
1981-82 to 1990-91	-0.95	-2.22
1990-91 to 2000-01	0.99	2.23
2000-01 to 2009-10	1.81	1.30

Source: As in Table 12.1.

MSP of rice was lower than that of wheat. The annual changes reveal that the MSP increased significantly in the first few years after the reforms were introduced. Again it rose substantially during 2006-07 to 2009-10. Rice and wheat prices have risen respectively by 62 per cent and 54 per cent during this period. The intercrop price parity between rice and wheat shows that the ratio of paddy to wheat increased from 0.89 in 1981-82 to around 1.0 in 1989-90 (Table 13.5). It ranged between 0.94 and 1.04 during 1989-90 to 1996-97. The ratio declined significantly in

Table 13.5

Intercrop Price Parity of MSP

Year	*Common Paddy/Wheat*	*Grade A Paddy/Wheat*	*Year*	*Common Paddy/Wheat*	*Grade A Paddy/Wheat*
1981-82	0.89	na	1996-97	1.00	1.04
1982-83	0.86	na	1997-98	0.87	0.94
1983-84	0.87	na	1998-99	0.86	0.92
1984-85	0.90	na	1999-2000	0.89	0.95
1985-86	0.90	na	2000-01	0.88	0.93
1986-87	0.90	0.93	2001-02	0.87	0.92
1987-88	0.90	0.93	2002-03	0.89	0.94
1988-89	0.93	0.98	2003-04	0.89	0.94
1989-90	1.01	1.07	2004-05	0.89	0.94
1990-91	0.95	1.00	2005-06	0.89	0.94
1991-92	1.04	1.09	2006-07	0.89	0.93
1992-93	0.98	1.02	2007-08	0.88	0.91
1993-94	0.94	1.00	2008-09	0.90	0.93
1994-95	0.97	1.03	2009-10	0.93	0.95
1995-96	1.00	1.04			

Note: MSP includes bonus.

Source: As in Table 12.1.

1997-98 because of a sharp rise in MSP for wheat. The MSP of wheat increased by 25 per cent compared to 12.7 per cent rise for rice in that year. This increase in the form of bonus for wheat distorted the intercrop price parity. It was below 0.90 from 1997-98 to 2007-08. Only in the last two years had the ratio reached 0.90 and beyond. Similar trends can be seen for the ratio of grade A paddy to wheat.

Trends in Prices Realised by Farmers

Farmers are more concerned with the prices they realise rather than the MSP *per se*. The ratio of price realised to MSP was higher than 1.0 for rice and wheat almost during the entire period (Table 13.6). Only in the case of rice, it was lower than 1.0 during 2000-01 to 2003-04. In the subsequent years, the ratio was closer to one. On the other hand, the prices realised by farmers were more than MSP for wheat in all the years (except 2001-02) during the period 1981-82 to 2007-08.

Growth rates of prices realised in real terms show that rice prices had a declining trend in both periods (Table 13.7), while wheat prices showed a positive growth rate and increased in the second period. In other words, prices realised by wheat farmers have been higher and increasing as compared to that of rice farmers.

Regional Disparities in Price Realisation

There are significant regional disparities when we consider the ratio of price realised to MSP. There was a decline in the ratio in the triennium ending 2006-07 at the all-India level and in several states excluding Punjab, HP and Haryana for rice. It was much lower in states like Odisha, Bihar, Assam, West Bengal and UP (Table 13.8). In the case of Haryana, the ratio was higher by 32 per cent in the same triennium, which means that the realised price is 32 per cent higher than respective support price. The ratio for wheat was much higher than for rice. For example, the realised price for wheat was 22 per cent higher as compared to MSP at all-India level in the TE 2007-08. The higher ratio for wheat is true for all the reported states.

Relationship between Costs, Prices Realised and MSP

In this section, we compare the trends in costs, realised prices, MSP and wholesale prices. The trends in CoP and price realised for rice show that the latter moved faster than the former till around 2000-01 (Figure

13.1). Later the prices realised were almost similar to the CoP without any margin except in 2006-07. On the other hand, the prices realised by farmers for wheat have always been higher than the CoP (Figure 13.2). Particularly, the margins have been higher since the mid-1990s and more so in the last three years of the study, i.e., 2005-06 to 2007-08.

Table 13.6

Price Realised in Relation to MSP in Rice and Wheat

Years	*Price Realisd (₹/Quintal)*		*Ratio of Price Realised to MSP*	
	Rice	*Wheat*	*Rice*	*Wheat*
1981-82	121	151	1.05	1.16
1982-83	151	165	1.24	1.16
1983-84	151	160	1.14	1.06
1984-85	145	165	1.06	1.09
1985-86	163	173	1.15	1.10
1986-87	162	175	1.11	1.08
1987-88	191	202	1.27	1.22
1988-89	199	214	1.24	1.24
1989-90	211	221	1.14	1.21
1990-91	221	257	1.08	1.20
1991-92	283	332	1.20	1.48
1992-93	289	345	1.07	1.25
1994-95	363	388	1.07	1.11
1995-96	385	413	1.07	1.15
1996-97	416	531	1.09	1.40
1997-98	429	517	1.03	1.09
1998-99	494	563	1.12	1.10
1999-2000	516	612	1.05	1.11
2000-01	477	586	0.94	1.01
2001-02	484	589	0.91	0.97
2002-03	511	625	0.93	1.01
2003-04	516	626	0.94	1.01
2004-05	557	648	0.99	1.03
2005-06	561	761	0.98	1.19
2006-07	609	898	0.98	1.28
2007-08	na	1,018	na	1.20

Note: na: not available.

Source: See Table 13.1.

Table 13.7

Trend Growth Rates of Price Realised in Rice and Wheat

(in % per year)

Period	Rice			Wheat			
	Madhya Pradesh	Punjab	All India	Haryana	Madhya Pradesh	Punjab	All India
1981-82 to 1992-93	1.04	-0.92	-0.64	-1.01	-0.07	-1.41	-0.51
1994-95 to 2006-07	0.88	0.50	-0.35	1.74	2.36	1.71	1.71

Notes: The growth rates for wheat in case of the second and third periods go up to 2007-08.

Source: See Table 13.1.

Table 13.8

Price Realised Relative to MSP in Rice and Wheat in Different States (%)

State	Rice			Wheat		
	TE 1984-85	TE 1996-97	TE 1984-85	TE 2006-07	TE 1996-97	TE 2007-08
Andhra Pradesh	107	110	104	-	-	-
Assam	103	105	94	-	-	-
Bihar	147	109	86	-	137	121
Chhattisgarh	-	-	102	-	-	138
Gujarat	-	-	-	-	156	124
Himachal Pradesh	110	-	127	124	127	121
Haryana	109	122	132	105	111	116
Jharkhand	-	-	-	-	-	-
Kerala	-	-	122	-	-	123
Karnataka	124	-	110	-	-	-
Madhya Pradesh	110	110	114	123	135	140
Odisha	116	101	85	-	-	-
Punjab	106	106	107	105	111	116
Rajasthan	-	-	-	119	132	127
Tamil Nadu	-	-	101	-	-	-
Uttar Pradesh	103	105	98	106	121	118
Uttarakhand	-	-	-	-	-	112
West Bengal	127	112	95	-	-	109
All India	115	108	99	110	122	122

Source: See Table 13.1.

Figure 13.1

CoP and Price Realised in Rice during 1981-82 to 2006-07
(₹ at current prices)

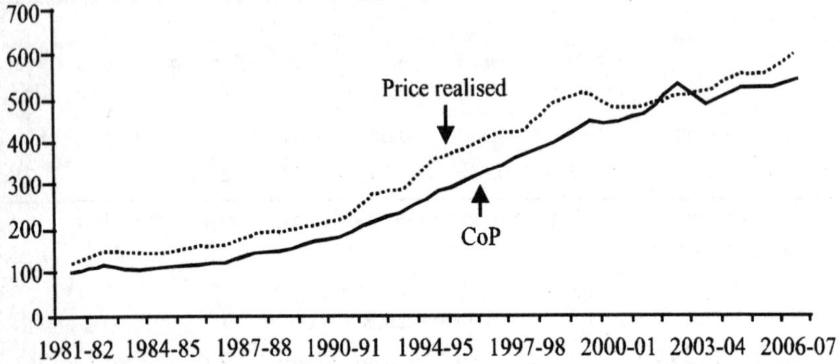

Source: Calculated using data from CACP reports.

Figure 13.2

CoP and Price Realised in Wheat during 1981 to 2006-07
(₹ at current prices)

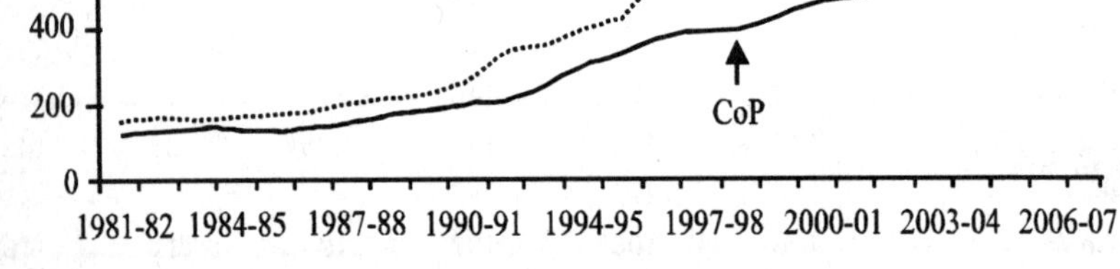

Source: Calculated using data from CACP reports.

Another issue is growth in CoP relative to the respective wholesale price indices (WPI). The WPI for rice increased from 100 in 1981-82 to 478.5 in 2006-07. The index of CoP shows that it was moving almost on par with the WPI till 2001-02. In the last five years of the study, i.e., 2002-03 to 2006-07, the CoP has risen faster than WPI (Figure 13.3). Here rice farmers were in difficult situation in terms of CoP compared to

WPI. The index of MSP of rice increased from 100 in 1981-82 to 539.1 in 2006-07. The growth in MSP is almost similar to that in CoP till 2001-02 after which spikes in CoP are much higher relative to the MSP (Figure 13.3). As shown later, the increase in MSP in 2007-08 and 2008-09 was much higher than costs and WPI.

Figure 13.3

Indices of CoP, MSP and WPI in Rice

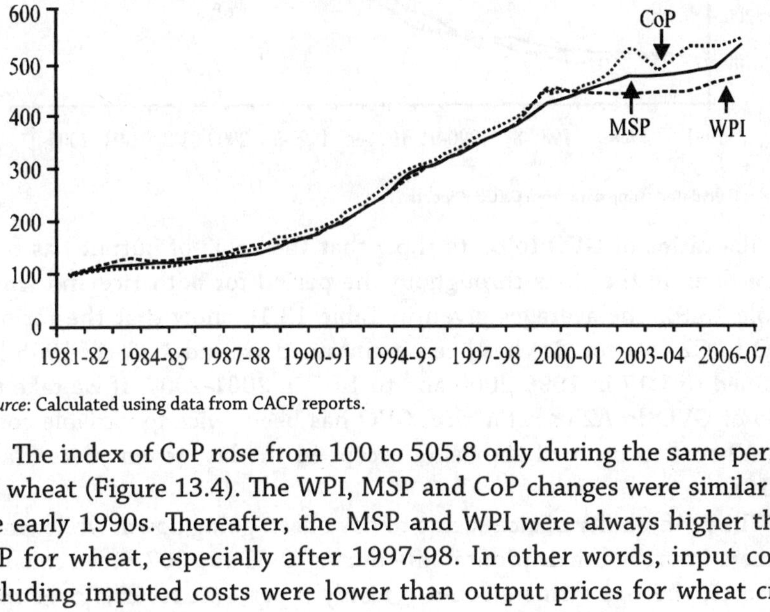

Source: Calculated using data from CACP reports.

The index of CoP rose from 100 to 505.8 only during the same period for wheat (Figure 13.4). The WPI, MSP and CoP changes were similar till the early 1990s. Thereafter, the MSP and WPI were always higher than CoP for wheat, especially after 1997-98. In other words, input costs including imputed costs were lower than output prices for wheat crop and the margins were higher for wheat as compared to rice.

Returns to Farming

Ultimately, one has to look at the trends in profitability in order to examine the viability of farming. For this purpose, we have examined the trends in net income (gross value of output (GVO)-cost C2) and farm business income (GVO-cost A2). We also looked at trends in the ratio of GVO to C2 cost, the ratio of GVO to A2 cost, which gives the level of margin over total costs and variable costs, respectively.

Figure 13.4

Indices of CoP, MSP and WPI in Wheat

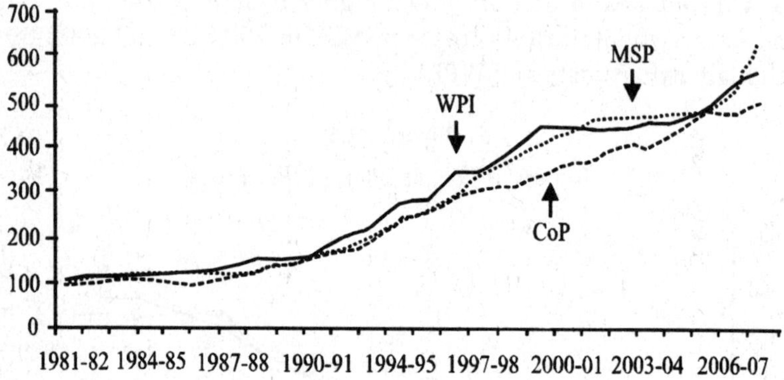

Source: Calculated using data from CACP Reports.

The ratios of GVO to costs show that the value of output has been more than all the costs throughout the period for both rice and wheat (Table 13.9). The averages given in Table 13.10 show that the ratio of GVO to C2 cost for rice has been maintained around 1.25 till 1995 but declined to 1.17 in 1996-2000 and to 1.07 in 2001-2007. If we take the ratio of GVO to A2 cost for rice, GVO has been twice to variable costs, *viz*, A2 cost in most of the years except in the last seven years (Table 13.10).

The profitability of rice seems to have been going down, while wheat farmers improved their profitability during 1981 to 2007. If we consider C2 costs, the rice farmers could get only 9 per cent returns over their total CoP in the TE 2006-07, when the wheat farmers got 26 per cent net returns over costs (Table 13.9). Significantly, the wheat farmers reaped more than 50 per cent margin over total costs in 2007-08. Although their counterparts in rice cultivation could get 13 per cent margin in 2006-07 and probably slightly higher in the later years, it still is nowhere near that for wheat farmers.

In contrast to rice, the ratio of GVO to C2 cost for wheat increased over time. The ratio increased from 1.21 in 1981-1985 to 1.33 in 1996-2000. The ratio of GVO to A2 cost has also risen as compared to the early 1980s. This profitability ratio was around 2.6 in the triennium ending in 2007-08 (Table 13.10). It may be noted that this ratio for wheat was 2.41 and much higher than that of rice at around 1.9 in the TE in 2006-07.

Table 13.9

All-India Costs and Returns in Rice and Wheat per hectare in Nominal Terms

(in ₹)

Year	Rice				Wheat			
	NI (₹)	FBI (₹)	GVO/ CoC	GVO/ A2 CoC	NI (₹)	FBI (₹)	GVO/ CoC	GVO/ A2 CoC
1981-82	561	1,748	1.19	2.03	558	1,872	1.17	1.96
1982-83	626	1,770	1.22	2.05	828	2,238	1.24	2.08
1983-84	1,058	2,451	1.32	2.25	486	1,909	1.14	1.94
1984-85	898	2,373	1.25	2.13	714	2,173	1.19	2.11
1985-86	1,326	3,078	1.36	2.57	1,152	2,775	1.29	2.19
1986-87	1,049	2,526	1.28	2.13	1,044	2,711	1.26	2.13
1987-88	1,262	3,088	1.27	2.09	1,181	3,230	1.24	2.16
1988-89	1,838	3,906	1.32	2.07	942	3,286	1.17	2.00
1989-90	1,143	3,944	1.18	2.11	1,131	3,540	1.20	2.05
1990-91	1,137	3,929	1.17	2.05	1,400	4,472	1.20	2.18
1991-92	2,026	5,748	1.26	2.38	3,053	6,443	1.40	2.50
1992-93	1,643	5,370	1.21	2.36	2,869	6,854	1.33	2.42
1994-95	3,170	8,014	1.28	2.26	2,757	8,301	1.25	2.52
1995-96	2,686	7,569	1.24	2.20	2,622	8,203	1.22	2.34
1996-97	2,603	8,551	1.21	2.28	4,984	11,818	1.36	2.71
1997-98	1,985	8,320	1.15	2.15	3,876	10,260	1.29	2.50
1998-99	3,513	10,298	1.23	2.18	5,403	12,450	1.38	2.71
1999-2000	2,737	10,440	1.16	2.13	6,161	14,582	1.37	2.81
2000-01	1,389	8,957	1.08	1.91	4,312	12,692	1.25	2.45
2001-02	1,023	9,060	1.05	1.85	3,905	12,127	1.23	2.34
2002-03	-9.0	8,236	1.00	1.75	3,606	12,598	1.19	2.24
2003-04	1,661	10,256	1.08	1.93	3,919	12,801	1.21	2.24
2004-05	1,382	10,277	1.07	1.87	3,215	12,228	1.16	2.10
2005-06	1,561	10,897	1.07	1.92	4,656	15,086	1.21	2.29
2006-07	2,867	12,472	1.13	1.99	9,655	20,982	1.40	2.64
2007-08	na	na	na	na	13,244	25,590	1.52	2.94

Note: NI: net income; FBI: farm business income; FL: family labour.

Source: As in Table 13.1.

Table 13.10

Ratios of GVO to Costs (Averages)

Period	Rice		Wheat	
	GVO/C2 CoC	GVO/A2 CoC	GVO/C2 CoC	GVO/A2 CoC
1981-82 to 1985-86	1.27	2.21	1.21	2.06
1986-87 to 1990-91	1.24	2.09	1.21	2.10
1991-92 to 1995-96	1.25	2.30	1.30	2.45
1996-97 to 2000-01	1.17	2.13	1.33	2.64
2001-02 to 2006-07	1.07	1.89	1.23	2.31
1981-82 to 1992-93	1.25	2.19	1.24	2.14
1994-95 to 2006-07	1.13	2.03	1.29	2.49
1981-82 to 2006-07*	1.19	2.11	1.26	2.33

Note: * The ratios of GVO with C2 and A2 CoC for wheat are 1.27 and 2.40, respectively during 2001-2008.

Source: As in Table 13.1.

Profitability across States

The returns over C2 costs show that the states like Assam, Bihar, Karnataka, MP, Odisha, Tamil Nadu, UP, and West Bengal witnessed negative returns for rice in the latest triennium (Table 13.11). On the other hand, all states covered all costs for wheat except for Jharkhand and West Bengal. The profitability improved for rice in AP, HP, Haryana and Punjab during the study period, while it declined for other states. On the other hand, returns for wheat rose for all the states considered in the study.

However, all the states cover variable costs (A2) in rice and wheat with the exceptions being Uttarakhand for wheat (Table 13.12). The situation in Jharkhand is also not remunerative enough to the farming community of wheat. The returns over variable costs for rice are much higher for HP, Punjab, Haryana and Chhattisgarh than other states. The returns for wheat are more than twice over A2 costs for the major wheat producing states. Figures 13.5 and 13.6 show that the ratio of returns over total costs (C2) and variable costs were higher for wheat as compared to rice since the mid-1990s.

The higher profitability for wheat as compared to rice can also be seen in the growth rates of returns in constant prices (Table 13.13). Rice recorded positive and high growth rates in net income, farm business income and farm investment income in the first period (1981-82 to 1992-93). However, it showed a negative growth rate in all these returns in the second period (1994-95 to 2006-07).

Table 13.11

Ratio of Returns to Total Costs in Rice and Wheat in Different States

State	Rice			Wheat		
	TE 1984-85	TE 1996-97	TE 2006-07	TE 1984-85	TE 1996-97	TE 2006-07
Andhra Pradesh	1.48	1.59	1.72	-	-	-
Assam	1.3	1.06	0.83	-	-	-
Bihar	1.34	1.1	0.97	-	1.23	1.34
Chhattisgarh	-	-	1.15	-	-	1.1
Gujarat	-	-	-	-	1.41	1.58
Himachal Pradesh	1.21	-	1.44	1.14	1.01	1.12
Haryana	1.07	1.06	1.2	1.12	1.37	1.38
Jharkhand	-	-	-	-	-	0.8
Kerala	-	-	1.01	-	-	-
Karnataka	1.48	-	1.19	-	-	-
Madhya Pradesh	1.21	1.13	0.92	1.32	1.17	1.37
Odisha	1.27	1.18	0.93	-	-	-
Punjab	1.15	1.19	1.33	1.17	1.21	1.39
Rajasthan	-	-	-	1.3	1.48	1.59
Tamil Nadu	-	-	0.91	-	-	-
Uttar Pradesh	1.13	1.29	0.98	1.16	1.3	1.34
Uttarakhand	-	-	-	-	-	1.11
West Bengal	1.19	1.17	0.93	-	-	0.95
All India	1.26	1.24	1.09	1.19	1.28	1.38

Note: The total costs are represented by C2 CoC.

Source: As in Table 13.1.

The growth rates of rice in farm business income were similar to those of wheat in the first period. However, the major point of distress for paddy farmers is that the returns over paid-out costs also declined in the second period at 1.15 per cent per annum. On the other hand, the growth rates in profitability for wheat recorded positive growth rates of more than 2 per cent in both net income and farm business income in the second period also. In spite of similar growth rates for yields, the profitability for wheat is much higher than that of rice. This could be partly due to better realisation of prices for wheat. At the state level, the growth rates in returns for rice in Punjab rose in the second period, while MP showed negative returns in the same period. The growth in rice for Punjab has risen in spite of the decline in yields for the second period, and this may be because of the high level of yields even with some decline and higher price realisation relative to the support prices. In the case of wheat, the growth rates for MP increased, while those of Haryana declined in the second period. Although the growth rates in returns declined for wheat in Punjab, they were nearly 3 per cent per annum in farm business income and above 2 per cent for net income in the second period.

Table 13.12

Ratio of Returns to Variable Costs in Rice and Wheat in Different States

State	*Rice*			*Wheat*		
	TE 1984-85	*TE 1996-97*	*TE 2006-07*	*TE 1984-85*	*TE 1996-97*	*TE 2006-07*
Andhra Pradesh	1.67	1.95	2.04	-	-	-
Assam	3.06	2.64	1.93	-	-	-
Bihar	3.16	2.24	1.67	-	2.31	2.21
Chhattisgarh	-	-	2.37	-	-	1.85
Gujarat	-	-	-	-	2.48	2.62
Himachal Pradesh	2.43	-	3.84	3.62	2.8	2.67
Haryana	1.75	2.23	2.26	1.85	3.04	2.96
Jharkhand	-	-	-	-	-	1.1
Kerala	-	-	1.44	-	-	-
Karnataka	2.8	-	1.9	-	-	-
Madhya Pradesh	2.43	2.28	1.8	2.58	2.32	2.81
Odisha	2.21	2.24	1.77	-	-	-
Punjab	1.82	2.18	2.49	1.94	2.31	2.78
Rajasthan	-	-	-	2.41	3.06	3.23
Tamil Nadu	-	-	1.47	-	-	-
Uttar Pradesh	2.19	2.84	1.89	1.95	2.47	2.39
Uttarakhand	-	-	-	-	-	0.91
West Bengal	2.23	2.39	1.81	-	-	1.59
All India	2.14	2.25	1.93	2.04	2.52	2.62

Note: The variable costs are represented by A2 CoC.

Source: As in Table 13.1.

Figure 13.5

Ratio of Returns to Total Costs in Rice and Wheat

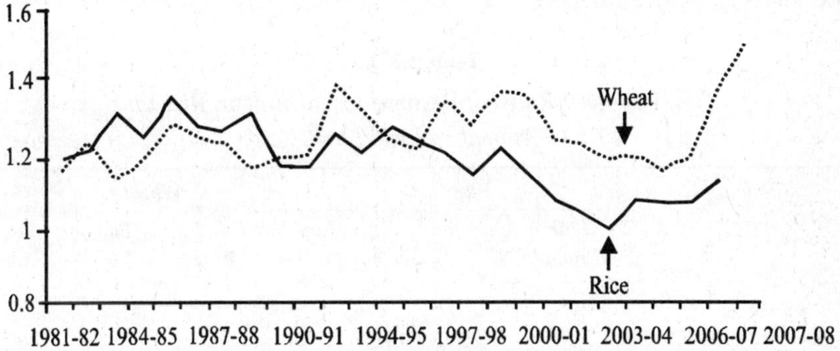

Source: As in Figure 13.1.

Figure 13.6

Ratio of Returns to Variable Costs in Rice and Wheat

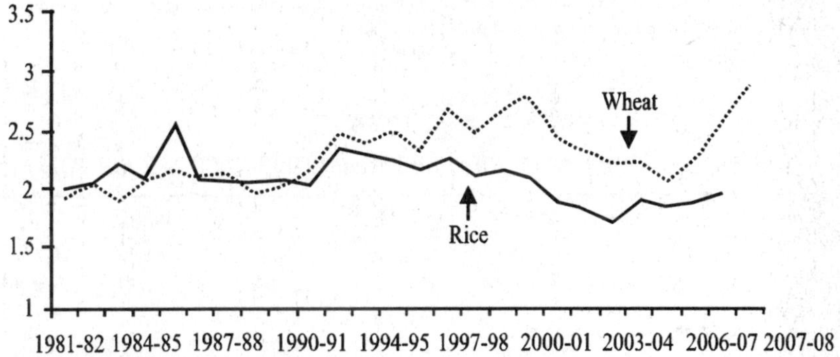

Source: As in Figure 13.1.

The data on costs and returns of crops from the cost of CS are available with a lag, and therefore, actual cost data for the years 2008-09 and 2009-10 are not available to compare with MSP data. Therefore, we have used the projected cost data which are used by CACP for recommending MSPs (Table 13.14). As can be seen from the table, the margin over cost declined over time for rice from 30.0 per cent in 1999-2000 to 7.6 per cent in 2005-06. But, the margin of MSP over cost for rice rose significantly from 14 per cent in 2006-07 to nearly 60 per cent in 2009-10. As compared to rice, the margins of MSP over C2 cost have been much higher for wheat except in 2009-10. The margin for wheat over cost was around 67 per cent in 2008-09. Therefore, it can be said that the recent increases in support prices have the effect of ameliorating the distress of rice farmers.

Table 13.13

Trend Growth Rates of Returns to Farming in Rice and Wheat in Real Terms

Period	Rice			Wheat			
	Madhya Pradesh	Punjab	All India	Haryana	Madhya Pradesh	Punjab	All India
Net income							
1981-82 to 1992-93	nc	2.06	1.00	17.01	-4.03	5.17	5.81
1994-95 to 2006-07	nc	7.15	-31.53	0.79	10.07	6.15	2.37
Farm business income							
1981-82 to 1992-93	1.06	0.71	2.56	6.96	0.93	3.59	3.67
1994-95 to 2006-07	-5.35	3.87	-1.15	1.30	5.06	3.14	2.05

Note: nc: Not calculated as the state witnessed negative returns during this period. The second period and the overall period go up to 2007-08 for wheat.

Source: See Table 13.1.

Table 13.14

Projected CoP and MSP: Rice and Wheat (1999-2000 to 2009-10)

Years	Rice			Wheat		
	Projected C2 Cost per qtl (in ₹)	MSP (in ₹)	MSP over Cost (%)	Projected C2 Cost per qtl (in ₹)	MSP (in ₹)	MSP over Cost (%)
1999-2000	400.6	520	29.8	415.9	550	32.2
2000-01	429.3	540	25.8	448.7	580	29.3
2001-02	471.7	560	18.7	478.9	610	27.3
2002-03	505.2	560	10.9	483.3	620	28.2
2003-04	525.2	580	10.5	496.8	630	27.0
2004-05	530.9	590	11.1	515.6	640	24.1
2005-06	557.6	600	7.6	541.5	700	29.3
2006-07	569.5	650	14.1	573.6	850	48.2
2007-08	595.0	775	30.3	624.5	1000	60.1
2008-09	619.0	930	50.2	648.6	1080	66.5
2009-10	644.9	1030	59.7	741.0*	1100	48.4

Note: * Refers to modified cost C2 including transportation, insurance premium and marketing charges.

Source: Various reports of CACP.

Increased Role of Price Policy

Agricultural price policy was earlier meant to mitigate the impact of any undue rises in prices on the vulnerable sections of the population. After the formation of the Agricultural Price Commission, it has always tried to maintain a balance between the interests of consumers and producers. Nevertheless, the limits of price policy in achieving these goals are recognised by the government and other non-price interventions are used primarily for the purpose. While a large network of the PDS ensures cheap food to the needy with appropriate levels of subsidy from time to time, many policy initiatives have been put in place to make farming profitable enough for farmers to invest sufficiently in technology for improving productivity per unit of land so that food security is not threatened. The policy aimed at encouraging higher production and that the resultant food produce should be available at lower prices. Both higher production and cheap food are considered necessary for food security. Thus, price policy remained subservient to the overall societal goal of poverty reduction on the whole until the new economic policies were introduced.

The higher emphasis and reliance on price policy in the 1990s altered the situation drastically,[3] as price interventions to the relative exclusion of non-price interventions marked the new regime as pointed out by Sen (2001). As a consequence, the earlier policy of 'low-input and low-output' prices shifted to 'high-input and high-output' prices (Acharya, 1997). On the other hand, public investments on irrigation, research, extension and other related infrastructure went down from 3.4 per cent of agricultural gross domestic product (GDP) in the early 1980s to 1.9 per cent in 2001-2003. Although private investments increased initially, it later stopped flowing due to the operation of complementarity between public and private investments, by the late 1990s. Technology development, dissemination and adoption received a major setback due to this.

As a result of this policy shift, growth rates in yields have gone down and eventually the CoP started rising. These rising costs necessitated higher support prices to sustain the long-run margin of 20 per cent over total costs. The analysis in the paper brings out this phenomenon clearly. The MSPs in real terms declined in the 1980s and still returns to farming did continue to be sufficient for the farming community. This is because the CoP of both rice and wheat fell during that period as productivity improved at more than 2.5 per cent per annum and outstripped growth in CoC. On the other hand, the CoP rose at the rate of nearly 1.5 per cent per annum in both the crops during the 1990s and beyond, making rising MSPs necessary to help the farmers maintain the same incomes.

It is important to note here that these higher support prices are meant to compensate the slowdown in yield growth and the consequent increase in CoP that is the result of dwindling non-price interventions through public investments. In this situation, if the MSPs are not hiked sufficiently as in case of rice in the late 1990s and early years of the new millennium, margins would have gone down and distress would have spread. The analysis in the paper shows that farm business income in real terms declined by 1.15 per cent per annum for rice farmers. To sum up, the farming community is not necessarily better off as a result of higher support prices, as these prices are meant to compensate for the rising CoP in the absence of yield increasing public investments.

The second major factor driving higher support prices is the operation of market forces in a liberal and open trade regime. Price policy faces different challenges in such a scenario. For example, low production can coincide with low prices with liberalised imports and exports. When the international market prices are higher and rising as a result of a supply shock, domestic prices of the respective commodity shoot up and procurement of sufficient quantities to the required levels to ensure food security becomes difficult. Therefore, the government will have to offer higher prices[4] as happened in 1997 and 2007 and 2008 in the case of wheat, making the gross margin more than 50 per cent. The pulls and pressures of democracy and farmer lobbies make it impossible to roll back these prices without very high political costs, even if global prices recede considerably. The forced unidirectional movement of support prices also has an advantage in that assured prices and continuity in price structure can only stimulate supply response for agricultural commodities.

The result of these higher support prices is that it hurts the consumers and has an adverse impact on poverty reduction.[5] It was estimated by Parikh *et al.* (2003) that a 10 per cent increase in MSPs of wheat and rice leads to a decline in overall GDP by 0.33 per cent, increase in aggregate price index by 1.5 per cent, reduction in investments by 1.9 per cent and has a minuscule impact on agricultural GDP. They also conclude that the bottom 80 per cent of the rural and all of urban population is worse off. The experience of the past few years clearly reveals that the option of trade for food security has limited scope in view of the huge demands of a large population of the country. This means that the balance between price and non-price interventions has to be struck as in earlier decades. Therefore, non-price interventions through public investments have to be accelerated to reduce the CoP, and thereby, the need for higher support prices. Also, a system of variable tariffs has to be implemented to insulate domestic prices from the impact of higher volatility in international food market.

Concluding Observations

Agricultural price policy has been largely successful in playing a major role in regard to providing reasonable level of margins of around 20 per cent over total costs to the farmers of both rice and wheat. In turn, it seems to have encouraged farmers' investments in yield increasing technology and in increasing production and enabling sufficient procurement for buffer stocks and providing physical access to food by achieving and maintaining self-sufficiency. The need to supply food to the PDS and various poverty alleviation programmes has also been increasing at a faster rate. The price policy could help in procuring 43 mt in TE 2008-09 compared to a mere 13 mt in TE 1982, providing buffer stocks for an offtake of 38 mt in TE 2008-09, which is a steep increase over just 14 mt in TE 1982. These huge tasks of production, procurement and distribution would not have been possible without the efficient working of the country's price policy. The country is, by and large, insulated from supply shocks because of its operation. For example, the prices of cereals increased by only 20 per cent while they spiked by 150 per cent in the international market during 2005-2008. This does not mean that there are shortcomings in its working, but only to highlight the fact its utility far outweighs any such problems to be rectified.

Nevertheless, agricultural price policy does face some new challenges in the current period with reduced non-price interventions in the form of public investments and also the percolation of some of the global price volatility through open trade. In fact, the analysis in this paper shows that these two are mainly responsible for higher support prices. The trend of declining CoP with higher growth in yields got reversed in the 1990s and beyond, and they went up to nearly 1.5 per cent per annum for rice and wheat. The returns over paid-out costs for rice farmers also declined at 1.15 per cent per annum in real terms leading to distress. This declining profitability seems to have discouraged them from increasing spending on yield augmenting technology as shown by the relatively declining growth rate of CoC.

The price intervention in enhancing MSPs for wheat in 1997-98, 2006-07 and 2007-08, keeping in view the fact that the market prices were higher, has distorted the intercrop price parity between rice and wheat. Although the CoP is similar for these two crops since the mid-1990s, the wheat MSP has been 14 per cent higher than that of paddy since then. Since 2000-01, rice farmers have also suffered from lower price realisation than the respective MSPs, lower (7%) returns over total costs compared to 27 per cent in wheat and a higher growth in CoP compared to the wholesale price indices between 2002-03 and 2006-07. On the whole, the analysis presented in the paper shows that there is some merit in the argument that the MSP of rice should be closer or slightly below that of wheat. The recent hikes in support prices for rice are therefore justified against this background.

The averages tend to mask regional variations and the impacts of price policy in a vast country like ours with divergent climatic conditions. The CoP is higher than the all-India average in some of the poorer states due to low productivity and prices realised do not cover all costs. But the price realisation does cover variable costs and leaves a reasonable margin over that in all the states. At the same time, the prices realised cover all costs in states producing efficiently at low cost.

To sum up, a higher emphasis has to be given to non-price interventions through public investments to supplement price policy measures.[6] They can help in increasing yields, reduce the exclusive reliance on prices for farm profitability and food security, and also hasten poverty reduction, as the history of poverty reduction in the country shows that the proportion of the poor declined at faster rates when food prices are low.[7] Decentralising the procurement operations by building necessary infrastructure in states like UP, Bihar, MP and Odisha is critical in achieving equity in this regard. Also, price support operations need to be extended to other crops like pulses and oilseeds to stimulate their production. The storage capacities at present for buffer stocks are sufficient to store less than 30 mt, while the actual needs often go beyond 50 mt. Therefore, measures to increase the storage capacities have to be initiated immediately and at the same time the quality of the stored grain needs to be given equal importance by upgrading the technology.

Notes

1. Rice and paddy are used interchangeably in the paper. Whenever we use rice it refers to paddy.
2. The year 1993-94 is excluded from analysis as too few surveys were done that year.
3. Rao (2001) provides a detailed exposition of the changes in the agricultural price policy.
4. It is also documented by some scholars. See for example Chand (2010).
5. Sen (1999) explains vividly the vicious circle of low public investments, low yield growth, higher support prices, lower poverty reduction in the 1990s quite well.
6. Several scholars have argued for yield increasing growth path for agricultural development to reduce an adverse impact on the poor (Dantwala, 1986; Krishnaji 1990; Rao 1994).
7. See for a detailed exposition Dev and Ranade (1998) and Dev and Ravi (2007).

References

Acharya, S.S. (1997). "Agricultural Price Policy and Development: Some Facts and Emerging Issues", *Indian Journal of Agricultural Economics* 52(1): 1-47.

Chand, Ramesh (2010). "Understanding the Nature and Causes of Food Inflation", *Economic & Political Weekly* 44(9): 10-13.

Dantwala, M.L. (1986). "Technology, Growth and Equity in Agriculture" in John W. Mellor and Gunvant M. Desai (ed.), *Agricultural Change and Rural Poverty*. Delhi: Oxford University Press.

Dev, S. Mahendra (2009). "Structural Reforms and Agriculture: Issues and Policies", Keynote Paper for the 92nd Annual Conference of the Indian Economic Association, 27-29 December, Bhubaneswar, Odisha.

Dev, S. Mahendra and Ajit Ranade (1998). "Rising Food Prices and Rural Poverty: Going Beyond Correlations", *Economic & Political Weekly* 33(39): 2529-36.

Dev, S. Mahendra and C. Ravi (2007). "Poverty and Inequality: All India and States, 1983-2005", *Economic & Political Weekly* 42(6): 509-21.

GoI (2008). *Eleventh Five Year Plan 2007-2012 III Volume: Agriculture, Rural Development, Industry, Services and Physical Infrastructure*, Planning Commission, Government of India. New Delhi: Oxford University Press.

Krishnaji, N. (1990). "Agricultural Price Policy: A Survey with Reference to Indian Foodgrain Economy", *Economic & Political Weekly* 25(26): A-54-A-63.

Parikh, Kirit S., A. Ganesh-Kumar and Gangadhar Darbha (2003). "Growth and Welfare Consequences of Rise in MSP", *Economic & Political Weekly* 38(9): 891-95.

Raghavan, M. (2008). "Changing Pattern of Input Use and Cost of Cultivation", *Economic & Political Weekly* 43(26&27): 123-29.

Rao, N. Chandrasekhara (2004). "Aggregate Agricultural Supply Response in Andhra Pradesh", *Indian Journal of Agricultural Economics* 59(1): 91-104.

———. (2006). "Agrarian Crisis in Andhra Pradesh", *Journal of Indian School of Political Economy* 18(1&2): 35-75.

Rao, C.H. Hanumantha (1994). *Agricultural Growth, Rural Poverty and Environmental Degradation in India*. New Delhi: Oxford University Press.

Rao, V.M. (2001). "The Making of Agricultural Price Policy: A Review of CACP Reports", *Journal of Indian School of Political Weekly* 13(1): 1-28.

Schiff, M. and C.E. Montenegro (1997). "Aggregate Agricultural Supply Response in Developing Countries: A Survey of Selected Issues", *Economic Development and Cultural Change* 45(2): 393-410.

Sen, Abhijit (1999). "Agricultural Price Policy: Achievements and the Emerging Problems" in Y.V. Krishna Rao (ed.) (1999), *New Challenges Facing Indian Agriculture*. Hyderabad: Visalandhra Publishing House.

———. (2001). "A Whole Crop of Uncertainties", *Frontline* 18(2): 8-10.

Sen, Abhijit and M.S. Bhatia (2004). *Cost of Cultivation and Farm Income in India*, Department of Agriculture and Cooperation, Ministry of Agriculture. New Delhi: Academic Foundation.

Singh, Manmohan (1995). "Inaugural Address at the 54th Annual Conference of the Indian Society of Agricultural Economics", *Indian Journal of Agricultural Economics* 50(1): 1-6.

Economic & Political Weekly XLV(26 & 27), 26 June 2010.

Part III

Industry

14

Policies and Performance in Industry

PART III , Chapters 14 to 21 contributed by R. Nagaraj, K.L. Krishna and Goldar, Aditya Bhattacharjea, M.H. Bala Subrahmanya, Vijay Kelkar, Nagesh Kumar, Dipak Mazumdar and Sandip Sarkar, is devoted to a discussion on policies and performance in Indian industry relating to growth, productivity, diversification; small scale industry, public sector; competition policy and foreign investment. While chapter 14 provides a broad overview of policy and performance of Indian industry since 1947. Nagaraj's essay (ch. 15) looks into industrial performance during 2001-2008. Krishna and Goldar (ch. 16) have reviewed studies on productivity in manufacturing, agriculture and services sector as well as for the aggregate economy. Public sector and the issue of Privatisation are discussed by Kelkar in chapter 19. Bala Subrahmanya (ch. 18) has discussed the policy changes relating to small industry, the impact of globalisation and domestic reforms since 1991 as well as the performance of the small scale sector. Bhattacharjea's essay with updated Post Script 2016 (ch. 17) is devoted to India's Competition Laws and government's handling of its competition laws. Policy towards FDI and FPI as evolved over time in tune with the requirements of the process of development in different phases has been discussed by Nagesh Kumar in chapter 20. Mazumdar and Sarkar (ch. 21) have looked into and analysed the problem of employment and the phenomenon of missing middle.

The Industrial Scene at Independence

The main features of the industrial scene in India on the eve of planning (1950) were as under:

1. There was the preponderance of consumer goods industries *vis-à-vis* producer goods industries resulting in lopsided industrial development. In 1953, the ratio of consumer goods to producer goods worked out to be 62:38.

2. The industrial sector was extremely underdeveloped with a very weak infrastructure.
3. The lack of government intervention in favour of the industrial sector was considered as an important cause of under-development.
4. Export orientation had been against the country's interests.
5. The structure of ownership was highly concentrated.
6. Technical and managerial skills were in short supply.

As a result, the national consensus was that economic sovereignty and economic independence lay in rapid industrialisation including particularly the promotion of industrial infrastructure.

Organised thinking concerning the direction of industrial development in India may be traced to the Statement of Industrial Policy, 1945; the Industrial Policy Resolution of 1948; the enactment of the Industries (Development and Regulation) Act, 1951; the First and Second Five Year Plan documents; and the Industrial Policy Resolution of 1956.

The First Five Year Plan stated that the objective of industrial planning was to make good the deficiencies in production of key industrial items and to initiate development which would enable the cumulative expansion of such basic production. The scope and need for the development of India's industries was felt to be so great that it was necessary for the public sector to develop those industries 'in which private enterprise is unable or unwilling to put up the resources required and to run the risk involved'. The idea was that the rest of the field could be left free for private enterprise.

The Industrial Policy Resolution of 1948 had identified a small number of industries to be reserved for production by the public sector. The production of arms and ammunition, production and control of atomic energy, and ownership and management of railways were to be the sole preserve of the central government. However, coal, iron and steel, aircraft manufacturing, ship-building, manufacture of telegraph and wireless equipment (except radios), and minerals were reserved for production by central or state government undertakings.

The 1956 list of industries reserved for the public sector is based on this 1948 list but includes a number of additional industries. The thinking concerning the public sector had changed during the course of the 1950s. The original thinking was concerned with the use of the public sector investment in industries which the private sector would find difficult to invest in. By 1956 this had changed towards an explicit preference for state ownership of industries that were termed as capturing the 'commanding heights of the economy'.

Although the Second Five Year Plan is always seen as the conceptual basis of Indian planning, a close reading of the First Five Year Plan suggests that the difficulty of directing a mixed economy was better appreciated by the earlier planners and policy makers. There was better appreciation of the need for indicative planning in the First Plan and the need for coordination of industrial planning with the formulation of other economic policies such as customs and excise tariff structure, import and export policy, investment and technology policy, monetary and financial policy. The Second Plan and later plans have been increasingly concerned with the allocation of public resources and much less with indications and policies to direct the whole economy in desired directions (Mohan, 1992).

Industrial Control Regime

The system of Indian industrial licensing, therefore, has its origins in a combination of thinking resulting from the exigencies and requirements of a war situation, Indian nationalistic aspirations and the socialistic leanings of some of the founding fathers of the country. The leaders of the private sector of the time were also in favour of strong governmental assertion. The industrial licensing system has operated in the country with the simultaneous operation of other schemes of governmental allocations and controls such as:

1. Five Year Plan documents.
2. Import and export controls.
3. Control of capital issues.
4. Control of foreign exchange.
5. Transport controls including allocation of raw materials.
6. Price controls.
7. Allocations of credit.

This suggests that the planners and policy makers in India understood the need for using a wide variety of instruments and controls to steer Indian industrial development in a desired direction. However, there has always been a mismatch between the intentions expressed and the licensing instruments available for realising these planning intentions. It should also be noted that whereas the original intention of licensing was to use this power selectively for the promotion of selected important industries, it was later used to control almost all industries with the result that regulation rather than development became the more important feature of the system.

Performance of the Industrial Licensing System

Until the recent industrial and trade policy reforms, the establishment and operation of an industrial enterprise in India required approvals from the central government at almost every step (see Paranjape, 1988). Before making an investment, an entrepreneur had to first obtain approval in principle from the Ministry of Industry. The granting of this approval resulted in the issuance of a Letter of Intent (LoI). Armed with this LoI, the entrepreneur could then tie up other requirements for setting up the project. If he needed to import a capital good, he had to obtain a capital goods import licence from the Chief Controller of Imports & Exports (CCI&E) in the Ministry of Commerce. The approval for the import, however, was given by a committee set up in the Ministry of Industry. If there was also need for a foreign technology collaboration agreement, the entrepreneur had to obtain a specific approval for this (a foreign collaboration—FC-approval) from a committee chaired by the Finance Secretary but serviced by the Ministry of Industry. In order to raise funds for the project, if an entrepreneur wanted to go to the capital market, he needed separate approval from the Controller of Capital Issues in the Ministry of Finance. For imports of raw material and components, separate licences had to be obtained on an annual basis from the CCI&E. In each case, an 'essentiality' and indigenous non-availability clearance had to be given by the technical wing of the Ministry of Industry (the Directorate General of Technical Development—DGTD). Once everything was tied up and the unit was about to go into production, the entrepreneur had to go back to the Ministry of Industry for an 'Industrial Licence'.

In addition to these approvals, since the enactment of the Monopolies and Restrictive Trade Practices (MRTP) Act in 1969, the firms covered under this needed to obtain separate MRTP clearances from the Department of Company Affairs. Further, resulting from the desire to promote small-scale industries, 836 items have been reserved for production in small-scale enterprises. Since 1956, there has also been a list of industries reserved for exclusive production in the public sector.

Since 1977, there has also been a ban on the location of industries in the largest 20-30 cities. In 1988, this ban was extended to include municipal areas of all towns and cities and to specified areas of influence around the largest 21 cities.

That this system was unsuited for directing investments has been well understood since the early 1960s. The most comprehensive description, evaluation and indictment of this system is that by Bhagwati and Desai (1970). The government appointed one committee after another in the 1960s to examine the industrial licensing system (The Swaminathan Committee, 1964; the Mahalanobis Committee, 1964; the Hazari Report, 1967; the Dutt Committee Report, 1969; and the Administrative Reform Commission, 1969). Despite the findings of most of these early committees, that the licensing mechanism was not serving its purpose of channelising investments into desired directions, there seems to have been a continuing inability of the government, until recently, to bring any substantative changes to the industrial licensing system.

It seems the promotion of a sheltered home market had a common appeal to the bureaucratic authoritarian state, urban manufacturers and multinationals that supplied technology and capital. Protection also met the state's objectives pursuing revenue and expenditure maximising activities through maximum revenue tariffs and export tariffs.

Thus, the interests of politicians, bureaucrats, multinationals, as well as domestic industrial houses all coincided to keep Indian industry sheltered through the operation of the industrial control system.

The stagnation of Indian industrial production between the mid-1960s up to the late 1970s induced some serious new thinking. Towards the end of the 1970s and by the early 1980s, there emerged a growing consensus that Indian industry was exhibiting a slowdown in industrial growth due to low productivity, high costs, low quality of production and obsolete technology (Ahluwalia, 1985). Three important committees were set up in the early 1980s: the Abid Hussain Committee on trade policy, the Narasimham Committee on the shift from physical to fiscal controls and the Sengupta Committee on the public sector. These committees clearly recommended an easing up of trade policy, the substitution of physical and quantitative controls by fiscal and other means of macroeconomic management, the promotion of greater public sector autonomy in business and operating decisions and the need for measures for enhancing productivity efficiency and modernisation.

The result of such thinking was that there was some progress in the process of deregulation during the 1980s, though perhaps not as significant as is often believed. Two kinds of delicensing activity took place. First, 32 groups of industries were delicensed without any investment limit. Second, in 1988, all industries were exempted from licensing except for a specified negative list of 26 industries. This exemption from licensing was, however, subject to investment and location limitations. As has often been done in the past, this announcement also contained further restrictions which reduced significantly the effectiveness of exemption from licensing that was provided in this announcement. On the trade policy front, the key change was increasing access of exporters to inputs at international prices. However, it seems that tariff protection to industry increased significantly during the 1980s relative to previous decades.

While the industrial licensing system underwent some changes in terms of threshold levels and types of products, it formed an essential part of government policy until the end of the 1980s.

The Policy Regime in the 1990s

A process of reflection and debate on the need for a change in policies had been set in motion in India in the second half of the 1970s, i.e., about the same time that China was preparing for a major change in policy. It is worth noting that while China went ahead with full force towards market orientation and doubled its GDP (gross domestic product) between 1978 and 1991, India used the decade of the 1980s for hesitant experimentation in domestic deregulation, retaining its highly protectionist trade policy regime and keeping its loss making public sector intact. The reform on the industrial policy front, however, coincided with a sharp deterioration in the fiscal accounts of the government. As the Government of India's (GoI) policies became increasingly expansionary to support growing levels of current government expenditures on sharply rising interest payments, defence and subsidies, the gross fiscal deficit of the government increased from 6.2 per cent of GDP in 1980-81 to 8.3 per cent by 1990-1991.

While the reorientation of industrial and trade policies evoked a better productivity response and led to substantially higher industrial growth in the 1980s, the deteriorating fiscal position and growing macro-economic imbalances posed a serious challenge to the sustainability of the higher growth of the 1980s. The Gulf War of 1990 provided the trigger, which brought the underlying economic crisis to the force.

The experience of the 1980s had a direct bearing on how the GoI responded to the crisis of 1990-91. Evidence of faster industrial growth and productivity in the 1980s was clear. Whether it was productivity-led growth or debt-led growth or a bit of both, most policy watchers agreed that the better industrial performance could not be sustained because of the growing macroeconomic imbalances during the 1980s. The response to the crisis therefore was two-fold—more domestic deregulation and foreign competition and striving to attain macroeconomic balance. In opening up the economy to foreign trade and foreign investment, the policies represented a more radical break with the past (Ahluwalia, 2006).

New Economic Policy

As Rangarajan has rightly stated, the year 1991 is an important landmark in the economic history of post-Independent India. The country went through a severe economic crisis triggered by a serious balance of payments (BoP) situation. The crisis was converted into an opportunity to introduce some fundamental changes in the content and approach to economic policy. The response to the crisis was to put in place a set of policies aimed at stabilisation and structural reform. While the stabilisation policies were aimed at correcting the weaknesses that had developed on the fiscal and the BoP fronts, the structural reforms sought to remove the rigidities that had entered into the various segments of the Indian economy. The structural reforms introduced in the early 1990s broadly covered the areas of industrial licensing, foreign trade, foreign investment, exchange rate management and the financial sector. From the point of view of industrialisation, changes in the areas of licensing and foreign trade and investment had important implications. Even before the onset of reforms, the problems associated with industrial licensing were well recognised. The approach document of the Eighth Plan (1991-1996) submitted in May 1990 had remarked:

> A return to the regime of direct, indiscriminate and detailed controls in industry is clearly out of question. Past experience has shown that such control system is not effective in achieving the desired objective. Also the system is widely abused and leads to corruption, delays and inefficiency (Government of India, 1990).

One early step that was undertaken as part of the structural reform process was to dispense with licensing. Changes in foreign trade policy focused on reducing the tariff rates and dismantling quantitative controls over imports. The tariff rates have been brought down in stages. Some caution in this regard had become necessary to enable the Indian industries set up behind high protective tariff walls to adjust to the changed situation. The policy towards foreign investment underwent a significant change with foreign investors given the freedom to own majority shareholding over a wide spectrum of industries.

Without going into details, the common thread running through the various policy measures introduced since 1991 has been the improvement of the efficiency of the system. The thrust of the New Economic Policy has been towards creating a more competitive environment in the economy as a means to improving the productivity and efficiency of the system. This was to be achieved by removing the barriers to entry and the restrictions on the growth of firms. While the Industrial Policy of 1992 sought to bring about a greater competitive environment domestically, the counterpart Trade Policy set out in the same year, sought to improve international competitiveness subject to the degree of protection offered by the tariffs. The private sector was to be given a larger space to operate inasmuch as some of the areas, reserved exclusively earlier for the public sector, were now to be opened to the private sector. In these areas, the public sector would have to compete with the private sector, even though the public sector might continue to play the dominant role in the foreseeable future. What was sought to be achieved was the improvement in the functioning of the various entities, whether they were in the private or in the public sector.

The industrial policy reforms during the 1990s were bold in doing away with numerous barriers to entry, e.g., removal of industrial licensing for investment, opening up all but a few strategic areas which were earlier reserved for investment only by the pubic sector, preparing to replace the earlier MRTP Act with a new Competition Law which would regulate anti-competitive behaviour. Even on the policy for reservation for the small-scale sector, a beginning was made by dereserving a number of items. However, the absence of institutional and legal reforms created barriers to exit. Delays in securing numerous permissions from state governments and environmental clearances from the GoI are also emerging as the new barriers to entry. A World Bank study (Dollar and Goswami, 2002) has highlighted the impact of these together with that of the availability of infrastructure and the quality of governance in determining the investment climate facing different states in India.

The 10 years from 1991 to 2001, therefore, marked a significant transition for the Indian economy from a policy regime with very high rates of protection and all-pervasive quantitative restrictions to moderate rates of protection and removal of quantitative restrictions. The degree of tariff protection, however, was still higher than in most developing economies.

Opening up to Foreign Investment

The reforms of the 1990s marked a significant break with the past in respect of the policy towards foreign investment. From a policy which was restrictive and selective and supported mainly technology transfers, foreign investment policy in the 1990s became more open and more proactive as the rules were liberalised over time with a view not only to gain better access to technology but also to build strategic alliances to penetrate world markets. Besides enlarging the scope for automatic approval over the years, the Foreign Investment Promotion Board was set up to expedite other applications for foreign investment. Specifically, liberal conditions were set up for attracting foreign investment in infrastructure sectors and export-oriented sectors. As of 2001, 100 per cent foreign ownership is allowed in a large number of industries and majority ownership in all but banks, insurance companies, telecommunications and airlines.

Public Sector Reforms, Privatisation and Infrastructure

A major gap in domestic policy reform has been in the area of public sector with maximum adverse effect on the infrastructure sectors with its consequences for the industrial sector as a whole. During the 1980s, while there was disillusionment with respect to the resource generation aspects of the public sector undertakings (PSUs), the objective of the public sector as the guiding spirit for development continued to be at the core of planning. Some effort was made to grant greater autonomy to the PSUs from the control of their administrative ministries, but even at the end of the 1980s, there was little improvement in the situation with respect to the operating surpluses of the PSUs.

Public sector reform remained an area of darkness in the 1990s. A significant practical approach was adopted in which the better performing PSUs were given the freedom to access capital markets on the strength of their own performance. They were also given more autonomy in shaping their future. The non-performing PSUs, on the other hand, languished for want of budgetary support or reform.

Privatisation was not pursued as an option in the early phase of reforms. Instead, government policy concentrated on selective disinvestments of public sector equity with a view to finance fiscal deficits rather than address the issue of improving the returns on the capital invested. In 1997, the GoI set up the Disinvestment Commission. The Commission gave a series of reports analysing around 50 cases of PSUs, which were referred to it and made detailed recommendations. Subsequently, the Commission was wound up and a Department of Privatisation was created.

Industrial Policy Objectives for the Twelfth Plan and Beyond[1]

Quoting the Twelfth Five Year Plan,

> Industrial policies, where they have succeeded, have generally not been an outcome of Centrally planned economies but of economies that have had the active involvement of private enterprises and other non-governmental stakeholders. Successful strategies evolve from ongoing productive interactions between government and producers. Therefore, the government must improve the process of interaction, collaboration and learning amongst producers and itself. This is very different from the paradigm of Indian industrial policy prior to India's economic reforms commencing in the 1980s. In that era, industrial planning was a topdown control activity with Government determining who should produce what, where and how much and also what technology they should use. The roadmap for the Twelfth Plan and beyond can definitely not be a return to this type of planning.

According to the Twelfth Plan document, in order to create a paradigm shift in the manufacturing sector, it is essential to consider the objectives over a longer time frame, such as 15 years. The National Manufacturing Policy, which was introduced in 2011, states these objectives and these are the underlying objectives that the Plan aims to achieve as well. These objectives are:

1. Increase manufacturing sector growth to 12–14 per cent over the medium term to make it the engine of growth for the

1. This section is drawn from Twelfth Five Year Plan 2012-2017, Vol. II, Ch. 13.

economy. The 2-4 per cent differential over the medium term growth rate of the overall economy will enable manufacturing to contribute at least 25 per cent of the national GDP by 2025.

2. Increase the rate of job creation in manufacturing to create 100 million additional jobs by 2025. Emphasis should be given to creation of appropriate skill sets among the rural migrant and urban poor to make growth inclusive.
3. Increase 'depth' in manufacturing, with focus on the level of domestic value addition, to address the national strategic requirements.
4. Enhance global competitiveness of Indian manufacturing through appropriate policy support.
5. Ensure sustainability of growth, particularly with regard to the environment.

The contribution of the manufacturing sector to Gross Value Added (GVA) has been hovering around 17 per cent for the last four years. The government has taken several measures to accelerate the growth of the industrial sector so as to strengthen and sustain the momentum of economic growth. These are primarily focused on simplification and rationalization of procedures and processes for boosting investment, adopting a more open Foreign Direct Investment (FDI) policy and measures for creating a conducive business environment.

Some of the recent reforms are: reducing the list of industries that can be considered defence industries requiring industrial licence; and amendments in FDI policy which include allowing FDI in defence up to 49 per cent, in railway infrastructure up to 100 per cent and in the insurance and pension sector up to 49 per cent. The investment limit requiring prior permission from the Foreign Investment Promotion Board (FIPB)/Cabinet Committee on Economic Affairs has been increased from R1200 crore to R3000 crore. The definition of investment by Non Resident Indians (NRI), Persons of Indian Origin (PIO) and Overseas Citizens of India (OCI) in the FDI policy has been revised.

The government has launched several programmes/initiatives such as ease of doing business, Make in India, Invest India, and e-biz Mission Mode Project under the National e-Governance Plan. Further, the Government of India is also building a pentagon of corridors across the country to boost manufacturing and to project India as a global manufacturing destination. The National Investment and Infrastructure Fund (NIIF) has been approved to extend equity support to infrastructure Non-Bank Financial Companies (NBFC). Issue of taxfree infrastructure bonds has been allowed for rail, roads and irrigation programmes (*Economic Survey 2015-16*, Vol.II)

Trends and Pattern of Industrial Growth

Having looked into the industrial control regime and the performance of the industrial licensing system under different policy regimes and the trade liberalisation and industrialisation policy reforms of the 1990s, and the policy objectives for the Twelfth Plan and beyond, let us now look at the industrial growth since Independence—the rate and pattern of growth and the structural changes.

Over the six decades between 1950 and 2010, industrial (or manufacturing) sector grew annually at 5.5 per cent, compared to the domestic output growth rate of 4.6 per cent (Table 14.1).[2] The growth is accompanied by output diversification, its regional composition, and organisational and ownership pattern. Until the end of the 1970s, the industry was the economy's leading sector; then it was manufacturing in the 1980s; but the services sector overtook it to become the leading sector since the 1990s.

Table 14.1

Long-term Growth Rates of Indian Economy and Its Principal Sectors: 1951 to 2010

(% per year)

Sector	1951-1980	1981-2010	1981-1991	1992-2010	1951-2010
1. Agriculture	2.2	3.0	3.1	2.7	2.6
2. Industry	5.4	6.4	7.0	7.0	5.5
2.1 Manufacturing	5.3	6.4	7.4	7.1	5.5
3. Services	4.6	7.6	7.0	8.5	5.8
4. GDP	3.6	6.0	5.6	6.8	4.6
5. GNP per capita	1.4	4.0	3.0	5.0	2.4

Notes: (a) Agriculture includes allied activities such as forestry, fishery, dairying; industry includes (i) mining, (ii) manufacturing, (iii) electricity, gas, and water, and (iv) construction.

(b) Services include (i) trade, hotels, and restaurants, (ii) transport, storage, and communications, (iii) banking and insurance, real estate, dwelling and business services, and (iv) community, social, and personal services.

Source: National Accounts Statistics, various issues.

2. All growth rates reported in the chapter are at constant prices obtained by computing log-linear trend growth rates, unless otherwise mentioned.

Evidently, Indian industry has underperformed (relative to its potential), or it has remained undersized, in a comparative perspective. The reasons behind this and policies to reverse the trend have engaged a lot of attention for quite some time now, which also form the main concerns of the present chapter.

Policy Regimes and Pattern of Growth[3]

The period since 1951 may be divided into five phases as in Table 14.2, according to policy regime:

- 1951-52 to 1966-67: Evolution of Industrial Development Strategy.
- 1967-68 to 1980-81: Inward orientation and Industrial Stagnation.
- 1981-82 to 1990-91: Deregulation, and Acceleration of Growth.
- 1991-92 to 2000-01: Economic Reforms and Service-led Growth.
- 2001-02 to 2010-11: Growth Resurgence and Global Crisis. The three-year period 2011-12 to 2013-14 is covered later in this section.

Table 14.2 presents growth rates of GDP and major sectors for two phases in the pre-Independence period and five phases in the post-independence period. In the first phase after independence, 1951-1966, the industrialisation strategy was evolved as part of the development planning process. The First Five Year Plan, 1951-1956, however, accorded primacy to agriculture, irrigation and infrastructure. Compared to the pre-independence era, growth performance, overall and in industry sector, was indeed impressive. The strategy in the Second Plan (1956-1961) based on the celebrated Mahalanobis model emphasised heavy industry and public sector dominance. Against a background of 'export pessimism,' import substitution industrialisation (ISI) strategy was pursued. The foreign exchange crisis in 1957 prompted re-imposition of exchange controls. As a consequence of border wars with China in 1962, with Pakistan in 1965 and 1966, development planning received a setback. Average annual growth rate during the Third Plan (1961-1966) was 2.8 per cent compared to 4.3 per cent in the Second Plan. However, the industry sector maintained the growth rate of over

3. This section draws upon Acharya *et al.* (2006).

Table 14.2

Annual Average Growth Rates of GDP and Major Sectors

	1900-01 to 1929-30	*1930-31 to 1946-47*	*1951-52 to 1966-67*	*1967-68 to 1980-81*	*1981-82 to 1990-91*	*1991-92 to 2000-01*	*2001-02 to 2010-11*
Agriculture and Allied	0.5	0.2	1.8	3.3	3.5	2.7	2.9
Industry	0.9	1.2	6.3	4.1	7.1	5.7	7.8
Services	1.6	1.7	4.8	4.3	6.8	7.6	9.4
GDP	0.8	0.8	3.4	3.8	5.6	5.6	7.9
GDP per Capita	0.4	-0.5	1.4	1.5	3.4	3.7	6.2

Source: Acharya *et al.* (2006, table 6) and Krishna (2012, Table 1).

Data Sources: Sivasubramonian (2000) and Central Statistical Organisation (2001) and EPW (2011).

6.5 per cent (Acharya *et al.*, 2006, table 3.16). The 1966 devaluation-cum-liberalisation episode proved unsuccessful and at the end of this first period, the anti-foreign trade pro-import substitution bias got entrenched. Rather than shift to outward oriented policies and exploit the export potential of labour-intensive products, as South Korea did in the early 1960s, India extended import substitution to a diverse set of goods including machinery. Entry barriers in the form of industrial investment licensing policy came in the way of domestic competition, and as a result, efficiency gains from competition could not be reaped. According to careful analysts (e.g., Panagariya, 2008), this was a colossal policy mistake responsible for the lack luster performance of Indian manufacturing in the second phase 1967-1980 (Krishna, 2015).

In the second phase, 1967-1980, with the strengthening of import substitution strategy and imposition of various government controls, namely, nationalisation of major banks and insurance in 1969-70, Foreign Exchange Regulation Act (FERA), small-scale industries reservations, Monopoly and Restrictive Trade Practices (MRTP) Act, the policy environment became increasingly statist. Industrial growth during this phase decelerated to around 4.1 per cent per annum from 6.3 per cent attained in the earlier phase, leading to doubts about the efficacy of the system of detailed controls on industry, foreign trade and payments (Acharya *et al.*, 2006).

The third phase, 1981-1990, witnessed a substantial acceleration of overall GDP growth from 3.8 per cent per annum to 5.6 per cent, industry GDP growth increased by 3 percentage points from 4.1 to 7.1 per cent. Efforts at industrial liberalisation during 1980s, and better agricultural performance as a result of Green Revolution, and increasingly expansionist fiscal policy seemed to be the factors behind the vastly improved growth performance in this phase. However, the end of the period witnessed a severe balance of payments (BoP) crisis in the wake of the 1990 Gulf War and oil price hike.

As a policy response to the crisis at the beginning of the 1990s, wide ranging reforms in industrial deregulation, foreign trade policy, exchange rate and payments regime, capital markets and the banking sector, fiscal consolidation were introduced. These major reforms of 1991-94 resulted in acceleration of GDP growth to above 7 per cent per annum and industry sector growth to above 9 per cent. However, the pace of reforms slackened in mid-1990s and fiscal balances worsened thereafter, investment and exports lost momentum and growth slowed after 1997. Agriculture experienced significant slowdown and year-to-year fluctuations. Industry growth too decelerated and displayed milder fluctuations (Ahluwalia, 2012).

In the recent phase, 2001-02 to 2010-11, in Table 14.2, industrial growth accelerated to 7.8 per cent per annum, services growth to about 9.4 per cent and GDP growth to 7.9 per cent per annum. Per capita GDP growth accelerated appreciably by 2.5 percentage points to 6.2 per cent. The five-year period 2003-04 to 2007-08 was remarkable for witnessing an average annual growth rate of 8.7 per cent in GDP and 10.3 per cent in industry. The growth rate in 2006-07 was 9.6 per cent in GDP and 12.7 per cent in industry, a very impressive performance. However, as a consequence of the economic crisis in developed countries, GDP growth rate in 2008-09 dropped to 6.7 per cent, but recovered in the following two years. The first decade of the New Millennium as a whole witnessed most impressive growth performance, especially in the services sector.

Balakrishnan (2010) econometrically estimates the years of structural breaks in the annual time series of GDP and sectoral GDP for the Indian economy for the post-1950-51 period. The growth phases thus delineated, and the annual growth rates for overall GDP, GDP in manufacturing, GDP in registered manufacturing and GDP in unregistered manufacturing in 1999-2000 prices are presented in Table 14.3 (Krishna, 2015).

It may be seen from Table 14.3 that the years 1978-79 and 1990-91 are the structural break years for the GDP series. GDP growth rate has accelerated from 3.5 per cent per year in Phase I to 4.4 per cent in Phase II, the period of deregulation and partial liberalisation, and to 5.9 per cent in Phase III, the period of major and wide-ranging liberalisation. Growth acceleration is higher from Phase II to Phase III, than from Phase I to Phase II.

Table 14.3

GDP Growth Rates in the Different Growth Phases: Economy and Manufacturing

		Overall GDP		
Phase	1950/51 to 1978/79	1979/80 to 1991/92	1990/91 to 2005/06	-
Growth rate (% p.a.)	3.48	4.38	5.89	
		Manufacturing GDP		
Phase	1950/51 to 1965/66	1966/67 to 1994/95	1995/96 to 2005/06	-
Growth rate (% p.a.)	5.93	4.75	6.59	
		Registered Manufacturing GDP		
Phase	1950/51 to 1965/66	1966/67 to 1982/83	1983/84 to 2005/06	-
Growth rate (% p.a.)	7.77	4.66	6.89	
		Unregistered Manufacturing GDP		
Phase	1950/51 to 1964/65	1965/66 to 1977/78	1978/79 to 1994/95	1995/96 to 2005/06
Growth rate (% p.a.)	4.79	3.83	3.46	5.18

Note: Growth phases have been econometrically delineated by Balakrishnan (2010).

Source: Balakrishnan (2010), appendix.

In the case of total manufacturing, the years of structural break were estimated to be 1965-66 and 1994-95. The growth rates in the three phases are 5.9 per cent, 4.8 per cent and 6.6 per cent. Growth rate decelerated by 1.1 percentage points from Phase I to Phase II. This phenomenon of deceleration in the mid-1960s has received considerable attention of researchers. It is gratifying to note that growth rate in the manufacturing sector has accelerated significantly to 6.6 per cent in the post-reform era from 4.7 per cent during the pre-reform phase 1966-67 to 1994-95.

As far as registered manufacturing sector is concerned, the second structural break occurred in 1982-83, during the period of deregulation. There has been no structural break in the post-reform period, however.

Unregistered manufacturing sector has witnessed three, rather than two, structural breaks, in 1964-65, 1977-78 and 1994-95. The growth rates are much smaller at 4.8 per cent, 3.8 per cent, 3.5 per cent and 5.2 per cent in the four phases compared to registered manufacturing. The extent of deceleration from Phase I to Phases II and III and the extent of acceleration from Phase III to Phase IV are also milder. Thus the growth patterns of the two segments of the manufacturing sector are rather dissimilar, and the registered segment has gained further in terms of output share.

In the most recent three-year period, 2011-12 to 2013-14, the industry sector witnessed steep deceleration in growth to an average of 3.4 per cent, compared to 7.8 per cent during the period 2001-02 to 2010-11. This is attributed to 'policy paralysis' (Krishna, 2015).

Recent Industrial Growth, 2008-09 to 2013-14

Recent industrial growth, measured in terms of IIP, shows fluctuating trends. Growth had reached 15.5 per cent in 2007-08 and then started decelerating. Initial deceleration in industrial growth was largely on account of the global economic meltdown. There was, however, a recovery in industrial growth from 2.5 per cent in 2008-09 to 5.3 per cent in 2009-10 and 8.2 per cent in 2010-11.

Thus post 2008-09, industrial sector, consisting of manufacturing, mining, electricity and construction, showed remarkable recovery and steady growth for three years but lost momentum thereafter owing to a combination of supply-side and demand-side constraints. Industrial performance in 2013-14 remained lackluster for the second successive year. Industry grew by just 1.0 per cent in 2012-13 and slowed further in 2013-14, posting a modest increase of 0.4 per cent.

Industrial-sector Performance Based on Revised GDP Estimates 2012-13 to 2015-16

The recently released new series of national accounts, revising the base year from 2004-05 to 2011-12 and applying changed methodology, gives considerably improved estimates of growth in the industrial sector in 2012-13 and 2013-14 as compared to those based on the 2004-05 series (Table 14.4). This is mainly due to much better performance in the mining and manufacturing sectors as per the new series. In 2013-14, manufacturing sector growth is estimated at 5.3 per cent as compared to the (-) 0.7 per cent estimated under the 2004-05 series. The Advance Estimates (AE) for the year 2014-15 show industrial growth of 5.9 per cent as per 2011-12 base year. The manufacturing, electricity, and construction sectors have grown remarkably while growth in the mining sector has declined as compared to 2013-14. The improved performance in manufacturing is attributed to the change in methodology and use of new data sources. The growth in electricity, gas, and water supply and construction shows marked improvement in 2014-15 as compared to the previous two years.

Table 14.4

IIP-based Growth Rates of Broad Sectors/Use-based Classification

(%)

	Weight	*2013-14*	*2014-15*	*2014-15*				*2015-16*			
				Q1	*Q2*	*Q3*	*Apr.-Dec.*	*Q1*	*Q2*	*Q3*	*Apr.-Dec.*
General	100.00	-0.1	2.8	4.5	1.3	2.0	2.6	3.3	4.8	1.5	3.1
Sectoral											
Mining	14.16	-0.6	1.5	3.0	0.5	2.1	1.8	0.4	3.1	3.3	2.3
Manufacturing	75.53	-0.8	2.3	3.9	0.4	1.1	1.8	3.7	4.7	0.9	3.1
Electricity	10.32	6.1	8.4	11.3	9.4	9.4	10.0	2.3	6.8	4.4	4.5
Use Based											
Basic goods	45.68	2.1	7.0	8.7	7.0	8.3	8.0	4.7	4.4	1.3	3.4
Capital goods	8.83	-3.6	6.4	13.6	-0.5	3.2	5.1	2.0	13.4	-10.0	1.7
Intermediate goods	15.69	3.1	1.7	3.1	1.6	0.8	1.8	1.6	2.2	1.9	1.9
Consumer goods	29.81	-2.8	-3.4	-3.2	-5.4	-6.4	-4.9	2.5	2.7	6.8	4.0
Consumer durables	8.46	-12.2	-12.6	-9.5	-15.5	-20.9	-15.2	3.7	11.9	23.4	12.4
Consumer nondurables	21.35	4.8	2.8	1.4	2.3	3.2	2.3	1.7	-3.0	-1.6	-1.0

Source: Central Statistics Office (CSO).

Economic Survey 2015-16.

While the overall IIP has shown recovery, there is variation in the performance of some of the major industries during April-December 2015. While some sectors like electricity, coal, fertilisers, cement and passenger cars have shown positive growth, sectors like steel and aluminium have shown negative growth during April-December 2015. In terms of production, fertilisers and passenger cars have achieved higher levels during April-December 2015 as compared to the same period of the previous two years.

Why has Growth Moderated?

The moderation in industrial growth, particularly in the manufacturing sector, is largely attributed to sluggish growth of investment, squeezed margins of the corporate sector, deceleration in the rate of growth of credit flows and the fragile global economic recovery.

To these may be added the challenges caused, directly or indirectly by government policies. These according to Rajiv Kumar (2014) can be grouped under five headings: a difficult business environment; labour deployment rigidity and legacy issues related to labour; an extensive infrastructure deficit that affects the economy, especially the manufacturing sector; costs of time overruns and uncertainty in getting environment clearances and in land acquisition; and the high cost—when it's even available—of commercial bank credit, especially for small and medium enterprises (SMEs).

Challenges Arising from Government Policies

Difficult Business Environment

India ranked 134 out of the 189 countries in the World Bank's Ease of Doing Business survey in 2014, a deterioration from the rank of 131 in 2013. The ranking has declined in recent years, signifying a relative worsening of the business environment. India takes 27 days to start a company as against Singapore ranking No. 1 and Hong Kong No. 2 requiring 3 days to open a company (World Bank, July 2014).

Labour Deployment Rigidities

Indian industry has suffered in the past as well as presently on account of militant and competitive trade unionism and a plethora of labour legislation on the other. Although, in recent years militant unionism has ostensibly weakened, nevertheless, it is still present in major industrial centres and its infrequent but violent demonstration discourages foreign investors and induces others to keep employment to a minimum. India has nearly 50 laws, either at the central or state level, that in one way or the other affect labour conditions in India. Consequently, hardly any enterprise can claim to be in total compliance with the legal provisions governing labour conditions. It would not be unfair to say that this dysfunctional legal framework is perhaps the principal reason for the slow growth of large-scale and globally competitive manufacturing in India (Kumar, 2014).

Infrastructure Bottlenecks

India's infrastructure deficit in comparison to other economies is best captured by the summary statistics that India's per capita commercial energy consumption is about 760 kilowatt-hours (kWh), while that of China is nearly 3,000 kWh and that of the United States is 12,000 kWh. Peak power deficit in India is estimated at 7-8 per cent, and industry is not insulated from the resultant power cuts that are common across the country. A significant majority of large manufacturing units have to put up 100 per cent power backup capacities, which raises capital costs and also costs 40-50 per cent more than electricity consumed from the grid. As a result of the infrastructure deficit, Indian industry across the board bears a significantly higher price for infrastructure services and utilities than their global competitors (Ibid.).

Regulatory Delays and Lack of Transparency

Over time, a rather complex regulatory structure has been established in India to deal with land acquisition and change of land use, protection of natural forests, and safeguarding of the environment. According to one survey, there are in all (counting both the central and state governments) 1,240 regulations that apply to the industrial sector. This is far too severe a compliance requirement, especially for SMEs (Ibid.).

High Cost and Non-availability of Commercial Bank Credit

Normally, manufacturers in India face real capital costs (nominal lending charges minus inflation) exceeding 4-5 per cent compared with the 1-2 per cent costs for their global competitors. This has been mitigated recently, with the government permitting external commercial borrowing of up to 200 per cent of a company's net worth. But this measure has helped only the very large manufacturing units, and even for them the foreign exchange risk raises the real cost of capital. It is reported that in a survey, more than two-third of SMEs preferred not to utilise commercial bank credit because of the long and complicated processing times and large volume of collateral demanded by banks. The owners preferred to secure credit from the informal markets at higher rates but with less onerous conditions that did not leave them personally vulnerable. This defeats the avowed aim of the government's selective credit control policy that requires banks to earmark 10 per cent of their credit to SMEs.

India needs a rapidly growing manufacturing sector both to meet its rising demand for industrial products and even more so for absorbing the one million per month new entrants to the workforce. This will require that the current slowdown in the sector be decisively reversed and the sector be put on a path of sustained rapid growth—higher growth than the overall rate of GDP growth. This requires both industry and government (central and states) to implement a reform agenda together. This agenda would in essence increase competition, reduce the extent of dualism in the manufacturing sector, make the regulatory process more transparent, and reduce the compliance burden.

The reforms necessary for the manufacturing sector expansion must be undertaken urgently. For if the country is to achieve its strategic and development objectives, it cannot afford to have a shrinking manufacturing sector.

We now take up the uniqueness aspect of Indian industrial development. In a very insightful analysis of Indian industrialisation since Independence, Kochhar *et al.* (2006) argue that India pursued an 'idiosyncratic' pattern of development which resulted in direct shift of labour from agriculture sector to the service sector, bypassing the intermediate stage (industrial sector) to a considerable extent. Within manufacturing, India has emphasised skill-intensive rather than labour-intensive industries and industries with typically higher average scale. Analysing the pattern of growth of fast-moving Indian states in the reform era, they come to the conclusion that it is unlikely that India will adopt the pattern of development followed by other countries. This prediction has serious implication for the employment potential of the manufacturing sector in the years to come.

Organisation for Economic Co-operation and Development (OECD) (2007) notes that India has followed a unique development path with the share of manufacturing in total GDP not increasing with economic growth, and attributes this feature to 'deeply rooted problems' in the manufacturing sector constraining its growth, although some of these have been eased with reforms. Manufacturing firms were not able to fully exploit their comparative advantages of low-labour costs and have remained very small in scale—yet capital-intensive—limiting productivity gains as well as job creation. In recent years, there has been some employment expansion due to some liberalisation of labour laws, but many of the new jobs are of low quality. Large firms still face obstacles to restructuring employment, constraining their ability to compete effectively.

The analysis reported in OECD (2007) for 21 Indian states on product market regulations (PMR) and employment protection legislation (EPL) shows that the PMR indicator is negatively correlated with state level labour productivity, while EPL indicator is negatively correlates with the extent of job turnover, suggesting that both types of regulations, PMR and EPL, adversely affect economic performance in India.

Micro, Small and Medium Enterprises (MSMEs)

The MSME sector has emerged as a highly vibrant and dynamic sector of the Indian economy over the last few decades.

With 3.6 crore units spread across the country, that employ 8.05 crore people, Micro, Small and Medium Enterprises (MSME) have a contribution of 37.5 per cent to the country's GDP. The sector has huge potential for helping address structural problems like unemployment, regional imbalances, unequal distribution of national income and wealth across the country (*Economic Survey 2015-16*, Vol. II).

It is estimated that this sector contributes about 45 per cent of manufacturing output and 40 per cent of total exports of the country and employs about 69 million persons in over 29 million units throughout the country. Within the MSME sector, there is a significant concentration of micro enterprises, both in terms of working enterprises and employment. There are over 6,000 products ranging from traditional to high-tech items manufactured by the MSMEs. The sector also covers the enterprises established in *khadi* and village industries and coir sector (plans for these sectors are detailed in *Twelfth Five Year Plan*, Vol. II, Ch. 13).

The real importance of the SMEs, however, can be seen in China where over 68 per cent of the exports come from the SMEs. China has created more SMEs in the last 20 years than the total number of SMEs in Europe and the US combined. Their numbers have increased from about 1 million private sector SMEs in the 1990s to 40 million in 2004. In China, an industrial SME is defined as having up to 2,000 employees, while a small business has less than 300 employees and a medium-size business has employees between 301 and 2,000 (Ibid.).

Role of MSEs in Indian Economy

To Generate Large-scale Employment

Not only do MSEs generate the highest employment per capita investment, they also go a long way in checking rural-urban migration by providing villagers and people living in isolated areas with a sustainable source of employment. Among the MSEs in India, the dispersed food products sector generates maximum employment (13.7% of total employment in the MSE sector), followed by non-metallic mineral products (10.9%) and metal products (10.2%). In chemicals and chemical products, machinery parts except electrical parts, wood products, basic metal industries, paper products and printing, hosiery and garments, repair services, and rubber and plastic products, the contribution ranges from 9 per cent to 5 per cent. In all other industries, the contribution is less than 5 per cent.

To Sustain Economic Growth and Increase Exports

Non-traditional products account for more than 95 per cent of the SSI exports. The performance of garments, leather, and gems and jewellery units has been remarkable in the last decade. The SSI sector dominates in export of sports goods, ready-made garments, woollen garments and knitwear, plastic products, processed food and leather products. The US, Europe and West Asia are the major export destinations.

There is tremendous potential to expand the quantum of exports from traditional MSEs because they are handcrafted and hence, eco-friendly and exclusive. Further, while MSEs are unable to take advantage of economies of scale, they are ideal for meeting small order quantities—a bonus in industries such as ready-made garments, home furnishings, etc.

MSEs often act as ancillary industries for LSIs providing them with raw materials, vital components and backward linkages. For instance, large cycle manufacturers of Ludhiana rely heavily on the small MSEs of Malerkotla which produce cycle parts. MSEs also promote eco-friendly growth, especially in difficult terrains and the ecologically sensitive areas. In large tracts of barren desert land in Barmer and Kutch, in the scattered *dhanis* of Udaipur, in the hilly hamlets of J&K, Ladakh, Himachal and the North-east, in the tribal hinterlands of central India, they are the only source of livelihood.

For Making Growth Inclusive

The MSE sector is a microcosm of all vulnerabilities—it touches upon the lives of women, children, minorities, SCs and STs in the villages, in the urban slums and in the deprived pockets of flourishing towns and cities. For many families, it is the only source of livelihood. For others, it supplements the family income. Thus, instead of taking a welfare approach, this sector seeks to empower people to break the cycle of poverty and deprivation. It focuses on people's skills and agency.

The Twelfth Plan has listed the following as the objectives for the MSME sector:

1. Promoting competitiveness and productivity in the MSME space.
2. Making the MSME sector innovative, improving technology and depth.
3. Enabling environment for promotion and development of MSMEs.
4. Strong presence in exports.
5. Improved managerial processes in MSMEs.

Status and Key Challenges

There are some inherent challenges faced by the sector which have a strong impact on its growth. These relate to (i) availability of credit and institutional finance, (ii) outdated technology and innovation, (iii) need for skill development and training, (iv) inadequate industrial infrastructure, and (v) marketing and procurement.

State governments are formulating and implementing heterogeneous sets of regulations. Apart from inspections and compliances, insolvency provisions make it difficult to restructure and rehabilitate sick and dying businesses in the SMEs sector. Procedures to buy and acquire land are costly. Registration of land sale and purchase deeds, transfer of title, and acquiring of construction permits are complicated and time-consuming procedures. While some states have taken steps to promote ease of doing business in recent years, the majority of states are still far from having a friendly eco system for small businesses.

Public Sector

The declared social objective of the Indian development strategy since Independence has been growth with social justice which was sought to be achieved within the democratic political framework and for which India adopted the concept of mixed economy. The expansion of the public sector was considered to be a major instrument with which the state in a mixed economy operating under the democratic framework can influence the pace as well as the composition of economic activity with a view to pursuing the social objective. However, a large part of the economic activity will remain market based, decentralised in nature and in the private sector.

The Rationale

In India, the rationale for the public sector has been explicit or implicit in all plan documents as well as policy statements, although the emphasis has changed in degrees depending upon the constraints faced and the emerging major issues of the time.

It was in the context of the Mahalanobis strategy that the approach to the public sector got further crystallised. The long-term growth orientation in an import-substitution dominated strategy required that the domestic capacity creation be biased in the direction of producing capital goods to produce more capital goods. According to (late) Prof. Tendulkar, the distinct preference for the public sector in this strategy can be traced to the following reasons.

First, the concentration of economic power that would result from the uncontrolled operation of the market forces can be reduced through the extension in the public ownership of means of production.

Secondly, private investors may demand a higher risk premium for investment in certain industries than would be socially justified. Off-shore drilling of oil is one example in this connection.

Thirdly, the scale of investment efforts in certain heavy industries may be beyond the capital-raising capacity of the private sector e.g., steel mills, heavy electrical machinery.

Fourthly, the public sector, through the appropriate price policy for its output will generate investible surpluses for further investment in the economy.

Fifthly, by production as well as distribution of certain universal intermediate inputs like coal, steel, electricity etc., the state will be able to control the composition of private economic activity in a socially desirable direction.

Finally, the public sector would assume the role of a model employer and its employment and wage policies would have a moderating influence on the corresponding policies in the private sector.

Analysing these reasons, one finds that public sector was expected to fulfil varied and sometime conflicting objectives. The generation of investible surplus was bound to conflict with subsidies involved in keeping the prices of certain universal intermediates at low levels as well as the public sector's role as a model employer.

In the 1960s and 1970s, the public sector policy has been largely guided by the Industrial Policy Resolution of 1956 which gave the public sector a strategic role in the economy. Massive investments have been made to build a public sector which had a commanding role in the economy. Many key sectors of the economy are today dominated by mature public enterprises that have successfully expanded production; opened up new areas of technology and built up a reserve of technical competence in a number of areas.

The public sector in India, in its broadest measure as recorded in the National Accounts Statistics (NAS), currently contributes to about a quarter of the GDP increasing from slightly less than one-tenth in 1960-61 (the earliest year with firm estimates). The gross value added of the administrative departments, broadly representing Adam Smith's "duties of the sovereign", accounts for 8-9 per cent of GDP; natural monopolies such as the railways and the postal system add another 3-4 per cent. But the largest share of public sector gross value added, 12-13 per cent of GDP, comes from the non-departmental enterprises (NDEs), producing many private goods and services, but mainly from utilities and infrastructure, owned and operated by the central, state and local governments. NDEs are further disaggregated into: (i) financial enterprises that are part of the financial sector (including the RBI), and (ii) the non-financial enterprises, which account for much of the growth in public sector output during the last half century.

Performance of Central Public Sector Undertakings

The Central Public Sector Enterprises (CPSE) have played a significant role in India's growth process. Out of 298 CPSEs under the administrative control of various ministries/departments, 235 were in operation and 63 under construction up to December 2015. Financial investment (paid-up capital + long-term loans) in all the CPSEs taken together stood at R10,96,057 crore as on 31 March 2015, showing an increase of 10.48 per cent over 2013-14. The net profit of profit making (157) CPSEs stood at R1,30,363 crore in 2014-15, while net loss of loss-making (77) CPSEs stood at R27,360 crore. ONGC Ltd, Coal India Ltd, NTPC Ltd, the National Mineral Development Corporation (NMDC) Ltd and Power Finance Corporation Ltd were the top five profit-making CPSEs during 2014-15, whereas Bharat Sanchar Nigam Ltd, Air India Ltd, Mahanagar Telephone Nigam Ltd, Hindustan Photo Films Manufacturing Company Ltd and Mangalore Refinery and Petrochemicals Ltd were the top five lossmaking CPSEs (*Economic Survey 2015-16*, Vol. II).

CPSEs contribute to the central exchequer by way of dividend payment, interest on government loans and payment of taxes and duties. Their contribution to the central exchequer, however, decreased from R2,20,981 crore in 2013-14 to R2,00,584 crore in 2014-15. This was mainly on account of a decrease in their contribution to dividend, corporate tax and custom duty in 2014-15. There was, however, an increase in their contribution to excise duty, dividend tax, sales tax and service tax.

Privatisation

Privatisation may be broadly defined as the transfer of various activities from the public to the private sphere. Specifically, it could mean the sale by government or state-owned enterprises (SOEs) to private economic agents. It could refer to a sale that is effected in full or in part. It can also mean a partnership between the public and private sectors through a transfer of responsibilities from the public to private sector. In terms of broad political economy, it could also simply mean a shrinking of the welfare state (Nayak, 2007).

Privatisation: Indian Experience since 1991

In 1991, when the government embarked on a comprehensive process of economic reform and liberalisation, the public sector in India accounted for more than one-fifth of the country's GDP. Since a large number of public-sector enterprises (PSEs) regularly showed negative profit margins, the government was keen on a programme of privatisation, calling it disinvestment instead.

The Rangarajan Committee report on the Disinvestment of Shares in PSEs in April 1993 emphasised the need for substantial disinvestment, and recommended that the percentage of equity to be divested could go up to 49 per cent for industries especially reserved for the public sector. It recommended that in exceptional cases, such as enterprises that had a dominant market share or where separate identity had to be maintained for strategic reasons, the target public ownership level could be kept at 26 per cent, that is disinvestment could take place to the tune of 74 per cent. In all other cases, it recommended 100 per cent divestment of the government stake. Holding of 51 per cent or more equity by the government was recommended only for six scheduled industries, namely: (i) coal and lignite, (ii) mineral oils, (iii) arms, ammunitions and defence equipment, (iv) atomic energy, (v) radioactive minerals, and (vi) railway transport.

In 1996, the government set up the Disinvestment Commission with a view to formulate procedures so that any decision to disinvest would be taken and implemented in a transparent manner. The revenues generated from such disinvestment were to be allocated for education and health and for creating a fund to strengthen PSEs. By August 1999, the Disinvestment Commission made recommendations on 58 PSEs. The recommendations indicated a shift from public offerings to strategic/trade sales, with transfer of management. The Commission also observed that the essence of a long-term disinvestment strategy should be not only to enhance budgetary receipts, but also to minimise budgetary support to unprofitable units while ensuring their long-term viability. By 1998, government was of the view that 'in the generality of cases its shareholding in PSEs will be brought down to 26 per cent'. In PSEs involving strategic considerations, namely arms and ammunitions, atomic energy and railway transport, government was to retain majority voting.

By 2000-01, the government's policy regarding privatisation and public-sector restructuring comprise the following considerations:

restructure and revive potentially viable PSEs, close down PSEs that cannot be revived, bring down government equity in all strategic PSEs to 20 per cent or lower, if necessary, and fully protect the interests of workers. The entire receipt from disinvestments and privatisation was to be used for meeting expenditure in social sectors, restructuring of PSEs and meeting public debt.

The Ministry of Disinvestment was converted into a department under the Ministry of Finance with effect from 27 May 2004 after the UPA (United Progressive Alliance) government headed by Dr. Manmohan Singh as Prime Minister assumed office. From this point on, the disinvestment programme had to be in conformity with the National Common Minimum Programme. All privatisations were from now on to be considered on a transparent and consultative case-by-case basis. It was made explicit that the UPA would retain the existing *navaratna* companies, which include the BHEL (Bharat Heavy Electricals Limited), in the public sector and that these will be permitted to raise resources from the capital market. The government constituted a 'National Investment Fund' in January 2005 into which the realisation from sale of minority shareholding of the government in profitable PSEs would be channelised. This fund would be maintained outside the Consolidated Fund of India and the income from this fund would be used for the following purposes: (i) invest in social sector projects that promote education, health care and employment and (ii) capital investment in selected profitable and revivable PSEs that yield adequate returns, in order to enlarge their capital base to finance expansion or diversification (Nayak, 2007).

According to Kelkar (2010), disinvestment is an area of economic policy with multiple objectives. The most important objective should be that of increasing the efficiency with which the labour and capital, that is in existing PSUs, is converted into GDP. In addition, other auxiliary goals include enhancing investment in the country, creating new traditions of corporate governance catering to consumer interests by maximising competition in product markets, and reducing the stock of public debt. An important positive impact of disinvestment upon our fiscal problems would flow through a higher GDP growth.

Regarding the policy for deployment of resources generated through disinvestment/privatisation which is currently channelised from the National Investment Fund, Kelkar argues that this is a restrictive policy and we should liberalise this fully by allowing the government to use these resources as a part of the budgetary resources to create new public capital assets—whether in the form of better urban infrastructure by providing capital grants to our cities or for revamping the country's energy base through an ambitious solar energy programme or the expansion of rural road network or for recharging the country's depleting water bodies and cleaning of rivers. This would require the union government sharing the proceeds from disinvestment or privatisation with the state governments on a systematic basis on the lines of the Finance Commission's devolution formula for the sharing of union taxes with the states.

For coming decades, water, environment and urban infrastructure are going to be the key binding constraints on India's growth ambition. To remove these binding constraints, we will require large investments to accelerate the country's march towards high quality growth. Disinvestment and privatisation policy has now assumed strategic importance in our country.

According to Kelkar (2010), India's future lies in building a new institutional architecture with government as regulator and with the private sector doing investment. If we think of the next 25 years, a very substantial portion of the investment in all regulated industries in India is going to come from the private sector. It makes more sense for the government to reorganise itself, shifting into the role of the umpire and away from the role of the player.

To sum up, we need a bold and imaginative programme for disinvestment and privatisation calling for restructuring of the portfolio of the country's 'public capital assets'. It does not mean a retreat of the state but essentially a re-engineering of its portfolio of public capital assets. This will help our country meet the challenges of the first half of the 21st century just like our PSUs helped the country in the second half of the 20th century to overcome our industrial backwardness (Kelkar, ch. 19).

In conclusion, we may quote (late) Minhas (1991) which is very relevant even today.

> The choice between the public sector enterprises and private firms is not a simple either/or question. While there may be eminently good reasons for promoting public sector production under certain circumstances, nevertheless there is no basis whatever for the doctrine of the so-called commanding heights. The Indian economy is struggling in the deep swamps of inefficiency. Its deliverance from this inefficiency trap can be vastly facilitated if both the public sector

and private firms are exposed more and more to global competition and the arbitrary bureaucratic controls for the regulation of entry and freedom of exit of firms are substantially rolled back.

There is certainly no clear superiority of private *vis-à-vis* public ownership from the standpoint of economic theory. More than ownership, it would seem that the degree of competition and the regulatory environment are more relevant to productive efficiency. The empirical evidence presents a mixed picture. As the world environment gets more competitive, it would be necessary to put the sizeable assets of the PSEs in countries like India to more productive use. Ultimately, it is this consideration that should be of relevance rather than the simplistic presumption that the public sector is necessarily inefficient or that privatisation is an all-purpose panacea (Nayak, 2007).

Foreign Direct Investment (FDI)

Foreign direct investment (FDI is an important driver of economic growth as it leads to productivity enhancement and is a major source of non-debt financial resources and employment generation. FDI inflows are critical for sustaining a high growth rate. The government is playing a proactive role in investment promotion through a liberal FDI policy. A favourable policy regime and sound business environment have facilitated increase in FDI flows into the country.

With a view to liberalizing and simplifying the FDI policy to provide ease of doing business climate in the country that will also lead to larger FDI inflows, the government has undertaken various reforms. A number of sectors have been liberalized, including defence, construction, broadcasting, civil aviation, plantation, trading, private sector banking, satellite establishment and operation and credit information companies. During 2015-16, FDI policy in the pension sector has been revised to permit foreign investment up to 49 per cent, with 26 per cent under automatic route. Manufacturing of medical devices and white label ATM operations have been opened up to 100 per cent FDI under automatic route (*Economic Survey 2015-16*, Vol.II).

The various reforms in the FDI sector have led to a significant increase in FDI inflows into India. During April-November 2015, total FDI inflows were US$34.8 billion as compared to US$27.7 billion during April-November 2014, showing a 26 per cent surge. FDI equity inflows also increased from US$18.9 billion during April-November 2014 to

US$24.8 billion during April-November 2015, showing 31 per cent growth. There were FDI inflows into sectors like computer software and hardware, services, trading, automobile industry, construction (infrastructure) activities, chemicals (other than fertilizers) and telecommunications. FDI statistics of the last fifteen years reveal that the services sector has accounted for the highest inflows (17.6% of total FDI inflows into India), followed by construction development (8.8%), computer hardware and software (7.2%), telecommunications (6.6%) and the automobile industry (5.2%).

There are wide variations in the FDI inflows into India from different countries. However, Singapore, Mauritius, Netherlands and the USA account for the major share. Out of FDI equity inflows of US$24.8 billion during 2015-16 (April- November), more than 60 per cent have come from two geographically small countries named Singapore and Mauritius. These inflows need perhaps to be examined more closely to determine whether they constitute actual investment or are diversions from other sources to avail of tax benefits under the Double Tax Avoidance Agreement that these countries have with India (*Economic Survey 2015-16*).

A country-wise analysis of the FDI inflows in major sectors from 2011 to 2015 (till November) from top five countries are given in Table 14.5.

Table 14.5

FDI Inflows to Major Sectors from Top Five Host Countries (in %) from 2011-12 to 2015-16 (November)

Sectors	*Singapore*	*Mauritius*	*Netherlands*	*US*	*Japan*
Services sector	18.6	18.9	15.4	19	20
Computer software and hardware	13.8	6.2	3.2	9.8	1
Trading	11.8	2.4	10	3.2	4.6
Telecommunications	8.6	11.5	0.3	2	0.1
Drugs & pharmaceuticals	6.6	1.0	0.6	2	3
Power	5.0	6.1	2.7	4	0.3
Construction (infrastructure)	3.5	3.9	0.2	3.5	0.5
Hotel tourism	2.3	10.6	0.6	0.8	0.1
Automobiles	1.9	1.5	8.7	17.8	21
Chemicals	NA	1.6	8.9	1.8	2.7
Petroleum and natural gas	0.7	1.1	8.4	0.1	1.2

Source: Economic Survey 2015-16.

The Government of India has taken a series of measures to improve 'Ease of Doing Business' in the country. Existing rules have been simplified and information technology introduced to make governance more efficient and effective. Large improvements in World Economic Forum and World Bank rankings testify to the reforms implemented in this regard. Reflecting the better economic performance and the commitment of the government to reforms, the global perception about India's competitiveness has improved as per the Global Competitiveness Index of the World Economic Forum. Significantly, at position 55, India went up 16 rungs in 2015-16, which is the largest gain among the major economies (*Economic Survey 2015-16*, Vol.II).

References

Ahluwalia, Isher J. (2006). "Trade Liberalisation and Industrial Performance: A Disaggregated View of Indian Manufacturing in the 1990s", in S.D. Tendulkar *et al.* (eds.) (2006), *India: Industrialisation in a Reforming Economy: Essays for K.L. Krishna*. New Delhi: Academic Foundation.

———. (1985). *Industrial Growth in India: Stagnation since the Mid-Sixties*. Oxford University Press.

———. (1991). *Productivity and Growth in Indian Manufacturing*. Oxford University Press.

Bhagwati, Jagdish and Arvind Panagariya (2012). *India's Tryst with Destiny*. New Delhi: Collins Business.

Bhagwati, Jagdish and Padma Desai (1970). *India: Planning for Industrialization*. Oxford University Press.

Desai, Ashok V. (2002). "A Decade of Reforms", in Raj Kapila and Uma Kapila (eds.) (2002), *A Decade of Economic Reforms in India: The Past, The Present and The Future*. New Delhi: Academic Foundation.

Government of India, *Economic Survey*, various issues including 2011-12, 2012-13, 2013-14, 2014-15, 2015-16.

Kapila, Uma (ed.) (2012). *Two Decades of Economic Reforms*. New Delhi: Academic Foundation.

Kelkar, Vijay (2010). "On Strategies of Disinvestment and Privatisation", (26th Sir Purshotamdas Thakurdas Memorial Lecture, January 29, Mumbai) in Sameer Kochhar and M. Ramachandran (eds.) (2010), *Building from the Bottom: Infrastructure and Poverty Alleviation*, New Delhi: Academic Foundation.

Krishna, K.L. (2010). "Industrial Growth and Diversification", in Uma Kapila (ed.) (2010), *Indian Economy since Independence*, 21st edition. New Delhi: Academic Foundation.

———. (2015). "Industrial Development and Policies Since Independence: Growth without Employment", in Uma Kapila (ed.) (2015), *Indian Economy since Independence*, 26st edition. New Delhi: Academic Foundation.

Kumar, Rajiv (2014). "Revisiting Manufacturing Policy", in Bibek Debroy, Ashley J. Tellis and Reece Trevor (eds.) (2014), *Getting India Back on Track: An Action Agenda for Reform*. Random House India.

Mohan, Rakesh (1992). "Industrial Policy and Controls", in Bimal Jalan (ed.) (1992), *The Indian Economy, Problems and Prospects*. Viking Penguin India.

Nagaraj, R. (2006). *Aspects of India's Economic Growth and Reforms*. New Delhi: Academic Foundation.

———. (2011). "Trends and Patterns in Industrial Growth: A Review of Evidence and Explanations", *Indian Industrialisation*. New Delhi.

Nayak, Pulin (2007). "Privatisation", in Kaushik Basu (ed.) (2007), *Oxford Companion to Economics in India*. New Delhi: OUP.

Nayyar, Deepak (1996). "Economic Liberalisation in India: Analytics Experiences and Lessons", R C Dutt Lectures. Orient Longman.

Planning Commission (2012). *Twelfth Five Year Plan 2012-2017*, Vol. II.

———. (2010). *Mid Term Appraisal, Eleventh Five Year Plan.*

———. (2008). *Eleventh Five Year Plan 2007-2012*, Vol. III.

———. (2005). *Mid-Term Appraisal of the Tenth Five Year Plan* (June).

———. (2002). *Tenth Five Year Plan* (2002-07) (December).

Rangarajan, C. (2003). Select Essays on Indian Economy (Vol.1). Academic Foundation.

Reserve Bank of India, Report on Currency and Finance, 2001-02, 2005-06.

Tendulkar, S.D., Arup Mitra, K. Narayanam and Deb Kusum Das (2006). *India: Industrialisation in a Reforming Economy: Essays in Honour of Prof. K.L. Krishna*. New Delhi: Academic Foundation.

15

R. NAGARAJ

Industrial Performance, 1991-2008

*A Review**

Introduction

In 1990-91, industry (manufacturing) contributed 26 per cent of India's gross domestic product (GDP) (15%), employing 15 per cent (12%) of the workforce and using 39 per cent (24%) of the economy's net renewable capital stock.[1] In the 1980s, industry was the economy's 'leading' sector, growing annually at over 6 per cent, while the domestic output grew annually at around 5.5 per cent and exports (two-third of which were manufactures) at 8.5 per cent (in current dollar terms). The decade witnessed modernisation of the production structure with a step up in infrastructure, de-licensing of investment and output controls, and a shift in trade policy from quotas to tariff. However, in 1991, the economy faced a liquidity crisis on account of (i) the Gulf War (leading to the drying up of inward remittances and project exports), (ii) collapse of the Soviet Union (then India's largest trading partner) and (iii) the domestic political uncertainty, paralysing policy making.

Encouraged by the industrial and export boom of the 1980s, the orthodox economic reforms initiated in 1991 sought to (i) make a bonfire of the remaining output and investment controls that are said to have throttled private initiative; (ii) cut back public investment as it is believed to have 'crowded out' private investment; (iii) undermine the protective and promotional measures for small-scale industries that are claimed to have bred inefficiency and failed to expand labour-intensive manufactures; and (iv) sell minority equity holding in public

---

* The author is grateful to K.L. Krishna, K.V. Ramaswamy, and C. Veeramani for their comments and suggestions on an earlier draft of the chapter.

sector enterprises (called 'disinvestments') to reduce government's fiscal deficit. Policy makers apparently perceived an opportunity in the crisis to quickly undo India's state-led, inward-oriented industrialisation strategy, as it is claimed to have delivered neither adequate growth nor measurable equity—unlike in East Asia and China that have succeeded in export-oriented industrialisation following market friendly policies.

Surely, disenchantment with the regulatory mechanism in India had been growing for quite a while. Starting with R.K. Hazari's evaluation of the industrial licensing system in the mid-1960s to the Dagli Committee report (1979) on controls and subsidies in the late 1970s, there were compelling official evidence against the dysfunctional and discretionary policies, buttressing the critique of India's industrialisation strategy, starting with Bhagwati and Desai's (1970) contribution.

There was, however, an equally persuasive scepticism of the virtues of unbridled play of market forces in a large, diverse and unequal agrarian economy. Liberal trade and investment regime could be a recipe for a flood of imports, decimating domestic enterprise and retrenching workers; domination of foreign capital resulting in de-industrialisation, compelling the nation to revert to exporting primary products that face cyclical fluctuations and adverse terms of trade in the long run. Serious apprehensions were also expressed that the reforms could undermine the domestic market-driven independent path of industrialisation, denting the long-term growth prospects—as had happened in much of Latin America and Africa after the debt crisis in the 1980s. In other words, while the market-oriented reforms were espoused on the promise of faster and labour-intensive (hence equitable) growth, critics feared debt, deflation and de-industrialisation.

After nearly two decades of the reforms, it is perhaps an opportune moment to ask: how does the industrial performance measure up against these expectations and apprehensions? This chapter offers a brief answer, mostly using the official aggregate statistics. Excluding the introduction and conclusion, the chapter has three sections: the next section describes the industrial performance. The section that follows it makes a critical assessment of the competing perspectives on the reforms, and the section thereafter outlines possible policy options.

Industrial Performance After 1991-92

Figure 15.1 plots the annual growth rates in industrial output as measured by (i) the index of industrial production (IIP) and (ii) GDP in industry since 1990-91; both the indices show the same trend. After an expected dip in 1991-92 on account of the crisis and adjustment, output boomed for four years, peaking in 1995-96 at 13 per cent—following the predicted 'J' curve, vindicating the reform stance. For a variety of reasons, however, the boom petered out quickly, followed by a steep deceleration for seven years until 2002-03. The next boom lasted for five years, from 2003-04 to 2007-08.

Figure 15.1

Industrial Growth, 1991-2009

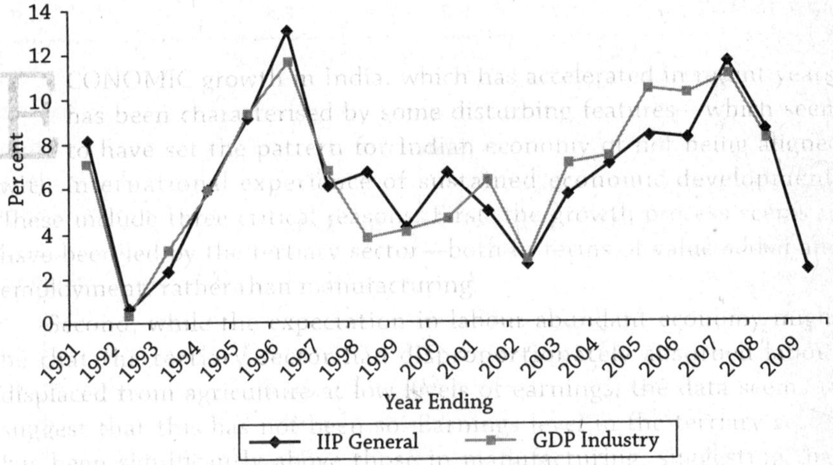

Source: *Economic Survey* and National Accounts Statistics , various issues.

So, the average of annual growth rate over the 17-year period since 1991-92 is 6.6 per cent. During this period, consumer durables grew the fastest at 8.1 per cent per year (weight in the index in 1993-94, 2.6%), followed by capital goods at 7.4 per cent per year (weight 16.4%) (Table 15.1). By two-digit industry groups, beverages (National Industrial Classification [NIC 22]) recorded the fastest growth at 12 per cent per year (Table 15.2). However, capital goods, hurt by the sharp reduction in tariffs, stagnated during the first boom but bloomed in the next one, growing annually at nearly 15 per cent during 2003-2008, led by automobiles (NIC 37).

How does the industrial growth after the reforms reported earlier compare with the 1980s? Table 15.3 reports the trend growth rates for two-digit industry groups for total manufacturing GDP using the

Table 15.1

Industrial Output Growth, 1991-92 to 2007-08
(Average of Annual Growth Rates)

	IIP General	IIP-Manufacturing	Use-based Classification of IIP				Consumer Goods	
			Basic	Capital	Intermediate	Consumer Goods	CDs	CNDs
1992-1996	6.2	6.1	7.8	0.3	8.0	5.8	7.3	3.7
1997-2002	5.2	5.6	3.9	5.8	6.2	5.6	9.6	4.3
2003-2008	8.2	8.9	6.5	14.8	6.6	9.0	7.2	9.7
1992-2008	**6.6**	**6.9**	**5.9**	**7.4**	**6.8**	**7.7**	**8.1**	**6.0**

Note: CDs: consumer durables; CNDs: Consumer non-durables.
Source: *Economic Survey*, various issues.

Table 15.2

Industrial Output Growth by Two-Digit Industry Groups, 1991-92 to 2007-08
(Average of annual percentage growth rates)

NIC	Industry Group	1992-1996	1997-2002	2003-2008	1992-2008
20–21	Food	4.6	2.7	4.5	3.9
22	Beverages	9.2	11.6	14.3	11.9
23	Cotton Textiles	6.8	2.4	4.9	4.6
24	Silk, Wool Textiles	10.7	9.0	4.3	7.8
25	Jute	1.3	–0.2	4.3	1.8
26	Textile Products	0.6	3.8	10.3	5.2
27	Wood	5.0	–4.3	7.2	2.5
28	Paper	7.4	5.4	7.3	6.6
29	Leather	1.2	8.3	1.2	3.7
30	Rubber	3.1	6.7	6.4	5.6
31	Chemicals	6.6	8.0	9.2	8.0
32	Non-metallic Minerals	8.9	9.0	6.6	8.1
33	Basic Metals	13.6	3.0	12.4	9.4
34	Metal Products	–2.2	6.4	3.4	2.8
35–36	Electrical and Non-electric machinery	3.0	6.4	12.1	7.4
37	Transport Equipment	8.0	7.6	11.0	8.9
38	Other Manufacturing	3.5	4.8	13.2	7.4
2–3	**Manufacturing**	**6.1**	**5.6**	**8.9**	**6.9**

Source: *Economic Survey*, various issues.

National Accounts Statistics (NAS). In the aggregate, there is hardly any difference in growth rate in the two periods. However, machinery manufacturing (NIC 31 and 32) grew faster in the 1980s at 12.7 per cent per year, while transport equipment fared better after the reforms of 1991.

Table 15.3

Comparing Industrial Growth: 1981-1991 and 1992-2008

NIC-98	*Industry Description*	*Growth Rate*	
		1981-1991	*1992-2008*
151-154	Food Products	6.6	5.2
155+16	Beverages and Tobacco	4.4	8
171-173+181+014505	Textiles	4.6	5.2
182+19	Leather and Fur	3.4	4.4
20+361	Wood	-2.7	-1.5
21+22	Paper and Printing	9.1	3.9
23+25	Rubber and Petroleum	13.6	5.8
24	Chemicals	9.3	8.3
26	Non-metallic Mineral Products	8.7	7.3
271+272+2731+2732	Basic Metals	5.8	7.9
28+29+30	Metal Products and Machinery	6	5.6
31+32	Electric Machinery	12.7	10.3
33+369	Other Manufacturing	10.6	8.5
34+35	Transport Equipment	5.5	8.6
	GDP manufacturing	6.3	6.5

Source: *Economic Survey*, various issues.

How does the forgoing performance measure up against the alternative perspectives discussed earlier? In spite of the dismantling of the much criticised 'permit licence raj', industrial growth rate has not accelerated, nor has the growth rate of labour-intensive consumer goods gone up, but there has been no de-industrialisation either, as the critics feared: the shares of industrial employment and output in the total have not declined (as had happened in Latin America and Africa after the debt crisis in the 1980s) (Figure 15.2 and Table 15.4). The structural transformation of workforce has continued at the same pace after the reforms, though the workforce has gone into the services, not manufacturing (Table 15.4). Within industry, the incremental workforce has gone into construction (not shown here). Measured by investment, the reforms were not a setback for industrialisation, as the manufacturing sector's share in total fixed investment has gone up from around 27 per cent in the 1980s to about 40 per cent in the current decade (Figure 15.3).

Table 15.4

Employment and Output Share of Principal Sectors, 1983 to 2004-05

(%)

	Employment			GDP		
	1983	1993-94	2004-05	1983	1993-94	2004-05
1. Agriculture	68.5	64.0	56.5	37.1	30.0	20.2
2. Industry	13.8	15.0	18.7	24.3	25.2	26.2
2.1 Manufacturing	10.7	10.6	12.2	14.5	14.5	15.1
3. Services	17.6	21.1	24.8	38.6	44.8	53.6

Sources: NAS, various issues; National Sample Survey (NSS) *Employment and Unemployment Surveys*, various rounds.

Figure 15.2

Shares of Industry and Manufacturing in GDP

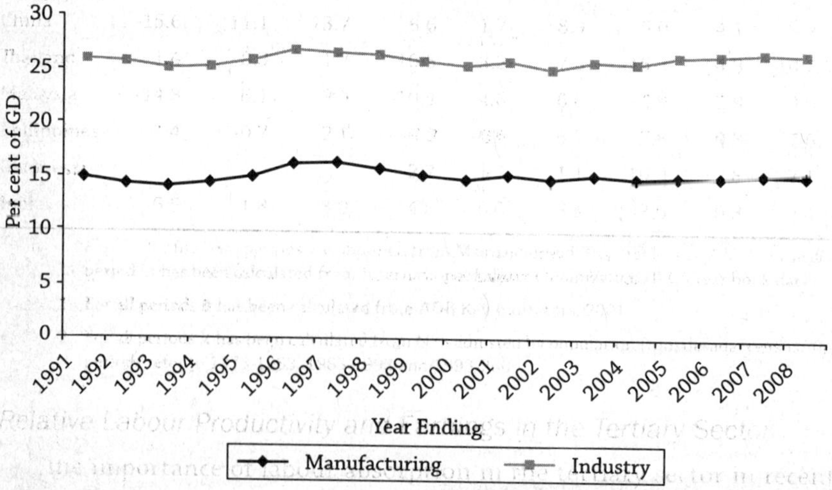

Source: NAS, various issues.

Figure 15.3

Investment Shares, 1991-2008

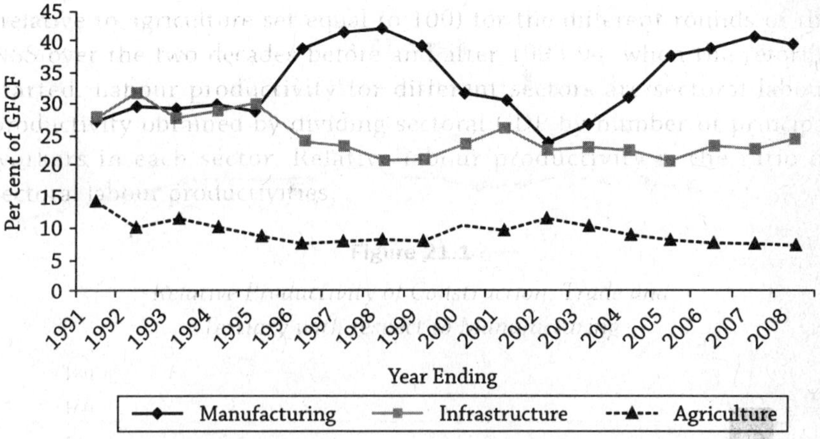

Source: NAS, various issues.

The proponents and the critics of the reforms alike expected the share of capital goods in output and investment to fall, as it was considered emblematic of the state-led import substitution industrialisation. But its growth rate went up modestly after the reforms (mainly automobiles in the current decade). India's export basket has got diversified after the reforms, mainly into services—surprising the proponents and critics of the reforms alike. This is perhaps an unintended outcome of the India's sustained investments in capital goods and high-technology industries made earlier on, along with the nurturing of scientific and technical education. However, within merchandise exports, the share of manufactures has fallen from 80 per cent in the 1990s to 64 per cent in 2007-08 as primary exports (mainly iron ore) also boomed in the current decade.

While the foregoing account represents a broad picture of continuity with change, on a closer look, there are some causes of concern. While there is no de-industrialisation, industry or manufacturing sector's share in domestic output has practically stagnated and its export share has declined; by implication, primary sector's share in merchandise exports has risen (Figures 15.2 and 15.4). Arguably, the rising share of primary exports is almost entirely due to iron ore exports to China (propelled largely by the Beijing Olympics-related construction), as India rode the commodity boom, perhaps out of the necessity to finance burgeoning petroleum imports. This was perhaps avoidable, if the much-anticipated expansion of labour-intensive manufacturing was realised.

Figure 15.4

India's Trade Balance, 1991-2008

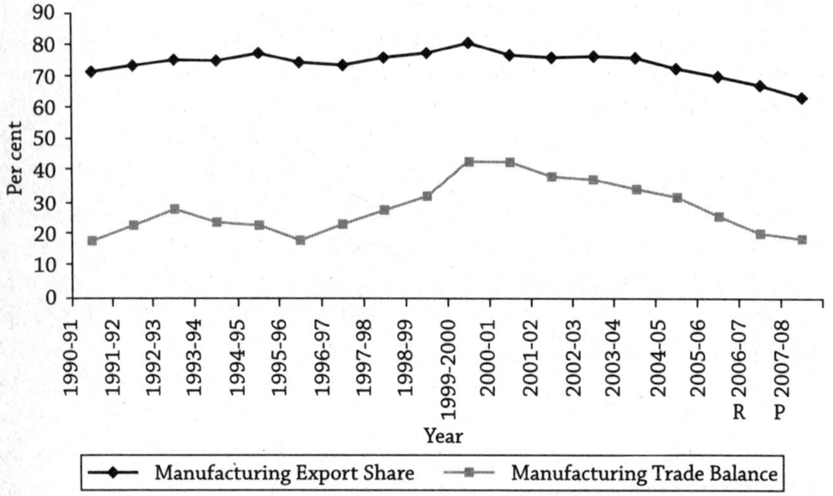

Source: *Economic Survey* and NAS, various issues.

Why did manufacturing sector's share in total employment stagnate, despite a respectable trend growth of over 6.5 per cent per year? *Prima facie*, it represents the failure of the reforms to promote labour-intensive manufacturing in spite of doing away with the import substitution bias in the industrial policy. Partly, growing capital intensity of production in general perhaps explains the employment stagnation, as it has become much easier to import the latest labour-saving equipment in an open trade regime with modest tariffs (if any).

There could, however, be some deeper structural reasons as well, with increasing sub-contracting (outsourcing) of manufacture of parts and auxiliary services to the unorganised sector, and forging of close supply-chain networks. Such an organisation of production is quite the opposite of the vertically integrated production structures that were common in the early years of industrialisation. After the reforms, with increased competitive pressure, under the liberalised rules of resource use, and with lax enforcement of labour laws, firms have apparently restructured their production processes by shedding labour. Conceivably, some of the employment lost in the organised sector would have reappeared in the unorganised sector, though no direct evidence for it is available. [2] Therefore, while the stagnation of the industrial employment share is a cause for concern, it perhaps represents an outcome of the changing market conditions, organisation of production and technology in an open labour-surplus economy.

Thus, what emerges from the foregoing (mainly) statistical account is a nuanced picture of industrial change. While India has managed to averted de-industrialisation, its output growth rate has not accelerated. Manufacturing sector's share in GDP has stagnated; its share in merchandise exports has declined in favour of primary products—perhaps suggesting signs of weaknesses of the domestic capability, as the critics of the reforms have contended. Yet, the sustained growth in output and exports, and a rising share in the economy's fixed investment are reassuring that the reforms have not damaged, in any essential sense, India's industrialisation prospects.

Other Aspects of Industrial Change

The reforms have increased the effective competition in the domestic market with easier imports and entry of new firms, though it would be hard to quantify these effects.[3] Perhaps, for the first time, there is a buyers' market in industrial goods, with improved quality, variety and after-sales service—as evident from the decline in the relative price of capital goods, making fixed investment more productive. The flip side of it is the rising import intensity of production: import share in manufacturing (economy) went up from 12.9 per cent (10.5%) in 1993-04 to 16.8 per cent (12.6%) in 1998-99—reversing the declining trend up the 1980s (Bhat *et al.*, 2007).

Arguably, increased import competition, especially in capital goods, would have enhanced productivity. Yet, the evidence of its impact on total factor productivity growth is not conclusive, though labour productivity has climbed steadily (Balakrishnan *et al.*, 2000).

With the reduction in the entry barriers for foreign-owned firms, their share in manufacturing GDP has gone up from 5 per cent in 1991 to about 8 per cent in 2007—probably an underestimate.[4] With the decline in public investment, the share of public sector enterprises in total manufacturing GDP has halved to 8 per cent between 1991 and 2008 (Figure 15.5).

Figure 15.5

Public Sector's and Foreign Films' Share in GDPmfg

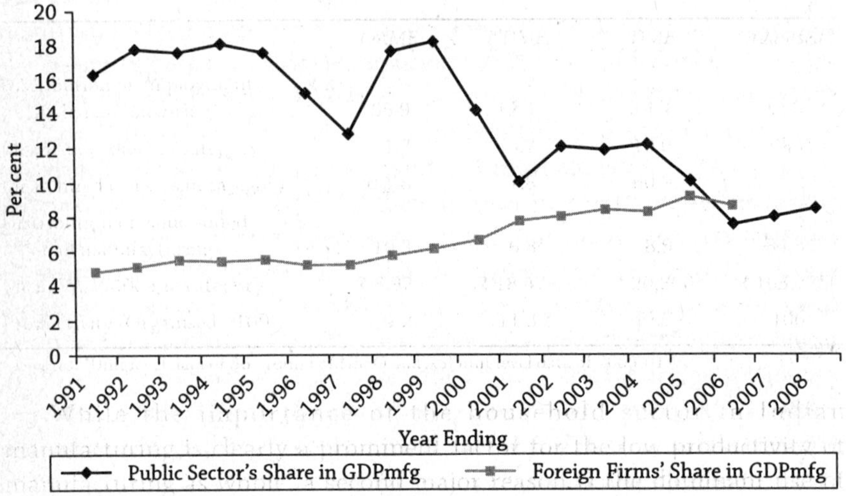

Source: NAS; Corporate Sector , CMIE, various issues.

In the 1990s, the manufacturing sector underwent painful restructuring—plant closures, sell offs of productive assets and relocations, and unprecedented lay offs and retrenchments—that is yet to be adequately documented. In the end, however, it has apparently improved production efficiency to face the increased competition, especially from China. Although research and development (R&D) investments have contracted as a proportion of the domestic output, the restructuring and competitive pressure seem to have spurred innovation and product development—perhaps best exemplified by Tata Indica, followed more recently by Tata Nano, making India the sixth country in the world to design and manufacture passenger cars domestically—a sure sign of industrial maturity (Mani, 2009).[5]

The growing strength and stature of Indian industry and enterprise are also evident from their ability to acquire and manage factories and firms in developed economies in relatively advanced manufacturing industries. For instance, Tata group's exports apparently account for 15-20 per cent of its sales, and (as per the group's website)[6] it earned 61 per cent of its annual revenue from international operations. Moreover, the growing outward foreign direct investment (FDI) by large private Indian firms in the recent boom, estimated at $17.6 billion cumulative stock as in 2008 (UN, 2009)—to leverage their domestic manufacturing capability and use it as a short-cut to acquire technology—is yet another testimony of the coming of age of Indian business (Nagaraj, 2006a; Nayyar, 2008).

Why Did the Reforms Fail to Deliver the Expected Results?

Yet the principal question remains unanswered: why did the speeding up of the reforms after 1991 not yield faster output, employment and labour-intensive growth? The protagonists would contend that the reforms have remained incomplete, with the persistence of the labour market rigidities (lack of entrepreneurial freedom to hire and fire workers at will), infrastructure bottlenecks and incomplete financial integration, including full convertibility of the currency (Kocchar *et al.*, 2006; Panagariya, 2008; Krueger, 2009, among others).

Based on cross-country analysis, Kocchar *et al.* argue that India has followed idiosyncratic policies in promoting skill-intensive industries, discouraging labour-intensive manufactures—a pattern that has not changed after the reforms because of the labour market rigidities. These scholars also contend that on an average Indian firms tend to be small because workers cannot be fired, preventing them from reaping the advantages of economies of scale in production. But, since skilled workers and professionals are outside the purview of trade unions, India has specialised in skill-intensive industries.

Following Little (1987), Krueger (2009), on the other hand, has argued the opposite: industrial productivity is low in India because of the dominance of large-sized factories in manufacturing industries, representing vestiges of inward-looking state-dominated industrialisation. Krueger believes that Indian factories are either too large (employing 1,000 or more workers) or too small (less than 10 workers, in the unregistered sector), both of which are said to be inefficient, while the middle-sized factories (100-500) are the most efficient. She has also identified poor agricultural productivity growth, inadequate infrastructure and labour market rigidities as the other reasons for poor industrial growth.

What then are the facts of the matter? The average factory size in registered manufacturing in 2004-05 was 35 workers per factory, declining steadily over the last half century from over 140 workers (Nagaraj, 1985). Krueger's observation was correct for the 1950s but not any more, with the growth of factories in the intermediate-sized classes. At the other end of the scale, household manufacturing has become marginal with the expansion of smaller-sized workshops and factories. These are long-term trends of industrial change, unaffected by the reforms.

But looking closely at the product level, India surely has many large-sized, international standard factories. For instance, the world's largest bicycle factory (Hero cycles), largest motorcycle plant (Hero Honda), and the second largest petroleum refinery (Reliance refinery in Jamnagar) are all here. However, at the two-digit industry groups, India has a long tailed distribution of firms that makes the average size small (Desai, 1985). But this in itself need not be a sign of inefficiency, if there exist dense intra-industry transactions between large and small firms. Therefore, the relationship between size and efficiency can be ambiguous in principle and practice, as it could depend on a number of other factors like financial structure and aspects of industrial organisation (Tybout, 2000). Thus, without further probing, the argument that the size structure of factories in India is *per se* inimical to efficiency is perhaps difficult to sustain.

The contention that large factories in consumer goods industries in China (like textile weaving or knitting) represent efficient production scale is debatable. Historically, in light manufactures, the average factory size usually tended to be small, with dense inter-firm relationship in small geographical locations. For example, in Japan in early 20th century, or in Taiwan more recently, a lot of light manufactures were produced in small and household enterprises, but were sold world over by large trading houses (especially the Japanese Sogo-Soshos), which provided them with credit, technical assistance and marketing expertise. Such an industrial organisation is predicated on reasonably well-functioning product and credit markets.

But in China, perhaps because of inadequate development of these market-based relationships, firms have often sought to internalise their functions in vertically integrated plants. So, the large-sized factories in China are probably not a sign of a superior or more efficient production organisation but perhaps a symptom of its weakness (Nagaraj, 2007b). Therefore, to hold up China as the model to follow and to find fault with India on this count is perhaps an incorrect reading of the comparative experience.

Labour Market Rigidity Hypothesis

The reformists believe that India's labour laws are the most protective of the organised labour, which makes firing of workers almost impossible, rendering labour a quasi-fixed capital, leading to substitution of capital for labour, yielding little employment growth. Such a reading of the labour law is perhaps facile as it overlooks the 'fine print' of exemptions and loopholes that are built into them. By now, there is abundant evidence to question such a simplistic view.[7] Perhaps it is suffice to present the telling evidence that between 1987 and 2004, 1.3 million workers, or 1 in 6 workers in registered manufacturing, lost their jobs without a murmur of protest or industrial unrest (Nagaraj, 2004). Moreover, in the current economic crisis (since 2008), the labour ministry's quick surveys reported on its website show that during the last financial year (2008-09), 3.7 lakh workers lost their jobs, mostly in export-oriented textiles and gems and jewellery industries—an ample testimony to the fallacy of the labour market rigidity hypothesis, at least in the aggregate.[8]

Infrastructure Bottlenecks

The fact that infrastructure bottlenecks are throttling industrial progress is undisputed. But on how to overcome them and why the progress is so meagre despite much official rhetoric, there can be widely differing diagnoses and prescriptions. Until 1991, public sector provided much of the infrastructure, as in most industrialising economies. But its poor supply was often blamed on lack of resources, enormous cost and time overruns in project completion, and poor public management in general.

Attributing these problems to public ownership, the reforms have encouraged entry of private and foreign capital in these industries. Infrastructure services, by definition, have a long gestation period and are capital intensive, with low rates of return spread over a long period. They are often networked industries, where efficiency of an individual plant or a firm depends on the performance of the entire network, and financial returns depend on output pricing, which are public policy decisions. In such industries, foreign investment is fraught with risk, as evidence world over can testify (Wells and Gleason, 1995). Closer home, the nation has paid dearly for the misadventures like the Enron's Dabhol power project, but policy makers seem to have learnt few lessons from it (Mehta, 1999).[9]

What Should Be Done Now?

If the foregoing critique is valid, what then is the alternative? The reforms implicitly assume that the policy-induced restrictions on supply are holding back output growth. Surely, there is some truth in this, as industrial regulation had degenerated into an inefficient and dysfunctional system. But were these the binding constraints on long-term growth, as the reformists claim? Probably not.

The reforms, in our view, failed to deliver because they ignored the demand factors. Careful analytical work and econometric evidence have suggested that long-term industrial growth in India is constrained by supply as well as demand factors, which, it seems, runs on the twin engines of public investment and agriculture productivity (Chakravarty, 1979; Storm, 1993). Moreover, in a large agrarian economy, public investment removes constraints on productivity growth in agriculture, creating demand for industrial goods—a crucial insight that the writings on the reforms have inadequately appreciated—a view also endorsed by Krueger (2009). Surely, the creative function of competitive industrial structure is to spur efficiency, but it need not necessarily translate into faster and labour-intensive growth, as argued in the mainstream economic literature. As the experience of the 1980s has demonstrated, gradual deregulation of industrial markets, along with stepping up of public infrastructure investment and rising agriculture productivity perhaps provided the right demand and supply conditions for industrial turnaround.

Arthur Lewis famously said that if a nation wants to industrialise, it should enrich its farmers. But farmers have got impoverished after the reforms as the growth rate of crop production has decelerated (Figure 15.6). This seems to get reflected in the widespread phenomenon of farmers committing suicide (under debt burden), which is not just a crisis of production but also a serious humanitarian problem. The agrarian distress has also manifested itself in a political crisis, fuelling rural violence, as evident from the spread of left-wing radical movements, engulfing nearly one-third of the districts in the country.

Proponents of the reforms would probably contend that agriculture has lost the capacity to absorb labour and, in any case, India is saddled with excess food stocks. Both are probably half-truths, as best. As Table 15.5 shows, India's land productivity in all major crops is a modest fraction of the world average, so the argument that agriculture has little scope for absorbing labour to increase productivity is simply incorrect. As is widely acknowledged, overflowing food stocks are not a measure of food self-sufficiency when a large proportion of the poor cannot demand food for lack of purchasing power. So, the argument that agriculture cannot absorb labour is patently false. If we believe that the pace of workforce transformation depends on agriculture productivity to sustain non-agricultural employment, then poor agricultural growth is surely retarding industrial progress.

Figure 15.6

Trends in Agriculture Production, 1981-2007

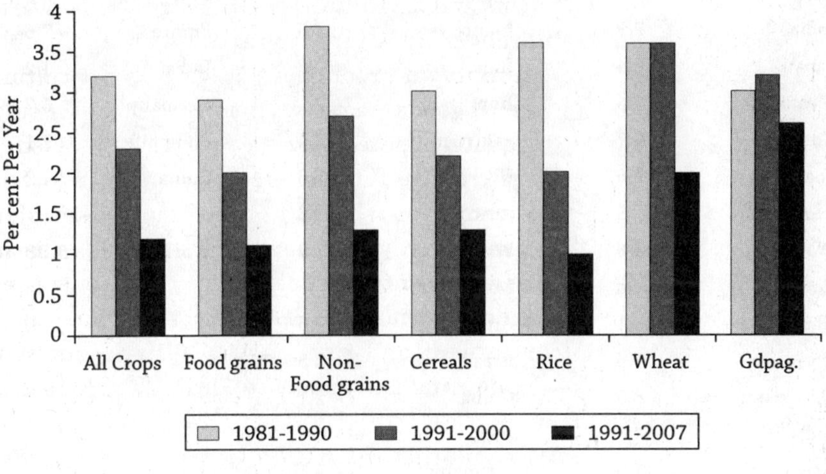

Source: *Economic Survey*, various issues.

The other extreme view—of agrarianism and anti-industrialisation mainly emanating from the recent West Bengal experience—that agriculture alone can cure all the ills of unemployment and underemployment is perhaps equally false, as the 'excess' growth of agriculture can choke industrialisation *via* rising wages in the industrial sector and lack of industrial inputs in agriculture.[10] Therefore, what is needed, as Lewis argued long ago, is balanced growth.[11] Surely, rising demand from rural economy can boost industrial output, but unless industry modernises to augment exports, economy may face external imbalance. Therefore, what is also required after reaching a certain level of economic development, as Kaldor (1967) argued, is growing exports of manufactures to meet finance import requirements. As India has more or less completed import substitution phase, what it now needs to vigorously pursue is export of labour-intensive goods to finance its burgeoning import requirements (especially of oil) to lubricate the engine of domestic market-led growth. This requires modern infrastructure and long-term credit at reasonable interest rates.

Table 15.5

International Comparisons of Yield in Selected Commodities in 2004-05

(Metric tonnes/hectare)

Rice/Paddy	*Yield*	*Wheat*	*Yield*	*Maize*	*Yield*
Egypt	9.8	China	4.3	USA	9.2
India	2.9	France	7.6	France	7.6
Japan	6.4	India	2.7	India	1.2
Myanmar	2.4	Iran	2.1	Germany	6.7
Korea	6.7	Pakistan	2.4	Philippines	2.1
Thailand	2.6	UK	7.8	China	4.9
USA	7.8	Australia	1.6		
World	**3.96**	**World**	**2.9**	**World**	**3.38**
Cotton	Yield	Major Oilseeds			
China	11.1	Argentina	2.5		
USA	9.6	Brazil	2.5		
Uzbekistan	8.0	China	2.1		
India	4.6	India	0.9		
Brazil	11.0	Germany	4.1		
Pakistan	7.6	USA	2.6		
World	7.3	World	1.0		

Source: *Economic Survey*, 2008-09, Ministry of Finance, Government of India (GoI), New Delhi.

But we are now in a peculiar situation: even after steady improvement in the financial performance of public sector enterprises (PSEs) over the last two decades (Nagaraj, 2006b), rising tax-GDP ratio, and a steep increase in domestic saving rate (Nagaraj, 2008), policy makers continue to favour private sector over public sector in infrastructure development due to fiscal orthodoxy. It is true that in the period after the mid-1960s to 1980, excessive and discretionary regulation stifled private initiative. However, it is equally true that leaving infrastructure to private initiative after the reforms did not lead to faster investment and output growth. Therefore, what is needed, as Hazari (1985) insightfully noted, is a judicious rebalancing between the *babu* and *bania*, to achieve the national goals—a balance needs to be pragmatically re-assessed from time to time.

Conclusions

Ending the strategic role of the state-led import-substituting industrialisation, the two decades of industry and trade policy reforms have dismantled the output and investments controls. Many lines of manufacture have become more competitive with a marginal rise in India's share in world merchandise trade to 1 per cent in 2005 (*Economic Survey*, 2007-08). Quality and variety of goods produced have improved; relative price of capital goods has declined (enhancing the productivity of fixed investment), although the import content in domestic production has risen. The unintended boom in the export of services in information technology and related services can be clearly seen as a consequence of investments early on in heavy industry and scientific and technical education. A growing number of Indian firms have gained technical expertise to run factories and firms across the globe, leveraging their domestic competence and, in turn, to acquire technology to enhance their domestic capabilities.

Yet, these achievements have not translated into faster and labour-intensive industrial growth or growth in industrial exports, as compared to the 1980s. As a result, the services sector has replaced manufacturing as the economy's leading sector. Although India did not witness de-industrialisation, as the critics of the reforms apprehended, industry's share of domestic output and employment has stagnated; its share in merchandise export has declined, with rising exports of primary exports (mainly of iron ore). Why did the reforms fail to deliver a faster and equitable industrial growth? In other words, why did the reforms fail to promote labour-intensive growth and manufactured exports, as in East Asia and China?

Mainstream economists point to the remaining distortions, mainly the alleged rigidities in the labour market, inadequate infrastructure and the incomplete financial sector reforms. Labour market rigidities hypothesis does not hold water, with over a million manufacturing jobs lost during 1997-2004 and unprecedented job losses during the current downturn, without a murmur of protest.

There is, however, a great unanimity on the need for stepping up infrastructure investment, but not on how to achieve it. With the rising tax revenue and domestic saving as proportions of the domestic output, and with a steady improvement in public sector's physical and financial performance, lack of resources and organisation are no longer the binding constraints on augmenting infrastructure. The real stumbling block, therefore, appears to be the policy makers' commitment to (i) fiscal orthodoxy and (ii) encourage private and foreign investment in infrastructure provision. Such persistence to the means rather than the ends seems galling, even in the face of the disaster with Enron's Dabhol power project in the 1990s and worldwide experience in large infrastructure investment.

The principal drawback of the reforms is its exclusive focus on removing supply constraints at the neglect of demand. There is a growing consensus on the need to raise agriculture productivity to find markets for industrial goods, but the view has no serious takers as (i) there are enough buffer stocks to ward off any emergency and to maintain price stability, and (ii) there is a growing belief that agriculture has lost the capacity to absorb labour. Both the arguments are fallacious since the nation's food needs are far from fulfilled (though enough to meet demand) and the agriculture productivity in most crops is only a small fraction of the world average.

Notes

1. Industry includes mining, manufacturing, electricity, gas and water, and construction. Unless otherwise mentioned, all growth rates reported in this chapter are at constant prices, estimated using long-linear trend equation.
2. Such a shift, in principle, should lead to a more than proportionate rise in employment, given higher labour intensity in the unorganised sector. But as the length of the working day is generally more and intensity of supervision greater, such an employment expansion may not materialise.
3. Desai (1985) had shown that most Indian industries were competitive, with a small number of firms having dominant market shares but a large number of firms with marginal market shares. In such a situation, entry of a few foreign firms may not alter the usual measures of concentration, but the effectiveness of competition is likely to have gone up.
4. Value added in manufacturing by foreign-owned firms is based on the estimates of the Centre for Monitoring Indian Economy (CMIE). This is probably an underestimate as much of the recent entry of foreign firms into India is in the form of private limited companies, branch plants, and offices whose legal status does not warrant full disclosure of their operations, which makes it hard to get their balance sheets and estimate their value addition.
5. Ashok Parthasarathy, a careful observer of industrial technology, recently stated, "If we are talking of "technological innovation", I would put India ahead of both China and Brazil" (Parthasarathy 2009).

6. *http://www.tata.co.in* (accessed on 14 October 2009).
7. For a review of the relevant literature, see Bhattacharjea (2006) and Nagaraj (2007a).
8. As the job losses reported seem to refer only to the organised sector, they could be much higher in the unorganised sector, which accounts for an increasingly larger share of consumer goods and labour-intensive exports.
9. During the first United Progressive Alliance (UPA) government (2004-2009), there were serious shortfalls in the targets for additions to electricity-generating capacity and road construction (after a reasonably successful record in laying the Golden quadrilateral in the preceding five years), despite the much advertised 'Bharat Nirman' programme. Why? One suspects that this was because of the policy of public-private partnership, of introduction of private partners, and development of private markets.
10. Political difficulties faced in West Bengal to acquire agriculture land for large industrial projects like Tata Motor's car plant have given rise to intellectual arguments against modern industrialisation as a means of long-term economic development.
11. To quote Lewis, "If we assume that the subsistence sector is producing more food, while we escape the Scylla of adverse terms of trade we may be caught by the Charybdis of real wages rising because the subsistence sector is more productive. We escape both Scylla and Charybdis if rising productivity in the subsistence sector is more than off set by improving terms of trade. However, if the subsistence sector is producing food the elasticity of demand for which is less than unity, increase in productivity will be more than off set by reduction in prices" (1954: 174).

References

Balakrishnan, Pulapre, K. Pushpangadan and M. Suresh Babu (2000). "Trade Liberalisation and Productivity Growth in Manufacturing", *Economic and Political Weekly* 35(41).

Bhagwati, Jagdish and Padma Desai (1970). *India: Industrialisation*. Delhi: Oxford University Press.

Bhat, T.P., Atulan Guha, Mahua Paul and Partha Pratim Sahu (2007). "Estimation of Import Intensity in India's Manufacturing Sector: Recent Trends and Dimensions", Institute for Studies in Industrial Development (ISID) Working Paper No. 2007/8.

Bhattacharjea, Aditya (2006). "Labour Market Regulation and Industrial Performance in India: A Critical Review of the Empirical Evidence", *The Indian Journal of Labour Economics* 49(2): 211-32. Available at *http://ssrn.com/abstract=954908*.

Chakravarty, S. (1979). "Keynes, 'Classics' and the Development Economics", in C.H. Hanumantha Rao and P.C. Joshi (eds.) (1979), *Reflections on Economic Development and Social Change*. Delhi: Allied Publishers, pp.75-89.

Dagli Committee (1979). *Report of the Committee on Controls and Subsidies*. Ministry of Finance, Government of India.

Desai, Ashok (1985). "Market Structure and Technology: Their Interdependence in Indian Industry", *Research Policy* 14.

Hazari, R.K. (1985). "Rents of Misdelivery: A Case for Modernisation of Industrial Planning" (Review Article), *Economic and Political Weekly* 20(28): 1177-84.

Kaldor, Nicholas (1967). *Strategic Factors in Economic Development*. Ithaca, New York: Cornell University.

Kocchar, Kalpana, Utsav Kumar, Raghuram Rajan, Arvind Subramanian and Ioannis Tokatlidis (2006). "India's Pattern of Development: What Happened and What Follows?", *Journal of Monetary Economics* 53(5): 981-1019.

Krueger, Anne (2009). "The Missing Middle", *Working Paper* No. 230. New Delhi: ICRIER.

Lewis, W. Arthur (1954). "Economic Development with Unlimited Supply of Labour", *Manchester School of Economic Studies* , May, reprinted in A.N. Agarwala and S.P. Singh (eds.) (1963), *The Economics of Underdevelopment* . Delhi: Oxford University Press, pp.400-49.

Little, I.M.D (1987). "Small Manufacturing Enterprises in Developing Countries", *The World Bank Economic Review* 1(2): 203-35.

Mani, Sunil (2009). "Is India Becoming More Innovative since 1991?", *Mimeo*, Centre for Development Studies, Thiruvananthpuram.

Mehta, Abay (1999). *Power Play: A Study of the Enron Project* . Hyderabad: Orient Longman.

Nagaraj, R. (1985). "Fall in Organised Manufacturing Employment: A Brief Note", *Economic and Political Weekly* 20(8): M26-M32.

———. (2004). "Fall in Organised Manufacturing Employment: A Brief Note", *Economic and Political Weekly* 39(30): 3387-90.

———. (2006a). "Indian Investments Abroad: What Explains the Boom?", *Economic and Political Weekly* 41(46): 4716-18.

———. (2006b). "Public Sector Performance since 1950: A Closer Look", *Economic and Political Weekly* 41(25): 2551-7.

———. (2007a). "Are Labour Regulations Holding up India's Growth and Exports? A Review of Analysis and Evidence", paper prepared for National Commission for Unorganised Sector Enterprises.

———. (2007b), "Industrial Growth in China and India: A Preliminary Comparison", in K.L. Krishna and A. Vaidyanathan (eds.) (2007b), *Institutions and Markets in India's Development* , *Essays for K.N. Raj*. New Delhi: Oxford University Press, chapter 9, pp.178-204.

———. (2008), "India's Recent Economic Growth: A Closer Look", *Economic and Political Weekly* 43(15): 55-61.

Nayyar, Deepak (2008). "The Internationalisation of Firms from India: Investment, Mergers and Acquisitions", *Oxford Development Studies* 36(1): 111-31.

Panagariya, Arvind (2008). *India: The Emerging Giant*. New Delhi: Oxford University Press.

Parthasarathy, Ashok (2009). "Who Says We Have Not Innovated?", *Business Standard*, 18 March.

Storm, Servaas (1993). *Macroeconomic Considerations in the Choice of an Agricultural Policy: A Study into Sectoral Interdependence with Reference to India*. Aldershot: Avebury.

Tybout, James (2000). "Manufacturing Firms in Developing Countries: How Well Do They Do, and Why?", *Journal of Economic Literature* 38(1): 11-44.

United Nations (UN) (2009). *World Investment Report 2009*. Geneva: UNCTAD.

Wells, Louis T. and Eric S. Gleason (1995). "Is Foreign Direct Investment Still too Risky?", *Harvard Business Review*, September-October, pp.44-55.

D.M. Nachane (ed.) (2011). *India Development Report 2011*. Chapter 6. Indira Gandhi Institute of Development Research and Oxford.

16

K.L. KRISHNA and BISHWANATH GOLDAR

Productivity Growth Performance in India

Review and New Approach

1. Introduction

Productivity of an input is the average product of the input. It is the ratio of a volume measure of output to a volume measure of the input. Productivity may refer to a firm, an industry or the total economy. Productivity growth in the economy is the basis for improvement in the standards of living of the citizens in the economy. Measures of productivity growth and productivity levels are important economic indicators. Productivity growth, which involves the comparison of productivity of a given economic entity over time is easier to measure compared to comparison of productivity levels between countries which requires adjustment for differences in cost of living or level of prices based on purchasing power parity (PPP). The data for PPP adjustments need to be assembled through special field surveys. Much of the extant productivity literature deals with productivity growth.

Productivity measures can be classified as partial or total. Labour productivity and capital productivity are partial measures. The ratio of value added to a weighted combination of labour and capital is total factor productivity (TFP). Another distinction is between productivity measures based on value added or gross output. Table 16.1 presents the different commonly used productivity measure for the two measures of output, gross output (GO) and value added (VA) and different types of input, namely, labour (L) capital (K) and three intermediate inputs, energy (E), materials (M) and services (S).

Table 16.1

Different Commonly used Productivity Measures

	Input Measure (s)			
Output Measure	*Labour (L)*	*Capital (K)*	*K and L*	*K,L,E,M and S*
Gross Output (GO)	Labour Productivity based on GO = GO/L	Capital Productivity based on GO = GO/K	K-L TFP (MFP) based on GO	KLEMS TFP
Value Added (VA)	VA/L	VA/K	K-L TFP based on VA	—
	Partial (single) factor productivity measures		Total or multi-factor productivity (TFP/measures MFP)	

Note: MFP denotes multi-factor productivity

Source: Adapted from Schreyer (2001)

The OECD productivity manual published in 2001 provides a comprehensive and up-to-date treatment of various issues in productivity measurement of the industry level and aggregate productivity. Schreyer (2001) is a concize guide to the somewhat voluminous OECD manual. Schreyer discusses two important issues:

i) the choice between gross output and value-added-based productivity measures, and
ii) questions associated with measuring labour and capital inputs.

The India KLEMS productivity research project taken up in a latter section of this essay pays attention to the issues raised by Schreyer.

Interpretation of Productivity Measures

Labour productivity, defined as output (GO or GVA in constant prices) per unit of labour input (number of persons or hours worked), is an important and easily understood measure of productivity. Labour productivity at the economy level, defined as GDP per worker is an important determinant of living standards, measured as per capita income. However, labour productivity is a partial measure. It depends on the capital labour ratio and technology.

To capture the role of all factors of production total factor productivity (TFP), defined as the ratio of output to total factor input, a weighted combination of all inputs is used (see Table 16.1 for details).

"TFP" is a catch-all term that reflects any factor that influences the efficiency with which different inputs are combined to produce output. At the economy level, TFP defined as the ratio of GDP to a weighted combination of labour and capital input, includes the effects of technology, geography, institutions and government policies and errors of measurement. Due caution is therefore necessary in interpreting TFP measures as an indicator of productive efficiency or technological progress.

TFP growth is usually measured as a residual in the decomposition of output growth using the growth accounting methodology (see Box 16.3 in section 3).

The plan of the rest of this essay is as follows: Section 2 presents the evolution of the productivity literature in India. The conventional methodology of productivity measurement is outlined in section 3. Studies on productivity in manufacturing, agriculture and services sectors are reviewed in sections 4, 5 and 6, respectively. The inter-sectoral perspective is covered in section 7. Several productivity studies for the Aggregate Economy are presented in section 8. The India KLEMS productivity project is outlined in section 9. The main findings of the project for the period 1980-81 to 2008-09 are given in section 10. The current phase of the project for the 3-year period 2015 to 2017 is outlined in section 11. The summary and conclusions are presented in section 12.

2. Evolution of the Productivity Literature in India

Early productivity studies were undertaken for manufacturing industries from 1950s onwards. Studies for the agricultural sector appeared some two decades later. Studies for the sub-sectors of the services sector are more recent. Although the first study on the sources of growth in the Indian economy appeared around 1975, it is during the 2000s decade that several such studies have been published (e.g., Bosworth *et al.*, 2007). Some of these studies of recent vintage have worked out productivity growth estimates for major sectors (two or three) in the economy. Several studies attempting to assess the impact of economic reforms on economic growth in India have taken recourse to productivity measurement at the appropriate level. Within the manufacturing sector, the unorganised segment (units employing less than 10 workers with power or less than 20 workers without power) which accounts for bulk of the employment has not been studied adequately due to lack of annual data series. Nor has the unorganised segment of the services sector been studied. Here, again, the reason is the lack of data.

Box 16.1

Early Research on Productivity in India

Early productivity research in India focussed on Indian industry. The very first two studies, Dutt (1955) appeared in *Sankhya*, and Murty and Sastry (1957) in *Econometrica*. Both are cross-sectional production function studies. Reddy and Rao (1962), published in *Artha Vijnana*, was the first major study on total factor productivity growth in Indian industry. This study covered the period 1946 to 1957.

Banerji (1975) was the first comprehensive study on productivity, returns to scale and elasticity of substitution in Indian industry undertaken at the Delhi School of Economics and completed in 1969. Careful price adjustments were made in construction of the capital series. Banerji covered the period 1946-64 and used CMI (*Census of Indian Manufactures*) and ASI (*Annual Survey of Industries*) data.

Another study on productivity in Indian industry undertaken around that time is by S.R. Hashim and M.M. Dadi (1973), who also covered the period 1946-64. This study is notable for the care taken in arriving at a series of gross capital stock in constant prices from the series on book values.

3. Conventional Methodology of Productivity Measurement

In the productivity studies undertaken for India, growth accounting has been the most commonly used methodology in productivity measurement (or, to be more precise, total factor productivity (TFP) measurement). Econometric methodology has also been applied extensively for measuring productivity. Panel data models are increasingly becoming more popular. There have been a number of studies for Indian manufacturing industries or manufacturing firms or plants in which the production function has been econometrically estimated. Some recent studies have taken the Levinsohn-Petrin or Olley-Pakes approach to the production function estimation which helps in controlling for certain estimation biases in the conventional methodology of production function estimation (e.g., Topalova, 2004; Sivadasan, 2008; Pattnayak and Thangavelu, 2009; Maiti, 2013).

Growth accounting is based on the assumptions of constant returns to scale, profit maximisation (or cost minimisation) and factors of production being paid according to their marginal product. These assumptions are hard to justify for developing countries' conditions because of the presence of various imperfections in the product and factor markets caused among other factors by the interventions of the government. Econometric estimation of production function does not require the above mentioned assumptions and thus has an advantage in this respect. But, the econometric methodology has disadvantages of its own, and has therefore not found as much favour of Indian researchers as growth accounting. A small section of econometric studies have taken the cost function approach to the analysis of productivity growth (e.g. Hashim, 2003, 2004). This requires the assumptions of cost minimisation and factors of production being paid according to their marginal product, but has an advantage that the contributions of technical change and scale economies to productivity growth can be separated.

Box 16.2

Value Added Function versus Gross Output Function

Much of the productivity measurement in India has been undertaken in the framework of the value added production function. This framework does not take explicit account of the role of materials, energy and services. The biases inherent in the use of value added function in place of the more appropriate gross output function are known and have been noted in several Indian productivity studies (e.g., Mohan Rao, 2006). Some recent productivity studies have been based on the gross output KLEM (capital-labour-energy-materials) framework. There have been two Indian studies (Banga and Goldar, 2007; Veeramani and Goldar, 2005) for manufacturing in the KLEMS (capital-labour-energy-materials-services) framework. This forward step was taken before the India KLEMS project, launched in 2009 and discussed in some detail in a latter section.

Data Envelopment Analysis (DEA) has also been gaining ground in productivity research in India (e.g., Ray, 2002; Sinha and Chatterjee, 2008; Deb and Ray, 2014). DEA is different from the econometric methodology in that it is non-parametric. It is also different from growth accounting, since it does not require the assumption of factors being paid according to their marginal product. A number of studies have employed the DEA technique for assessing productivity increases in banking. It has been used for manufacturing and agriculture too. By using DEA, it is possible to compute the Malmquist index of productivity change, decomposed into changes in pure technical efficiency, changes in scale efficiency (i.e. economies and diseconomies of scale) and technical change.

Box 16.3

Growth Accounting Approach: Translog Index of TFP Growth

Consider the case, where there is one output (real value added) and two inputs (labour and capital). Let V denote output (real value added) and L and K be the two inputs. Let S_L and S_K be the income shares of labour and capital respectively. The Translog index of technical change or TFP growth between the years *t*-1 and *t* may be written as:

$$\Delta \ln TFP(t) = \Delta \ln V(t) - \left[\frac{S_L(t)+S_L(t-1)}{2} \times \Delta \ln L(t)\right] - \left[\frac{S_K(t)+S_K(t-1)}{2} \times \Delta \ln K(t)\right] \quad \text{... (16.1)}$$

where *t* represents year, $\Delta \ln V(t) = \ln V(t) - \ln V(t-1)$, and $\Delta \ln TFP(t), \Delta \ln L(t) \text{ and } \Delta \ln K(t)$ are defined similarly. It should be noted that a simple average of the income shares of the inputs in years *t* and *t*-1 is taken. The index is implicitly based on a Translog production function and thus has the advantage of flexibility of the Translog production function. Extending this to the case where there is one output (Q) (represented by the value of gross output at constant prices) and five inputs: capital (K), labour (L), energy (E), materials (M) and services (S), the Translog index of TFP growth may be written as (x_j denotes j'th input):

$$\Delta \ln TFP(t) = \Delta \ln Q(t) - \left[\Sigma \frac{S_j(t)+S_j(t-1)}{2} \times \Delta \ln x_j(t)\right]$$

$$j = K,L,E,M,S \quad \text{... (16.2)}$$

Two crucial assumptions underlying the Translog index of TFP growth are (a) constant returns to scale and (b) perfectly competitive product and factor markets (factors of production being paid according to their marginal product).

4. Productivity in Manufacturing

Most studies on productivity in manufacturing have used the Annual Survey of Industries (ASI) (Central Statistics Office, Government of India) as the database (available 1959 onwards). Some studies done in the 1970s or earlier combined ASI with the Census of Indian Manufactures (CMI) or used only CMI. The use of such databases made it necessary that the analysis be done at the level of individual industries or at higher levels of aggregation, say broad industry divisions or the aggregate manufacturing sector. Also, these data sources did not cover the unorganised manufacturing enterprises which account for over 85 per cent of manufacturing employment. For this reason, productivity study for unorganised manufacturing had to be done by using of other data sources. Due to limited availability of data for unorganised manufacturing, there have been only a small number of studies on productivity growth in unorganised manufacturing (e.g., Prakash, 2004; Kathuria *et al.*, 2010). These studies make use of NSS (National Sample Survey) data for unorganised manufacturing which are available with an interval of about five years.

Chronologically, productivity studies on Indian manufacturing can be divided into three groups. The first generation studies which include the studies undertaken by Reddy and Rao, Banerji, Goldar and Ahluwalia, came up with estimates of TFP growth which indicate that TFP growth in Indian manufacturing in the period 1951 to 1979 was slow or negative. Ahluwalia (1985), for instance, found a growth rate of TFP of -0.4 per cent per annum in the period 1959-1979. These studies used a value added function with labour and capital as two inputs. Single deflated value added (deflating nominal value-added figures by the price index for gross output) was taken as the measure of output.

The second generation studies drew attention to the biases in productivity estimates arising from the use of value added function and particularly the use of single deflated value added. Two prominent studies belonging to this group are Balakrishnan and Pushpangadan (1994) and Mohan Rao (1996). These studies contested the assertion made by Ahluwalia (1991) that there was a marked acceleration in TFP growth in manufacturing after 1980 which she attributed to liberalisation of economic policies. Ahluwalia had relied on the single-deflation (SD) procedure. The more appropriate double-deflation (DD) procedure by Balakrishnan and Pushpangadan resulted in TFPG estimates which contradicted Ahluwalia's claim. Mohan Rao's results based on the (i) double deflation in the case of value added production function and (ii) Gross output production function as well as those of Pradhan and Barik (1998) using the Gross Output function lend support to the contention of Balakrishnan and Pushpangadan that there was no turn-around in productivity growth in manufacturing in the 1980s.[1]

The third generation studies have mostly focussed on the productivity growth in the post-reform period (i.e. the period since 1991). How the industrial and trade policy reforms have impacted industrial productivity has been a key question. Some of these studies (e.g., Trivedi, *et al.*, 2000; Goldar and Kumari, 2003; Goldar, 2004; Das, 2004; Banga and Goldar, 2007) have used ASI data and analysed productivity at the industry level (or for aggregate manufacturing). Some other studies have used firm level data to analyse productivity growth (e.g., Srivastava, 1996; Srivastava *et al.*, 2001). Also, there have been several studies that have used firm level data to estimate technical efficiency and analyse how it has changed over time. The overall conclusion one may draw from the findings of these studies is that there has been no improvement in the rate of TFP growth in Indian manufacturing in the post-reform period compared to the growth rate achieved in the 1980s. Rather, TFP growth has slowed down. Goldar (2004), for instance, reports that the rate of TFP growth in manufacturing was 2.14 per cent annum during 1979 to 1990 which declined to 1.57 per cent per annum in the period 1991 to 1999.[2]

The third generation studies have in most cases used the gross output function for the measurement of TFP. This takes care of the key methodological issues raised by Balakrishnan and Pushpangadan (1994) and Mohan Rao (1996). The study by Banga and Goldar (2007) distinguishes itself by taking services as an input along with capital, labour, materials and energy for estimating total factor productivity growth in Indian manufacturing.

As regards the unorganised manufacturing sector, there have been only a couple of productivity studies. Prakash (2004) finds that TFPG was 10.3 per cent per annum during 1985-1995 and it declined precipitously to 6.9 per cent per annum during 1995-2001. An earlier study by Unni *et al.* (2001) had, however, found a downward trend in TFP. They reported that the growth rate in TFP in the unorganised manufacturing sector was -2.66 per cent per annum during 1978 to 1990 and -3.13 per cent per annum during 1990 to 1995. In a more recent study, Kathuria *et al.* (2010) again report a fall in TFP in unorganised manufacturing. The average rate of growth across industries and states is reported to be about -4 per cent per annum during 1994-2001 and about -16 per cent per annum during 2001-2005. These rates of fall in productivity are rather high, and it is difficult to understand why and how this could have happened. Obviously, further probing is needed.[3]

The volume of 14 essays edited by Kathuria, Raj and Sen (2014) provides a very comprehensive, scholarly and informative treatment of a wide range of aspects of measurement of productivity growth in Indian manufacturing. The troika of editors have contributed chapters 1, 2 and 6 of this 14-chapters volume based on an international conference held at the Indian Institute of Technology, Bombay in 2011. In chapter 6, the three authors attempt an empirical comparison of three major methodologies, namely, growth accounting (GA) (non-parametric), production function estimation with correction for endogenesity Levinsohn-Petrin (LP) (semi-parametric) and stochastic production frontier (SFA) (parametric), for both organised and unorganised segments of the manufacturing sector using real world data from 1989-90 to 2005-06. The estimates are found to be sensitive to the methodology employed. Also, the TFP growth estimates for the organised and unorganised segments are found to be different. The authors conclude that, "there is no unambiguous picture emerging on the direction of change in TFP growth in post-reform India".

Goldar in chapter 4 and the three editors in chapter 2 provide detailed reviews of a large number of productivity studies of the Indian manufacturing sector for the post-reform period. Some of the other essays in the volume deal with industries such as chemicals, petroleum refining, rubber, metals and minerals food and beverages, textiles, transport, machinery and equipment. The regional aspect and the organised unorganised dichotomy have also received due attention in the volume.

As Kathuria, Raj and Sen point out, the manufacturing sector is vital for the Indian economy, from the stand point of employment generation, poverty reduction, modernisation and technological developments. The government of India finalised and notified in 2011 the National Manufacturing Policy (NMP), which aims at rapid growth of the manufacturing sector with the goal of raising the share of manufacturing in GDP to 25 per cent by 2025. The "Make in India" drive of the present government reiterates the objectives of NMP. In this context, productivity and competitiveness have much policy relevance.

The contributions in the volume provide "a mixed assessment of the effects of the economic reform process". They open up avenues for further research building upon the lessons learnt. The volume deserves a careful study by the Indian economics profession.

Box 16.4

Factors Influencing Industrial Productivity

A number of studies have looked into the effect of trade liberalisation on industrial productivity in India. Goldar and Kumari (2003), Topalova (2004) and Sivadasan (2008) find a favourable effect of tariff reduction on productivity, while Das (2006) finds a favourable effect of removal of non-tariff barriers. In a recent paper, Topalova and Khandelwal (2011) find that both lowering of tariff on final goods and improved access to inputs due to lowering of tariff on intermediate inputs have increased firm-level productivity in India. Ghose and Biswas (2014) find that the impact of effective rate of protection, import coverage ratio and import-penetration ratio and real effective exchanges rate on TFPG is industry-specific.

There have been studies also on the effect of increasing domestic competition on productivity. From their analysis of variations in productivity at three-digit industry level in different states of India for the period 1985 to 1997, Bhaumik, Gangopadhyay and Krishnan (2006) find that the rate of entry of new firms (i.e. increased competition) had a favourable effect on productivity growth. Analysing TFP variation across plants (based on ASI unit level data), Dougherty, Herd and Chalaux (2009) find that inter-plant dispersion in TFP came down somewhat between 1993-94 and 2003-04. They attribute the observed fall in inter-plant TFP dispersion to increased competition among firms. They also note that the increase in TFP between 1993 and 2003 was relatively greater in larger firms than in smaller firms. The study identifies a set of distortions that depress productivity. These distortions exist at different levels and reflect constraints in the reallocation of labour across sectors, excessively small scale of firms, exit barriers, poor market integration, high concentration and dominant state ownership.

contd...

.contd...

In a recent study covering the period 1990-91 to 2009-10, Das (2016) examines the effect of trade liberalization on manufacturing productivity in India and finds that lowering of tariff protection in this period improved TFP of Indian manufacturing. However, his empirical analysis indicates that the impact of the liberalization of domestic industrial policy on TFP was relatively much greater. In this context it may be mentioned that Topalova and Khandelwal (2011) find that the favourable effect of tariff reform on industrial productivity gets magnified if it is accompanied by industrial reforms.

That infrastructure endowments exert a significant influence on technical efficiency and productivity growth of manufacturing industries in India is shown by Mitra *et al.* (2002, 2012). Aghion and Burgess (2003) show that labour market rigidities adversely affect productivity in industries. The effect of investment climate (which includes both infrastructure facilities and labour market conditions) on industrial productivity is examined by Veeramani and Goldar (2005) who find a positive correlation between investment climate and industrial productivity and conclude that a market friendly investment climate is essential for achieving a higher level of productivity.

5. Productivity in Agriculture

During the past 20 years or so, research on productivity growth in Indian agriculture has evolved (literature reviewed by Krishna, 2006; Kumar and Mittal, 2006; Kumar *et al.*, 2008). Estimates of TFP growth are available for aggregate agriculture, crop sector, livestock sector and even individual crops such as rice, wheat, maize and sugarcane. Estimates have also been worked out at the state level for major crops. Concerns have been expressed on the basis of available evidence that agricultural growth is becoming unsustainable as a result of resource (soil) degradation.

Box 16.5

Productivity Growth in Indian Agriculture in an Inter-Country Perspective

Avila and Evenson (2004a) compared the performance of India with that of three other South Asian countries—Bangladesh, Nepal and Sri Lanka, during 1961-1980 and 1981-2001, and found that Indian performance was the best both in the crop sector and livestock sector. In India, the translog measure of TFPG in the crop sector accelerated from 1.5 per cent per annum during 1961-1980 to 2.3 per cent during 1981-2001. TFPG in the livestock sector was around 2.6 per cent per annum in both the periods. According to the productivity estimates given in Avila and Evenson (2004b), TFPG in agriculture (crop and livestock sectors combined) during 1981 to 2001 was 0.98 per cent per annum in the middle-east Asian countries (average across countries) and 0.61 per cent per annum in south-east Asian countries. India's performance was relatively better at 2.41 per cent per annum. India, however, performed worse than Pakistan (2.54% per annum), China (4.76% per annum) and Vietnam (3.26% per annum).

According to the estimates made by Rao and Coelli (2004), the global average annual rate of growth of TFP in agriculture over the period 1980 to 1995 was 2.7 per cent per annum, the technical efficiency (TE) change and technical progress (TP) components being 1.5 per cent and 1.2 per cent respectively. For India, TFP growth was 1.6 per cent, TE change and TP change being 1.0 per cent and 0.6 per cent respectively. The corresponding figures for China are 6.8 per cent, 5.1 per cent and 1.6 per cent. Thus, India lagged far behind China and even the all-country average, in regard to TFP growth in agriculture.

Pratt, Yu and Fan (2008) compare TFP growth in the agricultural sectors of India and China by using the Malmquist index, and find that efficiency improvement played a more dominant role in raising TFP in China whereas in India the major source of productivity advance was technical change.

Rada (2013) examines farm productivity growth for 59 crops and four livestock products between 1980 and 2008 in six regions and at the national level. The annual rate of growth for India was 1.9 per cent. It varied between 1.4 per cent in the North region and 2.8 per cent in the South region.

To mention here briefly the estimates TFP growth obtained in some of the studies undertaken, Mukherjee and Kuroda (2003) report that the growth rates in TFP in Indian agriculture was 1.45 per cent per annum during 1973-1980, 2.33 per cent per annum during 1981-1988 and 1.21 per cent per annum during 1989-90. During the entire period, 1973 to 1993, the average rate of growth in TFP was 2.02 per cent per annum. Joshi *et al.* (2003) estimate the growth rate in TFP for rice and wheat cultivation in Indo-Gangatic plains as 3.5 and 2.44 per cent per annum respectively during 1980-1990, and 2.08 and 2.14 per cent per annum respectively during 1990-1999. An average annual growth rate of TFP in Indian agriculture in the range of 1 to 2 per cent has been reported in the studies undertaken by Evenson, *et al.* (1999) for the period 1956 to 1987 and by Fan *et al.* (1999) for the period 1970 to 1994.

6. Productivity in Services

There have been several productivity studies on specific sub-sectors of services. Indian Railways, for example, has been studied by Sailaja (1988) and Alivelu (2006). The output of Indian Railways is classified as freight kilometres (NTKM) and passenger kilometres (PKM). Tornquist aggregation of output is constructed. Labour input is divided into three categories: skilled-management personnel (groups A and B), semi-skilled employees (group D). A Tornquist index of labour input is constructed. Similarly indices of capital input, energy input and material input are constructed. Finally, the translog index of TFP is constructed.

Similarly, productivity in Indian airlines has been studied by Hashim (2003), productivity in the insurance industry by Sinha (2007), and productivity of information technology industry by Mathur (2007).

In comparison with other sub-sectors of services, a much larger number of studies of productivity and efficiency have been undertaken for Banks. To outline one study to illustrate the type of analysis undertaken, De (2004) undertook an econometric study of technical efficiency (TE) of banks in India belonging to three different ownership categories, namely, public sector, domestic private sector and foreign sector. Using panel data for 165 banks for the years 1985 to 1995-96, he estimated a stochastic frontier function of the Cobb-Douglas form. Allowance was made for time variant technical efficiency. The study found that the average TE of the banking industry was rather low, around 58 per cent and it declined slightly after financial liberalisation in the early 1990s. Foreign owned banks as a group achieved higher average TE than the other two groups.

To discuss another study on banks, Sinha and Chatterjee (2008) compare operating performance and total factor productivity growth of 30 selected Indian commercial banks (20 public sector, eight private sector and two foreign commercial banks) for the five year period 2000-01 to 2004-05 using DEA and Malmquist total factor productivity index. The public sector commercial banks exhibit relatively higher Malmquist TFP Index than the private sector banks. Decomposition of TFP growth into technical efficiency change and technical change components reveals that across the groups the commercial banks exhibit rising technical efficiency but negative technical change.

Unlike manufacturing, there is hardly any comparative productivity study that covers the entire range of services, providing detailed estimates of TFPG for different services. This is done to a limited extent by Virmani (2004) and Goldar and Mitra (2010). These studies make use of National Accounts time series data on real value added and real investment/real capital stock. Labour series used in these studies are based on NSS data for employment and estimates of working age population. The estimates of TFP growth presented in the two studies indicate that there was a marked acceleration in TFP growth in services after 1980 (Table 16.2). The growth rate in TFP in the period after 1991 appears to be high in all three major sub-sectors of services. It would be useful to analyse productivity trends at a finer division of the services sector.

Table 16.2

TFP Growth in Services, by Groups

(% per annum)

<table>
<tr><th rowspan="2">Sub-sectors/groups</th><th colspan="3">Virmani (2004)</th><th colspan="2">Goldar and Mitra (2010)</th></tr>
<tr><th>1965-1979</th><th>1980-1991</th><th>1992-2003</th><th>1960-1979</th><th>1980-2006</th></tr>
<tr><td>Trade, hotels and restaurants</td><td>-3.0</td><td>1.6</td><td>3.6</td><td>-3.4</td><td>2.9</td></tr>
<tr><td>Transport, storage and communication</td><td>1.5</td><td>2.8</td><td>4.9</td><td>2.0</td><td>3.0</td></tr>
<tr><td>Financing, insurance, real estate and business services</td><td rowspan="2">2.4</td><td rowspan="2">4.1</td><td rowspan="2">4.7</td><td>2.0</td><td>3.9</td></tr>
<tr><td>Public administration and other community, social and personal services</td><td>1.1</td><td>3.5</td></tr>
</table>

Sohini Sahu (2015) uses to CMIE data on service sector companies to show that the extent of resource misallocation has declined in the sector in the post reform period resulting in acceleration of TFP growth in the service sector.

7. Inter-Sectoral Perspective

The literature on economic development has the premise that productivity growth in agriculture is lower than in non-agriculture (manufacturing). There is also an impression that productivity growth in services is likely to be less than that in manufacturing since the latter has a greater scope for improving productivity by introducing new technology (see Banga, 2005 for a discussion on this issue). It is believed that because of their labour intensive nature, service-sector activities cannot be made more efficient through capital accumulation, innovation, or economies of scale. How do the productivity growth performance of the three sectors in Indian economy compare with one another?

Sivasubramonian (2004) and Dholakia (2002), covering the periods 1950-2000 and 1960-2001, respectively, provide TFPG estimates for the agricultural and non-agricultural sectors in India. In the first study, the rate of TFPG was equal at 1.13 per cent per year in both the sectors over the 50-year period. However, the contribution of TFPG to output growth was 43 per cent in agriculture compared to 20 per cent in non-agriculture. During the sub-periods 1980-1990 and 1990-2000, the non-agriculture sector experienced marginally higher rates of TFPG than the agricultural sector. In the Dholakia study, non-agriculture witnessed higher TFPG than agriculture. The estimated growth rate in TFP in the agriculture and non-agriculture sectors in the period 1960-1985 are 0.36 and 0.62 per cent per annum respectively, and those for the period 1985-2000 are 1.34 and 3.39 per cent per annum respectively.

Bosworth *et al.* (2007) present sources of economic growth during 1960-2005, for the three sectors, agriculture, industry and services, as well as total economy. Going by their estimates (Table 16.3) the productivity performance of the services sector was the best in both the sub-periods 1960-1981 and 1981-2005. Overall, the performance was unsatisfactory in all the three sectors during the first sub-period.

The estimates of productivity presented in Bosworth and Maertens (2010) show a pattern very similar to that in Bosworth *et al.* (2007). The growth rate of TFP in services exceeds that in industry and agriculture in the periods 1980-1990, 1990-2000 and 2000-2004 (Figure 16.1).

The gap in the TFP growth rates between services and other sectors is relatively much greater in the period 1990 to 2000.

Table 16.3

Growth of Output and TFP, Sector-wise, 1960-1981 and 1981-2005

(% per annum)

Sector	*Output Growth*	*TFP Growth*
Agriculture		
1960-1981	1.9	-0.1
1981-2005	2.8	1.1
Industry		
1960-1981	4.7	-0.4
1981-2005	6.4	1.0
Services		
1960-1981	4.9	0.4
1981-2005	7.6	2.9
Total Economy		
1960-1981	3.4	0.2
1981-2005	5.8	2.0

Source: Bosworth *et al.* (2007).

Figure 16.1

Total Factor Productivity Growth, India, by Broad Sectors of the Economy

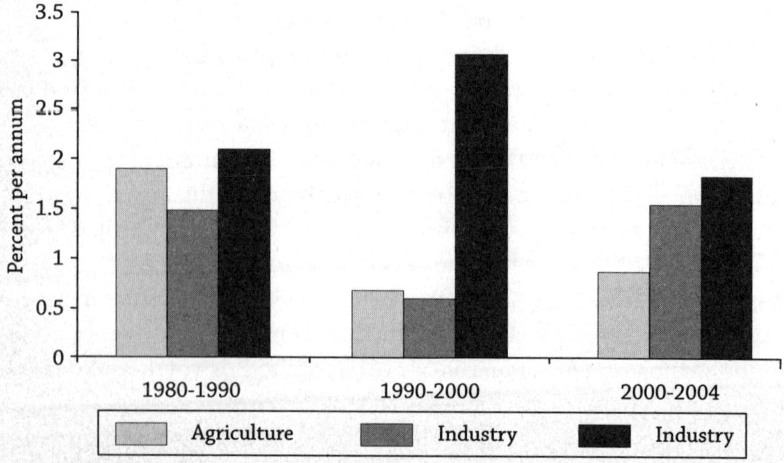

Source: Based on TFP estimates in Bosworth and Maertens (2010).

8. Productivity Studies for the Aggregate Economy

Four major recent studies on sources of growth of the Indian economy are Dholakia (2002), Sivasubramonian (2004), Virmani (2004), and Bosworth *et al.* (2007). Estimates of TFP growth in the Indian economy are presented also in Bosworth and Collins (2008) which makes a comparison between India and China, in Bosworth and Maertens (2010) which makes a comparison between Indian and Pakistan and in Jorgenson and Vu (2005) which examines productivity growth in a number of countries including seven major world economies (Germany, Japan, United States, etc.) and seven major developing and transition economies (Brazil, China, India, Indonesia, Medico, Russian Federation, and South Korea).

Sivasubramonian's study is the most detailed one, covering the 50-year period 1950-2000. Dholakia in the previous study done in 1974 followed Denison (1962) methodology and Dholakia (2002) revisited the subject. Sivasubramonian (2004) too followed the Denison methodology quite meticulously and gave a detailed account of the data sources and data adjustments. Bosworth *et al.* (2007) drew upon the data adjustment procedures developed by Sivasubramonian and improved upon them, by incorporating revisions in the official data.

Table 16.4 shows the estimates of TFP growth for the aggregate economy obtained in various studies. The broad conclusion one may draw from the productivity growth estimates presented in the studies is that the rate of TFP growth in the Indian economy accelerated sharply after 1980. Also, there is indication that the rate of growth in TFP in the post-reform period has been higher than that achieved in the 1980s. The source of this acceleration does not lie in manufacturing since a number of studies have shown that the rate of TFP growth in manufacturing has gone down in the post-reform period. The acceleration in TFP growth at the aggregate economy level seems to be rooted in an improved productivity performance of the services sector.

The estimates of TFPG obtained by Virmani (2004), Bosworth *et al.* (2007) and Bosworth and Collins (2008) indicate that the rate of TFP growth in the Indian economy in the period after 1990 was higher than that during the 1980s. The estimate of Bosworth and Maertens (2010), however, does not show any increase. Rather, a slight fall in the growth rate in TFP is indicated.

Table 16.4

Estimates of TFP Growth in the Indian Economy

Author(s)	*Method*	*Period*	*Estimated TFP Growth Rate (% per annum)*
Dholakia (2002)	Value added function (land included as an input)	1960-1985	0.79
		1985-2000	2.85
Sivasubramonian (2004)	Value added function (land included as an input); estimates for non-residential sector	1950-1960	1.81
		1960-1970	1.20
		1970-1980	0.16
		1980-1990	2.02
		1990-1999	2.01
		1950-1964	1.42
Virmani (2004)	Value added function	1950-1964	1.9
		1965-1979	0.1
		1980-1991	2.5
		1992-2003	3.6
Jorgenson and Vu (2005)	Value added function (contribution of ICT investment taken into account)	1989-1995	2.06
		1995-2003	2.49
Bosworth, Collins and Virmani (2007)	Value added function (land included as an input)	1960-1980	0.2
		1980-2004	2.0
		1983-1993	1.7
		1993-1999	2.8
		1999-2004	2.0
Bosworth and Collins (2008)	Value added function (land included as an input)	1978-1993	1.1
		1993-2004	2.3
		1978-2004	1.6
Bosworth and Maertens (2010)	Value added function (land included as an input)	1980-1990	2.2
		1990-2000	1.8
		2000-2006	2.1

Comparisons of TFP growth rates at the economy level presented in Bosworth and Collins (2008) and Jorgenson and Vu (2005) reveal that TFP growth in China has been higher than that in India (Figure 16.2). However, there are indications that the gap in TFP growth rate has narrowed since the mid-1990s. Indeed, the estimates obtained by

Jorgenson and Vu for the period 1995-2003 show that the TFP growth rates attained by the two countries were equal in this period.

Figure 16.2

TFP Growth Rate, Aggregate Economy, India and China

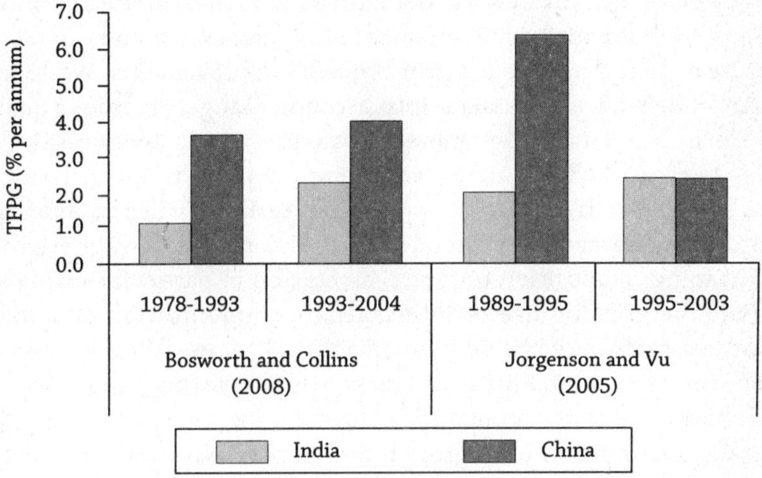

Source: Based on TFP estimates of Bosworth and Collins (2008) and Jorgenson and Vu (2005).

9. Improving on Past Productivity Research: The India KLEMS Project*

India KLEMS Study is aimed at improving on the past productivity research in India on several counts. While a majority of the past studies were concerned with a sector or a sub-sector of economy, the present study has a comprehensive coverage. Arguably, studies undertaken by Virmani (2004) and Bosworth *et al.* (2007) also have comprehensive coverage, but they have not divided the economy into as many sub-sectors or industries as done here. The estimation of productivity at detailed sectoral level for a comparable time period will provide much greater insight into the source of productivity growth than what an aggregate level productivity analysis as, for instance, done by Virmani (2004) and Bosworth *et al.* (2007), can provide. The second advantage

* The core research team for the project consisted of B. Goldar (as Advisor), D.K. Das, who was also the co-ordinator, S. Aggarwal and A.A. Erumban. It was assisted by Kuhelika De, Sreerupa Sengupta and Pilu Das. An Advisory Committee of top-level experts and representatives of RBI and CSO monitored the work continuously. K.L. Krishna chaired the Advisory Committee.

of the present study is that the industrial classification and the methods of measurement of output and inputs have been so chosen as to render international comparability of the productivity estimates. This will make it possible valid international comparisons of productivity growth for a large number of sub-sectors or industries in India. In this regard, many earlier studies have a handicap. The third point is that careful attention is paid in this study to the measurement of inputs, labour and capital. The measure of labour input takes care of quality improvements. While some earlier studies have also taken into account changes in labour quality, this has by and large been ignored in the past productivity research in India. As regards capital input, an attempt is made to estimate capital service rather than use capital stock as all earlier studies in India have done. The measurement of capital services is done by taking into account the changing composition of capital assets and in particular taking into account the growing use of information-communication technology in various sectors of the Indian economy. This greatly improves the measurement of capital input and thus helps in getting a more accurate measure of total factor productivity growth.

Work on India KLEMS growth and productivity was launched in 2009 at ICRIER (Indian Council for Research on International Economic Relations) New Delhi, with funding from the Reserve Bank of India. The major objective of the project was to construct time series data on output and inputs (KLEMS) at disaggregate industry level for the Indian economy to facilitate productivity measurement and analysis. The project is in the framework of the World KLEMS initiative established at the first world KLEMS conference at Harvard in August 2010. The researches of Jorgenson and Griliches (1967), Jorgenson, Gollop and Fraumem (1987) and Jorgenson, HO and Stiroh (2005) were the forerunners for the World KLEMS Initiative and the EU KLEMS project. The industrial classification and the concepts adopted in the India KLEMS project were on the lines of EU KLEMS located at the Groningen Growth and Development Centre in the Netherlands.

The data sets of India KLEMS constructed at ICRIER during 2009-2013 were submitted to RBI in late 2013 along with a Report and these were officially put on a RBI website in July 2014 under the title "Estimates of Productivity Growth for the Indian Economy". See *http://www.rbi.in/scripts/publication Report Details as px? Urlpage=&ID=785*.

The Indian data sets are available also on the Asia KLEMS and World KLEMS websites. Japan, India, South Korea and Taiwan are four Asian countries with KLEMS-type data sets. The Chinese data set is yet to be officially released.

The data set uses a 26-industry classification with six broad sectors, namely, 1. Agriculture, Forestry and Fishing, 2. Mining and Quarrying, 3. Manufacturing, 4. Electricity, Gas and Water Supply (EGW), 5. Construction, and 6. Services. The Manufacturing sector consists of 13 industries (3-15) and services sector consists of 9 industries (18-26). Annual time series from 1980-81 (1980) to 2008-09 (2008) on gross output (GO), gross value added (GVA) and primary inputs, Capital (K), labour (L), and intermediate inputs, energy (E), materials (M) and services (S) for the 26 industries with 1999-2000 as the base year are in the data set. Labour input has two components: number of persons employed and labour quality or composition based on the education of the person. Capital input is measured in terms of capital services taking into account differences in the depreciation rates for different asset types.

For constructing the data sets, the project has relied on official data sources, such as NAS (National Accounts Statistics), Employment-unemployment surveys of NSSO, ASI (Annual Survey of Industries) and follow-up NSSO surveys on unorganised industry. The official input-output tables have been used for constructing data series on energy (E), materials (M) and services (S) inputs.

In building annual time series on gross output (GO) and five inputs and factor income shares from less frequent data series, some assumptions have been made. Therefore, some caution in the interpretation of the results as called for.

TFP growth at the industry level is computed using both the GVA and the GO frameworks and using the growth accounting methodology. Appropriate aggregation formulae have been applied to compute TFP growth at sectoral and economy levels.

10. Some Major Findings from the India KLEMS Report for the Period 1980-2008

1. The Indian economy registered a TFP growth rate of 1.4 per cent per annum during 1980-2008. There was improvement during the sub-period 2000-2008 with TFP growth of 2.3 per cent per annum compared to 1.1 per cent during the sub-period 1980-1999.

2. Three broad sectors, manufacturing, services and EGW sector experienced increase in TFP growth in the 2000s. The productivity growth in agriculture sector and mining and quarrying sector suffered decline in the 2000s. In the case of the construction sector, the observed fall in TFP during 1980-1999 was arrested during 2000-2008. Eight of the 13 manufacturing industries showed acceleration of productivity growth in the 2000s.
3. TFP growth in the services industries tended to be higher than that in industries in other sectors. The TFP growth contribution of post and telecommunication industry and public administration and defence industry to output growth was the highest.
4. As regards labour productivity, the median growth rate was 4.1 per cent per year during 1980-2008, with higher growth rates in some manufacturing industries, service industries and EGW sector.

The decomposition of GVA growth in the six broad sectors and the economy are given in the Table 16.5.

Table 16.5

Components of GVA Growth by Sector, 1980-2008

Sector	*GVA Growth Rate*	*Contribution of*			
		Labour (no. of persons)	*Labour Quality (Education)*	*Capital Services*	*TFPG*
(1)	(2)	(3)	(4)	(5)	(6)
Agriculture	3.03	0.37	0.15	0.99*	1.52
Mining and quarrying	4.75	0.68	0.38	3.93	-0.24
Manufacturing	7.22	0.68	0.44	5.37	0.73
EGW	7.44	0.66	0.34	3.49	2.96
Construction	3.48	5.21	0.21	1.37	-3.31
Services	7.11	1.73	0.53	3.00	1.84
Economy	5.82	0.84	0.69	2.69*	1.40

Note: * includes the contribution of land capital.

EWG - Electricity, Gas and Water supply.

The results in Table 16.5 reveal the following points:

The annual growth rate of GVA in the economy during 1980-2008 was 5.82 per cent. The capital input's contribution was highest at 2.69 percentage points. TFPG contribution was rather low at 1.40 per cent points. The two components of labour input persons employed and labour quality were even lower at 0.84 and 0.69 per cent points.

In the manufacturing sector capital input's contribution was highest at 5.37 per cent and that of TFP growth quite low at 0.73 per cent points. The agriculture sector with a GVA growth of a little over 3 per cent achieved comparatively good TFPG contribution at 1.52 per cent points. The services sector received highest contribution to GVA growth from employment and labour quality.

11. Further Work in the India KLEMS Project

The India KLEMS productivity project with the same research team and further financial support from the Reserve Bank of India(RBI), for three years, 2015, 2016, and 2017, is now located at the Centre for Development Economics (CDE),Delhi School of Economics. A Steering Committee consisting of National and International experts, nominees of RBI, CSO, and CDE is monitoring work. Some important details of the work completed so far and the work in progress are given below.

1. The industrial classification now has 27 industries, with Business Services as a separate industry.
2. The work on the updation of the data sets for the years 1980-81(1980) to 2011-12 (2011), with 2004-05 as the base year was completed. This up-dated data set is referred to as "India KLEMS Data Set, Version 2015". Further updation for post 2011-12 years is in progress. The shift of the base year to 2011-12 (and incorporating the new National Accounts series of the CSO with base 2011-12) is contemplated.
3. The updated data set has been utilized by the members of the research team to develop analytical papers on a variety of productivity-related themes. Some of the themes are: Employment Potential at the detailed industry level, the dynamics of Service-led Growth, the Industrial Origins of Economic Growth and the contribution of Reallocation of labour and capital inputs to Growth, Comparison of productivity growth and level of the Organized and Unorganized segments

of the Manufacturing sector in India, and Comparison of productivity growth in India and South Korea.

4. Members of the research team made two presentations at the Third Asia KLEMS Conference in Taipei, Taiwan, in August 2015, and two more at the Fourth World KLEMS Conference in Madrid, Spain, in May 2016 on the research done during 2015 and 2016.
5. Some preliminary work on comparing growth and productivity in China and India in collaboration with Prof Harry Wu was one of the presentations in Madrid. This work has to be pursued in the coming months. Work on comparison of productivity levels for selected industries in the two countries is on the agenda of the project.
6. Construction of series on ICT (information and communication technology) capital at the industry level is also on the agenda for the year 2016.

There is much need to consolidate the research outputs of the Project and bring out Working Papers as soon as possible. This is part of the agenda for 2016.

12. Summary and Conclusions

This essay has dealt with two aspects of productivity growth performance in India:

(i) a comprehensive review of the literature that has evolved since 1950s, with a focus on the literature for the post-reform period, and

(ii) an introduction to a new approach to productivity measurement, the so-called KLEMS approach, largely a development of the twenty-first century. The India KLEMS productivity research project, on the lines of similar studies for the United States, and European Union, aims at analysis of productivity at the disaggregated industry level and international comparability of the estimates. Sections 9, 10 and 11 of the essay are on India KLEMS research.

The extant literature on productivity in India is quite vast, especially for the organised manufacturing sector. Two important studies for this sector by Ahluwalia (1985) and Goldar (1986) and another by Ahluwalia (1991) gave rise to a lively methodological debate among researchers in mid-1990s, on single *versus* double deflation of value added in manufacturing. The verdict of the debate went in favour of double deflation (DD). DD made a difference to the productivity growth estimates. Some studies using the gross output framework in preference to the value added framework were published in mid-1990s. One of the studies highlighted the contribution of the services input to gross ouput. Another study in the KLEM framework examined the impact of tariff rates on industrial productivity.

The literature for the post-reform period is quite extensive, Goldar's review in chapter 4 and the editors' three essays in Kathuria *et al.* (2014) together cover all the major issues related to the manufacturing sector in India. The reader gets acquainted with all the important methodologies and empirical evidence on the issues covered, from the different chapters in the volume. Unfortunately, the results of comparison of the major methodologies attempted by the editors are not conclusive. Another limitation of the recent literature is the inadequate attention given to the unorganised segment of the manufacturing sector, the segment which accounts for the bulk of the employment in the sector. Goldar *et al.* (2016) in their presentation at the Fourth World KLEMS conference in Madrid attempted a comparison of productivity between organised and unorganised segments for 13 industries comprising the manufacturing sector. The issue of promoting labour-intensive manufacturing and enhancing employment opportunities for the semi-skilled labour force deserves more attention.

The essay has reviewed the literature for the agriculture and service sectors, but somewhat less extensively. Productivity growth in the services industries is being studied in the India KLEMS project, with ten services industries, classified into market services and non-market services. Some results are available. They need to be disseminated.

Bosworth *et al.* (2007), reviewed in the current essay, attempts a comparison of the productivity (TFP) growth in agriculture, industry, and services sectors in two sub-periods 1960-1981 and 1981-2005 (Table 16.3). There is improvement in productivity in the aggregate economy and in the three sectors. The improvement is most pronounced in the services sector. The India KLEMS project has the promise of comparing the productivity growth performance between broad sectors and disaggregate industries on the basis of India KLEMS data sets for the year 1980-81 onwards.

In the 2000s, seven productivity studies for the aggregate economy have been published, some of them with long temporal coverage since 1950 or 1960. Some of them cover the early reform period. Together they provide a wealth of evidence on the productivity growth performance of the Indian economy. The India KLEMS project with continual data updation and bottom-up approach to measurement of productivity for broad sectors and aggregate economy will be a useful supplement to the seven studies reviewed in this essay.

Some work on international comparisons of productivity using the India KLEMS data sets is in progress. A preliminary comparison of the manufacturing sectors in India and South Korea was presented at the Fourth World KLEMS conference in May 2016. An attempt was made to compare productivity growth in China and India at the conference. This type of work has to be continued and extended to other aspects. Comparison of competitiveness at the level of specific industries is on the agenda of the India KLEMS project.

Note

1. See Balakrishnan and Pushpangadan (1998) for a review of these and other such studies in the 1990s. See also Goldar (2002) on the question whether productivity growth in manufacturing was faster in the 1980s than in the 1970s.
2. Several studies have found that the growth rate in TFP in India's organized manufacturing accelerated in the 2000s (e.g., Virmani and Hashim, 2011; Goldar, 2015a; and Goldar and Sengupta, 2016). An acceleration in TFP growth in the 2000s has been reported also for India's unorganized manufacturing (Goldar, 2015b; Goldar and Sengupta, 2016).
3. By contrast, Goldar (2015b) and Goldar and Sengupta (2016) find a positive growth rate of TFP in India's unorganized manufacturing of more than one percent per annum in the period 1999-2000 to 2011-12. It seems there has been a marked improvement in productivity growth in unorganized manufacturing in the 2000s.

References

Aghion, Philipe and Robin Burgess (2003). "Liberalisation and Industrial Performance: Evidence from India and the UK", (available on line at *www.ycsg.yale.edu/activities/files/Aghion-Burgess%20Paper.pdf.* accessed 24th September 2010).

Ahluwalia, I.J. (1985). *Industrial Growth in India: Stagnation since the Mid-Sixties*. New Delhi: Oxford University Press.

———. (1991). *Productivity and Growth in Indian Manufacturing*. New Delhi: Oxford University Press.

Alivelu, G. (2006). *Analysis of Productivity and Costs across the Indian Zonal Railways 1981-82 to 2002-03*, unpublished Ph.D. thesis, Centre for Economic and Social Studies and Dr. B.R. Ambedkar Open University, Hyderabad.

Avila, A.F. and R.E. Evenson (2004a). "TFP Calculation from FAO Data", Unpublished.

———. (2004b). "Total Factor Productivity Growth in Agriculture: The Role of Technological Capital". New Haven, CT: Yale Economic Growth Center.

Balakrishnan, P. and K. Pushpangadan (1994). "Total Factor Productivity Growth in Manufacturing Industry: A Fresh Look", *Economic and Political Weekly* 29: 2028-35, July 23.

———. (1998). "What Do We Know about Productivity Growth in Indian Industry", *Economic and Political Weekly* 33: 2241-46. August 15-22.

Banerji, Asit (1975). *Capital Intensity and Productivity in Indian Industry.* Delhi: Macmillan India.

Banga, Rashmi (2005). "Critical Issues in India's Services Led Growth", *ICRIER Working Paper* No. 171. New Delhi: Indian Council for Research on International Economic Relations.

Banga, Rashmi and Bishwanath Goldar (2007). "Contribution of Services to Output Growth anhd Productivity in Indian Manufacturing: Pre- and Post-Reforms", *Economic and Political Weekly* 42(26): 2769-77. June 30.

Bhaumik, S.K., S. Gangopadhyay and S. Krishnan (2006). "Reforms, Entry and Productivity: Some Evidence from the Indian Manufacturing Sector", *Indian Development Foundation Working Paper* No. 0602 and IZA Discussion Paper No. 2086.

Bosworth, B., S. Collins and A. Virmani (2007). "Sources of Growth in Indian Economy", *NBER Working Paper* No. 12901, National Bureau of Economic Research.

Bosworth, Barry and Susan M. Collins (2008). "Accounting for Growth: Comparing China and India", *Journal of Economic Perspectives* 22(1): 45-66. Winter. American Economic Association.

Bosworth, Barry and Annemie Maertens (2010). "Economic Growth and Employment Generation: The Role of the Service Sector", in Ejaz Ghani (ed.), *The Service Revolution in South Asia*. New Delhi: Oxford University Press.

Das, Deb Kusum (2016). Trade Policy and Manufacturing Performance: Exploring the Level of Trade Openness in India's Organized Manufacturing in the Period 1990-2010, Study no. 41, Development Research Group, Department Economic and Policy Research, Reserve Bank of India.

Das, Deb Kusum (2004). "Manufacturing Productivity under Varying Trade Regimes, 1980-2000", *Economic and Political Weekly* 39(5): 423-33. January 31.

———. (2006). "Improving Industrial Productivity: Does Trade Liberalisation Matter? Evidence from Indian Capital and Intermediate Goods Sectors", in S. Tendulkar *et al.* (ed.), *India: Industrialisation in a Reforming Economy: Essays for K.L. Krishna*. New Delhi: Academic Foundation.

De, P.K. (2004). "Technical Efficiency, Ownership and Reform: An Econometric Study of Indian Banking Industry", *Indian Economic Review, Special Issue on Productivity and Efficiency* 39(1). (January-June).

Deb, A.K. and S.C. Ray (2014). "Total Factor Productivity Growth in Indian Manufacturing: A Biennial Malmquist Analysis of Inter-State Data", *Indian Economic Review* 49(1): 1-25.

Dholakia, B. (2002). "Sources of India's Accelerated Growth and the Vision of the Indian Economy in 2020", *Indian Economic Journal* 49(4): 27-46.

Dougherty, S.M., R. Herd and T. Chalaux (2009). "What is holding back Productivity Growth in India? Recent Micro Evidence", *OECD Journal: Economic Studies* (1).

Dutt, M.M. (1955). "The Production Function for Indian Manufacture", Sankhya, 15.

Ghose, A. and P.R. Biswas (2014). "Impact of Trade Policy on Manufacturing Productivity in India: Evidence using a Non-parametric Approach", in Kathuria, V. et al. (eds.), *Productivity in Indian Manufacturing*. New Delhi: Routledge.

Evenson, R.E., C. Pray and M.W. Rosegrant (1999). "Agricultural Research and Productivity Growth in India", *Research Report* No. 109. Washington, D.C.: International Food Policy Research Institute.

Fan, S., P.B.R. Hazell and S. Thorat (1999). "Linkages between Government Spending, Growth, and Poverty in Rural India", *Research Report* No. 110. Washington, D.C.: International Food Policy Research Institute.

Goldar, Bishwanath (1986). Productivity Growth in Indian Industry. New Delhi: Allied Publishers.

———. (2002). "TFP Growth in Indian Manufacturing in the 1980s", *Economic and Political Weekly* 37(49): 4966-68.

———. (2004). "Indian Manufacturing: Productivity Trends in Manufacturing in Pre- and Post-Reform Periods", *Economic and Political Weekly* 39(46/47): 5033-43. November 20.

———. (2014). "Productivity in Indian Manufacturing in the Post-Reform Period: A Review of Studies", in V. Kathuria *et al.* (eds.), *Productivity in Indian Manufacturing*. New Delhi: Routledge.

———. (2015a). "Productivity in Indian Manufacturing (1999-2011): Accounting for Imported Materials Input", *Economic and Political Weekly* 50 (29): 104-111.

———. (2015b). "Sustaining a High Rate of Industrial Growth in India in the Next 10 Years", in Pradeep Agrawal (ed.), *Reviving Growth in India*. Cambridge University Press, Delhi. pp. 47-81.

Goldar, Bishwanath and Arup Mitra (2002). "Total Factor Productivity Growth in Indian Industry: A Review of Studies", in B.S. Minhas (ed.), *National Income Accounts and Data Systems*. New Delhi: Oxford University Press.

———. (2010). "Productivity Increase and Changing Sectoral Composition: Contribution to Economic Growth in India", in Pulin B. Nayak, Bishwanath Goldar and Pradeep Agrawal (eds.), *India's Economy and Growth: Essays in Honour of V.K.R.V. Rao*. New Delhi: Sage.

Goldar, Bishwanath and Anita Kumari (2003). "Import Liberalisation and Productivity Growth in Indian Manufacturing Industries in the 1990s", *Developing Economies* 41(4): 436-60.

Goldar, Bishwnath and Sreerupa Sengupta (2016). "Post-Reforms Trends in Growth and Productivity in Indian Manufacturing", in C. Veeramani and R. Nagaraj (eds.), *International Trade and Industrial Development in India*. New Delhi: Orient BlackSwan. pp.45-102.

Hashim, S.R. and M.M. Dadi (1973). Capital-Output Relations in Indian Manufacturing. Baroda: M.S. University of Baroda.

Hashim, Danish A. (2003). "A Comparative Analysis of Productivity and Cost in Indian Airlines: 1964-99". Delhi: Institute of Economic Growth. Available on line at *http://iegindia.org/dis_hash_67.pdf.* accessed September 30, 2010.

———. (2004). "Cost & Productivity in Indian Textiles: Post MFA Implication", *ICRIER Working Paper* No. 147. New Delhi: Indian Council for Research on International Economic Relations.

Jorgenson, D.W. and Z. Griliches (1967). "The Explanation of Prodictivity Change", *Review of Economic Studies* 34: 249-283.

Jorgenson, D.W. *et al.* (1987). *Productivity and U.S. Economic Growth*. Cambridge: Harvard University.

———. (2005). *Information Technology and American Growth Resurgence*. Cambridge: MIT Press.

Joshi, P.K., L. Joshi, R.K. Singh, J. Thakur, K. Singh and A.K. Giri (2003). Analysis of Productivity Changes and Future Sources of Growth for Sustaining Rice-Wheat Cropping System. National Agricultural Technology Project (PSR 15; 4.2). New Delhi: National Centre for Agricultural Economics and Policy Research (NCAP). August.

Kathuria, Vinish, S.N. Rajesh Raj and Kunal Sen (2010). "Organised versus Unorganised Manufacturing Performance in the Post-Reform Period", *Economic and Political Weekly* 65: 55-64.

———. (eds.) (2014). *Productivity in Indian Manufacturing.* New Delhi: Routledge.

Krishna, K.L. (1987). "Industrial Growth and Productivity in India", in P.R. Brahmananda and V.R. Panchamukhi (eds.), *The Development Process of the Indian Economy*. Bombah: Himalaya.

———. (2006). "Some Aspects of Total Factor Productivity in Indian Agriculture", in R. Radhakrishna *et al.* (eds.), *India in a Globalisation World, Essays in Honour of C.H. Hanumantha Rao.* New Delhi: Academic Foundation.

———. (2007). "What do we know about the Sources of Economic Growth in India?", in A. Vaidyanathan and K.L. Krishna (eds.), *Institutions and Markets in India's Development: Essays for K.N. Raj.* New Delhi: Oxford University Press.

Kumar, Praduman and Surabhi Mittal (2006). Agricultural Productivity Trends in India: Sustainability Issues, Agricultural Economics Research Review 19 (Conference No.): 71-88.

Kumar, Praduman, Surabhi Mittal and Mahabub Hussain (2008). "Agricultural Growth Accounting and Total Factor Productivity in South Asia: A Review and Policy Implications", *Agricultural Economics Research Review* 21: 145-172. (July-December).

Maiti, Dibyendu (2013). "Market Imperfections, Trade Reform and Total Factor Productivity Growth: Theory and Practices from India", *Journal of Productivity Analysis* 40(2): 407-18.

Mathur, Somesh (2007). "Indian IT and ICT Industry: A Performance Analysis Using Data Envelopment Analysis and Malmquist Index", *Global Economy Journal* 7(2).

Mitra, Arup, Aristomene Varoudakis and Marie-Ange Veganzones-Varoudakis, "Productivity and Technical Efficiency in Indian States' Manufacturing: The Role of Infrastructure", *Economic Development and Cultural Change* 50(2): 395-426.

Mitra, A., C. Sharma and M. Veganzones-Varoudakis (2012). "Estimating Impact of Infrastructure on Productivity and Efficiency of Indian Manufacturing", *Applied Economics Letters* 19(8): 779-783.

Mohan, Rao, J. (1996). "Manufacturing Productivity Growth: Method and Measurement", *Economic and Political Weekly* 31(44): 2927-36. November 2.

Mukherjee, Anit N. and Yoshimi Kuroda (2003). "Productivity Growth in Indian Agriculture: Is there Evidence of Convergence Across States?" *Agricultural Economics* 29: 43-53.

Murthy, V.N. and V.K. Sastri (1957). "Production Functions for Indian Industry", *Econometrica* 25.

Pattnayak, Sanja Samirana and Shandre M. Thangavelu (2009). "Economic Liberalisation in India: Productivity and Learning-by-export", *CCAS Working Paper* no. 21. Centre for Contemporary Asian Studies, Donisha University.

Prakash, B.S. (2004). "Structural Change and Productivity Trends in Unorganised Manufacturing Sector 1984-2001", *IAMR Report* No. 2.

Pradhan, G. and K. Barik (1998). "Fluctuating Total Factor Productivity in India: Evidence from Selected Polluting Industries", *Economic and Political Weekly* 33: M25-M30. February 28.

Pratt, A.N., B. Yu and S. Fan (2008). "The total factor productivity in China and India: New Measures and Approaches", *China Agricultural Economic Review* 1(1): 9-22.

Rada, N.E. (2013). "Agricultural Growth in India: Examining the Post-Green Revolution Transition", paper presented at the Agricultural and Applied Economics Associations Joint Meeting, Washington, D.C.

Ray, Subhash C. (2002). "Did India's Economic Reforms Improve Efficiency and Productivity? A Nonparametric Analysis of the Initial Evidence from Manufacturing", *Indian Economic Review* 37(1): 23-57. January.

Reddy, M.G.K. and S.V. Rao (1962). "Functional Distribution in the Large Scale Manufacturing Sector in India", *Artha Vijnana* 4(3): 189-96.

Rao, D.S.P. and T.J. Coelli (2004). "Catch-up and Convergence in Global Agricultural Productivity", *Indian Economic Review* 39(1): 123-48. Special Issue, January-June.

Sahu, S. (2015). "Source of Service Sector TFP Growth in India: Evidence from Micro-data", *South Asian Journal of Macro economics and Public Finance* 4(1): 62-96.

Sailaja, M. (1988). *Productivity in the Service Sector: The Case of Indian Railways*, 1950-51 to 1985-86, unpublished Ph.D. thesis, Delhi School of Economics, Delhi.

Schreyer, P. (2001). "The OECD Productivity Manual: A Guide to the Measurement of Industry-Level and Aggregate Productivity", *International Productivity Monitor* 2, spring 2001.

Sinha, Ram Pratap (2007). "Premium Income of Indian Life Insurance Industry: A Total Factor Productivity Approach", *IUP Journal of Financial Economics* 5(1): 61-69.

Sinha, Ram Pratap and Biswajit Chatterjee (2008). "Fund-Based Activity of Indian Commercial Banks: A Malmquist Approach", *Indian Economic Review* 43(1): 83-102.

Sivadasan, Jagadeesh (2008). "Barriers to Competition and Productivity: Evidence from India" available on line at *http//webuser.but.umich.edu/jagadees/papers/pml_dec08_all.pdf*, accessed September 30, 2010.

Sivasubramonian, S. (2004). *The Sources of Economic Growth in India: 1950-51 to 1999-2000*. New Delhi: Oxford University Press.

Srivastava, Vivek (1996). *Liberalisation, Productivity and Competition: A Panel Study of Indian Manufacturing*. Delhi: Oxford University Press.

Srivastava, Vivek, Pooja Gupta and Arindam Datta (2001). *The Impact of India's Economic Reforms on Industrial Productivity, Efficiency and Competitiveness: A Panel Study of Indian Companies, 1980-1997*. Report, National Council of Applied Economic Research, New Delhi.

Topalova, Petia (2004). "Trade Liberalisation and Firm Productivity: The Case of India", *IMF Working Paper*, International Monetary Fund.

Topalova, P. and A. Khandelwal (2011). "Trade Liberalisation and Firm Productivity: the Case of India", *Review of Economics and Statistics* 93(3): 995-1009.

Trivedi, P., A. Prakash and D. Sinate (2000). "Productivity in Major Manufacturing Industries in India: 1973-74 to 1997-98", Development Research Group Study No. 20, Department of Economic Analysis and Policy, Reserve Bank of India, Mumbai.

Unni, Jeemol, N. Lalitha and Uma Rani (2001). "Economic Reforms and Productivity Trends in Indian Manufacturing", *Economic and Political Weekly* 36(41): 3914-3922. October 13-19.

Veeramani, C. and Bishwanath Goldar (2005). "Manufacturing Productivity in Indian States: Does Investment Climate Matter?" *Economic and Political Weekly* 40(24): 2413-20. June 11.

Virmani, A. (2004). "Sources of India's Economic Growth", *ICRIER Working Paper* No. 131. New Delhi: Indian Council for Research on International Economic Relations.

Virmani, A. and D.A. Hashim (2011). "J-Curve of Productivity and Growth: Indian Manufacturing Post-Liberalisation", *IMF Working Paper* No. WP/11/163, International Monetary Fund.

17

ADITYA BHATTACHARJEA

Of Omissions and Commissions

India's Competition Laws

Introduction

On 1 September 2009, almost unnoticed by the media, an era came to an end with the repeal of the 40 year old Monopolies and Restrictive Trade Practices (MRTP) Act. Drawing upon several high-quality studies by various authors in this journal over the past four decades, as well as my own research, Section 2 of this article provides an unsentimental obituary of the Act, ending with its prolonged and messy demise. I argue that, despite being one of the oldest competition laws in the developing world, the way in which the Act was originally drafted and subsequently amended, interpreted and enforced ensured that it could not really function as a competition law. Consequently, it did not bequeath a body of expertise that could help in the implementation of its successor, the Competition Act, which is very demanding in terms of economic analysis. Section 3 offers a critical assessment of the latter Act, whose enforcement began in 2009, nearly seven years after its enactment. This section summarises and updates my earlier writings, some of which, as I point out below, seem to have had a modest impact on the final shape of the Competition Act. This time, however, the focus will be as much on law and (mis)governance as on economics, and so this article should appeal to a wider readership.

With that wider readership in mind, I begin with a brief introduction to the relevant economic principles. Modern competition law (also known as anti-trust law) is primarily concerned with the prohibition or regulation of certain kinds of behaviour by market participants that might have an adverse effect on competition. These include agreements or mergers between firms as well as activities of individual firms. The agreements that may need to be scrutinised are in turn subdivided into two categories. 'Horizontal' agreements between competitors selling the same or similar products may result in a cartel that collusively fixes prices, restricts output, divides up markets, or makes collusive bids in an auction or procurement process. 'Vertical' agreements between firms at different stages in the production and distribution chain may also limit competition, for example by requiring distributors not to sell a competitor's product, not to sell outside a particular territory, or to maintain resale prices imposed by the producer. The behaviour of a dominant single firm may also be regarded as anti-competitive if its primary motivation is to drive out rivals or deter potential competitors from entering the market. This 'abuse of dominance' may involve temporarily charging 'predatory' prices below costs so as to drive out competitors who are unable to sustain losses. Or it could take the form of tying the sale of a product in which the firm has a dominant share of the market (e.g., computer hardware, printers or cars) to another product or service provided by the same firm for which there are many competing suppliers (the corresponding examples would be software, printer cartridges, and spare parts and servicing).

Cartels harm consumers while seldom yielding any efficiency gains, and therefore in most countries evidence of a cartel agreement is sufficient to condemn it, without further investigation of its effects. The other actions described above may, however, be approved on a case-by-case basis under a 'rule of reason' if they provide offsetting benefits. For example, a merger reduces the number of competitors, but may result in synergies or economies of scale that reduce costs. Vertical restrictions may be necessary to encourage distributors to invest in proper display facilities and customer support, and may thus enhance competition with other brands. Tying the sale of complementary products may be required to ensure performance or safety. These cases require careful analysis of the efficiency gains and the degree of competition in the relevant market, which must be defined taking into account potential competition from new suppliers and substitutable products. In cases where the efficiency gains do not outweigh the injury to competition, the competition authority may block the merger or issue an injunction to terminate the impugned agreement or behaviour, together with a deterrent fine. But it may also order a modification of the merger, agreement or behaviour, so as to preserve its benefits while minimising adverse effects on competition. All this requires subtle analysis of the firms' conduct and the market in question.

In light of the preceding discussion, it should be clear that the objective of modern anti-trust is to prevent market players from restricting competition in ways that are on balance harmful to efficiency and consumer welfare. It targets abuse of a dominant position in the market, not firm size or dominance as such, and it does not seek directly to control prices or profits: it only strives to preserve conditions which would allow market forces to keep them in check.[1] It does not attempt to fulfil social objectives such as protecting employment. In fact, attempting to promote competition and efficiency may actually result in job losses. There is therefore a case for exempting small firms from some provisions of the law. But this should be done as a matter of policy rather than selectively dispensing social justice through individual decisions of the competition authority. Furthermore, it should be kept in mind that condoning anti-competitive behaviour does imply that higher prices and poorer quality will be inflicted on buyers, who may also be small producers or poor consumers. Conversely, competition law can protect these vulnerable sections of society from anti-competitive conduct by powerful firms—provided that it is vigorously and impartially enforced.[2] Let us now evaluate India's old and new competition laws against these standards.

The MRTP Act, 1969-2009

The MRTP Act was a product of another era. It covered three categories of competition matters, superficially corresponding to those described above, but dealt with them in ways that departed from standard anti-trust treatment. Chapter III, on concentration of economic power, originally applied to firms that were either large (those whose assets together with those of their 'interconnected undertakings' exceeded ₹ 20 crore) or 'dominant' (whose assets exceeded ₹ 1 crore and whose share of the market exceeded one-third, later reduced to one-fourth in 1982). All such 'MRTP companies' were required to register themselves and thereafter obtain government permission for mergers, amalgamations and takeovers—but also for establishment of new undertakings and substantial expansion of old ones, thus reinforcing the then-prevailing system of industrial licensing. Chapter IV, on monopolistic trade practices (MTPs), originally applied to 'monopolistic' undertakings that were either dominant (as defined above) or commanded half or more of the market along with not more than two other independent undertakings. An inquiry could be ordered if it appeared that a monopolistic undertaking was 'unreasonably' limiting competition or technical development, which would today be called abuse of dominance—but also if it appeared to be 'unreasonably' maintaining or increasing prices and limiting investment, which are usually not anti-trust concerns. The government was armed with the authority to prohibit MTPs, if necessary by regulating prices, production, distribution and quality. It could refer Chapter III applications or complaints about MTPs to the MRTP Commission, but did not have to accept its opinion.

Chapters V and VI of the Act, based on the British Restrictive Practices Act of 1956, targeted restrictive trade practices (RTPs). Certain specific types of inter-firm horizontal and vertical agreements, including those described in the first section of this article, had to be registered with the Commission, which would review them to ensure that they did not restrict competition. However, as in the UK, the firms could defend agreements on specified grounds, known as 'gateways'. These included benefits to consumers—but also maintenance of employment or exports. Unlike Chapter III and IV matters, the Commission was authorised to entertain complaints on RTPs and give decisions, although it could only issue 'cease and desist' orders.

Promoting competition was thus only one of many objectives of the MRTP Act, and the corrective measures that were prescribed were similar to those of the then-prevailing licence-permit-control raj. But even in the heyday of so-called socialism, most of the firms that should have been covered by Chapter III did not register. A firm could have a market share exceeding one-third for a particular product, but still not be classified as dominant because product categories were defined broadly for purposes of the Act. Similarly, a company could be connected with others in a business group such that their combined assets exceeded ₹ 20 crore, but might not register because complex patterns of inter-corporate shareholdings made it almost impossible for the government and MRTP Commission to establish interconnection (Oza, 1971; Chandra, 1977). In any case, especially after the first few years, applications under Chapter

III were seldom referred to the MRTP Commission. In a few merger cases that were reviewed by the Commission in the 1970s, reduction of foreign-owned equity, rather than competition and efficiency, was a major consideration for recommending approval (Chandra, 1977).

By the mid-1980s, policy makers came to realise that, like industrial licensing, the Act's restraints on concentration of economic power were preventing the growth of firms to optimal scales and their entry into new activities. In 1985, the asset threshold of ₹ 20 crore was quintupled to ₹ 100 crore, taking hundreds of firms out of the purview of Chapter III approval. The requirement for approval was deleted altogether as part of the liberalising reforms of 1991, so for nearly two decades there has been no merger review in India. Agarwal and Bhattacharjea (2006) have shown that both the 1985 and 1991 reforms were followed by significant increases in the number of mergers, but firms that remained under the purview of Chapter III after 1985 were actively involved only after merger review was completely abolished in 1991. Most mergers involving these erstwhile MRTP companies were between firms belonging to the same business group, indicating that the restrictions imposed by the MRTP Act had allowed (or perhaps encouraged) business houses to set up nominally independent firms but had prevented them from merging.

The chapter on MTPs can be dismissed briefly. With MTPs being defined in such general terms, competition analysis was rare. Amendments in 1984 made the chapter essentially unworkable by deleting the concept of a monopolistic undertaking and dictating that any MTP would henceforth be 'deemed to be prejudicial to the public interest' unless it was authorized by the government. Thus, almost any firm could in principle be hauled up for normal business decisions having no bearing on competition. Fortunately, there were very few inquiries, and they were either dropped or stayed by the courts (Singh, 2000). As the accompanying Table 17.1 shows, the number of MTP inquiries has dwindled further in the last decade (although the sudden upsurge in the last year of the Commission's life is surprising). However, I shall show that inquiries into 'unreasonable' pricing were initiated under a different section of the Act.

As regards RTPs, the Commission in its earlier cases ruled that many of the types of agreement listed in the Act, such as tying, exclusive dealerships, resale price maintenance, and of course price-fixing, were illegal *per se* (Chandra, 1977). This was consistent with international

Table 17.1

Inquiries under Various Sections of the MRTP Act, 1972-2009

	Inquiries Instituted and Applications Received							Pending in 2009	
	1972-91 (Annual Average)	2001	2004	2005	2006	2007	2008-2009	March	August
RTP inquiries resulting from:									
Complaint from any trade association, consumer or consumer association	8.6	44	21	26	39	19	45	211	
Reference from central or state governments	0.1	1	0	0	1	1	0	1	
Application from Director General of the MRTP Commission	109.3	37	0	2	11	5	4	47	
Commission's own knowledge or information	55.8	11	2	3	8	6	16	32	
TOTAL RTP INQUIRIES.	173.7	93	23	31	59	31	65	291	291
TOTAL MTP INQUIRIES.	0.8	0	0	0	0	0	4	7	5
UTP inquiries resulting from:									
Complaint from any trade association, consumer or consumer association		90	80	81	54	56	128	435	
Reference from central or state governments		5	0	0	0	0	0	0	
Application from Director General of the MRTP Commission		5	0	0	6	2	15	19	
Commission's own knowledge or information		14	6	7	46	93	115	292	
TOTAL UTP INQUIRIES	259.2	114	86	88	106	151	258	746	80
Applications for compensation from loss or damage caused by an MTP/ RTP/UTP		229	71	77	114	79	353	1155	1186

Notes: For RTP inquiries, annual averages in the first column are computed by dividing by 20 the total number of inquiries under various sections of the MRTP Act during 1972-91 given in Sandesara (1994: table 3). For UTP inquiries, Sandesara (1994: 2084) gives a figure of "nearly 1900", which I divide by 7.33 as the UTP chapter was inserted into the MRTP Act only with effect from August 1984, and I assume that inquiries were initiated a month later. Figures in the last column are from the statement of the Minister of Corporate Affairs in the Rajya Sabha on 16 December 2009 (see n 8 below for citation). Figures in the remaining columns are taken from the annual reports of the Department of Company Affairs (later renamed the Ministry of Corporate Affairs) for the respective years. Where the report gives no figure for inquiries initiated, it is computed by subtracting the number of inquiries brought forward from the preceding year from the number reported to be under consideration during the year under review.

practice at the time. However, a rule of reason gradually began to take shape after a remarkable 1977 Supreme Court judgement which drew upon very recent economic thinking while discussing the efficiency benefits of vertical restraints, and argued that in certain circumstances they could actually promote competition.[3] But, as with MTPs, an ill-advised 1984 amendment dictated that all agreements of the kind that were specifically listed in the Act would henceforth be deemed to be restrictive, thus absolving the Commission from having to analyse their anti-competitive effects.

Despite this apparent strengthening of the Commission's hands, there was a sharp fall in the proportion of RTP inquiries resulting in cease and desist orders in 1982-1991 as compared to the preceding decade (Sandesara, 1994). One reason for this could have been that the 1984 Amendment Act inserted a new chapter (V-B) to protect consumers from 'unfair' trade practices (UTPs), including misrepresentation about the nature of goods or services and misleading prize and promotional schemes. It also inserted new sections allowing the Commission to award compensation for losses arising out of RTPs, MTPs or UTPs. Together, these new provisions attracted a large number of complaints about defective products and deficiency in service. As the accompanying Table shows, such cases came to dominate the Commission's workload. The UTP chapter was retained even after the enactment of the Consumer Protection Act (COPRA) in 1986 with very similar coverage.

The reforms of the 1990s further attenuated what little genuine anti-trust enforcement was being undertaken in India. Chapter III review was formally abandoned, and the Commission struggled to enforce the remaining sections of the Act. It was understaffed, underfunded, without a chairman for long periods of time, and usually functioned with far fewer than the eight members provided for in the Act. According to one study, in 2000 its budget as a proportion of total government expenditure was much less than those of the competition agencies of Pakistan, Sri Lanka, Brazil, Kenya or South Africa.[4] To complete this picture of official neglect, the Table shows that inquiries were seldom initiated by references from the central or state governments.

With the Commission's limited resources being increasingly diverted to cases involving UTPs, the number of RTP inquiries declined sharply in the 1990s, and many of these did not involve the potentially anti-competitive agreements listed in Chapter V. Instead, an increasing proportion invoked a general definition in the Act, according to which an RTP included any practice that "tends to bring about manipulation of prices or conditions of delivery ... in such manner as to impose on the consumers unjustified cost or restrictions". This was taken out of context and used to condemn 'unfair' pricing, underutilisation of capacity, delayed delivery, changes in payment terms or discriminatory treatment of dealers. Thus, by the late 1990s, the majority of cases before the Commission were not competition matters at all, but involved extraneous issues, including consumer complaints that should have been taken up under COPRA and contractual disputes that should have been resolved in civil courts.

Fortunately, this tendency of the Commission to stray into areas it should have avoided was curbed in the early years of the new century by a series of Supreme Court judgments insisting that an RTP must involve a restriction of competition. This forced the Commission to terminate many long-pending inquiries that did not fit this description.[5] But overburdened with UTP compensation cases, it did not take up more competition-related matters. In the entire period 1991-2007, only seven cases involving seller cartels were decided, three of which were dismissed for lack of evidence.[6] In one case, an inquiry into price fixing by cement manufacturers began in 1990—and a cease and desist order was handed down in 2007. In another case, in which evidence of cartelisation by foreign suppliers was found, the Commission prohibited the imports, which from a competition perspective was a remedy worse than the disease. This judgment was overturned by the Supreme Court, which unfortunately went to the other extreme by holding that the Act could not be applied to firms outside India even if their conduct had an effect in India, unless the agreement involved an Indian party.[7] This meant that India could not take action against international cartels, whose activities have been brought to light by hundreds of cases in the United States, Canada and Europe in the past two decades, resulting in multi-million dollar/euro fines being imposed on some giant corporations.

With the passing of the Competition Act in 2002, it seemed that the end of the MRTP era was imminent. Section 66 of the new Act provided for the repeal of the MRTP Act, the dissolution of the MRTP Commission, and the disposal of pending cases. UTP cases and investigations (other than those involving "false or misleading facts disparaging the goods, service or trade of another person") were to be transferred to the National Commission constituted under the COPRA, to be decided in accordance with the latter Act. The remaining cases were to be transferred to the Competition Commission of India (CCI), a new body to be set up under the Competition Act, but would be decided under the MRTP Act. I discuss the Competition Act separately below, but the MRTP story did not end as scripted. Section 66 and the substantive sections of the new legislation could not be brought into force because a writ petition in the Supreme Court raised issues about the separation of powers between the judiciary and the executive in the selection and composition of the CCI. Only administrative sections of the Act were notified, under which a single member and a small staff began functioning in 2003, without being able to take up any cases or investigations. Disposing of the writ petition in early 2005, the Supreme Court took note of the government's promise to make suitable amendments to the Act. But it was not until September 2007 that Parliament passed an amendment Act, allowing for the creation a new Competition Appellate Tribunal (Compat), to be headed by a judge. The amending Act also made far-reaching changes throughout the Competition Act, including a proviso to section 66, extending the life of the MRTP Commission by two years so as to dispose of pending cases. UTP cases (other than those relating to false disparagement) remaining undecided after two years would go to the National Commission, as originally provided in the 2002 Act, but the other cases would now go to the Compat rather than the CCI. As provided for in the original Act, pending investigations relating to UTPs would immediately be transferred to the National Commission, with the rest going to the CCI.

There were, however, more twists in the tale. The government got around to making appointments to the CCI only in early 2009, and notified most of the remaining provisions of the Competition Act in May that year. Section 66, repealing the MRTP Act, was notified in September, and the MRTP Commission's two-year extension was to commence at that point. But by then, natural attrition had resulted in the Commission having no Chairman and only two members—both of whom came to the end of their terms of office within a month. More than 2000 cases remained pending, some dating back to the 1980s. The government claimed that it was unable to find suitable persons to fill the vacancies, and so in October it promulgated an ordinance, doing away with the two-year extension and transferring cases immediately to the

Compat and the National Commission. But the National Commission expressed its inability to accept the UTP cases because unlike the MRTP Commission, it had no staff to handle investigations, and the COPRA under which it functioned had a different definition of 'consumer' as compared to the MRTP Act. In the final act of this sorry tale, the government got Parliament to pass another amendment act in December 2009. Apart from replacing the ordinance with legislation as required by the Constitution, it transferred the orphaned UTP cases, investigations and all compensation applications to the Compat, which would now adjudicate all the cases left pending by the MRTP Commission.[8]

Thus ended the four-decade old MRTP era. No tears need be shed, except for the opportunity that was missed in building up a body of expertise after India enacted one of the earliest competition laws in the developing world. Despite a promising start in the 1970s, at least in respect of RTPs, the 1984 and 1991 amendments closed the door to competition analysis and thrust an expanding workload of UTP cases on the Commission, which diverted it from what remained of its anti-trust mandate. Consequently, it could not bequeath a body of expertise in competition analysis that could help in the enforcement of the much more economically informed Competition Act, to which I now turn.

The Competition Act, 2002

The new Act, whose enforcement belatedly began in May 2009, appears on the surface to conform more closely to the principles of modern anti-trust economics. It covers the usual three areas discussed in the first section of this article: anti-competitive agreements between firms, abuse of dominance by a single firm and 'combinations' (i.e., mergers, amalgamations or acquisitions of control). Wisely, it does not deal with 'unfair' trade practices, which distracted the MRTP Commission. It defines terms that were left open-ended in the MRTP Act, and lays down several economic criteria that the CCI should apply in deciding cases, as well as detailed time-bound steps for reviewing combinations. Unlike the MRTP Act, the new Act empowers the Commission, rather than the government, to decide on combinations and also on abuse of dominance (the counterpart of MTPs in the earlier Act). The CCI can block or undo a combination, but it can also require that it be modified so as to allow it to proceed while taking care of competition concerns. The Competition Act explicitly asserts jurisdiction over foreign combinations and the conduct of firms based abroad having anti-competitive effects in India. This restores India's ability to act against foreign cartels, and to follow the European Commission in taking action against Microsoft for bundling applications software with its Windows operating system. Unlike the MRTP Act, the Competition Act provides for substantial monetary penalties on firms who infringe it or fail to comply with CCI orders, and a leniency programme that allows for reduced penalties to induce cartel members to provide evidence that can be used against others. The CCI, unlike its predecessor, can call on outside experts and also undertake advocacy to spread awareness of competition principles. Apart from these positive features of the Act itself, the CCI has been constituted with its full complement of members, a much larger staff, and a website, which the MRTP Commission never had.[9]

I should also acknowledge that the government has responded favourably to constructive criticism. Commenting on the draft amendment bill in my 2006 article in this journal, I had noted tongue in cheek that officials in the Ministry of Company Affairs who were responsible for drafting the law seem to read EPW, for one of the proposed amendments deleted the provision in the original Act which allowed the CCI to impose an injunction prohibiting the import of goods—an absurd measure from a competition perspective, as I had pointed out in Bhattacharjea (2003). That paper also suggested some modifications to make the cartel leniency programme effective. Changes to this effect were incorporated into the amending Bill, but as I pointed out in Bhattacharjea (2006), the scheme was still too permissive and unpredictable to be of much use. I was gratified when these arguments appeared in the report of the Parliamentary Standing Committee on Finance that reviewed the Bill,[10] and thereafter suitable changes were made and passed in the 2007 Amendment Act. The CCI subsequently published 'Lesser Penalty Regulations' containing well-structured guidelines for implementing the leniency programme that are consistent with international best practice.

Despite these improvements, the Act remains riddled with loopholes and ambiguities, creating unnecessary legal uncertainty and thus favouring lawyers and the large firms that can hire them. As I have discussed most of these problems in detail in my earlier articles, I shall only summarise and update some key objections. First, the Act allows the CCI to take into account the "relative advantage, by way of the contribution to the [sic] economic development" of a combination or an enterprise abusing its dominant position. This is meaningless and potentially dangerous. The relationship between competition and development, and even the meaning of development itself, is controversial. This clause may enable large firms to justify blatantly anti-competitive practices in the name of 'development'.

Second, in its treatment of anti-competitive agreements, the Act requires more analysis and gives greater discretionary power to the CCI than is available to far more experienced agencies in developed countries. In most anti-trust regimes, cartel agreements are treated as illegal *per se*, without any inquiry into their effects. In section 3(3) of the Competition Act, however, such agreements are only presumed to have an 'appreciable adverse effect on competition' (AAEC). It is well established under Indian law that a presumption can be rebutted, and section 19(3) of the Act allows the CCI, while determining whether an agreement has an AAEC, to consider its possible benefits to consumers, improvement of production of goods and provision of services, and promotion of technical, scientific and economic development. Cartels may thus be dealt with under a rule of reason, in which positive as well as negative effects can be taken into account.

The guidance provided by the Act for determining whether an agreement has an AAEC is unsatisfactory. Section 19(3) is similar to Article 101(3) [formerly numbered 81(3)] of the Treaty of the European Union, but in order to be condoned under the latter, an agreement must share the benefits with consumers, must not involve restrictions that are unnecessary to attaining the efficiency objective, and must not substantially eliminate competition. None of these conditions is required under the Indian Competition Act. Unlike the MRTP Act, it does not even require that the benefits be balanced against the losses inflicted on other parties. Besides, unlike in the EU, the Act does not contain any provision for 'block exemption' for small firms involved in certain categories of agreements that are likely to have positive effects. This means that the CCI will have to evaluate each agreement individually. And while the Act provides numerous loopholes for business agreements, it does not exempt trade unions or cooperatives, which on a literal reading could be regarded as price-fixing agreements by associations of persons.[11] Anti-trust laws of most countries explicitly exempt trade unions and cooperatives, as did the MRTP Act.

Third, the Competition Act's provisions on abuse of dominance, which also selectively adapt several phrases from the EU Treaty, leave much to be desired. These could work either in favour or against big business. On the one hand, the Act favours cash-rich firms by allowing them to charge below-cost prices to 'meet the competition' without attracting penalties for predatory pricing. This defence is not permitted in the EU. On the other hand, the Act authorises the CCI to break up a firm to ensure that it does not abuse its dominant position, without requiring evidence that it has done so. Moreover, evidence of an AAEC is not required to prove abuse. This will invite allegations of unfair or discriminatory pricing or conditions in a contract, of the kind that were entertained under the MRTP Act but which are not competition concerns. The five decisions so far reported on the CCI website relate to cases of this nature, and it is encouraging that the Commission has dismissed them on the grounds that dominance was not established and/or competition was not affected. Such clear precedents will have to be set in other areas where the law is ambiguous.

Fourth, the Act's revival of merger review remains controversial. The original Act provided for voluntary notification of combinations in which the assets or turnover of the combined entity would exceed certain threshold levels, specified separately for assets or turnover within India and worldwide. But on the recommendations of a Parliamentary committee, the amending Act of 2007 made notification of such combinations mandatory. It also sensibly inserted a sub-threshold, in terms of the combined assets or turnover of the parties within India, so that foreign combinations exceeding the thresholds for global assets or turnover but having little or no 'local nexus' with the Indian market would not have to be notified to the CCI. However, powerful interests were still not satisfied. After protests by Indian industry as well as memoranda from the American Bar Association and International Bar Association, the CCI published Draft Regulations in 2008, specifying further sub-thresholds for assets and turnover in India for each party individually. This would save firms from the paperwork involved in filing applications for mergers that are unlikely to have an AAEC, and the CCI from having to devote resources to investigate them. But it would also mean turning a blind eye to mergers in which foreign firms with no current Indian business enter the Indian market by taking over local firms, instead of competing through exports or foreign direct investment (FDI). The Draft Regulations thus ignored potential competition, which is taken into account in merger cases in the US and Canada.[12] This issue has become salient recently with several large Indian pharmaceutical companies being acquired by multinationals. But as of early July 2010, the sections of the Act dealing with regulation of combinations had not yet been brought into force, and the related Draft Regulations had disappeared from the CCI website.

Fifth, some institutional issues give rise to disquiet. There is likely to be conflict with sectoral regulators (such as the Telecommunications Regulatory Authority of India), some of whom also have mandates to regulate competition. The Act also compromises the autonomy of the CCI by giving the government powers to supersede and reconstitute it if it fails to discharge its functions, to comply with policy directives, or even 'in the public interest'. In order to divest the CCI of powers that are judicial in nature, the 2007 amendment created multiple points at which its decisions can be held up or reversed: not just the Compat, but also tax authorities for levying monetary penalties and a magisterial court for awarding jail terms for failure to comply with CCI orders.

Finally, there is the issue of expertise to implement the Act, which is replete with technical concepts requiring fairly advanced knowledge of modern industrial economics. As pointed out above, on anti-competitive agreements the Act leaves much more to the Commission's analysis and discretion than competition regimes in countries with far greater experience. As I argued in the preceding section, four decades of enforcement of the MRTP Act yielded very little relevant experience. To make matters worse, all the personnel appointed to the CCI between 2003 and 2008, who immersed themselves in learning the relevant concepts even though they could not take up any cases, are no longer with the agency. Some were transferred to other government departments; others resigned and joined law firms, where their skills will now be deployed on behalf of private parties against the CCI, which is staffed entirely with recent appointees. No regular appointment was made for more than a year to the key post of Director General, responsible for overseeing investigations. And of the 185 professionals who were to be appointed in the first year, only 35 positions had been filled, mainly on deputation from other government departments, as of May 2010. This personnel deficit in the Commission is believed to be responsible for its inability to decide more than a handful of cases in its first year of functioning.[13]

To conclude, the government's handling of its competition laws can be faulted on several counts. It took 32 months to enact the relevant amendments after the Supreme Court cleared the way for appointments to the CCI in January 2005, and another 20 months to make appointments and notify the enforceable provisions of the Act, ensuring that the CCI would lose all the expertise built up since 2003. A further year elapsed without a regular Director General at the helm. With the CCI unable to decide cases, the government failed to make fresh appointments to the MRTP Commission, allowing its ranks to be depleted, further weakening whatever anti-trust enforcement was being undertaken, and allowing cases to pile up. After the MRTP Commission was finally wound up, the government tossed pending UTP cases and investigations into the lap of the National Commission, whose inability to handle them was known well in advance.[14] After unnecessarily delaying the disposal of the remaining cases with these missteps, it steered them to the Compat, which was never envisaged as a body that would supervise investigations or hear the UTP cases that constitute the majority of the huge MRTP backlog.

Was all this simply the result of ineptness, or was the government really not keen on having a well-staffed anti-trust agency that would make life difficult for powerful corporate interests, especially in the run-up to the 2009 Lok Sabha elections? Whatever be the reason, the two new bodies have made a good beginning despite their unfortunate inheritance. The Compat has made steady progress in clearing the backlog of MRTP cases. And according to media reports, the CCI has recently made out a *prima facie* case of predatory pricing against the National Stock Exchange (NSE), and another of tying faulty meters with electricity connections against Delhi's power distribution companies, which are owned by two of the biggest business houses in the country. It remains to be seen, however, whether these allegations can be sustained in the regular hearings that will now take place, and what kind of analysis these two bodies will undertake in deciding the more complex cases that are before them.

Notes

1. In sectors where technology and heavy capital costs make competition infeasible (e.g., in local electricity distribution, landline telephone networks, oil pipelines, or ports and airports), monopoly may be allowed, with a sectoral regulator to award licences and regulate prices, quantities and quality of service. Anti-trust issues may still arise if the monopolist owns

or merges with a firm that is a buyer of its services in a market in which there are actual or potential competitors. (The corresponding examples would be power generation, mobile telephony, oil refining, shipping and air transport.) The monopolist may overcharge or deny access to competitors in the 'downstream' activity, thus abusing its upstream monopoly power in favour of its downstream subsidiary.

2. In section III of Bhattacharjea (2003), I discuss the importance of broader social objectives, the relatively recent application of the efficiency standard in the competition regimes of the US and UK, and the possibility of balancing efficiency with distributional concerns.
3. TELCO vs Registrar of Restrictive Trade Agreements, 2 SCC 55 (1977). This judgement actually preceded by a few months a judgment of the U.S. Supreme Court (Continental TV vs GTE Sylvania) which is regarded as a landmark in the anti-trust treatment of vertical restraints.
4. Approaches to Competition Policy in South Asian Countries (Jaipur: CUTS-CIER 2003).
5. The preceding analysis is based on my reading of 52 Commission orders on RTPs between 2001 and 2007, as well as several Supreme Court judgements. More details and citations for the major cases are provided in Bhattacharjea (2008).
6. This is based on my updating of the meticulous study by De (2005), who examined all cartel cases reported in journals or law textbooks since 1970. The contrast with the Commission's early years is stark: the first RTP inquiries were initiated in 1972, and just five years later Chandra (1977) was able to identify seven price-fixing cases, most of them resulting in cease and desist orders.
7. Haridas Exports vs All India Float Glass Manufacturers' Association, 6 SCC 600 (2002). This judgment and its background are extensively analysed in Bhattacharjea (2003, 2008).
8. This paragraph is based on the Statement of Objects and Reasons appended to the Competition (Amendment) Bill, 2009, and the record of the debate in the Rajya Sabha on the Bill on 16 December 2009, from *http://164.100.47.5/newdebate/218/16122009/16.00 pmTo17.00 pm.pdf* (last viewed 1 June 2010).
9. See Ghosh and Ross (2008) for a broader overview of the Act, and a discussion of its strengths and weaknesses that partially overlaps with this paper.
10. Lok Sabha Secretariat (2006: 38-39). The government also implemented some (but not all) of the other recommendations of the committee.
11. The absence of a trade union exemption was pointed out by Ghosh and Ross (2008).
12. The argument is spelt out in detail, with examples, in Agarwal and Bhattacharjea (2008).
13. See *http://www.financialexpress.com/news/Competition-panel-to-increase-headcount-for-quicker-redressal/613534/*, and *http://www.livemint.com/2010/05/19232645/One-year-on-CCI-still-doesn.html*, viewed 12 June 2010. As pointed out above, the CCI has posted orders on five cases on its website, although according to a more recent news report, it has decided 19 out of the 94 cases that it has taken up, including 50 transferred from the MRTP Commission: see *http://www.business-standard.com/india/news/corporate-houses-keep-cci-busy/399770/*, viewed 29 June 2010.
14. The Parliamentary committee that reviewed the 2006 amendment bill was well aware of this problem, and directed the government to make suitable amendments in the Consumer Protection Act (Lok Sabha Secretariat, 2006: 54-6). The government's assurances to this effect were not fulfilled.

References

Agarwal, M. and A. Bhattacharjea (2006). "Mergers in India: A Response to Regulatory Shocks", *Emerging Markets Finance and Trade* 42(3): 46-65.

———. (2008). "Are Merger Regulations Diluting Parliamentary Intent?", *Economic and Political Weekly* 43(26/27): 10-13.

Bhattacharjea, A. (2003). "India's Competition Policy: An Assessment", *Economic and Political Weekly* 38(34): 3561-74.

———. (2006). "Amending India's Competition Act", *Economic and Political Weekly* 41(41): 4314-17.

———. (2008). "India's New Competition Law: A Comparative Assessment", *Journal of Competition Law and Economics* 4(3): 1-30. To be reprinted in Eleanor Fox and Abel Mateus (eds.), *Economic Development: The Critical Role of Competition Law and Politics*. Edward Elgar, forthcoming.

Chandra, N.K. (1977). "Monopoly Legislation and Policy in India", *Economic and Political Weekly*, 12(33/34): 1405-18, reprinted in The Retarded Economies, N.K. Chandra (ed.), Bombay: OUP, 1988.

De, O. (2005). "Identifying Cartels in India", M.Phil. dissertation, University of Delhi.

Ghosh, S. and T.W. Ross (2008). "The Competition (Amendment) Bill 2007: A Review and Critique", *Economic and Political Weekly* 43(51): 35-40.

Lok Sabha Secretariat (2006). Standing Committee on Finance (2006-07), Fourteenth Lok Sabha, Ministry of Company Affairs, Competition (Amendment) Bill, 2006, Forty-Fourth Report, December 2006.

Oza, A.N. (1971). "Putting Teeth into the Monopolies Act", *Economic and Political Weekly* 6(31-32): 1703-08.

Sandesara, J.C. (1994). "Restrictive Trade Practices in India, 1961-91: Experience of Control and Agenda for Further Work", *Economic and Political Weekly* 29(32): 2081-94.

Singh, J. (2000). "Monopolistic Trade Practices and Concentration of Economic Power: Some Conceptual Problems in MRTP Act", *Economic and Political Weekly* 35(50): 4437-44.

→ → →

Economic and Political Weekly XLV(35), 28 August 2010.

Postscript (2016)

In the six years since this article was written, the Competition Commission of India (CCI) has decided over 400 cases that involved allegations of anti-competitive agreements and abuse of dominance. It has imposed substantial fines on some leading corporate entities, especially in the cement, pharmaceuticals and real estate sectors, and in government procurement. An assessment of some of the early cartel cases is available in Aditya Bhattacharjea and Oindrila De, "Cartels and the Competition Commission", *Economic and Political Weekly*, 1 September 2012. However, many of these decisions have recently been overturned on procedural grounds by the Competition Appellate Tribunal (COMPAT). In some other cases, the COMPAT has drastically reduced the penalties on the grounds that the firms are small-scale industries and first-time offenders.

The section of the Competition Act on combinations was brought into effect in June 2011, along with new and much better regulations. Since then, the CCI has cleared over 350 mergers and acquisitions. It has so far not blocked any proposed deal, but has ordered modifications to preserve competition in a few cases. For an assessment of the CCI's record on merger review, see Aditya Bhattacharjea, "Recent Trends in Mega-mergers in India and Lessons for Competition Policy: Insights from Merger Cases under the Competition Act", in C. Veeramani and R. Nagaraj (eds), *International Trade and Industrial Development in India: Emerging Trends, Patterns and Issues*. New Delhi: Orient Blackswan, 2016. Finally, for a detailed assessment of competition issues and competition policy (including horizontal and vertical agreements, intellectual property issues, as well as combinations) in the Indian pharmaceuticals sector, see Aditya Bhattacharjea and Fiyanshu Sindhwani, "Competition Issues in the Indian Pharmaceutical Sector", Project Report submitted to CUTS-CIRC, January 2014, *http://www.cuts-ccier.org/Compeg/PDF/Report-Pharmaceutical_Sector_Study.pdf*.

18

M.H. BALA SUBRAHMANYA

Small-scale Industrialisation under Globalisation

Is the Tide Turning Around?

Introduction

Small-scale industries (hereafter SSI) play a significant role in the economic development of nations (Deo, 2013). However, the role that SSI plays in both developed and developing economies has been undergoing remarkable transformation since the early 1990s. This is primarily due to the intensification of globalisation—the opportunities as well as the challenges emerging out of it, specific to SSI (Ibid.). Empirical evidence reveals that globalisation has impacted small and medium enterprises (SMEs) in different economies differently (Smeral, 1998; Acs *et al.*, 2001; Asiedu and Freeman, 2007; Abdullah *et al.*, 2009; Vladimirov *et al.*, 2013). But the competitiveness of SMEs of least developed countries (LDCs), which may not have adequate capabilities to handle challenges, might deteriorate relatively as well as absolutely (Awuah and Amal, 2011).

SSI development has been one of the major planks of India's economic development strategy since Independence. An exclusive institutional framework and a host of policies and programmes had emerged for the protection and promotion of SSI since then (Bala Subrahmanya, 1998). As a result, SSI contribution to employment, industrial production and total exports grew considerably over the period. By 1990, SSI accounted for 35 per cent of the gross value of output in the manufacturing sector and over 40 per cent of the total exports from the country, apart from providing employment to around 12 million people (Ministry of Industry, 1991).

However, with the beginning of 1990s, the policy environment for SSI has undergone dramatic changes due to national macroeconomic policy reforms covering that of SSI, coinciding with that of international policies. As a result, there were indicators to argue that SSI performance has suffered initially, in the 1990s (Bala Subrahmanya, 2004). Since then, both policies and competitive environment for SSI have changed further. Against this backdrop, this paper attempts to examine the following three sets of research questions (RQs):

RQ1: What are the major policy changes that have occurred, nationally as well as internationally, which have implications for SSI performance? What kind of an impact they have made on the SSI so far?

RQ2: How has Indian SSI responded to these policy changes and performed since 1991? How far the SSI has been able to cope with the emerging challenges and exploit the growing global opportunities?

RQ3: What are the current policy focus and its implications for SSI? How far will it enable the sector to overcome its challenges and enhance its competitiveness in the future?

In this paper, official definitions of an SSI unit pursued from time to time by the Government of India (GoI) under the Industries Development & Regulation (IDR) Act, 1951 (till Micro, Small and Medium Enterprises (MSME) Development Act, 2006, was enacted) are followed. Prior to 2006 an SSI unit was defined as one having original investment in plant and machinery, whether held on ownership terms or on lease/hire purchase basis, not exceeding ₹100 million (Ministry of SSI, 2006).

Globalisation and Domestic Economic Reforms: Implications and Impact on the SSI

Since the beginning of 1990s, policy changes have been taking place at three different levels—global, national and sectoral, which have implications for SSI functioning and performance in India. The first and the foremost development is the 'globalisation' process at the international level. Globalisation refers to the worldwide phenomenon of technological, economic, political, and cultural exchanges among nations, organisations and private individuals. These exchanges, which have led to interdependencies at all levels (national, firm and private individual levels), are complex and multifaceted (Fischer, 2003).

Since the early 1990s, we are moving away from a world where national economies were relatively self-contained entities, isolated from each other by barriers to cross-border trade and investment towards a world where barriers to cross-border trade and investment are tumbling, and perceived distance is shrinking due to advances in transportation and telecommunications technology. Globalisation has resulted in the integration of economies and has prompted a rapid increase in the movement of products, capital and labour across borders (Abdullah *et al.*, 2009). Globalisation allows firms to sell their products and services to consumers beyond the borders of their country of origin. Globalisation is literally removing the boundaries to potential customers in a worldwide market.

But the question is what drives the globalisation of business? Three forces drive this globalisation of business (Acs *et al.*, 2001). The first is the explosive growth in low-cost technology connecting people and locations. Better information processing and communications technology creates a greater awareness of international economic opportunities. It also lets firms divide their production processes more and spread it over a wider geographical region, beyond the national borders. A second driving force behind the globalisation of business is the steady dismantling of the trade barriers the world erected just before and during the Great Depression of the 1930s. A third force motivating the globalisation of business is the widespread economic restructuring and liberalisation that followed the fall of socialism in Russia and Eastern Europe.

International trade and foreign direct investment (FDI) are two important aspects of globalisation (Asiedu and Freeman, 2007). Reduced trade barriers can affect SSI in the international market as well as in the domestic market in two different ways. A steady increase in world exports can pose new challenges to some SSI, while creating new opportunities for some others (particularly, the innovative ones) in the international market (Acs *et al.*, 2001). Similarly, a steady increase in domestic imports (particularly raw materials and intermediates) can generate more competition to some SSI, while enabling access to new technologies (capital goods) to the local SSI and thereby contribute to the building of their competitiveness.

The formation of World Trade Organization (WTO) in 1995 accelerated the process of scaling down trade barriers through a steady reduction of tariff and non-tariff restrictions on imports. India, as a member of the WTO substantially reduced its quantitative and non-quantitative restrictions by 1 April 2001 (Ministry of Finance, 2002). This would have made Indian industry, particularly SSI, to face much stronger international competition (Planning Commission, 2002). The process of removal of quantitative and non-quantitative restrictions across countries had led to freer movement of goods between countries including India. As a result, world exports grew in constant dollar terms at an average rate of 4.58 per cent during 1990-2005 as against the average rate of 2.97 per cent during 1975-1990 (Ministry of Finance, 2007). The reduction of restrictions on the movement of goods between countries and the subsequent increase in world exports would have benefited multinational corporations (MNCs) more than SSI.

The other dimension of trade is domestic imports, which can be broadly classified under (i) raw materials & intermediates, and (ii) capital goods. India's import of raw materials and intermediates [excluding petroleum, oil and lubricants (POL)] grew (in constant dollar terms) by 9.39 per cent per annum during 1990-2005 as compared to 2.20 per cent per annum during 1970-1990, whereas the import of capital goods increased (in constant dollar terms) by 6.84 per cent per annum during 1990-2005 as compared to 6.06 per cent per annum during 1970-1990 (Ibid.). An increase in the former would have posed more competition, whereas an increase in the latter might have proved beneficial to the SSI in the domestic market.

While import liberalisation would have contributed to the growth of both kinds of imports, it was the phasing out of Phased Manufacturing Program (PMP) in the 1990s (Bala Subrahmanya, 2009), which would have specially encouraged both domestic large firms and newly entered MNCs to import both raw materials and intermediate goods rather than procure them from the domestic-market-based SSI. Perhaps, this would explain why the import of raw materials & intermediates grew faster than that of capital goods. But the liberalisation of capital goods imports would have benefited SSI as much as large firms by enabling them to acquire sophisticated technologies from abroad. In fact, there has been a significant shift away from Indian made technologies towards foreign made technologies in the machinery industry of Bangalore, in the era of liberalisation (Bala Subrahmanya *et al.*, 2014).

In economic terms, FDI is probably the most important and possibly the most visible aspect of globalisation in many regions (Deo, 2013).

Since 1991 till 2006, on an average, 68 countries across the world have introduced more than 100 favourable regulatory changes to FDI (UNCTAD, 2006). As a result, global FDI inflow increased initially marginally from 21.7 per cent per annum during 1986-1990 to 22.0 per cent per annum during 1990-1995 and considerably to 40.0 per cent per annum during 1995-2000. Global FDI inflows grew by 31.60 per cent in 2004 and by 27.40 per cent in 2005 (Ibid.). The sectoral and industrial pattern of global FDI inflows reveals that it has been shifting towards services accompanied by a decline in the share of FDI in natural resources and manufacturing. The services sector, which accounted for about 2/5 of the total FDI inflows in the late 1980s, accounted for about 3/5 of the total by the late 1990s and after. The shift towards services is more pronounced in the case of developing and transition economies (Ibid.).

The global upswing in FDI inflows has been experienced by Indian economy as well: the FDI inflow to India increased (in constant US dollars) by 31.94 per cent per annum during 1991-2005 (NCAER, 2009). Further, the shift in FDI inflows towards services sector has been observed, though not to the same extent, in the Indian context as well: while manufacturing industry accounted for a majority of the FDI inflows in the 1990s, its share declined to about 41 per cent by 2005 (NCAER, 2009; Rao and Dhar, 2011). Whereas the share of services sector (including financial services, consultancy, housing and real estate, construction, hotel and tourism, etc.) increased from less than 20 per cent in the 1990s to about 40 per cent of the total FDI inflows during 2000-2009. What is more significant is that FDI in manufacturing sectors has penetrated not only metro cities but also small cities, thus generating linkages with suburban and rural regions of India (NCAER, 2009).

Globally, FDI has the potential for negative displacement/competition effects as well as positive knowledge spill over and linkage effects on the survival of new business start-ups and existing small firms (Deo, 2013). There are at least three channels through which FDI can affect the performance of domestic firms: competition, labour market and linkages (Asiedu and Freeman, 2007). The product market competition from MNCs might affect local firms but, at the same time, the 'learning by competition' analogy applies: the pressure to survive may speed up the adoption of new technologies and thereby enhance the productivity of domestic firms. This is substantiated by the experience of Bangalore-based machinery industry SMEs, which went for acquiring external technologies due to 'competition-related factors' much more than to overcome 'technological obsolescence' in the era of globalisation (Bala Subrahmanya *et al.*, 2014).

In the labour market, the entry and operations of MNCs might attract more productive workers towards them and thereby lowering of the employee pool available to domestic firms and possibly reducing average productivity levels (Asiedu and Freeman, 2006). This has been empirically observed in the context of auto component manufacturing SMEs in Bangalore. Fresh technically qualified degree and diploma holders treat SMEs as 'training centres' in the initial part of their career and subsequently join large enterprises including MNCs for better remuneration. As a result, the turnover rate of skilled and semi-skilled employees in SMEs is relatively high and therefore they are forced to hire these employees more than 'optimally.' The skill accumulation made in the course of innovations carried out by SMEs is lost to MNCs in due course of time. As a result of all these, innovations undertaken by the SMEs had a positive impact on employment growth but not on productivity growth (Bala Subrahmanya, 2010).

MNC presence, however, can have a positive effect on the performance of domestic firms. The linkages between MNCs and domestic firms create business opportunities and enhance the technological know-how and productivity of domestic firms (Javorick, 2004). This is because MNCs often outsource parts of their production to domestic firms or utilise local firms as suppliers of services and raw materials, thus creating business opportunities for domestic firms. Also, MNCs tend to provide training, equipment and technology to their local suppliers (Asiedu and Freeman, 2007). The strong forward and/or backward linkages of major FDI receiving sectors have been observed in the Indian economy. The sectors with strong backward and forward linkages include construction, fuels, chemicals and metallurgical industries; the sectors with strong backward linkages include electrical equipment, drugs and pharmaceuticals, food processing, textiles, among others; service sectors, telecommunications and consultancy services have strong forward linkages (NCAER, 2009).

At the micro level, auto component SMEs, which are subcontractors of automobile MNCs located in Bangalore, are able to receive product-related and purchase process assistance from the latter, which facilitated the former to carry out technological innovations and improve their economic performance. The higher the degree of assistance, the higher will be the levels of innovations and economic performance. Thus subcontracting relationship with MNCs has proved beneficial to local SMEs as a means of technological innovations and enhanced economic performance (Kumar and Bala Subrahmanya, 2010).

At the domestic industry level, the de-reservation of industries reserved exclusively for public sector enterprises (PSEs) has led to the shrinkage of industrial space reserved for PSEs, whereas industrial de-licensing and removal of restrictions on FDI has substantially enlarged the scope for private investments, both domestic and foreign (Bala Subrahmanya, 2009). PSEs form an important and reliable market segment for SSI. This is due to the continued operations of two policy measures for SSI promotion, among others, even in the period of globalisation: (i) purchase preference policy: about 360 items manufactured by SSI are reserved for exclusive purchase to be made by government departments and PSEs, and (ii) price preference policy: Price preference up to 15 per cent over the lowest quotation of the large-scale units will be given to the products of SSI by government departments and PSEs, if the product quality is comparable (DCMSME, 2014). Both the policies have to be implemented by the PSEs. Given this, the number of PSEs, its composition in terms of profit making and loss making, and their total turnover would make a difference to the performance of SSI.

While the total number of central PSEs increased in 1990-91 compared to 1980-81, it has decreased marginally between 1990-91 and 2005-06, whereas the proportion of profit making enterprises in total PSEs has gone up and the proportion of loss making PSEs has declined considerably after 1990-91 (Table 18.1). This is attributed to the introduction of memorandum of understanding (MoU) system, among others. MoU have enhanced not only commercial profitability but also have enhanced operational efficiency of the central PSEs (Seema Gupta *et al.*, 2003). A detailed analysis of the performance of central PSEs concluded that central PSE performance has improved in the liberalisation period compared to the pre-liberalisation period (Singh and Chittedi, 2011). The better central PSE performance in the liberalisation period would have only benefited the SSI.

Table 18.1

Central Public Sector Enterprises: Composition of Profit/Loss Making Units

Year	Number of PSEs		
	Profit Making	Loss Making	Total*
1981-82	104 (55.32)	83 (44.15)	188 (100.00)
1990-91	124 (52.54)	109 (46.19)	236 (100.00)
2005-06	157 (70.00)	58 (26.00)	225 (100.00)

Note: * The sum total of profit making and loss making PSEs will not add up to the total because it includes PSEs which did not submit financial returns or no-profit/no-loss enterprises.

Source: *Public Enterprises Survey*, various issues.

The remarkable shift in India's SSI policy since 1991, in tune with the overall trend of economic liberalisation, represents the sector-specific dimension of the change in the macroeconomic policy environment for SSI. The most visible plank of SSI protection policy prior to 1991 was the reservation of product lines for exclusive manufacturing in the SSI sector. The policy was introduced in 1947 with a list of 47 items which was expanded steadily to comprise 504 items in 1977, and after the recast of the list based on National Industrial Classification (NIC) codes, the list of items increased to 807 in 1978. By 1991, the list included 836 items (Bala Subrahmanya, 1995). Since then, however, the list of reserved items for exclusive manufacturing has been curtailed steadily. Today, the list of items reserved for the SSI sector comprises only 20 items (DCMSME, 2014). To the extent of 816 de-reserved items from the list, the SSI sector would have been exposed to intense competition *vis-à-vis* large firms, in the era of globalisation. On the positive front, to enhance the competitiveness of SSI, the government has introduced several policy measures backed by institutions to provide better access to finance, technology and marketing, among others (Ministry of MSMEs, 2010).

The above discussion brings out that policy changes that have taken place since 1991 at the global, national and sectoral levels and their implications for SSI present a mixed bag of challenges and opportunities. The limited, location-specific, empirical research findings reveal that SSI has gained on different fronts whereas lost on some other fronts. Overall, it would be appropriate to conclude that globalisation and domestic economic liberalisation together would have considerably contributed to the intensification of competitive environment for Indian SSI locally as well as globally.

In the process, less competitive ones would have suffered whereas more competitive ones would have gained. Further, a considerable number of SSI enterprises would have responded to the emerging competitive environment by enhancing their competitiveness, by taking advantage of the market forces on the one hand, and policy intervention, on the other, wherever appropriate. The overall growth performance and contribution of SSI to the national economy in the era of globalisation have to be analysed against this backdrop.

SSI Performance in the Globalisation Era

The SSI sector in India comprises two sub-sectors: registered and unregistered. The registered SSI sector comprises factories registered under Indian Factories Act, 1948, and those registered with the District Industries Centres (DICs) in the states and union territories of India, among others. The unregistered SSI, on the other hand, includes non-factory enterprises and those which are not registered with the DICs, among others (Ministry of MSMEs, 2012).

The Ministry of MSMEs, GoI, provides two kinds of data on the SSI: (i) annual time-series data on the number of enterprises, employment, output and exports, for the SSI sector and country as a whole, and (ii) comprehensive data on the number of enterprises, employment, value of output, number of exporting enterprises, value of exports, value of raw materials, value of energy inputs, value of gross value added, etc., industry-wise and state-wise, based on the census for the registered sector and based on a sample survey for the unregistered sector (Ministry of MSMEs, 2013). The first SSI Census was conducted in 1972/73, followed by the second Census in 1987/88, and the third Census in 2001/02. The fourth Census, conducted in 2006/07, was broader in coverage as it included medium enterprises as well (DCSSI, 1992; Ministry of MSMEs, 2012).

Given the above, the performance of SSI can be evaluated based on (i) aggregate annual time-series data for the SSI sector as a whole and (ii) aggregate census-based data for the registered SSI sector. Based on the former, the compound average growth rate (CARG) is calculated for units, employment, output and exports (both at 2004/05 prices) for the pre-liberalisation period (1973/74-1989/90) as well as the liberalisation period (1990/91-2006/07). Subsequently, the annual growth rates of number of units, employment, output and exports (both at 2004/05 prices) of SSI are graphically presented and the trend lines are set, for the pre-liberalisation period as well as the liberalisation period. The slope of the trend lines for each of the variables for both the periods is estimated by means of regression analysis, using time as the explanatory variable for the four dependent variables (units, employment, output and exports, respectively). Further, a t-test is conducted to ascertain whether the annual growth rates of units, employment, output and exports experienced in the liberalisation period are significantly different from that of the pre-liberalisation period.

The registered SSI sector represents a more developed/modern segment of the SSI, as it primarily includes factories and those registered with the DICs. Therefore, examining its growth performance and contribution to the national economy (based on census data) might be more meaningful. Therefore, registered SSI performance has been examined in terms of (i) growth of units, exporting units, employment, values of output and exports (both at 2004/05 prices), (ii) relative contribution of registered SSI to national income, organised sector employment and total exports, (iii) degree of internationalisation, (iv) growth of ancillarisation, and (v) growth of sickness, from 1987/88 to 2001/02 and from 2001/02 to 2006/07.

Performance of the SSI Sector: Pre-liberalisation Period versus Liberalisation Period

The growth performance of SSI units, employment, output and exports for the pre-liberalisation period and for the liberalisation period (Figure 18.1) as well as for the decades from the 1970s to 2000s is presented in Table 18.2. The growth rate of SSI, on an average, has declined considerably in terms of units and even employment, but has improved marginally in terms of output and exports, in the liberalisation period compared to the pre-liberalisation period. The decade-wise performance provides more insights. The growth of SSI units declined in the 1980s compared to that of the 1970s, and it declined further in the 1990s but remained steady in the 2000s compared to that of the 1990s.

The growth of SSI employment, similar to that of SSI units, declined in the 1980s compared to that of the 1970s, and it declined further in the 1990s but improved marginally in the 2000s compared to that of the 1990s. The growth of output, unlike units and employment, improved marginally in the 1980s compared to that of the 1970s, but declined sharply in the 1990s and improved remarkably in the 2000s compared

Table 18.2

Growth Performance of SSI: Pre-Liberalisation versus Liberalisation

Period		*Units*	*Employment*	*Output*	*Exports*
Pre-liberalisation	1973/74-1989/90	9.67	7.14	3.66	12.09
Liberalisation	1990/91-2006/07	4.06	4.34	4.34	12.62
1970s	1973/74-1980/81	11.19	8.66	3.36	13.95
1980s	1980/81-1989/90	8.51	5.97	3.89	10.66
1990s	1990/91-2000/01	4.06	4.21	0.11	12.87
2000s	2000/01-2006/07	4.06	4.56	11.78	12.20

Source: Ministry of MSMEs.

Figure 18.1

SSI Growth Performance in the Pre-Liberalisation and Liberalisation Periods

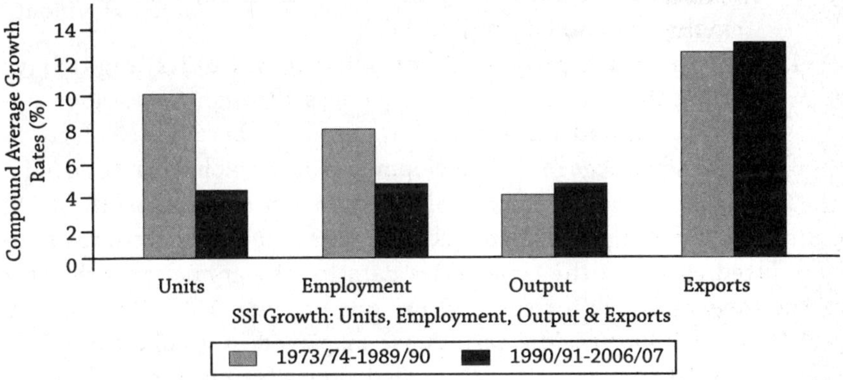

to the earlier decades. The growth of exports, unlike units, employment and output, has remained, more or less, steady all through the pre-liberalisation and liberalisation periods. Although the growth of exports declined in the 1980s compared to that of the 1970s, it improved modestly in the 1990s but declined marginally in the 2000s compared to that of the 1990s. On the whole, it may be appropriate to conclude that while SSI growth suffered in terms of units and employment, in terms of output, SSI has improved, and in terms of exports it could hold on to its ground to a large extent, in the liberalisation period relative to the pre-liberalisation period. The question is why this has happened. The possible reasons could be the following:

1. New SSI units might not have come up as significantly in the liberalisation period as compared to the pre-liberalisation period due to the threat of competition. This would have affected directly SSI employment generation as well (Bala Subrahmanya, 2007).
2. Those new SSI units that have come up in the liberalisation period might be much more capital-intensive than those that have come up in the past. Even some proportions of the existing SSI units might have modernised themselves, to rely less on labour. This was one of the objectives of technology upgradation and modernisation achieved by some of the machinery SMEs in Bangalore (Bala Subrahmanya *et al.*, 2014).
3. Those SSI units which lacked access to basic infrastructural facilities and which could not strengthen their competitiveness would have exited from the market, thereby affecting SSI employment and output initially.
4. A significant proportion of existing SSI units might have strengthened their competitiveness through technology upgradation and modernisation, among others, particularly to take advantage of the developments in the global market (Ibid.).

To further probe the impact of globalisation on the growth of SSI units, employment, output and exports, linear least square lines have been fitted based on the time series data for the annual growth rates of the four variables for the two periods of time: 1973/74-1989/90 and 1990/91-2006/07. The results are displayed in graphs from A to D, in Figure 18.2. None of the estimated slopes (except for the slope of the growth of SSI units in the pre-liberalisation period) is statistically significant implying that there is no consistent trend in the performance of SSI either in the pre-liberalisation period (excluding SSI unit growth) or in the liberalisation period. Further, we carried out paired t-tests for the annual growth rates of units, employment, output and exports for the pre-liberalisation period (1973/74-1989/90) and the liberalisation period (1990/91-2006/07) to ascertain whether the growth trends of the four variables in the liberalisation period are different from those of the pre-liberalisation period. The results of t-test analysis (carried out with stata 11 software) are presented in Table 18.3.

Figure 18.2

The Influence of Globalisation on SSI Units, Employment, Output and Exports

A1

Growth of SSI Units: Pre-Liberalisation Period

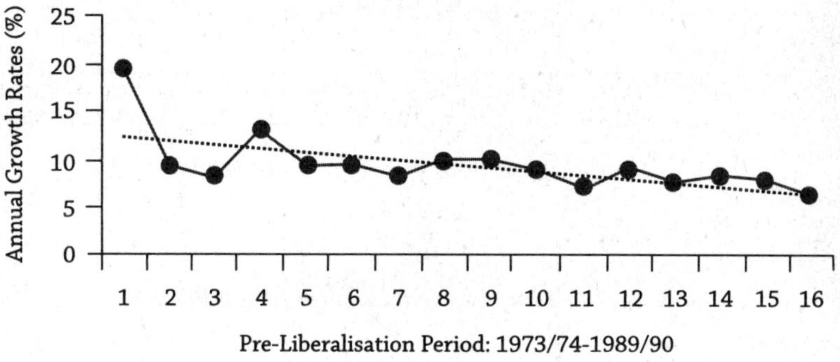

Slope: -0.41 (Significant at 0.01 level)

A2

Growth of SSI Units: Liberalisation Period

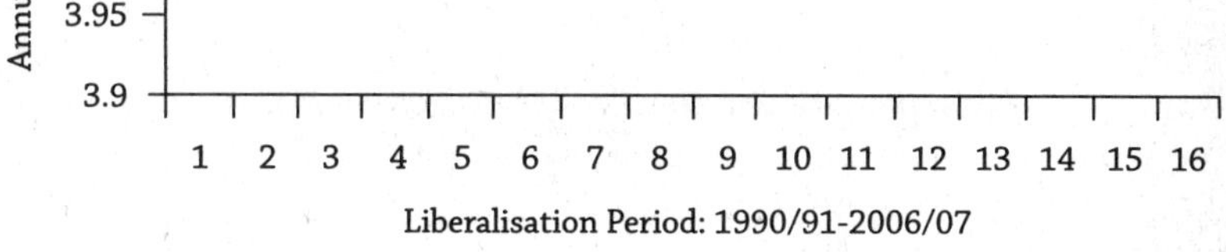

Slope: 0.00*

B1

Growth of SSI Employment: Pre-Liberalisation Period

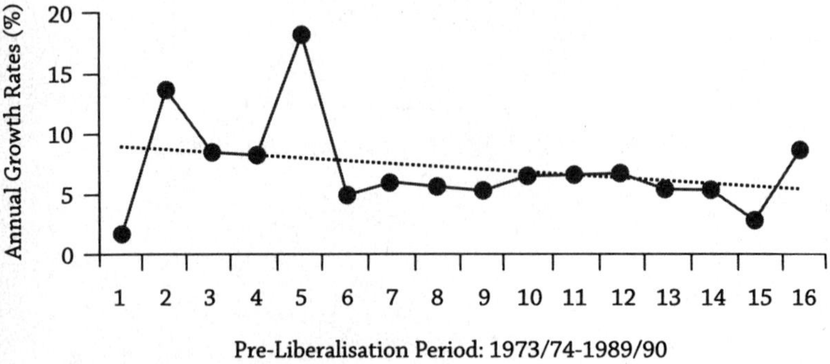

Slope: -0.24*

B2

Growth of SSI Employment: Liberalisation Period

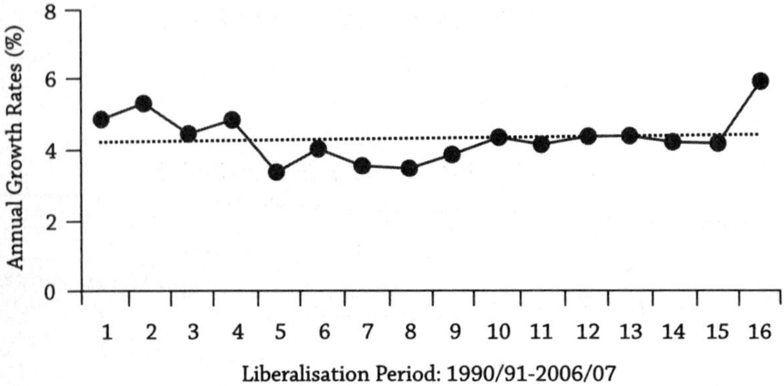

Slope: 0.01*

C1

Growth of SSI Output: Pre-Liberalisation Period

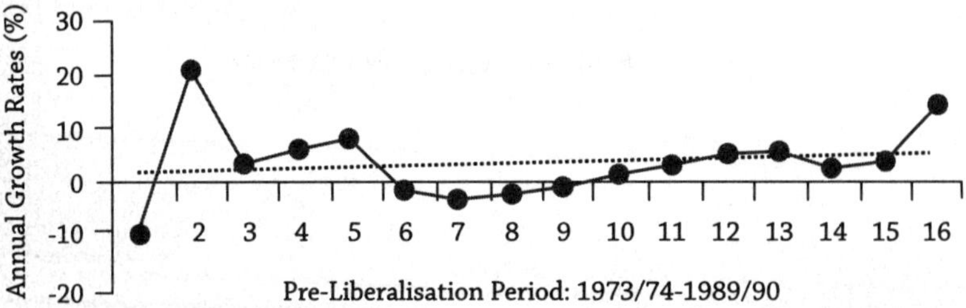

Slope: 0.21*

C2

Growth of SSI Output: Liberalisation Period

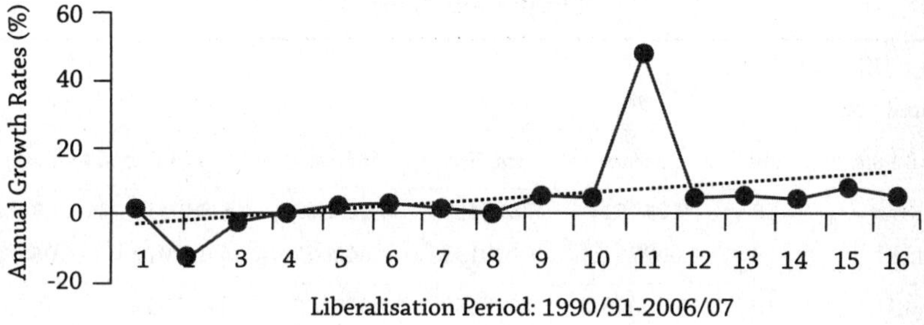

Slope: 1.06*

D1

Growth of SSI Exports: Pre-Liberalisation Period

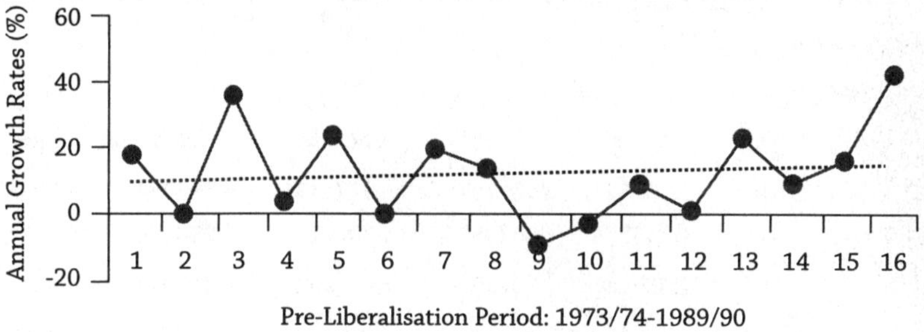

Slope: 0.35*

D2

Growth of SSI Exports: Liberalisation Period

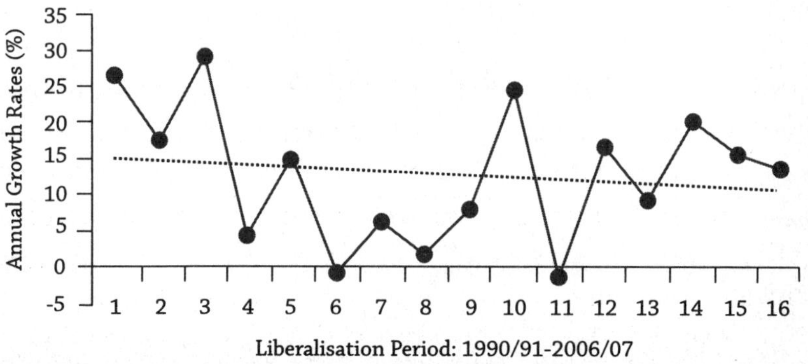

Slope: -0.30*

Note: * Statistically not significant.

Table 18.3

Paired t-Test Results for the Growths of SSI Units, Employment, Output and Exports

.ttest UG == LUG

paired t test

variable	*obs*	*Mean*	*Std. Err.*	*Std. Dev.*	*[95% conf. Interval]*	
UG	16	9.712611	.7616405	3.046562	8.089213	11.33601
LUG	16	4.0622315	.0100133	.040053	4.040972	4.083658
diff	16	5.650296	.7662769	3.065108	4.017016	7.283577

mean (diff) = mean (UG-LUG) t = 7.3737

HO : mean (diff) = 0 degrees of freedom = 15

Ha : mean (diff) < 0	Ha: mean (diff) 1 = 0	Ha: mean (diff) > 0
Pr (T < t) = 1.0000	Pr (|T| > |T| = 0.0000	Pr (T > t) = 0.0000

.ttest EG == LEG

paired t test

variable	*obs*	*Mean*	*Std. Err.*	*Std. Dev.*	*[95% conf. Interval]*	
EG	16	7.201541	.90867871	3.947149	5.098254	9.304828
LEG	16	4.344354	01676878	.6707512	3.986936	4.701772
diff	16	2.857187	.9979979	3.991992	.7300045	4.984369

mean (diff) = mean (EG-LEG) t = 2.8629

HO : mean (diff) = 0 degrees of freedom = 15

Ha : mean (diff) < 0	Ha: mean (diff) 1 = 0	Ha: mean (diff) > 0
Pr (T < t) = 0.9941	Pr (|T| > |T| = 0.0119	Pr (T > t) = 0.0059

.ttest OG == LOG

paired t test

variable	*obs*	*Mean*	*Std. Err.*	*Std. Dev.*	*[95% conf. Interval]*	
OG	16	3.87089	1.73553	6.942119	.1716957	7.570084
LOG	16	4.924069	3.107289	12.42916	-1.69896	11.5471
diff	16	-1.053179	3.805329	15.22131	-9.164945	7.057687

mean (diff) = mean (OG-LOG) t = -0.2768

HO : mean (diff) = 0 degrees of freedom = 15

Ha : mean (diff) < 0	Ha: mean (diff) 1 = 0	Ha: mean (diff) > 0
Pr (T < t) = 0.3929	Pr (|T| > |T| = 0.7857	Pr (T > t) = 0.6071

contd...

...contd...

.ttest XG == LXG

paired t test

variable	*obs*	*Mean*	*Std. Err.*	*Std. Dev.*	*[95% conf. Interval]*	
XG	16	12.88808	3.513771	14.05508	5.398652	20.3775
LXG	16	12.99107	2.376685	9.506738	7.925291	18.05686
diff	16	-.1029971	3.677881	14.71152	-7.942214	7.73622

mean (diff) = mean (XG-LXG) t = -0.0280

HO : mean (diff) = 0 degrees of freedom = 15

Ha : mean (diff) < 0	Ha: mean (diff) 1 = 0	Ha: mean (diff) > 0
Pr (T < t) = 0.4890	Pr (|T| > |T| = 0.9780	Pr (T > t) = 0.5110

Notes: 1. UG = Growth rates of SSI units from 1973/74 to 1989/90.
2. LUG = Growth rates of SSI units from 1990/91 to 2006/07.
3. EG = Growth rates of SSI employment from 1973/74 to 1989/90.
4. LEG = Growth rates of SSI employment from 1990/91 to 2006/07.
5. OG = Growth rates of SSI output from 1973/74 to 1989/90.
6. LOG = Growth rates of SSI output from 1989/90 to 2006/07.
7. XG = Growth rates of SSI exports from 1973/74 to 1989/90.
8. LXG = Growth rates of SSI exports from 1990/91 to 2006/07.

The results indicate that the SSI growth performance in terms of annual growth rates of units and employment has declined in the liberalisation period compared to the pre-liberalisation period and is statistically significant. However, SSI growth performance in terms of annual growth rates of output and exports though has increased in the liberalisation period relative to the pre-liberalisation period, it is not statistically significant. The possible factors for the declined growth of SSI units and employment have been reasoned out adequately above. Given this, if there is no corresponding decline in terms of SSI output and exports, this itself would mean higher productivity, higher degree of internationalisation (penetration of international markets) and 'enhanced competitiveness' of SSI in India. Overall, it may be appropriate to conclude that there is no adequate evidence to indicate that globalisation is continuing to affect SSI performance adversely. Against this backdrop, it is appropriate to examine the performance and contribution of registered SSI (based on census data) to Indian economy in the liberalisation period.

Performance of the Registered SSI in the Liberalisation Period: 1987/88-2006/07

The growth performance of registered SSI sector in terms of units, exporting units, employment, values of output and exports (both at 2004/05 prices) for the liberalisation period is presented in Table 18.4. The growth of registered SSI units has suffered in the 2000s compared to that of the 1990s, but employment has grown considerably in the 2000s, and output growth was much more impressive, whereas export orientation of the registered SSI sector (in terms of exporting units and value of exports) has improved remarkably in the 2000s. Broadly, this would corroborate the overall SSI growth performance that we have observed earlier. It appears that SSI growth performance (in terms of employment, output and exports) might have suffered initially but it has been able to recover impressively subsequently.

Table 18.4

Registered SSI Performance: Census Data: 1987/88-2006/07

Period	*Units*	*Employment*	*Output*	*Exporting Units*	*Exports*
1987/88-2001/02	6.33	3.78	3.57	3.47	3.87
2001/02-2006/07	3.22	9.55	27.20	58.21	46.82

How did the registered SSI contribution to the national economy change in the liberalisation period? This is the other pertinent issue essential to examine. The relative contribution of registered SSI to gross domestic product (GDP) [in terms of gross value added (GVA)], organised sector employment and total exports is given in Table 18.5. The share of registered SSI in India's GDP has more than doubled from 3.35 per cent to 6.73 per cent between 1987/88 and 2006/07, and its share in total organised sector employment increased marginally from 20 per cent to about 23 per cent between 1987/88 and 2001/02 but increased considerably to more than 34 per cent between 2001/02 and 2006/07. Although the share of registered SSI exports declined sharply from about 16 per cent in 1987/88 to about 6 per cent in 2000/01, it bounced back and doubled to reach almost 12 per cent in 2006/07. These statistics imply that though the registered SSI growth performance and contribution might have suffered in the initial decade of economic liberalisation, the sector appeared to have turned the corner in the decade of 2000s.

Table 18.5

Registered SSI Contribution to GDP, Employment and Total Exports

Year	GDP	Organised Sector Employment	Total Exports
1987/88	3.35	20.00	15.94
2001/02	NA	22.65	5.90
2006/07	6.73	34.13	11.88

The improved economic health of registered SSI sector is reflected in another parameter, i.e., industrial sickness. While the second SSI Census did not provide figures relating to SSI sickness, the subsequent two census provided these figures. Sickness in the registered SSI sector has declined both absolutely and relatively (Table 18.6). The number of sick SSI units reduced to almost one-half in 2006/07 compared to 2001/02, and even as a percentage of total registered SSI units, sick SSI units declined to less than half of the figure of 2001/02 in 2006/07. This reduction in sickness could be attributed to two factors: (i) sickness has been cured and (ii) fresh sickness has not emerged as intensively as in the past. This might be the outcome of improvements in SSI internal strength and favourable external environment, since the identified causal factors for SSI sickness comprised both internal and external factors (such as management deficiencies, insufficient financial control, inadequate attention to research & development (R&D), obsolete technology, inadequate demand, shortage of raw materials, inadequate working capital, infrastructural bottlenecks, etc.) which often operated in combination (DCSSI, 2002). Therefore, sickness reduction may be considered another indicator of an improvement in the SSI performance.

Table 18.6

Sickness in SSI: 2001/02-2006/07

Year	Total SSI Units	Sick SSI Units	% of Sick SSI Units
2001/02	1374974	192328	13.98
2006/07	1561000	101270	6.49

There are two more issues concerning SSI performance, namely, (i) ancillarisation and (ii) degree of internationalisation. The promotion of inter-firm linkages between large firms and SSI through subcontracting and ancillarisation in both public and private sectors has been an important dimension of India's SSI Policy. Accordingly, Small Industries

Development Organisation (SIDO) resorted to proactive promotion of ancillarisation through vendor development programmes and subcontracting exchanges as early as in the 1980s (DCSSI, 1989). In 1995, government introduced a scheme to encourage subcontracting exchanges by SSI associations (Bala Subrahmanya, 1998). The merits of subcontracting relationship, in addition to assured marketing, though to a lesser degree, covered technical assistance, finance, supply of raw materials and training (Sahu, 2007). Therefore, any growth of ancillarisation and subcontracting relationship between SSI and large firms would be advantageous to the performance of the former.

The second and third Censuses of SSI provide data on ancillary units but not the fourth Census. There was a considerable increase in the number of ancillary units between 1987/88 and 2001/02, and as a result, the percentage of ancillary units increased from <1 per cent to >5 per cent (Table 18.7). Since then, the number of ancillary units might have gone up further. But this figure takes into account only formal sub-contracting relationships, whereas a significant proportion of SSI in states like Karnataka (particularly, in cities like Bangalore) has informal sub-contracting relationships with large firms including MNCs (Bala Subrahmanya *et al.*, 2001; Kumar and Bala Subrahmanya, 2010). The growing inter-firm linkages, formal as well as informal, would have benefited the economic performance of SSI. Empirical evidence in the context of Bangalore has revealed that SMEs, which have internal technical competence and obtain external support from their large enterprise customers, among others, are able to enhance their innovation performance and thereby their economic performance (Bala Subrahmanya, 2013a).

Table 18.7

SSI and Ancillarisation: 1987/88-2001/02

Year	*Ancillary Units*	*Total SSI Units*	*% of Ancillary Units*
1987-88	3028	582368	0.52
2001-02	69848	1374974	5.08
2006-07	NA	1561000	NA

How does SSI respond to the growing global opportunities is another important issue having implication for its performance. With increasing global competition, falling barriers to international trade and improved international information and communication technology

(ICT) networks, globally active SMEs are emerging in considerably large numbers across the world and it is expected to gain further momentum in the future (Ruzzier *et al.*, 2006). An export strategy has been the primary foreign-market entry mode adopted by SMEs in their internationalisation efforts (Wolff and Pett, 2000). This is because exporting fits the capabilities of SMEs by offering them a greater degree of flexibility and minimum resource commitments combined with minimum risk exposure (Young *et al.*, 1989). The growing trend of SSI entering the international markets through exports can be observed in the Indian context as well (Table 18.8).

Both exporting SSI units and value of SSI exports have increased considerably between 1987/88 and 2006/07, absolutely as well as relative to the total SSI units and total SSI output. The degree of internationalisation in terms of units (exporting SSI units as a percentage of total SSI units) though declined to 0.53 per cent in 2001/02 from 0.78 per cent in 1987/88, increased to 2.95 per cent in 2006/07. The degree of internationalisation in terms of export value (value of SSI exports as a percentage of total SSI output) marginally went up from 5.82 per cent in 1987/88 to 6.06 per cent in 2001/02 and further to 9.60 per cent in 2006/07 (Table 18.8). At the national level, several factors would have contributed to this increasing trend of SSI internationalisation. Of them, the most notable one is the structural shift in the composition of SSI exports from traditional to non-traditional items (Bala Subrahmanya, 2011). Among the factors which facilitated the growth of SSI internationalisation, MNCs and E-Commerce as the modes of entry stood out significantly, in the context of Bangalore (Bala Subrahmanya, 2013b).

Table 18.8

Degree of Internationalisation

Year	*Exporting Units*	*Total Units*	*DOI**	*Value of Exports (at 2004/05 prices)*	*Total Output (at 2004/05 prices)*	*DOI***
1987/88	4554	582368	0.78	249902	14180777	5.82
2001/02	7344	1374974	0.53	1230826	23171027	6.06
2006/07	46012	1561000	2.95	NA	60649632	--
2006/07#	46675	1563974	2.98	6791400	67925307	9.60

Notes: DOI* = Percentage of exporting units in total SSI units.
DOI** = Percentage of value of SSI exports in the value of total output.
Includes medium enterprises.

In brief, the overall SSI growth performance indicators revealed that the growth pattern in the liberalisation period is not significantly different from that of the pre-liberalisation period, with the exception of the growth rates of units and employment. Although the growth rates of SSI units and employment, more or less, steadily declined in the pre-liberalisation period, on an average, the growth rates of units and employment were much higher in the pre-liberalisation period compared to that of the liberalisation period, which did not exhibit any definite pattern of growth. Although the average growth rates of output and exports are higher in the liberalisation period relative to the pre-liberalisation period, the differences in the annual growth rates between the two periods of time are not statistically significant.

However, the performance indicators of the registered SSI sector are more pronounced. Although its growth rates (in absolute terms) were lower in the 1990s, it recorded a substantial recovery thereafter. Its contribution to national income and organised sector employment increased significantly. Further, there are indicators of its improved performance in terms of reduced sickness, improved linkages with large firms, and better penetration of the international market. Given the 'encouraging' performance of registered SSI, the key policy initiatives were introduced by the GoI subsequent to the Micro, Small and Medium Enterprises Development (MSMED) Act, 2006, to strengthen the SSI/SME sector further, and its implications need to be examined.

Inferences and Conclusions (in the Context of Recent Policy Initiatives)

Globalisation and domestic economic liberalisation have radically changed the economic environment for the operations of SSI in India since 1991. Increased imports and FDI inflow in the domestic market, increased exports in the global market, improved performance of the public sector despite curtailed space, de-reservation of the vast list of items reserved for exclusive SSI manufacturing represent the major dimensions of policy-related developments. As a result, new challenges as well as opportunities have emerged for Indian SSI. The performance of SSI has been evaluated against this backdrop.

The analysis of SSI performance indicates that SSI sector is undergoing transformation with an initial suffering and a subsequent recovery, and the recovery is more pronounced in the case of registered SSI. Its performance in terms of employment generation, output growth as well as export growth, its relative contribution to national GDP, organised sector employment and total exports are considerable and significant, particularly in the early 2000s. There are further indicators of improved economic health of SSI in the form of (i) reduced industrial sickness, (ii) improved linkages with large firms, and (iii) increasing degree of internationalisation, with its resultant benefits. This lends credence to the observation made earlier that,

> irrespective of the degree of support extended by the government and irrespective of the amount of efforts put in by SSI and their associations, India is going to experience the emergence of SSI sector, which is qualitatively superior, technologically vibrant and internationally competitive, in the next five to ten years because the 'inefficient ones' are likely to vanish gradually (Bala Subrahmanya, 2004).

However this could be largely true with respect to the registered SSI, which accounted for just about 6 per cent of the total MSMEs in 2006/07, whereas the remaining 94 per cent of the enterprises belonged to the unregistered sector (GoI, 2010).

The unregistered SSI would predominantly comprise micro enterprises, particularly confined to rural India, operating with obsolete technology, limited access to institutional finance, and limited marketing/management expertise. Given this, how to transform the huge unregistered SSI into the registered SSI and how to enhance the competitiveness of the overall SSI are the two foremost challenges confronted by the policy makers.

The shift in the SSI policy emphasis from protection to promotion of competitiveness began with the introduction of an exclusive policy for SSI in 1991 (Ministry of Industry, 1991). Since then, the policy support in the 1990s and early 2000s has been largely to enable the SSI to overcome the key challenges to their performance and growth, namely, finance, technology and marketing, among others (Bala Subrahmanya, 2004). Since 2005/06, several major policy initiatives have been taken by the GoI to promote SSI competitiveness, which are as follows (Ministry of MSMEs, 2010):

- The promulgation of MSMED Act 2006, which clubbed micro and small enterprises with medium enterprises and provided a common legal framework, for their integrated development and enhancing competitiveness.
- As part of the National Manufacturing Competitiveness Programme (NMCP), 10 specific initiatives were taken in

2007/08 to enhance the competitiveness of the entire value chain of the MSME sector.

- Limited Liability Partnership (LLP) Act, 2008, was introduced to enable early corporatisation of MSMEs and tap the capital market for fund raising. Accordingly, SME platforms are created in Bombay Stock Exchange (BSE) and National Stock Exchange (NSE) in 2012 (Ministry of MSMEs, 2013).
- To develop a road map for the development and promotion of MSMEs, a Task Force was created by the Prime Minister of India in 2009 (GoI, 2010). The Task Force, which comprised, among others, six specific theme-based sub-groups (on credit, marketing, infrastructure/technology/skill development, exit policy, labour and taxation) submitted its report in 2010 suggesting (i) immediate policy measures, (ii) medium-term institutional measures, and (iii) legal and regulatory structures to create a conducive environment for entrepreneurship and growth of MSMEs.
- The Working Group on MSMEs Growth for 12th Five Year Plan (2012-2017) made recommendations on six thematic verticals: (i) finance, including credit, (ii) infrastructure, (iii) technology, (iv) marketing and procurement, (v) skill development and training, and (vi) institutional structure. The Working Group reinforced the recommendations made by the Task Force earlier (Ministry of MSMEs, 2012).
- The Inter-Ministerial Committee for Accelerating Manufacturing in Micro, Small and Medium Enterprises made recommendations on (i) the promotion of start-ups, (ii) facilitating operation and growth (covering credit, technology and marketing), (iii) closure and exit, and (iv) labour laws and regulations (Ministry of MSMEs, 2013).

These policy initiatives are clear and consistent, aimed at transforming the ecosystem for the MSME sector by influencing their (i) birth (encouraging start-ups), (ii) operations and growth (by simplifying laws and regulations, and facilitating their access to credit, better technology and dynamic markets, apart from skilled labour and reliable infrastructure), and (iii) orderly and easy exit. Thus, the emerging focus of India's MSME policy aims at covering the entire life cycle of MSMEs to ensure a healthy, vibrant and competitive MSME sector. To conclude, the 'appropriate policy information diffusion and effective penetration of policy support' amongst the MSMEs can have a desirable impact on the competitiveness, particularly, of registered SSI, slowly and steadily in the years to come.

References

Abdullah, H., S. Azis and M.K. Mat (2009). "Globalisation: How it Affects Small & Medium Enterprises?" *Working Paper*, Universiti Teknologi Mara, Selangor.

Acs, Z.J., R.K. Morck and B. Yeung (2001). "Entrepreneurship, Globalisation and Public Policy", *Journal of International Management* 7: 235-51.

Asiedu, E. and J. Freeman (2007). "The Effect of Globalisation on the Performance of Small and Medium Enterprises in the US: Does Owners' Race/Ethnicity Matter?" Paper presented at the *AEA Conference in Chicago*, January 5-7, 2007.

Awuah, G.B. and M. Amal (2011). "Impact of Globalisation: The Ability of Less Developed Countries' (LDCs') firms to Cope with Opportunities and Challenges", *European Business Review* 23(1): 120-32.

Bala Subrahmanya, M.H., Z. Hussain and A. Chand (2014). "External Technology Acquisition of SMEs in the Machinery Industry of Bangalore", *Asian Journal of Innovation and Policy* 3(1): 50-71.

Bala Subrahmanya, M.H., M. Mathirajan, P. Balachandra and M.N. Srinivasan (2001). *Research & Development in Small Scale Industries in Karnataka*, Research Project Report, Department of Science and Technology, New Delhi.

Bala Subrahmanya, M.H. (2013a). "External Support, Innovation and Economic Performance: What Firm Level Factors Matter for High-tech SMEs? How?" *International Journal of Innovation Management* 17: 1-26.

———. (2013b). "Internationalisation Motivation, Pattern and Process of Indian SMEs: Why? How? How Fast?" Paper presented at the *Workshop on Internationalization of Business Groups: Illustrations from China and India*, 5-6 December 2013 held at National University of Singapore.

———. (2011). "Small Scale Industry Development for Export Promotion: India's Experience under Liberalisation", in Keshab Das (ed.), *Micro and Small Enterprises in India: The Era of Reforms.* New Delhi: Routledge India, Chapter 3, pp.46-66.

———. (2010). "Auto SMEs in Bangalore: Does Innovation Promote Employment and Labour Productivity?" *Economic and Political Weekly* 45: 59-66.

———. (2009). *Industrial Policy & Management*, ISTE-WPLP Learning Material Series. Bangalore: Indian Society for Technical Education, Working Professionals Learning Project.

———. (2007). "Development Strategy for Indian SMEs: Promoting Linkages with Global Transnational Corporations", *Management Research News* 30: 762-74.

———. (2004). "Small Industry and Globalisation: Implications, Performance and Prospects", *Economic and Political Weekly* 39: 1826-34.

———. (1998). "Shifts in India's Small Industry Policy", *Small Enterprise Development* 9(1): 35-45. March.

———. (1995). "Reservation Policy for Small Scale Industry: Has it Delivered the Goods?" *Economic and Political Weekly* 30: M 51-M 54.

DCMSME (2014). *http://www.dcmsme.gov.in/policies/preseve.htm*

DCSSI (1989). *Annual Report 1988-1989*. New Delhi: Ministry of Industry, Government of India.

DCSSI (1992). *Report on the Second All India Census of Small Scale Industrial Units, 1987/88*. New Delhi: Ministry of Industry.

———. (2002). *Small Scale Industries in India: An Engine of Growth*. New Delhi: Ministry of SSI, Government of India.

Deo, S. (2013). "The Impact of Globalisation on Small Business Enterprises (SBEs)", *26th Annual SEAANZ Conference Proceedings*, 11-12, Sydney 2013.

Fischer, S. (2003). "Globalisation and Its Challenges", *The American Economic Review* 93(2): 1-30.

Government of India (2010). *Report of the Prime Minister's Task Force on Micro, Small and Medium Enterprises*. New Delhi.

Gupta, Seema, P.K. Jain and S.S. Yadav (2011). "Impact of MoU on Financial Performance of Public Sector Companies in India", *Journal of Advances in Management Research* 8: 263-84.

Javorick, B. (2004). "Does Foreign Direct Investment Increase the Productivity of Domestic Firms? In Search of Spill-overs through Backward Linkages", *American Economic Review* 94(3): 605-27.

Kumar, R.S. and M.H. Bala Subrahmanya (2010). "Influence of Subcontracting on Innovation and Economic Performance of SMEs in Indian Automobile Industry", *Technovation* 30(11/12): 558-69.

Ministry of Finance (2002). *Economic Survey 2001-02*. New Delhi: Government of India.

———. (2007). *Economic Survey 2006-07*. New Delhi: Government of India.

Ministry of Industry (1991). *Policy Measures for Promoting and Strengthening Small, Tiny and Village Enterprises*. New Delhi: Government of India.

Ministry of MSMEs (2010). *Micro, Small and Medium Enterprises in India: An Overview*. New Delhi: Government of India, New Delhi.

———. (2012). *Report of The Working Group on Micro, Small & Medium Enterprises (MSMEs) Growth for 12th Five Year Plan (2012-2017)*. New Delhi: Government of India.

———. (2013). *Recommendations of the Inter-Ministerial Committee for Accelerating Manufacturing in Micro, Small & Medium Enterprises Sector*. New Delhi: Government of India.

NCAER (2009). *FDI in India and its Growth Linkages*. Study Report, New Delhi.

Planning Commission (2002). *Tenth Five Year Plan (2002-2007)*, Vol. 2. New Delhi: Government of India.

Rao, K.S.C. and B. Dhar (2011). "India's FDI Inflows: Trends and Concepts", *Working Paper* No: 2011/01. New Delhi: Institute for Studies in Industrial Development.

Ruzzier, M, R.D. Hisrich and B. Antoncic (2006). "SME Internationalisation Research: Past, Present and Future", *Journal of Small Business and Enterprise Development* 13(4): 476-97.

Sahu, P.P. (2007). "Subcontracting in India's Small Manufacturing Enterprises: Problems and Prospects", *Working Paper* No: 2007/01. New Delhi: Institute for Studies in Industrial Development.

Singh, J. and K.R. Chittedi (2011). "Performance of Public Sector Enterprises in India: A Macro-Level Analysis", *IUP Journal of Managerial Economics* IX(3): 7-25.

Smeral, E. (1998). "The Impact of Globalisation on Small and Medium Enterprises: New Challenges for Tourism Policies in European Countries", *Tourism Management* 19(4): 371-80.

UNCTAD (2006). *World Investment Report 2006*. Geneva.

Vladimirov, Z., R.S. Ganeva and K. Ganev (2013). "Significance of Globalisation-specific Factors for SME Competitiveness: A Conceptual Model and an Empirical Test", *Business Systems Review* 2: 1-25. July-December.

Wolff, J.A. and T.L. Pett (2000). "Internationalization of Small Firms: An Examination of Export Competitive Patterns, Firm Size, and Export Performance", *Journal of Small Business Management* 38: 34-47.

Young, S., J. Hamill, C. Wheeler and J.R. Davies (1989). *International Market Entry and Development*. Englewood Cliffs, NJ: Prentice-Hall.

October, 2014.

19

VIJAY KELKAR

On Strategies for Disinvestment and Privatisation

THE conceptual foundation of India's industrialisation strategy was laid by the Bombay Plan, which envisaged a strategic role to the public sector enterprises. Over the years, the size of the public sector has increased and currently, there are 473 central public sector undertakings (PSUs) including banks and insurance companies. Out of these, 104 are listed and 369 unlisted, while at the state level there are 1,160 PSUs. It is estimated by informed financial analysts that the valuation of the central PSUs on P/E basis for the listed companies and P/B basis for the unlisted companies is now placed at $450-$500 billion or 40-45 per cent of the country's GDP (gross domestic product).

However, according to the Centre for Monitoring Indian Economy (CMIE) data, the net profits of the central PSUs work out to be only 2.2 per cent of their total assets. It is true that this ratio is higher for the oil companies such as Oil and Natural Gas Corporation (ONGC) and Oil India, but in general, the net return on the capital employed in PSUs seems to be lower than for the India's private corporate sector. If one includes the state-level PSUs, then the private corporate sector would show significantly higher returns on the capital employed. While the public sector or the state-led entrepreneurship played an important role in triggering India's industrialisation, our evolving development needs, comparatively less than satisfactory performance of the public sector enterprises, the maturing of our private sector, a much larger social base now available for expanding entrepreneurship and the growing institutional capabilities to enforce competition policies would suggest that the time has come to review the role of public sector, particularly the structural composition of the portfolio of public sector or in other words, of the country's 'public capital assets.'

What should the composition of state assets be? The answer to this critical question can provide an important perspective on the issue of disinvestment and privatisation. Very often, this question is not seen in the correct light. Many people in the policy discourse advocate State ownership of one more enterprise. Each of these proposals might appear to make sense in the small. But budget constraints are a harsh reality of life. Ultimately, there is a budget constraint in terms of the overall assets of the state. When the state chooses to own ₹ 1 of something, this comes at the cost of owning ₹ 1 of something else.

Public *versus* Private Ownership

The interesting and important question that we should all be asking ourselves is: what should the portfolio composition of the government be? What assets should be held by the state? We need to think about this question, and once we have a consensus and clarity about what the portfolio composition ought to be, we should embark on a set of adjustments that take us to a different, and hopefully better, asset composition.

The portfolio composition of the state is not something that should remain static at all times. A few decades ago, India was in a very different setting. After Independence, the Bombay Plan was drafted by the business community. It envisaged government investment in capital-intensive and technologically complex problems of the time, such as production of steel or electricity. In the 1970s, the argument was made that if the government did not run an airline, then the private sector could not.

Some of the choices made in this period reflected the needs of the developmental state and this was a useful part of the early growth trajectory of a country. But those compulsions are no longer with us. The private sector is now fully able to muster the capital and technology required to produce steel or electricity. The landscape has changed and our thinking must change too.

So what assets should the government own and control? Most of us would agree that the airline industry works quite well as a purely private affair. All over the world, governments have got out of airlines. The decades of losses and poor performance of Alitalia airline is commonly held up as an example of what goes wrong when a firm is brought under public ownership. At the opposite end, most of us would agree that rural roads have to be on the balance sheet of the state. These roads typically do not have adequate traffic, and tolling would not generate adequate revenues. If the government did not own rural roads, these roads would not exist. Similarly, the public health capital in our towns and cities will need to come from the public sector. Equally, the preservation and improvement of forest cover will have to be a new priority for the public sector assets.

So there is a spectrum of assets, ranging from airlines to rural roads, where government ownership is inadvisable for airlines but required for rural roads or public health infrastructure. How should we think about where each problem falls? I would like to describe two broad categories where I think the story is quite clear.

The first area where we have a good understanding is goods and services in ordinary competitive markets. An example is steel. Now that India has near-zero tariffs on steel, it is a globally competitive market. Many private companies produce steel. The old argument—about capital and technology required for steel companies being out of reach for the private sector—is no longer convincing. We are now seeing Indian firms exporting steel into the global market—which demonstrates that there is no gap in technology. And, we are also seeing Indian companies turning into multinationals and buying up global steel companies—which demonstrates that there is no gap in capital availability for Indian companies.

Under these conditions, private ownership works best. This should be seen at different levels. First, under ordinary circumstances, private ownership generates the best incentives for cost-minimisation, innovation and dynamic adjustment of corporate strategy. This is not an ideological position. An extensive research literature has examined privatisation experiences from all across the world, and the findings suggest big gains in productivity from private ownership.

The second aspect of public *versus* private ownership concerns the issues that arise when a company approaches bankruptcy. In the private sector, bankruptcy is taken seriously. The fear of bankruptcy generates drastic responses in terms of selling off parts of the company, modifying business strategy, etc. These are healthy responses from the viewpoint of the economy. When an unhealthy company sells off a factory to a strong company, the control of assets of the economy moves into the best hands.

Output and employment are optimised through these adjustments. In contrast, in the public sector, managers have a tendency to be relatively relaxed about the prospect of bankruptcy. Drastic adjustments when faced with extinction do not take place, because the managers know that there is no real danger of extinction. Public sector companies are always able to access capital from the taxpayer. So, there are two problems. Adjustments do not take place because of the lack of fear of extinction, and the taxpayer suffers from periodic claims on resources every time the company gets into trouble. There is also a deeper problem here. If in the market place, one of the participants like a PSU is operating under a 'soft budget constraint' and that too with deep pockets, then it can adversely affect the performance and fortunes of even efficient private sector companies operating in that sector and such a market structure will systematically misallocate resources.

The second area where private ownership is clearly desirable is in regulated industries. In India, we are now seeing numerous regulated industries, ranging from finance to infrastructure, where a government agency performs the function of regulation and multiple competing firms are located in the private sector. Here, the simple and clean solution—government as the umpire and the private sector as the players—is what works best. This configuration is used in every advanced country, and we in India also face the challenge of setting up this architecture of government as regulator with massive investment coming in from the private sector which builds multiple competing firms.

In many of these industries, we have a legacy of government ownership either directly by government departments or in the form of PSUs. The problems described above are very much there: productivity tends to be lower in public sector companies, the fear of bankruptcy is absent, and the risk of asking for money from the taxpayer is ever present. There is an additional issue. This is the conflict of interest between government as an owner and government as the regulator. For instance, the formulation and implementation of competition policy will be much vigorous and fair if government companies are not out of action. Look at the recent example of government's various policy measures to support Air India. Many of these can be construed as anti-competitive as these vitiate the playing field for our private airlines.

India's future lies in building a new institutional architecture with government as regulator and with the private sector doing investment.

There is a problem when the government is conflicted. If the private sector feels that the regulator will not be an unbiased umpire in the competitive process, because a ward of the government is one of the players, then this makes the private sector feel uncomfortable. In the eyes of the private sector, this is a political risk. To pay for higher risk, the private sector demands a higher return. Fewer projects are implemented; the magnitude of investment goes down. With a higher rate of return on capital demanded by the private sector, user charges go up.

If we think of the next 25 years, a very substantial portion of the investment in all regulated industries in India is going to come from the private sector. It would be myopic for the government to have a regulator who is conflicted, which reduces the quantum of investment and drive up user charges. It makes more sense for the government to reorganise itself, shifting into the role of the umpire and away from the role of the player. We must move towards a simple and clean solution: government as an umpire and the private sector as players.

There are other areas where there are shades of grey or complexities, for instance, natural resource-based industries such as upstream hydrocarbons sector. Here, there is a strategic issue as well as the issue of optimal appropriation of the underlying vast resources rent. Similarly, the role of government *vis-à-vis* universities is also complex. Barring such a few but key areas, we can confidently set about reformulating the activities of the state in the following two key areas. Firstly, the state should not be producing things which can be produced in competitive markets—this covers areas like steel or aluminium or cars. And secondly, the state should not be a player in regulated industries—this covers areas like airlines, railways, shipping, telecom, banking or insurance.

A useful way to visualise this is essentially as a balance sheet adjustment. Suppose the government undertakes a portfolio adjustment, where ₹ 10,000 crore of shares of Air India is sold and used to build 2,000 kilometres of highway. Let us trace through the full implications of this. Even if ₹ 10,000 crore of shares of Air India constitute a minority sale (i.e., 'disinvestment' in the Indian jargon), then also certain efficiency gains are obtained. We now have our own empirical evidence which shows that the mere act of listing induces improved productivity. Four channels seem to be at work: listing induces increased transparency, the stock market brings pressure on senior managers by doing daily performance evaluation, corporate governance is typically improved after listing, and to the extent that employees are given some shares, they become more aligned towards the growth and success of the organisation.

If ₹ 10,000 crore of shares of Air India constitutes a majority sale (i.e., 'privatisation'), then even bigger efficiency gains are obtained. Extensive international evidence shows that productivity goes up strongly after privatisation. The increase in India's GDP because of a better-run Air India is the first gain from the proposed portfolio adjustment. The second gain from the proposed portfolio adjustment lies in obtaining an additional 2,000 kilometres of highway. The benefits for India of this public asset are simply enormous. The 2,000 kilometres of highway that we do not have is the opportunity cost that we suffer every year owing to an investment of ₹ 10,000 crore in Air India.

In short, it makes a lot of sense for India to undertake this portfolio adjustment of public sector assets to switch from owning Air India to owning highways or public health infrastructure or augmenting 'environmental capital.' The motivation for disinvestment or privatisation should not be narrowly seen as being only about maximising the proceeds from the sale of assets. The real big gains come from the full picture. We gain when the private sector obtains higher productivity (and this happens even with mere disinvestment, but it happens much more strongly with privatisation). We gain when the private sector becomes more comfortable bringing capital into investing in India in regulated industries. And, we gain when the government is able to build highways and canals, metro systems and railroad, which are crucial for India's growth and legitimately belong on the government's balance sheet.

Privatisation

We may embark on disinvestment today, but we have to think about the end-game which is privatisation, where the government fully gets out of the picture. How do we want to approach the ownership and governance of PSUs? The two broad approaches that can be adopted for privatisation are 'strategic sales' (where a controlling stake is sold to one buyer) or 'open market sales' (where shares are sold to the public at large).

There are three arguments which favour strategic sales:

- In some situations, the buyer brings in essential new technology or expertise.
- The buyer can exert sound governance inputs into the firm, and has incentives to do so owing to the large stake and
- The buyer can decisively displace government as the controller of the firm.

Other arguments in favour of strategic sales are somewhat suspect. For example, the argument that strategic sales fetch higher prices raises concerns. If the valuation of the buyer is solely driven by expectations of improved dividends from the firm, then there is no difference between his valuation of shares as compared with those of the broad public. If a buyer is willing to pay much more than the wide public, this would generally mean that the buyer plans to extract private benefits (i.e., steal) from the company, at the expense of minority shareholders. Such a transaction needs to be questioned.

Strategic sales of large public sector companies such as Vizag Steel or Hindustan Petroleum Corporation Limited (HPCL) are more likely to encounter operational and political difficulties. They yield reduced competition when existing incumbents take over such large PSUs. Most importantly, strategic sales serve to increase the concentration of power and wealth in the hands of a few hundred families of the country.

Strategic sales are often attractive owing to the perception that they yield higher proceeds. Perhaps, in the case of smaller public sector companies operating in competitive markets, strategic sales may be an easier option. However, as emphasised earlier, the full impact of privatisation lies in its impact on GDP growth and not just on maximisation of proceeds. There are other dimensions of the privatisation process in which strategic sales fare poorly.

Apart from strategic sales, open-market sales are an important instruments for disinvestment, and should not be overlooked in our policy efforts. Open-market sales are the path to obtaining dispersed share ownership, widely held, professionally managed companies, and creation of widespread shareholder wealth. A disinvestment strategy based on open-market sales would strengthen institutions and corporate governance in the country.

At the simplest, in cases where a strategic sale has been completed, and a new management team is clearly in the saddle, government can eliminate the residual shareholding by selling in the open market. For firms where no strategic sale has taken place, government can privatise through open-market sales designed to deliberately disperse share ownership over a very large number of households, and create professionally managed, widely-held companies.

India has now a growing experience of good corporate governance by professional management teams with widely dispersed shareholding, where no one family has a controlling stake in the company. Some of the best-run and most respected companies in India, such as HDFC, Infosys and L&T, lead by an example.

According to CMIE data, there are 300 companies in India today where the 'promoters' control below 10 per cent. In each of these companies, the managing director and the rest of the top management team do not own a controlling stake in the company, yet these companies continue to function without being captured by other firms or individuals. This suggests that we do have significant skills and institutions in the country in the creation and operation of professionally managed, widely held firms.

The disinvestment or privatisation programme could explicitly target conversion of the larger PSUs into widely held, professionally managed companies, as an alternative to strategic sales which explicitly give over control of the company to a narrowly defined buyer. There could be provisions in the disinvestment mechanism that creeping acquisitions—which are currently regulated by SEBI—would not be permitted for a few years. For instance, there could be a rule requiring that no one individual or firm could own more than 5 per cent of the firm for a period greater than five years. This would give time for the professional management team to develop modern corporate governance mechanisms. Such an approach can be also applied to disinvestment in our banking sector.

India already knows quite a bit about having well-run widely held and professionally managed companies. PSUs which turn into private, widely held, professionally managed companies could perform a valuable role in economic policy by strengthening this crucial part of the economy.

There is another dimension in which dispersed share-holding makes a lot of sense, and that is the political economy. If the disinvestment process is designed appropriately, it can lead to dispersed share ownership amongst millions of households. This could have enormous economic and political consequences. It would help in sharing the benefits of disinvestment with the people of India; it would improve support for the reforms process, and improve the stake in the functioning of the country as seen by households. The significance of dispersed ownership is not limited to the economy. Dispersed ownership would also have beneficial impact upon democracy. An exclusive reliance on strategic sales would greatly increase the wealth and power of a few hundred families in the country. Dispersed ownership, spread across millions of households, would spread wealth across a much larger slice of the country.

As an example of an international experience, it has been argued that the exclusive use of strategic sales in the privatisation process of some large Latin American countries was detrimental to obtaining dispersion of wealth and income in the country. We should seek to avoid such an outcome in India.

In the international experience, open-market sales have been widely used in all major countries which have strong capital markets and democratic institutions. Among OECD countries as a whole, in the decade of the 1990s, two-thirds of privatisation proceeds were obtained using public offerings of shares in the stock market. The stock market in India has made enormous progress in technology, whereby millions of investors now access the market using tens of thousands of satellite terminals and Internet trading. Mutual funds, banks and foreign institutional investors (FIIs) also exclusively trade through these computer screens. In the future, we could see foreign investments brought into India for FDI purposes become indirectly deployed into purchasing shares in the disinvestment process also.

Thus, selling shares through these screens is a powerful tool for accessing a very large investor base, which includes Indian retail households, Indian institutional investors such as banks, insurance companies and mutual funds, and foreign institutional investors. This is in contrast with the narrow group of buyers who interact with government on strategic sales. When shares are sold in India, they are accessible to foreign buyers of shares through the FII route. This channel can be strengthened by further liberalisation of the entry rules into FII status, and increasing the fraction of shares which can be held by FIIs. In contrast, when shares are sold in London or New York through the

Global Depository Receipt (GDR) or American Depository Receipt (ADR) route, they are not accessible to domestic buyers. Hence, disinvestment within India is the channel through which the largest possible investor base can be accessed.

The primary market in India is a large conduit for selling shares and bonds. The disinvestment process could creatively exploit the sale of convertible bonds, exchangeable bonds or exchange-traded warrants, thus better catering to the needs of retail investors and current market conditions. From an international perspective, strategic sales have been heavily used in countries which lack domestic capital markets, such as the erstwhile communist countries. This is not a constraint that India suffers from. The National Stock Exchange (NSE) and the Bombay Stock Exchange (BSE) are now amongst the largest exchanges in the world, measured by the number of trades per year where they occupy ranks 3rd and 7th respectively. The stock market mechanism in India today—using electronic trading, clearing corporation, depository and T+3 settlement coupled with vibrant equity derivatives markets—is now up to the best international standards.

The incentives of employees of PSUs could be influenced by sale of shares, and employee stock option plans (ESOPs), whereby every employee in the company would end up having a stake in obtaining a higher stock price. This would serve to align the interests of employees with the interests of owners, and encourage support for the disinvestment process on the part of employees. This is another attractive feature of the strategy of selling shares widely, instead of doing strategic sales to a few.

One of the important areas where the disinvestment process should seek to make continued progress lies in the domain of companies where the first listing has been achieved, and a clear secondary market benchmark price exists. For these companies, there is no impediment to establishing a steady and ongoing mechanism for government to gradually reach zero per cent shareholding.

There are concerns about the impact upon prices when government sells shares of (say) CMC (Computer Maintenance Corporation Pvt. Ltd.), which is listed on the stock market today. However, it is important to see that the valuation of CMC is fundamentally driven by the growth prospects of dividends paid by CMC. When the ownership of shares changes from government to some other hands, it does not (in itself) alter the number of shares, and it does not alter the prospects for dividend growth. Hence, sales by government are fundamentally different from fresh equity issuance, which dilutes the cash flows of the company and diminishes share prices.

A transaction where government sells shares could have a temporary impact upon market prices. This can be contained using two tools: the call auction and a sequence of pre-announced small transactions.

Call Auction

The call auction is a computerised market mechanism through which buyers and sellers discover a single price which clears demand and supply. It is used, for instance, to discover the NYSE (New York Stock Exchange) opening price. The call auction is very effective at clearing large blocks of supply and demand, while giving all transactions a single price (i.e., zero 'impact cost').

It is possible for the NSE to build software which runs the call auction. Once that is done, the NSE opening and closing prices would come out of call auctions. This would offer government a mechanism to steadily sell shares using the routine processes of the secondary market, using a market mechanism specially designed to absorb large transactions without incurring market impact cost.

Pre-announcement

A key element which should play a role here is a pre-announced schedule of sales. Government can make a public announcement about a programme of future sales using the call auction. For example, government could announce that on the 1st of every month, 100,000 shares of VSNL would be sold on the NSE pre-opening call auction. This would serve as advance notice for myriad prospective buyers of VSNL (Videsh Sanchar Nigam Ltd.) shares to flock to the NSE trading screens on the 1st, thus generating demand for those shares. These sales would realise a value which is close to prevailing market prices.

Through such a programme of pre-announced sales, government can engage in a steady selling of shares in simple, depoliticised way. Markets become volatile when they are surprised; by doing full pre-announcement of all future transactions, there would be minimal disruptive effects upon the market.

There is yet another instrumentality, particularly for partial disinvestment and this relates to the sale of underperforming or underutilised assets of the PSUs. A prominent example of such assets is 'land.' Many of our PSUs have large tracts of land which have become very valuable with creeping urbanisation and with growing reluctance to make land available to new industrial units. One central PSU alone in Bangalore has as much as 2,000 acres of such underutilised land. In cooperation with the state governments, such land assets can be leveraged by the PSUs by making them available to new units. This will remove one of the new constraints faced by Indian industries. When one includes such land assets of the departmental enterprises such as Railways and Port Trusts, a mind boggling amount of resources will be available for the government for restructuring its balance sheet and for further industrialisation and alleviating housing constraints. This is also true for the state-level public sector enterprises.

There is one additional point, and this relates to the policy for deployment of resources generated through disinvestment/privatisation. According to current policy, this is to be channelised through the National Investment Fund (NIF). It may be argued that this is a restrictive policy and we should liberalise this fully by allowing the government to use these resources as a part of the budgetary resources to create new public capital assets—whether in the form of better urban infrastructure by providing capital grants to our cities or for revamping the country's energy base through an ambitious solar energy programme or the expansion of rural road network or for recharging the country's depleting water bodies and cleaning of rivers. This would require the Union government sharing the proceeds from disinvestment or privatisation with the state governments on a systematic basis on the lines of the Finance Commission's devolution formula for the sharing of union taxes with the states.

For coming decades, water, environment and urban infrastructure are going to be the key binding constraints on India's growth ambition. To remove these binding constraints, we will require large investments to accelerate the country's march towards high quality growth. Disinvestment and privatisation policy has now assumed strategic importance in our country.

We should recognise that disinvestment is an area of economic policy with multiple objectives. The most important objective should be that of increasing the efficiency with which the labour and capital, that is in existing PSUs, is converted into GDP. In addition, other auxiliary goals include enhancing investment in the country, creating new traditions of corporate governance, catering to consumer interests by maximising competition in product markets, and reducing the stock of public debt. An important positive impact of disinvestment upon our fiscal problems would flow through a higher GDP growth.

Policies on disinvestment must be particularly mindful of its ramifications to the political economy. The disinvestment process can lead to dispersed share ownership amongst millions of households. This would disperse wealth in the country. It would help create a middle-class constituency which has a stake in the profits of PSUs and (more generally) in the economic well-being of the country. This could have larger ramifications for the reforms programme. The design of disinvestment policy needs to cater to these multiple goals. In particular, a narrow focus upon maximising proceeds is unlikely to yield sound policies on disinvestment.

In terms of implementation, the recent successes with strategic sales have been a very important achievement of the disinvestment programme. At the same time, open-market sales are also a useful instrument in pursuing disinvestment. Strategic sales are attractive in decisively displacing government from the driver's seat, but suffer from many other important weaknesses which I have already outlined. Dispersed public ownership of PSUs particularly of our large PSUs is attractive in many ways, but requires obtaining sound governance. Towards this, we need to guard against a risk of PSUs being captured by managers, which can happen if control is not contestable and governance is weak.

There is a strong role for utilising asset management companies (AMCs) for managing the disinvestment process, and for performing corporate governance functions for PSUs pending complete disinvestment. There is also a need for building a consensus around extending the domain of disinvestment to PSUs in the financial sector. In a recent thoughtful article, Dr Ajit Ranade has persuasively argued for such a strategy as there is a dire need to capitalise our banking sector. Undoubtedly, a relatively undercapitalised banking sector will considerably slow down the Indian economy.

To sum up, we need a bold and imaginative programme for disinvestment and privatisation calling for restructuring of the portfolio of the country's 'public capital assets.' It does not mean a retreat of the state but essentially a re-engineering of its portfolio of public capital assets. This will help our country meet the challenges of the first half of the 21st century just like our PSUs helped the country in the second half of the 20th century to overcome our industrial backwardness.

26th Sir Purshotamdas Thakurdas Memorial Lecture, Mumbai, January 29, 2010.

20

NAGESH KUMAR

Foreign Direct and Portfolio Investments Flows and Development

A Perspective on Indian Experience

The Context

Foreign capital flows have emerged as key channels of global economic integration all across the world over the past two decades. While foreign direct investment (FDI) flows have been undertaken for a long time by multinational enterprises (MNEs) in the course of their overseas expansion, foreign portfolio investments (FPIs) representing equity and debt flows unaccompanied by management control have become highly visible and often dominant components of the foreign capital flows in recent years with the rise of foreign institutional investors (FIIs) and sovereign wealth funds on the horizon that seek to make quick returns through short-term speculative activities abroad.

FDI flows represent longer-term investments made abroad bringing together with capital and entrepreneurship, technology and managerial know how and sometimes even market access, hence are seen by developing countries as catalysts of development. Therefore, most developing countries actively seek to attract FDI flows with different policy instruments. FPIs, in contrast, tend to have limited potential of contributing to development, if at all, given their short-term and speculative nature. Their distribution across countries is highly uneven as they target only the fast growing emerging economies and those with deep capital markets to benefit from their dynamism. In fact they are often seen to be bringing volatility to the financial and exchange rate

Revised August, 2014.

markets. Hence, a number of emerging market economies are seeking to moderate their volatility through a variety of capital controls.

Recent years have also seen the rise of FDI and FPI flows in India. This can be partly attributed to substantial liberalisation of the policy regime since 1991 and with her economy embarking on robust growth trajectory in the new millennium, India also begun to attract increasing attention of MNEs as well as FIIs as destination for investments. The past decade also marked the emergence of India as sources of outward investments. Indian enterprises have begun to use outward FDI as a strategic tool for strengthening their international competitiveness. As a result, FDI flows are increasingly of bi-directional in nature rather than only one sided with India playing host.

Against that background, this paper summarises the Indian experience in attracting FDI and FPI and reviews the recent trends, patterns and prospects for these flows and their developmental impact. As the country also emerges as a source of FDI as well, the paper also briefly touches upon the trends in these flows. It concludes with some policy lessons.

Evolution of Policy Regime Towards FDI and FPIs in India

Indian government policy towards FDI has evolved over time in tune with the requirements of the process of development in different phases (see Kumar, 2005a). Soon after Independence, India embarked on a strategy of import substituting industrialisation in the framework of development planning with a focus on encouraging and improving the local capability in heavy industries including the machinery-manufacturing sector. As the domestic base of 'created' assets *viz.*, technology, skills, entrepreneurship was quite limited, the attitude towards FDI was increasingly receptive. FDI was sought on mutually advantageous terms, though the majority local ownership was preferred. The government adopted a more restrictive attitude towards FDI in the late 1960s as the local base of machinery manufacturing capability and local entrepreneurship developed and as the outflow on account of remittances of dividends, profits, royalties, and technical fees, etc., abroad on account of servicing of FDI and technology imports grew sharply. Restrictions were put on proposals of FDIs unaccompanied by technology transfer and those seeking more than 40 per cent foreign ownership. From 1973 onwards, the further activities of foreign companies (along with those of local large industrial houses) were restricted to a select group of core or high priority industries. The Foreign Exchange Regulation Act (FERA) of 1973 required all foreign companies operating in India to register under Indian corporate legislation with up to 40 per cent foreign equity. Exceptions from the general limit of 40 per cent were made only for companies operating in high priority or high technology sectors, tea plantations or those producing predominantly for exports.

In the 1980s, the attitude towards FDI began to change as a part of the strategy of modernisation of industry with liberalised imports of capital goods and technology, exposing the Indian industry to foreign competition, and assigning a greater role to MNEs in the promotion of manufactured exports. The policy changes adopted in the 1980s covered liberalisation of industrial licensing (approval) rules, a host of incentives, and exemption from foreign equity restrictions under FERA to 100 per cent export-oriented units and a degree of flexibility concerning foreign ownership.

After pursuing a restrictive policy towards FDI over the four decades with a varying degree of selectivity, India changed tracks in 1990s and embarked on a broader process of reforms designed to increase her integration with the global economy. Among the reform measures implemented included a departure from the restrictive policy towards FDI, a much more liberal trade policy besides reforms of capital market and exchange controls. The New Industrial Policy (NIP), announced on 24 July 1991, marked a major departure with respect to FDI policy with the abolition of industrial licensing system except where it is required for strategic or environmental grounds, creation of a system of automatic clearance of FDI proposals fulfilling the conditions laid down, such as the ownership levels of 50 per cent, 51 per cent, 74 per cent and 100 per cent foreign equity, and opening of new sectors such as mining, banking, insurance, telecommunications, construction and management of ports, harbours, roads and highways, airlines, and defence equipment, to foreign-owned companies subject to sectoral caps. Foreign ownership up to 100 per cent is permitted in most manufacturing sectors—in some sectors even on automatic basis—except for defence equipment where it is limited to 26 per cent and for items reserved for production by small-scale industries where it is limited to 24 per cent. The dividend balancing and the related export obligation conditions on foreign investors, which applied to 22 consumer goods industries, were withdrawn in 2000 (Kumar, 2005a). In September 2012, India allowed FDI in multibrand retail and in civil aviation. Sectoral caps were revised upwards in July 2014 in some sectors like telecom to 100 per cent, in insurance to 49 per cent, and in defence equipment beyond 26 per cent on a case-by-case basis.

In September 1992, the Indian government announced guidelines for investments by FIIs in the Indian capital market. FIIs were now welcome to invest in all types of securities traded on the primary and secondary market with full repatriation benefits and without restrictions on either volume of trading or lock-in period. This liberalisation has led to considerable inflows of portfolio inflows making the country one of the most exposed to portfolio inflows. In June 2013, FII investments were reclassified as FPI which is subject to their holding in a company within 10 per cent of its equity. Any holdings beyond 10 per cent will qualify as FDI.

Recognising the importance of outward investment for competitiveness of enterprises, the policy governing outward FDI has also been liberalised since 1991. With the build-up of foreign exchange reserves, the limits for outward investments have been gradually relaxed and Indian enterprises are now permitted to invest abroad up to 100 per cent of their net worth on automatic basis.

India has also entered into 88 Double Taxation Avoidance Treaties, and Bilateral Investment Promotion and Protection Agreement (BIPAs) with 82 countries.

Foreign Direct Investment Flows and Their Quality

Trends in FDI Inflows

FDI inflows to India have been growing since 1991, but the big break came in 2006 when annual inflows to the country nearly tripled in one year from $7.6 billion to $20 billion and increased from that level peaking to $47 billion in 2008 before declining to $27 billion in 2010 in the wake of the global financial crisis but recovering to $36.5 billion in 2011 (Table 20.1A). With the slowdown of Indian economy since 2011, however, it declined again and was at $28 billion in 2013. India's share in global FDI inflows nearly doubled over 2005-06 and again between 2006 and 2009 to nearly 2.9 per cent before declining to little 2.1 per cent in 2011 (Table 20.1, Figure 20.1A). The relative importance of the flows in relation to gross fixed investment has also risen from 2.9 per cent in 2005 to 6.6 per cent in 2006. The share of FDI in gross fixed investments

Table 20.1

Inward Foreign Direct Investment Flows, Annual, 2001-2013

(Million US$)

A. Inward FDI flows, annual 2001-2013, million USD

Year	*2001*	*2002*	*2003*	*2004*	*2005*	*2006*	*2007*	*2008*	*2009*	*2010*	*2011*	*2012*	*2013*
World	837748	628760	604303	737682	996714	1481561	2001987	1818834	1221840	1422255	1700082	1330273	1451965
Developing Economies	226164	172323	197459	284619	341428	432869	591161	668758	532580	648208	724840	729449	778372
Developing Economies: Asia	125212	99007	130810	170522	231822	296849	365822	396025	323683	409021	430622	415106	426355
Southern Asia	6837	10568	8419	10875	14182	28590	34557	56692	42427	35038	44372	32442	35561
India	5478	5630	4321	5778	7622	20328	25350	47139	35657	27431	36190	24196	28199
Share of India in Developing Asia	4.4%	5.7%	3.3%	3.4%	3.3%	6.8%	6.9%	11.9%	11.0%	6.7%	8.4%	5.8%	6.6%
Share of India in Developing Economies	2.4%	3.3%	2.2%	2.0%	2.2%	4.7%	4.3%	7.0%	6.7%	4.2%	5.0%	3.3%	3.6%
Share of India in World	0.7%	0.9%	0.7%	0.8%	0.8%	1.4%	1.3%	2.6%	2.9%	1.9%	2.1%	1.8%	1.9%

B. FDI Inflows as a per cent of Gross Fixed Capital Formation

Year	*2001*	*2002*	*2003*	*2004*	*2005*	*2006*	*2007*	*2008*	*2009*	*2010*	*2011*	*2012*
World	11.6	8.6	7.3	7.8	9.5	12.8	15.1	12.5	9.1	9.7	10.3	7.8
Developing Economies	13.8	10.1	10.0	11.9	12.1	12.9	14.3	13.3	10.1	10.2	9.8	9.1
Developing Economies: Asia	11.0	7.9	8.8	9.4	10.9	11.8	11.9	10.6	7.9	8.3	7.4	6.5
Southern Asia	3.9	5.5	3.7	3.6	3.9	6.8	6.4	9.4	6.9	4.6	5.2	3.9
India	4.7	4.6	2.8	2.7	2.9	6.6	6.2	10.8	7.9	4.8	5.6	4.0

Source: Author's compilation from United Nations Conference on Trade and Development (UNCTAD) online data base (2014), *www.unctad.org*.

Figure 20.1

India's Attractiveness as a Destination of FDI Inflows

A: India's Share in Global Inflows

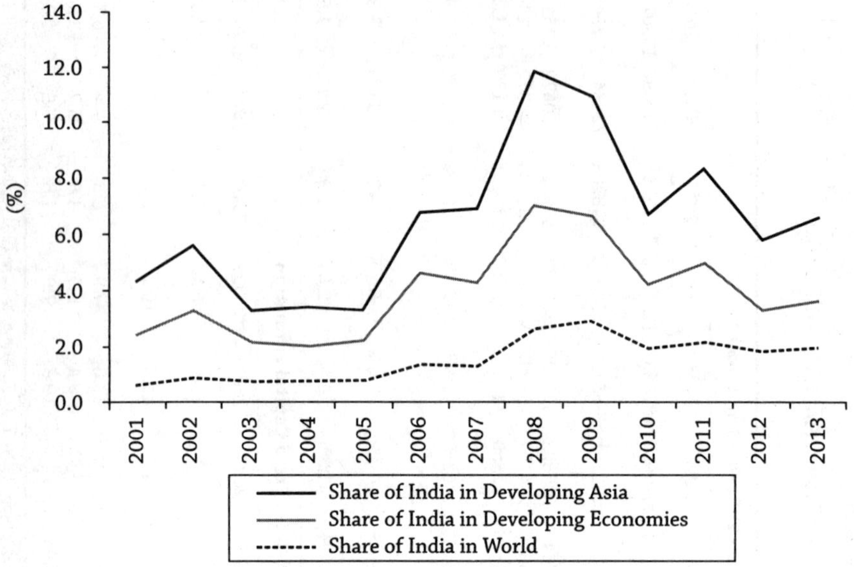

B: Share of FDI in Gross Fixed Capital Formation in Developing Asian Economies and India

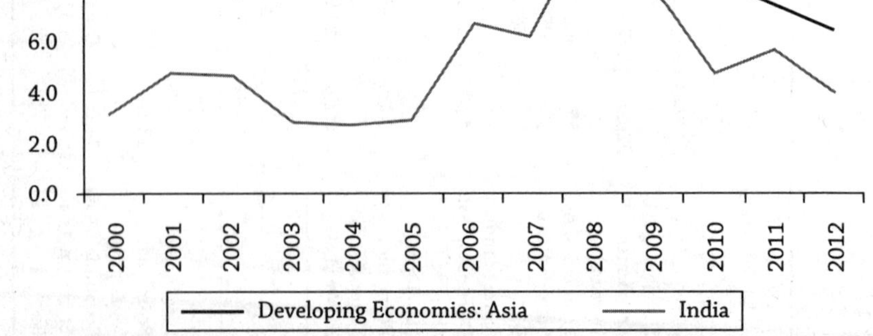

Source: Author's calculations based on Table 30.1.

in India has been lower than for other developing countries but was catching up. In 2008 when FDI inflows peaked in India, this ratio at 10.8 per cent was quite close to that for developing Asia at 10.6 per cent. Afterwards it has declined in the wake of financial crisis indicating the potential for a rise in the future (Table 20.1B and Figure 20.1B)

Investment Climate and Prospects for FDI Inflows

The empirical studies of determinants of FDI inflows have found an important role of market size, extent of urbanisation, quality of infrastructure, geographical and cultural proximity with major sources of capital, and policy factors, e.g., tax rates, investment incentives, performance requirements, among other factors (Kumar, 2000). In the light of these findings, while India's large population base may be an advantage, relatively low income levels, low levels of urbanisation and relatively poor quality of infrastructure are disadvantages. Furthermore, India also does not have the benefit of geographical and cultural proximity with major sources of FDI such as the US, Europe or Japan. However, over time the relative attractiveness of the country is improving with rapid growth that is expanding market size and other aspects of macroeconomic performance. A recent inter-temporal analysis for India has found a broad correspondence between the industrial growth rates in a year and FDI inflows received in the following year (Kumar, 2005a). Apparently, good industrial performance tends to crowd-in FDI inflows as well.

The recent rise in FDI inflows since 2006 reflects improving investment climate in India with the acceleration of growth rate since 2003, the rise of a sizeable middle class with purchasing power, and with the recognition of India's comparative advantage in knowledge-based industries. This is not only evident from the rising magnitudes of FDI inflows but also from investor surveys conducted by global consultancy organisations. In the FDI Confidence Index published by AT Kearney, a global consultancy organisation, covering 25 top destinations for FDI, India has moved up from 6th place in 2003 to 2nd in 2005 and stayed there before swapping the 3rd rank with the US in 2010 (Table 20.2). In 2012, it again regained the second position in the global rankings (AT Kearney, 2012). In 2013, India moved down to the 5th rank globally as the US moved up to the 1st rank as the prospects for growth improved and as their natural resources bases helped Brazil (3) and Canada (4) moved up. Among the Asian developing countries, India continues to remain 2nd after China. Similar upgrading in India's ranks has been reported by the surveys of investors conducted by the Japanese Bank of International Cooperation (JBIC) as well as in UNCTAD's *World Prospects Survey 2013-2015*, where India is ranked as the 3rd most preferred FDI location (UNCTAD, 2014). Recent reforms adopted by the country to allow FDI in multibrand retail and civil aviation and large infrastructure projects such as Delhi-Mumbai Industrial Corridor are also likely to help in realising its potential for FDI inflows. This is in sharp contrast to the World Bank's studies on Ease of Doing Business based on perception surveys that tend to put India at a very poor rank of 132. It is clear therefore that foreign investors get attracted to a country by the potential of benefiting from its dynamism and are willing to put up with hardships rather than going to countries with easier business conditions but with poorer prospects of making profits. FDI inflows may also assist in manufacturing-oriented structural transformation of the economy and technological upgrading of exports that India needs by bringing technologies and other resources working together with local entrepreneurs.

Table 20.2

Select Asian Ranking in FDI Confidence Index

	2003	*2004*	*2005*	*2007*	*2010*	*2013*
China	1 (1.97)	1 (2.03)	1 (2.19)	1 (2.21)	1 (1.93)	2 (2.02)
India	6 (1.04)	3 (1.4)	2 (1.95)	2 (2.09)	3 (1.64)	5 (1.85)
Thailand	16 (0.83)	20 (0.87)	20 (1.05)	..	..	17 (1.63)
Singapore	28 (0.91)	18 (1.07)	18 (1.75)	7 (1.19)	24 (1.77)	10
Malaysia	23 (0.67)	15 (0.92)	..	16 (1.63)	21 (1.22)	25 (1.60)
Hong Kong	22 (0.69)	8 (0.99)	10 (1.21)	5 (1.78)	14 (1.28)	.. ..

Note: Index values are in parentheses.

Source: Author's calculation based on AT Kearney, Foreign Direct Investment Confidence Index, different years.

Quality of FDI Inflows

There can be several indicators of quality of FDI inflows (see Kumar, 2002). In what follows, we discuss India's performance in terms of a few such indicators.

Sectoral Composition

One of the indicators of quality is the sectoral composition of FDI inflows. It matters whether FDI is going to the modern technology-intensive sectors and building productive capabilities or to conventional sectors crowding out domestic investments. In terms of the sectoral composition of FDI inflows, there is a shift since 1991 in India's case. Earlier the bulk of FDI inflows used to be directed to manufacturing especially the high technology industries through a selective policy. After the liberalisation, a substantial proportion of FDI inflows has been directed to services. Manufacturing has accounted for only about 40 per cent of inflows in the post-1991 period with services accounting for about 35 per cent share. Furthermore, among the manufacturing subsectors, FDI stock in the post-1991 period is also more evenly distributed between food and beverages, transport equipment, metals and metal products, electricals and electronics, chemicals and allied products, and miscellaneous manufacturing. This stands in contrast to the situation prior to 1990 when there was a very heavy concentration in relatively technology-intensive sectors *viz.*, machinery, chemicals, electricals, and transport equipment (Kumar, 2005a).

In China, on the other hand, the bulk of FDI inflows have been directed by the government policy to manufacturing (of the export-oriented type) and very little has gone to services (Yongding, 2006). Of the FDI in manufacturing in China, 11 per cent has gone in electronics and telecommunication equipment helping it emerge as the leading producer and exporter of these products. A policy guiding FDI inflows to manufacturing has helped in China's emergence as a global factory. Therefore, FDI inflows in China have been directed to assist in industrial development of the industry that has made China a global factory, generating in the process billions of dollars of output and exports and millions of jobs.

Impact of FDI on Growth and Domestic Investment

FDI inflows could contribute to growth rate of the host economy by augmenting the capital stock as well as with infusion of new technology. However, high growth rates may also attract more FDI inflows by enhancing the investment climate in the country. Therefore, the FDI-growth relationship is subject to causality bias given the possibility of two-way relationship. What is the nature of the relationship in India? A recent study has examined the direction of causation between FDI and growth empirically for a sample of 107 countries for the 1980s and 1990s period. In the case of India, the study finds a Granger neutral relationship as the direction of causation was not pronounced (see Kumar and Pradhan, 2005, for more details of the methodology and results).

It has also been shown that sometimes FDI projects may actually crowd-out or substitute domestic investments from the product or capital markets with the market power of their well-known brand names and other resources and may thus be immiserizing (see Fry, 1992; Agosin and Mayer, 2000, for evidence). Therefore, it is important to examine the impact of FDI on domestic investment to evaluate the impact of FDI on growth and welfare in the host economy. An earlier study to examine the effect of FDI on domestic investment in a dynamic setting, however, did not find a statistically significant effect of FDI on domestic investment in the case of India (see Kumar and Pradhan, 2005). It appears, therefore, that FDI inflows received by India have been of mixed type combining some inflows crowding-in domestic investments while others crowding them out, with no predominant pattern emerging in the case of India. In the case of East Asian countries such as South Korea and Thailand, the relationship was clearly indicating FDI crowding-in domestic investments (Ibid.). Therefore, the quality of FDI in India in respect to its impact on growth and on domestic investment is of mixed type and leaves scope for improvement.

The empirical studies on the nature of the relationship between FDI and domestic investments suggest that the effect of FDI on domestic investment depends on host government policies. Governments have extensively employed selective policies and imposed various performance requirements such as local content requirements (LCRs) to deepen the commitment of MNEs to the host economy. The Indian government had imposed a condition of phased manufacturing programmes (or LCRs) in the auto industry to promote vertical inter-firm linkages and encourage development of the auto component industry (and crowding-in of domestic investments). A case study of the auto industry where such a policy was followed shows that these policies (in combination with other performance requirements *viz.*, foreign exchange neutrality) have succeeded in building an internationally competitive vertically integrated auto sector in the country (Ibid.). The Indian experience in this industry, therefore, is in tune with the experiences of Thailand, Brazil and Mexico as documented by Moran (1998).

FDI and Export-platform Production

A number of developing countries have used FDI to exploit the resources of MNEs such as globally recognised brand names, best practice technology or by increasing integration with their global production networks, among others, for expanding their manufactured exports. In this respect, China has had a considerable success in exploiting the potential of FDI for export-oriented production. A very substantial (55%) proportion of manufactured exports of China are undertaken by foreign invested enterprises, which account for as much as 80 per cent of all technology-intensive exports (UNCTAD, 2005). Foreign enterprises while setting up export-oriented production bases created 23 million jobs by 2003 making China a global factory. Export-oriented FDI also helps in bringing world's best practice technology as the affiliate has to compete globally right from the beginning. It also enhances the chances of FDI inflows crowding in domestic investments and reducing the chances of crowd-out as the foreign affiliate would be mainly catering to the outside markets rather than eating into domestic firms' markets. It would also create fresh possibilities of market information spillovers for domestic firms on export possibilities.

Unlike the East Asian countries, India has not been able to exploit the potential of FDI for export-oriented production. The bulk of FDI inflows in India are market-seeking coming for tapping the domestic market with the share of foreign affiliates in exports around 10 per cent. Therefore, the quality of FDI in respect of export orientation is poorer compared to FDI received by East Asian countries. In this respect, two observations can be made. The first is that recent studies of export performance are beginning to indicate a relatively superior performance of foreign enterprises in terms of export orientation compared to early studies suggesting a poorer performance of foreign companies (see Kumar and Joseph, 2007). Therefore, MNEs are beginning to exploit the potential of India as base for export-oriented production.

The second observation is about the role of host country policies in exploiting the potential of FDI for export-oriented production. A quantitative study analysing the determinants of the patterns of export orientation of MNE affiliates across 74 countries in seven branches of industry over three points of time has shown that in host countries with large domestic markets, the export obligations were effective for promoting export orientation of foreign affiliates to third countries (see Kumar, 1998).

Export obligations have also been employed fruitfully by many countries to prompt MNE affiliates to exploit the host country's potential for export platform production. For instance, in China which has succeeded in expanding manufactured exports with help of MNE affiliates, regulations stipulate that wholly owned foreign enterprises must undertake to export more than 50 per cent of their output (Rosen, 1999: 63-71). As a result of these policies, the proportion of foreign enterprises in manufactured exports has steadily increased to over 55 per cent as observed above.

India has not imposed export obligations on MNE affiliates except for those entering the products reserved for SMEs. However, indirect export obligations in the form of dividend balancing have been imposed for enterprises producing primarily consumer goods (since phased out in 2000). Under these policies, a foreign enterprise was obliged to earn the foreign exchange that it wished to remit abroad as dividend so that there was no adverse impact on host country's balance of payment (BoP). Sometimes a condition of foreign exchange neutrality has been imposed where the enterprise is required to earn foreign exchange enough to even cover the outgo on account of imports. Therefore, these regulations have acted as indirect export obligations prompting foreign enterprises to export to earn the foreign exchange required by them. The evidence that is available suggests that such regulations have prompted foreign enterprises to undertake exports. In the case of auto industry, in order to comply with their export commitments to comply with foreign exchange neutrality condition, foreign auto majors have undertaken export of auto components from India which have not only opened new opportunities for Indian component manufacturers but also in that process found profitable opportunities for business (Kumar, 2005). Hence, exports of auto components from India are now growing rapidly and exceeding the obligations several times over. These regulations have acted to remove the information asymmetry existing about the availability of quality components in India among the foreign auto majors. In that respect, India's experience is very similar to that of Thailand that has emerged as the major auto hub of Southeast Asia (as documented by Moran, 1998, and Kumar, 2005).

R&D and Other Knowledge-based Activities and Local Technological Capability

A comparison of R&D (research & development) intensity of foreign firms in India and in other countries has not been possible due to lack of data. Within the country, foreign firms appear to be spending more on R&D activity in India than local firms, although gap between their R&D intensities has tended to narrow down. A study analysing the R&D activity of Indian manufacturing enterprises in the context of liberalisation has found that after controlling for extraneous factors, MNE affiliates reveal a lower R&D intensity compared to local firms, presumably on account of their captive access to the laboratories of their parents and associated companies. The study also observed differences in the nature or motivation of R&D activity of foreign and local firms. Local firms seem to be directing their R&D activity towards absorption of imported knowledge and to provide a backup to their outward expansion. MNE affiliates, on the other hand, focus on customisation of their parents' technology for the local market (Kumar and Agarwal, 2005).

An important issue is diffusion and absorption of technology brought by foreign firms in the host countries. Some governments have imposed technology transfer requirements on foreign enterprises, e.g., Malaysia. However, such performance requirements do not appear to have been very successful in achieving their objectives (UNCTAD, 2003). Instead, other performance requirements such as local content requirements or domestic equity requirements may be more effective in transfer of technology. As observed above, local content requirements and export performance requirements have prompted foreign enterprises to transfer and diffuse some knowledge to domestic enterprises in order to comply with their obligations. Similarly, the domestic equity requirements may facilitate the quick absorption of the knowledge brought in by foreign enterprises which is an important pre-requisite of the local technological capability, as is evident from case studies of Indian two-wheeler industry where Indian joint ventures with foreign firms were able to absorb knowledge brought in by the foreign partner and eventually become self-reliant not only to continue production but even to develop their own world-class models for domestic market and exports on their own (see Kumar, 2005). Some have expressed the view that domestic equity requirements may adversely affect the extent or quality of technology transfer (Moran, 2001). However, it has been shown that MNEs may not transfer key technologies even to their wholly owned subsidiaries abroad fearing the risk of dissipation or diffusion through mobility of employees. Furthermore, even if the content and quality of technology transfer is superior in the case of a sole venture than in the case of a joint venture, from the host country point of view, the latter may have more desirable externalities in terms of local learning and diffusion of the knowledge transferred.

FPI Inflows and Their Impact

The rapid rise in inflows of portfolio investments in India since 2003-04 is summarised in Table 20.3. Large magnitudes of portfolio investments in the form of short-term equity investments by FII have flowed in as the Indian economy gathered momentum and capital markets started giving attractive returns. The annual net inflows, however, are highly volatile.

Table 20.3

FDI and Foreign Portfolio Investment Flows to India

	Gross Inflows/ Gross Investments	*Direct Investment to India*	*FDI by India*	*Net FDI*	*Net Portfolio Investment*	*Total (in million USD)*
2000-01	4029	4029	759	3270	2590	5860
2001-02	6130	6125	1391	4734	1952	6686
2002-03	5035	4976	1819	3157	944	4101
2003-04	4322	4322	1934	2388	11377	13765
2004-05	6051	5986	2274	3712	9291	13003
2005-06	8961	8900	5867	3033	12492	15525
2006-07	22826	22739	15046	7693	6947	14640
2007-08	34843	34727	18836	15891	27434	43325
2008-09	41873	41707	19364	22343	-14032	8311
2009-10	37745	33108	15143	17965	32396	50361
2010-11	34847	27829	16524	11305	30292	41597
2011-12	46556	32957	11097	22860	17171	39031
2012-13	34298	26953	7134	19819	26891	46710

Source: Extracted from RBI's *Handbook of Statistics on Indian Economy*, 2013, and *www.rbi.org.in*.

FII inflows rose to a sizeable $27 billion in 2007-08 that led to not only stock prices booming, with BSE Sensex more than doubling from under 10,000 to 20,000, but also the rupee exchange rate appreciating sharply from ₹47 in 2006 to ₹38 to a US dollar in 2008. In 2008-09, in the wake of global financial crisis, there was a net outflow of FII to the tune of $14 billion that brought down the BSE Sensex from nearly 20,000 points to less than 9,000 points in the early part of 2009. Much more importantly it led to a sharp depreciation of rupee by nearly 25 per cent in early 2009. The depreciation would have been greater had the Reserve Bank of India (RBI) not intervened in the market by selling dollars. This depleted the RBI's foreign exchange reserves by $58 billion to about $252 billion from $310 billion from 2007-08 to 2008-09. However, as FIIs returned quickly to the market in the wake of recovery, the FII inflows to the country in 2010 were of the order of $32 billion bringing the Sensex back above 20,000 points in October 2010. Despite the RBI's market intervention to offset the subsequent exchange rate pressure, the rupee appreciated by nearly 8 per cent, although foreign exchange reserves were augmented to about $284 billion. FII inflows have become primary determinants of the movements in the stock exchange indices and the exchange rate of the rupee (see Kumar, 2011). As there are sharp movements in these inflows linked to global developments, they become channels of transmission of instability to the country's financial system. As a result, the rupee has been on a roller coaster ride: from ₹44 per dollar in January 2007 to ₹39 in January 2008 to increase again to ₹49 per dollar in January 2009 to ₹44 in October 2010. The rupee fluctuated around ₹54 in 2012 and early 2013 and after May 2013 depreciated sharply to cross ₹60 to a dollar, as there was outflow of FIIs in anticipation of roll back of quantitative easing policy by Federal Reserve in the US and as concerns about India's rising current account deficit (CAD) mounted.

Besides the volatility, FII inflows have a very high servicing burden. Among foreign resources such as FDI, foreign borrowings, non-resident Indian (NRI) deposits, American Depositary Receipts (ADRs), global depositary receipts (GDRs), FII investments are most expensive in terms of servicing burden (Kumar, 2011). This is because they come to chase primarily good returns at the stock markets and exchange rate speculation. In 2007-08, Indian stock markets were giving around 44 per cent return. That means for every dollar India received in FII flows, it became liable to pay $1.44 in one year. As they are stock price makers rather than takers, they manage to exit safely before major crashes of markets thereby precipitating the declines.

One may argue that FII inflows help a country to build foreign exchange reserves. What is not appreciated very well is the fact that exposure to these inflows also enhances the need to have large foreign exchange reserves due to their highly volatile nature. Therefore, developing countries such as India should rely for their foreign resource needs more on FDI inflows and where possible raise ADRs/GDRs and deposits from NRIs rather than relying on the FIIs. In view of their high cost and their other deleterious effects such as volatility, a number of emerging economies such as Brazil, South Korea and Indonesia have recently imposed capital controls to moderate their volatility. The unprecedented injection of liquidity by the governments in developed countries in the wake of global financial crisis is likely to find its way to emerging economies of Asia like India to take advantage of higher returns. There is now a growing consensus on the relevance of capital controls as aspects of the policy tool kit for the governments in emerging economies (UN-ESCAP, 2010; Ostry *et al.*, 2010). The benefits of maintaining open capital accounts, if any, are ambiguous.

India as an Emerging Source of FDI Outflows

Another important emerging trend with respect to FDI in India is its emergence as a significant source of FDI outflows. Like FDI inflows the major turnaround in their outflows came in 2006 when outflows more than quadrupled in one year to $14 billion and peaked to nearly $20 billion in 2007 before declining to around $15 billion in subsequent years in the wake of global financial crisis (Table 20.4). The big break came with Indian enterprises using their outward investments to acquire larger companies in the advanced economies as a part of their effort to augment their bundles of strategic assets including known brand names, proprietary knowledge and global marketing networks in order to jump start their global orientation. The past few years have seen several multi-billion dollar acquisitions of western firms by Indian companies including Tata Steel-Corrus, Tata Motors-Jaguar/Land Rover, Handalco-Novelis, among others. During 2012 and 2013, outward FDI flows declined dramatically as Indian companies struggled with slowdown of Indian economy (Table 20.4).

A recent analysis of India's outward FDI flows has shown that among the emerging markets,the relative scale of India's outward FDI was quite significant (Kumar, 2008). The emergence of Indian enterprises on the global scene is striking considering their origin in a lower middle-income country. Their ability to acquire much larger enterprises in the developed world reflects their confidence in managing the newly acquired entities successfully. It has been argued that the source of their ownership or competitive advantage lies in their accumulation of skills for managing large multi-location operations across diverse cultures in India and in their ability to deliver value for money with their 'frugal engineering skills' honed up while catering to the larger part of income pyramid in India (Ibid.).

Table 20.4

Foreign Direct Investment Outflows Originating in India

(Million USD)

	World	*Developing Economies*	*Developing Economies: Asia*	*India*
2001	747657	83087	49155	1397
2002	528496	47484	34987	1678
2003	570679	46668	23961	1876
2004	925716	122792	91404	2175
2005	888561	132507	86425	2985
2006	1415094	239336	151400	14285
2007	2198025	316863	228154	19594
2008	1969336	328121	223116	19257
2009	1175108	268476	210925	15927
2010	1451365	400144	273033	13151
2011	1711652	422582	304293	12456
2012	1346671	440164	302130	8486
2013	1410810	454067	3261013	1679

Source: Extracted from UNCTAD database, 2014.

Considering that nearly all the Indian enterprises undertaking outward investments had their origins in import-substitution based industrialisation strategies and the selective FDI policy regime, it would appear that the policy of infant industry protection with supportive institutional framework can assist in enterprise development by giving to them access to domestic market to grow and build capabilities (Ibid.). However, the protection needs to be phased out once the capabilities are built up to expose the enterprises to international competition and sharpen their competitiveness. In fact, the reforms of 1991 have sparked of a considerable restructuring of Indian industry which emerged from it leaner, more efficient and competitive. The exposure also gave to the Indian firms global ambitions and also the confidence to pursue them. In some ways, the Indian experience follows in the Japanese and Korean tradition of enterprise development policies and may have lessons for other developing countries.

The acquisition-based strategy of internationalisation adopted by Indian enterprises in the recent years by acquiring strategic assets, such as technology, known brands, access to customers and global footprints for jump starting their internationalisation, is challenging as it involves managing across diverse cultures and win over the confidence of workforce to successfully exploit the synergies. Indian enterprises can face this challenge by relying on their experience and their skills in cross-cultural management honed in India, their emphasis on corporate social responsibility and their sensitivities to workers' rights from the beginning (Ibid.).

Concluding Remarks and Policy Lessons

The above discussion has reviewed the India's experience with FDI and FPI inflows. These inflows to India have grown in the recent years in response to policy liberalisation and as the country's economy picked up momentum. Although starting from a low base, India has also been able to increase its share in FDI inflows received by developing countries especially in the past few years and is catching up with Southeast Asian countries in terms of share of these inflows in capital formation. India is also attracting large magnitudes of portfolio equity flows from FIIs which are highly volatile.

The above discussion also shows that even though India may be attracting increasing magnitudes of FDI inflows, they are yet to harness their development potential fully. The empirical studies suggest that the country has received FDI inflows of mixed quality and the developmental impact has been uneven. India can learn a great deal from the experiences of China and other Southeast Asian countries in this regard. China has had a much greater success in harnessing the potential of FDI for building high technology export-oriented industrial base using a variety of policy instruments and performance requirements. On the other hand, India is getting exposed in a significant manner to the FPI flows that are not only highly volatile but are expensive in terms of servicing burden.

Policy Lessons

In general, the above analysis brings out the role of government policy in attracting and benefiting from FDI inflows for development. In light of this discussion, we may now draw a few policy lessons for the region and other similarly placed developing countries.

First of all, liberalisation of FDI policy may be necessary but not sufficient for expanding FDI inflows. The overall macroeconomic performance continues to exercise a major influence on the magnitude of FDI inflows by acting as a signaling device for foreign investors about the growth prospects for the potential host economy. Hence, paying attention to macroeconomic performance indicators such as growth rates of industry through public investments in socioeconomic infrastructure and other supportive policies, and creating a stable and enabling environment would crowd-in FDI inflows. Studies have shown that policies that facilitate domestic investments also pull in FDI inflows. While investment incentives may not be efficient, active promotion of FDI by developing certain viable projects and getting key MNEs interested in them could be useful in attracting investments in desirable directions.

The evidence suggests that the government policies play an important role in determining the quality or developmental impact of FDI and in facilitating the exploitation of its potential benefits by host country's development. The various performance requirements such as phased manufacturing programmes, export performance requirements and domestic ownership requirements have also been employed by the governments to achieve their developmental policy objectives. Even with liberalised policy, some policy direction to FDI is desirable as has been demonstrated by the case of East Asian countries.

One way to maximise the contribution of FDI to the host development is to improve chances of FDI crowding-in domestic investments and minimise the possibilities of it crowd-out domestic investments. In this context, the experiences of Southeast Asian countries such as Malaysia, Korea, China and Thailand in channelling FDI into export-oriented manufacturing through selective policies and export performance requirements imposed at the time of entry deserve careful consideration (see Kumar, 2005b, for evidence). The export-oriented FDI minimises the possibilities of crowding-out of domestic investments and generates favourable spillovers for domestic investments by creating demand for intermediate goods. Another policy that can help in maximising the contribution of FDI inflows is to push them to newer areas where local capabilities do not exist as that minimises the chances of conflict with domestic investments. Some governments such as Malaysia have employed pioneer industry programmes to attract FDI in industries that have the potential to generate more favourable externalities for domestic investment (see UNCTAD 1999; 2001, for examples). Similarly because MNE entry through acquisition of domestic enterprises is likely to generate less favourable externalities for domestic investment than greenfield investments, some governments discourage acquisitions by foreign enterprises (see Agosin and Mayer, 2000, for examples).

Another sphere where governmental intervention may be required to maximize gains from globalisation is in diffusion of knowledge brought in by foreign enterprises. An important channel of diffusion of knowledge brought in by MNEs in the host economy is vertical inter-firm linkages with domestic enterprises. Many governments—in developed as well as developing countries alike—have imposed local content requirements on MNEs to intensify generation of local linkages and transfer of technology (see Kumar, 2005b, for evidence). The host governments could also consider employing proactive measures that encourage foreign and local firms to deepen their local content as a number of countries, e.g., Singapore, Taiwan, Korea and Ireland, have done so successfully (see Battat *et al.*, 1996). The knowledge diffusion could also be accomplished by creating sub-national or sub-regional clusters of inter-related activities which facilitate the spillovers of knowledge through informal and social contacts among the employees besides traditional buyer-seller links. UNCTAD (2001) also highlights the policy measures employed by different governments in promoting linkages.

Investments made by governments in building local capabilities for higher education and training in technical disciplines, centres of excellence, and in other aspects of national innovation systems have substantial favourable externalities as is demonstrated by the case study of FDI in India's knowledge-based industries.

Finally, rising CAD poses an important challenge for policy makers and need urgent attention. With widening merchandise trade deficits driving this trend, immediate attention needs to be paid to reviving export growth and exploiting the opportunities for import substitution. For reviving exports, attention needs to be paid to strengthening their competitiveness by addressing exchange rate distortions. Export competitiveness needs to be strengthened by maintaining relative exchange rate stability with a slight tendency towards depreciation rather than appreciation. Besides that, policy distortions such as inverted duty structures need to be removed and flow of trade finance needs to be strengthened (see Kumar and Joseph, 2007, for an inventory of policy support measures). In a situation of slowdown of the global economy as at present, a major expansion of exports can be challenging given an environment of excess capacities throughout the Asia-Pacific region, the growing threat of protectionism and the temptation of dumping by those with deep pockets. In such circumstances, it might be also critical to look at new opportunities for, strategic import substitution. As observed earlier, while large bulk imports of fuels and raw materials may be price inelastic, attention should be paid to very large and fast growing imports of electronics, non-electrical machinery, and defence equipment, among others, that provide opportunities for strategic import substitution. An effort needs to be made to start domestic manufacture of these products leveraging India's large domestic market size and by targeting MNEs to set up local manufacturing facilities through creation of incentives for pioneering industries, as has been done in East Asian countries like Malaysia, besides incentives in public procurement like 'buy America' programmes. These policies are part of industrial policies and infant industry protection that have been widely practised in different developed and emerging economies (Kumar and Gallagher, 2007). The strategic import substitution will also lead to a more balanced structural change by creating more manufacturing jobs which is critical for poverty reduction (Kumar, 2013).

References

Aggarwal, Aradhna and Nagesh Kumar (2012). "Structural Change, Industrialisation and Poverty Reduction: The Case of India", *ESCAP-SSWA Development Papers* 1206. *http://sswa.unescap.org/meeting/documents/Dev-Challenges/SSWA_Development_Papers_1206_October2012.pdf*

Agosin, M.R. and Ricardo Mayer (2000). "Foreign Investment in Developing Countries: Does it Crowd in Domestic Investment?" *UNCTAD Discussion Paper*, No. 146, Geneva: UNCTAD.

AT Kearney (2013). *FDI Confidence Index 2013*, *www.atkearney.com* and previous years.

Battat, Joseph, Isiah Frank and Xiaofang Shen (1996). *Suppliers to Multinationals: Linkage Programmes to Strengthen Local Capability in Developing Countries*. Washington, DC: FIAs.

Freire, C. (2012). "Structural Transformation for Inclusive Development in South and South-West Asia", *ESCAP-SSWA Development Papers* 1204; *http://sswa.unescap.org/meeting/documents/Dev-Challenges/SSWA_Development_Papers_1204_August2012.pdf*

Fry, Maxwell J. (1992). "Foreign Direct Investment in a Macroeconomic Framework: Finance, Efficiency, Incentives and Distortions", *PRE Working Paper*, Washington, DC: The World Bank.

Kumar, Nagesh (1998). "Multinational Enterprises, Regional Economic Integration, and Export-Platform Production in the Host Countries: An Empirical Analysis for the US and Japanese Corporations", *Weltwirtschaftliches Archiv* 134(3): 450-83.

———. (2000). "Explaining the Geography and Depth of International Production: The Case of US and Japanese Multinational Enterprises", *Weltwirtschaftliches Archiv* 136(3): 442-76.

———. (2001). "Determinants of Location of Overseas R&D Activity of Multinational Enterprises: The Case of US and Japanese Corporations", *Research Policy* 30: 159-74.

———. (2002). *Globalization and the Quality of Foreign Direct Investment*. Delhi: Oxford University Press.

———. (2005). "Performance Requirements as Tools of Development Policy: Lessons from Experiences of Developed and Developing Countries", in Kevin Gallagher (ed.) (2005), *Putting Development First: The Importance of Policy Space in the WTO and International Financial Institutions*. London: Zed Press. pp.179-94.

———. (2005a) "Liberalization, Foreign Direct Investment Flows and Development: Indian Experience in the 1990s", *Economic and Political Weekly* 40(14): 1459-69. April 2.

———. (2008). "Internationalization of Indian Enterprises: Patterns, Strategies, Ownership Advantages and Implications", *Asian Economic Policy Review* 3(2): 242-61.

———. (2009). *Mid-year Review of Indian Economy 2008-09: Challenges of Susutaining Dynamism in the Context of Global Financial Crisis*. New Delhi: Shipra Publications for India International Centre.

———. (2011), "Capital Flows and Development: Lessons from South-Asian Experiences", in Raghabendra Jha (ed.) (2011), *Handbook of South Asian Economies*. London and New York: Routledge.

———. (2013). "Trade, Capital Flows and the Balance of Payments: Trends, Challenges and Policy Options for India", *UNESCAP-SSWA Development Paper* 1303. Available at *http://sswa.unescap.org/pdf/SSWA_Development_Papers_1303_March2013.pdf*

Kumar, Nagesh and N.S. Siddharthan (1994). "Technology, Firm Size and Export Behaviour in Developing Countries: The Case of Indian Enterprises", *Journal of Development Studies* 31(2): 289-309.

Kumar, Nagesh and Aradhna Agarwal (2005). "Liberalization, Outward Orientation and In-house R&D Activity of Multinational and Local Firms: A Quantitative Exploration for Indian Manufacturing", *Research Policy* 34(4): 441-60.

Kumar, Nagesh and J. Pradhan (2005). "Foreign Direct Investment, Externalities and Economic Growth in Developing Countries: Some Empirical Explorations", in Edward M. Graham (ed.) (2005), *Multinationals and Foreign Investment in Economic Development*, Palgrave. pp.42-84.

Kumar, Nagesh and Kevin P. Gallagher (2007). "Relevance of 'Policy Space' for Development: Implications for Multilateral Trade Negotiations", *RIS Discussion Papers # 120*, *http://www.ris.org.in/publications/discussion-papers/508*

Kumar, Nagesh and K.J. Joseph (eds.) (2007). *International Competitiveness and Knowledge Based Industries*. New Delhi: Oxford University Press and RIS.

Moran, Theodore H. (1998). *Foreign Direct Investment and Development*. Washington, DC: Institute for International Economics.

———. (2001). *Parental Supervision: The New Paradigm for Foreign Direct Investment and Development*. Washington, DC.

Ostry, Jonathan D., Atish R. Ghosh, Karl Habermeier, Marcos Chamon, Mahvash S. Qureshi, and Dennis B.S. Reinhardt (2010). "Capital Inflows: The Role of Controls", *IMF Staff Position Note* SPN/10/04.

RBI (2012). *Handbook of Statistics on Indian Economy 2012*. Mumbai: Reserve Bank of India. *www.rbi.gov.in*

Rodrik, D. (2004). "Industrial Policy for the Twenty-First Century", *CEPR Discussion Paper* 4767, November.

Rosen, D. (1999). *Behind the Open Door: Foreign Enterprise Establishment in China*. Washington, DC: Institute for International Economics.

UNCTAD (2003). *Use and Effectiveness of Performance Requirements: Select Case Studies*. New York: United Nations.

———. (2005). *World Investment Report 2005*. New York: United Nations.

———. (2014). *World Investment Report 2014*. New York: United Nations.

UN-ESCAP (2010). *Economic and Social Survey of Asia and the Pacific*. Bangkok: UN-ESCAP.

UN-ESCAP-SSWA (2012). *Regional Cooperation for Inclusive and Sustainable Development: South and South-West Asia Development Report 2012-13*. New York, New Delhi and London: UN Publications and Routledge.

Yongding, Yu (2006). 'The Experience of FDI Recipients: The Case of China", in Shujiro Urata, Chia Siow and Fukunari Kimura (eds.) (2006), *Multinationals and Economic Growth in East Asia*. London and New York: Routledge. pp.423-52.

21

DIPAK MAZUMDAR and SANDIP SARKAR

The Employment Problem in India and the Phenomenon of the Missing Middle

ECONOMIC growth in India, which has accelerated in recent years, has been characterised by some disturbing features—which seem to have set the pattern for Indian economy of not being aligned with international experience of sustained economic development. These include three critical reasons. First, the growth process seems to have been led by the tertiary sector—both in terms of value added and employment, rather than manufacturing.

Second, while the expectation in labour-abundant economy might be that the tertiary sector had disproportionately absorbed labour displaced from agriculture at low levels of earnings, the data seems to suggest that this has not been so. Earnings level in the tertiary sector has been significantly above those in manufacturing, suggesting that growth in the tertiary sector has been productivity-led rather than employment-led.

Third, the manufacturing sector in India has been characterised by the persistence of 'dualism.' There has been a strong bi-modal distribution in employment—even when we confine our attention to the non-household sub-sector in manufacturing—with strong concentration of employment at the small and large size-groups of establishments, with a conspicuous 'missing middle.' A related point is that the productivity (and wage) gap between the two extreme size groups is much larger in India than in other Asian economies.

It is our contention that these three phenomena are inter-related. It is the 'dualism' in the manufacturing sector which has slowed down the expected dynamic role of this sector in the growth of the economy. The bias towards the tertiary sector in the growth and the productivity gap in its favour can also be traced to the persistence of dualism in manufacturing. Section I of the paper documents the empirical evidence of the bias towards the tertiary sector in Indian development in the context of international experience. In Section II, we set out the evidence on dualism in the manufacturing sector—again stressing the extreme position of India compared to top other Asian economies. Section III develops the argument as to why this type of 'dualism' is a problem and a drag on the growth experience. Section IV explores some hypotheses about the origins and persistence of dualism in Indian manufacturing. Section V concludes.

I

Trends in the Industrial Structure of Employment

Historically speaking, structural change in employment in India has been very slow. But it seems to have accelerated a bit in the post-reform decade. Table 21.1 gives the industrial distribution of employment from the quinquennial National Sample Surveys (NSS) for the two decades ending in the 61st round (2004-05). We present the data for employment by Usual Principal Status (UPS).[1] It can be seen from Table 21.1 that the share of employment of agriculture in the post-reform decade of 1993/94 to 2004-05 had declined by 6.5 percentage points—nearly double the decline in the pervious decade. Barely 1.1 per cent of this decline was absorbed by manufacturing. The tertiary sector, along with construction accounted for the bulk of the relative change in the industrial structure.

Two points regarding the increase in tertiary employment need to be stressed. First, in many developing countries, the public sector has taken the lead in creating employment in government and related services. This is, however, not so in the post-reform India. It can be seen that after contributing as much as a third to the increase in the relative share of employment in non-agriculture sector in the pre-reform decade, the public and community services had quite a significant decline in the share of employment in the decade following the reform of the 1990s. Second, much attention has been paid to the development of the IT (information Technology) sector and outsourcing in recent years. The direct contribution to employment in these sub-sectors, however, has been quite small. It can also be seen from Table 21.1 that the sub-sector 'transport, storage and communication'—which include these IT-related activities contributed no more than a sixth of total employment in the tertiary sector, although its incremental share was quite high. 'Trade, hotel and restaurants' continued to play a dominant role in employment in this sector, and its relative growth in the post-reform decade seems to have been higher than the average for the sector as a whole.

Table 21.1

Distribution of Employment across Sectors over the Years (UPS)

	Share of UPS Employed across Sectors				
Sector	*1983-84*	*1987-88*	*1993-94*	*1999-2000*	*2004-05*
Agriculture	64.9	62.5	61.1	58.5	54.6
Mining & quarrying	0.7	0.8	0.8	0.6	0.7
Manufacturing	11.3	11.5	11.0	11.0	12.1
Electricity, gas and water supply	0.4	0.4	0.5	0.3	0.3
Construction	2.7	4.2	3.7	4.9	6.4
Trade, hotels and restaurants	6.9	7.6	8.0	9.3	11.2
Transport, storage and communication	3.0	3.0	3.3	4.1	4.5
Financial, insurance, real estate and business services	0.7	0.7	1.1	1.3	1.8
Community, social and personal services	9.4	9.3	10.5	10.0	8.5
Tertiary sector (ALL)	20.0	20.6	23.0	24.7	25.9

Employment Growth in the Tertiary Sector in India in a Comparative Context

The growth of the tertiary sector in India seems to be somewhat out of line with international experience of recent decades. Table 21.2 brings together the data for sectoral changes in the shares of employment for several Asian countries over the last three decades of the 20th century.

The newly industrialising countries of Asia—Korea and Taiwan—had their share of employment in manufacturing increasing much faster than that of the tertiary sector during their initial period of growth in the 1970s. In the next decade, tertiary sector employment grew faster, but the magnitude of the increase relative to manufacturing was not as high as was observed in India during this decade. Only in the 1990s, after Taiwan and

Korea had developed into mature industrialised economies, their tertiary sector become the dominant provider of employment outside agriculture. By contrast India's share of employment growth in the tertiary sector in the 1970s was already 60 per cent higher than in manufacturing. Since then, the decades of 1980s and the 1990s have seen a virtual stagnation in the share of employment in manufacturing, with the tertiary sector virtually absorbing the entire loss of employment share by agriculture. The figures also show that other developing countries of Asia—Thailand, Malaysia and Indonesia—do have larger shares of employment in the tertiary sector, but the contrast with India is that none of them have a stagnant share in manufacturing in any decade. On the contrary, something between a third and one half of the often large decline in the share of employment in agriculture was taken up by manufacturing. The only country in the sample with an experience close to that of India is the Philippines.

Table 21.2

Changes in Sectoral Share of Employment in Selected Asian Countries (1970-2000)

Country	*1971-1980*			*1980-1991*			*1990-2000*		
	Agri.	*Manu.*	*Tertiary*	*Agri.*	*Manu.*	*Tertiary*	*Agri.*	*Manu.*	*Tertiary*
Rep. of Korea	-14.4	8.3	6.0	-17.3	5.0	12.9	-7.6	-6.7	14.5
Taiwan, China[1]	-15.6	11.1	3.7	-6.6	1.7	8.9	-5.0	-4.1	9.2
Thailand	-1.4	0.3	1.7	-10.5	3.2	7.3	-15.3	4.3	10.2
Malaysia	-14.8	6.1	9.9	-10.4	4.6	6.6	-7.9	2.9	3.0
Philippines[1]	-1.4	-0.7	2.1	-6.2	-0.6	6.7	-7.8	0.3	7.6
Indonesia				-2.7	1.3	1.1	-10.9	2.8	7.1
India[2]	-5.5	1.8	3.0	-4.6	0.0	3.4	-3.6	0.3	2.4

Note: Figures for first two periods are obtained from Masumdar and Basu, table 3.2, p.38. For the last period, it has been calculated from International Labour Organization (ILO) Year book data.

1. For all periods it has been calculated from ADB Key Indicators, 2001.
2. For all periods it has been calculated from NSS adjusted by population from decadal census. The periods refer to 1973-1983, 1983-1993 and 1993-2000.

Relative Labour Productivity and Earnings in the Tertiary Sector

The importance of labour absorption in the tertiary sector in recent Indian development begs the question: At what level of earnings is this labour being absorbed in the sector? Is labour being 'pushed' into it as the 'employer of last resort' or is it being 'pulled' into it at higher relative earnings?

Figure 21.1 gives the relative productivity of different sectors (relative to agriculture set equal to 100) for the different rounds of the NSS over the two decades before and after 1993-94, when the reforms started. Labour productivity for different sectors are sectoral labour productivity obtained by dividing sectoral GDP by number of principal workers in each sector. Relative labour productivity is the ratio of sectoral labour productivities.

Figure 21.1

Relative Productivity of Construction, Trade and Tertiary with respect to Manufacturing

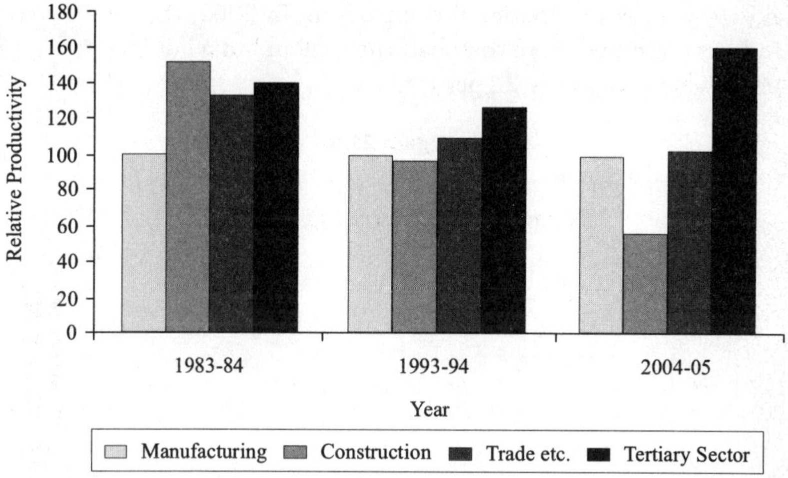

It is seen that the mean productivity of labour has been higher throughout the tertiary sector relative to manufacturing, and might have increased somewhat over the post-reform decade. Even manufacturing does not perform better than the least productive sub-sector of tertiary activities (trade, etc.) which are supposed to be relatively free entry sector, allowing labour displaced from agriculture to push down earnings. The tertiary sector contrasts dramatically with the experience of the construction sector.

Construction is another sector which has registered a large increase in employment in the post-reform decade. If we include construction in the secondary sector, along with manufacturing, as is usual in international practice, the relative productivity of the tertiary sector would be even higher and increasing over time.

Relative Productivity of the Broad Sectors in International Perspective

Papola (2005) compared the experience of changing shares of GDP and employment over the period 1960-2002 in five Asian countries—China, Indonesia, Thailand, Malaysia and India (Mazumdar and Sarkar 2008). The significant point to emerge was that that the share of workforce in industry increased along with the share of GDP in all countries including India, but it produced a much larger share of GDP in all Asian developing countries other than India. It implied that the relative sectoral productivity of labour in Indian manufacturing has been strikingly low by international comparison. In 2002, the tertiary sector in India contributed more than half the GDP in India but its contribution to employment was only 22 per cent.

Figure 21.2

Relative Productivity in Services vis-à-vis Industry, Various Asian Countries (1960-2000)

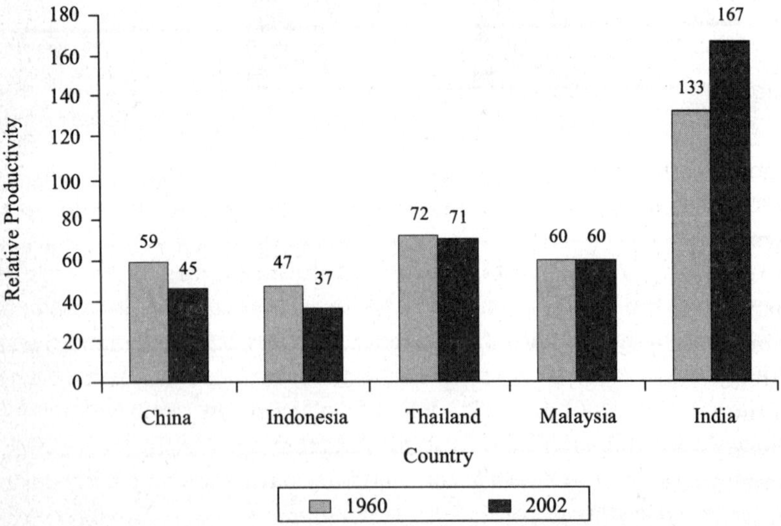

Source: Papola (2005). The original source of the data is the *World Development Report*, various years.

Figure 21.2 brings out the striking point that it is only in India—among all the countries represented—that the relative productivity in services has increased over the 40-year period. A second important point to note is that it is only India where the productivity in services exceeds that in industry in both years and also by a substantial percentage.

It shows that service sector growth in India has been productivity led and not employment led contradicting views of some economists that employment grew in services because this sector has been a repository of low income labour 'pushed out' of agriculture. The heart of the employment problem in India would thus seem to be not an excess absorption of labour in the tertiary sector, but the low productivity of the manufacturing sector, and its persistence over time. It is this low performance of manufacturing which has prevented it from being the dynamic sector—playing a central role in productivity growth as well as the reallocation of labour as in other countries in the history of successful economic development. It will now be argued that this disappointing role of the manufacturing sector can be traced, at least to a significant part, to the persistence of dualism in the sector; and which perpetuates the tremendous difference in relative labour productivity between the small (informal) and large (formal) size groups. The very low level of labour productivity in the manufacturing sector can be traced to this dualism.

II

Dualism in Indian Manufacturing

Indian manufacturing is characterised by the prevalence of a large 'unorganised sector' existing side by side with the formal or organised sector. Three sub-categories within the unorganised sector include: (i) own-account manufacturing enterprises (OAME) which are household enterprises making use only of family labour; (ii) non-directory manufacturing establishments (NDME) who employ at least one wage (hired) worker and have between two to five workers in total; and (iii) Directory manufacturing establishments (DME) employing between six to nine workers in total of which at least one would be a hired worker. These three sub-categories co-exist with the formal or organised sector which are statistically defined (by the Factory Act) to be employing 10 or more workers. Table 21.3 provides a statistical profile of the manufacturing sector in India distinguished by the above four categories of establishments. The dominance of the household sector as well as its low productivity is apparent from the table.

Table 21.3

Employment and Value Added in Manufacturing by Type of Establishment (2000-01)

	OAME	*NDME*	*DME*	*Organised*
Distribution of employment (% of all manufacturing)	55.9	12.4	14.4	17.3
Mean all workers in category	1.7	3.2	10.0	63.9
Mean hired workers in category	0 1.8	7.8	60.9	
Distribution of value added (% of all manufacturing)	10.3	6.8	8.9	84.3
Mean VA/Worker in category	₹ 6,929	₹ 18,479	₹ 20,800	₹ 163,775
Productivity (Organised =100)	4.2	11.3	12.7	100

Sources: Unit level data of 56th round of NSSO and ASI unit level data of 2000-01.

While the importance of the household sector in Indian manufacturing is clearly a prominent factor for the low productivity of manufacturing as whole, a second major reason is the dominant use of hired labour for employment in the enterprises. This includes both the DME and the organised sector as defined under the Factory Act [and covered by the Annual Survey of Industries (ASI)].

The DME establishments of 6-9 workers include the small enterprises in modern manufacturing. In international statistical practice, they are generally included in surveys or censuses covering the Factory Manufacturing sector (the cut-off point being generally five workers). To put in perspective the Indian size distribution in modern manufacturing, we can include these enterprises along with the ones in the formal sector covered by the ASI. When we do this, a striking result emerges from the international comparison. Among the Asian countries, India has 'dualistic' structure with a bi-polar distribution. There are two strong modes in the distribution of employment in modern manufacturing: in the 500 and more category and the 5-9 category with the proportion of employment in the intermediate middle size groups being conspicuously small. This phenomenon—sometimes characterised as that of the 'missing middle'—is contrasted with other Asian countries, e.g., Korea, Hong Kong, Taiwan, Malaysia and Thailand. A few of other Asian countries like Taiwan, Hong Kong, Japan and post-1990 Korea have strong presence of small enterprises in the five to nine class but the proportion of employment in this group is never as much as in the large enterprises, and of course the intermediate size groups are well represented. A further striking difference between India and the other Asian countries with a strong small-scale sector in manufacturing is that the productivity gap between the small and the large units in modern manufacturing is much larger in India. The gap in labour productivity between the large and the small size groups in India is 8:1, as against 3:1 in Japan, Korea and Taiwan (and even smaller in Hong Kong).[2] The two aspects of 'dualism'—the bi-polar distribution of employment within the formal manufacturing sector, and the productivity gap between the smallest and the largest—are portrayed in Figures 21.3 and 21.4 for India and a few Asian countries. They bring out strongly the peculiarity of the Indian case relative to the other countries in the mid-eighties.

Figure 21.3

The Missing Middle: Employment by Size Groups in Manufacturing Firms—India Compared to Other Countries

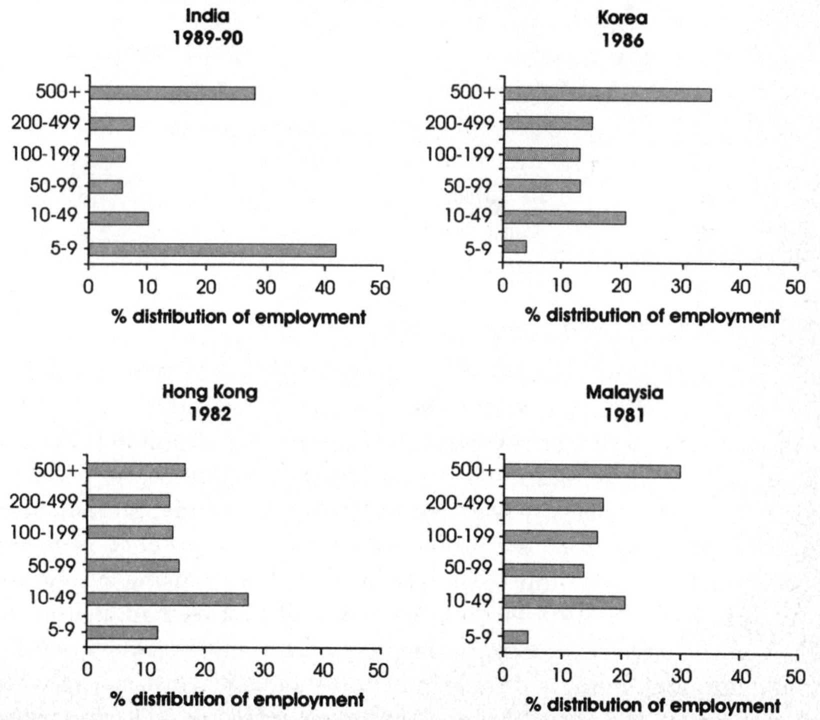

Source: Mazumdar (2003).

Figure 21.4

Productivity Differential by Size Groups—India Compared to Other Countries (Productivity of 500+ Equals 100)

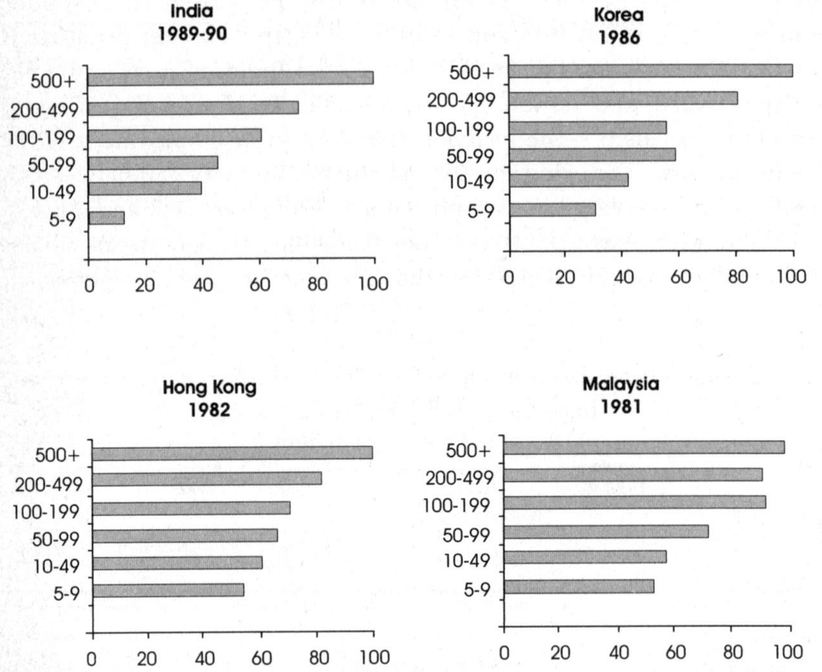

Source: Mazumdar (2003).

The Post-Reform Experience in India

The package of reforms in the last decade could be expected to have made a serious impact on the structure of manufacturing. First, the traditional policy of reservation of a long list of products for the small-scale industry was dismantled. Second, liberalisation of import controls, particularly on a range of consumer goods, should have reduced the strength of the protective umbrella for production in the small establishments. Third, the relaxation of the licensing system for large-scale industrial units could be expected to have had significant effect on the large-scale sector in moving away to more labour-intensive production and giving encouragement to middle-sized firms. What is the evidence to the effect of these developments on the size structure of manufacturing?

The first point to note is in spite of the increase in the growth rate of the formal or organised sector, labour absorption in this sub-sector has been quite low. Employment elasticity in organised manufacturing has experienced a cyclical pattern along with the cycles of boom and relative stagnation in manufacturing output.[3] But over-all the employment elasticity in the pre-reform period—1973-1990 and 1990-2005—has been 0.27 and 0.16 respectively, even as the output (value added) growth has increased from 6.6 per cent to 7.0 per cent over these two broad periods. It seems that the organised manufacturing sector has been reluctant to increase labour use per unit of output even as state policy has moved in the direction of lessening of controls. The increase in employment in all manufacturing—which we do observe—has been almost entirely due to the increase in employment in the unorganised sub-sector (Table 21.4).

Table 21.4

Changes in Employment in Different Segment of Indian Manufacturing

Size Group of Manufacturing	*Number of Workers (1994-95)*	*Number of Workers (2000-01)*	*Increase in Employment*
OAME[1]	20,512,449	25,061,244	4,548,795
NDME (1-5)	4,124,179	5,561,633	1,437,454
DME (6-9)	5,478,046	6,457,911	979,865
Organised (10+)	7,716,029	7,779,961	63,932

Note: 1. Does not employ any hired labour.

Taking the DME and the ASI sub-sectors together, the problem of 'dualism' identified above has remained largely unchanged (Table 21.5). As far as the distribution of employment is concerned, the only change over the period covered seems to have been a significant change in the number of workers employed in very large firms (1,000 and above). The distribution is, however, still bipolar with strong modes at the employment size groups at the two extremes (6-9 and 500+).

The productivity differentials by size groups seem to have changed even less. If anything the extreme 'dualism' noticed in India compared to other Asian countries seems to have worsened since 1984-85, much of the deterioration occurred in the first half of the 1980s (Table 21.6).

Table 21.5

Percentage Distribution of Employment in Different Size Classes

Type & Size	1984-85	1994-95	2000-01
6-9	40.27	44.91	41.52
10-49	9.47	10.34	10.42
50-199	11.83	13.31	15.34
200-499	8.27	8.56	9.49
500-999	7.65	7.02	8.87
1000 and above	22.52	15.85	14.35
All	100.00	100.00	100.00

Source: NSS, different rounds.

Table 21.6

Indices of Labour Productivity by Size Groups (500+ = 1.00)

Type & Size	1984-85	1994-95	2000-01
6-9	0.19	0.12	0.10
10-49	0.42	0.35	0.37
50-199	0.53	0.47	0.49
200-499	0.86	0.77	0.84
500-999	1.06	0.98	1.02
1000 and above	0.98	1.01	0.99

Source: NSS, different rounds.

III

Why is Dualism a Problem for Manufacturing Growth?

Why should the phenomenon of 'dualism' in manufacturing be regarded as a drag on the growth and performance of the manufacturing sector? The important relevant points in this regard are:

- The impact on allocative efficiency and wage inequality.
- The dynamic impact on the growth of skilled labour and entrepreneurship.
- The stagnation in the growth of markets for manufactured goods.

Allocative Efficiency and Inequality

The large gap in productivity between the firms in the two extreme size groups, as presented above in the data on manufacturing , suggests the existence of a large gap in the marginal products of labour and capital between the two classes of firms. We know from independent evidence that large firms have access to capital supplied by the formal financial institutions, while small firms mostly have to depend on local informal sources of finance and the interest rate differential between these sources can be huge (Little *et al.*, 1987). It is also well known that wage levels follow differences in labour productivity and large firms have a wage per worker which, even after we have controlled for measurable human capital attributes, are much higher in the large firms. Again the detailed study of a specific labour market (Bombay City); reported in Little *et al.*, 1987) revealed that, after allowing for the effect of education, training, occupation and knowledge of English, wage per man of manual workers in the largest size class of factories employing 1,000+ workers was almost twice the level in 'small' enterprises with less than 10 workers. Two conclusions are suggested by this evidence of size-related factor price differentials: First, the larger the differential, the larger is the loss in welfare in terms of static allocative efficiency theory. Second, since employment in the 'dualistic' pattern is concentrated in the smallest and the largest size groups, there is great inequality in the distribution of wage per worker.

Impact on Dynamic Efficiency

In a more dynamic sense, the missing middle implies a weak process of graduation of small firms and the development of entrepreneurship. It is arguable that the dispersion of entrepreneurship as well as industrial technology over a wide spectrum of spatially and economically distributed regions is dependant on the mushrooming of medium-scale enterprises, into which the small units are able to graduate.

Similarly dualism slows down the growth of the labour force with industrial skills. This is particularly true in developing economies in which many of the skill requirements of modern industry (including discipline in the workplace) are acquired by on-the-job-training rather than education in schools. The slow growth of the skilled work force in its turn has an impact on the choice of technology. It has been established that capital-intensive techniques have been adopted in economies or sectors more in response to a shortage of skilled rather than unskilled labour. Thus, a potential shortage of skilled labour needed by modern manufacturing could dampen the value of employment elasticity and slow down the rate of growth of employment in the industrial sector.

An important result in our research project on Indian manufacturing was the evidence that although employment elasticity varied with the economic cycles, it did not exceed 0.33 in the best period of the post-reform upswing. As analysed in the research, there are several important reasons for the low employment elasticity, but a perceived shortage of labour of the requisite skill and efficiency is one of them.

Dampening the Growth of Markets

While the last two points emphasise problems created on the supply side, 'dualism' might also affect the growth of manufacturing through its impact on the demand side—on the expansion of markets for industrial goods. The medium-sized establishments have been lauded in the literature for having the desired amount of flexibility and enterprise to seek out new export markets in new industries. But their importance in the expansion of domestic markets also needs to be emphasised. Dualism strengthens and perpetuates product market segmentation. The market for industrial products is split into low-quality products catering to the need of low-income consumers and supplied by small-scale local producers on the one hand, and the higher quality segments which the large establishments supply to a limited number of high-income consumers. The lack of integration of markets could be a bottleneck in the development of mass markets for manufactured consumer goods.

IV

Causes of the Emergence and Persistence of Dualism

What are the major factors causing the emergence of dualism in its two aspects—the phenomenon of the 'missing middle' and the unusual productivity gap between the small and the large units? What are the reasons for its persistence over time, even when the reform process reducing some of the strength of the proximate causes of dualism has been eroded?

- Labour legislation has been traditionally at the top of the list of the proximate causes of the phenomenon. The Factory Act applies to all workers in the 'registered' sector which covers units employing 10 or more workers using power. Additionally, job security legislation (discussed in Section IV) kicks in for units with employment size of 100 or more workers. Both types of legislation would impose costs on units increasing beyond the threshold sizes.

- Education polices as have been implemented in India over the years have been biased towards the promotion of tertiary education and have neglected basic primary and low secondary education. It has been maintained in the literature (e.g., in the work of Adrian Wood among others) that modern manufacturing requires a minimum of basic education for enabling workforce to perform up to minimum standards. Small- and medium-sized units—adopting comparatively labour-intensive technology—benefits from an ample supply of such labour. This is in contrast to tiny units which could use nearly unskilled labour with less than primary education for low grade production, but would find it difficult to grow beyond a certain scale with such labour. The relatively plentiful supply of skilled labour with higher education biases production to less labour-intensive industry and modes of production. Large units have a comparative advantage in using such labour which smaller units cannot afford.
- The protection of small-scale units has been an important aspect of Indian industrial policy since independence. It has taken the form of reservation of large number of items for production in exclusively small units and the provision of incentives—fiscal, financial and legislative—as long as the units stayed below a certain size. The threshold size was first defined in terms of the traditional employment size of five workers. It was in later years changed to a definition based on capital size and was increased somewhat over the years. Nevertheless, the policies have always provided an incentive for entrepreneurs to expand horizontally with more small units, rather vertically with larger middle-sized units.
- Hysteresis: The policy of reservation for the small-scale units was largely ended in the post-1991 reform process. But we have seen that the impact on the size structure of establishments in manufacturing has been minimal. This limited impact might be due to widely recognised processes in which a socio-economic system established over a long period of time tends to persist even after the original causes have disappeared. This persistence is not just due to inertia. Economic agents and

institutions acquire characteristics which sustain the system. For example, entrepreneurs develop with ambitions to think in terms of horizontal rather than vertical growth. Marketing channels, financial institutions and infrastructure are geared more to supporting small units with limited market rather than dynamic units growing into larger sizes and different markets.

V

Conclusion

An important objective of further policy-oriented research is to see what is the relative importance of the factors outlined in the last section. This can be done only with the help of enterprise level surveys in key industries and districts. Perhaps much can also be learnt by contrasting the experience of different states of India which have had different trajectories of manufacturing development.

Notes

1. The NSS records employment by the activity in which the individual spent most of its time in the reference period (last 365 days)—called UPS—as well as by the activity in which he or she spent only a part of the time—called SS secondary status. The total and the industrial distribution of the latter are subject to short-term fluctuations.
2. See Mazumdar (2003) for the detailed statistical evidence and a discussion of the comparative Asian scenario.
3. See Mazumdar and Sarkar (2008) for details. Also see, the contribution in Kanbur and Sverner (ed.) for an updated and more theoretical discussion.

References

Little, Ian, Dipak Mazumdar and John Page (1987). *Small Manufacturing Enterprises*. New York: Oxford.

Mazumdar, Dipak (2003). "Small and Medium Enterprise Development in Equitable Growth and Poverty Alleviation", in Christopher M. Edmonds (ed.), *Reducing Poverty in Asia; Emerging Issues in Growth, Targeting and Measurement*. Chaltenham, UK: Edward Elgar & Asian Development Bank.

Mazumdar, Dipak and Sandip Sarkar (2008). *Globalisation, Labour Markets and Inequality in India*. London: Routledge.

Papola, T.S. (2005). '"Emerging Structure of Indian Economy—Implications of Growing Inter-Sectoral Imbalances", Presidential address of *88th Annual Conference of Indian Economic Association*. 27-29 December. Vishakhapatanam.

Vasudeva-Dutta, P. (2004). "Trade Liberalisation and the Industry Wage Structure in India", *Department of Economics Discussion Paper*. University of Sussex.

Indian Journal of Labour Economics 52(1). January-March 2009.

Part IV

Services

22

Trends and Performance in Services

The services sector has emerged as the most dynamic sector of the world economy, contributing almost one-third of world gross value added, half of world employment, one-fifth of global trade and more than half of the world foreign direct investment flows. It remains the key driver of India's economic growth, contributing almost 66.1 per cent of its gross value added growth in 2015-16, important net foreign exchange earner and the most attractive sector for foreign direct investment inflows. However, the global slowdown has cast a shadow even on this promising sector. (Economic Survey 2015-16).

Introduction

The services sector covers a wide range of activities from the most sophisticated information technology (IT) to simple services provided by the unorganised sector, such as the services of the barber and plumber. National Accounts Classification (NAC) of the services sector incorporates trade, hotels and restaurants; transport, storage and communication; financing, insurance, real estate and business services; and community, social, and personal services. In World Trade Organization (WTO) and Reserve Bank of India (RBI) classifications, construction is also included.The phenomenal expansion of services worldwide led to services being regarded as an engine of growth and even as a necessary concomitant of economic growth. Development economics suggests that development is a three-stage process. The dominance of the services sector in the growth process is usually associated with the third stage of growth. During the 1980s and 1990s, services accounted for a share of about 70 per cent of GDP in industrialised countries and about 50 per cent in developing countries.

In India growth of services picked up in the 1980s, and accelerated in the 1990s, when it averaged 7.5 per cent per annum, thus providing an impetus to industry and agriculture, which grew on average by 5.8 per cent and 3.1 per cent respectively. Growth in the services sector has also been less cyclical and more stable than the growth of industry and agriculture (in the sense of having the smallest coefficient of variation).

A notable feature of the structural transformation of the services sector has been the growth of skill intensive and high value added sectors, i.e., software, communication and financial services. The rapid growth of services can be attributed, *inter alia*, to the advent of IT and the knowledge economy. This has enhanced the growth of the high productivity segment of the services sector as well as a variety of service activities involving low productivity activities catering to a large mass of people. The phenomenal growth of low skilled service activities has occurred due to reduced opportunities in the manufacturing sector, particularly in the unorganised sectors.

Some of the activities in the services sector are multidimensional, being part of industry as well as services, such as IT and construction. Service statistics in most countries including India provide information on value-addition of various activities of business services, hotels, trade, financial services, etc. For an empirical analysis, sub-sectors including trade, transport and communication, financing, insurance, real estate and business services can be categorised as producer services with hotels and restaurants and other services as consumer services. Government services comprise public administration and defence services. During 1999-2000, producer services accounted for about 70 per cent of the total services followed by consumer services (17%) and government services (13%). The high share of producer services reflects the strong inter-linkages between services and goods producing sectors of the economy.

Table 22.1

Sectoral Growth Rates

	Average Growth (in % per annum)		
	1951-1980	*1981-1990*	*1991-2000*
Agriculture	2.1	4.4	3.1
Industry	5.3	6.8	5.8
Services	4.5	6.6	7.5
GDP	3.5	5.8	5.8

Source: Gordon and Gupta, 2003.

Rapid growth of the service sector is not unique to India. The existing literature shows that as an economy matures, the share of services in output increases consistently. To begin with, the increase occurs along with an increase in the share of industry. Thereafter, the service share grows more rapidly, accompanied by a stagnant or declining share of the industrial sector. Cross-country experience suggests that the first stage occurs until the country reaches lower middle income status, while the second stage commences once it becomes an upper middle income country.

Consistent with the trend observed in other countries, India's growth experience has been characterised by a decline in the share of agriculture in GDP and an increase in the shares of industry and services. Between 1950 and 1990, agriculture's share in the GDP declined by around 25 per cent with the corresponding increase in the share of services and industry being distributed roughly evenly. However, since the 1990s, the share of industry in overall GDP has remained at around 27 per cent while the entire decline in the share of agriculture from 32 per cent to 22 per cent of GDP has been matched by a corresponding rise in the share of services in the economy. This is in contrast to other developing economies, where the decline in the share of agriculture in GDP has been followed by a corresponding rise in the share of industry, in particular manufacturing, and later in services. Thus, India seems to be an aberration in terms of the service sector having a much greater role in its economy than in other countries at similar or even higher levels of income. It appears to have leapfrogged from the primary to the tertiary sector.

The service sector has played an important role in enabling improved economic performance on the domestic growth as well as external fronts during the post-reform period. Services have been the fastest-growing sector of the Indian economy over the past decade and have thus, helped accelerate the overall growth rate of the economy. Services have also facilitated India's integration with the world economy through trade and capital flows. The phenomenal growth and export performance witnessed in services like information technology (IT) and business process outsourcing (BPO) have placed India on the global map as a major supplier of knowledge-based services. Services have also helped improve productivity in other sectors of the economy, thus contributing to an improvement in overall competitiveness (Chanda, 2007).

Growth and Sectoral Shares, Cross-Country Evidence and Indian Experience

The evolution of sectoral shares in output, consumption and employment as economies grow has been studied by economists for well over 50 years. During the 1950s and 1960s, research by Kuznets and Chenery suggested that development would be associated with a sharp decline in the proportion of GDP generated by the primary sector, counter-balanced by a significant increase in industry, and by a more modest increase in the service sector. Sectoral shares in employment were predicted to follow a similar pattern.

With the benefit of more data on development than was available to Kuznets and Chenery, recent literature has tended to emphasise the growing importance of service sector activity (Inman, 1985; Kongsamut *et al.*, 2001). For example, Kongsamut *et al.*, (2001) analyse a sample of 123 countries for 1970-1989 and show that rising per capita GDP is associated with an increase in services and a decline in agriculture both in terms of share in GDP and employment. In other words, the sectoral share given up by agriculture as the economy matures goes more to the services sector and less to industry than the Kuznets-Chenery work had suggested. The modern view is that as an economy matures, the share of services (in output, consumption and employment) grows along with a decline in agriculture. By contrast, the share of industry first increases modestly, and then stabilises or declines (Gordon and Gupta, 2003).

Share of Services in GDP

Such a pattern of growth is visible in the cross-country data on shares in GDP (Table 22.2). These data suggest two stages of

Table 22.2

Sectoral Shares in GDP in 2001, Global Averages

(% of GDP)

	Agriculture	*Industry*	*Services*	
Low income	24	32	45	Stage I
Lower middle income	12	40	48	
Upper middle income	7	33	60	Stage II
High income	2	29	70	Stage III

Note: Definition: low income: per capita GDP<$745; lower middle: $746-2975; upper middle: $2976-9205; and high: >$9206.

Source: World Bank's *WDI*, 2003, Table 4.2.

development. In the first, both industry and services shares increase as countries move from low income to lower middle income status, while in the second, the share of industry declines and that of services increases as the economy moves to upper middle and higher income levels.

Services GDP: International Comparison

In the US$ 74.0 trillion world gross value added (GVA) in 2014, the share of services (at current prices), and growth rate (at constant prices), improved marginally to 66.0 per cent and 2.5 per cent respectively over 2013. But in the last thirteen years, the share of services in world GVA has declined by 2.7 percentage points (pp). Among the world's top 15 countries in terms of gross domestic product (GDP), the US ranks first in both services GVA and overall GDP, followed by China in second and Japan in third position. India ranked ninth in terms of overall GDP and tenth in terms of services GVA in 2014, climbing one rung in both rankings. However, among these top 15 nations, in the period 2001-13, the maximum increase in services share to GVA was recorded by Spain (9.7 pp), followed by India (7.8 pp) and China (6.8 pp).

As in the case of overall GDP, services GVA also did not fully recover from the impact of the 2008 global financial crisis with a general slowdown trend in the growth rate of services for the world and across nations (except Brazil) in the post crisis period (2010-14) compared to the pre-crisis period (2001-8). Brazil was an exception, showing good growth in services in 2012 and 2013, which in turn was due to very high growth in the wholesale, retail trade, restaurants and hotels category. The compound annual growth rate (CAGR) of world services in the post crisis period (2010-14) at 2.5 per cent was lower than the 3.0 per cent in the precrisis period (2001-8). Despite the slowdown in the post crisis period, India showed the fastest service sector growth with a CAGR of 8.6 per cent, followed by China at 8.4 per cent. In 2014 India's service sector growth at 10.3 per cent was noticeably higher than that of China at 8.0 per cent (Table 22.3) (*Economic Survey 2015-16*).

World Services Trade

After growing robustly in the last 12 years from 2001 to 2013 with a CAGR of 9.9 per cent, world services export growth has been seeing a see-saw movement. It was at 0.1 per cent in 2001, reached a high of 21.5 per cent in 2004, fell steeply to a negative 9.4 per cent in 2009,

Table 22.3

Performance in Services: International Comparision

Country	*Rank in*		*Services Growth Rate*						*Share of Services in*						*Services Export Growth*					
	Overall GDP	*Services GVA*	*(%) Y-o-Y*				*CAGR 2001-2008*	*CAGR 2010-2014*	*GVA*		*Employment*		*Total Exports*		*(%) Y-o-Y*				*CAGR 2001-2008*	*CAGR 2010-2014*
			2001	2009	20013	2014			2001	2014	2001*	2014*	2001	2014	2001	2009	2013	2014		
US	1	1	2.0	-2.0	0.9	2.3	2.2	1.8	77.4	78.4	75.0	81.2	27.2	29.8	-3.6	-4.2	5.1	3.7	9.5	6.1
China	2	2	10.2	11.1	8.2	8.0	11.7	8.4	40.9	47.7	12.7	47.0	11.0	9.0	9.1	-13.4	-3.9	12.4	25.9	7.9
Japan	3	3	1.3	-3.1	1.3	0.1	0.9	0.9	69.0	72.0	63.9	69.1	13.6	18.8	-6.9	-14.6	1.2	19.2	11.8	5.2
Germany	4	4	3.1	-3.0	0.4	1.3	1.4	1.3	68.7	69.0	64.6	70.4	12.8	15.0	5.6	-8.5	8.4	4.3	15.8	4.9
UK	5	5	3.5	-2.6	2.8	2.8	2.9	2.6	73.6	78.4	73.7	79.1	30.1	40.0	-0.8	-13.8	2.3	7.9	14.5	5.8
France	6	6	1.9	-2.0	0.8	0.7	1.8	1.2	74.7	78.9	69.9	75.8	19.8	31.4	-0.5	-13.6	7.4	5.3	15.8	7.4
Brazil	7	8	2.3	2.1	11.9	1.1	3.9	6.9	68.2	71.0	59.4	76.6	13.0	14.8	-2.7	-8.9	-1.7	4.7	18.6	6.8
Italy	8	7	2.3	-2.7	-1.1	0.0	0.8	-0.6	70.5	74.3	63.1	69.5	18.9	18.0	2.1	-16.3	4.8	3.6	10.5	3.8
India	9	10	7.2	10.7	8.9	10.3	9.3	8.6	45.2	53.0	24.0	28.7	27.9	32.6	4.8	-12.5	2.2	5.0	30.1	7.5
Russia	10	12	3.3	-5.1	2.2	1.0	7.6	2.6	55.9	60.0	58.6	65.8	9.9	11.5	17.3	-19.8	12.4	-6.1	26.0	7.5
Canada	11	9	3.5	1.2	1.9	2.4	2.9	2.3	65.9	69.9	74.8	78.2	12.7	15.2	-3.6	-8.7	-0.1	-4.0	9.9	3.0
Australia	12	11	3.8	1.8	2.8	2.6	3.4	2.8	69.9	70.1	67.9	69.5	21.8	18.1	-8.9	-7.6	-0.8	1.5	13.3	3.9
S. Korea	13	14	4.9	1.4	2.9	3.1	4.2	3.0	59.0	59.4	62.6	69.5	16.3	15.6	-4.9	-20.5	0.2	3.1	17.4	6.6
Spain	14	13	4.0	-0.9	-0.8	1.1	3.9	0.4	65.3	75.1	62.0	76.3	32.2	29.2	6.0	-14.8	5.0	4.3	13.2	4.6
Mexico	15	15	1.1	-3.7	2.3	2.0	3.6	3.4	57.6	59.0	56.1	62.4	7.2	5.0	-7.5	-16.1	24.6	4.6	5.3	8.4
World			2.6	-0.8	2.2	2.5	3.0	2.5	68.7	66.0	35.9	50.9	19.4	20.6	19.9	-10.9	5.4	4.9	15.0	6.4

Notes: Rank and share are based on current prices (2014); growth rates are based on constant prices (US$); construction sector is excluded in services GDP.

* For employment data in 2001 and 2014, the available data of nearest preceding years is used.

Source: Computed from UN National Accounts Statistics for GDP/GVA, World Bank database for employment and World Trade Organization (WTO) database for services trade. *Economic Survey 2015-16*.

rebounded quickly to 9.8 per cent in 2010 and 12.2 per cent in 2011, but decelerated to 2.2 per cent in 2012. It has again picked up to 5.5 per cent in 2013.

The impact of the global financial crisis was more pronounced in services trade than services GVA, with the CAGR of world commercial services exports during the postcrisis period decelerating to 6.4 per cent compared to the 15.0 per cent during the precrisis period. In the pre-crisis period, among the top 15 services producer countries, the services exports CAGR of India was the fastest at 30.1 per cent, followed by China at 25.9 per cent. However, during the post crisis period, it decelerated in both India and China, with Mexico registering the highest growth at 8.4 per cent, followed by China at 7.9 per cent and India at 7.5 per cent.

The growth story overall and services of world and India in the 2000s began from almost the same level of around 4-5 per cent in 2000. But over the years, India's overall and services growth rates have outpaced those of the world. Interestingly, unlike world services growth, which has been moving in tandem with its overall growth with mild see-saw movements over the years, India's services growth has been consistently above its overall growth in the last decade except for 2003 (when the former was marginally lower than the latter). Thus, for more than a decade, this sector has been pulling up the growth of the Indian economy with a great amount of stability.

In 2014, the growth of the US$ 4.9 trillion world commercial services exports contributing almost one-fifth of total trade, decelerated to 4.9 per cent from 5.4 per cent in 2013. While, services exports of the United States, the largest exporter of commercial services, decelerated to 3.7 per cent in 2014, those of Japan, China, and the UK, accelerated to 19.2 per cent, 12.4 per cent and 7.9 per cent respectively, due to base effect. India's services exports also accelerated to 5.0 per cent.

As per the latest World Trade Organization (WTO) data for 2015, services trade growth is in negative territory from Q1 to Q3 for the world and in Q2 and Q3 for India. The situation is similar in many important services trading countries. Merchandise trade growth figures show a steeper fall than services trade growth in Q1 to Q3 of 2015 as in 2009 for both the world and India. In the first three quarters of 2015, there was negative growth in world commercial services exports at - 4.9 per cent, - 8.1 per cent and - 6.6 per cent respectively. During these periods, services export growth of the US was positive for two quarters and negative for one quarter at 3.4 per cent, -0.8 per cent and 1.3 per cent respectively, whereas for the EU, it was highly negative at -10.1 per cent, -12.3 per cent and -9.4 per cent respectively. Significant declines in exports and imports of EU in 2015 are due two depreciation of the euro against the US dollar. India's services trade growth was negative at - 1.4 per cent and - 0.1 per cent in Q2 and Q3 of 2015, but services export growth, though low, was positive at 2.3 per cent, 0.4 per cent and 1.0 per cent in Q1, Q2 and Q3 of 2015 respectively (*Economic Survey 2015-16*).

Factors Underlying the Services Growth

What are the factors behind the dynamism of the services sector in India, one explanation suggested in the literature for fast growth in services is that the income elasticity of demand for services is greater than one. Hence, the final demand for services grows faster than the demand for goods and commodities as income rises.

A rising share of services in GDP is regarded as an outcome of higher income elasticity of demand for services. The empirical studies have shown that the income elasticity of demand for services could be greater than or equal to unity (Gemmell, 1982; Summers, 1985; Bergstand, 1991; Falvey and Gemmell, 1991). Income elasticity of demand for services increases with rising income which favours the fulfilment of more sophisticated desires. During the development process, distribution of GDP and employment registers sectoral shifts. Such shifts may occur on account of the hierarchy of needs, distinguished into basic needs for food and shelter and needs for other material and non-material goods including services (Maslow, 1970). According to this view, income elasticity of demand depends on per capita income and differs across various sectors.

The empirical estimates of price and income elasticity for various categories of services in India are summarised in Table 22.4. It is important to mention that the actual behaviour of the services sector in real GDP depends on the relative strength of the coefficients of income and price elasticity.

The income elasticity of demand is greater than unity and price elasticity is negative and significant for the total services, producer services and government services. In other words, demand for overall services rises with increase in per capita GDP and decreases with increase in prices of services. The higher income elasticity of demand in the case of producer services underscores its forward linkages. This is corroborated by the emergence of producer services comprising advertising, publicity, marketing and other IT-related activities in the recent period as important service industries in India. Therefore, producer services can be regarded as a major source of economic growth.

Table 22.4

Income and Price Elasticities for the Services Sector

Sector	*Income Elasticity*	*Price Elasticity*
1	*2*	*3*
Services	1.20 *	-0.68 *
1. Producer services	1.22 *	-0.78 *
2. Consumer services	1.00 *	-0.10
3. Government services	1.41 *	-1.05 *

Note: * : Statistically significant at 1 per cent.

Another explanation is that technical and structural changes in an economy make it more efficient to contract out services that were once produced in the industry. This type of outsourcing has been called the 'splintering' of industrial activity. Splintering results in an increase in net input demand for services from the industrial sector, as well as the services sector growing proportionately faster than other sectors.

The empirical evidence (Gordon and Gupta, 2003) shows that while splintering and high income elasticity of demand for services have served to stimulate services growth in India, it is necessary to look beyond these factors to fully explain the growth acceleration since the 1990s. In particular, important roles also seem to have been played by economic reforms, the advent of the IT era, and growing external demand for services exports. Industrial sector reforms have also been carried out in India and the question arises why the industrial sector has not experienced the same sustained high level of growth that the service sector has experienced. This could be because industrial growth is more dependent on infrastructure development (such as roads and ports), which have acted as a bottleneck to growth. Labour restrictions and small-scale reservations may also have disadvantaged industry more than services. In addition, the faster growing services activities seem to be more intensive in skilled labour, with which India is well endowed.

A number of studies have attempted to explain the fast growth in the share of service activity observed in cross-country data. The literature draws a distinction between demand and supply factors.

On the supply side, the share of services can be boosted by a switch to a more service-input intensive method of organising production. Such a change in production methods can arise as a result of increasing specialisation as the economy matures. For example, over time, industrial firms may make greater use of specialist sub-contractors to provide services that were previously provided by the firms themselves. Legal, accounting and security services are obvious candidates to be contracted out. Bhagwati (1994) calls this process of specialisation splintering. Kravis (1982) points out that splintering will lead to growth in the share of services in GDP, even when GDP itself is not growing.

On the demand side, an increase in the output share of services can arise from rapid growth in the final demand for services. This could be from domestic consumers with a high income elasticity of demand for services, or from foreign consumers with a growing demand for the country's service exports. Demand-led growth of this type is likely to result, at least initially, in higher prices of services, as well as a shift of resources into the production of services.

Both demand-side and supply-side factors have been shown to have played important roles in this 'services revolution' (Rakshit, 2007). Two types of demand for services are the final demand from consumers (both domestic and exports) and the intermediate demand for services from the other two sectors of the economy of industry and agriculture. Faster growth of the final demand for service sector output is indicated by growth in private household consumption expenditure and a rapid growth of export of services. During the time period 1995-2005, private consumption of services grew at an average of 8.6 per cent and export of services grew at 19.1 per cent that are much higher than the growth rate of services GDP (8.0%). Household income elasticity demand for services averaged 1.5 per cent for the 10-year period (Rakshit, 2007). A key supply-side factor widely mentioned has been the 'splintering' of production activity. This refers to 'outsourcing' of activities previously carried out 'in house' by industrial firms like marketing, legal services, transport, security, repair and maintenance. This outcome of the splintering process gets reflected in the greater service input per unit of output (intensity of use of services) in industry. Available evidence suggests that the intensity with which services are used in industry and agriculture has not changed much over time (Eichengreen and Gupta, 2011). Therefore, the growth in the intermediate demand for services is largely attributed to increasing output and not to outsourcing by manufacturing firms. A supply factor of importance has been technological change or total factor productivity growth (TFPG) in the service sector. Indirect evidence in support of this factor is the declining incremental capital-output ratio and increasing labour productivity growth in the service sector since 1995. Real GDP estimates by sector are not available separately for rural and urban segments in India. However, as most of the manufacturing and services activities are dominated by the urban sector, it can be safely assumed that similar high output growth rates were achieved in the urban sector as a whole.

Service activity can also be stimulated by technological advances, whereby new activities or products emerge as a result of technological breakthrough—such advances are likely to be particularly relevant in the case of the IT sector (e.g., the Internet), telecommunication (cellular phone services) and to some extent in financial services (credit cards, ATMs, etc.).

Economic reform measures initiated since 1991 also impacted on the performance of the services sector. First, reforms in the domestic industrial environment which resulted in rising manufacturing growth provided synergies to the services sector in the form of increased demand for producer services. Second, the liberalisation of the financial sector provided an environment for faster growth of the financial services. Third, reforms in certain segments of infrastructure services also contributed to the growth of services. Consequently, the services sector posted a much higher growth during the reform period as compared with the pre-reform period with its share touching the 50 per cent mark.

Services GDP and Gross Capital Formation

In 2015-16, as per the advance estimates (AE), the services sector accounting for 53.3 per cent of India's GVA at basic prices (current prices), grew by 9.2 per cent (constant prices), marginally lower than in 2014-15. The slight slowing down was mainly due to the deceleration in growth of the combined category of public administration, defence and other services to 6.9 per cent from 10.7 per cent in 2014-15.

As in the case of total gross capital formation (GCF) to GVA, the rate of GCF to GVA at current (2011-12) prices in the services sector also declined marginally from 40.1 per cent in 2013-14 to 39.3 per cent in 2014-15. However, the share of the services sector in the GCF has increased consistently over the last four years from 53.3 per cent in 2011-

Table 22.5

Share and Growth of India's Services Sector (GVA at Basic Price)

(%)

	GVA			GCF	
	2013-14	2014-15®	2015-16#	2013-14	2014-15®
Total Services	50.9(7.8)	52.6(10.3)	53.3 (9.2)	56.5(5.1)	58.3(8.7)
Trade, repair, hotels and restaurants	11.5(7.2)	11.8(10.7)	18.6 (9.5)*	7.4(-26.9)	8.9(25.0)
Trade & repair services	10.5(7.7)	10.7(10.8)	NA	6.7(-28.4)	7.5(18.9)
Hotels & restaurants	1.0(2.4)	1.1(9.5)	NA	0.8(-10.6)	1.3(77.2)
Transport, storage, communication & services related to broadcasting	6.7(8.7)	6.9(8.4)	NA	8.9(24.2)	8.9(4.8)
Railways	0.8(6.0)	0.8(7.7)	NA	1.2(6.9)	1.4(22.4)
Road transport	3.2(6.2)	3.2(6.3)	NA	1.8(-46.4)	0.8(-50.4)
Air transport	0.1(8.7)	0.2(12.8)	NA	0.1(-16.1)	0.2(94.1)
Financial services	5.8(4.8)	5.7(7.9)	20.6(10.3)^	0.9(-3.4)	1.2(35.3)
Real estate, ownership of dwelling & professional services	14.3(12.5)	14.9(11.8)	NA	25.3(7.2)	23.8 (-1.0)
Public administration and defence	5.9(3.2)	6.2(9.8)	14.1 (6.9)@	8.6(14.9)	9.9(21.2)
Other services	6.7(5.6)	7.2(11.4)	NA	5.3(19.0)	5.7(14.0)
Construction	9.0(4.6)	8.8(4.4)	8.2(3.7)	5.4(-28)	5.4(4.6)
Total services (+ construction)	59.8(7.3)	61.4(9.4)	61.5(8.4)	62.0(1.0)	63.7(8.4)
TOTAL (All Sectors)	100.0(6.3)	100.0(7.1)	100.0 (7.3)	100(2.1)	100(5.6)
GDP (market price constant 2011-12)	(6.6)	(7.2)	(7.6)		

Notes: Shares are in current prices and growth in constant 2011-12 prices; Figures in parentheses indicate growth rate; ® First RE; #AE for 2015-16; * Also includes transport, storage, communication & services related to broadcasting; ^ Also includes real estate and professional services; @ Also includes other services.

Source: Central Statistics Office (CSO).. *Economic Survey 2015-16.*

12 to reach 58.3 per cent in 2014-15, with services GCF growing at 8.7 per cent in 2014-15 compared to total GCF growth of 5.6 per cent (*Economic Survey 2015-16*).

State-wise Comparison of Services

Out of the 33 states and union territories(UT) for which data is available, the services sector is the dominant sector contributing more than half of the gross state domestic products (GSDP) in 21 states and UTs and more than 40 per cent in all states except Sikkim and Arunachal Pradesh. The major services in most of the states are trade, hotels and restaurants, followed by real estate, ownership of dwellings and business services. Out of the 23 states and UTs for which data is available for 2014-15, Delhi is at the top in services GSDP with a share of 87.5 per cent followed by Maharashtra at 63.8 per cent, with growth rates of 8.2 per cent and 5.7 per cent respectively. Puducherry had the highest services growth at 16.3 per cent followed by Meghalaya at 13.2 per cent, owing to increase in growth rate of high weighted sectors like trade, hotels and restaurants and real estate and business services in the case of the former and other services in the case of the latter. Jammu and Kashmir had the lowest services growth at 2.0 per cent, mainly due to low and negative growth in most of the sectors except public administration. Bihar's services sector growth was among the fastest with a consistent double-digit growth in the last seven years due to high growth in the high weighted sectors like trade, hotels and restaurants, and real estate and business services besides transport by other means. (*Economic Survey 2015-16*).

India's Services Employment

The pattern of the sectoral share of employment has changed over the last two decades with the share of agriculture falling and of industry and services rising steadily. Services share in employment at 28.5 per cent in 2011-12 is higher than in industry at 24.4 per cent. Among the different services sectors, from 1993-94 to 2011-12, there was continuous increase in employment share in trade, hotels, and restaurants; transport, storage, and communication; and financial, insurance, real estate and business services. Employment share in community, social, and personal services has fallen continuously except in 2011-12 when there was an increase compared to 2009-10 and 2004-05. Employment elasticity has increased for both services and industry in 2009-10 to 2011-12 compared

Table 22.6

Sector-wise Employment Trends (UPS)

	Absolute number (million) (Share in percent given in parentheses)					*Employment Elasticity*			
	1993-94	*1999-00*	*2004-05*	*2009-10*	*2011-12*	*1993-94 to 1999-00*	*1999-00 to 2004-05*	*2004-05 to 2009-10*	*2009-10 to 2011-12*
Agriculture	204.3 (61.1)	214.7 (58.5)	226.8 (54.5)	220.5 (51.6)	204.4 (47.1)	0.3	0.7	-0.2	-0.5
Industry	53.5 (16.0)	61.7 (16.8)	81.0 (19.5)	93.1 (21.8)	106.1 (24.4)	0.4	0.9	0.3	0.9
Services	76.6 (22.9)	90.6 (24.7)	108.0 (26.0)	113.7 (26.6)	123.9 (28.5)	0.3	0.5	0.1	0.5
Trade, hotels, and restaurants	26.8 (8.0)	34.1 (9.3)	46.5 (11.2)	48.4 (11.3)	50.5 (11.6)	0.4	0.8	0.1	0.3
Transport, storage, and communication	11.0 (3.3)	15.0 (4.1)	18.7 (4.5)	19.9 (4.6)	22.8 (5.2)	0.5	0.4	0.1	0.6
Financial, insurance, real estate and business services	3.7 (1.1)	4.8 (1.3)	7.5 (1.8)	9.4 (2.2)	10.7 (2.5)	0.5	1.6	0.4	0.6
Community, social, and personal services	35.1 (10.5)	36.7 (10.0)	35.3 (8.5)	36.1 (8.4)	39.9 (9.2)	0.1	-0.2	0.1	1.1
Total	334.4 (100.0)	367.0 (100.0)	415.7 (100.0)	427.4 (100.0)	434.4 (100.0)	0.2	0.4	0.1	0.1

Note : Employment elasticity is calculated by CAGR method, Employment elasticity = (CAGR employment)/(CAGR GDP at FC constant 2004-05 prices) for the respective period. UPS- usual principal status

Source : Based on data from National Sample Survey Office (NSSO) different round reports and CSO.

to 2004-05 to 2009-10, though industry had relatively higher employment elasticity. Among services, employment elasticity was the highest in 'financial, insurance, real estate, and business services' and 'transport, storage, and communication' (Table 22.6) (*Economic Survey 2014-15*).

India's Services Trade

Services exports have been a dynamic element of India's trade and globalization in recent years. WTO data shows that India's services exports grew from US$16.8 billion in 2001 to US$155.6 billion - which constitutes 7.5 per cent of the GDP - in 2014, making the country the eighth largest services exporter in the world. The share of India's services exports in global services exports at 3.2 per cent in 2014, is nearly double its share of merchandise exports in global merchandise exports at 1.7 per cent. The overall openness of the economy reflected by total trade including services as a percentage of GDP shows a higher degree of openness at 50 per cent in 2014-15 compared to 38 per cent in 2004-5. The openness indicator based only on merchandise trade stood at 38 per cent in 2014-15 compared to 28 per cent in 2004-5.

Sector-wise performance of services exports in 2014-15 and H1 of 2015-16 has been uneven, with some sectors exhibiting a turnaround and higher growth while others registered considerable decline. With significant moderation in foreign tourist arrivals (FTAs), travel receipts with a 12.9 per cent share in services exports in 2014-15, witnessed a decelerated growth of 4.1 per cent in H1 of 2015-16 compared to 13.5 per cent in 2014-15 and 18.0 per cent in H1 of 2014-15. Transportation services export growth was negative at - 17.0 per cent in H1 of 2015-16 as against a growth of 0.6 per cent in 2014-15 and 7.6 per cent in H1 of 2014-15, reflecting the slowdown in international trade. Growth in computer services, accounting for around 46.4 per cent of total services exports in 2014-15, improved marginally to 5.8 per cent in H1 of 2015-16 from 5.3 per cent in 2014-15 and 5.1 per cent in H1 of 2014-15. Other business services, another major services export segment with a share of 18.0 per cent in 2014-15, posted modest growth of 6.3 per cent in H1 of 2015-16 compared to negative growth of - 0.2 per cent in 2014-15 and - 3.9 per cent in H1 of 2014-15. Of this, growth in professional and management services clocked up to 9.4 per cent in H1 of 2015-16 from negative growth of - 6.9 per cent in 2014-15 and - 6.7 per cent in H1 of 2014-15, while export of technical, trade-related and other business services grew by a paltry 1.1 per cent in H1 of 2015-16 compared to 7.5

per cent in 2014-15 and - 1.4 per cent in H1 of 2014-15 (Table 22.7). (*Economic Survey 2015-16*).

Table 22.7

Export Performance of Major Services

	Value (US$ bn)	*Share (%)*	*Growth Rate (%)*			
	2014-15	*2014-15*	*2013-14*	*2014-15*	*2014-15 H1*	*2015-16 H1*
Total services exports	157.70	100.0	4.0	4.1	4.5	0.7
Transport	17.49	11.1	0.3	0.6	7.6	-17.0
Travel	20.33	12.9	-0.4	13.5	18.0	4.1
Financial, insurance & pension services	7.9	5.0	22.2	-10.3	-12.0	-0.9
Telecommunications services	2.00	1.3	43.0	-17.1	-22.2	15.4
Computer services	73.11	46.4	5.4	5.3	5.1	5.8
Other business services	28.42	18.0	0.1	-0.2	-3.9	6.3
R&D services	1.26	0.8	24.0	9.7	6.2	22.9
Professional and management consulting services	14.43	9.1	10.4	-6.9	-6.7	9.4
Technical, trade-related, and others	12.73	8.1	-12.2	7.5	-1.4	1.1
Total services imports	81.11	100.0	-2.8	3.3	5.4	4.2
Net services	76.59	-	12.4	5.0	3.5	-3.1

Source: RBI's Balance of Payments (BoP) data (BPM-6).
Economic Survey 2015-16.

The growing role of software and business services in India's services-sector exports reflects India's comparative advantage in skill and knowledge-intensive labour-based services.

India's growing presence in global BPO services is based on its huge labour endowment, varied skill sets and low-cost but quality manpower coupled with a rapidly growing domestic IT industry. According to the *Financial Times*, half of the world's largest 500 companies and many government agencies contract out IT and business process work to India across a wide range of services, including medical and legal tranacriptions, customer support, human-resource management and administration, financial and accounting processes, technical suport, logistics, sales, and research and development (R&D), to name a few.

Apart from software and BPO services, there are emerging export opportunities in various other services, such as health, education, and tourism. There are concerted effors underway to establish India as a hub for medical tourism services. Similarly, there is growing interest among Indian higher-education institutions in exporting education services throuygh establishment of offshore campuses as well as twining and partnership arrangements. It is again worth noting that trade data on services are subject to problems of coverage and classification. Information is not available from the balance of payments at a sufficiently disaggregated level, particularly in the category of other services, to gauge trends and prospects for individual activities.

There are numerous domestic and external barriers to India's services exports. The main domestic barriers are in the form of infrastructural, financial, regulatory, technical, and standard-related constraints. The main external barriers are in the form of immigration and labour-market regulations, which limit India's ability to deliver on-site services. In addition, there has recently been a backlash against outsourcing in key markets like the US and introduction of domestic regulations such as data privacy laws, which could affect India's BPO exports (Chanda, 2010).

Foreign Direct Investment in India's Service Sector

There has been a significant growth in FDI inflows in 2014-15 and 2015-16. (Apr-Oct) in general and to the services sector in particular. Though there is ambiguity in the classification of FDI in services, the combined FDI share of the top 10 service sectors such as financial and non-financial services under services sector, telecommunications, trading, computer hardware and software, construction, hotels and tourism, hospital and diagnostic centres, consultancy services, sea transport, information and broadcasting can be taken as the best estimate of services FDI, though it could include some non-service elements. This share is 53.3 per cent of the cumulative FDI equity inflows during the period April 2000-October 2015 and 53 per cent during 2014-15. If the shares of some other services or service-related sectors like retail trading, ports, agriculture services, education, and air transport are included, then the total share of cumulative FDI inflows to the services sector would increase to 55.6 per cent and 54.5 per cent respectively for the above two periods (Table 22.8).

Table 22.8

FDI Equity Inflows in the Services Sector

Sr	Sub-Sectors	Value (in US$ million)			Percentage to total		Growth rate (%)	
		2014-15	2015-16 (Apr. to Oct.)	April 2000 to Oct. 2015	2014-15	April 2000 to Oct. 2015	2014-15	2015-16 (Apr. to Oct.)
1	Services sector*	4443.3	3874.1	46586.8	14.4	17.2	99.7	134.5
2	Telecommunications	2894.9	949.6	18007.7	9.4	6.7	121.5	-61.6
3	Trading	2728.0	2372.1	10432.5	8.8	3.9	103.1	52.5
4	Computer software & hardware	2296.0	4122.5	19139.8	7.4	7.1	103.9	530.9
5	Construction #	1639.4	1151.0	28649.5	5.3	10.6	-4.2	33.6
6	Hotel & tourism	777.0	714.6	8631.0	2.5	3.2	59.8	46.0
7	Hospital & diagnostic centres	567.9	377.2	3322.4	1.8	1.2	-17.1	67.2
8	Consultancy services	458.1	384.8	3194.1	1.5	1.2	60.3	11.2
9	Sea transport	333.2	295.7	1841.6	1.1	0.7	1526.3	119.9
10	Information & broadcasting	255.0	515.1	4484.5	0.8	1.7	-40.5	813.7
Top 10 service categories (1-10)		16392.8	14756.9	144289.9	53.0	53.3	70.4	74.7
Total FDI equity		30930.5	21873.7	270506.8	100.0	100.0	27.3	26.1

Note: * Financial, banking, insurance, non-financial business, outsourcing, R&D, courier, technology testing and analysis, other; #Combined with infrastructure activities and townships, housing, built-up infrastructure and construction-development projects.

Source: Based on Department of Industrial Policy and Promotion (DIPP) data. *Economic Survey 2015-16.*

In 2014-15, while total FDI equity inflows grew by 27.3 per cent to US$ 30.9 billion, FDI equity inflows to the services sector (top 10 services including construction) grew by a whopping 70.4 per cent to US$16.4 billion (*Economic Survey 2015-16*).

Liberalisation of Services in India

Services have been a critical part of the overall economic reform and liberalisation process in India. Much of the recent structural and institutional reforms as well as the liberalisation/deregulation strategies have involved the opening up of key services such as telecommunications, banking, and insurance to attract much-needed foreign capital and technology, and to encourage competition and efficiency in these areas to induce positive externalities for the rest of the economy. Many services, including construction, tourism, health, and computer-related services, for instance, have been put on automatic approval route for FDI. Government monopoly in many critical services has been eliminated, with further liberalisation planned or already announced.

Telecommunication services have experienced the greatest amount of liberalisation. Today, fully owned foreign firms are allowed in some segments of telecom sector, government monopoly in long-distance telephony and Internet has been eliminated, and there is no restriction on the number of providers. FDI in voice telephony services has been permitted with a ceiling of 49 per cent foreign-equity participation and a proposal to raise the equity cap to 74 per cent. Similarly, government monopoly in the insurance-services sector has been eliminated and the sector has been opened up to private players, with a foreign-equity ceiling of 26 per cent through joint ventures and possibly 49 per cent in the near future. Banking services have also been liberalised with a 74 per cent ceiling on foreign equity in private banks and a 20 per cent ceiling on FDI and portfolio investment in public sector banks (World Bank 2004).

Evidence suggests that services that have been liberalised most have typically experienced higher growth rates. Figure 9 indicates the positive correlation between the degree of liberalisation in the services sector with regard to trade and FDI policies and its access to external markets, and the growth exhibited in that sector with regard to output and employment opportunities. Areas such as business services (mainly IT and IT-enabled services), communication, banking, and insurance, which have been liberalised, have exhibited higher growth rates, wich wider efficiency and growth benefits to the rest of the economy. On the other hand, services with limited opening, like air-transport, legal, and real-estate services, have grown much more slowly, with likely adverse effects on economy-wide competitiveness and growth performance.

Productivity estimates also corroborate the role played by competition and integration with global markets in improving efficiency in the services sector. Estimates by McKinsey indicate that telecommunications and software services have much higher productivity levels than other services sectors in India, owing to factors such as global and domestic competition and changes in ownership structure, which have in turn enabled technological externalities, knowledge spillovers, improved management practices, and technology diffusion. In addition, liberalisation in certain services has also impacted positively on export opportunities.

For instance, the opening up of areas like telecommunications to FDI has had a positive impact on export opportunities in IT and BPO services. Evidence also indicates increased usage of services in manufacturing and resulting productivity gains in India's manufacturing sector. Further liberalisation of the services sector is likely to yield sector-specific and economy-wide gains in terms of growth, export, efficiency, and competitiveness.

India and Trade Negotiations in Services

India is actively involved in the World Trade Organisation (WTO) negotiations on services. In view of the various barriers that affect India's key modes of export interest, India has taken a proactive position in the services negotiations on temporary cross-border movement of service providers (mode 4) and cross-border supply of services (mode 1) under the General Agreement on Trade in Services (GATS). It has made a joint submission along with some other developing countries for a Service Provider Visa under GATS, which would expand and ensure more predictable and transparent market access for intracompany transferees, contractual service suppliers, and independent professionals. It has also submitted a joint proposal for securing market access in outsourcing through binding commitments in mode 1 across a wide range of services so as to pre-empt further protectionism in this areas.[1]

There is in turn growing pressure on India by the main developed countries to make binding and more liberal commitments on commercial presence (GATS mode 3) across a wide range of services India has received requests to multilaterally bind in the liberalisation it has undertaken autonomously in sectors such as banking, insurance, and telecommunications and also to schedule other sectors such as distribution and education services, which it had not committed earlier. Several developed countries have requested India to open up areas like retail distribution, higher education, legal, and accountancy services to foreign commercial presence. Thus far India has taken a quid pro quo approach to the services negotiations, that is, exchanging commitments on foreign commercial presence against securing its market access interests in modes 1 and 4. However, in its latest services offer under the Doha round of services negotiations, India has significantly improved upon its earlier commitments on commercial presence, despite its failure to secure its market-access interests in mode 4. India also endorsed plurilateral negotiations in services following the 2005 Hong Kong Ministerial Conference so as to expedite services negotiations.

The preceding discussion clearly highlights that the service sector has not only outperformed other sectors of the Indian economy, but has also played an important role in India's integration with world trade and capital markets. There is, however, growing debate within the country about the sustainability of a services-led growth process. No country in history has been able to grow rapidly in a sustained manner based on services alone. The manufacturing sector has always been part of the growth success. Hence it remains to be seen whether this model of growth also holds for India or not. The prevailing view today is that India needs broad-based growth as its services sector is largely driven by external demand. If high growth is to be sustained within services, then creation of internal demand is necessary and this is only possible with a vibrant manufacturing sector.; Moreover, employment concerns cannot be addressed without concomitant growth in manufacturing since, as highlighted earlier, the faster-growing services are those that are not generating sufficient growth in employment opportunities for the masses. More broad-based growth within the services sector is required. Services such as trade and distribution, tourism, and construction, which have high employment intensities and large backward and forward linkages with other sectors need to grow more rapidly. In this regard, further infrastructural and regulatory reforms and FDI liberalisation in services can help diversify the sources of growth within India's services sector and provide the required momentum (Chanda, 2010).

The government has taken a number of policy initiatives to promote services exports which include the Service Exports from India Scheme (SEIS) for increasing exports of notified services from India; organizing Global Exhibitions on Services (GES) and services conclaves to augment exports of various services and position India as a key player in world services trade; besides some initiatives in sectors like tourism and shipping. Given the potential of India's services exports, services-sector negotiations both at multilateral and bilateral/regional levels are of vital importance to India (See Box 22.1).

Box 22.1

WTO Services Negotiations and Bilateral Negotiations including Services Trade

WTO negotiations

- The 10th session of the WTO Ministerial Conference was held in Nairobi, Kenya, from 15 to 18 December 2015. In the area of services trade, the conference took decisions such as implementation of preferential treatment in favour of services and service suppliers of least developed countries (LDC) and increasing LDC participation in services trade; and moratorium on payment of customs duties on electronic transmissions until 2017.
- Preferential treatment for LDCs: So far, 21 members, including India, have notified preferential treatment to LDCs in services trade. India has offered this in respect of: (i) article XVI of the General Agreement on Trade in Services (GATS) (Market Access); (ii) technical assistance and capacity building; and (iii) waiver of visa fees for LDC applicants applying for Indian business and employment visas. The fee waiver will be valid until 31 December 2030. India is the only member which has offered waiver of visa fees. This is a unique and almost path-breaking offer by India. So far, visa issues have remained untouched in the WTO/free trade agreements (FTA). India's offer should give significant advantage to service suppliers from LDCs *vis-à-vis* service suppliers from any other country.
- E-commerce: The WTO Members agreed to maintain the current practice of not imposing customs duties on electronic transmissions until the next Ministerial Conference which will be held in 2017.

Bilateral agreements:

- India has signed comprehensive bilateral trade agreements, including trade in services, with the governments of Singapore, South Korea, Japan and Malaysia. An FTA in services and investment was signed with the Association of South East Asian Nations (ASEAN) in September 2014, which came into effect from 1 July 2015.
- India has joined the Regional Comprehensive Economic Partnership (RCEP) plurilateral negotiations. The RCEP is a proposed FTA which includes the 10 ASEAN countries and its six FTA partners, viz. Australia, China, India, Japan, South Korea and New Zealand. The RCEP is the only mega-regional FTA of which India is a part.

contd...

.contd...

- India is also engaged in bilateral FTA negotiations including trade in services with Canada, Israel, Thailand, the EU, the European Free Trade Association (EFTA), Australia and New Zealand. Dialogue is under way with the US under the India-US Trade Policy Forum (TPF), with Australia under the India-Australia Joint Ministerial Commission (JMC), with China under the India-China Working-Group on Services, and with Brazil under the India-Brazil Trade Monitoring Mechanism (TMM).

Source: Based on inputs from the Department of Commerce, Government of India.

Conclusion

The services sector is like an uncharted sea with plenty of opportunities that have not been fully tapped. A targeted policy of removing bottlenecks in major and potential services can result in large dividends in the form of higher services growth and services exports, which in turn can help in pulling up the economy to higher growth levels (Box 22.1).

India's services sector, which showed resilient growth after the recovery of the global economy following the global financial crisis, has been showing subdued performance in recent times. Despite the slowdown, the prospects continue to be bright for many segments of the sector. Looking ahead, the government's focus on infrastructure development, favourable regulatory policies like liberalization of FDI norms, increasing number of multimodal logistics service providers, growing trend of outsourcing logistics to third party service providers and entry of global players are expected to provide impetus to logistics services. Though shipping services are at a low key at present, with increased imports of POL (petroleum, oil and lubricants) for stocks build up to take advantage of low crude oil prices, containerization of export and import cargo and modernization of ports with private sector participation, recovery of the shipping and port services sector can be expected (*Economic Survey 2015-16*).

Note

1. Discussion of India's strategic interests in the WTO negotiations on services and proposals submitted is based on Chanda (2004).

References

Acharya, Shankar (2002a). "India's Medium-term Growth Prospects", *EPW*, July 13.

Banga, R. (2005). "Critical Issues in Services-led Growth", *Working Paper* No. 171. New Delhi: Indian Council for Research on International Economic Relations.

Bhagwati, Jagdish (1984). "Splintering and Disembodiment of Services and Developing Nations", *World Economy* 7(2):133-43.

Bhattacharya, B.B. and Arup Mitra (1990). "Excess Growth of Tertiary Sector in Indian Economy, Issues and Implications", *EPW*, November 3, pp. 2445-50.

Budget Speech 2014-15 (July 10, 2014).

Chanda, Rupa (2007). "Services" in Kaushik Basu (ed.) (2007), *The Oxford Companion to Economics in India*. New Delhi: Oxford University Press.

———. (2010). "Services" in Kaushik Basu and Annemie Maerttens (ed.) (2010), *The Concise Oxford Companion to Economics in India*. New Delhi: Oxford University Press.

Gordon, Jim and Poonam Gupta (2003). "Understanding India's Services Revolution", Paper prepared for the IMF-NCAER Conference *A Tale of Two Giants: India's and China's Experience with Reform*, November 14-16, New Delhi.

Government of India. *Economic Survey,* various issues including 2011-12, 2012-13, 2013-14, 2014-15, 2015-16.

Hansda, Sanjay Kumar (2002a). *Services Sector in the Indian Economy: A Status Report*. RBI Staff Studies, Department of Economic Analysis and Policy.

Inman, Robert P. (1985). "Introduction and Overview", in *Managing the Service Economy: Prospects and Problems*. Cambridge: Cambridge University Press.

Kongsamut, Piyabha, Sergio Rebelo and Danyang Xie (2001). "Beyond Balanced Growth", *IMF Working Paper*, WP/01/85.

Planning Commission. *Tenth Five Year Plan 2002-2007*.

———. *Eleventh Five Year Plan 2007-2012*.

Reserve Bank of India. *Annual Reports* 2005-06, 2006-07, 2009-10, 2011-12.

———. (2002). *Report on Currency and Finance 2000-01*.

United Nations (2004). *World Investment Report 2004: The Shift towards Services*. New York and Geneva.

World Bank (2004). *Sustaining India's Services Revolution: Access to Foreign Markets, Domestic Reform and Internatioanl Negotiations*. New Delhi.

The editor gratefully acknowledges Jim Gordon and Poonam Gupta, and Rupa Chanda from whose papers on Services, the editor has liberally drawn in this chapter.